T0183290

Lecture Notes in Computer Science   11859

More information about this series at http://www.springer.com/series/7412

Zhouchen Lin · Liang Wang ·
Jian Yang · Guangming Shi ·
Tieniu Tan · Nanning Zheng ·
Xilin Chen · Yanning Zhang (Eds.)

Pattern Recognition and Computer Vision

Second Chinese Conference, PRCV 2019
Xi'an, China, November 8–11, 2019
Proceedings, Part III

 Springer

Editors
Zhouchen Lin
School of EECS
Peking University
Beijing, China

Jian Yang
Nanjing University of Science
and Technology
Nanjing, China

Tieniu Tan
Institute of Automation
Chinese Academy of Sciences
Beijing, China

Xilin Chen
Chinese Academy of Sciences
Beijing, China

Liang Wang
Institute of Automation
Chinese Academy of Sciences
Beijing, China

Guangming Shi
Xidian University
Xi'an, China

Nanning Zheng
Institute of Artificial Intelligence
Xi'an Jiaotong University
Xi'an, China

Yanning Zhang
Northwestern Polytechnical University
Xi'an, China

ISSN 0302-9743   ISSN 1611-3349 (electronic)
Lecture Notes in Computer Science
ISBN 978-3-030-31725-6   ISBN 978-3-030-31726-3 (eBook)
https://doi.org/10.1007/978-3-030-31726-3

LNCS Sublibrary: SL6 – Image Processing, Computer Vision, Pattern Recognition, and Graphics

This Springer imprint is published by the registered company Springer Nature Switzerland AG
The registered company address is: Gewerbestrasse 11, 6330 Cham, Switzerland

Preface

Welcome to the proceedings of the Second Chinese Conference on Pattern Recognition and Computer Vision (PRCV 2019) held in Xi'an, China!

PRCV merged from CCPR (Chinese Conference on Pattern Recognition) and CCCV (Chinese Conference on Computer Vision), which are both the most influential Chinese conferences on pattern recognition and computer vision, respectively. Pattern recognition and computer vision are closely inter-related and the two communities are largely overlapping. The goal of merging CCPR and CCCV into PRCV is to further boost the impact of the Chinese community in these two core areas of artificial intelligence and further improve the quality of academic communication. Accordingly, PRCV is co-sponsored by four major academic societies of China: the Chinese Association for Artificial Intelligence (CAAI), the China Computer Federation (CCF), the Chinese Association of Automation (CAA), and the China Society of Image and Graphics (CSIG).

PRCV aims at providing an interactive communication platform for researchers from academia and from industry. It promotes not only academic exchange, but also communication between academia and industry. In order to keep track of the frontier of academic trends and share the latest research achievements, innovative ideas, and scientific methods in the fields of pattern recognition and computer vision, international and local leading experts and professors are invited to deliver keynote speeches, introducing the latest advances in theories and methods in the fields of pattern recognition and computer vision.

PRCV 2019 was hosted by Northwestern Polytechnical University and was co-hosted by Xi'an Jiaotong University, Xidian University, and Shaanxi Normal University. We received 412 full submissions. Each submission was reviewed by at least three reviewers selected from the Program Committee and other qualified researchers. Based on the reviewers' reports, 165 papers were finally accepted for presentation at the conference, including 18 oral and 147 posters. The acceptance rate is 40%. The proceedings of the PRCV 2019 are published by Springer.

We are grateful to the keynote speakers, Prof. Kyros Kutulakos from the University of Toronto in Canada, Prof. Licheng Jiao from Xidian University, Prof. Tinne Tuytelaars from the University of Leuven in Belgium, and Prof. Kyoung Mu Lee from Seoul National University in South Korea.

We give sincere thanks to the authors of all submitted papers, the Program Committee members and the reviewers, and the Organizing Committee. Without their contributions, this conference would not be a success. Special thanks also go to all of the sponsors and the organizers of the special forums; their support made the conference a success. We are also grateful to Springer for publishing the proceedings and especially to Ms. Celine (Lanlan) Chang of Springer Asia for her efforts in coordinating the publication.

We hope you find the proceedings enjoyable and fruitful.

November 2019

Tieniu Tan
Nanning Zheng
Xilin Chen
Yanning Zhang
Zhouchen Lin
Liang Wang
Jian Yang
Guangming Shi

Organization

Steering Committee Chair

Tieniu Tan   Institute of Automation, Chinese Academy of Sciences,
                              China

Steering Committee

Xilin Chen   Institute of Computing Technology, Chinese Academy
                              of Sciences, China
Chenglin Liu   Institute of Automation, Chinese Academy of Sciences,
                              China
Long Quan   The Hong Kong University of Science
                              and Technology, SAR China
Yong Rui   Lenovo, China
Hongbin Zha   Peking University, China
Nanning Zheng   Xi'an Jiaotong University, China
Jie Zhou   Tsinghua University, China

Steering Committee Secretariat

Liang Wang   Institute of Automation, Chinese Academy of Sciences,
                              China

General Chairs

Tieniu Tan   Institute of Automation, Chinese Academy of Sciences,
                              China
Nanning Zheng   Xi'an Jiaotong University, China
Xilin Chen   Institute of Computing Technology, Chinese Academy
                              of Sciences, China
Yanning Zhang   Northwestern Polytechnical University, China

Program Chairs

Zhouchen Lin   Peking University, China
Liang Wang   Institute of Automation, Chinese Academy of Sciences,
                              China
Jian Yang   Nanjing University of Science and Technology, China
Guangming Shi   Xidian University, China

Organizing Chairs

Jianru Xue   Xi'an Jiaotong University, China
Peng Wang   Northwestern Polytechnical University, China
Wei Wei   Northwestern Polytechnical University, China

Publicity Chairs

Shiguang Shan   Institute of Computing Technology, Chinese Academy
                      of Sciences, China
Qiguang Miao   Xidian University, China
Zhaoxiang Zhang   Institute of Automation, Chinese Academy of Sciences,
                      China

International Liaison Chairs

Jingyi Yu   ShanghaiTech University, China
Jiwen Lu   Tsinghua University, China
Zhanyu Ma   Beijing University of Posts and Telecommunications,
                      China

Publication Chairs

Xiang Bai   Huazhong University of Science and Technology,
                      China
Tao Yang   Northwestern Polytechnical University, China

Special Issue Chairs

Ming-Ming Cheng   Nankai University, China
Weishi Zheng   Sun Yat-sen University, China

Tutorial Chairs

Deyu Meng   Xi'an Jiaotong University, China
Yuxin Peng   Peking University, China
Feiping Nie   Northwestern Polytechnical University, China

Workshop Chairs

Huchuan Lu   Dalian University of Technology, China
Yunhong Wang   Beihang University, China
Qingshan Liu   Nanjing University of Information Science
                      and Technology, China

Sponsorship Chairs

Tao Wang	iQIYI, China
Jinfeng Yang	Civil Aviation University of China, China
Xinbo Zhao	Northwestern Polytechnical University, China

Demo Chairs

Huimin Ma	Tsinghua University, China
Runping Xi	Northwestern Polytechnical University, China

Competition Chairs

Nong Sang	Huazhong University of Science and Technology, China
Wangmeng Zuo	Harbin Institute of Technology, China
Hanlin Yin	Northwestern Polytechnical University, China

PhD Forum Chairs

Junwei Han	Northwestern Polytechnical University, China
Xin Geng	Southeast University, China
Si Liu	Beihang University, China

Web Chairs

Guofeng Zhang	Zhejiang University, China
Di Xu	Northwestern Polytechnical University, China

Financial Chairs

Jinqiu Sun	Northwestern Polytechnical University, China
Lifang Wu	Beijing University of Technology, China

Registration Chairs

Yu Zhu	Northwestern Polytechnical University, China
Shizhou Zhang	Northwestern Polytechnical University, China

Area Chairs

Xiang Bai	Huazhong University of Science and Technology, China
Songcan Chen	Nanjing University of Aeronautics and Astronautics, China
Jian Cheng	Chinese Academy of Sciences, China

Jinfeng Yang	Civil Aviation University of China, China
Xucheng Yin	University of Science and Technology Beijing, China
Xiaotong Yuan	Nanjing University of Information Science and Technology, China
Zhengjun Zha	University of Science and Technology of China, China
Changshui Zhang	Tsinghua University, China
Daoqiang Zhang	Nanjing University of Aeronautics and Astronautics, China
Zhaoxiang Zhang	Chinese Academy of Sciences, China
Weishi Zheng	Sun Yat-sen University, China
Wangmeng Zuo	Harbin Institute of Technology, China

Additional Reviewers

Peijun Bao	Jiaqing Fan	Rui Huang
Jiawang Bian	Qingnan Fan	Sheng Huang
Jinzheng Cai	Jianjiang Feng	Rongrong Ji
Ziyun Cai	Wei Feng	Kui Jia
Xiangyong Cao	Jingjing Fu	Ming Jiang
Yang Cao	Xueyang Fu	Shuqiang Jiang
Boyuan Chen	Chenqiang Gao	Tingting Jiang
Chusong Chen	Jin Gao	Yu-Gang Jiang
Dongdong Chen	Lin Gao	Liang Jie
Juncheng Chen	Shaobing Gao	Lianwen Jin
Songcan Chen	Shiming Ge	Xin Jin
Tianshui Chen	Xin Geng	Jianhuang Lai
Xilin Chen	Guoqiang Gong	Chenyi Lei
Yingcong Chen	Shuhang Gu	Chunguang Li
Jingchun Cheng	Xiaojie Guo	Kai Li
Ming-Ming Cheng	Yiwen Guo	Shijie Li
Li Chi	Yulan Guo	Stan Li
Yang Cong	Zhenhua Guo	Wenbo Li
Peng Cui	Chunrui Han	Xiangyang Li
Daoqing Dai	Hu Han	Xiaoxiao Li
Yuchao Dai	Tian Han	Xin Li
Cheng Deng	Yahong Han	Yikang Li
Weihong Deng	Huiguang He	Yongjie Li
Chao Dong	Fan Heng	Yufeng Li
Jiangxin Dong	Qibin Hou	Zechao Li
Weisheng Dong	Tingbo Hou	Zhanqing Li
Xiwei Dong	Changhui Hu	Zhizhong Li
Lijuan Duan	Lanqing Hu	Wei Liang
Lixin Duan	Qinghua Hu	Minghui Liao
Bin Fan	Xiaowei Hu	Zicheng Liao
Dengping Fan	Qingqiu Huang	Shuoxin Lin

Weiyao Lin
Zhouchen Lin
Bing Liu
Bo Liu
Chenchen Liu
Chenglin Liu
Dong Liu
Guangcan Liu
Jiawei Liu
Jiaying Liu
Liu Liu
Mengyuan Liu
Miaomiao Liu
Nian Liu
Qingshan Liu
Risheng Liu
Sheng Liu
Shuaicheng Liu
Si Liu
Siqi Liu
Weifeng Liu
Weiwei Liu
Wentao Liu
Xianglong Liu
Yebin Liu
Yiguang Liu
Yu Liu
Yuliang Liu
Yun Liu
Xihui Liu
Yaojie Liu
Mingsheng Long
Cewu Lu
Jiang Lu
Sihui Luo
Bingpeng Ma
Chao Ma
Huimin Ma
Lin Ma
Zhanyu Ma
Zheng Ma
Lin Mei
Deyu Meng
Qiguang Miao
Weiqing Min
Yue Ming

Yadong Mu
Feiping Nie
Yuzhen Niu
Gang Pan
Jinshan Pan
Yu Pang
Xi Peng
Yuxin Peng
Xiaojuan Qi
Yu Qiao
Jianfeng Ren
Jimmy Ren
Min Ren
Peng Ren
Wenqi Ren
Nong Sang
Mingwen Shao
Dongyu She
Shuhan Shen
Tianwei Shen
Lu Sheng
Boxin Shi
Jian Shi
Yukai Shi
Zhenwei Shi
Tianmin Shu
Dongjin Song
Xinhang Song
Jian Sun
Ke Sun
Qianru Sun
Shiliang Sun
Zhenan Sun
Ying Tai
Mingkui Tan
Xiaoyang Tan
Yao Tang
Youbao Tang
Yuxing Tang
Jun Wan
Changdong Wang
Chunyu Wang
Dong Wang
Guangrun Wang
Hanli Wang
Hanzi Wang

Hongxing Wang
Jian Wang
Le Wang
Liang Wang
Limin Wang
Lingjing Wang
Nannan Wang
Qi Wang
Tao Wang
Weiqun Wang
Wenguan Wang
Xiaosong Wang
Xinggang Wang
Xintao Wang
Yali Wang
Yilin Wang
Yongtao Wang
Yunhong Wang
Zilei Wang
Hongyuan Wang
Xiushen Wei
Junwu Weng
Kwanyee Wong
Yongkang Wong
Baoyuan Wu
Fei Wu
Jianlong Wu
Jianxin Wu
Lifang Wu
Shuzhe Wu
Xiaohe Wu
Xinxiao Wu
Yihong Wu
Guisong Xia
Fanyi Xiao
Xiaohua Xie
Xianglei Xing
Peixi Xiong
Yu Xiong
Xiangyu Xu
Yongchao Xu
Yuanlu Xu
Zheng Xu
Jianru Xue
Shipeng Yan
Sijie Yan

Hao Yang
Jufeng Yang
Meng Yang
Shuang Yang
Wei Yang
Yang Yang
Jingwen Ye
Ming Yin
Dongfei Yu
Gang Yu
Jiahui Yu
Tan Yu
Yang Yu
Zhenbo Yu
Ganzhao Yuan
Jiabei Zeng
Dechuan Zhan
Daoqiang Zhang
He Zhang
Juyong Zhang
Lei Zhang

Lin Zhang
Runze Zhang
Shanshan Zhang
Shengping Zhang
Shiliang Zhang
Tianzhu Zhang
Wei Zhang
Xiangyu Zhang
Xiaoyu Zhang
Yongqiang Zhang
Yu Zhang
Zhaoxing Zhang
Feng Zhao
Jiaxing Zhao
Kai Zhao
Kaili Zhao
Qian Zhao
Qijun Zhao
Qilu Zhao
Tiesong Zhao
Ya Zhao

Yue Zhao
Haiyong Zheng
Wenming Zheng
Guoqiang Zhong
Yiran Zhong
Chunluan Zhou
Hao Zhou
Jiahuan Zhou
Xinzhe Zhou
Yipin Zhou
Siyu Zhu
Chao Zhu
Guangming Zhu
Tyler (Lixuan) Zhu
Xiaoke Zhu
Yaohui Zhu
Liansheng Zhuang
Nan Zhuang
Dongqing Zou
Qi Zou
Wangmeng Zuo

Contents – Part III

Computer Vision Applications

Data Analysis and Optimization

Modality Consistent Generative Adversarial Network for Cross-Modal Retrieval

Zhiyong Wu[1], Fei Wu[1(✉)], Xiaokai Luo[1], Xiwei Dong[1],
Cailing Wang[1], and Xiao-Yuan Jing[2]

[1] College of Automation, Nanjing University of Posts and Telecommunications,
Nanjing, China
wuzybarskish@163.com, wufei_8888@126.com,
wangcl@njupt.edu.cn
[2] School of Computer, Wuhan University, Wuhan, China
jingxy_2000@126.com

Abstract. Cross-modal retrieval, which aims to perform the retrieval task across different modalities of data, is a hot topic. Since different modalities of data have inconsistent distributions, how to reduce the gap of different modalities is the core of cross-modal retrieval issue. Recently, Generative Adversarial Networks has been used in cross-modal retrieval due to its strong ability to model data distribution. We propose a novel approach named Modality Consistent Generative Adversarial Network for cross-modal retrieval (MCGAN). The network integrates a generator to generate synthetic image features from text features, a discriminator to classify the modality of features, and followed by a modality consistent embedding network that projects the generated image features and real image features into a common space for learning the discriminative representations. Experiments on two datasets prove the performance of MCGAN on cross-modal retrieval, compared with state-of-the-art related works.

Keywords: Generative adversarial network · Cross-modal retrieval

1 Introduction

Nowadays, a large amount of multimedia data with different modalities, e.g., image, text, video, etc., is mixed together to gain a comprehensive understanding of the real world. The existence of the huge multi-modal data repository greatly stimulates the demand for cross-modal retrieval in search engines or digital libraries, such as returning concerned results from image as response to query of text or vice versa. Cross-modal retrieval provides queries against any modality to find relevant information with different modalities [1].

The main task of cross-modal retrieval is to bridge the modality gap. A large body of traditional cross-modal retrieval methods have been proposed to learn linear projections by optimizing the statistical values from different modalities into a common semantic space and explore the correlation, like canonical correlation analysis

---

The first author is a student.

© Springer Nature Switzerland AG 2019
Z. Lin et al. (Eds.): PRCV 2019, LNCS 11859, pp. 3–14, 2019.
https://doi.org/10.1007/978-3-030-31726-3_1

(CCA)-based methods [2]. Deep learning technology is widely used in image recognition, natural language processing and object dictation [3, 4]. Deep neural network can also play a good role in the field of cross-modal retrieval. Deep neural network (DNN)-based methods [5–7] construct multilayer network to conduct nonlinear projection. The correlation learning error across different modalities is minimized for bridging the gap of different modalities and learning the common representation. Recent works have shown that generative adversarial networks (GANs) [8] have the advantage of modeling data distribution. Inspired by GANs, the heterogeneous gap of different modalities can be reduced through the adversarial mechanism, and some GAN-based cross-modal retrieval methods are proposed [9, 10].

1.1 Motivation and Contribution

Although many methods were proposed focusing on cross-modal retrieval research, how to better bridge the gap of different modalities and improve the accuracy of retrieval are still concerned [11]. Most of existing methods [12, 13] project data from different modalities into a common semantic space in which the similarity measurements are made. However, these methods directly project data from different modalities into common semantic space to reduce the gap, which will lead to the loss of semantic information in both image and text modalities. How to effectively reduce the heterogeneous gap and retain the semantic information of each modality as much as possible has not been well studied.

Inspired by [14] that leverages GANs as a powerful model to convert cross-modal data to single-modal data for zero-shot learning, we propose a novel approach named Modality Consistent Generation Adversarial Network for cross-modal retrieval (MCGAN). The contributions of our study are three-fold:

(1) We design a new generative adversarial network to generate image features with the input text features, which projects text features into the image feature space. In this way, the cross-modal retrieval problem is converted into a single-modal retrieval problem. The gap of different modalities is bridged while the image semantic information is preserved as much as possible.
(2) We project the generated image features and real image features into a common space via a sub-network, and utilize label information to model both the inter- and intra-modal similarity, such that features are semantically discriminative in both inter- and intra-modal aspects.
(3) MCGAN is evaluated on two widely used datasets, i.e., Wikipedia dataset [2] and NUS-WIDE-10 k dataset [5]. The experimental results show that it can outperform related state-of-the-art works.

2 Related Work

2.1 Non-GANs-Based Cross-Modal Retrieval Methods

There exist many methods proposed to bridge the heterogeneity gap between different modalities, which focus on learning common representation of different modalities and measuring similarities to correlate the heterogeneous data [15].

Traditional cross-modal retrieval methods usually linearly project cross-modal data into a common space to generate the common representation. The similarity measurement of features in the common space can maximize the correlation between modalities. Based on canonical correlation analysis (CCA) [16], some representative methods are developed for cross-modal retrieval. Rasiwasia et al. [2] project text features and image features into a low-dimensional common subspace and investigate the correlation between two modalities through CCA. After [2], plenty of extensions, for example [17] adopts kernel function to pursue features and incorporate the semantic labels for learning correlation between two modalities. Besides, Wang et al. [12] present a method learning coupled feature spaces (LCFS) to learn a coupled feature space by coupled linear regression, and the selection of discriminant and relevant features is considered in the space. Furthermore, joint feature selection and subspace learning (JFSSL) [18] method integrates graph regularization and label information to make inter- and intra-modalities features close to relevant labels while far away from irrelevant labels.

Recently, deep neural network promotes the development of cross-modal retrieval due to its great nonlinear fitting ability and self-learning ability [19]. Deep learning based methods non-linearly project the data of each modality to independent semantic space for feature extraction. Feng et al. [5] propose correspondence autoencoder (Corr-AE), which takes representation learning and correlation learning into account to establish a robust model. Since the convolutional neural network (CNN) can fit the image well to get the visual features, Wei et al. [13] provide a deep semantic matching (Deep-SM), which adopts CNN to get deep visual features, validating the superiority of CNN for improving the performance of cross-modal retrieval. Cross-media multiple deep network (CMDN) presented by Peng et al. [6] obtains separate representation of each media type through a model that combines intra- and inter-media representations hierarchically to get the shared representations.

2.2 Generative Adversarial Networks (GANs)-Based Cross-Modal Retrieval Methods

Generative Adversarial Networks proposed by Goodfellow et al. [8] is an unsupervised learning model, which is used to generate desired image from random noise. After several years of development, it has been used in many applications, such as image style transformation, object detection, zero-shot learning including cross-modal retrieval. The original GANs can been divided into two models: generator G and discriminator D. The two models carry out alternating iterative training in the way of minimax game and finally enable generator G to learn the data distribution of real images. Generator G receives random noise, obtains the distribution of real images and outputs the generated images, while the discriminator D aims to distinguish whether the input image is real or not.

However, the original GANs has the problems of unstable training, gradient disappearance and mode collapse, which makes the generated results unsatisfactory. In order to solve these problems, Arjovsky et al. [20] put forward Wasserstein GAN training strategy and adopt gradient penalty to train the model. Condition generative adversarial networks (CGANs) [21] is proposed to add constraint conditions for GANs.

The data is labeled in the generative model and discriminative model respectively, so as to increase the clarity of the images generated by GANs. Radford et al. propose deep convolutional generative adversarial networks (DCGAN) [22], which applies the convolutional neural network to GANs to make the generated images more precise. Recently, Wang et al. [10] apply GANs to cross-modal retrieval and propose adversarial cross-modal retrieval (ACMR), which projects features of different modalities into common space through the minimax training strategy to obtain discriminative feature representations.

These non-GANs-based methods and GANs-based methods directly project data of different modalities into common semantic space to reduce the gap, which will lead to the loss of semantic information in both image and text domain. Different from them, our method effectively transforms the cross-modal retrieval issue into the single-mode retrieval issue, and retains the semantic information of each modality while reducing the heterogeneous gap of different modalities. In addition, we use the label information to model the similarity between and within modality, and obtain semantically more discriminative feature representations.

3 Our Approach

3.1 Problem Formulation

Let $\Omega = \{o_n, y_n\}_{n=1}^{N}$ be a set of N instances of paired image and text, where each instance $o_n = (v_n, t_n)$ includes an image feature vector $v_n \in \mathbb{R}^{d_v}$ and a text feature vector $t_n \in \mathbb{R}^{d_t}$, d_v and d_t denote the feature dimension of two modalities, and n is the number of training samples. Let $V = [v_1, \ldots, v_N]$ and $T = [t_1, \ldots, t_N]$ be the training sets of image features and text features, respectively. $y_n = [y_{n1}, \ldots, y_{nC}]^T$ denotes the semantic category label vector corresponding to o_n, where $y_{nc} = 1$ if $o_n = (v_n, t_n)$ is from the cth class while $y_{nc} = 0$ otherwise. The generator G is designed to learn synthetic image feature representations $\tilde{V} = G(T; \theta) = [\tilde{v}_n]_{n=1}^{N} \in \mathbb{R}^{d_v \times N}$ for text modality. To explore the correlation between modalities, we adopt a common two layers feed-forward sub-networks to nonlinearly project V and $\tilde{V}$ into a common space for learning the correlative representations, by $V_s = f(V; \phi) = [s_v^n]_{n=1}^{N} \in \mathbb{R}^{d_s \times N}$ and $\tilde{V}_s = f(\tilde{V}; \phi) = [s_{\tilde{v}}^n]_{n=1}^{N} \in \mathbb{R}^{d_s \times N}$, where $f(\cdot; \phi)$ is the mapping function.

The objectives of our approach can be summarized as two points: (1) the text features can be effectively converted into the space of image features through adversarial mechanism; (2) the learned features should be semantically discriminative. We alternately and iteratively train the generator G, discriminator D and common embedding network respectively. Figure 1 shows the overall framework of MCGAN.

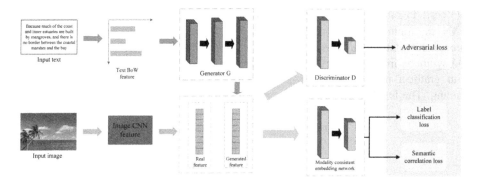

Fig. 1. Our MCGAN overall framework. The architecture of MCGAN consists of two parts. (1) A generative adversarial network is composed of generative model G and discriminative model D: the generative model G takes the text features as input and outputs the generated features near to the real image features; the discriminative model tries to distinguish the real and generated image features via the adversarial loss. (2) A modality consistent embedding network is a two feed-forward sub-network, which models both the intra-modal semantic similarity via label classification loss and the inter-modal semantic similarity via semantic correlation loss.

3.2 Generative Model

Our generative adversarial networks (GANs) defines a minimax game between two competing components: a generator G that captures the image feature distributions from text features for synthesizing image features, and a discriminator D that is learned to distinguish the real image features from synthetic features. Specifically, text features T which are extracted by a well-known bag-of-words (BoW) vector with the TF-IDF weighting scheme, are accepted as input by three-layer feed-forward networks, and the generated image features $\tilde{V} = G(T; \theta)$. In the minimax game, the goal of generator G is to make the synthetic image features approximate to the real image features through the adversarial training strategy. Inspired by Wasserstein GAN that is stable to synthesize great images, the loss of generator is defined as:

$$L_G = -E_{T \sim p_T}[D(G(T; \theta); \omega)] \tag{1}$$

where θ and ω denote the parameters of generator and discriminator respectively, p_T is the distribution of text features.

3.3 Discrimination Model

The discriminator D is actually a modality classifier used to distinguish whether the input features are real image features or not. In generative adversarial networks, the discriminator D plays the role of adversary, distinguishing input feature by minimizing the classification error of probabilities $D(V; \omega)$ and $D(\tilde{V}; \omega)$. As shown in Fig. 1, we build a modality classifier with a two-layer sub-network, which takes as input either a real image feature or a generated image feature and the outputs are $D(V; \omega)$ and

$D(\tilde{V};\omega)$. In other to solve the problems of unstable training and mode collapse of GAN, the training strategy of Wasserstein GAN is adopted to train the discriminator through calculating the Wasserstein distance of the distribution of real image features and synthetic image features as loss. Furthermore, a differentiable Lipschitz constraint with gradient penalty is added to prevent the gradient from disappearing during training. The loss for the discriminator is formulated as:

$$L_D = E_{T \sim p_T}[D(G(T;\theta);\omega)] - E_{v \sim p_v}[D(V;\omega)]$$
$$+ \lambda E_{\hat{V} \sim p_{\hat{V}}}\left[\left(\left\|\nabla_{\hat{v}}D(\hat{V};\omega)\right\|_2 - 1\right)^2\right] \tag{2}$$

where $\hat{V}$ is the linear interpolation of real image feature V and generated image feature $\tilde{V}$. The first two terms approximate Wasserstein distance of distribution of real image feature V and generated image feature $\tilde{V}$. The third term is the gradient penalty to enforce the Lipschitz constraint with λ being the penalty coefficient.

3.4 Modality Consistent Embedding Network

Though we have obtained the distribution of image features through the generative adversarial network and have converted the cross-modal retrieval issue into single-modal retrieval issue, the similarity measurement of paired features is also what we should focus on. In other to capture more discriminative features semantically, we propose a modality consistent embedding network, which is a two-layer sub-network, mapping paired features into a common space, and then label information is used to model the inter- and intra-modal semantic similarity.

Intra-modal Semantic Similarity Modeling
To make the paired features to be semantically discriminative, a feed-forward one-layer sub-network activated by Softmax is adopted as a classifier, such that when the output of feature embedding network $s_{v_n} = f(v_n;\phi)$ or $s_{\tilde{v}_n} = f(\tilde{v}_n;\phi)$ is the input of classifier, the corresponding probability distribution of semantic categories, i.e., $\hat{p}_n(s_{v_n})$ or $\hat{p}_n(s_{\tilde{v}_n})$ can be output. We define the following label classification loss:

$$L_C = -\frac{1}{N}\sum_{n=1}^{N} y_n(\log \hat{p}_n(s_{v_n}) + \log \hat{p}_n(s_{\tilde{v}_n})) \tag{3}$$

where y_n is the ground-truth label of each feature, which is expressed as an one-hot vector.

Inter-modal Semantic Similarity Modeling
The embedding features of two modalities in the common space have superior intra-modal semantic similarity through the combination of GAN and feature embedding network. Furthermore, in order to get better classification results, the embedding features should also show good inter-modal semantic similarity. Motivated by [14], we design a modality consistent semantic correlation term to calculate the similarity of

features with the same semantic category. We provided the following semantic correlation loss:

$$L_m = \frac{1}{C} \sum_{c=1}^{C} \left\| E_{s_{v_c} \sim p_v^c[s_{v_c}]} - E_{s_{v_c} \sim p_{\bar{v}}^c[s_{v_c}]} \right\|^2 \tag{4}$$

where C is the number of classes, s_{v_c} is the embedding image feature of class c and $s_{\bar{v}_c}$ is the embedding generated feature of class c. For each modality, the centroid of the cluster of embedding features should be defined, so we adopt the empirical expectation $E_{x_c \sim p_x^c[x_c]}$ to calculate the centroid of the embedding features of class c. We define the following formulas as:

$$E_{s_{v_c} \sim p_v^c}[s_{v_c}] = \frac{1}{U_c} \sum_{i=1}^{U_c} s_{v_c}^i$$

$$E_{s_{\bar{v}_c} \sim p_{\bar{v}}^c}[s_{\bar{v}_c}] = \frac{1}{M_c} \sum_{i=1}^{M_c} s_{\bar{v}_c}^i \tag{5}$$

where the first formula is the expectation of embedding image features, which is approximated by averaging the embedding image features for class c, and U_c is the number of samples in class c. Similarity, the second formula is the expectation of embedding generated features, and M_c is the number of embedding generated features for class c.

By combining the Eqs. (4) and (5), we obtain the optimization loss of the modality consistent embedding network for learning discriminative features as follows

$$L_{emb} = L_C + \zeta L_m \tag{6}$$

where ζ is a parameter to balance two terms.

3.5 Optimization

The overall framework proposed in this paper is composed of two components: a generative adversarial network to generate the generated image features that are close to real image features, and a modality consistent embedding network to obtain more discriminative features. The optimal features can be obtained by integrating the loss functions in Eqs. (2), (3) and (7). The optimization problems for discriminator D, generator G and modality consistent embedding network are respectively defined as follows:

$$\left(\hat{\omega} \right) = \arg \min_{\omega} (L_{emb} + \alpha L_D) \tag{7}$$

$$\left(\hat{\theta} \right) = \arg \min_{\theta} (L_{emb} + \beta L_G) \tag{8}$$

$$\left(\hat{\phi}\right) = \arg\min_{\phi}(L_{emb}) \tag{9}$$

where α and β are tradeoff parameters. Each part of the network is updated separately though the optimization objectives above. The parameters ω, θ and ϕ can be effectively optimized through the automatic differential back propagation of Pytorch. Algorithm 1 summarizes the process of our approach.

Algorithm 1 Optimization procedure of MCGAN

1. **Input:** mini-batch image features $V = [v_1,...,v_N]$ and text features $T = [t_1,...,t_N]$, the semantic category label $y_n = [y_{n1},...,y_{nC}]^T$ and number of training epoch S.

2. **Training procedure:**
   (1) Initialize generative network G, discriminative network D and modality consistent embedding network;
   (2) **for** $i = 1$ to S **do**

   $\tilde{V} \leftarrow G(T;\theta)$; $s_{v_n} = f(v_n;\phi)$; $s_{\tilde{v}_n} = f(\tilde{v}_n;\phi)$;

   Compute $L_{emb} + \alpha L_D$ using Eqs. (2) and (6);

   Update ω by $Adam(\nabla_\omega L_{emb} + \alpha L_D)$;

   Compute $L_{emb} + \beta L_G$ using Eqs. (1) and (6);

   Update θ by $Adam(\nabla_\theta L_{emb} + \beta L_G)$;

   Compute L_{emb} using Equation (6);

   Update ϕ by $Adam(\nabla_\phi L_{emb})$;

   end for

3. **Output:** Optimized parameters ω, θ, ϕ.

---

4 Experiments

4.1 Datasets

We evaluate our proposed approach on the widely used Wikipedia dataset [2] and NUS-WIDE-10 k dataset [5].

Wikipedia dataset is collected from Wikipedia featured articles, and there are 2,866 image-text pairs. Each pair of image and text is extracted from the same articles. All image-text pairs are from 10 semantic classes, and each pair is labeled with only one class label. Following [2], 2,173 pairs of samples are used for training, 231 pairs for validation and 462 pairs for testing. For image modality, 4,096-dimensional features are extracted by fc7 layer of VGGnet, and each text is represented by a 3,000-demensional Bag-of-Word feature.

NUS-WIDE-10 k dataset consists of 10,000 web images including 10 semantic concepts download from Flicker website. Following [5], this dataset is split into three subsets: the training set with 8,000 pairs, the validation set with 1,000 pairs, and the testing set with 1,000 pairs. For each image, 4,096-dimensional feature is extracted by the fc7 layer of VGGnet, and for each text, 1,000-dimensional Bag-of-Word feature vector is extracted.

4.2 Evaluation Measure and Compared Methods

In this paper, we use mean Average Precision (mAP) to evaluate the cross-modal retrieval performances.

$$mAP = \frac{1}{N} \sum_{i=1}^{N} AP(q_i) \tag{10}$$

where $AP(\cdot)$ computes the average precision, N is the number of query samples and q_i represents the ith query sample. The larger the mAP value is, the better the retrieval performance is.

For comparison, we compare our proposed MCGAN approach with six representative cross-modal retrieval methods: (1) traditional cross-modal retrieval methods: CCA [2] and LCFS [12]; (2) deep learning-based methods: Deep-SM [13], Corr-AE [5] and MCSM [23]; (3) GAN-based method: ACMR [10]. We report the experimental results of the compared methods according to the published results in their papers or the codes provided by the authors to implement the evaluation.

In experiment, we perform two types of experiments, namely retrieving images with text and retrieving text with images.

4.3 Implementation Detail

Our proposed MCGAN approach and relevant experiments are implemented on Torch framework. The implementation details of our generative adversarial network and the modality consistent embedding network are as follows: our generative adversarial network consists of two components, the generative model is a 3-layer network, which is composed of three fully connected layers to learn the generated image features from text features. The number of neurons in each layer is 3500, 4000, 4096, and the activation function is Tanh. The discriminative model consists of two fully connected layers: the number of neurons in the first layer is 1000, the number of neurons in the second layer is 2, and the subsequent activation function is ReLU. In addition, Softmax activation is added after the last layer to conduct the modality classification. For the modality consistent embedding network, two fully connected layers with dimensional [1000, 10] activated by Tanh are used to project both the generated image features and the real image features into a common semantic space to learn the discriminative feature representations.

In our training procedure, the mini-batch size is 128, and the tradeoff parameters λ, ζ, α and β are set up by grid search. The good results are achieved with $\lambda = 10$, $\zeta = 1$, $\alpha = \beta = 0.1$.

4.4   Result and Discussion

Table 1 tabulates the Map results of compared methods on Wikipedia and NUS-WIDE-10 k datasets. In can be seen from the table that in both image to text and text to image retrieval tasks, GAN-based methods such as MCSM and ACMR outperform the non-GAN-based cross-modal retrieval methods including CCA, LCFS, Corr-AE, CMDN and Deep-SM on the benchmark datasets. Furthermore, our MCGAN can always outperform all compared methods. Specifically, for the retrieval task of image to text and text to image on the Wikipedia dataset, MCGAN improves the mAP results at least by $0.004 = (0.522 - 0.518)$, $0.013 = (0.471 - 0.458)$. Similarly, for the retrieval task of image to text and text to image on the NUS-WIDE-10 k dataset, our approach improves the mAP scores at by $0.019 = (0.563 - 0.544)$, $0.01 = (0.551 - 0.541)$. The results show that by turning text features into image features through generative adversarial network, semantic information can be effectively preserved while the gap of different modalities can be bridged. Besides, the more discriminative features learned from the inter- and intra-modal discrimination are helpful to improve the retrieval performance.

Table 1. The mAP cross-modal retrieval results on two datasets

Method	Wikipedia			NUS-WIDE-10 k		
	Img2txt	Txt2img	Average	Img2txt	Txt2img	Average
CCA	0.258	0.250	0.254	0.202	0.220	0.211
LCFS	0.455	0.398	0.427	0.383	0.346	0.365
Corr-AE	0.402	0.395	0.399	0.366	0.417	0.392
CMDN	0.488	0.427	0.458	0.492	0.515	0.504
Deep-SM	0.458	0.345	0.402	0.389	0.496	0.443
MCSM	0.516	0.458	0.487	0.543	0.541	0.542
ACMR	0.518	0.412	0.465	0.544	0.538	0.541
MCGAN	**0.522**	**0.471**	**0.497**	**0.563**	**0.551**	**0.557**

In the modality consistent embedding network, label classification loss and semantic correlation loss are defined to promote semantically discriminative feature learning. To demonstrate whether they can contribute to improving the retrieval performance, the version of MCGAN without label classification loss (MCGAN-C), the version of MCGAN without semantic correlation loss (MCGAN-m) are proposed to evaluate the role of each component. From the Table 2, the mAP results of MCGAN-C, MCGAN-m and MCGAN show that the label classification loss and semantic correlation loss are contributed to promoting semantically discriminative feature learning and improve the retrieval performance.

Table 2. The mAP results of cross-modal retrieval with fully MCGAN, MCGAN without L_C, and MCGAN without L_m.

Method	Wikipedia			NUS-WIDE-10 k		
	Img2txt	Txt2img	Average	Img2txt	Txt2img	Average
MCGAN	**0.522**	**0.471**	**0.497**	**0.563**	**0.551**	**0.557**
MCGAN-C	0.234	0.188	0.211	0.203	0.181	0.192
MCGAN-m	0.480	0.422	0.451	0.511	0.506	0.508

5 Conclusion

In this paper, we present a novel approach named MCGAN that is able to convert the cross-modal retrieval issue into single-modal retrieval issue on image domain via generative adversarial network. In this way, the semantic information of image modality can be preserved effectively. Furthermore, a modality consistent embedding network is designed to project both the image features and generated image features to a common semantic space and utilize label information to model both the inter- and intra-modal similarity via two defined loss functions. Extensive empirical results demonstrate that MCGAN can achieve significantly better retrieval performance than several state-of-the-art related methods.

Acknowledgements. The work in this paper was supported by National Natural Science Foundation of China (No. 61702280), Natural Science Foundation of Jiangsu Province (No. BK20170900), National Postdoctoral Program for Innovative Talents (No. BX20180146), Scientific Research Starting Foundation for Introduced Talents in NJUPT (NUPTSF, No. NY217009), and the Postgraduate Research & Practice Innovation Program of Jiangsu Province KYCX17_0794.

References

1. Li, D., Dimitrova, N., Li, M., et al.: Multimedia content processing through cross-modal association. In: ACM International Conference on Multimedia, Berkeley, 2–8, pp. 604–611 (2003)
2. Rasiwasia, N., Costa Pereira, J., Coviello, E., et al.: A new approach to cross-modal multimedia retrieval. In: ACM International Conference on Multimedia, pp. 251–260 (2010)
3. Fan, D.P., Wang, W., Cheng, M.M., et al.: Shifting more attention to video salient object detection. In: IEEE Conference on Computer Vision and Pattern Recognition, pp. 8554–8564 (2019)
4. Zhao, J.X., Cao, Y., Fan, D.P., et al.: Contrast prior and fluid pyramid integration for RGBD salient object detection. In: IEEE Conference on Computer Vision and Pattern Recognition (2019)
5. Feng, F., Wang, X., Li, R.: Cross-modal retrieval with correspondence autoencoder. In: ACM International Conference on Multimedia, pp. 7–16 (2014)
6. Peng, Y., Huang, X., Qi, J.: Cross-media shared representation by hierarchical learning with multiple deep networks. In: International Joint Conference on Artificial Intelligence, pp. 3846–3853 (2016)

7. Huang, X., Peng, Y., Yuan, M.: Cross-modal common representation learning by hybrid transfer network. In: International Joint Conference on Artificial Intelligence, pp. 1893–1900 (2017)
8. Goodfellow, I., Pouget-Abadie, J., Mirza, M., et al.: Generative adversarial nets. In: Advances in Neural Information Processing Systems, pp. 2672–2680 (2014)
9. Peng, Y., Qi, J.: CM-GANs: cross-modal generative adversarial networks for common representation learning. ACM Trans. Multimed. Comput. Commun. Appl. 15(1), 22 (2019)
10. Wang, B., Yang, Y., Xu, X., et al.: Adversarial cross-modal retrieval. In: ACM International Conference on Multimedia, pp. 154–162 (2017)
11. Yan, F., Mikolajczyk, K.: Deep correlation for matching images and text. In: IEEE Conference on Computer Vision and Pattern Recognition, pp. 3441–3450 (2015)
12. Wang, K., He, R., Wang, W., et al.: Learning coupled feature spaces for cross-modal matching. In: IEEE International Conference on Computer Vision, pp. 2088–2095 (2013)
13. Wei, Y., Zhao, Y., Lu, C., et al.: Cross-modal retrieval with CNN visual features: a new baseline. IEEE Trans. Cybern. 47(2), 449–460 (2017)
14. Zhu, Y., Elhoseiny, M., Liu, B., et al.: A generative adversarial approach for zero-shot learning from noisy texts. In: IEEE Conference on Computer Vision and Pattern Recognition, pp. 1004–1013 (2018)
15. Wu, F., et al.: Cross-project and within-project semisupervised software defect prediction: a unified approach. IEEE Trans. Reliab. 67(2), 581–597 (2018)
16. Hardoon, D.R., Szedmak, S., Shawe-Taylor, J.: Canonical correlation analysis: an overview with application to learning methods. Neural Comput. 16(12), 2639–2664 (2004)
17. Ranjan, V., Rasiwasia, N., Jawahar, C.V.: Multi-label cross-modal retrieval. In: IEEE International Conference on Computer Vision (2015)
18. Wang, K., He, R., Wang, L., et al.: Joint feature selection and subspace learning for cross-modal retrieval. IEEE Trans. Pattern Anal. Mach. Intell. 38(10), 2010–2023 (2016)
19. Wu, F., et al.: Intraspectrum discrimination and interspectrum correlation analysis deep network for multispectral face recognition. IEEE Trans. Cybern. 1–14 (2018)
20. Arjovsky, M., Chintala, S., Bottou, L.: Wasserstein generative adversarial networks. In: International Conference on Machine Learning, pp. 214–223 (2017)
21. Isola, P., Zhu, J.Y., Zhou, T., et al.: Image-to-image translation with conditional adversarial networks. In: IEEE Conference on Computer Vision and Pattern Recognition, pp. 1125–1134 (2017)
22. Radford, A., Metz, L., Chintala, S.: Unsupervised representation learning with deep convolutional generative adversarial networks. arXiv preprint arXiv:1511.06434 (2015)
23. Peng, Y., Qi, J., Yuan, Y.: Modality-specific cross-modal similarity measurement with recurrent attention network. IEEE Trans. Image Process. 27(11), 5585–5599 (2018)

Retrieval by Classification: Discriminative Binary Embedding for Sketch-Based Image Retrieval

Yufeng Shi[1], Xinge You[1,2]([✉]), Wenjie Wang[1], Feng Zheng[3], Qinmu Peng[1], and Shuo Wang[1]

[1] School of Electronic Information and Communications,
Huazhong University of Science and Technology, Wuhan, China
{yufengshi17,youxg}@hust.edu.cn
[2] Research Institute of Huazhong University of Science and Technology in Shenzhen, Shenzhen, China
[3] Department of Computer Science and Engineering,
Southern University of Science and Technology, Shenzhen, China

Abstract. Sketch-based image retrieval (SBIR) intends to use free-hand sketch drawings as query to retrieve correlated real-world images from database. Hashing based methods gradually become the mainstream approaches in SBIR with its low memory usage and high query speed. Existing hashing based methods are incapable of guiding hash codes to preserve inter-class relationship and improving object recognition ability of hash functions simultaneously, which limits the higher performance. Hence, we propose Discriminative Binary Embedding (DBE), a novel algorithm of considering inter-class relationship and object recognition ability in a joint manner by treating retrieval as classification. Specifically, we apply NLP methods to encode category labels as binary embedding and then build classifiers for images and sketches, so as to obtain hash codes of instances based on binary embedding of predicted labels. Experimental results on two benchmarks show that DBE outperforms several state-of-the-arts.

Keywords: Sketch-based image retrieval · Hashing · Cross modal

1 Introduction

Ubiquitous touch screens provide convenience for people to describe instances as free-hand sketches, which creates a new type of query entrance to retrieve images. Since sketches have lower hardware requirements than natural images and convey information more vividly than words, sketch-based image retrieval (SBIR) [7, 13,18,30] are more competitive compared with text-based image retrieval or content-based image retrieval, which attracts universal attention in computer vision and information retrieval community.

Y. Shi—Student Author.

© Springer Nature Switzerland AG 2019
Z. Lin et al. (Eds.): PRCV 2019, LNCS 11859, pp. 15–26, 2019.
https://doi.org/10.1007/978-3-030-31726-3_2

SBIR is a challenging problem due to the heterogeneity between free-hand sketches and real-world images. To remove heterogeneity, substantial efforts have been made [13,18,22,32]. As the request of large-scale data, hashing based methods, which intend to project data into a common hamming space, gradually become the mainstream approach in this area with their low memory usage and high query speed [11,19,27].

Among these methods, the first deep hashing method specialized in SBIR is Deep Sketch Hashing (DSH) [13]. DSH adopts edge structures extracted from real-world images (i.e., sketch-tokens), as bridges to mitigate the image-sketch geometric distortion. Benefiting from the rapid development of Generative Adversarial Networks (GAN) [9], it is feasible to transfer representation from one domain to another. Following this idea, Generative Domain-Migration Hashing (GDH) [32] employs cycleGAN [34] to generate synthetic natural images which are migrated from sketches to eliminate the sketch-image heterogeneity. Despite significant performance obtained by them, as shown in Fig. 1, they still can not get rid of heterogeneity completely. There exists discrepancy in the details not only between sketch-tokens and free-hand sketches, but also between synthetic images and real-world images.

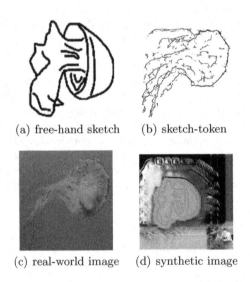

(a) free-hand sketch   (b) sketch-token

(c) real-world image   (d) synthetic image

Fig. 1. Sketch-tokens usually contain more details than free-hand sketches. Moreover, the synthetic images often ignore the rich details of real-world images.

Hence, the semantic-level bridge should be considered to connect sketches and images instead of instance-level bridges (e.g., sketch-tokens or synthetic natural images). Intuitively, the retrieval performance will be better if the various data from the same category have completely same binary codes, which regards category-labels as the bridge to cross the heterogeneity. Therefore, the discriminative hashing methods [14,26,29] are proposed. These methods transform category-labels as binary codes and build hash functions as the regression from instances to hash codes. Based on semantic-level bridge, these methods are robust to the instance-level variation.

However, the simple one-hot encoded category labels can not express the semantic distances among categories (e.g. in daily life, "tiger" and "zebra" appear together more frequently than "tiger" and "cake"), which makes most existing methods can not build hash codes to indicate inter-class relationship correctly. In addition, the neglect of object recognition during hash functions learning results in false hash codes mapping in the testing phase. Consequently, a discriminative hashing method that can make binary codes preserve inter-class relationship and improve object recognition ability of hash functions is demanded.

To overcome the problems discussed above, we propose Discriminative Binary Embedding (DBE) algorithm for SBIR to take into account inter-class relationship and object recognition ability in a joint manner by treating retrieval as classification, leading to discriminative binary embedding and hash functions with high object recognition ability. Specifically, the proposed DBE first applies NLP methods to encode category labels as binary embedding and then builds classifiers for images and sketches. At the end, hash codes of instances are binary embedding corresponding to predicted labels. Extensive experiments on two benchmark datasets demonstrate that the proposed DBE algorithm outperforms other baselines methods for SBIR.

The remainder of this paper is organized as follows. Section 2 introduces related work and Sect. 3 presents the proposed DBE. Experimental results are provided in Sect. 4. Finally, Sect. 5 concludes this paper.

2   Related Work

In view of instance representation type, existing methods can be divided into real-value representation methods and methods.

Real-value representation methods [1,7,20,22,33] usually aim to find a common subspace where sketches and images can be represented as real-value vectors. Early works [7,22] focus on designing representative features and base on them to measure similarity. To accelerate the retrieval speed, some works [1,33] introduce hierarchical database index structure to organize data. Nevertheless, high storage capacity of database structure still perplexes the practical applications of SBIR.

To tackle this problem, hashing based methods [13,24,32] which intend to project multisource data into a common hamming space emerge in SBIR. As the first deep hashing method specialized in SBIR, DSH extracts edge structures from images to remove heterogeneity. Afterwards GDH generates synthetic images based on sketches to cross the sketch-image gap. While SBIR is a specific form of cross-modal retrieval, the cross-modal hashing methods [5,12,15,31] can just be applied.

3   Discriminative Binary Embedding

In this section, we first present the notation and problem definition, and then bring in semantic binary embedding and retrieval by classification to preserve inter-class relationship and improve object recognition ability of hash functions.

3.1   Notation and Problem Definition

Scalars are denoted by lowercase letters (e.g., x). Matrices and vectors used in this paper are represented as boldface uppercase letters (e.g., $\mathbf{X}$) and boldface lowercase letters (e.g., $\mathbf{x}$), respectively.

Let $\boldsymbol{X}^1 = \left\{\boldsymbol{x}_i^1\right\}_{i=1}^{N_1}$ and $\boldsymbol{X}^2 = \left\{\boldsymbol{x}_j^2\right\}_{j=1}^{N_2}$ be images and sketches, where $\boldsymbol{x}_i^1 \in \boldsymbol{R}^{d_1}$, $\boldsymbol{x}_j^2 \in \boldsymbol{R}^{d_2}$. And, $\boldsymbol{Y} = \left\{y^k\right\}_{k=1}^{N_3}$ is their category labels. Given the code length c, the cross-modal hashing is to build specific hash functions $f^1\left(\boldsymbol{x}^1\right) : \boldsymbol{R}^{d_1} \rightarrow \{-1,1\}^c$ and $f^2\left(\boldsymbol{x}^2\right) : \boldsymbol{R}^{d_2} \rightarrow \{-1,1\}^c$ for images and sketches. Meanwhile, the Hamming distance $D\left(\boldsymbol{h}_i^1, \boldsymbol{h}_j^2\right)$ between hash codes $\boldsymbol{h}_i^1 = f^1\left(\boldsymbol{x}_i^1\right)$ and $\boldsymbol{h}_j^2 = f^2\left(\boldsymbol{x}_j^2\right)$ indicates the semantic correlation between $\boldsymbol{x}_i^1$ and $\boldsymbol{x}_j^2$.

3.2   Framework

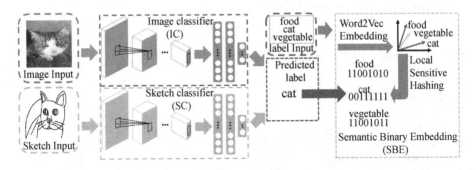

Fig. 2. Our proposed DBE algorithm for SBIR. First, SBE applies NLP methods to embed category labels into Hamming space. Then IC and SC predict labels of images and sketches. Finally, each instance is encoded based on binary embedding of labels.

Figure 2 illustrates the overall flow of our proposed DBE, which mainly consists of two parts: Semantic Binary Embedding (SBE) and specialized classifiers (e.g., IC and SC). For SBE, its mission is to encode category labels as c length hash code while preserve inter-class relationship. Specialized classifiers IC and SC, intend to classify instances accurately and preserve intra-class relationship. Moreover, because hash codes of instances are binary embedding corresponding to predicted labels, the trained-well classifiers improve object recognition ability of hash functions markedly.

Semantic Binary Embedding. The binary embedding of semantics (i.e. category labels) is primary in semantic hashing methods. Obviously, the distances between category labels are identical in semantic space. To reveal inter-class relationship, category labels are embedded as binary codes according to their frequency of co-occurrence in natural languages.

The first step of SBE is to translate the category labels (e.g. mushroom) into real-valued vectors in semantic space. The NLP toolbox Word2vec [17] trained on part of Google News dataset[1] (about 100 billion words) is used to accomplish it. With the Word2Vec model, each category label is projected into a 300-dim semantic space where the cosine distance can measure the frequency of co-occurrence in natural languages. So the real-valued vectors of labels are inter-class relationship preserving.

Once labels are vectorized, the next step is to convert the cosine distance relationship in the 300-dim semantic space into the Hamming distance relationship in c-dim Hamming space. Proved by [2], Local Sensitive Hashing (LSH) [21] is competent at this job. Therefore, the hash function of n-th bit is defined as following:

$$h_n\left(\boldsymbol{u}\right) = \begin{cases} 1, & \boldsymbol{u} \cdot \boldsymbol{r}^T \geq 0 \\ -1, & \boldsymbol{u} \cdot \boldsymbol{r}^T < 0 \end{cases}, \tag{1}$$

where $\boldsymbol{u}$ is the real-valued vector of label in semantic space and $\boldsymbol{r}$ is a vector sampled randomly from the Gaussian distribution whose dimension is the same as $\boldsymbol{u}$. The c-bit hash function consists of two parts: randomly sample c vectors and operate every bit following Eq. (1). After its processing of the real-valued vectors of category labels, category labels are embedded as binary codes.

Retrieval by Classification. Once the binary embedding of semantics is done, building hash functions that project instances into hash codes corresponding to their semantics ensues. Similarly, classification devotes to fitting the corresponding relationship between instances and semantics (i.e. category labels). If semantics in classification is embedded as binary codes, the fitting relationship in classification can be directly treated as hash function in retrieval. With the help of classification, we build hash functions in retrieval task. Specifically, we first classify instances to predict their semantics and then obtain hash codes by mapping semantics to their binary codes. In this case, object recognition ability of hash functions is improved.

For images and sketches, two modified CNN-F [3] are implemented as classifiers IC and SC respectively. To accommodate different datasets, the last fully-connected layer in origin CNN-F is changed to N_3-node fully-connected layer with no activation functions. To classify instances, the softmax-loss is applied, which can be formulated as:

$$\min_{\theta_m} L^m = -\sum_{i=1}^{N_m} \log\left(\frac{\exp\left(f_{y_i}\left(\theta_m; \boldsymbol{x}_i^m\right)\right)}{\Sigma_k \exp\left(f_{y_k}\left(\theta_m; \boldsymbol{x}_i^m\right)\right)}\right), \tag{2}$$

---

[1] https://code.google.com/archive/p/word2vec/.

where $m = 1, 2$ indicates images or sketches, and $f_{y_i}(\theta_m; \boldsymbol{x}_i^m)$ is the output of classifier corresponding to category label y_i. In the operating process, category labels $\left\{ y^k \right\}_{k=1}^{N_3}$ are expressed as one-hot vectors for network training. The Eq. (2) is derivable, so Back-propagation algorithm (BP) with mini-batch stochastic gradient descent (mini-batch SGD) method is applied to update it. When IC and SC are well-trained, instances are labeled according to the maximum of predicted vectors. For classification task where semantics are expressed as multi-labels, the non-redundant multi-label labels can be transformed into multi-class labels and use the aforementioned multi-class classification method to handle. As a result, the semantics of instances are acquired by classification.

Then, as illustrated in Fig. 1, the last part of hash functions is just to map semantics of instances to their binary embedding so as to obtain hash codes. Concurrently, the convenient mapping also avoids the approximation loss for binarization processing which limits the higher retrieval performance in deep hashing methods.

4   Experiments

Several experiments are conducted to evaluate our DBE on two benchmark datasets. The retrieval performance are measured by Hamming ranking and hash lookup. The effect of each component is also explored in our method using an ablation study and the discriminability of binary embedding is evaluated based on t-SNE visualization [16].

4.1   Implementation Details

We implement our method with Tensorflow and run the algorithm in a server with one NVIDIA 1080ti GPU. The CNN-F pretrained on ImageNet [4] are used to initialize the first seven layers of classifiers IC and SC. The other weights of networks are randomly initialized. We apply mini-batch SGD with a learning rate within $10^{-2} \sim 10^{-3}$ and set batch size as 128 to learn θ_1 and θ_2.

4.2   Datasets

Tu-Berlin Extension [13] is a dataset extended from Tu-Berlin [6]. It contains 20,000 free-hand sketches and 204,489 real-world images across 250 categories. **Sketchy** [23] includes 75,471 free-hand sketches of 12,500 objects (images) from 125 categories. Another 60,502 real-world images from ImageNet collected by [13] are used to construct the real-world image set which amounts to 73,002 images.

4.3   Evaluation Protocol and Baselines

The dataset splitting strategy is consistent with DSH [13] and GDH [32]. For **Tu-Berlin Extension**, 10 free-hand sketches are randomly selected from every category as query set and the remaining 17,500 free-hand sketches are used for training. For **Sketchy**, the query set consists of 6250 free-hand sketches (50 sketches per category) and the remaining 69,221 free-hand sketches serve as sketch training set. For both datasets, all real-world images are used as retrieval set and image training set. Because shallow-structure-based baselines require pairwise data with corresponding labels as input, similar to DSH [13] and GDH [32], we randomly select non-redundant 17,500 and 30,000 sketch-image pairs for **Tu-Berlin Extension** and **Sketchy** as their training set, respectively.

Evaluation Metrics. To evaluate retrieval performance, Hamming ranking and hash lookup are both utilized as protocols. Mean Average Precision (MAP) and TopN-precision curves are adopted to measure the Hamming ranking which sorts the data points in retrieval set based on their Hamming distance to the given query point. The hash lookup intends to return retrieval data in radius of a certain Hamming distance to the given query point. Precision-recall curve and the precision of Hamming distance with radius 2 (HD2) are used to evaluate its accuracy.

Baselines. Several state-of-the-art cross-modal hashing methods are selected for comparison with our DBE, including: Collective Matrix Factorization Hashing (CMFH) [5], Semantic Correlation Maximization (SCM) [31], Semantic Topic Multimodal Hashing (STMH) [25], Semantics-Preserving Hashing (SePH) [12], Composite Correlation Quantization (CCQ) [15], Deep Sketch Hashing (DSH) [13], Generative Domain-Migration Hashing (GDH) [32]. Meanwhile, the other three cross-view feature embedding methods including Canonical Correlation Analysis (CCA) [10], Learning Coupled Feature Spaces (LCFS) [28] and Partial Least-squares Regression (PLSR) [8] are also used for comparison with our DBE. To make fair comparisons with shallow-structure-based baselines, 4096-dimensional features for sketches and images are extracted by the well-trained SC and IC networks for Tu-Berlin Extension and Sketchy, separately.

4.4 Results and Discussions

Results For Hamming ranking, the MAP and TopN-precision curves of our DBE and other baselines are presented in Table 1 and Fig. 3, which illustrate that our DBE outperforms others with significant margin. From Table 1, compared with the state-of-the-art method GDH, our DBE achieves absolute increase of **7.23%** and **6.03%** on **Tu-Berlin Extension** and **Sketchy**. Meanwhile, the TopN-precision curves of DBE in Fig. 3 embody its high quality of Hamming ranking, which also demonstrate better performance for DBE across different datasets.

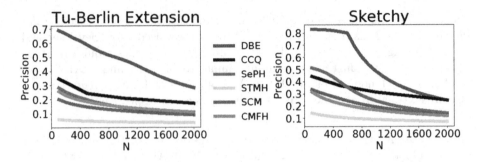

Fig. 3. TopN-precision curves for DBE and other five baselines with 32 bits.

Table 1. Mean average precision (MAP) comparison on Tu-Berlin extension and sketchy datasets. The results of methods marked by (*) are reported from the reference papers, while the others are obtained by running the released code.

Method		TU-Berlin Extension			Sketchy		
		32 bits	64 bits	128 bits	32 bits	64 bits	128 bits
Cross-modality hashing methods (binary codes)	CMFH [5]	0.123	0.171	0.210	0.176	0.229	0.280
	SCM [31]	0.119	0.208	0.300	0.227	0.361	0.415
	STMH [25]	0.031	0.058	0.096	0.081	0.140	0.216
	SePH [12]	0.155	0.234	0.307	0.362	0.478	0.544
	CCQ [15]	0.142	0.189	0.225	0.274	0.337	0.373
	DSH* [13]	0.358	0.521	0.570	0.653	0.711	0.783
	GDH* [32]	0.563	0.690	0.651	0.724	0.811	0.784
Cross-view feature learning methods (real-valued vectors)	CCA [10]	0.114	0.149	0.171	0.321	0.449	0.498
	LCFS [28]	0.078	0.159	0.299	0.190	0.379	0.705
	PLSR [8]	0.163 (4096d)			0.164 (4096d)		
Our DBE		**0.703**	**0.705**	**0.713**	**0.834**	**0.831**	**0.835**

The precision-recall curves in Fig. 4 and the precision of HD2 in Fig. 5 reflect the performance of our DBE and other baselines in hash lookup. Since the corresponding curves of our DBE locate above others in Figs. 4 and 5, our DBE achieves superior results on both datasets.

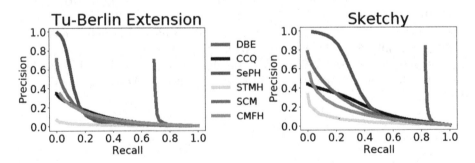

Fig. 4. Precision-recall curves for DBE and other five baselines with 32 bits.

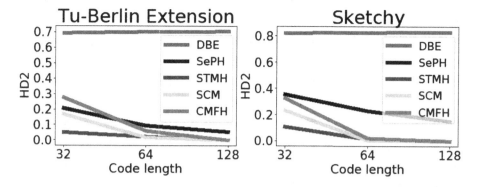

Fig. 5. HD2 precision for DBE and other four baselines with 32 bits.

Discussion. Two experiments including ablation study and visualization are used to further analyze the efficiency of our DBE.

In ablation study, experiments are conducted to evaluate the influence of problems solved by our DBE, specifically including inter-class relationship and object recognition ability. The curve marked as **label** in Fig. 6 represents the solution that instances are directly encoded as their predicted labels (e.g. 125-dim predicted labels in Sketchy). And the origin DBE is marked as **hash code** curve in Fig. 6. From Fig. 6, the mAPs of **label** on two datasets across three bits are higher than those of the state-of-the-art method GDH, which accounts for the significance of object recognition ability. The inter-class relationship also plays an vital role to further improve retrieval performance, since it makes **hash code** curves locate above **label** curves in Fig. 6.

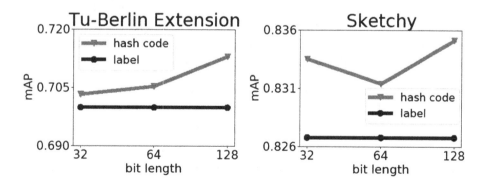

Fig. 6. The influence of inter-class relationship and object recognition ability.

To study the discriminability of our DBE, as shown in Fig. 7, t-SNE projection is applied to visualize the binary embedding of ten categories in retrieval set from the two datasets. The binary embedding of instances from the same category gathers together while different clusters are far away from each other in Fig. 7. Hence, the binary embedding of our DBE are discriminative.

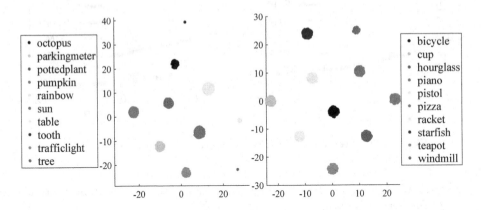

Fig. 7. The t-SNE visualizations of hash codes in ten categories from Tu-Berlin Extension and Sketchy retrieval set, respectively. Better view in color version. (Color figure online)

5   Conclusion

This paper introduced Discriminative Binary Embedding (DBE), a supervised deep model for category-level Sketch-Based Image Retrieval (SBIR), composed of Semantic Binary Embedding (SBE) and specialized classifiers (e.g., IC and SC). To guide hash codes to preserve inter-class relationship and improve the recognition ability of hash functions simultaneously, we treated retrieval as classification. Specifically, the SBE encoded category labels as hash codes while preserved inter-class relationship. Specialized classifiers IC and SC, intended to classify instances accurately to improve the recognition ability of hash functions and also preserved intra-class relationship. Experimental results on two benchmark datasets demonstrated the superiority of DBE compared with the state-of-the-art methods.

Acknowledgments. This work was supported partially by the Key Science and Technology of Shenzhen (JCYJ20180305180637611), the Shenzhen Research Council (JCYJ20180305180804836 and JSGG20180507182030600), the Key Science and Technology Innovation Program of Hubei Province (2017AAA017), the Natural Science Foundation of Hubei Province (2018CFB691), the Special Projects for Technology Innovation of Hubei Province (2018ACA135), the National Natural Science Foundation of China (61571205 and 61772220) and the key research and development program of China (2016YFE0121200).

References

1. Cao, Y., Wang, H., Wang, C., Li, Z., Zhang, L., Zhang, L.: MindFinder: interactive sketch-based image search on millions of images. In: Proceedings of the 18th ACM International Conference on Multimedia, pp. 1605–1608. ACM (2010)
2. Charikar, M.S.: Similarity estimation techniques from rounding algorithms. In: Proceedings of the Thiry-Fourth Annual ACM Symposium on Theory of Computing, pp. 380–388. ACM (2002)
3. Chatfield, K., Simonyan, K., Vedaldi, A., Zisserman, A.: Return of the devil in the details: delving deep into convolutional nets. arXiv preprint arXiv:1405.3531 (2014)
4. Deng, J., Dong, W., Socher, R., Li, L.J., Li, K., Fei-Fei, L.: ImageNet: a large-scale hierarchical image database. In: 2009 IEEE Conference on Computer Vision and Pattern Recognition, pp. 248–255. IEEE (2009)
5. Ding, G., Guo, Y., Zhou, J.: Collective matrix factorization hashing for multimodal data. In: Proceedings of the IEEE Conference on Computer Vision and Pattern Recognition, pp. 2075–2082 (2014)
6. Eitz, M., Hays, J., Alexa, M.: How do humans sketch objects? ACM Trans. Graph. **31**(4), 44–1 (2012)
7. Eitz, M., Hildebrand, K., Boubekeur, T., Alexa, M.: An evaluation of descriptors for large-scale image retrieval from sketched feature lines. Comput. Graph. **34**(5), 482–498 (2010)
8. Geladi, P., Kowalski, B.R.: Partial least-squares regression: a tutorial. Anal. Chim. Acta **185**, 1–17 (1986)
9. Goodfellow, I., et al.: Generative adversarial nets. In: Advances in Neural Information Processing Systems, pp. 2672–2680 (2014)
10. Hardoon, D.R., Szedmak, S., Shawe-Taylor, J.: Canonical correlation analysis: an overview with application to learning methods. Neural Comput. **16**(12), 2639–2664 (2004)
11. Jiang, Q.Y., Li, W.J.: Asymmetric deep supervised hashing. In: Thirty-Second AAAI Conference on Artificial Intelligence (2018)
12. Lin, Z., Ding, G., Hu, M., Wang, J.: Semantics-preserving hashing for cross-view retrieval. In: Proceedings of the IEEE Conference on Computer Vision and Pattern Recognition, pp. 3864–3872 (2015)
13. Liu, L., Shen, F., Shen, Y., Liu, X., Shao, L.: Deep sketch hashing: fast free-hand sketch-based image retrieval. In: Proceedings of the IEEE Conference on Computer Vision and Pattern Recognition, pp. 2862–2871 (2017)
14. Liu, L., Qi, H.: Discriminative cross-view binary representation learning. In: 2018 IEEE Winter Conference on Applications of Computer Vision (WACV), pp. 1736–1744. IEEE (2018)
15. Long, M., Cao, Y., Wang, J., Yu, P.S.: Composite correlation quantization for efficient multimodal retrieval. In: Proceedings of the 39th International ACM SIGIR Conference on Research and Development in Information Retrieval, pp. 579–588. ACM (2016)
16. Maaten, L.V.D., Hinton, G.: Visualizing data using t-SNE. J. Mach. Learn. Res. **9**(Nov), 2579–2605 (2008)
17. Mikolov, T., Sutskever, I., Chen, K., Corrado, G.S., Dean, J.: Distributed representations of words and phrases and their compositionality. In: Advances in Neural Information Processing Systems, pp. 3111–3119 (2013)

18. Parui, S., Mittal, A.: Similarity-invariant sketch-based image retrieval in large databases. In: Fleet, D., Pajdla, T., Schiele, B., Tuytelaars, T. (eds.) ECCV 2014. LNCS, vol. 8694, pp. 398–414. Springer, Cham (2014). https://doi.org/10.1007/978-3-319-10599-4_26

19. Peng, Y., Huang, X., Zhao, Y.: An overview of cross-media retrieval: concepts, methodologies, benchmarks, and challenges. IEEE Trans. Circuits Syst. Video Technol. **28**(9), 2372–2385 (2018)

20. Qi, Y., Song, Y.Z., Zhang, H., Liu, J.: Sketch-based image retrieval via Siamese convolutional neural network. In: 2016 IEEE International Conference on Image Processing (ICIP), pp. 2460–2464. IEEE (2016)

21. Ravichandran, D., Pantel, P., Hovy, E.: Randomized algorithms and NLP: using locality sensitive hash functions for high speed noun clustering. In: Proceedings of the 43rd Annual Meeting of the Association for Computational Linguistics (ACL 2005), pp. 622–629 (2005)

22. Saavedra, J.M., Barrios, J.M., Orand, S.: Sketch based image retrieval using learned keyshapes (LKS). In: BMVC, vol. 1, p. 7 (2015)

23. Sangkloy, P., Burnell, N., Ham, C., Hays, J.: The sketchy database: learning to retrieve badly drawn bunnies. ACM Trans. Graph. (TOG) **35**(4), 119 (2016)

24. Tseng, K.Y., Lin, Y.L., Chen, Y.H., Hsu, W.H.: Sketch-based image retrieval on mobile devices using compact hash bits. In: Proceedings of the 20th ACM International Conference on Multimedia, pp. 913–916. ACM (2012)

25. Wang, D., Gao, X., Wang, X., He, L.: Semantic topic multimodal hashing for cross-media retrieval. In: Twenty-Fourth International Joint Conference on Artificial Intelligence (2015)

26. Wang, D., Gao, X., Wang, X., He, L., Yuan, B.: Multimodal discriminative binary embedding for large-scale cross-modal retrieval. IEEE Trans. Image Process. **25**(10), 4540–4554 (2016)

27. Wang, J., Zhang, T., Sebe, N., Shen, H.T., et al.: A survey on learning to hash. IEEE Trans. Pattern Anal. Mach. Intell. **40**(4), 769–790 (2018)

28. Wang, K., He, R., Wang, W., Wang, L., Tan, T.: Learning coupled feature spaces for cross-modal matching. In: Proceedings of the IEEE International Conference on Computer Vision, pp. 2088–2095 (2013)

29. Xu, X., Shen, F., Yang, Y., Shen, H.T.: Discriminant cross-modal hashing. In: Proceedings of the 2016 ACM on International Conference on Multimedia Retrieval, pp. 305–308. ACM (2016)

30. Yu, Q., Liu, F., Song, Y.Z., Xiang, T., Hospedales, T.M., Loy, C.C.: Sketch me that shoe. In: Proceedings of the IEEE Conference on Computer Vision and Pattern Recognition, pp. 799–807 (2016)

31. Zhang, D., Li, W.J.: Large-scale supervised multimodal hashing with semantic correlation maximization. In: Twenty-Eighth AAAI Conference on Artificial Intelligence (2014)

32. Zhang, J., et al.: Generative domain-migration hashing for sketch-to-image retrieval. In: Proceedings of the European Conference on Computer Vision (ECCV), pp. 297–314 (2018)

33. Zhou, R., Chen, L., Zhang, L.: Sketch-based image retrieval on a large scale database. In: Proceedings of the 20th ACM International Conference on Multimedia, pp. 973–976. ACM (2012)

34. Zhu, J.Y., Park, T., Isola, P., Efros, A.A.: Unpaired image-to-image translation using cycle-consistent adversarial networks. In: Proceedings of the IEEE International Conference on Computer Vision, pp. 2223–2232 (2017)

Robust Subspace Segmentation via Sparse Relation Representation

Lai Wei[1(✉)] 🆔 and Hao Liu[2]

[1] Shanghai Maritime University,
Haigang Avenue 1550, Shanghai, People's Republic of China
`weilai@shmtu.edu.cn`
[2] Wuhan Digit Engineering Institute,
Canglong North Road 709, Wuhan, Hubei, People's Republic of China
`sjupiter83@hotmail.com`

Abstract. Spectral clustering based algorithms are powerful tools for solving subspace segmentation problems. The existing spectral clustering based subspace segmentation algorithms use original data matrices to produce the affinity graphs. In real applications, data samples are usually corrupted by different kinds of noise, hence the obtained affinity graphs may not reveal the intrinsic subspace structures of data sets. In this paper, we present the conception of relation representation, which means a point's neighborhood relation could be represented by the rest points' neighborhood relations. Based on this conception, we propose a kind of sparse relation representation (SRR) for subspace segmentation. The experimental results obtained on several benchmark databases show that SRR outperforms some existing related methods.

Keywords: Subspace segmentation · Low-rank representation · Sparse relation

1 Introduction

Spectral clustering based algorithms have been proven to be powerful tools for solving subspace segmentation problems such as motion segmentation [1,2], face clustering [3,4] and so on. Among the existing spectral clustering based methods, sparse subspace clustering (SSC) [5] and low-rank representation (LRR) [6] are the two most representative ones. The two algorithms divide the subspace segmentation procedure into three steps: firstly, they compute a reconstructive coefficient matrix for a data set, then construct an affinity graph by using the obtained coefficient matrix, finally produce the segmentation result by means of a kind of spectral clustering (e.g. Normalize cut (N-cut) [7]). Because of the excellent performances showed by SSC and LRR, a lot of subsequent researches have been proposed.

By analyzing SSC and LRR related works, we could find that most of them hope to enhance the abilities of SSC and LRR for revealing subspace structures

© Springer Nature Switzerland AG 2019
Z. Lin et al. (Eds.): PRCV 2019, LNCS 11859, pp. 27–37, 2019.
https://doi.org/10.1007/978-3-030-31726-3_3

of data sets by adding additional constraints on the reconstructive coefficient matrices. For example, Li et al. devised an adaptive weighted sparse constraint for a reconstructive coefficient matrix obtained by SSC and proposed a structured SSC method (SSSC) [8]. Chen et al. developed a within-class grouping constraint for a reconstructive coefficient matrix and introduced it into SSSC [9]. Zhuang et al. claimed that SSC tends to discover the local structure of a data set and LRR could discover its global structure. Hence, they combined SSC and LRR together and proposed a non-negative low-rank and sparse representation method (NNLRSR) [10]. Tang et al. generalized NNLRSR algorithm and designed a structured-constrained LRR method (SCLRR) [11]. Lu et al. presented a graph-regularized low-rank representation (GLRR) [12] which could strength the group effect of a coefficient matrix obtained by LRR.

According to the corresponding references, the above mentioned algorithms have shown to be superior to the classical SSC and LRR. However, we could find these algorithms follow the same methodology of SSC and LRR as we mentioned in the first paragraph.

In this paper, we reconsider the data representation problem and present the concept and technique of *relation representation*. Based on these new propositions, we propose a new algorithm, termed sparse relation representation (SRR), for subspace segmentation. We claim that SRR could find both the local and global structures of data sets. The experimental results obtained on different subspace segmentation tasks illustrate that SRR dominates the existing SSC and LRR related algorithms.

The rest of the paper is organized as follows: we briefly review SSC and LRR algorithms in Sect. 2. In Sect. 3, we introduce the idea of relation representation and present sparse relation representation (SRR) method. The optimization algorithm for solving SRR problem is described in Sect. 4. Experiments on benchmark data sets are conducted in Sect. 5. Section 6 gives the conclusions.

2   Preliminary

For a data set $\mathbf{X} \in \mathcal{R}^{d \times n}$, both SSC and LRR hope to find a reconstruction matrix $\mathbf{C} \in \mathcal{R}^{n \times n}$ which satisfies $\mathbf{X} = \mathbf{XC} + \mathbf{E}$. Here, $\mathbf{E} \in \mathcal{R}^{d \times n}$ indicates the reconstruction residual matrix. With different techniques, SSC expects $\mathbf{C}$ to be a sparse matrix and the l_1 norm of $\mathbf{E}$ to be minimal, while LRR tends to minimize the rank of $\mathbf{C}$ and the $l_{2,1}$ norm of $\mathbf{E}$ simultaneously. Because of the different constraints imposed on the coefficient matrix, SSC and LRR tends to reveal the local and global structures of a data set respectively. The objective function of SSC and LRR could be precisely expressed as the following Eqs. 1 and 2 respectively:

$$\min \quad \|\mathbf{C}\|_1 + \lambda \|\mathbf{E}\|_1, \\ s.t. \ \mathbf{X} = \mathbf{XC} + \mathbf{E}, [\mathbf{C}]_{ii} = 0, i = 1, 2, \cdots, n, \tag{1}$$

$$\min \|\mathbf{C}\|_* + \lambda \|\mathbf{E}\|_{2,1}, \\ s.t. \quad \mathbf{X} = \mathbf{XC} + \mathbf{E}, \tag{2}$$

where $[\mathbf{C}]_{ii}$ represents the (i,i)-th element of $\mathbf{C}$ and $\lambda > 0$ is a parameter which is used to balance the effects of the two terms. The above two problems could be solved by using the alternating direction method (ADM) [13]. Once the reconstructive coefficient matrix $\mathbf{C}$ is gotten, an affinity matrix $\mathbf{W}$ satisfying $[\mathbf{W}]_{ij} = ([\mathbf{C}]_{ij} + [\mathbf{C}]_{ji})/2$ could be constructed. Then the final segmentation result could be produced by using N-cut.

3   Motivation

3.1   Relation Representation

From the above descriptions, we could find that SSC and LRR (actually all the related algorithms) use a data set itself to compute the reconstruction coefficient matrix. However, in real applications, data samples usually is corrupted by different kinds of noise, so the obtained coefficient matrix may not be able to reveal the subspace structure of a data set.

As we know, the relationships between an object and its neighbors could usually define the object itself. And two similar objects will often have similar neighbors with similar relationships (See Fig. 1). Based on these evidences, for a data set, we consider to use the relations between a data sample and its neighbors to represent the data sample firstly, then reconstruct the neighborhood relation of a data sample by using the neighborhood relations of other samples. Hence, the reconstruction coefficient vector corresponding to each data sample's neighborhood relation could be acquired. We call this strategy "relation representation".

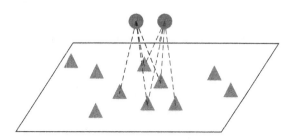

Fig. 1. Two similar objects (red points) and their neighbors (blue triangles) (Color figure online)

3.2   Sparse Relation Representation (SRR)

Now we discuss how to compute the relations between a data sample and its neighbors. Actually, many skills could handle this problem. For example, K nearest neighbors method (KNN) [14] can find each data sample's K neighbors, then linear reconstruction method [15] or Gaussian kernel [14] could be used to compute the similarities between the data sample and its K neighbors. However, the neighborhood scale K in KNN is usually difficult to choose for different data sets. And an improper K will degenerate the performance of corresponding algorithm sharply.

It has been proven that sparse representation (SR) technique [16] is capable of adaptively choosing the neighbors of a data sample and getting the corresponding reconstruction coefficient simultaneously. Therefore, for a data sample $\mathbf{x}_i \in \mathbf{X}$, its neighborhood relation vector $\mathbf{c}_i$ could be achieved by using the following SR problem:

$$\min_{\mathbf{c}_i} \|\mathbf{c}_i\|_1 + \alpha \|\mathbf{x}_i - \mathbf{X}\mathbf{c}_i\|_1. \tag{3}$$

We hope the reconstruction residual $\mathbf{x}_i - \mathbf{X}\mathbf{c}_i$ also to be sparse. Then for the whole data matrix $\mathbf{X}$, we could get its neighborhood relation matrix $\mathbf{C}$ by solving the following problem:

$$\begin{aligned} &\min_{\mathbf{C}} \|\mathbf{C}\|_1 + \alpha \|\mathbf{X} - \mathbf{X}\mathbf{C}\|_1, \\ &s.t. \quad [\mathbf{C}]_{ii} = 0, i = 1, 2, \cdots, n \end{aligned} \tag{4}$$

Similar to SSC, we could find that $\mathbf{C}$ will discover the local structure of the original data set.

Then according to the relation representation technique (described in Sect. 3.1), a data sample $\mathbf{x}_i$'s neighborhood relation $\mathbf{c}_i$ could be represented by the neighborhood relations of other data samples, namely $\mathbf{c}_i \simeq \mathbf{C}\mathbf{z}_i$, where $\mathbf{z}_i \in \mathcal{R}^n$ is the reconstruction coefficient. Consider the whole data set, we could obtain the following problem:

$$\min_{\mathbf{Z}} \|\mathbf{Z}\|_* + \beta \|\mathbf{C} - \mathbf{C}\mathbf{Z}\|_F^2 \tag{5}$$

where $\mathbf{Z} = [\mathbf{z}_1, \mathbf{z}_2, \cdots, \mathbf{z}_n]$ is the reconstruction coefficient matrix to the neighborhood relation matrix $\mathbf{C}$. We here use the nuclear norm minimization constraint to help $\mathbf{Z}$ to discover the global structure of $\mathbf{C}$. Moreover, Because $\mathbf{C}$ is a good representation of original data matrix $\mathbf{X}$, we aim to minimize the Frobenius norm of the reconstruction error. Finally, we combine Eqs. 4 and 5 together and let $\mathbf{E}_1 = \mathbf{X} - \mathbf{X}\mathbf{C}, \mathbf{E}_2 = \mathbf{C} - \mathbf{C}\mathbf{Z}$, then the sparse relation representation problem (SRR) could be defined as follows:

$$\begin{aligned} &\min_{\mathbf{C}, \mathbf{Z}, \mathbf{E}_1, \mathbf{E}_2} \|\mathbf{C}\|_1 + \|\mathbf{Z}\|_* + \alpha \|\mathbf{E}_1\|_1 + \beta \|\mathbf{E}_2\|_F^2, \\ &s.t. \quad \mathbf{E}_1 = \mathbf{X} - \mathbf{X}\mathbf{C}, \\ &\qquad \mathbf{E}_2 = \mathbf{C} - \mathbf{C}\mathbf{Z}, \\ &\qquad [\mathbf{C}]_{ii} = 0, i = 1, 2, \cdots, n. \end{aligned} \tag{6}$$

For a data set $\mathbf{X}$, because $\mathbf{C}$ characterizes the local structure of $\mathbf{X}$ and $\mathbf{Z}$ discovers the global structure of the neighborhood relation matrix $\mathbf{C}$, $\mathbf{Z}$ actually could reveal both the global and local structure of a data set.

4 Optimization and Analyses

4.1 Optimization

For solving Problem 6, we firstly covert it into the following equivalent problem:

$$
\begin{aligned}
\min_{\mathbf{C},\mathbf{Z},\mathbf{M},\mathbf{J},\mathbf{E}_1,\mathbf{E}_2} & \ \|\mathbf{M}\|_1 + \|\mathbf{J}\|_* + \alpha\|\mathbf{E}_1\|_1 + \beta\|\mathbf{E}_2\|_F^2, \\
s.t. \quad & \mathbf{E}_1 = \mathbf{X} - \mathbf{XC}, \\
& \mathbf{C} = \mathbf{M}, [\mathbf{M}]_{ii} = 0, i = 1, 2, \cdots, n, \\
& \mathbf{E}_2 = \mathbf{C} - \mathbf{CZ}, \\
& \mathbf{Z} = \mathbf{J}.
\end{aligned}
\tag{7}
$$

The above could be solved by using ADM method [13]. The augmented Lagrangian function of Eq. 7 can be described as follows:

$$
\begin{aligned}
\mathcal{L} =\ & \|\mathbf{M}\|_1 + \|\mathbf{J}\|_* + \alpha\|\mathbf{E}_1\|_1 + \beta\|\mathbf{E}_2\|_F^2 + \langle \mathbf{Y}_1, \mathbf{X} - \mathbf{XC} - \mathbf{E}_1\rangle + \langle \mathbf{Y}_2, \mathbf{C} - \mathbf{M}\rangle \\
& + \langle \mathbf{Y}_3, \mathbf{C} - \mathbf{CZ} - \mathbf{E}_2\rangle + \langle \mathbf{Y}_4, \mathbf{Z} - \mathbf{J}\rangle + \tfrac{\mu}{2}\Big(\|\mathbf{X} - \mathbf{XC} - \mathbf{E}_1\|_F^2 + \|\mathbf{C} - \mathbf{M}\|_F^2 \\
& + \|\mathbf{C} - \mathbf{CZ} - \mathbf{E}_2\|_F^2 + \|\mathbf{Z} - \mathbf{J}\|_F^2 \Big),
\end{aligned}
\tag{8}
$$

where $\mathbf{Y}_1, \mathbf{Y}_2, \mathbf{Y}_3$ and $\mathbf{Y}_4$ are four Lagrange multipliers, $\mu > 0$ is a parameter. Then by minimizing $\mathcal{L}$, the variables $\mathbf{C}, \mathbf{Z}, \mathbf{M}, \mathbf{J}, \mathbf{E}_1, \mathbf{E}_2$ could be optimized alternately. The detailed updating process for each variables presented as follows:

1. **Update M with fixed other variables.** By collecting the relevant terms of $\mathbf{M}$ in Eq. 8, we have:

$$
\begin{aligned}
& \min_{\mathbf{M}} \|\mathbf{M}\|_1 + \langle \mathbf{Y}_2, \mathbf{C} - \mathbf{M}\rangle + \mu/2\|\mathbf{C} - \mathbf{M}\|_F^2 \\
& = \min_{\mathbf{M}} \|\mathbf{M}\|_1 + \mu/2\|\mathbf{C} - \mathbf{M} + \mathbf{Y}_2/\mu\|_F^2,
\end{aligned}
\tag{9}
$$

then the solution to Eq. 9 could be obtained as

$$
[\mathbf{M}^{opt}]_{ij} = \begin{cases} \max(0, [\mathbf{C} + \mathbf{Y}_2/\mu]_{ij} - 1/\mu) + \min(0, [\mathbf{C} + \mathbf{Y}_2/\mu]_{ij} + 1/\mu), & i \neq j; \\ 0, & i = j. \end{cases}
\tag{10}
$$

2. **Update C with fixed other variables.** By picking the relevant terms of $\mathbf{C}$ in Eq. 8, we have:

$$
\begin{aligned}
& \min_{\mathbf{C}} \langle \mathbf{Y}_1, \mathbf{X} - \mathbf{XC} - \mathbf{E}_1\rangle + \langle \mathbf{Y}_2, \mathbf{C} - \mathbf{M}\rangle + \langle \mathbf{Y}_3, \mathbf{C} - \mathbf{CZ} - \mathbf{E}_2\rangle \\
& + \tfrac{\mu}{2}\Big(\|\mathbf{X} - \mathbf{XC} - \mathbf{E}_1\|_F^2 + \|\mathbf{C} - \mathbf{M}\|_F^2 + \|\mathbf{C} - \mathbf{CZ} - \mathbf{E}_2\|_F^2 \Big) \\
& = \min_{\mathbf{C}} \|\mathbf{X} - \mathbf{XC} - \mathbf{E}_1 + \mathbf{Y}_1/\mu\|_F^2 + \|\mathbf{C} - \mathbf{M} + \mathbf{Y}_2/\mu\|_F^2 \\
& + \|\mathbf{C} - \mathbf{CZ} - \mathbf{E}_2 + \mathbf{Y}_3/\mu\|_F^2
\end{aligned}
\tag{11}
$$

We take the derivation of Eq. 11 w.r.t. $\mathbf{C}$ and set it to $\mathbf{0}$, the following equation holds:

$$
\begin{aligned}
& \big(\mathbf{X}^t\mathbf{X} + \mathbf{I}_n\big)\mathbf{C}^{opt} + \mathbf{C}^{opt}\big(\mathbf{I}_n - \mathbf{Z}\big)\big(\mathbf{I}_n - \mathbf{Z}^t\big) - \mathbf{X}^t\big(\mathbf{X} - \mathbf{E}_1 + \mathbf{Y}_1/\mu\big) \\
& -\mathbf{M} + \mathbf{Y}_2/\mu - \big(\mathbf{E}_2 - \mathbf{Y}_3/\mu\big)\big(\mathbf{I}_n - \mathbf{Z}^t\big) = 0,
\end{aligned}
\tag{12}
$$

where $\mathbf{I}_n$ is an $n \times n$ identity matrix and $\mathbf{X}^t$ and $\mathbf{Z}^t$ are the transposes of $\mathbf{X}$ and $\mathbf{Z}$ respectively. Equation 12 is a Sylvester equation w.r.t. $\mathbf{C}^{opt}$, so it can be solved by the Matlab function lyap().

3. **Update J with fixed other variables.** By abandoning the irrelevant terms of $\mathbf{J}$, minimizing Eq. 8 becomes to the following problem:

$$\begin{aligned}
\min_{\mathbf{J}} \|\mathbf{J}\|_* + \langle \mathbf{Y}_4, \mathbf{Z} - \mathbf{J} \rangle + \mu/2 \|\mathbf{Z} - \mathbf{J}\|_F^2 \\
= \min_{\mathbf{J}} \|\mathbf{J}\|_* + \mu/2 \|\mathbf{Z} - \mathbf{J} + \mathbf{Y}_4/\mu\|_F^2.
\end{aligned} \tag{13}$$

Then the optimal solution to Eq. 13, $\mathbf{J}^{opt} = \mathbf{U}\Theta_{1/\mu}(\mathbf{S})\mathbf{V}$, where $\mathbf{USV}$ is the SVD of matrix $\mathbf{Z} + \mathbf{Y}_4/\mu$ and Θ is a singular value thresholding operator [17].

4. **Update Z with fixed other variables.** By dropping the irrelevant terms w.r.t $\mathbf{Z}$ in Eq. 8, we have:

$$\begin{aligned}
\min_{\mathbf{Z}} \langle \mathbf{Y}_3, \mathbf{C} - \mathbf{CZ} - \mathbf{E}_2 \rangle + \langle \mathbf{Y}_4, \mathbf{Z} - \mathbf{J} \rangle + \mu/2 \Big(\|\mathbf{C} - \mathbf{CZ} - \mathbf{E}_2\|_F^2 + \|\mathbf{Z} - \mathbf{J}\|_F^2 \Big) \\
= \min_{\mathbf{Z}} \|\mathbf{C} - \mathbf{CZ} - \mathbf{E}_2 + \mathbf{Y}_3/\mu\|_F^2 + \|\mathbf{Z} - \mathbf{J} + \mathbf{Y}_4/\mu\|_F^2
\end{aligned} \tag{14}$$

We also take the derivation of Eq. 14 w.r.t. $\mathbf{Z}$ and set it to $\mathbf{0}$, then the following equation holds:

$$\left(\mathbf{C}^t \mathbf{C} + \mathbf{I}_n\right)\mathbf{Z}^{opt} = \mathbf{C}^t\left(\mathbf{C} - \mathbf{E}_2 + \mathbf{Y}_3/\mu\right) + \mathbf{J} - \mathbf{Y}_4/\mu. \tag{15}$$

Hence, $\mathbf{Z}^{opt} = \left(\mathbf{C}^t \mathbf{C} + \mathbf{I}_n\right)^{-1}\left[\mathbf{C}^t\left(\mathbf{C} - \mathbf{E}_2 + \mathbf{Y}_3/\mu\right) + \mathbf{J} - \mathbf{Y}_4/\mu\right]$.

5. **Update $\mathbf{E}_1$ with fixed other variables.** By abandoning the irrelevant terms of $\mathbf{E}_1$, then minimizing Eq. 8 equals solving the following problem:

$$\begin{aligned}
\min_{\mathbf{E}_1} \alpha\|\mathbf{E}_1\|_1 + \langle \mathbf{Y}_1, \mathbf{X} - \mathbf{XC} - \mathbf{E}_1 \rangle + \mu/2\|\mathbf{X} - \mathbf{XC} - \mathbf{E}_1\|_F^2 \\
= \min_{\mathbf{E}_1} \alpha\|\mathbf{E}_1\|_1 + \mu/2\|\mathbf{X} - \mathbf{XC} - \mathbf{E}_1 + \mathbf{Y}_1/\mu\|_F^2.
\end{aligned} \tag{16}$$

Similar to computing the optimal value of $\mathbf{M}$, we could get $[\mathbf{E}_1^{opt}]_{ij} = \max(0, [\mathbf{X} - \mathbf{XC} + \mathbf{Y}_1/\mu]_{ij} - \alpha/\mu) + \min(0, [\mathbf{X} - \mathbf{XC} + \mathbf{Y}_1/\mu]_{ij} + \alpha/\mu)$.

6. **Update $\mathbf{E}_2$ with fixed other variables.** By gathering the relevant terms of $\mathbf{E}_2$ in Eq. 8, we have

$$\begin{aligned}
\min_{\mathbf{E}_2} \beta\|\mathbf{E}_2\|_F^2 + \langle \mathbf{Y}_3, \mathbf{C} - \mathbf{CZ} - \mathbf{E}_2 \rangle + \mu/2\|\mathbf{C} - \mathbf{CZ} - \mathbf{E}_2\|_F^2 \\
= \min_{\mathbf{E}_2} \beta\|\mathbf{E}_2\|_F^2 + \mu/2\|\mathbf{C} - \mathbf{CZ} - \mathbf{E}_2 + \mathbf{Y}_3/\mu\|_F^2.
\end{aligned} \tag{17}$$

We take the derivation of Eq. 17 w.r.t. $\mathbf{E}_2$ and set it to $\mathbf{0}$, then the following equation holds:

$$(2\beta + \mu)\mathbf{E}_2^{opt} = \mu\left(\mathbf{C} - \mathbf{CZ} + \mathbf{Y}_3/\mu\right). \tag{18}$$

Hence, $\mathbf{E}_2^{opt} = \mu/(2\beta + \mu)\left(\mathbf{C} - \mathbf{CZ} + \mathbf{Y}_3/\mu\right)$.

7. **Update parameters with fixed other variables.** The precise updating schemes for parameters existed in Eq. 8 are summarized as follows:

$$\begin{aligned}
\mathbf{Y}_1^{opt} &= \mathbf{Y}_1 + \mu(\mathbf{X} - \mathbf{XC} - \mathbf{E}_1), \\
\mathbf{Y}_2^{opt} &= \mathbf{Y}_2 + \mu(\mathbf{C} - \mathbf{M}), \\
\mathbf{Y}_3^{opt} &= \mathbf{Y}_3 + \mu(\mathbf{C} - \mathbf{CZ} - \mathbf{E}_2), \\
\mathbf{Y}_4^{opt} &= \mathbf{Y}_4 + \mu(\mathbf{Z} - \mathbf{J}), \\
\mu^{opt} &= \min(\mu_{max}, \rho\mu),
\end{aligned} \tag{19}$$

where μ_{max} and ρ are two given positive parameters.

4.2 Algorithm

The algorithmic procedure of SRR is summarized in Algorithm 1. For a data set, once the solutions to SRR are obtained, SRR defines an affinity graph $[\mathbf{W}]_{ij} = ([\mathbf{Z}]_{ij} + [\mathbf{Z}]_{ji})$, then N-cut is performed on the graph to get segmentation result.

Algorithm 1. Sparse relation representation (SRR)

Input:

Data set $\mathbf{X} = [\mathbf{x}_1, \mathbf{x}_2, \cdots, \mathbf{x}_n] \in \mathcal{R}^{D \times n}$, parameters α, β, the maximal number of iteration $Maxiter$;

Output:

The two coefficient matrices $\mathbf{Z}^{opt}, \mathbf{C}^{opt}$, and two noise term $\mathbf{E}_1^{opt}, \mathbf{E}_2^{opt}$;

1: Initialize the parameters, i.e., $\mathbf{Y}_1^0 = \mathbf{Y}_2^0 = \mathbf{Y}_3^0 = \mathbf{Y}_4^0 = 0, \mu^0 = 10^{-2}, \mu_{max} = 10^{30}, \rho = 1.1, \varepsilon = 10^{-8}, k = 0$ and $\mathbf{M}^0 = \mathbf{C}^0 = \mathbf{J} = \mathbf{Z}^0 = 0.$

2: **while** $\|\mathbf{X} - \mathbf{X}\mathbf{C}^k - \mathbf{E}_1^k\|_\infty > \varepsilon$, $\|\mathbf{C}^k - \mathbf{C}^k\mathbf{Z}^k - \mathbf{E}_2^k\|_\infty > \varepsilon$ and $k < Maxiter$ **do**

3:    Update $[\mathbf{M}]_{ij}^{k+1} = \max(0, [\mathbf{C}^k + \mathbf{Y}_2^k/\mu^k]_{ij} - 1/\mu^k) + \min(0, [\mathbf{C}^k + \mathbf{Y}_2^k/\mu^k]_{ij} + 1/\mu^k)$ when $i \neq j$, else $[\mathbf{M}]_{ij}^{k+1} = 0$;

4:    Update $\mathbf{C}^{k+1}$ by using Matlab function lyap() to solve $(\mathbf{X}^t\mathbf{X} + \mathbf{I}_n)\mathbf{C}^{k+1} + \mathbf{C}^{k+1}(\mathbf{I}_n - \mathbf{Z}^k)(\mathbf{I}_n - (\mathbf{Z}^k)^t) - \mathbf{X}^t(\mathbf{X} - \mathbf{E}_1^k + \mathbf{Y}_1^k/\mu^k) - \mathbf{M}^{k+1} + \mathbf{Y}_2^k/\mu - (\mathbf{E}_2^k - \mathbf{Y}_3^k/\mu)(\mathbf{I}_n - (\mathbf{Z}^k)^t) = 0$;

5:    Update $\mathbf{J}^{k+1} = \mathbf{U}\Theta_{1/\mu^k}(\mathbf{S})\mathbf{V}$, where $\mathbf{USV}$ is the SVD of matrix $\mathbf{Z}^k + \mathbf{Y}_4^k/\mu^k$ and Θ is a singular value thresholding operator ;

6:    Update $\mathbf{Z}^{k+1} = ((\mathbf{C}^k)^t\mathbf{C}^k + \mathbf{I}_n)^{-1}[(\mathbf{C}^k)^t(\mathbf{C}^k - \mathbf{E}_2^k + \mathbf{Y}_3^k/\mu^k) + \mathbf{J}^{k+1} - \mathbf{Y}_4^k/\mu^k]$;

7:    Update $[\mathbf{E}_1^{k+1}]_{ij} = \max(0, [\mathbf{X} - \mathbf{X}\mathbf{C}^{k+1} + \mathbf{Y}_1^k/\mu^k]_{ij} - \alpha/\mu^k) + \min(0, [\mathbf{X} - \mathbf{X}\mathbf{C}^{k+1} + \mathbf{Y}_1^k/\mu^k]_{ij} + \alpha/\mu^k)$;

8:    Update $\mathbf{E}_2^{k+1} = \mu^k/(2\beta + \mu^k)(\mathbf{C}^{k+1} - \mathbf{C}^{k+1}\mathbf{Z}^{k+1} + \mathbf{Y}_3^k/\mu^k)$

9:    Update $\mathbf{Y}_1^{k+1}, \mathbf{Y}_2^{k+1}, \mathbf{Y}_3^{k+1}, \mathbf{Y}_4^{k+1}, \mu^{k+1}$ by following the updating schedule in Eq. 19;

10:   set $k = k + 1$;

11: **end while**

12: **return** the coefficient matrix $\mathbf{Z}^{opt} = \mathbf{Z}^k, \mathbf{C}^{opt} = \mathbf{C}^k, \mathbf{E}_1^{opt} = \mathbf{E}_1^k, \mathbf{E}_2^{opt} = \mathbf{E}_2^k.$

4.3 Analyses

Now we discuss the complexity of Algorithm 1. Suppose the data matrix $\mathbf{X} \in \mathcal{R}^{D \times n}$, the complexity of Algorithm 1 is mainly determined by the updating of six variables: $\mathbf{M} \in \mathcal{R}^{n \times n}, \mathbf{C} \in \mathcal{R}^{n \times n}, \mathbf{J} \in \mathcal{R}^{n \times n}, \mathbf{Z} \in \mathcal{R}^{n \times n}, \mathbf{E}_1 \in \mathcal{R}^{D \times n}, \mathbf{E}_2 \in \mathcal{R}^{n \times n}$, We analyze the computational burden of updating these variables in each step.

First, updating $\mathbf{M}$ and $\mathbf{E}_1$ both need to compute each element of an $n \times n$ matrix, hence their computation burden is $O(n^2)$. Secondly, it takes $O(n^3)$ time to solve a Sylvester equations for updating $\mathbf{C}$. Third, by performing SVD, the update of $\mathbf{J}$ is $O(n^3)$. Fourthly, updating $\mathbf{Z}$ needs to compute the pseudo-inverse of an $n \times n$ matrix, whose complexity is $O(n^3)$. Fifthly, it can be easily to find that the computation burden for updating $\mathbf{E}_2$ is $O(n^2)$. Hence, we can see that the time complexity of Algorithm 1 in each iteration taken together is $O(n^3)$, which is same to that of LRR. Suppose the number of iterations is N, then the total complexity of Algorithm 1 should be $N \times O(n^3)$.

5   Experiments

In this section, subspace segmentation experiments will be performed to verify the effectiveness of SRR. Two types of data sets, such as Hopkins155 motion segmentation database [18], the extended Yale B [19] and ORL face images database [20] will be adopted. The related algorithms including SSC [5], LRR [6], SCLRR[1] [10] are chosen for comparisons.

5.1   Experiments on Hopkins 155 Database

Hopkins155 database [18] is a frequently used benchmark database to test the performances of subspace segmentation algorithms. It consists of 120 sequences of two motions and 35 sequences of three motions. Each sequence is a sole clustering task and there are 155 clustering tasks in total. The features of each sequence were extracted and tracked along with the motion in all frames, and errors were manually removed for each sequence. So it could be regarded that this database only contains slight corruptions. In our experiments, we projected the data to be 12-dimensional by using principal component analysis (PCA) [14]. Figure 2 presents two sample images of Hopkins 155 database.

We performed the four algorithms on Hopkins 155 database and recorded the detailed statistics of the segmentation errors of the four evaluated algorithms including Mean, standard deviation (Std.) and maximal error(Max.) in Table 1. From Table 1, we can see that (1) the mean of segmentation errors obtained by SRR are all slightly better than those of other algorithms; (2) the standard deviation on all data sets obtained by SRR is also superior to those of other algorithms; (3) all the best values are achieved SRR and SCLRR.

5.2   Experiments on Face Image Databases

The brief information of the extended Yale B and ORL face databases are introduced as follows:

The extended Yale B face database contains 38 human faces and around 64 near frontal images under different illuminations per individual. Some images in this database were corrupted by shadow. We just selected images from first 10 classes of the extended Yale B database to form a heavily corrupted subset.

---

[1] The reasons why we choose SCLRR for comparison are illustrated as follows: firstly, SCLRR is the generalization of NNLRSR; secondly, both SCLRR and NNLRSR impose the low-rank and sparse constraints on the reconstruction coefficient matrix to hope it could find the local and global structures of data sets.

(a) 1R2RC   (b) arm

Fig. 2. Sample Images of Hopkins 155 motion segmentation database. (a) 1R2RC, (b) arm.

Table 1. The segmentation errors (%) of different algorithms on Hopkins 155 database. The optimal values of different criterion are emphasized in bold style.

Method	2 motions			3 motions			ALL		
	Mean	Std.	Max.	Mean	Std.	Max.	Mean	Std.	Max.
SSC	4.02	10.24	41.59	11.16	11.00	37.56	5.63	10.81	41.59
LRR	3.13	7.45	30.20	6.56	7.49	23.41	3.93	7.57	30.20
SCLRR	2.96	6.42	31.09	**5.18**	7.24	24.68	3.49	8.49	**29.09**
SRR	**2.34**	**6.50**	**27.23**	5.67	**7.16**	**22.41**	**2.96**	**5.73**	29.23

Notice: The corresponding parameters in different algorithms varied in the interval $[0.01, 10]$. And the best result obtained by each evaluated algorithm on each sub-database was recorded.

ORL database contains 400 face images (without noise) of 40 persons. Each person has 10 different images. These images were taken at different times, varying the lighting, facial expressions (open/closed eyes, smiling/not smiling) and facial details (glasses/no glasses). In our experiments, all the images from the extended Yale B and ORL database are resized to 32×32 pixels. Moreover, for effective computation, the element value of each image vector was normalized into the interval $[0,1]$ by being divided 255. Some sample images from the two databases are shown in Fig. 3(a) and (b) respectively.

We performed subspace segmentation experiments on some sub-databases constructed from the above used two image databases. Each sub-database contains the images from q persons (q changes from a relative small number to the total number of class). Then the four algorithms are performed to obtain the subspace segmentation accuracies. In these experiments, all the corresponding parameters in each evaluated algorithm are varied from 0.001 to 20, and the best values corresponding to the highest accuracy of each evaluated algorithm are chosen. Finally, the segmentation accuracy curve of each algorithm against the number of class q are plotted in Fig. 4.

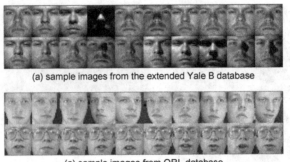

(a) sample images from the extended Yale B database

(a) sample images from ORL database

Fig. 3. Sample images from (a) the extended Yale B databases and (b) ORL.

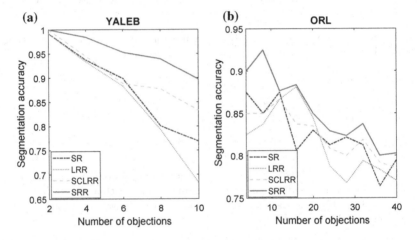

Fig. 4. The segmentation accuracies obtained by the evaluated algorithms versus the variations of number of class on different databases. (a) the extend Yale B (b) ORL databases.

Clearly, form Fig. 4, we can find that (1) in all the experiments, the best results are almost achieved by SRR; (2) the results of SRR are much better than those of other algorithms on the extended Yale B database.

6   Conclusion

We presented the relation representation conception in this paper and developed a kind of sparse relation representation (SRR) method for subspace segmentation. Different from the existing spectral clustering based subspace segmentation algorithms, SRR used the sparse neighborhood relation of each data sample to obtained the affinity graph for a data set. We claimed the obtained affinity graph could discover the subspace structure of the given data set more truthfully. The comparative experiments conducted on several benchmark databases showed that SRR dominated some related algorithms.

References

1. Rao, S., Tron, R., Vidal, R., Ma, Y.: Motion segmentation in the presence of outlying, incomplete, or corrupted trajectories. IEEE Trans. Pattern Anal. Mach. Intell. **32**(10), 1832–1845 (2010)
2. Ma, Y., Derksen, H., Hong, W., Wright, J.: Segmentation of multivariate mixed data via lossy coding and compression. IEEE Trans. Pattern Anal. Mach. Intell. **29**(9), 1546–1562 (2007)
3. Wei, L., Wu, A., Yin, J.: Latent space robust subspace segmentation based on low-rank and locality constraints. Expert Syst. Appl. **42**, 6598–6608 (2015)
4. Wei, L., Wang, X., Yin, J., Wu, A.: Spectral clustering steered low-rank representation for subspace segmentation. J. Vis. Commun. Image Represent. **38**, 386–395 (2016)
5. Elhamifar, E., Vidal, R.: Sparse subspace clustering. In: Proceedings of the IEEE Computer Society Conference on Computer Vision and Pattern Recognition, CVPR 2009, Miami, Florida, USA, pp. 2790–2797 (2009)
6. Liu, G., Lin, Z., Yu, Y.: Robust subspace segmentation by low-rank representation, In: Frnkranz, J., Joachims, T. (eds.) Proceedings of the 27th International Conference on Machine Learning, ICML 2010, Haifa, Israel, pp. 663–670 (2010)
7. Shi, J., Malik, J.: Normalized cuts and image segmentation. IEEE Trans. Pattern Anal. Mach. Intell. **22**, 888–905 (2000)
8. Li, C.-G., Vidal, R.: Structured sparse subspace clustering: a unified optimization framework. In: CVPR (2015)
9. Chen, H., Wang, W., Feng, X.: Structured sparse subspace clustering with within-cluster grouping. Pattern Recognit. **83**, 107–118 (2018)
10. Zhuang, L., Gao, H., Lin, Z., Ma, Y., Zhang, X., Yu, N.: Non-negative low rank and sparse graph for semi-supervised learning. In: CVPR, pp. 2328–2235 (2012)
11. Tang, K., Liu, R., Zhang, J.: Structure-constrained low-rank representation. IEEE Trans. Neural Netw. Learn. Syst. **25**, 2167–2179 (2014)
12. Lu, X., Wang, Y., Yuan, Y.: Graph-regularized low-rank representation for destriping of hyperspectral images. IEEE Trans. Geosci. Remote Sens. **51**(7–1), 4009–4018 (2013)
13. Lin, Z., Chen, M., Wu, L., Ma, Y.: The augmented Lagrange multiplier method for exact recovery of corrupted low-rank matrices, UIUC, Champaign, IL, USA, Technical report UILU-ENG-09-2215 (2009)
14. Duda, R.O., Hart, P.E., Stork, D.G.: Pattern Classification. Wiley, Hoboken (2001)
15. Roweis, S.T., Saul, L.K.: Nonlinear dimensionality reduction by locally linear embedding. Science **290**, 2323–2326 (2000)
16. Wright, J., Yang, A.Y., Ganesh, A., Sastry, S.S., Ma, Y.: Robust face recognition via sparse representation. IEEE Trans. Pattern Anal. Mach. Intell. **31**(2), 210–227 (2009)
17. Cai, J.F., Candes, E.J., Shen, Z.: A singular value thresholding algorithm for matrix completion. SIAM J. Optim. **20**(4), 1956–1982 (2010)
18. Tron, R., Vidal, R.: A benchmark for the comparison of 3D motion segmentation algorithms. In: CVPR (2007)
19. Lee, K., Ho, J., Driegman, D.: Acquiring linear subspaces for face recognition under variable lighting. IEEE Trans. Pattern Anal. Mach. Intell. **27**(5), 684–698 (2005)
20. Samaria, F., Harter, A.: Parameterisation of a stochastic model for human face identification (1994)

An Approach to the Applicability Evaluation of Moving Target Tracking Algorithm

Runping Xi[1,2,3(✉)], Shaohui Xue[1,2,3], Qianqian Han[1,2,3], and Jiaxin Chen[1,2,3]

[1] School of Computer Science, Northwestern Polytechnical University, Xi'an 710129, China
xrp@163.com
[2] National Engineering Laboratory of Integrated Aero-Space-Ground-Ocean Big Data Application Technology, Xi'an 710129, China
[3] Shaanxi Provincial Key Laboratory of Speech and Image Information Processing, Xi'an 710129, China

Abstract. Objective and effective algorithm performance evaluation results are an important basis for the selection of tracking algorithms. Problems in the existing performance evaluation of moving target tracking algorithms include an enlarge number of trials, and in particular, failure to consider the influence of algorithm performance on the multifactor combination scenario. This study proposes a method based on the orthogonal test to evaluate algorithms. First, the factors and levels of the tracking algorithm are analyzed, and an orthogonal test dataset is constructed by using an orthogonal table. Second, the experiments of the performance evaluation are arranged with the dataset and the results are analyzed via range analysis. Finally, evaluation results show that the strong–weak sequence of factors affect the performance of the algorithm and the combination of levels form the factors that can achieve enhanced algorithm performance. Experimental results show that the proposed method can evaluate algorithms comprehensively, objectively, and effectively with decreased test and data volume.

Keywords: Orthogonal test · Performance evaluation · Evaluation measures · Multifactor combination

1 Introduction

Moving target detection and tracking is an important research field in digital image processing and computer vision that has attracted considerable attention from researchers due to its potential economic benefits and important application value in human production and living [1–3]. Influenced by objective factors, such as complex environment and diversity of target motion state, an algorithm is generally applicable to specific environments or specific conditions. Therefore, performing objective performance evaluation for each algorithm under different environments and conditions is necessary.

© Springer Nature Switzerland AG 2019
Z. Lin et al. (Eds.): PRCV 2019, LNCS 11859, pp. 38–51, 2019.
https://doi.org/10.1007/978-3-030-31726-3_4

Several datasets, such as VIVID [4], CAVIAR [5], and PETS [6], are available for the performance evaluation of moving target tracking algorithms. In typical image sequences, the target is usually a person or a car. These datasets have neither considered the different levels of factors affecting the performance of the algorithm, nor have a common labeling box. At present, the mainstream algorithm evaluation platforms include object tracking benchmark (OTB) [7, 8] and VOT [9–12]. OTB uses a large number of image sequence combinations containing certain factors to obtain the performance of an algorithm under certain factors. VOT analyzes the relevance of the tracking algorithm evaluation criteria and obtains an appropriate evaluation measure. The updated VOT datasets even annotate the factors in every frame, thereby improving detection accuracy. However, the performance of the algorithm in a multifactor combination scenario is still neglected. Problems, such as large datasets and many trials in the algorithm evaluation, still exist.

The performance of the moving target tracking algorithm is affected by many factors, such as illumination changes, scale changes, and deformation. The multifactor impact analysis is commonly used in data analysis methods, such as simple comparison, grey correlation analysis, and orthogonal experimental design methods. The principle of simple comparison is straightforward, but different conclusions may be obtained in cases wherein other factors can change the values, especially when many factors exist. The Grey correlation analysis method [13] can apply a variety of dimensionless processing methods to calculate the closeness of each influencing factor. However, this method is unsuitable for multifactor and multilevel tests. The orthogonal experimental design method determines the factor level by selecting the factors that affect the test results, and selects the appropriate orthogonal table for the experimental design. The use of an orthogonal test design with horizontal combination of factors allows each factor to be evenly matched, thereby reducing both the number of trials and the accuracy of test results.

In this study, a method for evaluating the performance of the moving target tracking algorithm based on an orthogonal experiment is proposed. Taking the performance of TLD [14] and CXT [15] algorithms as an example, the orthogonal test method is used to analyze the different levels of factors affecting the algorithm. The primary and secondary relationships of each factor to the performance of the algorithm and the horizontal combination of factors when the algorithm performs optimally are obtained through analysis and discussion.

2   Datasets

The performance evaluation of the moving target tracking algorithm based on an orthogonal experiment uses the orthogonal principle to write a standardized orthogonal table, and then selects representative image sequences from the comprehensive experiment based on the orthogonality of the orthogonal table to be tested. The small number of trials has reached a comprehensive test result.

2.1 Test Factors and Levels

At present, the commonly used moving target tracking methods include tracking methods based on region, contour, target, and motion features. Tracking methods based on region features, such as Brox [16], use image segmentation results for moving target localization, and then use the location of the target position to correct the segmentation target of the image. This type of method performs well in a single background environment. However, the target motion, state, and external shape are complex and variable because of illumination changes, shape changes, and target rotation, in which case the matching of regional features cannot be achieved. Kass et al. [17] proposed the classical tracking method based on contour features called the snake model. The motion scene of the moving target often have occlusion problems, which cause the external contour to be obtained in real time. Achieving contour information matching is difficult, making it impossible to track the target effectively. The tracking method based on target features tracks the target by searching for the position of the target and matching one or several feature information of the target (such as target color, texture, and edge) [18]. Even if a part of the target is occluded, the target can be tracked by using feature points. In this method, regardless if the moving speed is uniform or not, some features will disappear when the target rotates, and the tracking effect is not ideal. Motion feature-based tracking methods, such as Kalman filtering [19] and particle [20] filtering algorithms, use the motion information of the target in the historical video frame to search within the entire image range, and find the target features in the previous video frame. According to the target range of the match, the search range is limited to a small range by using detection techniques.

Many different scenes exist for moving targets, and these scenes bring considerable challenges to moving target detection and tracking. For example, a striped background can cause the failure of edge feature based on the tracking algorithm, and when the background is similar to the color of the moving target, target tracking based on color features becomes difficult. Illumination changes are also a problem that must be addressed in moving target detection and tracking. Human targets appear in different colors under different lighting conditions, making the color-based tracking algorithm almost ineffective. Different color systems can be used to mitigate the effects of illumination changes on the algorithm. Occlusion is a common situation in which a target tracks a scene. Which appears as the gradual loss of target information, and the tracking algorithm aims to search enough target information to determine the target location. Thus, occlusion causes uncertainty to the reliability of the target tracking algorithm, possibly leading to unstable target tracking or even loss of target.

According to the aforementioned analysis and discussion, factors affecting the performance of the moving target tracking algorithm include environmental factors, target features, and tracking interference factors. Tables 1, 2, and 3 present the three types of common factors.

Table 1. Environmental factors

Feature classification	Feature description	Parameter description
Background	Background texture and color	Target feature similar background other background
Weather	Atmospheric transparency	Sunny day Foggy day
	Rainfall	Rainy day Snowy day
Brightness change	Shading	Occur

Table 2. Target characteristics

Feature classification	Feature description	Parameter description
Number of targets	Average number of targets per frame	Number of targets (ones)
	Maximum number of targets	Number of targets (ones)
Average target scale	Point target	Area value (pixels)
	Shaped target	Area value (pixels)
Speed feature	Uniform speed (fast/slow)	Speed value (pixels/s)
	Acceleration/deceleration	Acceleration value
	Short pause	Pause time (frames)
Direction feature	Turn/sudden turn	Angle value
	Target split	Occur
	Target consolidation	Occur
	In-plane rotation	Occur
	Out-of-plane rotation	Occur
Scale change feature	From far and near/from near and far	Proportional value
Shape change feature	Nonrigid deformation	Occur

Table 3. Classification of tracking interference factors

Feature classification	Feature description	Parameter description
Target occlusion	Target is obscured by the background	Occur
	Partial occlusion	Width ratio (target and obstruction)
	All occlusion	
	Target occlusion time	Frames
Occlusion between targets	Target crossing	Occur
Camera-induced interference	Camera shake	Occur

2.2 Selection of Image Sequences

Based on the above analysis. In this study, seven factors are selected for the performance evaluation of the moving target tracking algorithm, and the level (value of the factors) is appropriately categorized as follows:

Table 4. Factors affecting the performance of the algorithm

Level	A	B	C	D	E	F	G
1	Y	Y	Y	Y	Y	Y	Y
2	N	N	N	N	N	N	N

A. Illumination change level Yes/No, B. In-plane rotation level Yes/No, C. Out-of-plane rotation level Yes/No, D. Scale change level Yes/No, E. Similar to background level Yes/No, F. Target deformation level Yes/No, G. Target occlusion level Yes/No

2.3 Organization of Image Data Selection

Commonly used orthogonal tables can basically meet the needs. On the basis of the seven factors and two levels listed in Table 4, Table $L_8(2^7)$ [21] is used to arrange this test. Figure 1 shows the orthogonal table and the dataset.

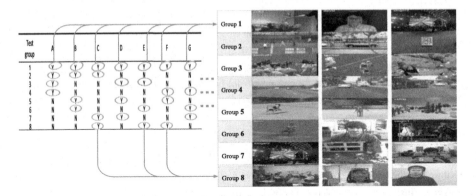

Fig. 1. Experimental dataset

The "Yes" in the table indicates that the set of image sequences clearly contains the influencing factors. Out of all the factors in the seventh data set, C, D, and G are the most significant. The trials are arranged according to a combination of factor levels in the orthogonal experimental tables. The image sequence of the partial factor level combination in Table is difficult to capture in actual situations, thus image synthesis [22] can be considered, that is, the target is merged into the background image to obtain an image that cannot be acquired. Orthogonal test method is a combination of complete and simple contrast tests. The selected data are representative. Therefore, the representative image sequence should be selected to evaluate the algorithm. In some cases, the experimental scene required for the combination of some factors cannot be obtained by shooting due to certain reasons or the acquisition of this part of the image sequence is costly. For example, in important military applications, missiles pursue aircraft targets. To improve the performance of missile pursuit targets, a large amount of aircraft image data is needed to experiment on and improve the algorithm. Image synthesis is an effective means to combine data sequences that are not easily available artificially. The key is to make it close to the real sequence of images. Therefore, image synthesis is crucial in image sequence motion target detection and tracking algorithm evaluation (Fig. 2).

Fig. 2. Intragroup test

2.4 Test Dataset Structure

Figure 1 shows the data selected for the experiment. The eight rows of data represent the test data for groups 1–8, and each group has three image sequences to avoid failure in the test caused by the extreme condition of the image sequence. The three image sequences selected in each group of experiments meet the requirements of experimental factors and horizontal combination, and the result of this group of experiments is obtained by using the weighted average sum method for the performance of the algorithm obtained in it. Figure 3 shows that the combination of several factors required by Table 5 in each selected image sequence combination is significant.

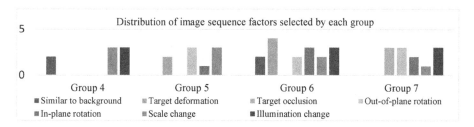

Fig. 3. Distribution of group factors

3 Orthogonal Test Evaluation Method

3.1 Evaluation Framework

After obtaining the test image sequence, the algorithm test and data analysis can be performed. Figure 3 shows the framework of the performance evaluation method for the moving target tracking algorithm based on the orthogonal test method. This framework and mainly includes the following processes:

(1) Data selection. According to the orthogonal table arrangement, eight sets of image data corresponding to the horizontal combination of orthogonal table factors are selected and combined.

(2) Algorithm testing. The algorithm is used to perform target tracking on eight sets of image data, and the results of each set of experiments are counted.

(3) Range analysis [23]. The range analysis method (referred to as the R method) uses the mathematical statistics method to calculate the magnitude of the change of the test index of the factor in the range of the orthogonal table. This range R value is used to assess the primary and secondary relationships of each factor and obtain the best algorithm performance and best combination of factors. If the value of Rj is large, then the factor has an enhanced influence on the test results.

$$K_{ij} = \frac{T_{ij}}{r}, \tag{1}$$

$$R_j = T_{ij(max)} - T_{ij(min)}. \tag{2}$$

(4) Verification test. The orthogonal test is a trial with a decreased number of generations. The combination of factors based on the test is not necessarily optimal, but it can obtain improved algorithm performance. The combination of the preferred factors obtained by the test analysis and the combination of factors of the optimal solution in the experiment are verified simultaneously to determine the advantages and disadvantages (Fig. 4).

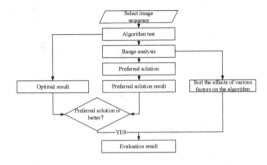

Fig. 4. Frame diagram of the performance evaluation method of the moving target tracking algorithm based on the orthogonal experiment

3.2   Selection and Construction of Evaluation Indicators

Various performance evaluation indicators, such as center error, area overlap rate, and accuracy, were used in the moving target tracking algorithm. Pixel error refers to the Euclidean distance between the center point of the predicted position and the center position of the mark. Tracking failure and size of the frame cause the meaning of the center to be unclear with the result of the index as a reference. The overlap rate S is measured by using the ratio of the overlap area.

$$S = \frac{r_t \cap r_a}{r_t \cup r_a} \qquad (3)$$

where r_t and r_a are the bounding boxes corresponding to the tracked and true obtained frames, respectively. A frame is considered successful when the overlap rate is greater than a certain threshold t_0 ($0 < t_0 < 1$). When the threshold changes between 0 and 1, the success rate of the tracking changes. The curve displayed in this process is called the success rate graph. The area under the success rate curve (AUC) [24] is equal to the average overlap rate. Hence, a large area indicates the enhanced performance of the algorithm. To verify the performance of the algorithm effectively, this study uses AUC as the test measure under the combination of factors of the group.

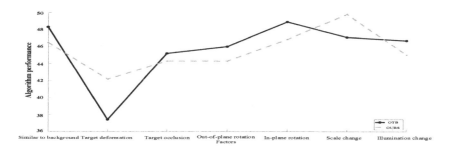

Fig. 5. Score performance of the CXT algorithm

The range R_j used in this paper indicates the magnitude of this factor's impact on the performance of the algorithm. A large R_j decreases the average overlap rate. The structural index is used as the score of the algorithm under this factor, indicating the relationship among the influencing factors.

$$Score_j = (1 - R_j) \times 50 \qquad (4)$$

When the value is set to 50, this value is basically close to the OTB indicator value. Figures 5 and 6 compare the test scores with the OTB-related results, and each point represents the score performance of the algorithm under this factor.

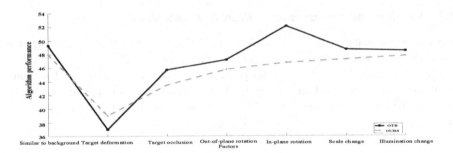

Fig. 6. Score performance of the TLD algorithm

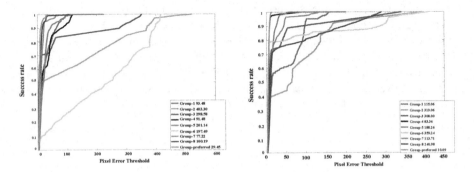

Fig. 7. Pixel error Performance of the TLD and CXT algorithms

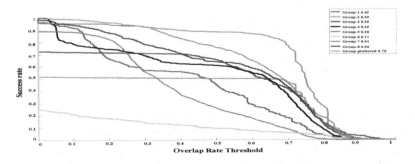

Fig. 8. Performance of the CXT algorithm

4 Experimental Results and Analysis

Figures 7, 8, and 9 show that the application algorithm was tested item by item on eight sets of datasets, which are eight sets of experimental results. The range analysis was performed based on these results.

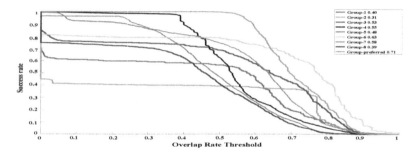

Fig. 9. Performance of the TLD algorithm

4.1   Range Analysis

See Table 5.

Table 5. Range analysis process

Test group		A	B	C	D	E	F	G	TLD–AUC (%)	CXT–AUC (%)
1		Y	Y	Y	Y	Y	Y	Y	0.40	0.42
2		Y	Y	Y	N	N	N	N	0.30	0.39
3		Y	N	N	Y	Y	N	N	0.52	0.50
4		Y	N	N	N	N	Y	Y	0.55	0.49
5		N	Y	N	Y	N	Y	N	0.48	0.36
6		N	Y	N	N	Y	N	Y	0.43	0.11
7		N	N	Y	Y	N	N	Y	0.58	0.61
8		N	N	Y	N	Y	Y	N	0.39	0.56
TLD	T_{1j}	1.77	1.61	1.67	1.98	1.74	1.82	1.96	–	–
	T_{2j}	1.88	2.04	1.98	1.67	1.91	1.83	1.69	–	–
	K_{1j}	0.4425	0.4025	0.4175	0.495	0.435	0.455	0.49	–	–
	K_{2j}	0.47	0.51	0.495	0.4175	0.4775	0.4575	0.4225	–	–
	R_j	0.0475	0.1075	0.0775	0.0775	0.0425	0.0025	0.0675	–	–
	Preferred	A2	B2	C2	D1	E2	F2	G1	–	–
CXT	T_{1j}	1.80	1.28	1.98	1.89	1.59	1.83	1.63	–	–
	T_{2j}	1.64	2.16	1.46	1.55	1.85	1.61	1.81	–	–
	K_{1j}	0.45	0.32	0.495	0.4725	0.3975	0.4575	0.4075	–	–
	K_{2j}	0.41	0.54	0.365	0.3875	0.4625	0.4025	0.4525	–	–
	R_j	0.04	0.22	0.13	0.085	0.065	0.055	0.045	–	–
	Preferred	A1	B2	C1	D1	E2	F1	G2	–	–

4.2   Analysis of Test Results

On the basis of the results of the range analysis in Table 6, the strong–weak relationship of the seven factors influence the performance of the algorithm. Target deformation has the greatest influence on the algorithm performance, followed by target occlusion, out-of-plane rotation, and illumination change, such as target scale changes, background similarity, and in-plane rotation have a relatively weaker influence on the performance of the algorithm. The value of the average overlap rate is the same as the AUC measurement. Table 7 shows that the evaluation result of the TLD algorithm, and the value shown in the comparison chart of Fig. 5 are substantially close to the average overlap rate.

Table 6. Algorithms in the object tracking benchmark and the performance of this test

Factor		A	B	C	D	E	F	G
OTB	TLD–average overlap	48.3	37.4	45.2	46.0	48.9	47.1	46.7
Ours	$TLD - Score_j$	47.6250	44.6250	46.1250	46.1250	47.8750	49.8750	46.6250
OTB	CXT–average overlap	49.3	37.0	45.7	47.2	52.1	48.7	48.5
Ours	$CXT - Score_j$	48	39	43.5000	45.7500	46.7500	47.2500	47.7500

Table 7. Optimal combination of factors in the algorithm performance (preferred result)

Algorithm	A	B	C	D	E	F	G
TLD	N	N	N	Y	N	N	Y
CXT	Y	N	Y	Y	N	Y	N

Based on the evaluation result of the algorithm in OTB, the algorithm has the lowest overlap rate under the target deformation factor. Thus, the target deformation factor has the greatest impact on the performance of the algorithm, followed by target occlusion, and out-of-plane rotation. The strength and weakness of the factors that influence the performance of the algorithm are consistent in this study.

Based on the preferred results, the TLD algorithm has the best performance in the case of illumination change and out-of-plane rotation, such that no scale change, target occlusion, target deformation, background similarity, and optimal combination of in-plane rotation are observed. The optimal combination is excluded from the orthogonal experimental design table. To verify the optimization results of the orthogonal experiment, the performance of the algorithm under the optimal combination condition is tested. On the basis of the preferred results, the combination of image sequences with the most significant factors of out-of-plane rotation and illumination variation is selected. Figure 10 shows the dataset with the optimal combination.

The algorithm has an accuracy of 0.71 in the optimal combination data, and the center error is 10.00, which is significantly lower than the other groups. Compared with the index values of each group in the orthogonal table, the optimized combination result obtained by the orthogonal experimental design method is effective.

The CXT algorithm also approximates OTB in terms of the relationship between factors and algorithm performance, and the preferred combination results outperform those of the other groups (Fig. 11).

Fig. 10. Dataset on the optimal combination scene of TLD algorithm

Fig. 11. Dataset on the optimal combination scene of TLD algorithm

5   Conclusion and Future Directions

This study proposed a performance evaluation method for moving target tracking algorithm based on an orthogonal experiment. By importing the orthogonal test design, the performance evaluation of TLD and CXT algorithms under different influencing factors and levels are completed comprehensively and objectively with less test and amount of data. The strong–weak relationship between the influencing factors and the application scenario (combination of different factors) of the algorithm are obtained. The experimental results show that the conclusions obtained by the method are consistent with actual results, thereby solving the existing problems in algorithm evaluation methods effectively, and the lack of factors that combine the performance of the algorithm is ignored.

The application of the orthogonal table designed for the performance evaluation of moving target tracking is an efficient, fast, and economical test method. In addition, the introduction of the orthogonal test method into the performance evaluation of moving target tracking algorithm also provides a reference for other image processing algorithms. In future studies, we will further consider the multilevel quantification of factor levels to optimize score accuracy and applicable scenarios.

Acknowledgement. This work is supported by the National Natural Science Foundation of China (No. 61572405) and the National High Technology Research and Development Program of China (863 Program) (No. 2015AA016402).

References

1. Li, Y., Zhu, J., Hoi, S.C.H., Song, W., Wang, Z., Liu, H.: Robust estimation of similarity transformation for visual object tracking. In: AAAI (2019)
2. Li, B., Wu, W., Wang, Q., Zhang, F., Xing, J., Yan, J.: SiamRPN++: evolution of siamese visual tracking with very deep networks. In: CVPR (2019)
3. Fan, H., Ling, H.: Siamese cascaded region proposal networks for real-time visual tracking. In: CVPR (2019)
4. Collins, R., Zhou, X., Seng, K.T.: An open source tracking Testbed and evaluation WebSite. In: IEEE International Workshop on Performance Evaluation of Tracking and Surveillance (2005)
5. Fisher, R.B.: The PETS04 surveillance ground-truth data sets. In: Proceedings of the IEEE International Workshop on Performance Evaluation of Tracking and Surveillance, pp. 1–5 (2004)
6. Ferryman, J., Shahrokni, A.: PETS2009: dataset and challenge. In: Twelfth IEEE International Workshop on PERFORMANCE Evaluation of Tracking and Surveillance, pp. 1–6. IEEE (2010)
7. Wu, Y., Lim, J., Yang, M.H.: Online object tracking: a benchmark. In: Computer Vision and Pattern Recognition, pp. 2411–2418. IEEE (2013)
8. Wu, Y., Lim, J., Yang, M.H.: Object tracking benchmark. IEEE Trans. Pattern Anal. Mach. Intell. 37(9), 1834–1848 (2015)
9. Kristan, Matej, et al.: The visual object tracking VOT2014 challenge results. In: Agapito, Lourdes, Bronstein, Michael M., Rother, Carsten (eds.) ECCV 2014. LNCS, vol. 8926, pp. 191–217. Springer, Cham (2015). https://doi.org/10.1007/978-3-319-16181-5_14
10. Kristan, M., Pflugfelder, R., Matas, J., et al.: The visual object tracking VOT2015 challenge results. In: IEEE International Conference on Computer Vision Workshop, pp. 564–586. IEEE (2016)
11. Kristan, M., Leonardis, A., Matas, J., et al.: The visual object tracking VOT2016 challenge results. In: IEEE International Conference on Computer Vision Workshops, pp. 98–111. IEEE Computer Society (2016)
12. Kristan, M., Eldesokey, A., Xing, Y., et al.: The visual object tracking VOT2017 challenge results. In: IEEE International Conference on Computer Vision Workshop (2017)
13. Cheng, Y.C., Zhang, P., Jiao, Y.B., et al.: Grey correlation analysis method to analyze the influence factors of attenuated performance of asphalt mixture under water-temperature-radiation cycle action. Appl. Mech. Mater. 361–363, 1857–1860 (2013)
14. Hare, S., Saffari, A., Torr, P.H.S.: Struck: structured output tracking with kernels. In: International Conference on Computer Vision, pp. 263–270. IEEE Computer Society (2011)
15. Dinh, T.B., Vo, N., Medioni, G.: Context tracker: exploring supporters and distracters in unconstrained environments. In: Computer Vision & Pattern Recognition. IEEE (2011)
16. Brox, T., Deriche, R., Weickert, J.: Colour, texture, and motion in level set based segmentation and tracking. Image Vis. Comput. 28(3), 376–390 (2010)
17. Kass, M., Witkin, A., Terzopoulos, D.: Snakes: active contour models. Int. J. Comput. Vis. 1(4), 321–331 (1988)

18. Xing, G.: Research on behavior detection and tracking algorithms for moving targets in intelligent monitoring. Chongqing University of Posts and Telecommunications (2013)
19. Liu, C., Shui, P., Li, S.: Unscented extended Kalman filter for target tracking. J. Syst. Eng. Electron. **22**(2), 188–192 (2011)
20. Sherrah, J., Ristic, B., Redding, N.J.: Particle filter to track multiple people for visual surveillance. IET Comput. Vis. **5**(4), 192–200 (2011)
21. Yu, Z.G.: A construction method of orthogonal table L $(p \sim 2)$ $(p\_(p-1)))$. J. Huazhong Norm. Univ. Nat. Sci. Ed.) **1982**(2), 35–49 (1982)
22. Na, L., Dan, W.: Image synthesis algorithm based on sampling matting and self-adaption color. Chin. J. Liq. Cryst. Displays **33**(2), 156–164 (2018)
23. Lei, L.M.: Analysis of variance in orthogonal experimental design. Northeast Forestry University (2011)
24. Fawcett, T.: An introduction to ROC analysis. Pattern Recognit. Lett. **27**(8), 861–874 (2006)

A Cooperative Particle Swarm Optimization Algorithm Based on Greedy Disturbance

Xing Huo[1], Fei Zhang[1], Chao Luo[1], Jieqing Tan[1], and Kun Shao[2(✉)]

[1] School of Mathematics, Hefei University of Technology, Hefei, China
[2] School of Software, Hefei University of Technology, Hefei, China
zzzf0214@163.com

Abstract. In this paper, an improved Particle Swarm Optimization Algorithm (GCPSO) is proposed to solve the shortcomings of the existing Particle Swarm Optimization Algorithm (PSO) which has low convergence precision, slow convergence rate and is easy to fall into local optimum when performing high-dimensional optimization in the late iteration. First, the whole particle swarm of the algorithm was divided into three sub-groups, and different ranges of inertia weight ω are set for balances global search and local search in each sub-group, which improves the algorithm's ability to explore. Then we add Gaussian perturbation with the greedy strategy to PSO to avoid the algorithm falling into local optimum and improve the convergence speed. And finally, the proposed algorithm is compared with Genetic Algorithm (GA), PSO and Grasshopper Optimization Algorithm (GOA) to analyse its performance and speed. Through experimental analysis, GCPSO has a significant improvement at convergence speed, convergence accuracy and stability.

Keywords: Optimization algorithm · Greedy strategy · PSO · GA · GOA

1 Introduction

Optimization problem often appears in scientific research, and many engineering problems ultimately boil down to optimization problems. It can be expressed as a mathematical problem. It generally refers to the question of how to find a specific factor (variable) under a given constraint to make the target reach the optimal value. The optimization algorithm is used to solve the optimization problem, and the objective function of the optimization problem is established as an optimization model to obtain the optimal value. For the more complex optimization problems of non-linear, multi-dimensional and global optimization, traditional optimization algorithms have been difficult to meet the needs. And various intelligent optimization algorithms that are inspired by bionics have a better solution in the complex optimization problem such as Genetic Algorithm (GA), Particle Swarm Optimization Algorithm (PSO), and Grasshopper Optimization Algorithm (GOA). And they have attracted the attention of many scholars. Because of the high efficiency and strong convergence of this kind of algorithm, more and more scholars have applied it to their respective fields and achieved good results [1–3]. Genetic Algorithm (GA) is a meta-heuristic algorithm proposed by Professor Holland [4] in 1975. Its principle on Darwin's evolutionary

© Springer Nature Switzerland AG 2019
Z. Lin et al. (Eds.): PRCV 2019, LNCS 11859, pp. 52–61, 2019.
https://doi.org/10.1007/978-3-030-31726-3_5

theory of survival of the fittest. Genetic Algorithm takes all individuals in a group as variable objects and represents the gene sequence in binary code form. The algorithm searches for the optimal value within the range of the coded variables through the genetic operations of selection, crossover and mutation, which retain the excellent individuals and eliminate the poor individuals, and then form a new population. And the optimal solution is obtained after repeated iterations. However, the convergence efficiency of GA is low, and it is easy to converge prematurely. Particle Swarm Optimization (PSO) is another metaheuristic algorithm proposed by Kennedy et al. [5]. This algorithm simulates the predation behaviour of a flock of birds. The solution of the optimization problem is compared to a bird in the search space which called "particles". And all particles are searched in the space of the variable range, and the fitness value is calculated by the optimized function to determine the distance of the current location to the food. The algorithm finds the global optimal by updating the individual historical optimal value and the overall population optimal value. The original PSO algorithm has the disadvantages of slow convergence speed and low convergence precision. In order to balance the local search ability and global search ability in the original PSO algorithm, Shi et al. [6] proposed an improved algorithm with inertia weight ω to adjust convergence and convergence speed dynamically which is called the standard PSO algorithm (For the convenience of description, PSO refers to the standard PSO algorithm in this paper). However, there are two problems with the algorithms: the algorithm is easy to fall into local optimization and has poor convergence precision when performing high-dimensional optimization; the convergence efficiency is low when entering the late iteration. For this reason, Li et al. [7] proposed an efficient and improved particle swarm optimization strategy, which divides the whole population into several sub-groups for the division of labor and information exchange to improve the local search ability and global search ability of the algorithm. Grasshopper Optimization Algorithm (GOA) is a new meta-heuristic algorithm proposed by Salemii et al. [8] in 2017. The basic idea is based on the regularity of grasshopper cluster activities and the model of group intelligence activities. The influencing factors are wind direction, gravity, effects of other grasshoppers in the population and the optimal position reached in the current population. However, GOA is not only easy to fall into local optimum but also has high design complexity and time-consuming. Therefore, it is necessary to improve the algorithm to get a better algorithm. And there are also some other metaheuristics such as Grey Wolf Optimization Algorithms [9], Whale Optimization Algorithms [10], etc.

Based on the work of Li, this paper improves PSO. The improved algorithm (GCPSO) uses the variation of inertia weight and adds a Gaussian perturbation strategy based on greedy thought to make the particles maintain strong vitality during the evolution process. The algorithm was carried out on the benchmark functions and compared with other intelligent optimization algorithms. Experiments show that GCPSO has a significant improvement at convergence speed, convergence accuracy and stability.

2 GCPSO Algorithm

Co-evolutionary algorithm establishes two or more populations to establish competition or cooperation between them [11]. Each population enhances its performance through its iterative strategy and interaction to achieve the purpose of population optimization. Traditional particle swarm optimization algorithm uses a single group iterative strategy. The algorithm has slow convergence speed and is easy to fall into local optimum when dealing with high-dimensional complex functions so that the satisfactory results cannot be obtained. This paper draws on the division strategy idea of the co-evolutionary algorithm, combines Gaussian perturbation strategy based on greedy thought [12], and proposes an algorithm (GCPSO) with the cooperative division of labor based on greedy disturbance. The algorithm effectively compensates for the defect. GCPSO is described as follows:

The whole particle swarm is divided into three subgroups: S1, S2 and S3. Each subgroup has different iterative strategies. The subgroup S1 adopts the traditional standard PSO iterative strategy, and the subgroup S2 adopts the global search to enhance the strategy gradually. The subgroup S3 only uses the "social experience" part, which considers the information sharing and cooperation between particles. Let x_i refers to the coordinate position of the particle i in the particle group, and v_i is the corresponding velocity, c_1 and c_2 are constant named learning factors, r_1 and r_2 are uniform random numbers between [0, 1]; $pbest_i$ is the individual historical optimum of the particle i and gbest is the global best value of the particle swarm. Let t be the current number of iterations and T be the maximum number of iterations. Then the iteration formula for each group is formulated as follows:

$$\text{Population S1}: \quad v_i = \omega_1 v_i + c_1 r_1 (pbest_i - x_i) + c_2 r_2 (gbest - x_i) \tag{1}$$

$$\text{Where,} \quad \omega_1 = \omega_{1max} - t * \frac{\omega_{1max} - \omega_{1min}}{T} \tag{2}$$

$$\text{Population S2} \quad v_i = \omega_2 v_i + c_1 r_1 (pbest_i - x_i) + c_2 r_2 (gbest - x_i) \tag{3}$$

$$\text{Where,} \quad \omega_2 = \omega_{2min} + t * \frac{\omega_{2max} - \omega_{2min}}{T} \tag{4}$$

$$\text{Population S3} \quad v_i = \omega_3 v_i + c_2 r_2 (gbest - x_i) \tag{5}$$

$$\text{Where,} \quad \omega_3 = \frac{\omega_1 + \omega_2}{2} \tag{6}$$

Among them, ω_1, ω_2, and ω_3 are iterative weights, ω_{1max}, ω_{1min} and ω_{2max}, ω_{2min} are the maximum and minimum values of the iterative weights, respectively. The larger iterative weight has better exploration ability and global convergence ability, while the smaller iterative weight makes stronger local convergence ability in the later stage, which can get more accurate results. At the same time, to prevent the algorithm from crossing the boundary, the boundary values v_{min} and v_{max} are set for the above velocity term.

The coordinate position x_i of the particle i in each of the above subgroups is updated by the formula:

$$x_i = x_i + v_i \tag{7}$$

To further avoid the algorithm falling into local optimum, a Gaussian perturbation is added to the global best position of the particles:

$$gbest = gbest * (c + gau) \tag{8}$$

Where gau represents White Gaussian Noise, and c represents the interference factor, which is a constant.

To increase the convergence rate, we add the greedy strategy idea and iterate multiple times in the Gaussian perturbation process:

$$
\begin{aligned}
&\text{for } i = 1 : M \\
&\quad gbest\_temp = gbest \times (a + gau) \\
&\quad gbest\_temp\_fit = f(gbest\_temp); \\
&\quad \text{if } gbest\_temp\_fit < gbest\_fit \\
&\quad\quad gbest = gbest\_temp; \\
&\quad \text{end} \\
&\text{end}
\end{aligned}
\tag{9}
$$

Where M represents the maximum number of iterations and f represents the function to be optimized, $gbest\_fit = f(gbest)$.

The working principle of GCPSO is to divide the whole group into several sub-groups and assign different evolution strategies to different sub-groups. Different sub-groups exchange information by sharing global best information gbest to complete group collaboration and accelerate the convergence speed. And Gaussian perturbation with greedy thought is added to prevent local optimum and achieve fast and accurate convergence. In GCPSO, the subgroup S1 is iterated according to the standard PSO. And the inertia weight value ω_1 of S1 is linearly decreased, representing particle optimization gradually evolves from the strong global convergence at the early stage to the strong local convergence at the later stage, and the accurate convergence results are obtained. The inertia weight value ω_2 of the subgroup S2 is linearly increased to improve the global search capabilities of whole particle swarm and avoid the local convergence of S1 in the later stage of the algorithm. The subgroup S3 only contains the "social experience" part, that is, it only searches near the current optimal position so that it can quickly converge to the current optimal position.

At the same time, to improve the convergence rate and further avoid the algorithm falling into local optimum, the disturbance with the thought of greedy strategy is added. GCPSO improves the efficiency and accuracy of optimization through the divide-and-conquer strategy of cooperative thinking and greedy disturbances. The pseudo code for GCPSO is given in Table 1.

Table 1. The procedure of GCPSO.

Procedure:

Input: Iterator times: T; Dimension: D; Three population sizes; Disturbance times: M

Output: The global best particle's position gbest and corresponding function value fbest

Initialize each particle i's position $x1_i$ and speed $v1_i$ in swarm1;

Initialize each particle j's position $x2_j$ and speed $v2_j$ in swarm2;

Initialize each particle l's position $x3_l$ and speed $v3_l$ in swarm3;

Set speed boundary v_{max} and v_{min}, inertia weight boundary $\omega_{1\,min}$, $\omega_{1\,max}$ and $\omega_{2\,min}$, $\omega_{2\,max}$;

Calculate the fitness of each particle;

Set $pbest1_i = x1_i$, $pbest2_j = x2_j$, $pbest_l = x3_l$ for each particle in three populations;

Update the gbest position of all particles in three populations;

While $(t \leq T)$

    Set inertia weight ω_1 using Eq.(2);

    For each particle in swarm1
        update the speed formula by the Eq.(1);
        update the position of the current particle by the Eq.(7);
    End For
    Calculate the fitness of each particle in swarm1;
    Update the position pbest1 for each particle in swarm1;

    Set inertia weight ω_2 using Eq.(4);

    For each particle in swarm2
        update the speed formula by the Eq.(3);
        update the position of the current particle by the Eq.(7);
    End For
    Calculate the fitness of each particle in swarm2;
    Update the position pbest2 for each particle in swarm2;

    Set inertia weight ω_3 using Eq.(6);

    For each particle in swarm3
        update the speed formula by the Eq.(5);
        update the position of the current particle by the Eq.(7);
    End For
    Calculate the fitness of each particle in swarm3;
    Update the position pbest3 for each particle in swarm3;

    Update the position gbest of all particles in three populations;

    For k=1 to M
        Update the gbest position by the operation (9);
    End For
    $t \leftarrow t+1$;

End While

Return gbest and fbest.

---

3 Experiments and Analysis

In this section, we focused on the effect of the improved particle swarm optimization algorithm in global optimization. Ten classical benchmark functions [13, 14] in Table 2 are used to test the algorithm. The functions $f_1 - f_6$ are unimodal functions, and the functions $f_7 - f_{11}$ are multimodal functions. The expressions and parameters of the functions are shown in Table 2. Dim represents the dimension of the function, and Range represents the range of values of each variable of the function, f_{min} represents the minimum value of the function, and D represents the dimension of the function f_7.

Table 2. Description of benchmark functions.

Fun	Dim	Range	f_{min}
$f_1(x) = \sum_{i=1}^{n} x_i^2$	30	$[-100, 100]$	0
$f_2(x) = \sum_{i=1}^{n} \lvert x_i \rvert + \prod_{i=1}^{n} \lvert x_i \rvert$	30	$[-10, 10]$	0
$f_3(x) = \sum_{i=1}^{n} \left(\sum_{j=1}^{i} x_j \right)^2$	30	$[100, 100]$	0
$f_4(x) = \max_i \{ \lvert x_i \rvert , \ 1 \le i \le n \}$	30	$[-100, 100]$	0
$f_5(x) = \sum_{i=1}^{n-1} [100(x_{i+1} - x_i^2)^2 + (x_i - 1)^2]$	30	$[-30, 30]$	0
$f_6(x) = \sum_{i=1}^{n} i x_i^4 + \text{random}[0 , 1)$	30	$[-1.28, 1.28]$	0
$f_7(x) = \sum_{i=1}^{n} -x_i \sin(\sqrt{\lvert x_i \rvert})$	30	$[-500, 500]$	$-418.9829*D$
$f_8(x) = \sum_{i=1}^{n} [x_i^2 - 10\cos(2\pi x_i) + 10]$	30	$[-5.12, 5.12]$	0
$f_9(x) = -20\exp(-0.2\sqrt{\frac{1}{n}\sum_{i=1}^{n} x_i^2})$ $-\exp(\frac{1}{n}\sum_{i=1}^{n} \cos(2\pi x_i)) + 20 + e$	30	$[-32, 32]$	0
$f_{10}(x) = \frac{1}{4000}\sum_{i=1}^{n} x_i^2 - \prod_{i=1}^{n} \cos(\frac{x_i}{\sqrt{i}}) + 1$	30	$[-600, 600]$	0
$f_{11}(x) = \frac{\pi}{n}\left\{ 10\sin(\pi y_1) + \sum_{i=1}^{n-1} (y_i - 1)^2[1 + 10\sin^2(\pi y_{i+1})] + (y_n - 1)^2 \right\}$ $+ \sum_{i=1}^{n} u(x_i, 5, 100, 4)$ where $y_i = 1 + \frac{x_i + 1}{4}$, $u(x_i, a, k, m) = \begin{cases} k(x_i - a)^m , & x_i > a \\ 0 , & -a \le x_i \le a \\ k(-x_i - a)^m , & x_i < -a \end{cases}$	30	$[-50, 50]$	0

The improved algorithm-GCPSO is compared with PSO, GA and GOA in function optimization experiments. For comparing the experimental performance of each algorithm quantitatively, the maximum number of iterations is set as 1000 in the experiment. The experimental parameters of each algorithm are given in Table 3.

Table 3. Parameter settings.

Algorithm	Parameter	Parameter value
GCPSO	Perturbation times: M	10
	Interference factor: a	0.5
	ω_{1min}, ω_{1max}	0.001, 0.9
	ω_{2min}, ω_{2max}	0.001, 0.9
	v_{min}, v_{max}	−4, 4
GA	Swarm size	300
	Crossover probability	0.6
	Mutation probability	0.001
PSO	Swarm size	300
	c_1, c_2	2, 2
	ω_{min}, ω_{max}	0.4, 0.9
	v_{min}, v_{max}	−4, 4
GOA	Swarm size	300
	c_{min}, c_{max}	0.00004, 1

3.1   Quality Analysis of Solutions

Table 4 shows the performance of GPSO, PSO, GA and GOA on different benchmark functions. F denotes the benchmark function, ave denotes the average optimal value of the function, std denotes the average standard deviation of the function value, and tim denotes the average running time of the algorithm on the function. And each benchmark function was run many times to generate these statistical results. The dimension of the experimental search space is 30-dimensional, and the population size is set to 300. The improved particle swarm optimization algorithm-GCPSO contains 100 particles per subpopulation, and each test function was run 30 times independently.

From the Table 4, we can see that the proposed algorithm-GCPSO takes a little shorter time than other algorithms except for PSO, but the mean value of the function is closer to the theoretical value than PSO. It indicates that GCPSO has advantages in solving high-dimensional function problems. It effectively solves the problem of poor convergence and local optimum of PSO in the later iteration period and improves the accuracy of the solution. At the same time, GCPSO has lower average standard deviation than PSO, which indicates that GCPSO improves the stability of the original algorithm. Comparing GCPSO with GA, we can see that GCPSO has better results in mean, standard deviation and running time for all functions except for a slight difference in the optimization of function f_{11}. This shows that the GCPSO proposed in this paper is much better than GA in convergence, convergence accuracy, optimization speed and robustness. Compared with GOA, except for the function f_7, GCPSO is also in a leading position in three statistical parameters for benchmark functions: the average time-consuming is short, indicating that GCPSO optimization speed is faster; the mean value of the function is closer to the theoretical value, indicating that GCPSO has better global convergence and convergence accuracy; the average standard deviation is lower, indicating that GCPSO has higher robustness than GOA.

Table 4. Comparison of optimization results.

F	GCPSO			PSO			GA			GOA		
	ave	std	tim	ave	std	tim	ave	std	tim	ave	std	tim
f_1	**5.8805e-230**	0	0.6725	0.1054	0.1749	0.5453	0.4606	0.1857	1.1866	0.0095	0.0045	357.4484
f_2	**4.9256e-118**	2.6887e-117	0.7178	2.4504	1.3186	0.5789	0.2848	0.0713	1.4102	0.0371	0.0563	348.2115
f_3	**4.1432e-118**	0	2.8946	5.5406	2.9889	2.7797	9.9922e+03	3.2617e+03	3.0920	10.9614	4.8229	349.2198
f_4	**7.5103e-118**	3.6256e-117	0.6809	1.2578	0.6080	0.5478	2.3943	0.5729	0.9109	0.2287	0.1603	339.9627
f_5	**28.4772**	0.2550	0.9670	165.8761	138.1158	0.9180	162.0951	70.7509	1.1970	44.9997	34.5939	345.7606
f_6	**8.6464e-05**	9.4700e-05	1.8967	0.0676	0.0368	1.7553	0.0027	9.4723e-04	2.0853	0.0214	0.0042	341.6339
f_7	-5.3806e+03	639.7023	1.0790	-6.4752e+03	697.6042	0.9488	-3.0650e+03	421.7024	1.1954	**-6.6520e+03**	852.6289	339.2142
f_8	**0**	0	0.7485	55.5829	16.1783	0.7485	26.0967	11.6551	1.0943	36.1833	34.0773	345.8481
f_9	**8.8818e-16**	0	0.7693	2.1103	0.6317	0.7515	10.1765	6.8661	1.5543	0.6351	0.7783	350.7806
f_{10}	**0**	0	1.0285	0.2342	0.2348	0.9198	1.0558	0.0163	1.6603	0.0223	0.0116	341.1963
f_{11}	0.0206	0.0306	4.1695	1.8660	1.2255	3.9015	**6.7226e-04**	3.2511e-04	4.8457	0.5705	1.3724	361.6257

3.2   Convergence Analysis of the Algorithm

Figure 1 shows the convergence curves of the function values varying with the number of iterations on the benchmark functions under different optimization algorithms. And the convergence curves for the functions $f_1 - f_{11}$ are arranged in the order from left to right and top to bottom. In the lower right corner of the figure, the enlargement effect in the yellow frame is given to show more clearly.

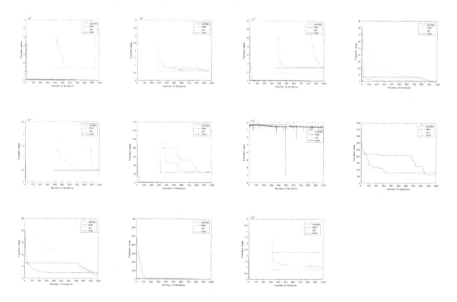

Fig. 1. Convergence curves.

It can be seen from the Fig. 1 that the final convergence values of GCPSO on the benchmark functions are the smallest except for the function f_7, which indicates that GCPSO has the best global convergence and high convergence precision, while the other algorithms fall into local convergence on the benchmark functions, resulting in low convergence and low convergence accuracy. Observing the convergence curves, GCPSO can reach the minimum in the number of iterations less than 50 on most functions, that is, the convergence rate is fast, and the PSO algorithm follows. This shows that the proposed algorithm-GCPSO not only improves the global search ability and convergence efficiency of PSO but also can find the optimal value more quickly. Compared with other algorithms, the proposed algorithm-GCPSO can converge to the optimal value stably and quickly, the global search ability of the algorithm is stronger, and the convergence results are better.

In conclusion, the proposed algorithm-GCPSO has the characteristics of high convergence efficiency, strong global convergence, high convergence accuracy and good robustness.

4   Conclusion

The algorithm-GCPSO proposed in this paper borrows the divide-and-conquer strategy of cooperative thinking to makes full use of the advantages of group division and cooperation. And the algorithm combines the perturbation based on the greedy strategy, which not only improves the convergence efficiency of the algorithm but also improves the convergence accuracy of the algorithm. Experiments of 11 benchmark functions show that GCPSO has great advantages in accuracy, speed and stability compared with other algorithms. Future research will focus on simplifying the initial parameters and more complex high-dimensional optimization problems to enhance the universality of the algorithm.

References

1. Hammouche, K., Diaf, M., Siarry, P.: A multilevel automatic thresholding method based on a genetic algorithm for a fast image segmentation. Comput. Vis. Image Underst. **109**(2), 163–175 (2008)
2. Sathya, P.D., Kayalvizhi, R.: PSO-based Tsallis thresholding selection procedure for image segmentation. Int. J. Comput. Appl. **5**(4), 39–46 (2010)
3. Sharma, A., Sharma, M., Rajneesh: SAR image segmentation using Grasshopper Optimization Algorithm. Int. J. Electron. **6**(12), 19–25 (2017)
4. Holland, J.H.: Genetic algorithms. Sci. Am. **267**(1), 66–73 (1992)
5. Kennedy, J., Eberhart, R.C.: Particle swarm optimization. In: IEEE International Conference on Neural Networks, pp. 1942–1948 (1995)
6. Shi, Y.H., Eberhart, R.C.: A modified particle swarm optimizer. In: Proceedings of the IEEE Conference on Evolutionary Computation, Anchorage, pp. 69–73 (1998)
7. Li, H.L., Hou, C.Z., Zhou, S.S.: High efficient algorithm of modified particle swarm optimization. Comput. Eng. Appl. **44**(1), 14–16 (2008)

8. Saremi, S., Mirjalili, S., Lewis, A.: Grasshopper optimization algorithm: theory and application. Adv. Eng. Softw. **105**, 30–47 (2017)
9. Mirjalili, S., Mirjalili, S.M., Lewis, A.: Grey wolf optimizer. Adv. Eng. Softw. **69**, 46–61 (2014)
10. Mirjalili, S., Lewis, A.: The whale optimization algorithm. Adv. Eng. Softw. **95**, 51–67 (2016)
11. Potter, M.A., De Jong, K.A.: A cooperative coevolutionary approach to function optimization. In: Davidor, Y., Schwefel, H.-P., Männer, R. (eds.) PPSN 1994. LNCS, vol. 866, pp. 249–257. Springer, Heidelberg (1994). https://doi.org/10.1007/3-540-58484-6_269
12. Pan, G., Li, K., Ouyang, A., et al.: Hybrid immune algorithm based on greedy algorithm and delete-cross operator for solving TSP. Soft. Comput. **20**(2), 555–566 (2016)
13. Yao, X., Liu, Y., Lin, G.: Evolutionary programming made faster. IEEE Trans. Evol. Comput. **3**(2), 82–102 (1999)
14. Digalakis, J.G., Margaritis, K.G.: On benchmarking functions for genetic algorithms. Int. J. Comput. Math **77**(4), 481–506 (2001)

Jointing Cross-Modality Retrieval to Reweight Attributes for Image Caption Generation

Yuxuan Ding[1], Wei Wang[1], Mengmeng Jiang[1], Heng Liu[1], Donghu Deng[2],
Wei Wei[3], and Chunna Tian[1(✉)]

[1] VIPS Lab, School of Electronic Engineering, Xidian University, Xi'an, China
chnatian@xidian.edu.cn
[2] Troops 95841 of PLA, Jiuquan, China
[3] School of Computer Science, Northwestern Polytechnical University, Xi'an, China

Abstract. Automatic natural language description for images is one of
the key issues towards image understanding. In this paper, we propose
an image caption framework, which explores specific semantics jointing
with general semantics. For specific semantics, we propose to retrieve
captions of the given image in a visual-semantic embedding space. To
explore the general semantics, we first extract the common attributes of
the image by Multiple Instance Learning (MIL) detectors. Then, we use
the specific semantics to re-rank the semantic attributes extracted by
MIL, which are mapped into visual feature layer of CNN to extract the
jointing visual feature. Finally, we feed the visual feature to LSTM and
generate the caption of image under the guidance of BLEU_4 similarity, incorporating the sentence-making priors of reference captions. We
evaluate our algorithm on standard metrics: BLEU, CIDEr, ROUGE_L
and METEOR. Experimental results show our approach outperforms the
state-of-the-art methods.

Keywords: Cross-modality retrieval · Image captioning · Semantic
attribute

1 Introduction

Image captioning aims to automatically describe an image with natural language
captions. It first grabs information of main objects, relationships among objects
and the scene context as well in the images, and then describes the information with natural languages. Thus, it involves the techniques of both computer
vision and natural language processing. However, how to well represent the visual
information of images and describe them reasonably are still challenging. Thus,
image captioning is still a hot research topic. A mass of methods are proposed
to address these issues in recent years.

The first author Yuxuan Ding is a Ph.D. candidate.

© Springer Nature Switzerland AG 2019
Z. Lin et al. (Eds.): PRCV 2019, LNCS 11859, pp. 62–74, 2019.
https://doi.org/10.1007/978-3-030-31726-3_6

Retrieval Based Caption: In retrieval base captioner, caption was retrieved from captions of similar images in the training set. As we can see, retrieval based methods need a large amount of annotated sentences for searching valid similar descriptions. Ordonez et al. [20] utilize global image representations to retrieve related captions from a large dataset and then transfer to the query image. Devlin et al. [7] find the visually similar k-Nearest Neighbor (k-NN) of the testing images in the training set, and then select best captions from the captions of k-NN images based on highest average lexical similarity. Kiros et al. [14] proposed an end-to-end method to train embedding mapping with triplet loss. Faghri et al. [9] uses rank loss to optimize the embedding, which has achieved the state-of-the-art performance in image-caption retrieval. However, these approaches cannot generate novel descriptions.

Encoder-Decoder Based Caption: Image captioning has big progress in recent years, because of deep learning based feature representation and sequential machine translation. Inspired by the end-to-end machine translation [2,6], Encoder-Decoder captioner extract the visual feature of images with Convolutional Neural Network (CNN) and then use Recurrent Neural Networks (RNN) to translate visual representation into natural language descriptions [13,19,26]. Mao et al. [19] propose a multimodal Recurrent Neural Network (m-RNN) model for generating captions, it consists of a CNN for image representation, a RNN for text embedding. Vinyals et al. [26] adopt GoogLeNet as an image encoder and apply LSTM [11] as the decoder. Karpathy et al. [13] attempt to align sentence fragments to image regions, and then aim at generating descriptions of visual regions using RNN. In the end-to-end translation framework, some approaches introduce an attention mechanism to improve the performance of image captioning [18,28]. Recently, Reinforcement Learning (RL) [24] has been applied to optimize the image captioning model by using the test metrics as rewards, such as BLUE in [1] or CIDEr in [22], which improve the results distinctively.

Visual Attribute: Feeding high-level semantic concepts to RNN usually results in better captioning results. Therefore, visual attributes are incorporated into image captioning in many ways [27,29,30], among which attribute extraction is one of the most successful method. Wu et al. [27] demonstrate that the high level visual concepts play an important role in image captioning. They feed the detected region-based attributes rather than CNN feature into the Decoder. Yao et al. [29] confirm that feeding image feature to LSTM at the first time step and feeding attributes at every step is the best choice. You et al. [30] use a Fully Convolutional Network (FCN) [23] selectively focus on visual semantic words while extracting image feature.

However, there are two issues need to be solved: (1) The detected attributes emphasize on the general attributes in the training set, which may not the most related to testing images; (2) Using attributes instead of visual features ignores the spatial layout and context of the attributes. Once the information is lost, it is hard to be recovered during decoding. To address these issues, we use cross-modal retrieval to find related captions for image. Considering the embedding space should align feature of both objects and scene, we concatenate the scene feature and object feature to build the multi-feature visual-semantic embedding (MVSE++) based cross-modal retrieval. Retrieved captions are used to re-rank the detected attributes, which pick the specific semantics. Then, we map attributes into the CNN to extract their visual feature. This feature contains objects, layout and context of general and specific semantic attributes. We adopt the Bleu_4 similarity in the decoding to further use the specific semantics, improving the performance of sentence generation. The framework of our method is illustrated as Fig. 1. The experimental results on MS-COCO show our method achieves the best performance on almost all evaluation metrics compared with the state-of-the-art methods, especially, the BLEU_4 reaches 0.342 and CIDEr reaches 1.058.

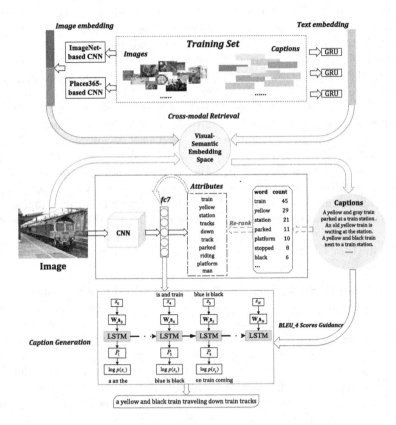

Fig. 1. The main framework of the proposed method.

2   Our Model

In this paper, we propose a retrieval based attribute model for captioning task. Our model consists of three parts: Attribute extraction by MIL detectors [10] to obtain the general semantics existing in the testing image for captioning, attributes re-ranking based on the specific semantics provided by MVSE++ retrieval and caption generation guided by BLEU_4 similarity. As the detectors were obtained from the whole dataset, we think they can represent general semantics of captions. We think specific semantics of an image can be provided by other images which correspond to it, so we called retrieval semantics as specific semantics.

2.1   Image-Caption Retrieval

We propose to retrieve the captions for the input image in a multi-feature visual-semantic embedding (MVSE++) space, which avoids the visual semantic miss-alignment on both aspects of objects and scene context. In the original VSE++ based cross-modal retrieval method, the visual feature is extracted by the CNN based object classifier trained on ImageNet dataset, which mainly focus on the objects in images and lacks the scene information. Thus, we joint the object-scene feature based visual-semantic embedding to retrieve the image specific captions. The feature of image and semantic features of captions, which are encoded by GRU as same as basic VSE++ method, which are mapped into the same space. Thus, we can get the candidates in another modality in this common space by finding near neighbors, which compose our specific semantics.

2.2   The General and Specific Semantics Jointed Visual Feature Extraction

First, we need figure out what are the generally happened semantics in image captions. Follow most attributes detection method, we analyze the distribution of word frequency in the training captions, and collect 1000 most frequently appearing words to build an attribute set $A = \{Att_1, Att_2, ..., Att_N\}, N = 1000$, as the common semantics. This set covers 92% words in all captions and acts as the initial semantic categories for 1000 attribute detectors, which is trained by a CNN based MIL model.

MIL views each training image as a bag of labels. An image **I** is a bag of semantic features. For one attribute Att_i, image is a positive sample if its caption contains Att_i, regions in the image build a positive bag, otherwise, it is a negative sample and we think it is a negative bag. The MIL detectors are alternatively optimized. Attributes usually describe complex and some of them cannot be demarcated boundaries clearly, such as "red", "holding" or "beautiful" etc. So we follow the work of Lebret et al. [15], detecting attributes with a noisy-OR version of MIL. We resize an image sample to 567×567 and feed into CNN, which is based on a modified VGG_16 network. Five convolution layers in front are kept, in order to maintain regional information for visual words extracting, we replace

fc layers by three convolutions then obtain a fully convolutional network. So, the penultimate convolution layer fc_7conv represents image feature reserving location information of original input image. After above steps, it generates a 12×12 coarse response map corresponding to slide the original CNN over image with stride of 32 and get fc_8conv's output on each location. For each image $\mathbf{I}$, $p_j^{Att_i}$ is the probability of sub-region j corresponding an attribute Att_i, then we calculate an integrated probability combine all regions probabilities in this image as follows

$$p^{Att_i} = 1 - \prod_{j \in \mathbf{I}} (1 - p_j^{Att_i})$$ (1)

We train the network with a multi-label classification task. The class is top 1000 frequent words and labels are built from the ground truth captions. This is our MIL detector.

Given a testing image $\mathbf{I}$, we detect a set of attributes $A = \{Att_1, Att_2, ..., Att_N\}$ by MIL detectors obtain the general semantics existing in the image for captioning. We obtain the specific semantics by retrieving top sentences in MVSE++ space. We count the frequency of attribute Att_i in A as c_{Att_i}, which is used to reweight the original attributes probabilities $\{p_{att}^{Att_1}, p_{att}^{Att_2}, ..., p_{att}^{Att_N}\}$ as follows.

$$p_{re-att}^{Att_i} = p_{att}^{Att_i} + \alpha * c_{Att_i}$$ (2)

In Eq. (2), α represents the weighting coefficient, means the proportion of retrieved words in the overall attributes. According to Eq. (2), we re-rank the attributes in A and selected top T attributes $\{Att_1, Att_2, ..., Att_T\}$, whose probabilities $\{p_{re-att}^{Att_1}, p_{re-att}^{Att_2}, ..., p_{re-att}^{Att_T}\}$ is defined as ρ, to maintain the testing-specific attributes and reduce the influence of uncorrelated attributes. Finally, we map the re-ranked attributes to fc_7conv layer of CNN to obtain the general and specific semantics collaborated visual feature. Corresponding visual features of the re-ranked attributes are extracted as follows.

$$\rho' = \sum_{i=1}^{T} \rho_i \mathbf{fc_8 w}_i$$ (3)

$$\mathbf{z}_{re-att} = \rho' \odot \text{GAP}(fc_7conv)$$ (4)

where $\mathbf{fc_8 w}_i$ is weight from fc_7conv to fc_8conv for Att_i, $\odot$ represents dot multiplication. GAP is global average pooling operation, which is a merging of region feature so it can provide more details in image. We consider the $\mathbf{z}_{re-att}$ as an importance-weighted visual feature with the most caption-relevant information. This feature is used as the input of LSTM to improve the accuracy of image captioning. These re-ranked attributes contain a variety types of word such as noun, adjective, verb and so on.

2.3   Image Caption Generator

We use the LSTM model as caption generator. At t time step, LSTM is formulated as below.

$$\mathbf{i}_t = \sigma\left(\mathbf{W}_{ix}\mathbf{x}_t + \mathbf{W}_{ih}\mathbf{h}_{t-1}\right) \tag{5}$$

$$\mathbf{f}_t = \sigma\left(\mathbf{W}_{fx}\mathbf{x}_t + \mathbf{W}_{fh}\mathbf{h}_{t-1}\right) \tag{6}$$

$$\mathbf{o}_t = \sigma\left(\mathbf{W}_{ox}\mathbf{x}_t + \mathbf{W}_{oh}\mathbf{h}_{t-1}\right) \tag{7}$$

$$\mathbf{c}_t = \mathbf{f}_t \odot \mathbf{c}_{t-1} + \mathbf{i}_t \odot \tanh(\mathbf{W}_{cx}\mathbf{x}_t + \mathbf{W}_{ch}\mathbf{h}_{t-1}) \tag{8}$$

$$\mathbf{h}_t = \mathbf{o}_t \odot \tanh(\mathbf{c}_t) \tag{9}$$

where $\mathbf{x}_t$, $\mathbf{h}_t$ and $\mathbf{c}_t$ are input vector, hidden state and cell state of LSTM. $\mathbf{W}$ represents the embedding matrix. σ is sigmoid function and tanh is hyperbolic tangent. $\odot$ represents dot multiplication of two vectors. $\mathbf{x}_t$, $\mathbf{h}_{t-1}$ and $\mathbf{c}_{t-1}$ are given at each time step. $\mathbf{i}_t$, $\mathbf{f}_t$, $\mathbf{o}_t$ are input gate, forget gate and output gate respectively.

Instead of feeding the simple image feature directly, we input the attributes re-ranked image visual feature $\mathbf{z}_{re-att}$ in Sect. 3.2 to LSTM as the "source language". Therefore, we establish a dependence relationship between words and sentences in the training dataset. The decoder maximizing the probability of the correct description is formulated by Eq. (10).

$$\theta^* = \arg\max_\theta \sum_{(\mathbf{I},S)} \log p(S|\mathbf{z}_{re-att}; \theta) \tag{10}$$

we define $S = \{S_1, S_2, ..., S_L\}$ as a sequence of words. It usually uses chain rule to model the joint probability of previously generated words as

$$\log p(S|\mathbf{z}_{re-att}) = \sum_{t=0}^{L} \log p(S_t|\mathbf{z}_{re-att}, S_0, ..., S_{t-1}), \tag{11}$$

where N is caption length and $\log p(S_t|\mathbf{z}_{re-att}, S_0, ..., S_{t-1})$ means the probability of generating the current word S_t conditioned on attribute based vector $\mathbf{z}_{re-att}$ and previously generated words.

During training, suppose we have image visual feature $\mathbf{z}_{re-att}$ and its description sequence $\{S_0, S_1, S_2, ..., S_N, S_{N+1}\}$, where S_0 is the start symbol and S_{N+1} is the end symbol. Each element in the sequence is a one-hot word vector, whose size is 11518. In the proposed approach, feature vector is mapped into H-dimensional space by the embedding matrixe $\mathbf{W}_f$. LSTM was initialized as follows.

$$\mathbf{h}_0 = \text{LSTM}(\mathbf{W}_f \mathbf{z}_{re-att}, \mathbf{0}) \tag{12}$$

The decoding procedure is given in Eqs. (13)–(15). After initializing LSTM, one-hot word vector is embedded by $\mathbf{W}_S$ as input vector. Hidden state $\mathbf{h}_t$ at each step is computed by LSTM and mapped into 11518-dimensional word space by $\mathbf{W}_h$. The generator is formulated to minimize the loss, which is the negative log likelihood in Eq. (17).

$$\text{init}\,(\mathbf{h}) = \mathbf{h}_0 \tag{13}$$

$$\mathbf{h}_t = \text{LSTM}(\mathbf{W}_S S_t, \mathbf{h}_{t-1}), t \geq 0 \tag{14}$$

$$p(S_t \mid \mathbf{z}_{re-att}, S_0, S_1, ..., S_{t-1}) = \text{Softmax}(\mathbf{W}_h \mathbf{h}_t) \tag{15}$$

Similar to Chen et al. [4], LSTM network infers image descriptions in the testing phase. We use retrieved sentences as references to guide the description generation by comparing the similarities between current generated sentence and top k retrieved captions. So during the generation of each sentence, it can correct the deviation of focus, making descriptions fit the evaluation metrics. Inspired by Devlin et al. [7], we introduce the consensus score concept that calculated by the descriptions of similar images from the training set. This consensus scoring function between image $\mathbf{I}$ and generated sentence S as

$$r(S, \mathbf{I}) = \frac{1}{k} \sum_{\omega=1}^{k} \varphi(S, \omega), \tag{16}$$

where S is current generated sentence and $\mathbf{I}$ is the given image, the k sentences $\{\omega_1, \omega_2, ..., \omega_k\}$ are retrieved by image $\mathbf{I}$ using cross-modal embedding, and $\varphi(S, \omega)$ is the similarity score between two captions: (S, ω). We choose BLEU_4 similarity function which measures 4-gram overlap. At each inference time step of LSTM, the probability of generating is decided by log likelihood Eq. (11) and consensus score Eq. (16) together. We use λ to balance these two terms, the final predict probability as follow.

$$l(S, \mathbf{z}_{re-att}) = \lambda \log p(S \mid \mathbf{z}_{re-att}) + (1 - \lambda) r(S, \mathbf{I}) \tag{17}$$

3   Experiments and Results

3.1   Datasets and Experimental Setup

MSCOCO contains 82,783 training images, 40,504 validation images and 40,775 testing images [17]. As MSCOCO is the most common dataset of image captioning task and many related works only evaluate on it, we also explore evaluation result of our model. Each image has five captions annotated by Amazon Mechanical Turk (AMT). Since the original testing set of is not completely available, we follow standard testing way of previous methods. For comparison with other approaches fairly, we split the training set and validation set together into three parts: training, validation and testing as Vinyals et al. [26] did. This split reserves 10% unused 5000 images of MSCOCO validation randomly for testing.

Network Architectures: As for feature extracting, we modify VGG_16 by keeping the convolutional layers $conv1_1$ to $conv5_3$ and replacing the fully connected layers fc_7 fc_8 with three fully convolutional layers. Finally, a MIL layer is followed for visual attributes prediction. We select all attributes with probabilities higher than 0.3 as candidate terms. For MVSE++, we implemented ResNet_152 CNN trained on ImageNet and Places365 datasets to obtain two

2048D feature vectors, which are concatenated as one 4096D visual feature. The top 20 retrieved sentences are used as the specific semantic prior to re-rank candidate attributes to weight layer and output a 4096D feature vector. We feed this feature to LSTM with a 512D state vector from Google NIC network for captioning. All these models are trained on NVIDIA Titan Xp.

Evaluation Metrics: The methods are evaluated on the standard metrics: BLEU_n [21], CIDEr [25], ROUGE_L [16] and METEOR [3] following coco-caption [5]. BLEU measures the similarity between two sentences in machine translation task, which is defined as the geometric mean of n-gram (up to 4) precision scores multiplied by a brevity penalty on short sentences. CIDEr measures the consensus between generated descriptions and the reference sentences, which is a specific evaluation metric designed for image captioning recently. METEOR is defined as the harmonic mean of precision and recall of unigram matches between sentences. For all the metrics, the higher is the better.

Baseline: In order to completely verify the effectiveness of our method, we use an original VGG_16 to extract image features as baseline, however, without attribute involves. We just make a common VGG Network to extract fc_7 feature as one 4096D vector which is fed into the LSTM directly.

3.2 Results and Analysis

For an intuitive presentation of our joint language retrieval attribute-conditional approach, we design the following experiment. Table 1 shows how the language retrieval results improve captioning accuracy. **ATTR** means an attribute based feature only mapping visual concepts on fc_7 fed into LSTM, its Bleu_4 score just reaches 0.256. **Re-ATTR** means the model combined attribute with the retrieval results, as we can see, Bleu_4 score rapidly increases to 0.32 while CIDEr increases from 0.765 to 1.001, nearly one-third. Other metrics have an excellent performance, too. **B4-Re-ATTR** model consists of visual attribute, MVSE++ retrieval based attribute distribution re-rank, and BLEU_4 similarity guidance caption generation, that achieves the best performance on all metrics obviously.

Table 1. Results comparison on variety of parameters, testing on MSCOCO dataset of 5000 images

Model	Bleu_1	Bleu_2	Bleu_3	Bleu_4	CIDEr	ROUGE_L	METEOR
Baseline	0.658	0.478	0.347	0.255	0.776	0.491	0.223
ATTR	0.663	0.481	0.347	0.256	0.765	0.491	0.226
Re-ATTR	0.730	0.561	0.423	0.320	1.001	0.540	0.260
B4-Re-ATTR	**0.749**	**0.586**	**0.446**	**0.337**	**1.051**	**0.548**	**0.260**

We report performance of our method and other state-of-the-art methods on MSCOCO in Table 2. The state-of-the-art algorithms are three main types: (1) The simple encode-decode based model Google NIC [26], LRCN [8] and m-RNN [19]. (2) Attention based methods such as Guiding LSTM [12] and Soft/Hard Attention [28], and 3. High level attributes based model ATT_FCN [30], ATT_CNN_LSTM [27], (3) LSTM-A [29]. Experiment demonstrates that our joint retrieval attribute-conditional approach achieves almost the excellent performance on metrics, BLEU_4 is a more convincing evaluation metrics that measures the matching degree between phrases. Our model has an outstanding performance in BLUE_4, it reaches to 0.342, outperforms all the compared state-of-the-art approaches. As for the specialized evaluation metric CIDEr, our 1.058 better than all the comparison methods, too. Soft/Hard Attention model performances better than other models because of the "attention" mechanism. However, our attribute model still has best results under most metrics. As the same type, our approach performs better than ATT_FCN, ATT_CNN_LSTM and LSTM-A, it is not difficult to judge that our cross-modal retrieval method provides effective scene context and spatial layout similarity of attributes for image caption task. And BLUE_4 similarity is a key supplement in generation stage.

Table 2. Performance of our proposed method and other state-of-the-art methods on MSCOCO

Model	Bleu_1	Bleu_2	Bleu_3	Bleu_4	CIDEr	ROUGE_L	METEOR
NIC [26]	0.666	0.451	0.304	0.203	0.855	0.491	0.237
LRCN [8]	0.628	0.442	0.304	0.210	-	-	-
m-RNN [19]	0.670	0.490	0.350	0.250	-	-	-
Soft Attention [28]	0.707	0.492	0.344	0.243	-	-	0.239
Hard Attention [28]	0.718	0.504	0.357	0.250	-	-	0.230
Guiding LSTM [12]	0.670	0.490	0.360	0.260	-	-	0.230
ATT_FCN [30]	0.709	0.537	0.402	0.304	-	-	0.243
ATT_CNN_LSTM [30]	0.740	0.560	0.420	0.310	0.940	-	0.260
LSTM-A [29]	0.730	0.565	0.429	0.325	0.986	0.538	0.261
Our model	0.730	0.561	0.423	0.320	1.001	0.540	0.260
Our B4 Model	**0.749**	**0.586**	**0.446**	**0.337**	**1.051**	**0.548**	**0.260**

Qualitative Analysis: In addition to the above exact results, we also draw a qualitative analysis chart as Fig. 2 to show the superiority of our method. It compares our model with the initial attributes model **ATTR**, two decoding networks use the same LSTM structure so the gap of results only depends on the differences of image features. We show some captioning examples from the validation set. As we can see, the visual words often corresponds to salient objects

Fig. 2. Qualitative analysis of attributes with caption retrieval result. The top line shows simple visual attributes feature captions. The bottom line shows retrieval reweighted descriptions.

or relationships of images. Since the retrieval based attributes provide both main objects and surroundings, the captions of our final network have more fine details, such as the type and number of objects, the color information and the spatial relationship between goals. All the above results illustrate that our attribute-conditional model guided by caption retrieval leads to an overall increase in caption generation performance.

4   Conclusions

In this paper, we propose a novel caption generation approach based on reweighted semantic attributes. We use cross-modality retrieval results to re-rank key visual attributes in image and obtain an attribute-conditional feature, on the other hand, retrieval results also provide BLEU_4 similarity information to guide caption generating for testing image. For attribute extraction, a MIL based VGG_16 network detects preliminary key attributes from sets of image regions as candidates, these attributes always pay more attention on the regions with richer semantic information in given image. For cross-modality retrieval, a MVSE++ model searches similar captions in joint visual-semantic embedding space. Then, we reweight the candidate attributes distribution according to the retrieved similar image captions from the training set, moreover, the retrieved captions also participate in sentence generating on the LSTM decoding stage. Experiments verify the accuracy of our method. It outperforms several state-of-the-art methods on MSCOCO 2014 dataset.

Acknowledgement. This work was supported in part by the National Natural Science Foundation of China under Grants 61571354 and 61671385. In part by China Post doctoral Science Foundation under Grant 158201.

References

1. Bahdanau, D., et al.: An actor-critic algorithm for sequence prediction. In: 5th International Conference on Learning Representations, ICLR 2017, Toulon, France, 24–26 April 2017, Conference Track Proceedings (2017)
2. Bahdanau, D., Cho, K., Bengio, Y.: Neural machine translation by jointly learning to align and translate. In: 3rd International Conference on Learning Representations, ICLR 2015, San Diego, CA, USA, 7–9 May 2015, Conference Track Proceedings (2015)
3. Banerjee, S., Lavie, A.: METEOR: an automatic metric for MT evaluation with improved correlation with human judgments. In: Proceedings of the Workshop on Intrinsic and Extrinsic Evaluation Measures for Machine Translation and/or Summarization@ACL 2005, Ann Arbor, Michigan, USA, 29 June 2005, pp. 65–72 (2005)
4. Chen, M., Ding, G., Zhao, S., Chen, H., Liu, Q., Han, J.: Reference based LSTM for image captioning. In: Proceedings of the Thirty-First AAAI Conference on Artificial Intelligence, San Francisco, California, USA, 4–9 February 2017, pp. 3981–3987 (2017)
5. Chen, X., et al.: Microsoft COCO captions: data collection and evaluation server. CoRR abs/1504.00325 (2015). http://arxiv.org/abs/1504.00325
6. Cho, K., et al.: Learning phrase representations using RNN encoder-decoder for statistical machine translation. In: Proceedings of the 2014 Conference on Empirical Methods in Natural Language Processing, EMNLP 2014, Doha, Qatar, 25–29 October 2014. A meeting of SIGDAT, a Special Interest Group of the ACL, pp. 1724–1734 (2014)
7. Devlin, J., Gupta, S., Girshick, R.B., Mitchell, M., Zitnick, C.L.: Exploring nearest neighbor approaches for image captioning. CoRR abs/1505.04467 (2015). http://arxiv.org/abs/1505.04467
8. Donahue, J., et al.: Long-term recurrent convolutional networks for visual recognition and description. IEEE Trans. Pattern Anal. Mach. Intell. **39**(4), 677–691 (2017)
9. Faghri, F., Fleet, D.J., Kiros, J., Fidler, S.: VSE++: improving visual-semantic embeddings with hard negatives. In: British Machine Vision Conference 2018, BMVC 2018, 3–6 September 2018, p. 12. Northumbria University, Newcastle, UK (2018)
10. Fang, H., et al.: From captions to visual concepts and back. In: IEEE Conference on Computer Vision and Pattern Recognition, CVPR 2015, Boston, MA, USA, 7–12 June 2015, pp. 1473–1482 (2015)
11. Hochreiter, S., Schmidhuber, J.: Long short-term memory. Neural Comput. **9**(8), 1735–1780 (1997)
12. Jia, X., Gavves, E., Fernando, B., Tuytelaars, T.: Guiding the long-short term memory model for image caption generation. In: 2015 IEEE International Conference on Computer Vision, ICCV 2015, Santiago, Chile, 7–13 December 2015, pp. 2407–2415 (2015)
13. Karpathy, A., Fei-Fei, L.: Deep visual-semantic alignments for generating image descriptions. IEEE Trans. Pattern Anal. Mach. Intell. **39**(4), 664–676 (2017)

14. Kiros, R., Salakhutdinov, R., Zemel, R.S.: Unifying visual-semantic embeddings with multimodal neural language models. CoRR abs/1411.2539 (2014). http://arxiv.org/abs/1411.2539
15. Lebret, R., Pinheiro, P.H.O., Collobert, R.: Simple image description generator via a linear phrase-based approach. In: 3rd International Conference on Learning Representations, ICLR 2015, San Diego, CA, USA, 7–9 May 2015, Workshop Track Proceedings (2015)
16. Lin, C.Y.: ROUGE: a package for automatic evaluation of summaries. Text Summarization Branches Out (2004)
17. Lin, T.-Y., et al.: Microsoft COCO: common objects in context. In: Fleet, D., Pajdla, T., Schiele, B., Tuytelaars, T. (eds.) ECCV 2014. LNCS, vol. 8693, pp. 740–755. Springer, Cham (2014). https://doi.org/10.1007/978-3-319-10602-1_48
18. Lu, J., Xiong, C., Parikh, D., Socher, R.: Knowing when to look: adaptive attention via a visual sentinel for image captioning. In: 2017 IEEE Conference on Computer Vision and Pattern Recognition, CVPR 2017, Honolulu, HI, USA, 21–26 July 2017, pp. 3242–3250 (2017)
19. Mao, J., Xu, W., Yang, Y., Wang, J., Yuille, A.L.: Deep captioning with multimodal recurrent neural networks (m-RNN). In: 3rd International Conference on Learning Representations, ICLR 2015, San Diego, CA, USA, 7–9 May 2015, Conference Track Proceedings (2015)
20. Ordonez, V., Kulkarni, G., Berg, T.L.: Im2text: describing images using 1 million captioned photographs. In: Advances in Neural Information Processing Systems 24: 25th Annual Conference on Neural Information Processing Systems 2011. Proceedings of a Meeting Held 12–14 December 2011, Granada, Spain, pp. 1143–1151 (2011)
21. Papineni, K., Roukos, S., Ward, T., Zhu, W.: BLEU: a method for automatic evaluation of machine translation. In: Proceedings of the 40th Annual Meeting of the Association for Computational Linguistics, 6–12 July 2002, Philadelphia, PA, USA, pp. 311–318 (2002)
22. Rennie, S.J., Marcheret, E., Mroueh, Y., Ross, J., Goel, V.: Self-critical sequence training for image captioning. In: 2017 IEEE Conference on Computer Vision and Pattern Recognition, CVPR 2017, Honolulu, HI, USA, 21–26 July 2017, pp. 1179–1195 (2017)
23. Shelhamer, E., Long, J., Darrell, T.: Fully convolutional networks for semantic segmentation. IEEE Trans. Pattern Anal. Mach. Intell. 39(4), 640–651 (2017)
24. Sutton, R.S., Barto, A.G.: Reinforcement Learning - An Introduction. Adaptive Computation and Machine Learning. MIT Press, Cambridge (1998)
25. Vedantam, R., Zitnick, C.L., Parikh, D.: Cider: consensus-based image description evaluation. In: IEEE Conference on Computer Vision and Pattern Recognition, CVPR 2015, Boston, MA, USA, 7–12 June 2015, pp. 4566–4575 (2015)
26. Vinyals, O., Toshev, A., Bengio, S., Erhan, D.: Show and tell: a neural image caption generator. In: IEEE Conference on Computer Vision and Pattern Recognition, CVPR 2015, Boston, MA, USA, 7–12 June 2015, pp. 3156–3164 (2015)
27. Wu, Q., Shen, C., Liu, L., Dick, A.R., van den Hengel, A.: What value do explicit high level concepts have in vision to language problems? In: 2016 IEEE Conference on Computer Vision and Pattern Recognition, CVPR 2016, Las Vegas, NV, USA, 27–30 June 2016, pp. 203–212 (2016)
28. Xu, K., et al.: Show, attend and tell: Neural image caption generation with visual attention. In: Proceedings of the 32nd International Conference on Machine Learning, ICML 2015, Lille, France, 6–11 July 2015, pp. 2048–2057 (2015)

29. Yao, T., Pan, Y., Li, Y., Qiu, Z., Mei, T.: Boosting image captioning with attributes. In: IEEE International Conference on Computer Vision, ICCV 2017, Venice, Italy, 22–29 October 2017, pp. 4904–4912 (2017)
30. You, Q., Jin, H., Wang, Z., Fang, C., Luo, J.: Image captioning with semantic attention. In: 2016 IEEE Conference on Computer Vision and Pattern Recognition, CVPR 2016, Las Vegas, NV, USA, 27–30 June 2016, pp. 4651–4659 (2016)

Pseudo Label Guided Subspace Learning for Multi-view Data

Shudong Hou$^{(\boxtimes)}$, Heng Liu, and Xiujun Wang

Anhui University of Technology, Maanshan 340122, China
{shudonghou,xjwang}@ahut.edu.cn, hengliusky@aliyun.com

Abstract. Multi-view spectral clustering methods could utilize the complementary information from different views to increase the robustness of clustering performances. Graph structures are usually revealed as affinity matrices. A pseudo label guided spectral embedding algorithm (PLGS) is proposed in this paper to enhance the consistence between graph matrices and spectral clustering results. Through iteratively estimating the pseudo labels of all samples and similarity matrices, the cluster assignment vector could be calculated with more confidence. Extensive experimental results on several benchmark datasets show promising performance and verify the effectiveness of our method.

Keywords: Spectral clustering · Pseudo label · Multi-view data · Unsupervised learning

1 Introduction

In recent years, multi-view learning methods [1] have received increasing attentions by exploring the consistency and complementary information of different views. It is difficult to fuse the heterogeneous properties from various representations together. If the relationships among different views are not modeled appropriately, the performance may be degraded compared to the best single one. The widely popular methods for multi-view learning are grouped into three main categories: co-training, multiple kernel learning and subspace learning.

As a classical representative paradigm, co-training method [2] utilizes the labeled data to train two classifiers, then categorizes unlabeled data separately. Then the predictive samples with great confidence are added to the labeled data to train the other classifier, and this procedure repeats. Multiple kernel learning [3] is originally proposed to learn a kernel matrix through optimizing a linear combination of kernel matrices. And it can be naturally extended to fuse heterogeneous data sources. Subspace learning-based approaches [4,5] aim to learn a common subspace shared by multiple views. The most typical method should be canonical correlation analysis (CCA) [6] that finds a latent space where the correlations of two projections are mutually maximized.

Different from pattern classification, data clustering aims at grouping vast unlabeled samples into several clusters in such a way that samples in the same

© Springer Nature Switzerland AG 2019
Z. Lin et al. (Eds.): PRCV 2019, LNCS 11859, pp. 75–83, 2019.
https://doi.org/10.1007/978-3-030-31726-3_7

cluster are more similar to each other and k-means clustering is the most well-known method [7]. Spectral clustering (SC) [8] constructs a graph similarity matrix and solves a relaxation of the normalized min-cut problem on this graph. It has gained lots of attention because of its robust performance. For multi-view data, it is assumed that all samples from different views share the same graph structure. Multi-view spectral clustering aims at discovering this intrinsic graph structure information exhibited by various data from several different views. Each view of the same object includes special features may not be described by other views. It is important to utilize the complementary information maximally and enhance the robustness of the final mixed clustering results. Hence co-regularized spectral clustering [9] find the consistent clusterings across the views through co-regularizing the clustering hypotheses. One challenging problems in spectral clustering methods is how affinity matrices are constructed.

Graph matrices are appeared in various methods when the local and global structure information is needed. The graph structure is described by encoding the pairwise similarities among all samples. However it is not reasonable to compute all distances between any two samples if they are far apart from each other. It is assumed that the data are satisfied with the local manifold structure. It is more robust to only compute the nearby several samples to construct the similarity matrix. Through a sparse similarity matrix, the local manifold structure could be better exhibited without lots of unnecessary links. The k-nearest and ε neighbours are widely adopted to compute similarity matrices since their simplicity and effectiveness. However it is hard to select the best k and ε values. Recently the graph matrix is optimized as a sub-problem when optimizing a unified global objective function instead of the original pre-computed similarity matrix [10]. Sparse [11,12] and low rank representation [13,14] could select the local samples by self-expressive abilities. It formulates the graph matrix automatically once the threshold is given. Multi-view low-rank sparse subspace clustering (MLRSSC) [15] learns a joint subspace representation imposing both sparse and low-rank constraint conditions. Kernel trick is utilized when the nonlinear extension is developed [16]. Multi-view learning with adaptive neighbors (MLAN) [17] performs clustering and learns the graph matrix simultaneously. The obtained optimized graph can be partitioned into the intrinsic clusters directly without a back-end processing. In [18], the common consensus information is leveraged instead of the weighted sum of different graphs. It is often happened that some values or views of one object are missing in practice. For traditional multi-view learning, this object is abandoned. By setting the connected weights corresponding to missing instances as 0, incomplete multi-view spectral clustering with adaptive graph learning (IMSC_AGL) [19] could flexibly handle kinds of incomplete cases and prove its effectiveness in incomplete multi-view learning.

Clustering with adaptive neighbors (CAN) [20] tries to acquire a fixed k-rank graph matrix and finish clustering using graph connected components without a back-end k-means method. It is said that the initialization of k-means is a big problem. However after the graph matrices is optimized, the initialization problem can be solved by repeating several times independently. And the restricted

k-rank constraint on graph matrices needs more iterations to balance the weighted factor. It is hard to judge which one costs more resources.

Inspired by learning to learn, a pseudo label guided multi-view spectral clustering method is proposed in this work. The consistence between data and models is maximally remained. If two samples do not share the same cluster assignment, the neighborhood relationship is not reliable. At the first step, we assume all paired samples have the same class label when the distance between them is more close than others. This operation may create some misleading linking edges. We hope to correct them by the following iterations. In each loop, only first k nearest samples with the same cluster assignment are selected as reliable neighbors. Then the similarity matrix is updated according to former spectral clustering results. The true label is approximately estimated after several repeats.

2 Related Work

In this section, we will first review the basic principles of multi-view spectral clustering. Then the CAN is revisited.

2.1 Spectral Clustering

Given a data set $X = \{x_1, \cdots, x_n\} \in \mathbf{R}^{d \times n}$, spectral clustering methods need to construct the graph matrix W first. Then the Laplace matrix is defined as

$$L = D - W \tag{1}$$

Thus the objective function of spectral clustering can be defined as

$$\min_{F} Tr(F^T L F) \tag{2}$$

$$s.t. \ F^T F = I$$

The optimal F is solved by eigen-decomposition. Then the final clustering is performed by using the formulated F as the low dimensional embedding of the raw data X.

2.2 Clustering with Adaptive Neighbors

Spectral clustering actually is a graph theory-based method. Thus the clustering task can be viewed as a graph cut problem. The ideal graph has exact c connected components for c-class clustering. Usually this strong constraint is difficult to satisfy due to the noisy and complex data distribution. For the sake of achieving the ideal graph cut, a reasonable low-rank constraint is added when constructing the similarity matrix S:

$$\min_{s_i \in \mathbf{R}^{n \times 1}} \sum_{i,j}^{n} \|x_i - x_j\|_2^2 s_{ij} + \alpha \|S\|_F^2$$

$$s.t. \ \forall i, s_i^T \mathbf{1} = 1, 0 \leq s_{ij} \leq 1, rank(L_S) = n - c \tag{3}$$

where s_i is a column vector with j-th element as s_{ij} and L_S is the Laplace matrix of S [17]. In each iterative loop, the value of α is adjusted to automatically select the local samples.

3   Methodology

The intuitive objective of multi-view clustering is mining the local common structure information. Since the unavoidable noise existed in each view, it requires more focus to balance the weights when fusing all graph matrices together. Different from CAN, our proposed PLGS iteratively estimates the pseudo label of all samples.

3.1   Model

For multi-view data, let $\mathcal{X} = \{\mathbf{X}^1, \mathbf{X}^2, \cdots, \mathbf{X}^V\}$ denotes the V-view feature sets where $\mathbf{X}^v \in \mathbf{R}^{n \times d_v}$ means the v-th feature set. In each feature set, the nearest k neighbors are selected to construct the similarity matrix S_i. Then the global similarity matrix S_g is calculated by integrating all S_i together. The classical spectral clustering method is performed based on S_g. Lastly, the nearest neighbors are corrected according to previous clustering results. Only the neighbors that are in the same cluster are remained in the similarity matrix, otherwise this pseudo label is not reliable and deleted. After the similarity matrix is updated, a new clustering result is generated again.

The integrated objective function is defined as:

$$\min_{S,Q} \quad Tr(Q^T L_g Q)$$
$$s.t. \quad \forall i \neq j, \quad cluster(q_i) = cluster(q_j)$$
$$\&\&S_{ij} \geq 0 \&\&(x_j \in K(x_i)||x_i \in K(x_j)) \tag{4}$$

where q_i is the i-th column of Q, L_g is the Laplace matrix of S_g, $K(x_i)$ represents the nearest neighbors for sample x_i and $cluster$ is the assignment vector calculated by SC methods. The main idea is finding a global optimized similarity matrix that is consistent with the spectral clustering result.

3.2   Optimization

To solve this challenging problem, an alternative iterative solution is adopted. The initial similarity matrix is constructed as follows:

$$S_{ij}^0 = \begin{cases} exp(-dist(x_i, x_j)^2/(2\sigma^2)), & x_j \in K(x_i)||x_i \in K(x_j) \\ 0, & otherwise \end{cases}$$
$$(i, j = 1, \cdots, n) \tag{5}$$

where $dist(x_i, x_j)$ means the distance between sample x_i and x_j. It is measured by the weighted average of all views. For simplicity the weights of all views are set to be the same $1/v$. Then the assignment vector *cluster* is acquired by spectral clustering (2).

Instead of the strictly matrix rank constraints, the k-means method is utilized to get the cluster assignment vector. Since its randomly initialization, the clustering results are different from each other for individual replicates. So the k-means are repeated for t times and the cluster assignment vector is computed as follows:

$$\begin{cases} cluster_f(x_i) = cluster_f(x_j), & if \ \#(cluster_k(x_i) == cluster_k(x_j)) \geq \theta \\ cluster_f(x_i) \neq cluster_f(x_j), & if \ \#(cluster_k(x_i) == cluster_k(x_j)) < \theta \end{cases}$$
$$(i, j = 1, \cdots, n, \ k = 1, 2, \cdots, t) \ (6)$$

where the function $\#$ means "the number of". It records how many times these two samples are in the same cluster. If this value is larger than the predefined threshold θ, we let them share the same cluster in the final assignment vector $cluster_f$. According to the new generated *cluster* assignment vector, the similarity matrix is corrected by deleting the inconsistent values.

$$S_{ij}^{(t+1)} = \begin{cases} S_{ij}^t, & if \ cluster(x_i) = cluster(x_j) \\ 0, & otherwise \end{cases} (i, j = 1, \cdots, n) \qquad (7)$$

Based on the above analysis, the overall algorithm for solving (4) is summarized in Algorithm 1.

Algorithm 1. PLGS Algorithm

Require:
  Multi-view data $\mathcal{X}$, the neighborhood size k and the repeat number t.
Ensure:
  The graph S_g and cluster assignment vector *label*.
  1: Construct the initial similarity matrix S according to (5).
  2: Formulate the global similarity matrix S_g by integrating all similarity matrices $\{S\}_{v=1}^V$ from all V views.
  3: **while** not convergence
  4:   Apply spectral clustering on S_g and get F by (2).
  5:   Perform t times k-means clustering and get assignment vector *label* using (6).
  6:   Update S_g by (7).
  7: **end while**

---

4 Experiments

In order to evaluate the effectiveness of the proposed method, extensive experiments are performed on several real-world multi-view datasets.

4.1 Datasets and Settings

The experimental results are reported on four real-world datasets: UCI Digits[1], Reuters, 3-sources[2] and Prokayotic. The detailed information of these datasets are listed in Table 1.

In the experiments, two evaluation metrics are used to verify the effectiveness of the proposed method. They are the accuracy and normalized mutual information (NMI). The clustering accuracy is defined as

$$accuracy = \frac{\#correct\ decisions}{\#total\ decisions} \tag{8}$$

And the NMI is defined as

$$NMI(\mu, \nu) = \frac{2\sum_{i=1}^{c}\sum_{j=1}^{\hat{c}} \frac{n_{ij}}{n} log \frac{n_{ij}n}{\sum_{i=1}^{c} n_i \sum_{j=1}^{\hat{c}} n_j}}{-\sum_{i=1}^{c} \frac{n_i}{n} log \frac{n_i}{n} - \sum_{j=1}^{\hat{c}} \frac{n_j}{n} log \frac{n_j}{n}} \tag{9}$$

where n_{ij} denotes the number of data in cluster i and class j, n_i and n_j denotes the data number belonging to the ground-truth (μ_i) and clustering result ν_j respectively.

Table 1. Statistics of the multi-view datasets

Dataset	Samples	Views	Clusters
UCI Digits	2000	6	10
Reuters	600	5	6
3-sources	169	3	6
Prokayotic	551	3	4

4.2 Experimental Results

Five methods, including spectral clustering, CAN, MLAN [17][3], MLRSSC and its kernel extension [15][4], are used for comparison. All parameters of these algorithms are set to values based on the respective source codes provided by their authors. The experimental results are shown in Table 2. For SC and CAN, the best single view result is reported.

Compare with spectral clustering, the performance of CAN is much better. This shows that the adaptive neighbors are more reliable than nearest neighbors. It is hard to adjust the parameter values of MLRSSC and its results are

---

[1] http://archive.ics.uci.edu/ml/datasets/Multiple+Features.
[2] http://mlg.ucd.ie/datasets/3sources.html.
[3] http://www.escience.cn/people/fpnie/papers.html.
[4] https://github.com/mbrbic/MultiViewLRSSC.

Table 2. Performance of different methods on four multi-view datasets.

Dataset	UCI digit		Reuters		3-sources		Prokaryotic	
	Accuray	NMI	Accuray	NMI	Accuray	NMI	Accuray	NMI
SC-best	85.45	88.44	56.00	42.54	88.76	75.06	60.25	9.26
CAN-best	86.65	89.61	37.33	32.82	70.41	61.69	75.32	47.96
MLRSSC	88.22	87.21	46.27	33.88	69.08	59.59	65.93	32.62
KMLRSSC	81.70	77.08	45.17	32.67	60.65	52.13	65.05	40.80
MLAN	97.20	93.60	55.33	41.35	92.31	81.87	**87.66**	58.21
PLGS	**98.15**	**95.72**	**60.17**	**43.86**	**92.90**	**83.84**	86.21	**59.92**

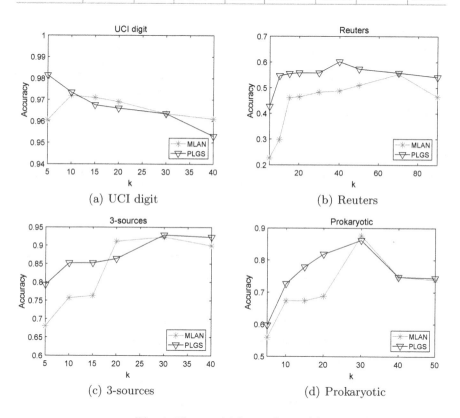

(a) UCI digit

(b) Reuters

(c) 3-sources

(d) Prokaryotic

Fig. 1. The sensitivity analysis of k

not satisfying. The rank-constraint is remained during the whole processing in MLAN while MLRSSC aims at optimizing a trace-norm minimization problem actually. Our proposed PLGS utilizes the k-nearest neighbors and pseudo labels of all samples to enhance the sparse and discriminative abilities of feature representations. Its promising clustering results are presented to demonstrate the effectiveness of PLGS.

4.3   Parameter Sensitivity

A predefined k value needs to be determined for MLAN and PLGS. To further verify the effectiveness of our proposed method, the sensitivity of k is analyzed in Fig. 1.

Although the neighbors in MLAN are selected adaptively, its clustering results are more sensitive compared with our PLGS. When the k value is large, two methods almost have the same performances. If the k value is small, PLGS usually performs better than MLAN.

5   Conclusion

In this paper, a pseudo label-guided clustering method is proposed to solve the multi-view clustering problem. Instead of solving a rank constraint optimization, we utilize a very simple idea to increase the sparse and discriminative abilities of feature representations. For PLGS, the global similarity matrix is calculated by average with the same weights. If the weights are carefully designed and iterative estimated, a better performance will be reached.

Acknowledgements. This work is partly supported in part by Natural Science Foundation of Anhui Province under Grant 1808085QF210 and Grant 1608085MF129. And in part by the Major and Key Project of Natural Science of Anhui Provincial Department of Education under Grant KJ2015ZD09 and Grant KJ2018A0043.

References

1. Xu, C., Tao, D., Xu, C.: A survey on multi-view learning. arXiv preprint arXiv:1304.5634 (2013)
2. Blum, A., Mitchell, T.: Combining labeled and unlabeled data with co-training. In: Proceedings of the Eleventh Annual Conference on Computational Learning Theory, pp. 92–100 (1998)
3. Lanckriet, G.R.G., Cristianini, N., Bartlett, P., El Ghaoui, L., Jordan, M.I.: Learning the kernel matrix with semidefinite programming. J. Mach. Learn. Res. **5**, 27–72 (2004)
4. Xu, C., Tao, D.: Multi-view intact space learning. IEEE Trans. Pattern Anal. Mach. Intell. **37**(12), 2531–2544 (2015)
5. Kan, M., Shan, S., Zhang, H., Lao, S., Chen, X.: Multi-view discriminant analysis. IEEE Trans. Pattern Anal. Mach. Intell. **38**(1), 188–194 (2016)
6. Hotelling, H.: Relations between two sets of variates. Biometrika **28**(3/4), 321–377 (1936)
7. MachQueen J.: Some methods for classification and analysis of multi-variate observations. In: Proceedings of 5th Berkeley Symposium on Mathematical Statistics and Probability, pp. 281–297 (1965)
8. von Luxburg, U.: A tutorial on spectral clustering. Stat. Comput. **17**(4), 395–416 (2007)
9. Kumar A., Rai P., Daume H.: Co-regularized multi-view spectral clustering. In: Proceedings of the 24th International Conference on Neural Information Processing Systems (NIPS 2011), pp. 1413–1421 (2011)

10. Pang, Y., Zhou, B., Nie, F.: Simultaneously learning neighborship and projection matrix for supervised dimensionality reduction. IEEE Trans. Neural Netw. Learn. Syst. (in press)
11. Elhamifar, E., Vidal, R.: Sparse subspace clustering: algorithm, theroy, and applications. IEEE Trans. Pattern Anal. Mach. Intell. **35**(11), 2765–2781 (2013)
12. Lu, C., Yan, S., Lin, Z.: Convex sparse spectral clustering: single-view to multi-view. IEEE Trans. Image Process. **25**(6), 2833–2843 (2016)
13. Liu, G., Lin, Z., Yan, S., Sun, J., Yu, Y., Ma, Y.: Robust recovery of subspace structures by low-rank representation. IEEE Trans. Pattern Anal. Mach. Intell. **35**(1), 171–184 (2013)
14. Lu, C., Feng, J., Yan, S., Lin, Z.: A unified alternating direction method of multipliers by majorization minimization. IEEE Trans. Pattern Anal. Mach. Intell. **40**(3), 527–541 (2018)
15. Brbić, M., Kopriva, I.: Multi-view low-rank sparse subspace clustering. Pattern Recogn. **73**, 247–256 (2018)
16. Houthuys, L., Langone, R., Suykens, J.A.K.: Multi-view kernel spectral clustering. Inf. Fusion **44**, 46–56 (2018)
17. Nie, Y., Cai, G., Li, J., Li, X.: Auto-wighted multi-view learning for image clustering and semi-supervised classification. IEEE Trans. Image Process. **27**(3), 1501–1511 (2018)
18. Zhan, K., Nie, N., Wang, J., Yang, Y.: Multiview consensus graph clustering. IEEE Trans. Image Process. **28**(3), 1261–1270 (2019)
19. Wen, J., Xu, Y., Liu, H.: Incomplete multiview spectral clustering with adaptive graph learning. IEEE Trans. Cybern. (in press)
20. Wang, Q., Qin, Z., Nie, F., Li, X.: Spectral embedded adaptive neighbors clustering. IEEE Trans. Neural Netw. Learn. Syst. **40**(3), 1265–1271 (2019)

MVB: A Large-Scale Dataset for Baggage Re-Identification and Merged Siamese Networks

Zhulin Zhang, Dong Li$^{(\boxtimes)}$, Jinhua Wu, Yunda Sun, and Li Zhang

Nuctech AI R&D Center, Beijing 100084, China
{zhangzhulin,li.dong,wujinhua,sunyunda,zhangli}@nuctech.com

Abstract. In this paper, we present a novel dataset named MVB (Multi View Baggage) for baggage ReID task which has some essential differences from person ReID. The features of MVB are three-fold. First, MVB is the first publicly released large-scale dataset that contains 4519 baggage identities and 22660 annotated baggage images as well as its surface material labels. Second, all baggage images are captured by specially-designed multi-view camera system to handle pose variation and occlusion, in order to obtain the 3D information of baggage surface as complete as possible. Third, MVB has remarkable inter-class similarity and intra-class dissimilarity, considering the fact that baggage might have very similar appearance while the data is collected in two real airport environments, where imaging factors varies significantly from each other. Moreover, we proposed a merged Siamese network as baseline model and evaluated its performance. Experiments and case study are conducted on MVB.

Keywords: Dataset · Re-Identification · Siamese networks

1 Introduction

At international airports, baggage from flights normally need to be scanned by security check devices based on X-ray imaging due to safety issues and customs declaration. To increase the customs clearance efficiency, X-ray security check devices have been deployed in BHS (Baggage Handling System) at many newly constructed airports. After flight arrivals, all check-in baggage will go through security check devices, which are connected with conveyor of BHS. Therefore, the X-ray image of each baggage is generated and inspected before baggage claim. Currently, the common practice is attaching RFID (Radio Frequency Identification) tags onto interested baggage right after security check devices, in order to indicate the baggage to be further manually unpacked and inspected. As passengers claim interested baggage with RFID tags and carry it to RFID detection zone, alarms will be triggered.

Nevertheless, RFID tag detection has certain drawbacks. First, tags might fall off in the process of transfer. Certain passengers might also deliberately tear

© Springer Nature Switzerland AG 2019
Z. Lin et al. (Eds.): PRCV 2019, LNCS 11859, pp. 84–96, 2019.
https://doi.org/10.1007/978-3-030-31726-3_8

off tags in order to avoid inspections. The loss of tags will directly result in detection failures of interested baggage. Second, tagging need to be conducted by manpower or certain equipment, which causes additional cost together with the tag itself and might affect customs clearance rate. Moreover, baggage of metal material surface will interfere with detection signal of RFID tags, thus it also leads to false negative cases.

Considering these defects, a security inspection approach that requires no physical tags will show great advantages in avoiding detection miss and metal interference, reducing costs, and increasing efficiency. An approach based on baggage appearance images is thus employed. Concretely, images of baggage appearance will be captured at BHS and bundled with inspection information before baggage claim. While passengers carrying the baggage and entering the customs checkpoint, i.e. the area for customs declaration and security check before leaving the airport, the appearance image will be taken again. These checkpoint images will be analyzed by comparing with those taken at BHS to identify whether certain baggage is of interest. Practically, passengers often place feature items such as stickers or ropes on baggage, which can serve as cues in distinguishing baggage, thus each baggage could be to be unique within certain time interval. Since the baggage is re-identified cross cameras, the process is referred as baggage ReID later in this paper.

Similar to the person ReID [1], the baggage ReID task also faces challenges such as object occlusion, background clutter, motion blurring and variations of lighting, pose, viewpoint, etc. Particularly, some of these aspects are even more challenging for baggage ReID. For instance, the baggage pose often differs between images captured at BHS and checkpoint, as well as per each baggage. It brings extra difficulties for applying part-based person image retrieval approaches [2,16] to baggage ReID, since pedestrian in video surveillance mostly remains canonical standing/walking pose. Meanwhile, similar to vehicle ReID [3,4], baggage images from different view-points vary much more than the case of person ReID. Furthermore, it is not uncommon that many baggage has very similar appearance thus are less distinctive compared with person. All these characteristics make baggage ReID a uniquely challenging task.

Recent years, research and application in computer vision have seen great development, especially with the help of deep learning. An important enabling factor of the rapid development of deep learning is the availability of large scale datasets [5,6,10]. Taking person ReID as example, datasets such as Market-1501 [7], MARS [8], CUHK03 [9], etc., have contributed to improving the state-of-the-art performance continuously [16,19]. These large-scale datasets played a key role to evolve the person ReID task from lab problem to real-world industrial application.

In this paper, a large-scale baggage ReID dataset called MVB (Multi View Baggage) is proposed. First, as a large-scale image dataset, MVB consists of 4519 baggage identities and 22660 annotated hand-drawn masks and bounding boxes, as well as surface material labels. Second, all baggage images are captured by specially-designed multi-view camera system to handle pose variation

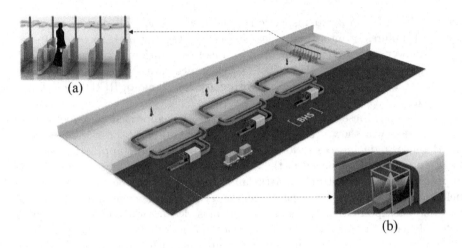

Fig. 1. Baggage ReID application and multi-view camera system at: (a) checkpoint (b) BHS.

and occlusion. The multi-view images contribute to obtaining 3D information of baggage surface as complete as possible, which is crucial to the ReID problem, since there could be notably different textures on specific area of baggage. Third, in real scenario at airports, the imaging factors like lighting, background, viewpoint, motion, etc., are quite different between BHS and checkpoint, making the baggage ReID task of our dataset tend to be a cross domain problem, which is more challenging and inspiring. Moreover, baggage might have very similar appearance thus are hardly distinctive. These aspects make our dataset have remarkable inter-class similarity and intra-class dissimilarity which domain adaptation approach [17,18] in person ReID could be applied. To the best of our knowledge, MVB is the first publicly available baggage ReID dataset, which will enable utilizing deep learning methods on baggage ReID and benefit research and application on general object ReID tasks. Additionally, we also propose baseline models using merged Siamese network with ablation study to understand how baggage ReID performance benefit from features like self-attention, hard example mining, foreground mask, etc.

This paper is organized as follows. In Sect. 2, MVB dataset will be introduced in detail. Task and evaluation method on MVB will be given in Sect. 3. Baseline models and corresponding experiment results will be shown in Sects. 4 and 5. In Sect. 6, a short conclusion will be summarized.

2 Dataset

2.1 Raw Data Collection System

As raw data, images containing baggage are all captured at an international airport. The baggage ReID application is illustrated in Fig. 1. The data collection process can be divided to two stages, i.e. BHS and checkpoint, both have multi-view image capture system deployed.

In BHS stage, after unloaded from landed airplanes, baggage is put on BHS conveyor and transferred to a security check device for X-ray scan in sequence. At the entrance of the device, a portal frame is set up over the conveyor. In order to get 3D information of baggage appearance as complete as possible, three cameras were placed on different position of the frame to capture multi-view images: right-front, top, and left-back respectively. These cameras receive the trigger signal as baggage passes by and take three images simultaneously. As the baggage being scanned by the device next to the frame, the generated X-ray image can be inspected by staff or algorithm in real-time, then the information of whether certain baggage is of interest is bundled with the multi-view images taken by the cameras.

Table 1. Annotation statistics.

	#Baggage images	#Full-sized images	Average views per identity
BHS	13028	13028	2.88
Checkpoint	9632	9237	2.13
Overall	22660	22265	5.01

The second stage for capturing multi-view images is at the checkpoint for customs clearance. According to procedure of customs clearance, passengers along with baggage are required to pass through gate at checkpoint after baggage claim. The checkpoint usually contains several gates. At each gate, four cameras are embedded for multi-view image capturing. Two pairs of cameras are located near the exit and entrance of the gate at each side, taking images against and along the passenger moving direction respectively. The two pairs of cameras are triggered in proper order to adapt many passenger actions such as pushing a baggage cart, dragging/pushing a mobile suitcase, etc. The intention of embedding four cameras is trying to capture baggage with different possible poses, such as lying on baggage cart and standing on ground, considering the fact that in some view the particular baggage might be heavily occluded by person or other baggage.

2.2 Data Annotation

Based on the multi-view image capturing system, raw image data were collected at an airport from actual flight during several days. In real case, a baggage ReID pipeline consists of two sequential steps, baggage detection and baggage retrieval. In this paper, the detection step is not considered in the pipeline of baggage ReID for mainly two reasons. First, we have trained Faster-R-CNN [11] based object detection models using annotated bounding boxes on full-sized images, it showed that using detection result for retrieval task has almost the same performance compared to using ground truth. Second, a baggage can be identified means it has at least one valid baggage image taken at BHS and checkpoint respectively. Since there could be many hold-on baggage also appeared in checkpoint image besides check-in baggage, the annotation for detection might bring the dataset many irrelevant baggage which are unable to identify. Therefore, we refer baggage retrieval as baggage ReID in our paper.

The annotation process can be described as follows. Images taken at BHS and checkpoint would be annotated if there is a valid baggage. Valid baggage denotes that one integrated surface of baggage is exposed at checkpoint or more than 50% of baggage surface is exposed at BHS. Each mask is a hand-drawn polygon and each corresponding bounding box is then cropped as minimum enclosing rectangle of annotated mask. Because there are four camera views at checkpoint and three camera views at BHS, the first annotation for ReID is to couple the same baggage separately based on time. The second step is finding the same identity between checkpoint and BHS, which is quite a time-consuming work. Therefore, a ReID model is trained based on a few identities and computed the scores of similarity between baggage at BHS and checkpoint, the ground-truth identity would be much easier to locate based on ranking. At last, the annotator confirms that each identity consists of images from BHS and checkpoint.

MVB consists of 4519 baggage identities and 22660 bounding boxes. Each identity is examined to be unique. For each bounding box, mask of baggage is also given as annotation information. 22660 baggage images (13028 at BHS, 9632 at checkpoint) are cropped from 22265 full-sized images (13028 at BHS, 9237 at checkpoint). Most identities have three baggage images taken at BHS. The number of baggage images at checkpoint gate for each identity fluctuates more. Most frequent occurrence of missing baggage image from certain view at BHS is due to missed camera capture, while at checkpoint is more often due to serious occlusion caused by passenger body parts or cloth, baggage cart, other baggage on cart or on ground. On average, each baggage identity has respectively 2.88 and 2.13 baggage images at BHS and checkpoint. The statistics of annotation is listed in Table 1.

For better baggage ReID evaluation, the dataset has also provided the attribute annotation of baggage surface material. The attribute labels of four categories are: hard (metal, plastic, etc.), soft (fabric, leather, etc.), paperboard and others (protective cover, etc.). Table 2 showed the sample baggage images and label distributions.

Table 2. Surface material annotation.

Categories	Hard	Soft	Paperboard	Others
#Identities	2767	1120	198	434
Sample Image				

Table 3. Samples of inter-class similarity on MVB. Images in each row are from one identity.

	Checkpoint		BHS		
	View1	View2	View1	View2	View3
a					
b					

Table 4. Samples of intra-class dissimilarity on MVB. Blank cell indicates corresponding view image is not valid. Images in each row represent the same identity.

	Checkpoint				BHS		
	View1	View2	View3	View4	View1	View2	View3
a							
b							
c							
d							
e							

2.3 Dataset Characteristics

In MVB dataset, each identity of baggage can be regarded as an individual class containing several images taken at BHS and checkpoint together. It is necessary to point out the characteristics of inter-class similarity and intra-class dissimilarity. For inter-class similarity, we have to admit that some baggage is naturally very hard to distinguish from each other according to their appearance, even more difficult than the case in person ReID. For instance, Table 3 gives two baggage that looks very similar but actually has different identities. The cues to distinguish them are hiding in detail of images. Meanwhile, the images of BHS and checkpoint are substantially different. The intra-class dissimilarity aspects are listed in Table 4.

Background: as most of images in Table 4 indicate, baggage images have quite different backgrounds between BHS and checkpoint. In BHS images, background mainly consists of black conveyor belt and security check device entrance. Meanwhile in checkpoint baggage images background varies from passenger body parts, clothes, baggage cart, floor, etc.

Occlusion: other baggage on cart can easily lead to heavy occlusion in checkpoint image as shown in Table 4d, while checkpoint image might be also partially invisible in BHS image because surface is at bottom, which corresponds to the case in Table 4c.

Viewpoint and pose: they are essentially unlike due to different locations of cameras, and baggage can be in various poses such as Table 4a showed.

Lighting: lighting conditions at BHS and checkpoint are not the same which often leads to color and reflection differences. For instance, Table 4b displays obviously different color characteristic at BHS and checkpoint.

Motion blur: as passengers walking through checkpoint gate at different speed, motion blur makes baggage image to be less distinctive, as shown in Table 4e.

All these above factors make baggage ReID on MVB a challenging and inspiring task between different domains.

3   Task and Evaluation Metric

The task of baggage ReID on MVB is to assign a baggage identity to a given probe by searching among gallery. In baggage ReID task on MVB, definition of probe and gallery are not exactly the same as person ReID based on application scenario. Due to the cross domain characteristic, probe and gallery are naturally separated. Specifically, baggage will be taken appearance images at BHS before the domain is transferred from BHS to checkpoint. Baggage will be detected in checkpoint domain and then searched in BHS domain. Therefore, baggage images captured at checkpoint and BHS are defined as probe and gallery respectively. During test, gallery images from different views of the same identity are supposed to be treated as a whole in identifying whether a probe corresponds to a certain identity. Specifically, for each probe, inference result is supposed to be a possibility rank of all identities rather than all gallery images. Information of which gallery images belong to the same identity is given in test set, which can be easily obtained due to the same trigger signal introduced in Sect. 2.1.

Among 4519 identities in MVB, 500 identities randomly selected from all identities are reserved for test, while all the rest 4019 identities can be used for training. For the 500 identities test set, there are 1052 probe images and 1432 gallery images. Each probe image will be matched with the 1432 gallery images and a 500 id-length result vector will be output, indicating the sorted baggage under certain similarity metric. How to incorporate matching results of probe with multiple gallery images within an identity to single similarity value is left to be determined by dataset user. CMC (Cumulated Matching Characteristics) is adopted as evaluation metric to measure the performance of baggage ReID on MVB since there is only one ground-truth identity among gallery of 500 identities. In this paper, CMC at rank1 till rank3 will be evaluated.

4 Baseline Method

One nature of dataset MVB lies in large number of identities yet limited number of images within each identity, which might make classification scheme less feasible. In this paper, verification scheme using deep neural network is adopted for baggage ReID task. A basic Siamese network and a merged Siamese network are introduced in Sects. 4.1 and 4.2 respectively.

4.1 Basic Siamese Network

Siamese network is originally put forward for verification of signatures [12]. Our basic Siamese network takes in two input images, processes these inputs using the same network architecture sharing parameters and subsequently produces two feature vectors. Ideally the distance under certain metric between the two output vectors indicates whether the two input vectors are from the same identity or not.

In the basic Siamese network adopted in our baggage ReID task, VGG16 [13] is used as backbone model to extract output feature vectors for input probe and gallery image. Euclidean distance between these two feature vectors is further calculated as similarity metric. In training phase, contrastive loss is adopted as loss function, with the intention of pushing Euclidean distance of same identity feature vectors near while pulling different identity feature vectors apart.

4.2 Merged Siamese Network

Our proposed merged Siamese network treats the verification problem as binary classification, as shown in Fig. 2. Concretely, feature maps for probe and gallery image are extracted after the last convolution layer of VGG16. Then an element-wise subtraction layer is conducted on the feature maps of two paths and the output is fed into the fully connected layers for binary classification. The classification part of network generates possibility of whether probe and gallery images are from the same baggage identity, cross-entropy loss is adopted as loss function in training.

Compared with the basic Siamese network, feature maps extracted after the last convolutional layer contain more spatial information for further merging. The motivation behind element-wise subtraction lies in that by such operation co-located similar features at feature maps are suppressed while prominent dissimilar features are emphasized, meanwhile the spatial information is reserved. The subtraction output is further fed into binary classification network with fully connected layers to learn a similarity metric, which has more nonlinearity compared with Euclidean distance metric. Given the remarkable difference

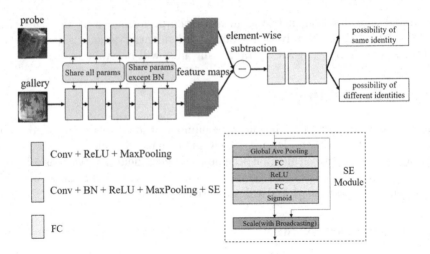

Fig. 2. Architecture of merged Siamese network.

between probe domain and gallery domain, batch normalization [15] is added in Conv4 and Conv5, and it should be noted that all parameters except batch normalization are shared for feature extraction of probe and gallery.

Considering that channels of feature map might have different representation power, a channel-wise module based on Squeeze-and-Excitation (SE) [14] is inserted after pooling layer in Conv4 and Conv5, aiming at learning weighted inter-channel relationship explicitly. The motivation behind Squeeze-and-Excitation module is to assign higher weight for more informative feature channels meanwhile lower weight for less informative ones. In baggage ReID problem specifically, feature channels can be reasonably assumed to be informative to different extent. For instance, channels in which more activated features are from background rather than baggage should be suppressed. Since no external information other than feature itself is needed, channel-wise attention in form of SE can be viewed as a self-attention mechanism. The parameters for SE module are shared between probe and gallery.

5   Experiments

The basic and merged Siamese networks that introduced in Sect. 4 are evaluated on MVB dataset. 4019 identities and 500 identities are employed for training and test respectively. Both Siamese networks are finetuned from a pretrained VGG16 model, setting parameters in Conv1 and Conv2 to be frozen. Training is performed on $4 \times$ NVIDIA Tesla P100 GPUs for 50k iterations with a minibatch of 128 image pairs. All probe and gallery images are resized to 256×256 and then randomly cropped to 224×224 in training phase.

For generating the pair data for Siamese network training, all positive pairs, i.e. pair of baggage images with the same identity, among 4019 identities are used as training data, meanwhile negative training pairs are randomly sampled among different identities, forming a training set balanced in positive and negative labels. The merged Siamese network is firstly trained on this balanced training set with a few epochs. Then the output model is utilized to inference each probe among 300 identities randomly sampled from 4019 identities for hard example mining. False positive pairs with high probability are filtered as supplement negative pairs then added to training set. The amount ratio of positive and negative pairs in the augmented training set is roughly 1:2, and total number of pairs is around 75k.

Training and evaluation are conducted on original baggage images and masked baggage images respectively. The masked baggage image is generated in a simple manner by keeping the pixel value inside the annotated polygon area and setting pixel value outside polygon area as zero.

At test time, distance and possibility are inferenced between probe and each image in gallery. For each identity, mean of nearest two distances is regarded as the distance between probe and corresponding identity. Similarly, in classification scheme, mean of highest two possibilities within each identity is regarded as the possibility of same identity. For the minority identities with only one gallery image, computing mean value is replaced with the only distance or possibility. At last, 500 identities will be sorted according to the mean value.

5.1   Performance and Ablation Study

Performance of proposed methods evaluated in form of CMC from Rank1 to Rank3 on MVB is shown in Table 5. As shown, merged Siamese network shows remarkably superior results compared to basic Siamese network, ca. 20% to 25% boost at Rank 1, Rank 2 and Rank 3. Augmenting training set (ATS) by hard example mining can effectively improve performance, ca. 1% to 2% for merged

Table 5. CMC of proposed methods at Rank 1, 2, 3 on MVB.

Siamese networks +				Rank1(%)	Rank2(%)	Rank3(%)
Merged	ATS	SE	Mask			
				20.15	34.51	43.92
	✓			24.24	39.16	48.00
			✓	22.05	36.22	44.01
	✓		✓	26.62	39.26	47.24
✓				44.39	60.27	68.54
✓	✓			46.39	58.46	65.49
✓			✓	47.91	**61.98**	**68.92**
✓	✓		✓	48.86	61.60	67.49
✓	✓	✓		47.72	59.60	67.30
✓	✓	✓	✓	**50.19**	61.31	68.73

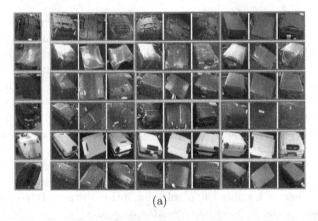

(a)

(b)

Fig. 3. Sample ReID results on MVB. Probe and Gallery images are not masked. Probe images are listed in the left in blue box. Gallery images are displayed in order of inferenced possibility. Gallery images with same identity as probe are bounded in green box, otherwise in red. (a) samples of baggage re-identified in top 3, (b) samples of baggage not re-identified in top 3. (Color figure online)

Siamese network at Rank 1 and ca. 3% to 5% for basic Siamese network at Rank 1, Rank 2 and Rank 3. Further superior performance, i.e. 50.19% at Rank 1 is obtained by augmenting training set and inserting SE module on masked bounding box. In real application, the most important metric is CMC Rank1, and the highest value of our baseline model is produced by combination of all model features.

5.2   Case Study

Sample baggage ReID results on MVB are shown in Fig. 3. As shown, our proposed network can effectively retrieve baggage with similar appearance from gallery and has detail discrimination ability to some extent. Nevertheless, there are still cases where our network fails to represent more distinguishable details in retrieving baggage at top ranks. One possible reason is that our proposed network mainly extracts a global rather than local feature vector for each probe and gallery image.

5.3 Future Work

Baggage ReID is a research problem toward real-world application, thus the data pipeline has been set up at certain airports and will be promoted to many others. It can be expected that the scale of dataset will be continuously growing and reaching to another order of magnitude within a short period of time. Meanwhile we are organizing an open contest based on MVB for technology improvements and suggestions of dataset usage. As shown in case study, a typical mismatch is related to failing to amplify some important detail information, which is caused by the feature extraction network mainly relying on global feature. Therefore, ReID performance could be possibly improved by making better use of salient details. Last but not least, the dataset potential as 3D object ReID should be further exploited. For instance, the probe and gallery image both can be 3D image, which is baggage 3D surface reconstructed by multi camera calibration and visual SLAM; also one can apply key point detection to understand the pose of baggage, then re-identify it based on 3D alignment with some geometric shape constrains.

6   Conclusion

A new baggage ReID dataset named MVB is proposed in this paper. MVB consists of 4519 baggage identities and 22660 bboxes along with mask and material annotations. All data is collected in real scenario using specially-designed multiview camera system. This paper also presented a merged Siamese network as a baseline model to work on the task of baggage ReID. Considering the large scale and the challenging factors of MVB, it will significantly contribute to further research on general 2D and 3D object ReID, especially with different domains. The performance of merged Siamese network is also evaluated as baseline model of the dataset. To access MVB dataset, please visit its corresponding contest website http://volumenet.cn/, any feedback is greatly appreciated.

References

1. Zheng, L., Yang, Y., Hauptmann, A.G.: Person re-identification: past, present and future. arXiv preprint arXiv: 1610.02984 (2016)
2. Cheng, D., Gong, Y., Zhou, S., Wang, J., Zheng, N.: Person re-identification by multi-channel parts-based CNN with improved triplet loss function. In: IEEE CVPR, pp. 1335–1344 (2016)
3. Liu, H., Tian, Y., Yang, Y., et al.: Deep relative distance learning: tell the difference between similar vehicles. In: IEEE CVPR, pp. 2167–2175 (2016)

4. Liu, X., Liu, W., Mei, T., Ma, H.: A deep learning-based approach to progressive vehicle re-identification for urban surveillance. In: Leibe, B., Matas, J., Sebe, N., Welling, M. (eds.) ECCV 2016. LNCS, vol. 9906, pp. 869–884. Springer, Cham (2016). https://doi.org/10.1007/978-3-319-46475-6_53

5. Deng, J., Dong, W., Socher, R., et al.: ImageNet: a large-scale hierarchical image database. In: IEEE CVPR, pp. 248–255 (2009)

6. Lin, T.-Y., et al.: Microsoft COCO: common objects in context. In: Fleet, D., Pajdla, T., Schiele, B., Tuytelaars, T. (eds.) ECCV 2014. LNCS, vol. 8693, pp. 740–755. Springer, Cham (2014). https://doi.org/10.1007/978-3-319-10602-1_48

7. Zheng, L., Shen, L., Tian, L., Wang, S., Wang, J., Tian, Q.: Scalable person re-identification: a benchmark. In: IEEE ICCV, pp. 1116–1124 (2015)

8. Zheng, L., et al.: MARS: a video benchmark for large-scale person re-identification. In: Leibe, B., Matas, J., Sebe, N., Welling, M. (eds.) ECCV 2016. LNCS, vol. 9910, pp. 868–884. Springer, Cham (2016). https://doi.org/10.1007/978-3-319-46466-4_52

9. Li, W., Zhao, R., Xiao, T., Wang, X.: DeepReID: deep filter pairing neural network for person re-identification. In: IEEE CVPR, pp. 152–159 (2014)

10. Cordts, M., Omran, M., Ramos, S., et al.: The cityscapes dataset for semantic urban scene understanding. In: IEEE CVPR, pp. 3213–3223 (2016)

11. Ren, S., He, K., Girshick, R., Sun, J.: Faster R-CNN: towards real-time object detection with region proposal networks. In: NIPS, pp. 91–99 (2015)

12. Bromley, J., Guyon, I., LeCun, Y., et al.: Signature verification using a "Siamese" time de-lay neural network. In: NIPS, pp. 737–744 (1994)

13. Simonyan, K., Zisserman, A.: Very deep convolutional networks for large-scale image recognition. arXiv preprint arXiv:1409.1556 (2014)

14. Hu, J., Shen L., Sun, G.: Squeeze-and-excitation networks. In: IEEE CVPR, pp. 7132–7141 (2018)

15. Ioffe, S., Szegedy, C.: Batch normalization: accelerating deep network training by reducing internal covariate shift. arXiv preprint arXiv:1502.03167 (2015)

16. Sun, Y., Zheng, L., Yang, Y., Tian, Q., Wang, S.: Beyond part models: person retrieval with refined part pooling (and a strong convolutional baseline). In: Ferrari, V., Hebert, M., Sminchisescu, C., Weiss, Y. (eds.) ECCV 2018. LNCS, vol. 11208, pp. 501–518. Springer, Cham (2018). https://doi.org/10.1007/978-3-030-01225-0_30

17. Wei, L., Zhang, S., Gao, W., et al. Person transfer GAN to bridge domain gap for person re-identification. In: IEEE CVPR, pp. 79–88 (2018)

18. Deng, W., Zheng, L., Ye, Q., et al.: Image-image domain adaptation with preserved self-similarity and domain-dissimilarity for person re-identification. In: IEEE CVPR, pp. 994–1003 (2018)

19. Wang, G., Yuan, Y., Chen, X., et al.: Learning discriminative features with multiple granularities for person re-identification. In: International Conference on Multimedia, pp. 274–282. ACM (2018)

Personalized Travel Recommendation via Multi-view Representation Learning

Yujun Zhang, Bin Han[(⊠)], Xinbo Gao, and Haoran Li

School of Electronic Engineering, Xidian University, Xi'an, China
yujunzhang96@163.com, bhan@xidian.edu.cn

Abstract. Personalized travel recommendation has become a significant approach for people to find attractions in line with their interests from explosive information. Existing personalized travel recommendation methods always focus on travel history records but attach limited attention to acquire the high-level representation of user's travel preferences from multi-view heterogeneous information. In this paper, we present a personalized travel recommendation approach based on multi-view representation learning. In the proposed approach, four-view representation obtained from rating, comment, image and regional popularity of attractions are exploited to acquire user's travel preferences by deep learning and pair-wise optimization. Specially, the aesthetic features are extracted to describe the visual appeal of image, and the regional popularity is introduced to represent the popularities of attractions in a region for personalized recommendation. Finally, an attention module is utilized to automatically learn the significances of four views to the user, and then the predicted preferences is obtained through a weighted average pooling strategy. Extensive experiments constructed on the real-world dataset we collected from tourism websites have demonstrated that the proposed method based on multi-view representation learning is effective and significantly improves the accuracy of personalized travel recommendation.

Keywords: Personalized travel recommendation · Multi-view representation learning · Multimodal information · Aesthetic attraction · Regional popularity

1 Introduction

Tourism has become an important lifestyle of public in recent years. It is troublesome for user to find attractions in line with their interests to enjoy a high-quality travel from explosive information [1–4], which is driving an urgent need for personalized attraction recommendation to provide smarter travel advice.

Existing travel recommendation methods can be classified into two categories: collaborative filtering (CF) [1, 8, 12] recommendation and content-based recommendation [3, 11, 14]. The performance of CF methods is significantly limited because of

The first author is a postgraduate. The authors would like to thank Zihen Zhou for his valuable advices in writing the paper. This work was supported by the National Natural Science Foundation of China (61603233).

© Springer Nature Switzerland AG 2019
Z. Lin et al. (Eds.): PRCV 2019, LNCS 11859, pp. 97–109, 2019.
https://doi.org/10.1007/978-3-030-31726-3_9

the sparse of user-attraction matrix based on travel records. The content-based methods can alleviate the data sparse problem, which employ various auxiliary content information of attractions for travel recommendation. Some existing methods [1, 2] combine additional information, e.g., tag of attractions, with matrix factorization to provide travel advice. STM [3] and ATCF [4] utilize latent dirichlet allocation (LDA) and author-topic model respectively to process textual data of users and attractions for travel location recommendation. However, these methods only use unimodal information but neglect multi-view information that affects user interest, such as the visual feature of attractions.

Previous studies [5, 16] have shown that multi-view data containing complementary information is able to infer user preferences from different aspects, which is benefit for personalized travel recommendation. For example, text comments can express user's opinions on various characteristics of attractions [17], and images can describe visual information of attractions [18]. However, the heterogeneity of multimodal multi-view information makes it difficult to be utilized in a uniform way for personalized recommendation. DTM [6] uses dynamic topic model and matrix factorization to excavate explicit feature and text information of attractions but ignore the image information of attractions. PSA [7] exploits image, text and score to obtain the similarity of attractions, with no consideration of the popularity of attractions influence on user's preferences. The difficulty in fusion multi-view heterogeneous information has become a vital problem that limits the accuracy of personalized travel recommendation.

In fact, user's travel decision is influenced by the regional popularity of attractions. Thus, user tends to show different interesting when they are visiting different regions. To handle the regional dynamic of user preferences, LSARS [10] incorporate uniform geographical influence with user interest. While, LSARS fails to identify the different influence of geographical factor on different travelers to provide personalized recommendation. In addition, the visual appeal of attractions is also an important factor which can influence the decision-making process of travelers. Most methods using attractions image only utilize low-level semantic features, such as the scale-invariant feature transform algorithm (SIFT features). The high-level aesthetic features which can describe the visual appeal of image has not yet been considered in travel recommendation.

In order to solve the problems, we propose a novel Personalized Travel Recommendation via multi-view representation learning (PTRMRL) approach to mimic the human decision process by fusing the information of rating, comment, image and regional popularity of attractions. In our approach, multi-view representation learning is adopted to learn more informative and compact representation of user and attractions by exploiting the complementarity of multiple views. The high-level representations of user preferences are acquired from multi-view heterogeneous information by deep learning, then an attention module is utilized to automatically learn the significance of each influencing factor on the user's decision-making process. Finally, user's travel preferences in the destination are predicted after a weighted average pooling. The model is optimized with the bayesian personalized ranking (BPR) optimization criterion [19].

The main contributions of this paper are summarized as follows:

1. A personalized travel recommendation approach via multi-view representation learning is proposed to infer user's travel preferences, which considers the content effects, visual effects and regional popularity of attractions effects in a unified way.
2. The aesthetic features describing visual appeal of attractions are leveraged to model the user's aesthetic preferences into user's travel preference to further improve the travel recommendation performance.
3. A real-world travel dataset with multimodal heterogeneous information is established, which includes three popular tourist destinations in China. Extensive experiments constructed on the dataset have demonstrated the effectiveness and superiority of the proposed method based on multi-view travel information.

2 Related Work

2.1 Deep Learning Based Recommender System

In recent years, deep learning has been gradually applied to recommendation systems [20]. He et al. [21] introduce a neural collaborative filtering framework to model the nonlinear relationship between user and item. Besides, deep networks are also adopted to learn user and item features from heterogeneous data sources for recommendation in some works. He et al. [22] utilize a trained (convolutional neural networks) CNN to extract visual features from product images and combined the features with BPR. Yu et al. [23] incorporate the clothing aesthetic features with a new neural tensor factorization model for clothing recommendation. Kim et al. [24] adopt CNN to process product's review and integrate it with probability matrix factorization model. Zheng et al. [25] proposed a novel deep cooperative neural network that can learn user behavior and project attributes from comments. In recent years, the attention network has been proved to be effective in improving the effect of personalized recommendation. Sidana et al. [26] designed an attention network to distinguish which historical items in a user profile are more important for item-based CF. Chen et al. [27] proposed a method consisting of a two-layered attention network to select project features and historical items.

2.2 Personalized Travel Recommendation

To provide smarter travel recommendation for user, numerous efforts have been made by researchers. Shi et al. [1] combine weighted matrix factorization and category-based regularization for landmark recommendation. Zhang et al. [15] exploit user collaborative filtering technology with trust friendship between users and geographic information. However, the performance of traditional CF method is limited when the user-attraction matrix is sparsity. Researchers explored richer auxiliary information to alleviate the problem. Jiang et al. [4] adopt author topic model to learn user preference from the textual description of attractions. These methods only use check-in data and text information neglected geographic information. Zhao et al. [9] incorporate co-geographical influence into a personalized pairwise preference ranking matrix factorization model for point-of-interest (POI) recommendation but ignored the content information of POI.

3 The Proposed PTRMRL Framework

3.1 Problem Definition

We introduce basic concepts and notations used in this paper.

Definition 1 (Attractions): An attraction v is specific geographical areas, such as parks, etc. Each attraction v contains information including images, texts, ratings.

Definition 2 (User Visit Activity): A visit activity c is represented as $c = (u, v_i, l, r_{ui})$, which means that user u has visited an attraction v_i in city l and writing a rating r_{ui}. We define a user-attraction interaction matrix as $R \in R^{m \times n}$, where m, n are the number of users and attractions respectively. r_{ui} denotes (u, i)-th entry of R. $r_{ui} = 1$ means that user u has visited attraction v_i, $r_{ui} = 0$ means that attraction v_j haven't been visited by user u.

Definition 3 (Attractions Recommendation): Given a target user u and a target city l he/she plans to visit (i.e., a query $q = (u, l)$), the target is to recommend a group of attractions in city l that user u would prefer to visit.

3.2 Architecture

Intuitively, we assume that when user choose an attraction to visit he/she will be affected by following factors: (1) the content of the attraction whether matches his/her interesting; (2) the visual of the attraction whether matches his/her aesthetic preferences; (3) the popularity of the attraction in the region. In addition, the factors mentioned above have different impact degree on users' decision-making process of travel. The proposed PTRMRL method modeling user preferences from four views with respect to user's content preferences, user's aesthetic preferences and user's rating preferences and the regional public's preferences. The framework of PTRMRL is depicted in Fig. 1.

Given a user u and attraction v which is located in region l, u^k and v^k denote the representations of user u and attraction v respectively in different views, $k \in K$, $K = \{s, t, p, l\}$. s represents rating view, t represents comment view, p represents image view, and l represents regional popularity view. Especially, u^l denote the representation of the public in region l. Finally, user-attraction preferences score is obtained by merge the representations of the user and the attraction in each view with an attention network and weighted average pooling strategy.

Objective Function. The proposed method is optimized with BPR pairwise optimization criterion, which models a triplet of one user and two items, where one of the item is visited attraction v_i and the other one is non-visited attraction v_j by user u. Then it is assumed that the user u prefers v_i over v_j. The objective function is shown as follow:

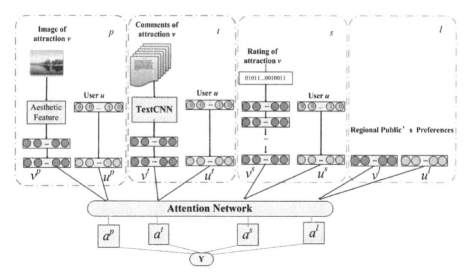

Fig. 1. Overview of the multi-view representation learning for personalized travel recommendation (PTRMRL) approach, p represents image view, t represents comment view, s represents rating view, l represents regional popularity view.

$$\arg \min \mathcal{L} = \sum_{u,i,j \in \mathcal{R}_B} \sum_{k \in K} \{-[\ln(\sigma(a_{ui}^k * \Phi(u^k, v_i^k) - a_{uj}^k * \Phi(u^k, v_j^k))] \\ + \lambda_k(||u^k||^2 + ||v_i^k||^2 + ||v_j^k||^2 + ||\theta^k||^2)\} \tag{1}$$

where θ^k is the network parameter in different views, a_{ui}^k and a_{uj}^k denotes user u's preference degree for v_i and v_j on view k respectively. Φ is the inner product function, λ_k is the regularization coefficient of different views to avoid overfitting. We employ end-to-end stochastic gradient descent to optimizing the objective function.

Inference. After we obtain the optimized user and attraction representation u^k and v^k in each view as well as the parameters of the attention network. Then the preferences score that user u will put on the attraction v_i can be predicted as:

$$Y = \sum_{k \in K} a_{ui}^k \Phi(u^k, v_i^k) \tag{2}$$

The recommendation of attractions reduced to ranking problem among all items in the destination based on the estimated score Y.

3.3   Multi-view User Preferences Representation

Image View: Aesthetic-Aware User Preferences Representation. The visual appeal of attractions is an important factor when a user chooses an attraction to visit. The CNN features or SIFT features of images used in traditional travel recommendation methods could not encode the visual appeal of images. While, the visual aesthetic quality of images can measure the visual appeal of images in the human eye. Therefore, we adopt the effective aesthetic neural network NIMA [13] to extract aesthetic features from attractions image, and then the output of penultimate fully connected layer of the network are obtained as attraction's aesthetic features, which is a feature vector of length 1024×1.

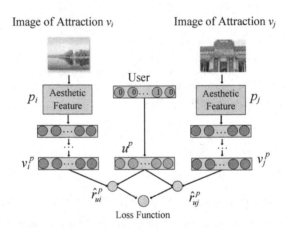

Fig. 2. The architecture of user's aesthetic preferences

Considering different user has different aesthetic preferences, we propose a neural network and personalized paired ranking model to learn the aesthetic-aware representations of users and attractions. As shown in Fig. 2, p_i and p_j denote aesthetic features of the attractions v_i and v_j respectively. The multi-layer neural network is adopted to map aesthetic features of attractions into a latent space and the user is mapped into the same latent space. The representations of the user u^p and the attraction v_i^p in this view were obtained by the BPR pairwise learning, then the user aesthetic preference score is predicted as: $\hat{r}_{ui}^p = \Phi(u^p, v_i^p)$. The objective function is as follow:

$$arg \min_{u,v,\theta} \sum_{u,i,j \in R_B} -ln(\sigma(\hat{r}_{ui}^p - \hat{r}_{uj}^p)) + \lambda_p(||u^p||^2 + ||v^p||^2 + ||\theta^p||^2) \qquad (3)$$

where θ^p is the network parameters. Only three hidden layers are used empirically. The objective function for the comment view and the rating view is similar if the view is used individually, we will not describe in detail in the following views.

Comment View: Content-Aware User Preferences Representation. In this section, we present the modeling of textual comment to obtain the content features of attractions and infer content-aware user's preferences. A CNN network, which refers to as TextCNN in the rest of this paper is adopted to process the reviews of attractions. More details can be referred to [25]. First, all the reviews of attraction v_i are merged into a single document, consisting of n words in total after flited stop words, then each word was mapped to n-dimensional distributed vectors by a trained word2vec model [28]. Then, reviews of attraction v_i are represented as a matrix of word embeddings T_i and inputted into TextCNN to learn an n-dimensional vector used in the next step. Finally, we added a prediction layer to catch the nonlinear interaction between a user and an attraction. The representations of the attraction v_i in this view are denoted as v_i^t,

$$v^t = f(\omega^t(TextCNN(T_i))) \tag{4}$$

where ω^t is the network parameter, and f is a non-linear activation function such as *sigmoid, tanh* or *relu*. Similar to the image view, let u^t denote the representation of user u in this view. The user's content preference score for the attraction v_i can be estimated as: $\hat{r}_{ui}^t = \Phi(u^t, v_i^t)$.

Rating View: Rating-Aware User Preferences Representation. In this subsection, we present the model for rating view. From the user-attraction matrix R, each attraction v_i is represented as a high-dimensional vector x_i, which represent attraction v_i's rating records among all users. Then x_i is put into a multi-layer neural network to learn the representation of attraction v_i in this view.

$$v_i^s = f(.. f(\omega_2^s f(\omega_1^s x_i + b_1^s) + b_2^s)) \tag{5}$$

where ω_i^s and b_i^s ($i = 1, 2.. .n$) denote the weights and biases of layer i. Only three hidden layers are used empirically. Similar to the image view, let u^s denote the representation of user u in this view, then the preference score can be predicted as: $\hat{r}_{ui}^s = \Phi(u^s, v_i^s)$.

Popularity View: Popular-Aware Regional Public's Preferences Representation. Popularity of attractions strongly influence user's visiting decisions. We use regional public's preferences to measure the attractiveness of popularity for user. This is the key model to solve the problem of a user interest varies in different destinations. The popularity of an attraction was reflected in the visited numbers by all travelers.

Given a region l, regional publics is all the users who have visited the region and were mapped into a latent space denote as u^l. The representations of the public u^l and the attraction v^l in region l were obtained by latent factor model and pairwise learning:

$$argmin \sum_{l,i,j \in \mathcal{R}_l} - \ln \sigma(\Phi(u^l, v_i^l) - \Phi(u^l, v_j^l)) + \lambda_l(\|U^l\|^2 + \|V^l\|^2) \tag{6}$$

For each attraction $v_i \in l$, an attraction $v_j \in l$ which is not as popular as v_i were selected as the corresponding negative sample. The training data are generated as follows:

$$R_l = \{(l, i, j) | l \in L \wedge i \in l \wedge j \in l \backslash i \wedge p^i > p^j)\} \tag{7}$$

where L represents the set of all destinations, p^i and p^j denote the popularity of attraction v_i and v_j respectively. The preference score of publics for attraction v_i is: $r_{ui}^l = \Phi(u^l, v_i^t)$.

3.4　The Attention Network

Considering the different impact degree of different influence factor in the user's decision-making process, we use an attention network to select important views for each user based on the assume that the attentive weight of each view is related with the embedding vectors of the user and the attraction in each view. The rationale is that the embedding vectors of users and attractions are supposed to encode the information of users and attractions. Then, for each user the attention score a^k of each view is:

$$a(u, i, k) = w_2 ReLU(w_u u^k + w_v v_i^k + b_1) \tag{8}$$

where w_u, w_v and b_1 are the parameters of first layer, w_2 is the parameter second layer. The final weight of each view is obtained by normalizing the above attention scores using SoftMax.

$$a(u, i, k) = \frac{exp(a(u^k, v_i^k))}{\sum_{h \in K} exp(a(u^h, v_i^h))} \tag{9}$$

4　Experiments

4.1　Dataset and Evaluation Protocols

Dataset Description. We collect a large amount of heterogeneous travel information from tourism websites-Mafengwo to build the dataset for following experiments. The dataset contains approximately 40000 user interactions (rating, review, etc.) on attractions and attractions' metadata (descriptions, image feature, geographic location, etc.) of three popular tourist destinations in China. The statistics of the dataset are shown in Table 1. To filter out noise records, attractions visited by less than 10 users and users reach less than two destinations are removed from the dataset. A typical picture of each attraction was selected form the dataset to obtain its visual feature. Finally, the dataset used for experiments contains 9157 users and 1407 attractions.

Table 1. Basic statistics of the experimental datasets

Destination	User (raw)	User (filtered)	Attractions (raw)	Attractions (filtered)	Comments (raw)	Comments (filtered)
Shanghai	25125	7051	750	403	108736	53853
Beijing	33658	8244	780	591	188268	94345
Shaanxi	24797	6308	867	413	108716	50598

Evaluation Protocols. In our experiments, the visited cities of each user were divided into two sets training cities and the test city by visiting time. Note that, the visiting time of training cities was earlier than the testing city. We provide top-N recommendation list for each user in the testing set. To appropriately evaluate the overall performance for ranking task, three representative top-N recommendation measures include Precision, Recall and NDCG with different cut-off value (e.g., P@5, P@10, R@5, R@10, NDCG@5 and NDCG@10) [16] are adopted to evaluate the performance of algorithms.

Implementation Details. We implemented our proposed method based on TensorFlow. The model parameters are randomly initialized according to the Gaussian distribution (with a mean of 0 and standard deviation of 0.01). The different views were pretrained independently and then merge the views with the attention network to train as a whole. The learning rate is 0.001, We primarily set the batch size to 256, and set the regularization coefficient as $\lambda_l = \lambda_p = 0.01$, $\lambda_p = \lambda_s = 0.001$.

4.2 The Impact of Embedding Dimension

The dimension of latent factor is an important parameter in latent factor model. Our model is an extension approach of latent factor model. In this experiment, we studied the effect of this parameter on the recommended performance by comparing our approach with two latent factor model BPRMF [19] and DTM [6]. Specially, we use BPRMF for model learning. The results are shown in Fig. 2. It can be seen from the experimental results that the linear BPRMF model is greatly affected by the parameter d. The DTM method can alleviate the influence of this parameter and improve the latent-factor model's stability to some extent due to the extra content regularization term. Our model is less affected by the parameter d and performance stable and robustness (Fig. 3).

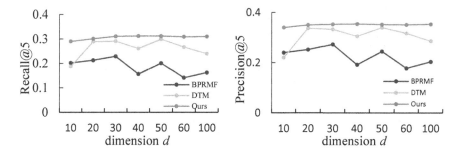

Fig. 3. The impact of the embedding dimension

4.3 Overall Comparison

To validate the effectiveness of our proposed method, we compared our method with several travel recommendation algorithms POP, UCF [12], BPRMF [19], ATCF [5],

STM [4], DTM [6] and deep learning-based recommendation method DeepCONN [25]. The POP method recommends attractions based on popularity of attractions and is non-personalized. Table 2 shows the performance of our method and other methods in terms of precision, recall, NDCG, when the parameters are set to optimal parameters.

It is observed that the proposed method PTRMRL achieves the best performances, which indicates that the recommendation accuracy can be greatly improved by acquires user's travel preference from multi-view heterogeneous information. From the experimental results, we can draw the following conclusions: the POP method performs the worst among all the methods, because the POP method only considers the popularity of attractions without considering individual user preference. The UCF and BPRMF performance worst among all personalized recommendation methods. Because of UCF and BPRMF method only utilize the travel history records and suffered from the data sparseness problem. ATCF added additional textual information in conjunction with CF methods and obtain better result than UCF, which indicates that additional content information is useful to alleviate the sparsity problem. DTM is superior to BPRMF model by combines with extra textual information regularization terms with MF.

Table 2. Performance comparison on Precision, Recall, NDCG

Methods	P@5	R@5	P@10	R@10	ndcg@5	ndcg@10
POP	0.128	0.135	0.097	0.183	0.175	0.184
UCF	0.282	0.247	0.225	0.349	0.369	0.382
BPRMF	0.229	0.273	0.229	0.354	0.331	0.357
ATCF	0.257	0.306	0.202	0.390	0.351	0.365
STM	0.265	0.270	0.208	0.375	0.343	0.361
DTM	0.333	0.291	0.277	0.447	0.394	0.430
DeepCONN	0.295	0.261	0.240	0.392	0.369	0.396
PTRMRL	**0.353**	**0.311**	**0.291**	**0.467**	**0.440**	**0.471**

Table 3. The effect of single-view data and multi-views data

Views	P@5	R@5	P@10	R@10	ndcg@5	ndcg@10
Rating view	0.203	0.173	0.210	0.339	0.213	0.278
Image view	0.329	0.280	0.282	0.455	0.416	0.456
Comment view	0.152	0.122	0.156	0.234	0.177	0.211
Image + Region	0.348	0.310	0.285	0.464	0.433	0.464
Rating + Region	0.346	0.304	0.289	0.465	0.424	0.460
Comment + Region	0.334	0.296	0.284	0.456	0.405	0.446
All	0.353	0.311	0.291	0.467	0.440	0.471

4.4 The Impact of Single-View Data on Recommendation Effects

The algorithm proposed in this paper utilized four views data include images, comments, rating and regional popularity to infer user preferences. In order to prove that multi-view information can effectively improve the travel recommendation performance, we analyze the performance of each view in the PTRMRL model. The results are shown in Table 3. The Rating + Region, Image + Region, Comment + Region means that adopt rating, image and comments view incorporate with regional popularity view respectively, all means all views are combined. It can be seen from the experimental results that image view performance better than comments and rating view, which indicates that attraction's appearance is an important factor for travel recommendation and user's aesthetic preferences plays an important role in the tourism decision-making process. The performance of the three single-view modules have been improved after adding regional public's preference, we can conclude that user's visiting record in the destination are deeply affected by popularity of attractions in the region. The research on travel recommendation should pay more attention on the geographical factors. Lastly, the performance is best when all views are combined, which indicates that the model learning user's travel preferences from multi-view data performance better than the model which only utilized unimodal information due to the complementarity of multiple views.

5   Conclusion

In this paper, we propose PTRMRL approach to model user's travel visiting behaviors, which considering user's aesthetic preferences, rating preferences, content preferences and the influence regional popularity at the same time. PTRMRL utilized multi-view travel information to alleviate the data sparse problem and effective improve the accuracy of personalized travel recommendation through exploiting the complementarity of multiple views. However, there are still many shortcomings of our paper-without considering the time, weather, as well as the user cold start problem, we will improve it in the later research.

References

1. Shi, Y., Serdyukov, P., Hanjalic, A., Larson, M.: Nontrivial landmark recommendation using geotagged photos. ACM Trans. Intell. Syst. Technol. 4(3), 47 (2013)
2. Shi, Y., Serdyukov, P., Hanjalic, A., Larson, M.: Personalized landmark recommendation based on geotags from photo sharing sites. In: International AAAI Conference on Weblogs and Social Media. AAAI (2011)
3. Xu, Z., Chen, L., Chen, G.: Topic based context-aware travel recommendation method exploiting geotagged photos. Neurocomputing 155, 99–107 (2015)
4. Jiang, S., Qian, X., Shen, J., Fu, Y., Mei, T.: Author topic model-based collaborative filtering for personalized POI recommendations. IEEE Trans. Multimedia 17(6), 907–918 (2015)
5. Li, Y., Yang, M., Zhang, Z.M.: A survey of multi-view representation learning. IEEE Trans. Knowl. Data Eng. 31, 1863–1883 (2018)
6. Xu, Z., Chen, L., Dai, Y., Chen, G.: A dynamic topic model and matrix factorization-based travel recommendation method exploiting ubiquitous data. IEEE Trans. Multimedia 19(8), 1933–1945 (2017)

7. Shen, J., Deng, C., Gao, X.: Attraction recommendation: towards personalized tourism via collective intelligence. Neurocomputing **173**, 789–798 (2016)
8. Kesorn, K., Juraphanthong, W., Salaiwarakul, A.: Personalized attraction recommendation system for tourists through check-in data. IEEE Access **5**, 26703–26721 (2017)
9. Zhao, S., King, I., Lyu, M.R.: Geo-pairwise ranking matrix factorization model for point-of-interest recommendation. In: Liu, D., Xie, S., Li, Y., Zhao, D., El-Alfy, E.-S.M. (eds.) ICONIP 2017. LNCS, vol. 10638, pp. 368–377. Springer, Cham (2017). https://doi.org/10.1007/978-3-319-70139-4_37
10. Wang, H., Fu, Y., Wang, Q., Yin, H., Du, C., Xiong, H.: A location-sentiment-aware recommender system for both home-town and out-of-town users. In: International Conference on Knowledge Discovery and Data Mining, pp. 1135–1143. ACM (2017)
11. Yin, H., Wang, W., Wang, H., Chen, L., Zhou, X.: Spatial-aware hierarchical collaborative deep learning for POI recommendation. IEEE Trans. Knowl. Data Eng. **29**(11), 2537–2551 (2017)
12. Hu, Y., Koren, Y., Volinsky, C.: Collaborative filtering for implicit feedback datasets. In: IEEE International Conference on Data Mining, pp. 263–272. IEEE (2008)
13. Talebi, H., Milanfar, P.: NIMA: neural image assessment. IEEE Trans. Image Process. **27**(8), 3998–4011 (2018)
14. Pazzani, M.J., Billsus, D.: Content-based recommendation systems. In: Brusilovsky, P., Kobsa, A., Nejdl, W. (eds.) The Adaptive Web. LNCS, vol. 4321, pp. 325–341. Springer, Heidelberg (2007). https://doi.org/10.1007/978-3-540-72079-9_10
15. Zhang, Z., Pan, H., Xu, G., Wang, Y., Zhang, P.: A context-awareness personalized tourist attraction recommendation algorithm. Cybern. Inf. Technol. **16**(6), 146–159 (2016)
16. Zhang, Y., Ai, Q., Chen, X., Croft, W.B.: Joint representation learning for top-N recommendation with heterogeneous information sources. In: Conference on Information and Knowledge Management, pp. 1449–1458. ACM (2017)
17. Chen, C., Zhang, M., Liu, Y., Ma, S.: Neural attentional rating regression with review-level explanations. In: International Conference on World Wide Web, pp. 1583–1592 (2018)
18. Wang, S., Wang, Y., Tang, J., Shu, K., Ranganath, S., Liu, H.: What your images reveal: exploiting visual contents for point-of-interest recommendation. In: International Conference on World Wide Web, pp. 391–400 (2017)
19. Rendle, S., Freudenthaler, C., Gantner, Z., Schmidt-Thieme, L.: BPR: Bayesian personalized ranking from implicit feedback. In: Conference on Uncertainty in Artificial Intelligence, pp. 452–461. AUAI Press (2009)
20. Zhang, S., Yao, L., Sun, A., Tay, Y.: Deep learning based recommender system: a survey and new perspectives. ACM Comput. Surv. **52**(1), 5 (2019)
21. He, X., Liao, L., Zhang, H., Nie, L., Hu, X., Chua, T.S.: Neural collaborative filtering. In: International Conference on World Wide Web, pp. 173–182 (2017)
22. He, R., McAuley, J.: VBPR: visual bayesian personalized ranking from implicit feedback. In: AAAI Conference on Artificial Intelligence. AAAI (2016)
23. Yu, W., Zhang, H., He, X., Chen, X., Xiong, L., Qin, Z.: Aesthetic-based clothing recommendation. In: International Conference on World Wide Web, pp. 649–658 (2018)
24. Kim, D., Park, C., Oh, J., Lee, S., Yu, H.: Convolutional matrix factorization for document context-aware recommendation. In: ACM Conference on Recommender Systems, pp. 233–240. ACM (2016)
25. Zheng, L., Noroozi, V., Yu, P.S.: Joint deep modeling of users and items using reviews for recommendation. In: ACM International Conference on Web Search and Data Mining, pp. 425–434. ACM (2017)

26. He, X., He, Z., Song, J., Liu, Z., Jiang, Y.G., Chua, T.S.: NAIS: Neural attentive item similarity model for recommendation. IEEE Trans. Knowl. Data Eng. **30**(12), 2354–2366 (2018)
27. Chen, J., Zhang, H., He, X., Nie, L., Liu, W., Chua, T. S.: Attentive collaborative filtering: Multimedia recommendation with item-and component-level attention. In: International ACM SIGIR conference on Research and Development in Information Retrieval, pp. 335–344. ACM (2017)
28. Mikolov, T., Sutskever, I., Chen, K., Corrado, G.S., Dean, J.: Distributed representations of words and phrases and their compositionality. In: Advances in Neural Information Processing Systems, pp. 3111–3119. Curran Associates Inc. (2013)

FollowMeUp Sports: New Benchmark for 2D Human Keypoint Recognition

Ying Huang[1(✉)], Bin Sun[2], Haipeng Kan[2], Jiankai Zhuang[3],
and Zengchang Qin[3]

[1] Alibaba Business School, Hangzhou Normal University, Hangzhou, China
yw155@buaa.edu.cn
[2] Keep Inc., Beijing, China
{sunbin,kanhaipeng}@keep.com
[3] Intelligent Computing and Machine Learning Lab, School of ASEE,
Beihang University, Beijing, China
{zhuangjk,zcqin}@buaa.edu.cn

Abstract. Human pose estimation has made significant advancement in recent years. However, the existing datasets are limited in their coverage of pose variety. In this paper, we introduce a novel benchmark "FollowMeUp Sports" that makes an important advance in terms of specific postures, self-occlusion and class balance, a contribution that we feel is required for future development in human body models. This comprehensive dataset was collected using an established taxonomy of over 200 standard workout activities with three different shot angles. The collected videos cover a wider variety of specific workout activities than previous datasets including push-up, squat and body moving near the ground with severe self-occlusion or occluded by some sport equipment and outfits. Given these rich images, we perform a detailed analysis of the leading human pose estimation approaches gaining insights for the success and failures of these methods.

Keywords: Pose estimation · Benchmark testing · Performance evaluation

1 Introduction

Human pose estimation is an important computer vision problem [1]. Its basic task is to find the posture of a person via recognising human joints and rigid parts from normal RGB images. The extracted pose information is essential to modelling and understanding the human behaviours, and can be used in many vision application problems, such as virtual/augmented reality, human-computer interaction, action recognition and smart perception.

Y. Huang, B. Sun, H. Kan and J. Zhuang—Equal contribution.
Y. Huang—The work was done at Keep Inc. The research was partially supported by the National Key Research and Development Program of China (2017YFB1002803).

© Springer Nature Switzerland AG 2019
Z. Lin et al. (Eds.): PRCV 2019, LNCS 11859, pp. 110–121, 2019.
https://doi.org/10.1007/978-3-030-31726-3_10

In the psst few years, pose estimation methods based on deep neural network techniques have achieved great progress [2–4]. Although the performance of some human pose estimation models (e.g. [5–7]) is almost saturated on the above mentioned datasets, applying these high-precision algorithms to the other specific industrial tasks shows a degradation in accuracy. For instance, one application case is workouts or sports scoring. In this case, lots of activities have severe self-occlusion or unusual postures, such as push-up and crunch. We find out the models [8–10] trained on the MS-COCO dataset [11] cannot correctly detect body joints with atypical postures, as shown in Fig. 1. In the top-right image of Fig. 1, the right knee is falsely detected as left knee. In the top-left and lower-part images of Fig. 1, some body joints, such as shoulders, knees and ankles, are missed in prediction. Since the pose estimation results of the same person in the standing posture are correct, we argue the false predictions are caused by the abnormal postures. Current datasets lack the corresponding samples [12,13].

We use the MS-COCO dataset [11] as an example to analyse the distribution of human postures. In our statistics, the number of human instances in standing posture achieves 102,495 (84.53%) while people in other postures only have 18,756 (15.47%) as shown in Fig. 2. The human instances in a horizontal position or an uncommon pose are extremely rare. This makes the model unable to learn the knowledge of irregular postures during training.

To improve the performance of human pose estimation in the certain sports situation, a large-scale human keypoints benchmark is presented in this paper. Our benchmark significantly advances state-of-the-art in terms of particular activities, and includes more than 16,000 images of people. We used the workout class videos as a data source and collected images and image sequences using queries based on the descriptions of more than 200 workout activity types. For each activity type, there are 3 different shot angles. This results in a diverse set of images covering not only different workout activities, but contrasting postures. This allows us to enhance the current human pose estimation methods.

2   Related Work

There are several human keypoints datasets presented in the past decades. Buffy dataset [14] and PASCAL stickmen dataset [15] only contain upper-bodies, but we need to process the full-body. In these two datasets pose variation is insignificant. The contrast of image frames is relatively low in the Buffy dataset.

The UIUC people dataset [16] contains 593 images (346 for training, 247 for testing). Most people in the images are playing badminton. Some people are playing jogging, Frisbee, standing, walking, etc. There are very aggressive pose and spatial variations. However, the activity type is limited in this dataset.

The sport categories of Sport image dataset [17] is more plentiful, which including soccer, cycling, acrobatics, American football, croquet, golf, horseback riding, hockey, figure skating, etc. The total number of images is 1299 (649 of them are split as training set and the rest as testing set).

Leeds Sports Poses (LSP) dataset [1] includes 2000 images, where one half for training and the other half for testing. The dataset shows people involved in various sports.

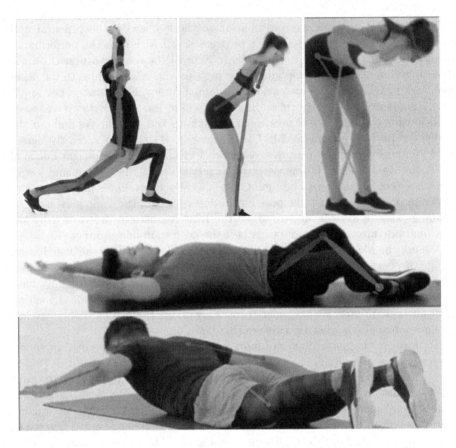

Fig. 1. Limitations of applying current pose estimation models on some workout postures, which have severe self-occlusion. Some body keypoints are falsely detected or missed in prediction even the background is plain.

The image parsing (IP) dataset [18] is a small dataset and contains 305 images of fully visible people, where 100 images for training and 205 images for testing. The dataset consists of various activities such as dancing, sports and acrobatics.

The MPII Human pose dataset [12] consists of 24,589 images, in which 17,408 images with 28,883 annotated people are split for training. During the testing stage, one image may contain multiple different evaluation regions that consist of a non-identical number of people. [20] defines a set of 1,758 evaluation regions on the test images with rough position and scale information. The evaluation metric deploys mean Average Precision (mAP) of the whole body joint prediction. The accuracy results are evaluated and returned by the staff members of the MPII dataset.

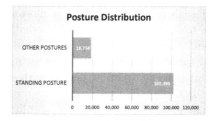

Fig. 2. The posture distribution of MS-COCO dataset. Around 85% human instances are standing with good, upright posture.

The MS-COCO keypoints dataset [11] includes training, validation and testing sets. On the COCO 2017 keypoints challenge, training and validation sets have 118,287 and 5000 images respectively, totally containing over 150,000 people with around 1.7 million labelled keypoints. In experiments, we perform ablation studies on the validation set. To analyse the effect of training, we also combine the COCO train set with the FollowMeUp train set to validate that new images will not affect the model's generality performance.

The DensePose-COCO dataset [19] has reannotated dense body surface annotations on the 50k COCO images. These dense body surface annotations can be understood as continuous part labels of each human body.

The PoseTrack dataset [13] includes both multi-person pose estimation and tracking annotations in videos. It can perform not only pose estimation in single frames, but also temporal tracking across frames. The dataset contains 514 videos including 66,374 frames in total. The annotation format defined 15 body keypoints. For the single-frame pose estimation, the evaluation metric uses mean average precision (mAP) as is done in [20].

3   The Dataset

3.1   Pose Estimation

The key motivation directing our data selection strategy is that we want to represent rare human postures that might be not easily accessed or captured. To this end, we follow the method of [21] to propose a two-level hierarchy of workout activities to guide the collection process. This hierarchy was designed according to the body part to be trained during the exercise. The first level is the body part interested to be trained, such as shoulder, whereas the second level is specific workout activities that can strengthen the muscles of shoulder.

Data Collection. We select candidate workout videos according to the hierarchy and filter out videos of low quality and those that people are truncated. This resulted in over 600 videos spanning over 200 different workout types with three shot angles. We also filter out the frames in which pose is not recognisable due to poor image quality, small scale and dense crowds. This step resulted to a total of 110,000 extracted frames from all collected videos. Secondly, since different exercises have disparate periods, we manually pick key frames with people from each video. We aim to select frames that either depict the whole one exercise period in a substantially different pose or different people with dissimilar appearance. The repeated or no significant distinction postures are ignored. Following this step we annotate 16,519 images. We rough randomly split the annotated images for training and use the rest for testing. Images from the same video are either all in the training or all in the test set. We last obtain the train set of 15,435 images and test set of 1,084 images.

Data Annotation. We follow the keypoint annotation format of COCO dataset, where 17 body keypoints are defined. This design facilitates us to utilise the common samples of COCO dataset during training. Following [11] the left/right joints in the annotations refer to the left/right limbs of the person. Additionally, for all body joints the corresponding visibility is annotated. At test time both the accuracy of joints localisation of a person along with the correct match to the left/right limbs are evaluated. The annotations are performed by in-house workers and inspected by authors. For some unqualified and incorrect annotations are modified continuously until totally correct. To maintain the quality of annotations, we arranged a number of annotation training classes for all annotation workers to unify the standard of annotation. We also supervise and handle some uncertain cases for workers during annotation.

Pose Estimation Evaluation Metrics. Some previous keypoints evaluation metrics rely on the calculation of body limbs' length, such as PCP, PCK and PCK_h used in [12]. However, the workout activities usually have specific postures where the limb's length may be near 0 if the limb is perpendicular to the image plane and the evaluation is not numeric stable in these cases. Therefore comparing the distance between points of groundtruth and prediction directly is more sensible. Here we follow the COCO keypoints dataset, using 5 metrics to describe the performance of a model. They are AP (i.e. average precision), $AP^{0.5}$, $AP^{0.75}$, AP^M and AP^L, as illustrated in Table 1. In the matching between predictions to groundtruth, a matching criterion called object keypoint similarity (OKS) is defined to compute the overlapping ratio between groundtruth and predictions in terms of point distribution [11]. If OKS is larger than one threshold value (e.g. 0.5), the corresponding groundtruth and prediction are considered as a matching pair and the correctness of predicted keypoint types is further analysed. Here OKS is similar to the intersection over union (IoU) in the case of object detection. Thresholding the OKS adjusts the matching criterion. Notice that in general applications, $AP^{0.5}$ gives a good accuracy already. When computing AP (averaged across all 10 OKS thresholds), 6 thresholds exceed 0.70 are over strict due to unavoidable jittering in annotations.

Table 1. Evaluation metrics on the COCO dataset.

Metric	Description
AP	AP at OKS* $= 0.50 : 0.05 : 0.95$ (primary metric)
$AP^{0.5}$	AP at OKS $= 0.50$
$AP^{0.75}$	AP at OKS $= 0.75$
AP^M	AP for medium objects: $32^2 < area < 96^2$
AP^L	AP for large objects: $area > 96^2$

*OKS–Object Keypoint Similarity, same role as IoU

4   Analysis of the State of the Art

In this section we first compare the leading human pose estimation methods on the COCO keypoints dataset, and then analyse the performance of these approaches on our benchmark.

The basis of the comparison is that we note that there is no uniform evaluation protocol to measure the performance of existing methods from a view of practical application. Although human pose estimation is one of the longest-lasting topics, and significant performance improvement has been achieved in the past few years, some reported accuracies in these approaches are obtained through several post-processing steps or some strategies used in the dataset challenge. For example, performing multi-scale evaluation, refining results by a different method, or precision is evaluated at one image scale while speed is recorded at another scale. These post-processing steps interfere the judgement in identifying the strength and weakness of an algorithm. Therefore, evaluating a method without any post-processing steps and strategies is more objective and more valuable for the research and practical application.

The aim of the analysis is to evaluate the generality of the current models on the different datasets and their performance to the unseen samples, identify the existing limitations and stimulate further research advances.

Currently, there are two main categories of solutions: top-down methods [7,22–26] and bottom-up methods [9,10,27–30]. Top-down methods can be seen as a two-stage pipeline from global (i.e. the bounding box) to local (i.e. joints). The first stage is to perform human detection and to obtain their respective bounding boxes in the image. The second stage is to perform single person pose estimation for each of the obtained human regions. [7] deploys multiple high-to-low resolution subnetworks with repeated information exchange across multi-resolution subnetworks. This design obtains rich high-resolution representations and leading more accurate result. [22] utilises a Symmetric Spatial Transformer Network to handle inaccurate bounding boxes. [24] uses simple deconvolution layers to obtain high-resolution heatmaps for human pose estimation. On the side of bottom-up methods, [9] proposes a limb descriptor and an efficient bottom-up grouping approach to associate neighbouring joints. [10] modifies the network architecture of [9] and optimises the post-processing steps to achieve real-time speed on the CPU devices. [30] designs two new descriptors based on [9] for body

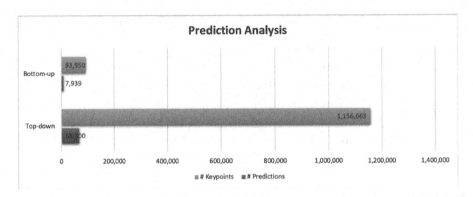

Fig. 3. The comparison of the numbers of effective instance predictions and body keypoints between top-down and bottom-up methods. The prediction number of top-down method is around 10 times higher than bottom-up method.

joints and limbs with the additional variable of object's spread. [28] presents a network to simultaneously output keypoint detections and the corresponding keypoint group assignments. [31] designs a feedback architecture that combining the keypoint results of other pose estimation methods with the original image as the new input to the human pose estimation network. In our analysis we consider 8 state-of-the-art multi-person pose estimation methods, which are listed in Table 2.

We compare the performance of each approach in terms of accuracy and speed on the COCO dataset and our novel FollowMeUp dataset. All the experiments are performed on a desktop with one NVIDIA GeForce GTX-2080Ti GPU. Since all testing approaches are trained and optimised on the COCO dataset, their open source codes have the corresponding configurations, we directly use their default parameters in our testing.

4.1   Comparisons of Approaches on the COCO Dataset

Table 2 presents the comparison results of testing approaches on the COCO dataset. The upper part of Table 2 are top-down approaches. [7] has the highest AP precision of 0.753. Note that the runtime costs around 50 ms as this only includes the part of pose estimation since this open source library uses the groundtruth of human bounding box as the human detection results on the COCO validation set. [24] and [22] have a relatively lower accuracy than [7] using smaller input sizes, which illustrates that the high-resolution and detailed representation is important for the task of human pose estimation. Note that some post-processing strategies, such as multi-scale and flip, are ignored to obtain the actual performance in the real application environments.

For the bottom-up methods, [9] achieves the fastest speed. [30] attains the highest precision in this group. The joint grouping part of [30] costs much longer time than [9]. [10] has around 7% degradation compared with [9] due to using a light-weight network architecture. We also see that the precision of bottom-up

Table 2. Comparisons of pose estimation results on the COCO 2017 validation set.

Type	Method	AP	$AP^{0.5}$	$AP^{0.75}$	AP^M	AP^L	Input size	Runtime
Top-down	HRNet [7]	**0.753**	**0.925**	**0.825**	**0.723**	**0.803**	384×288	0.049^*
	Xiao [24]	0.723	0.915	0.803	0.695	0.768	256×192	0.110
	RMPE [22]	0.735	0.887	0.802	0.693	0.799	320×256	0.298
Bottom-up	PAF [9]	0.469	0.737	0.493	0.403	0.561	432×368	**0.081**
	Osokin [10]	0.400	0.659	0.407	0.338	0.494	368×368	0.481
	PifPaf [30]	0.630	0.855	0.691	0.603	0.677	401×401	0.202
	AE [28]	0.566	0.818	0.618	0.498	0.670	$\mathbf{512 \times 512}$	0.260
	PoseFix [31]	0.411	0.647	0.412	0.303	0.559	384×288	0.250

*: without human detection

algorithms are lower than top-down methods. After detailed analysis, we find that the numbers of predicted effective keypoints of bottom-up methods are around 10 times less than top-down methods as illustrated in Fig. 3. We note that top-down methods correspond to performing single-person pose estimation on each detected human region. Single-person pose estimation can output all types of keypoints even the keypoint is occluded or truncated. However, for multi-person bottom-up methods, two or more overlapping keypoints with the same type can only be detected one due to depth information is not available on the RGB image. For the COCO dataset, there are a lot of crowded and occluded human instances. Therefore, the performance of bottom-up methods is weakened. In the FollowMeUp dataset, the crowding case is rare while most human instances have self-occlusion. We perform the same comparison on the FollowMeUp dataset and validate that bottom-up methods have comparable performance to top-down approaches in this circumstance.

4.2 Comparisons of Approaches on the FollowMeUp Dataset

Table 3 provides the comparison results of testing approaches on the COCO dataset. Since the open source libraries of [7] and [24] do not provide default human detection algorithm, using different human detector may bias the precision distribution, thus we do not test [7] and [24] on the FollowMeUp dataset. We are surprised that [22] obtains a very high precision value. However, the training set only including the COCO dataset of [9] just achieve the precision of 0.778. We argue that the training set of [22] may include other samples except the COCO dataset with particular postures. In this dataset, the precision of [10] decreases by 13% in $AP^{0.5}$ compared with [9], which indicates that the generality of [10] is also narrowed. We use the results of [9] as the initial poses of [31]. Through pose refinement, [31] improved the pose estimation results by 0.4%.

4.3 The Effect of Training on the FollowMeUp Dataset

To validate the effectiveness of samples with particular postures, we retrain the model on the COCO + FollowMeUp train set using the method of [9]. Testing

Table 3. Comparisons of pose estimation results on the FollowMeUp dataset.

Type	Method	$AP^{0.5}$	$AP^{0.6}$	$AP^{0.7}$	$AP^{0.8}$	$AP^{0.9}$
Top-down	RMPE [22]	0.975	0.948	0.885	0.787	0.421
Bottom-up	PAF [9]	0.778	0.728	0.625	0.474	0.326
	Osokin [10]	0.645	0.585	0.520	0.370	0.215
	PoseFix [31]	0.782	0.716	0.621	0.466	0.334

Table 4. Comparisons of pose estimation results on the FollowMeUp dataset.

Method	Train set	Test set	$AP^{0.5}$	$AP^{0.6}$	$AP^{0.7}$	$AP^{0.8}$	$AP^{0.9}$
PAF [9]	COCO	FollowMeUp	0.778	0.728	0.625	0.474	0.326
PAF [9]	COCO + FollowMeUp	FollowMeUp	0.964	0.959	0.926	0.876	0.691

Table 5. Comparisons of pose estimation results on the COCO dataset.

Method	Train set	Test set	AP	$AP^{0.5}$	$AP^{0.75}$	AP^{M}	AP^{L}
PAF [9]	COCO	COCO	0.465	0.740	0.447	0.379	0.597
PAF [9]	COCO + FollowMeUp	COCO	0.465	0.748	0.454	0.373	0.605

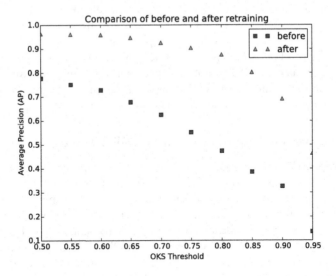

Fig. 4. Comparison of estimation accuracy before and after retraining on the FollowMeUp dataset. The accuracy of retrained model (marked as green triangles) has an obvious improvement. (Color figure online)

is performed both on the FollowMeUp test set and COCO validation set. The results of testing are provided in Table 4. We notice that the performance of the retrained model is greatly improved by around 20% in $AP^{0.5}$. While the threshold of AP becomes more strict, the AP value is decreased. Even in the most strict threshold of 0.9, the AP value attains 0.691, which is higher than the model before retraining by 37%. The accuracy comparison of before and after retraining on the FollowMeUp dataset is shown in Fig. 4. We also perform testing on the COCO validation set using before and after retraining models to check whether the model can maintain the performance on the COCO dataset. In Table 5 we see that before and after retraining the precision has no change. The generality of the retrained model is preserved. These results show that increasing some unusual samples which had not been learnt by the model before is an effective way to improve the accuracy in some specific scenes.

5   Conclusion

The problem of human pose estimation has obtained a great progress in recent years. This progress cannot be done without the development of large-scale human pose datasets. However, the existing human pose datasets are not sufficient for some particular application environments. In this paper, we propose a new large-scale workout activity human pose dataset, which provides a wide variety of sport exercise postures. We select 8 state-of-the-art multi-person pose estimation approaches and compare their performance on both the popular COCO keypoints dataset and our FollowMeUp dataset. The comparison results show that most methods trained on the COCO dataset do not have ideal performance on the FollowMeUp dataset. We also test the generality of the model using the data of both COCO and FollowMeUp datasets. The test results show that training on the data of both COCO and FollowMeUp datasets will not affect the performance of the model on the COCO dataset but the performance of the model on the FollowMeUp dataset is greatly improved. In the future, we will continue investigate pose tracking [32], multi-view action recognition [33], and light-weight network design [34] approaches on the FollowMeUp dataset.

References

1. Johnson, S., Everingham, M.: Clustered pose and nonlinear appearance models for human pose estimation. In: British Machine Vision Conference (BMVC), p. 5 (2010)
2. Wei, S.E., Ramakrishna, V., Kanade, T., Sheikh, Y.: Convolutional pose machines. In: Proceedings of the IEEE Conference on Computer Vision and Pattern Recognition (CVPR), pp. 4724–4732 (2016)
3. Newell, A., Yang, K., Deng, J.: Stacked hourglass networks for human pose estimation. In: Leibe, B., Matas, J., Sebe, N., Welling, M. (eds.) ECCV 2016. LNCS, vol. 9912, pp. 483–499. Springer, Cham (2016). https://doi.org/10.1007/978-3-319-46484-8_29
4. Luvizon, D.C., Picard, D., Tabia, H.: 2D/3D pose estimation and action recognition using multitask deep learning. In: Proceedings of the IEEE Conference on Computer Vision and Pattern Recognition (CVPR), pp. 5137–5146 (2018)

5. Chu, X., Ouyang, W.L., Li, H.S., Wang, X.G.: Structured feature learning for pose estimation. In: Proceedings of the IEEE Conference on Computer Vision and Pattern Recognition (CVPR), pp. 4715–4723 (2016)
6. Chu, X., Yang, W., Ouyang, W.L., Ma, C., Yuille, A.L., Wang, X.G.: Multi-context attention for human pose estimation. In: Proceedings of the IEEE Conference on Computer Vision and Pattern Recognition (CVPR), pp. 1831–1840 (2017)
7. Sun, K., Xiao, B., Liu, D., Wang, J.D.: Deep high-resolution representation learning for human pose estimation. arXiv preprint arXiv:1902.09212 (2019)
8. He, K.M., Gkioxari, G., Dollár, P., Girshick, R.: Mask R-CNN. In: Proceedings of the IEEE International Conference on Computer Vision (ICCV), pp. 2980–2988 (2017)
9. Cao, Z., Simon, T., Wei, S.E., Sheikh, Y.: Realtime multi-person 2D pose estimation using part affinity fields. In: Proceedings of the IEEE Conference on Computer Vision and Pattern Recognition (CVPR), pp. 7291–7299 (2017)
10. Osokin, D.: Real-time 2D multi-person pose estimation on CPU: lightweight Open-Pose. arXiv preprint arXiv:1811.12004 (2018)
11. Lin, T.-Y., et al.: Microsoft COCO: common objects in context. In: Fleet, D., Pajdla, T., Schiele, B., Tuytelaars, T. (eds.) ECCV 2014. LNCS, vol. 8693, pp. 740–755. Springer, Cham (2014). https://doi.org/10.1007/978-3-319-10602-1_48
12. Andriluka, M., Pishchulin, L., Gehler, P., Schiele, B.: 2D human pose estimation: new benchmark and state of the art analysis. In: Proceedings of the IEEE Conference on Computer Vision and Pattern Recognition (CVPR), pp. 3686–3693 (2014)
13. Andriluka, M., et al.: PoseTrack: a benchmark for human pose estimation and tracking. In: Proceedings of the IEEE Conference on Computer Vision and Pattern Recognition, pp. 5167–5176 (2018)
14. Ferrari, V., Marin-Jimenez, M., Zisserman, A.: Progressive search space reduction for human pose estimation. In: 2008 IEEE Conference on Computer Vision and Pattern Recognition, pp. 1–8 (2008)
15. Eichner, M., Ferrari, V., Zurich, S.: Better appearance models for pictorial structures. In: British Machine Vision Conference, p. 5 (2009)
16. Tran, D., Forsyth, D.: Improved human parsing with a full relational model. In: Daniilidis, K., Maragos, P., Paragios, N. (eds.) ECCV 2010. LNCS, vol. 6314, pp. 227–240. Springer, Heidelberg (2010). https://doi.org/10.1007/978-3-642-15561-1_17
17. Wang, Y., Tran, D., Liao, Z.C.: Learning hierarchical poselets for human parsing. In: Proceedings of the IEEE Conference on Computer Vision and Pattern Recognition (CVPR), pp. 1705–1712 (2011)
18. Ramanan, D.: Learning to parse images of articulated objects. In: Neural Information Processing Systems (NIPS) (2006)
19. Alp Güler, Rı., Neverova, N., Kokkinos, I.: DensePose: dense human pose estimation in the wild. In: Proceedings of the IEEE Conference on Computer Vision and Pattern Recognition (CVPR), pp. 7297–7306 (2018)
20. Pishchulin, L., et al.: DeepCut: joint subset partition and labeling for multi person pose estimation. In: Proceedings of the IEEE Conference on Computer Vision and Pattern Recognition (CVPR), pp. 4929–4937 (2016)
21. Ainsworth, B.E., et al.: 2011 compendium of physical activities: a second update of codes and MET values. Med. Sci. Sports Exerc. 43(8), 1575–1581 (2011)
22. Fang, H.S., Xie, S.Q., Tai, Y.W., Lu, C.w.: RMPE: regional multi-person pose estimation. In: Proceedings of the IEEE International Conference on Computer Vision (ICCV), pp. 2334–2343 (2017)

23. Papandreou, G., et al.: Towards accurate multi-person pose estimation in the wild. In: Proceedings of the IEEE Conference on Computer Vision and Pattern Recognition (CVPR), pp. 4903–4911 (2017)
24. Xiao, B., Wu, H., Wei, Y.: Simple baselines for human pose estimation and tracking. In: Ferrari, V., Hebert, M., Sminchisescu, C., Weiss, Y. (eds.) ECCV 2018. LNCS, vol. 11210, pp. 472–487. Springer, Cham (2018). https://doi.org/10.1007/978-3-030-01231-1_29
25. Chen, Y.L., Wang, Z.C., Peng, Y.X., Zhang, Z.Q., Yu, G., Sun, J.: Cascaded pyramid network for multi-person pose estimation. In: Proceedings of the IEEE Conference on Computer Vision and Pattern Recognition (CVPR), pp. 7103–7112 (2018)
26. Su, K., Yu, D.D., Xu, Z.Q., Geng, X., Wang, C.H.: Multi-person pose estimation with enhanced channel-wise and spatial information. In: Proceedings of the IEEE Conference on Computer Vision and Pattern Recognition (CVPR), pp. 5674–5682 (2019)
27. Insafutdinov, E., Pishchulin, L., Andres, B., Andriluka, M., Schiele, B.: DeeperCut: a deeper, stronger, and faster multi-person pose estimation model. In: Leibe, B., Matas, J., Sebe, N., Welling, M. (eds.) ECCV 2016. LNCS, vol. 9910, pp. 34–50. Springer, Cham (2016). https://doi.org/10.1007/978-3-319-46466-4_3
28. Newell, A., Huang, Z.A., Deng, J.: Associative embedding: end-to-end learning for joint detection and grouping. In: Proceedings of the Neural Information Processing Systems (NIPS), pp. 2277–2287 (2017)
29. Papandreou, G., Zhu, T., Chen, L.-C., Gidaris, S., Tompson, J., Murphy, K.: PersonLab: person pose estimation and instance segmentation with a bottom-up, part-based, geometric embedding model. In: Ferrari, V., Hebert, M., Sminchisescu, C., Weiss, Y. (eds.) Computer Vision – ECCV 2018. LNCS, vol. 11218, pp. 282–299. Springer, Cham (2018). https://doi.org/10.1007/978-3-030-01264-9_17
30. Kreiss, S., Bertoni, L., Alahi, A.: PifPaf: composite fields for human pose estimation. arXiv preprint arXiv:1903.06593 (2019)
31. Moon, G., Chang, J.Y., Lee, K.M.: PoseFix: model-agnostic general human pose refinement networkz. arXiv preprint arXiv:1812.03595 (2018)
32. Raaj, Y., Idrees, H., Hidalgo, G., Sheikh, Y.: Efficient online multi-person 2D pose tracking with recurrent spatio-temporal affinity fields. In: Proceedings of the IEEE Conference on Computer Vision and Pattern Recognition (CVPR), pp. 4620–4628 (2019)
33. Zhao, L., Peng, X., Tian, Y., Kapadia, M., Metaxas, D.N.: Semantic graph convolutional networks for 3D human pose regression. In: Proceedings of the IEEE Conference on Computer Vision and Pattern Recognition (CVPR), pp. 3425–3435 (2019)
34. Zhang, F., Zhu X.T., Ye, M.: Fast human pose estimation. In: Proceedings of the IEEE Conference on Computer Vision and Pattern Recognition (CVPR), pp. 3517–3526 (2019)

Partial Order Structure Based Image Retrieval

Zhuoyi Li[1,2], Guanghua Gu[1,2(✉)], and Jiangtao Liu[1,2]

[1] School of Information Science and Engineering, Yanshan University,
Qinhuangdao 066004, China
guguanghua@ysu.edu.cn
[2] Hebei Provincial Key Laboratory of Information Transmission and Signal
Processing, Qinhuangdao 066004, China

Abstract. Image retrieval plays an important role in the growing computer vision applications. The computation of the unrelated images in large scale image retrieval task seriously reduces the retrieval efficiency. In this paper, a new Partial Order Structure (POS) based image retrieval method is proposed. Partial order structure diagram is an effective visualization tool in Formal Concept Analysis (FCA) theory, including object partial order structure diagram and attribute partial order structure diagram. There are two contributions in this paper. First, we design an association rule according to the object partial order structure (OPOS) method to measure the correlation between the query image and the database, and then improve the database to be retrieved. Second, we perform a query expansion according to the attribute partial order structure (APOS) method to improve the generalization ability of the query information. Experimental results on two databases verify the effectiveness of the proposed algorithm.

Keywords: Image retrieval · Formal Concept Analysis · Partial order structure · Association rule · Query expansion

1 Introduction

Image retrieval is a significant part of computer vision applications. In the common retrieval methods, the retrieval process is to calculate the similarity between the feature descriptions of the query image and image database. However, many images unrelated to the query image are calculated for the similarity, which wastes a lot of time. To enhance the computation efficiency, we attempt to improve the database by removing the images with the unrelated semantics to the query image before the retrieval.

The partial order structure is a powerful visualization tool for the representational concept in Formal Concept Analysis (FCA) theory [1]. It contains the object partial order structure and the attribute partial order structure. In the object partial order structure diagram, nodes represent objects, and branches represent attributes. The cluster structure in the object partial order structure refers to the structural relationship of the objects containing the same or similar attributes. Such a structure has the role of clustering [2, 3]. In the object partial order structure, the attributes in the same cluster

---

The first author (Zhuoyi Li) is a student.

© Springer Nature Switzerland AG 2019
Z. Lin et al. (Eds.): PRCV 2019, LNCS 11859, pp. 122–134, 2019.
https://doi.org/10.1007/978-3-030-31726-3_11

have the higher similarity than the attributes in different clusters. So in this paper, we set an association rule to mine the similarities of the attributes based on the object partial order structure.

In the attribute partial order structure diagram, nodes represent attributes, and branches represent objects. The similarity of two branches can be calculated by the number of identical nodes on the branches. To make features of the query image more expressive, we use the attribute partial order structure to find the several top-ranked images by calculating the similarity between the query image and the database. The query image is expanded into the merged image of the top-ranked individuals.

The deep features have strong generalization ability, which can effectively capture the semantics of the image [4, 5]. The image features extracted by CNN model can globally represent the image [6]. When the deep neural network is applied to image feature extraction, the high-dimensional features show the great advantages in image processing. Many works [7, 8] focused on replacing the traditional hand-crafted descriptors with the deep features from the fully connected layers of a pre-trained CNN model for image classification. Other methods [9, 10] used the sum or max pooled convolutional features instead of the fully connected layer and achieved better results. Additionally, some methods first divided the image into several blocks [11, 12]. The features of the image blocks are obtained through the fully connected layer or the convolution layer, and the image blocks are encoded by the BOW model or the VLAD model [13, 14]. These methods used the local information of the image block. Although these methods were commonly used in image retrieval, extracting the CNN features of each image block is complicated and inefficient [15].

Feature maps are image features produced by the original image after convolution in a neural network. In this paper, the activations of the different neuron arrays across all feature maps in a convolutional layer are treated as local features. A single transfer of an image through CNN is sufficient to obtain its local features of blocks [16]. It avoids the block segmentation and the feature extraction such that the retrieval complexity is greatly reduced. We obtain the local features of the images in the database from the last convolutional layer in the VGG network. The visual semantics are obtained by clustering local features. In this paper, visual semantics are set as the attributes, and images are set as the objects to establish the formal background. The partial order structure is built based on the formal background. According to the object partial order structure, the association rule is designed to improve the image database that contains the same or similar semantics as the query image, that is, the unrelated images to the query image are removed. Meanwhile, the query expansion is performed based on the attribute partial order structure to complete the image retrieval.

2   Related Works

In the theory of Formal Conceptual Analysis (FCA), the human cognition consists of three basic elements: objects, attributes, and relationship between objects and attributes [17]. The objects are the individuals in the database. The attributes are the characteristics of the various objects. The relationship between attributes and objects indicates the corresponding connection of both [18], which is described by the formal background as shown in Table 1. Here, I_1–I_6 are 6 objects, and S_1–S_6 are 6 attributes. The formal background is a Boolean matrix including 1 or 0. Here 1 represents the object has the corresponding attribute, and 0 represents the non-correspondence.

Table 1. Formal background

	S_1	S_2	S_3	S_4	S_5	S_6
I_1	1	1	0	0	0	0
I_2	1	1	0	0	1	0
I_3	1	0	1	0	1	0
I_4	0	0	1	0	0	1
I_5	0	1	0	0	1	0
I_6	1	1	0	1	1	0

The formal background is the correspondence between objects and attributes. In this paper, we use VGG-f model to get the visual fuzzy semantics. Images are regarded as the objects and visual semantics are regarded as the attributes. The formal background is built by the objects and attributes, and then the partial order structure diagram is established. The partial order structure diagram contains the object partial order structure (OPOS) diagram and the attribute partial order structure (APOS) diagram. Both realize the hierarchical clustering of the data, which is useful to analyze the concept composition.

In the OPOS diagram, each node shows an object (image), and each branch under nodes indicates an attribute (visual semantic). OPOS brings together the objects with the similar attributes to generate a hierarchy of the database. In OPOS, the data filtering or data clustering can be completed according to the cluster structure. We put the clusters with more objects into the top of the hierarchy, and the clusters with less objects into the bottom of the hierarchy. The resulting hierarchical partial structure is helpful for data searching.

The generation process of the APOS diagram is similar to the OPOS diagram, but the node and the branch represent the opposite meaning. In the APOS diagram, each branch represents an object, and all attributes contained in this object correspond to all nodes on the branch. For an instance, the OPOS and APOS diagrams generated by the formal background in Table 1 are shown in Fig. 1.

Figure 1(a) shows an OPOS diagram. Here I_1–I_6 indicates 6 objects (images), and S_1–S_6 represents 6 attributes (fuzzy semantics). Each branch in Fig. 1(a) means an attribute. The number of attributes is the number of the clusters obtained by the clustering method. If two attributes contain more of the same images, the two visual semantics are more likely to appear at the same time. In other words, if the two visual semantics are more relevant, one is suitable for complementing the other. Figure 1(b) shows an APOS diagram in which each branch means an image and each node means a fuzzy semantic. If two branches have the more identical nodes, it means the branches have the higher similarity. In other words, the similarity between images can be determined by the number of identical nodes contained on the branch.

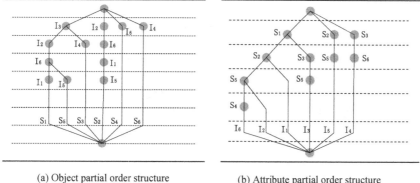

(a) Object partial order structure   (b) Attribute partial order structure

Fig. 1. An example for the OPOS diagram and APOS diagram

3 Image Retrieval Based on Partial Order Structure

The proposed method consists of three parts: Deep Feature Extraction (DFE), Partial Order Structure (POS) and Feature Similarity Metric (FSM). The main framework is shown in Fig. 2.

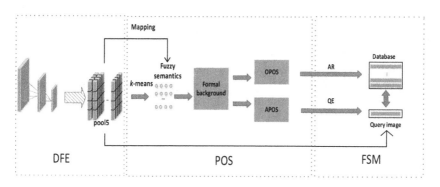

Fig. 2. Image Retrieval flowchart based on partial order structure

The DFE part contains the extraction of the local features in the network and the extraction of the global features from the full connect layer. The POS section is the primary step in the proposed method. It completes the adaptation of the database by using OPOS and association rule (AR). This part also expands the feature information of the query image, and improves the expressive ability of query images by using query expansion (QE) based on APOS. The FSM section computes the distance similarity metric between the query image and the database to generate the rank of the retrieval.

3.1   Visual Semantics

In convolutional neural network, the convolution kernel in the convolution layer acts on the receptive field [6]. The convolution calculation method is selected for each input image to form the image feature maps. Different feature maps represent different local features [19]. In the process of obtaining visual semantics, we extract the features by the last convolution layer (pool5) in the VGG-f network pre-trained on the ImageNet database. The network has not been fine-tuned. Each vector in the pool5 layer is treated as a local feature. An image extracts 6*6 local feature descriptions, each of which is 256-dimensional. It means that an image can be represented as the 36 local features with a dimension of 256.

Among the clustering methods, the k-means algorithm keeps scalability and high efficiency for dealing with the big data. In this paper, after obtaining the local features, we perform the k-means clustering to get the centers, which are regarded as the visual fuzzy semantics. Features of all images in database are mapped into the centers to form their visual fuzzy semantic representation [20]. We expect that each local feature can be properly mapped into the most appropriate cluster (i.e. the fuzzy semantics). As we all know, the number of k is essential for k-means. In this paper, a Davies Bouldin index (*DBI*) [21] method is used as a criterion to select the number of cluster centers.

3.2   Object Partial Order Structure

According to the OPOS diagram, we can remove the images on the branches that have no visual semantics of the query image. However, if we only leave the images with the same visual semantics as the query image, some images with the similar semantics may be ignored. It maybe leads to a bad recall rate. Therefore, it is necessary to find the similar semantics as the complementary semantics.

Some visual semantics often appear at the same time, such as airplane and sky. These simultaneous semantics are often used to complement the retrieval each other. It is necessary to calculate the association between the visual semantics by using the partial order structure, and get the related semantics of each visual semantic. This paper defines a semantic association rule to measure the degree of association between two semantics in Eq. 1.

$$D_a = \frac{num(Im(X) \cap Im(Y))}{num(G)} \tag{1}$$

Here X and Y represent two semantics respectively. $Im(X)$ and $Im(Y)$ represent the images containing the semantics X and Y, respectively. For instance, if X is S_1 and Y is S_5 in Fig. 1(a), $Im(X)$ represents the image set $\{I_3, I_2, I_6, I_1\}$ and $Im(Y)$ represents the image set $\{I_3, I_2, I_6, I_5\}$. $Im(X) \cap Im(Y)$ represents the common images $\{I_3, I_2, I_6\}$ from the vertex down. In the object partial order structure, there are some top clusters, that is, the branches under the nodes in the first level, for example the clusters under the nodes I_3, I_2, I_6 and I_4. So as to standardize the relevance of two semantics, avoided the influence of the number of pictures between different clusters on semantic relevance, we perform correlation metrics within clusters in a partial order structure and introduce

G as the denominator. In Eq. 1, G is the image set of the top cluster in which semantics X and Y are belonging, that is, $\{I_3, I_4, I_2, I_1, I_6, I_5\}$ in Fig. 1(a). The function num ($\cdot$) indicates the number of the image set.

As well known, in a database, a picture often has multiple semantics, the semantics are distributed across multiple clusters. For each semantic, we calculate the similarity between it and other semantics in a cluster and rank the similarity. The semantics that the similarity D_a is greater than the mean value within the cluster is considered to be the complementary semantics. The images on the branches with the higher similarity are merged to form the final image database to be retrieved. Figure 3 displays an example of the semantics complement.

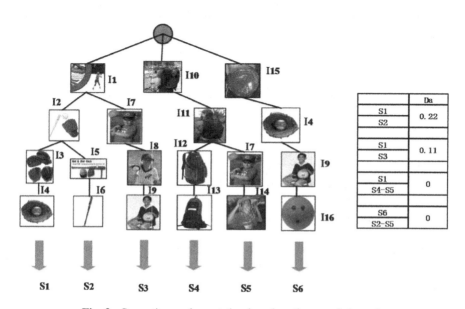

Fig. 3. Semantic supplementation based on the association rule

Suppose that the query image contains semantics S_1 and S_6, the association rule algorithm based on the OPOS diagram in Fig. 3 is as follows:

Input: Query image, database, and OPOS.

1. Get the branch $\{S_1, S_6\}$ of the query image from OPOS, and take the images on the branches as a new database DB $\{I_1-I_4, I_9, I_{15}-I_{16}\}$.
2. Calculate the degree of association D_a between $\{S_1, S_6\}$ and other semantics $\{S_2, S_3, S_4, S_5\}$ by Eq. 1.
3. Calculating the mean value (0.165) of the semantic similarity D_a in the cluster where S_1 is located.
4. Update DB by adding images on branches $\{S_2\}$, that is $\{I_1-I_6, I_9, I_{15}-I_{16}\}$.

End

In Fig. 3, the whole image database includes 16 images (i.e. I_1-I_{16}). The OPOS diagram has three top clusters corresponding to the node I_1, I_{10} and I_{15}, respectively.

Suppose the query image contains semantic S_1 and semantic S_6. The right of Fig. 3 is the D_a value of $\{S_1, S_6\}$ and other semantics. After the semantics complement by the association rule, the optimized image database includes 9 images (i.e. I_1–I_6, I_9, I_{15}–I_{16}), and images (I_7–I_8, I_{10}–I_{14}) are removed. If we do not perform the association rule, only the images on the branch S_1 and S_6 will be retrieved, and the images (such as I_5 and I_6) with the similar semantics as the query image will be missed. It will cause the missing of the retrieval.

3.3   Attribute Partial Order Structure

In the APOS diagram, nodes represent attributes (visual semantics), and branches represent objects (images). The degree of similarity between two branches is evaluated by the number of identical nodes on the branches (images) in the APOS diagram. As well known, the images contain more identical attributes means that they have the higher similarity. In this paper, we calculate the number of identical attributes on the corresponding branches between the database and the query image, and sort the images of the database. The features of the top-ranked N images and the query image are averaged to obtain a new feature that replaces the feature of query image for the subsequent image retrieval. The algorithm of query expansion based on the APOS diagram is as follows:

   Input: Query image, database and APOS.

1. Calculate the degree of association between query image and database according to the APOS diagram.
2. Sort the similarity of the query image and the database, and select the top N images that are most similar to the query image.
3. Average the features of the top-ranked N pictures and the feature of the query picture.
4. The obtained mean feature is used as the query feature for image retrieval.

   End

   The sorted result obtained by APOS is shown in Fig. 4, where the first column shows the query picture and the last is the top 5 pictures. It can be seen that most of the top 5 images are correctly retrieved. This paper performs the query expansion by selecting the top 5 images to improve the representation ability of the query image.

4   Experiments

4.1   Dataset

Two commonly used image databases, DupImage and Paris Buildings [22], are applied to evaluate the proposed retrieval method. DupImage database has 33 categories of icon images with a total number of 1188 images. Paris Buildings database contains 11 classes of building images with a total number of 6412 images. For DupImage database, all the images are used for the retrieval in the experiment. For Paris Buildings

Query image	Top 5 images

Fig. 4. The top 5 ranked results obtained by APOS

database, we randomly select 200 images for each category thus a total 2200 images to perform the image retrieval.

In Paris Buildings database, each query image has a groundtruth file which contains four types of labels: 'good', 'ok', 'junk' and 'bad'. The images with the four labels are manually classified according to the similarity between the database and the query image. Visually, the images with the 'good' and 'ok' labels are similar to the query image, while the images with the 'junk' and 'bad' labels are not similar. Many previous works only used 'good' and 'ok' labels for image retrieval. In order to highlight the filtering ability of the partial order structure, this paper treats all the images under the category of the query image as similar images instead of using the 'good' and 'ok' labels given by the database.

4.2 Setup

Suppose that there are M actual semantics for the database. After the clustering by the k-means method, k semantic centers are produced. If k is bigger than M, the semantics is over-clustering, that is, the semantics are not representative. If k is less than M, some actual semantics are merged, that is, some actual semantics are missing. Therefore, choosing an appropriate k value is necessary for the clustering. In this paper, we utilize Davies Bouldin index (DBI) to achieve the optimal k value automatically. The definition of DBI is as follows:

$$DBI = \frac{1}{k}\sum_{i=1}^{k}\max_{j\neq i}\left(\frac{\overline{C_i}+\overline{C_j}}{\left\|w_i - w_j\right\|_2}\right) \tag{2}$$

$$C_i = \frac{1}{T_i}\left(\sum_{p=1}^{T_i}\left|X_p - w_i\right|^2\right)^{1/2} \tag{3}$$

Here C_i represents the average distance between all the data points in the ith cluster and its center, which indicates the dispersion degree of the data points in clusters. X_P

represents the pth data point. T_i represents the number of data points in the ith cluster. w_i represents the clustering center of the ith cluster. The data clustering is performed on two databases to obtain the *DBI* curve and get the appropriate k value. To observe the best k value clearly, the data points are fitted to a curve as shown in Fig. 5.

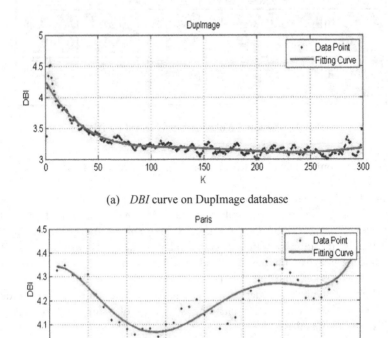

(a)   *DBI* curve on DupImage database

(b)   *DBI* curve on Paris Building database

Fig. 5.   *DBI* curves on two image databases

A smaller *DBI* value means a better clustering effect. From Fig. 5(a) we can see that the value of *DBI* in the DupImage database becomes smaller as the k value increases. When the k value reaches 100, the curve tends to be stable. From Fig. 5(b), when the k value is about 150, the *DBI* of the Paris Building database reaches the lowest value. Therefore, we take 100 and 150 as the best k values for the DupImages database and Paris Building database, respectively.

In this paper, the parameters including the mean Average Precisions (*mAP*), Precision (*P*), Recall (*R*) and *F*-measure (*F*) are taken as the evaluation indexes to test the proposed OPOS and APOS methods. The result is reported as the average of the results from the 5 individual runs. The definition of *F* is as follows:

$$F = \frac{2PR}{P+R} \tag{4}$$

4.3   Experimental Results

In this section, we randomly select five images for each category in the Paris Building and DupImage databases as the query images, that is, there are 55 query images for the Paris Building database and 165 query images for the DupImage database. To demonstrate the efficiency of the experiment, we calculate the mAP, P, R and F to evaluate the proposed OPOS and APOS methods.

The P-R curves on two databases are plotted in Fig. 6. We compare the retrieval performance of three methods, OPOS, OPOS+APOS and CNN. The OPOS method indicates the database adaption by the semantics association rule based on the OPOS diagram. The OPOS+APOS method means the OPOS method combined with the query expansion based on the APOS diagram. The CNN method directly measures similarity of features extracted by the fully connected layer in VGG-f network without the database adaption and the query expansion. The number of the returned retrieved images is ranging from 40 to 200 with an increment by 20 for the DupImage database, and ranging from 50 to 600 with an increment by 50 for the Paris Building database.

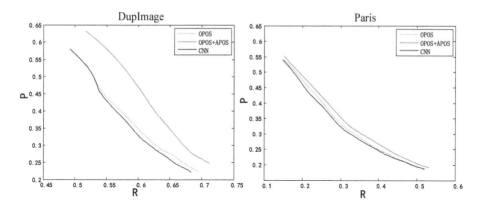

Fig. 6. P-R Statistical curves

From Fig. 6, the OPOS+APOS method outperforms other methods on two databases. The CNN method has the worst performance. Since the images in the different categories of the Paris Building database are highly similar, it is hard to increase the performance for the Paris Building database. From Fig. 6 we can see that the OPOS +APOS method improves better performance on DupImage database than Paris Building database.

In all, the OPOS method removes images that are not related to the query image and recalls some similar semantic images to improve the original image database, which indicates the clustering ability of partial order structure and the ability to filter association rules. The APOS method enhances the expressive ability of the query image according to query expansion based on attribute partial order structure, Table 2 shows the average of P, R and F for the first W returned retrieved images, where W is the number of images of each category in the database. For two databases, the F value of the OPOS+APOS method is better than that of CNN method by about 4%.

Table 2. Comparison of the P, R, F on two databases

	DupImage			Paris		
Method	CNN	OPOS	OPOS+APOS	CNN	OPOS	OPOS+APOS
P	0.58	0.59	0.62	0.32	0.33	0.35
R	0.45	0.46	0.49	0.30	0.31	0.33
F	0.51	0.52	0.55	0.31	0.32	0.34

To further verify the superiority of the OPOS and APOS methods, Table 3 displays the mAP values of the three methods on the two image databases. For two databases, the mAP of the OPOS+APOS method is better than that of CNN method by about 4%. Need to point out, in Paris Building database, Since this paper does not use the groundtruth file that the database has given, compared with some works that only returns 'good' and 'ok' images as the similar images of the query image, the mAP obtained in this paper is lower.

Table 3. Comparison of mAP values on two databases

	DupImage	Paris
OPOS+APOS	0.56	0.38
OPOS	0.53	0.36
CNN	0.52	0.34

5   Conclusion

To better explore the relationship between images and the corresponding visual semantics, in this paper, we construct the formal background and establish the object partial order structure and attribute partial order structure according to the image and the visual semantics. We filter the irrelevant images and supplement the similar semantic images from the original image database by using the object partial order structure to improve the efficiency of the image retrieval. Also, we use the attribute partial order structure diagram to expand the query information of the database, which generalizes the characteristics of the query image. Experimental results demonstrate the validity of the proposed image retrieval method based on Object Partial Order Structure (OPOS) and Attribute Partial Order Structure (APOS). However, there is still a problem to be solved. Because the visual semantics obtained by the clustering are ambiguous, a few similar semantic images as the query image may be lost in the filtering process.

Acknowledgements. This work was partly supported by National Natural Science Foundation of China (No. 61303128), Natural Science Foundation of Hebei province (F2017203169), Key Scientific Research Projects of Colleges and Universities in Hebei province (ZD2017080), and Science and Technology Foundation for Returned Overseas People of Hebei Province (CL201621).

References

1. Li, S., Song, J., Hong, W., et al.: Partially ordered structure loop: a new method for visualization of big data's partial ordered structure. J. Yanshan Univ. **5**, 409–415 (2014)
2. Fan, F., Hong, W., Song, J., et al.: A visualization method for Chinese medicine knowledge discovery based on formal concept analysis. Express Lett. Part B Appl. Int. J. Res. Surv. **4**, 801–808 (2013)
3. Ganter, B., Eklund, P., Wille, R., et al.: Formal Concept Analysis. Electron. Notes Discrete Math. **2**(3), 199–200 (1999)
4. Yan, Z., Zhang, H., Piramuthu, R., et al.: HD-CNN: hierarchical deep convolutional neural network for large scale visual recognition. In: ICCV (2015)
5. Wan, J., Wang, D., Hoi, S.C.H., et al.: Deep learning for content-based image retrieval: a comprehensive study. In: ACM International Conference on Multimedia (2014)
6. Ozeki, M., Okatani, T.: Understanding convolutional neural networks in terms of category-level attributes. In: Cremers, D., Reid, I., Saito, H., Yang, M.-H. (eds.) ACCV 2014. LNCS, vol. 9004, pp. 362–375. Springer, Cham (2015). https://doi.org/10.1007/978-3-319-16808-1_25
7. Babenko, A., Slesarev, A., Chigorin, A., Lempitsky, V.: Neural codes for image retrieval. In: Fleet, D., Pajdla, T., Schiele, B., Tuytelaars, T. (eds.) ECCV 2014. LNCS, vol. 8689, pp. 584–599. Springer, Cham (2014). https://doi.org/10.1007/978-3-319-10590-1_38
8. Razavian, A.S., Azizpour, H., Sullivan, J., et al.: CNN features off-the-shelf: an astounding baseline for recognition. In: CVPRW, pp. 512–519 (2014)
9. Babenko, A., Lempitsky, V.: Aggregating local deep features for image retrieval. In: ICCV, pp. 1269–1277 (2015)
10. Sharif Razavian, A., Sullivan, J., Maki, A., et al.: A baseline for visual instance retrieval with deep convolutional networks. In: ICLR (2015)
11. Liu, Y., Guo, Y., Wu, S., et al.: Deep index for accurate and efficient image retrieval. In: ICMR (2015)
12. Gong, Y., Wang, L., Guo, R., Lazebnik, S.: Multi-scale orderless pooling of deep convolutional activation features. In: Fleet, D., Pajdla, T., Schiele, B., Tuytelaars, T. (eds.) ECCV 2014. LNCS, vol. 8695, pp. 392–407. Springer, Cham (2014). https://doi.org/10.1007/978-3-319-10584-0_26
13. Jegou, H., Douze, M., Schmid, C., et al.: Aggregating local descriptors into a compact image representation. In: CVPR, pp. 3304–3311 (2010)
14. Arandjelović, R., Gronat, P., Torii, A., et al.: Net-VLAD: CNN architecture for weakly supervised place recognition. Trans. Pattern Anal. Mach. Intell. TPAMI **40**(6), 1437–1451 (2017)
15. Donahue, J., Jia, Y., Vinyals, O., et al.: DeCAF: a deep convolutional activation feature for generic visual recognition. In: ICML (2014)
16. Mohedano, E., Salvador, A., Mcguinness, K., et al.: Bags of local convolutional features for scalable instance search. In: ICMR (2016)

17. Hong, W., Luan, J., Zhang, T., et al.: Knowledge discovery based on partial ordered structure theory. J. Yanshan Univ. **5**, 395–402 (2016)
18. Zhang, T., Ren, H., Wang, X., et al.: A calculation of formal concept by attribute topology. ICIC Express Lett. Part B Appl. Int. J. Res. Surv. **4**, 793–800 (2013)
19. Liu, S., Deng, W.: Very deep convolutional neural network based image classification using small training sample size. In: ACPR, pp. 730–734 (2015)
20. Ng, Y., Yang, F., Davis, L.: Exploiting local features from deep networks for image retrieval. In: CVPRW, pp. 53–61 (2015)
21. Davies, L., Bouldin, W.: A cluster separation measure. IEEE Trans. Pattern Anal. Mach. Intell. **1**(2), 224–227 (1979)
22. Philbin, J., Chum, O., Isard, M., et al.: Lost in quantization: improving particular object retrieval in large scale image databases. In: CVPR (2008)

Computer Vision Applications

Semantic Object and Plane SLAM
for RGB-D Cameras

Longyu Zheng[1] and Wenbing Tao[1,2(✉)]

[1] National Key Laboratory of Science and Technology on Multi-spectral Information Processing, School of Artificial Intelligence and Automation, Huazhong University of Science and Technology, Wuhan 430074, China
{m201772502,wenbingtao}@hust.edu.cn
[2] Shenzhen Huazhong University of Science and Technology Research Institute, Shenzhen 518057, China

Abstract. Simultaneous Localization And Mapping (SLAM) is a fundamental problem in mobile robotics as well as in virtual reality (VR) and augmented reality (AR). Traditional visual-SLAM systems, such as ORB-SLAM, deal with sparse features extracted from high gradient image regions. While being robust and stable to light changing, camera rotation and scale changing to some extent, they are easy to accumulate drifts and cannot provide high-level information of the environment. To solve this problem, we take advantage of state of the art object detectors and a robust ICP method to build a map made up of objects providing semantic information as well as extra constraints to original point-based SLAM system. What's more, for indoor scenes where planar structures are common, we introduce plane landmarks into SLAM framework to reduce drift. Experiments show that the our method can build a semantically more meaningful map without reducing the original SLAM system's performance remarkably.

Keywords: SLAM · Object detection · Plane extraction · Semantic understanding

1 Introduction

Semantic understanding and Simultaneous Localization and Mapping (SLAM) [24] are two essential tasks in computer vision and robotics. Traditional visual-SLAM systems use low-level primitives (points, lines, patches, etc.) to represent the environment and localize the sensor. While being robust to light changing, camera rotation and scale changing to some extent, they are easy to accumulate drifts and lack high-level information of the environment. As the development of Convolutional Neural Network (CNN), the performance of image-based object detection has been improved enormously [31]. Incorporating object detection into

---

This is a student paper.

Z. Lin et al. (Eds.): PRCV 2019, LNCS 11859, pp. 137–148, 2019.
https://doi.org/10.1007/978-3-030-31726-3_12

SLAM and building a map made up of objects will greatly enhance robot intelligence for environment understanding and human-computer interaction, and the object landmark added can provide extra constraints for SLAM optimization. Some existing object SLAM [2,3,6] use object model pre-built for object detection and incorporate object landmarks into SLAM pipeline to get better SLAM performance. There are also frameworks [18,27,28] reducing scale drift by measuring the size of objects. CubeSLAM [4] and QuadricSLAM [5] firstly detect objects using CNN based object detectors and then represent them as geometric models. Planes are typical structures in man-made environments and can provide long-range constraint. Incorporating planes into a point-based SLAM framework will reduce drift that is typical for point-based SLAM and enhance the performance of SLAM where little point features can be seen.

In this work, we propose a SLAM framework incorporating objects and planes extracted from RGB-D images. The main contributions of the paper are as follows:

- Propose a method for object detection and matching to incrementally create a map made up of objects.
- Incorporate a robust ICP method for object pose estimation and add object poses into SLAM optimization.
- Utilize a Plane Detection method for plane mapping and incorporate plane landmarks into SLAM optimization.

In the following section, we discuss related work. In Sect. 3.1 we show our system framework. In Sect. 3.2 we present the object mapping module of our SLAM system. In Sect. 3.3 we introduce our method for plane extraction and matching. Section 3.4 describes the joint optimization of objects, planes, and points. Section 4 shows experimental results and comparisons. Finally, we summarize the contributions and discuss future work in Sect. 5.

2   Related Work

2.1   Object Detection

In recent years, algorithms based on deep learning (mainly convolutional neural network, CNN) had made great breakthroughs in various computer vision tasks, including object detection. With the mature application of the learning framework of the convolutional neural network (CNN), the technology of object detection had made remarkable progress. This was because deep learning had the ability to learn massive data and the ability to learn high dimensional features, which gave deep features excellent discrimination. Typical method for object detection was the R-CNN (Region with CNN features) proposed by Girshick et al., which combined the general candidate region algorithm and CNN classification framework. Faster R-CNN [34] was one of the most accurate deep neural networks with more than 80% mAP in the PASCAL VOC dataset, depending on region proposal algorithms. Redmon et al. designed a unified architecture for YOLO [29] and its improved model YOLOv2 [30], making YOLOv2 one of the fastest networks that could process images at 91 FPS with 69% mAP or 40 FPS with 78.6% mAP on PASCAL VOC dataset. Single Shot Multibox Object Detector (SSD) [31] was the first DNN-based real-time object detector that achieves above 70% mAP in PASCAL VOC dataset with 40 FPS in TitanX. This detector balanced speed and accuracy well, hence we deploy SSD as the detector module in our method.

2.2   Object SLAM

Sünderhauf *et al.* [7] proposed a semantic mapping system that used object detection and RGB-D SLAM to build a map containing objects. But the object models were not used to help localization. McCormac *et al.* [8] presented a system that fused multiple semantic predictions with a dense map reconstruction, but the semantic labels did not inform localization. SLAM++ [2] built object models by extracting meshes from TSDF volume and discretizing PPFs in search data structures for them, with the process accelerated by GPU. By dense ICP estimation, SLAM++ built a graph, where each node stored either the estimated SE(3) pose of object j to the world, or the pose of camera to each other. And finally the object pose and camera pose were optimized together. Dorian Gálvez-López *et al.* [3] used bags of binary words to describe objects. By incorporating objects into a monocular SLAM, real scale of the scene can be retrieved and more accurate trajectory can be obtained. Without prior models, the recent QuadricSLAM [5] and CubeSLAM [4] proposed two different object representation of mathematical model. Fusion++ [6] built TSDF volume for every object and did not rely on pre-built models. [9–11] optimized object mathematical models, points and planes together, which were most similar to our method. Probabilistic data association for object SLAM were addressed in [12,13]. PSfMO [15] solved SFM theoretically with ellipsoid object and affine cameras. [16] solved SFM by jointly optimizing camera poses, objects, points and planes. [17] and [18] represented object as spheres to correct the scale drift of monocular SLAM.

2.3   Planar SLAM

Planar SLAM utilized planes as landmark instead of point features for pose estimation and SLAM optimization. CPA-SLAM [22] used direct image alignment towards a keyframe and a global plane model in an EM framework and optimized the spatial constraints between keyframes and global plane model and alignment constraints between keyframes. DPPTAM [21] proposed a new initialization scheme for planar areas. By reconstructing high-gradient image areas as 3D points and low-gradient image areas as planes segmented using superpixels, DPPTAM improved the accuracy and density of semi-dense monocular SLAM. Lee [19] estimated the layout plane and point cloud registration iteratively to reduce RGBD mapping drift. Similarly, planes were shown to provide long-range constraints compared to points in indoor building environments [14,20]. Kaess [23] presented a novel minimal representation for planar features that are suitable for least-squares optimization by mapping from the standard homogeneous

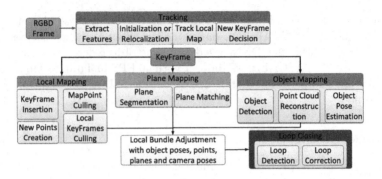

Fig. 1. Our method adds two more concurrent threads to ORB-SLAM2: (a) Plane Mapping, (b) Object Mapping. And the local bundle adjustment process will include object poses, points, planes additionally than just camera poses.

plane parametrization to a quaternion. KDP-SLAM [20] applied the keyframe-based framework in the planar SLAM solution, with keyframe poses and landmark planes optimized in a global factor graph using incremental smoothing and mapping (iSAM).

3 Method

3.1 System Overview

The pipeline of our system is shown in Fig. 1, which is built upon ORB-SLAM2. ORB-SLAM2 is a feature based visual SLAM system made up of three parallel threads: Tracking, Local Mapping and Loop Closing. The Tracking thread is in charge of tracking the pose of camera frame by frame. Local Mapping thread maintains a local map made up of several key frames and 3D points and performs local BA to optimize them. Loop Closing thread finds loops and corrects them. Compared to ORB-SLAM2, which is made up of three parallel threads, our system adds two more threads handling objects and planes: Object Mapping and Plane Mapping. To insure the performance, we run object mapping and plane mapping thread only on keyframes. The Object Mapping thread (Sect. 3.2) is responsible for building a map made up of objects. It first detects objects in 2D images and reconstructs corresponding point cloud for each object with depth image. The object pose w.r.t the world frame is initialized as identity in global frame. For data association, the object is compared to all objects already in the map to find the corresponding one. If there do exist corresponding one, we merge their point clouds, associated key points and per-class confidence scores, and estimate new object's pose w.r.t the former one in the global frame using a robust ICP method. Otherwise we create new object instance in the object map.

The Plane Mapping thread (Sect. 3.3) creates and maintains a global plane map. In each keyframe, we extract planes from depth images and find the corresponding plane landmark in the plane map. If there are no corresponding landmark in the global map, we create new plane landmark in the global map otherwise we add new constraint between global plane landmark and local plane for later optimization. We use infinite plane and its minimal representation to represent plane landmark, which is easy to be optimized and not affected by singularities.

3.2   Object Mapping

Object Detection. We use the SSD detector [31] and pre-trained model for object detection in each keyframe. Like [7], we build an object with the bounding box and confidence score from the RGB-D image. Each object instance is composed of point cloud C^O, object pose $T_{WO} \in SE(3)$, which maps the point cloud from object frame $\overrightarrow{\mathcal{F}}_O$ to World frame $\overrightarrow{\mathcal{F}}_W$, associated key points, and accumulated per-class confidence scores $\mathcal{C}$. For the robustness of the system, we only build static objects and exclude moving objects judged by their labels. What's more, we remove key points belong to moving objects in the SLAM process, which will enhance our system's performance in dynamic environments.

Point Cloud Reconstruction: We reconstruct an object's point cloud from 2D bounding boxes and depth image. In the k-th keyframe each detection i produces a binary mask M_i^k and we project all the masked image coordinates $\mathbf{u} = (u_1, u_2)$ in depth image into $\overrightarrow{\mathcal{F}}_W$,

$$_W\mathbf{p} = \mathbf{T}_{WC}^k \mathbf{K}^{-1} D_k(\mathbf{u})\mathbf{u} \tag{1}$$

where $\mathbf{K}$ denotes the 3×3 intrinsic camera matrix, $\mathbf{T}_{WC}^k \in SE(3)$ the camera pose estimate, and $D_k(\mathbf{u})$ the corresponding depth estimate of image coordinate $\mathbf{u}$.

2D-3D Data Association. Data association is important for our system in order to build a globally consistent object map. By data association, we find if a new object has corresponding object already existing in the object map. As we have the 2D bounding box and 3D point cloud for the object, we introduce a 2D-3D combined data association method. Like CubeSLAM [4], we first associate 2D key points to objects if those points are observed enough times (3 in our method) of belonging to the 2D object bounding box. Utilizing the 3D information, we find a fixed number of objects (5 in our method) in the object map that have the nearest distances with current object between point cloud centroid. Then in these fixed number object map objects, we find the object that has most shared associated key points with current object and judge if the number of shared key points exceeds a threshold (10 as [4] proposed). If not, new object instance will be created and if so, new object detection will be merged with the existing one.

Object Model Update. Every time we merge a new object and an object that already exists in the object map, we update the object model shown in Fig. 2. As illustrated in Fig. 2, every object in our map contains (i) the segmented colored 3D point clouds associated with that object by the data association step, (ii) assoiciated key points that are observed enough times of belonging to the object, (iii) a vector of object poses w.r.t. the world in the keyframes it has appeared, and (iV) the accumulated per-class confidences provided by the object detector. We add new 3D point cloud segments transformed into global coordinate into the object model. The key points found in the 2D bounding box are added to the object model for association. Key points not observed enough times of belonging to the object will be delete. If an object m is observed in keyframe i for the first time, the pose to world frame T_m^i is set to identity. When we merge object model m and new object n in keyframe j, we calculate global pose T_n^j of object n using ICP to its corresponding point cloud C^n and C^m. With the object observed in many keyframes we can define the least-square error of object poses and optimize it in the local BA:

$$e_{object} = T_{ij}^{-1}(T_m^i)^{-1}T_n^j \tag{2}$$

As described in [7] when a detection is associated with a map object, its per-class confidence scores $\mathcal{C}$ is updated according to $C_c = C_c + s$, where c and s are the class ID reported by object detector, and the associated confidence. The class label for an object is finally determined by the accumulated score $\mathbf{argmax}_c C_c$ and a final confidence σ can be assigned as $\sigma = maxC_c/n$ where n is the total number of observations for that object.

3.3 Plane Mapping

Plane Segmentation. Planes can provide long rang constraints to the SLAM progress as well as more semantic information of the environment. We extract planes from depth images captured by kinect style RGB-D cameras using the method of [25].

Plane Presentation. Inspired by [23], we use normalised homogeneous coordinate $\pi = (\pi_1, \pi_2, \pi_3, \pi_4)^T$ and its minimal representation ω to represent infinite plane π in the map. In projective space a point $\mathbf{p} = (p_1, p_2, p_3, p_4)^T$ lies on a plane $\pi = (\pi_1, \pi_2, \pi_3, \pi_4)^T$ iff

$$\pi^T \mathbf{p} = 0, \tag{3}$$

represented by homogeneous coordinate. Given the normal vector of the plane $\mathbf{n} = (n_1, n_2, n_3)^T$ and its distance d from the origin, we can get its homogeneous representation by (3)

$$\pi = (\frac{\mathbf{n}, -d}{\|\mathbf{n}, d\|})^T \tag{4}$$

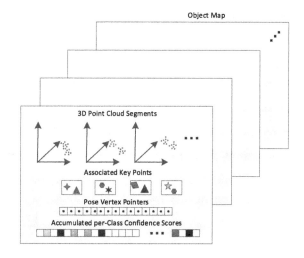

Fig. 2. Every object in our map contains (i) the segmented colored 3D point clouds associated with that object by the data association step, (ii) associated key points that are observed enough times of belonging to the object, (iii) a vector of object poses w.r.t. the world in the keyframes it has appeared, and (iV) the accumulated per-class confidences provided by the object detector.

To transform a plane from local frame to global frame, we can use the inverse transpose of the corresponding point transform T_{gx}:

$$\pi_g = T_{gx}^{-T} \pi_x \qquad (5)$$

Taking the minimal representation of plane proposed by [23], we can avoid rank-deficient information matrices in optimization. We use the mapping of $\mathbf{R}^3$ to S^3 to transform the 3-dimentional vector ω to quaternion π

$$exp\,(\omega) = \frac{1}{2}sinc(\frac{1}{2}\|\omega\|)\omega cos(\frac{1}{2}\|\omega\|), \qquad (6)$$

and the inverse mapping of S^3 to $\mathbf{R}^3$ to transform quaternion π to its minimal representation ω:

$$\omega = log(\mathbf{q}) = \frac{2cos^{-1}(q_w)}{\|\mathbf{q}_v\|}\mathbf{q}_v \qquad (7)$$

Finally, the error between two planes π and π' can be measured by the 3 dimentional vector:

$$e_{plane} = log(\mathbf{q}(\pi)^{-1}\mathbf{q}(\pi')) \qquad (8)$$

Plane Association. Every time we extract planes from the RGB-D images, we decide either to create new planes in the global map or to associate them to the ones already exist. We use the approach introduced in [23] with little change for data association. Planes detected in the current frame are matched against all plane landmarks in the global map instead of planes in some specific keyframes, with a threshold of angle (8°) and center distance (0.1 m). The local plane and global plane landmark that have distance and angle below given threshold will be seen as the same plane and new constraint between local plane and global plane landmark will be added into the local bundle adjustment. If there are no matching planes in the global plane map, we create a new plane landmark for detected plane in the global plane map.

3.4   Bundle Adjustment with Points, Objects and Planes

ORB-SLAM2 performs local BA and full BA to optimize camera pose and points together. In our method, we define object pose error in (2) and plane error in (8) for optimization. And we optimize these two error with point reprojection error together. The unified cost function is

$$E = \rho(e_{\text{reproj}}^{\text{T}} \Omega_{\text{reproj}}^{-1} e_{\text{reproj}} + e_{\text{object}}^{\text{T}} \Omega_{\text{object}}^{-1} e_{\text{object}} + e_{\text{plane}}^{\text{T}} \Omega_{\text{plane}}^{-1} e_{\text{plane}}) \qquad (9)$$

where ρ is the Huber robust cost function and $\Omega_{\text{reproj}}, \Omega_{\text{object}}, \Omega_{\text{plane}}$ are the covariance matrices.

4   Experiment

4.1   Experimental Settings

We implement our SLAM system on a desktop computer with an Intel Core i7-7500 processor, and GPU being used only for visualization, not computation. We use a pretrained SSD model as a deep detector and PEAC[1] as our plane detector. RGB-D based ORB-SLAM2 is used as our basic SLAM system for comparison. There are five separate threads in the system: Tracking, Local Mapping, Plane Mapping (include Plane Segmentation, Plane Matching), Object Mapping (include Object Detection, Point Cloud Reconstruction, Object Pose Estimation) and Loop Closing. Our implementation can run at nearly 15 fps. To evaluate the advantage of our method itself, we assess it on the TUM datasets [32] and ICL-NUIM datasets [33] by adding or removing one of the modules.

4.2   Results

Figure 3 shows a monitor and teddy bear reconstructed by our object mapping method. With the plane mapping thread closed, we test the performance of our object mapping thread on TUM datasets, which contain scenes of various objects. The result is shown in Table 1. Our object mapping method outperforms original ORB-SLAM2 in two scenes and is equal in other scenes.

---

[1] https://github.com/symao/PEAC.

Table 1. Comparison of ATE RMSE (unit: m) of our Object Mapping and original ORB-SLAM2 on the TUM datasets.

Method	fr1 _desk	fr1 _floor	fr1 _plant	fr1 _teddy	fr2 _pioneer	fr3 _sitting_static
ORB-SLAM2+ Object Mapping	0.018	0.015	**0.013**	0.050	**0.047**	0.008
ORB-SLAM2	0.016	0.014	0.018	0.044	0.048	0.007

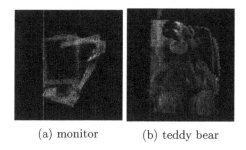

(a) monitor   (b) teddy bear

Fig. 3. Objects reconstructed by our method in TUM dataset

Table 2 shows the performance of object mapping method in scenes with moving objects. With the moving objects removed, the robustness of the SLAM system was improved. Figure 4 shows the planes extracted by plane mapping thread. Table 3 shows the performance of our plane mapping method compared to ORB-SLAM2 on ICL-NUIM datasets, where plane is the main structure in the scene. Our plane mapping method outperforms original version in all 4 scenes. To show the overall performance of ORB-SLAM2+Object Mapping+Plane Mapping, we run tests on ICL-NUIM datasets and compare it to other state of the art RGB-D SLAM. The result in Table 4 shows that our method is comparable to other methods.

Table 2. Comparison of ATE RMSE (unit: m) of our Object Mapping and original ORB-SLAM2 on the TUM datasets with moving objects.

Method	fr2_desk _with_person	fr3_sitting _halfsphere	fr3_sitting _rpy	fr3_sitting _static	fr3_walking _halfsphere	fr3_walking _static
ORB-SLAM2+ Object Mapping	0.008	**0.016**	0.020	**0.007**	**0.123**	**0.017**
ORB-SLAM2	0.006	0.031	0.020	0.008	0.360	0.114

Table 3. Comparison of ATE RMSE (unit: m) of our Plane Mapping and original ORB-SLAM2 on the ICL-NUIM datasets.

Method	lr kt0n	lr kt1n	lr kt2n	lr kt3n
ORB-SLAM2+Plane Mapping	**0.020**	**0.114**	**0.055**	**0.032**
ORB-SLAM2	0.021	0.153	0.060	0.034

Table 4. Comparison of ATE RMSE (unit: m) of our ORB-SLAM2+Object Mapping+Plane Mapping with other RGB-D SLAM systems

Method	lr kt0n	lr kt1n	lr kt2n	lr kt3n
our method	0.024	0.081	0.058	0.032
DVO SLAM [35]	0.104	0.029	0.191	0.152
RGB-D SLAM [36]	0.026	0.008	0.018	0.433
CPA-SLAM [22]	0.007	0.006	0.089	0.009
KDP-SLAM [20]	0.009	0.019	0.029	0.153

Fig. 4. Planes extracted by the plane mapping thread

5   Conclusions

We propose a new semantic SLAM system that combines object and plane information, which simultaneously optimizes semantic landmarks with SLAM process. We add two concurrent thread handling objects and planes. The object mapping thread creates object point cloud incrementally and add object pose into SLAM optimization. Plane mapping thread extracts planes from depth image and compares their angle and distance to existing plane landmarks. Every time we determine a corresponding relation of two planes, we add a constraint in the BA and optimize it latter. The experiment on TUM datasets and ICL-NUIM datasets prove that our method provides a semantically more meaningful map while enhancing SLAM system's performance.

Acknowledgment. This work was supported by the National Natural Science Foundation of China under Grant 61772213 and Grant 91748204 and in part by the Shenzhen Science and Technology Plan under Grant JCYJ20170818165917438 and the Wuhan Science and Technology Plan under Grant 2017010201010121.

References

1. Zhong, F., et al.: Detect-SLAM: making object detection and SLAM mutually beneficial, pp. 1001–1010 (2018)
2. Moreno, R.F.S., et al.: SLAM++: simultaneous localisation and mapping at the level of objects, pp. 1352–1359 (2013)
3. Gálvez-López, D., et al.: Real-time monocular object SLAM. Robot. Auton. Syst. **75**, 435–449 (2016)
4. Yang, S., Scherer, S.: CubeSLAM: monocular 3D object detection and SLAM without prior models. CoRR, abs/1806.00557 (2018)
5. Nicholson, L., Milford, M., Nderhauf, N.S.U.: QuadricSLAM: constrained dual quadrics from object detections as landmarks in semantic SLAM. CoRR, abs/1804.04011 (2018)
6. McCormac, J., et al.: Fusion++: volumetric object-level SLAM. CoRR, abs/1808.08378 (2018)
7. Sünderhauf, N., et al.: Meaningful maps with object-oriented semantic mapping, pp. 5079–5085 (2017)
8. McCormac, J., et al.: SemanticFusion: dense 3D semantic mapping with convolutional neural networks, pp. 4628–4635 (2017)
9. Hosseinzadeh, M., et al.: Towards semantic SLAM: points, planes and objects. CoRR, abs/1804.09111 (2018)
10. Yang, S., Scherer, S.: Monocular object and plane SLAM in structured environments. CoRR, abs/1809.03415 (2018)
11. Hosseinzadeh, M., et al.: Real-time monocular object-model aware sparse SLAM. CoRR, abs/1809.09149 (2018)
12. Mu, B., et al.: SLAM with objects using a nonparametric pose graph, pp. 4602–4609 (2016)
13. Bowman, S.L., et al.: Probabilistic data association for semantic SLAM, pp. 1722–1729 (2017)
14. Yang, S., et al.: Pop-up SLAM: semantic monocular plane SLAM for low-texture environments, pp. 1222–1229 (2016)
15. Gay, P., et al.: Probabilistic structure from motion with objects (PSfMO), pp. 3094–3103 (2017)
16. Bao, S.Y.Z., et al.: Semantic structure from motion with points, regions
17. Frost, D.P., Hler, O.K.A., Murray, D.W.: Object-aware bundle adjustment for correcting monocular scale drift, pp. 4770–4776 (2016)
18. Sucar, E., Hayet, J.B.: Bayesian scale estimation for monocular SLAM based on generic object detection for correcting scale drift, pp. 1–7 (2018)
19. Lee, J.K., et al.: Joint layout estimation and global multi-view registration for indoor reconstruction, pp. 162–171 (2017)
20. Hsiao, M., et al.: Keyframe-based dense planar SLAM, pp. 5110–5117 (2017)
21. Concha, A., Civera, J.: DPPTAM: Dense piecewise planar tracking and mapping from a monocular sequence, pp. 5686–5693 (2015)
22. Ma, L., et al.: CPA-SLAM: consistent plane-model alignment for direct RGB-D SLAM, pp. 1285–1291 (2016)

23. Kaess, M.: Simultaneous localization and mapping with infinite planes, pp. 4605–4611 (2015)
24. Mur-Artal, R., Tardós, J.D.: ORB-SLAM2: an open-source SLAM system for monocular, stereo, and RGB-D cameras. IEEE Trans. Rob. **33**(5), 1255–1262 (2017)
25. Feng, C., Taguchi, Y., Kamat, V.R.: Fast plane extraction in organized point clouds using agglomerative hierarchical clustering, pp. 6218–6225 (2014)
26. Tateno, K., et al.: CNN-SLAM: real-time dense monocular SLAM with learned depth prediction, pp. 6565–6574 (2017)
27. Frost, D.P., Prisacariu, V.A., Murray, D.W.: Recovering stable scale in monocular SLAM using object-supplemented bundle adjustment. IEEE Trans. Rob. **34**(3), 736–747 (2018)
28. Botterill, T., Mills, S., Green, R.D.: Correcting scale drift by object recognition in single-camera SLAM. IEEE Trans. Cybern. **43**(6), 1767–1780 (2013)
29. Redmon, J., et al.: You only look once: unified, real-time object detection, pp. 779–788 (2016)
30. Redmon, J., Farhadi, A.: YOLO9000: Better, Faster, Stronger, pp. 6517–6525 (2017)
31. Liu, W., et al.: SSD: single shot multibox detector. In: Leibe, B., Matas, J., Sebe, N., Welling, M. (eds.) ECCV 2016. LNCS, vol. 9905, pp. 21–37. Springer, Cham (2016). https://doi.org/10.1007/978-3-319-46448-0_2
32. Sturm, J.U.R., et al.: A benchmark for the evaluation of RGB-D SLAM systems, pp. 573–580 (2012)
33. Handa, A., et al.: A benchmark for RGB-D visual odometry, 3D reconstruction and SLAM dense visual SLAM for RGB-D cameras an evaluation of the RGB-D SLAM system, pp. 1524–1531, 2100–2106, 1691–1696 (2014)
34. Ren, S., et al.: Faster R-CNN: towards real-time object detection with region proposal networks. In: Cortes, C., et al. (eds.) Advances in Neural Information Processing Systems, vol. 28, pp. 91–99. Curran Associates, Inc. (2015)
35. Kerl, C., Sturm, J., Cremers, D.: Dense visual SLAM for RGB-D cameras. In: 2013 IEEE/RSJ International Conference on Intelligent Robots and Systems, Tokyo, pp. 2100–2106 (2013). https://doi.org/10.1109/IROS.2013.6696650
36. Endres, F., Hess, J., Sturm, J., et al.: 3-D mapping with an RGB-D camera. IEEE Trans. Rob. **30**(1), 177–187 (2014)

Crime Scene Sketches Classification Based on CNN

Kaixuan Wang⬭, Houlu Zhang⬭, and Yunqi Tang$^{(\boxtimes)}$⬭

School of Criminal Investigation and Forensic Science, People's Public Security
University of China, Beijing, China
wasd4119@163.com, zhanghoulu1996@gmail.com, tangyunqi@ppsuc.edu.cn

Abstract. Crime scene sketch plays a significant role in criminal investigation. In China, the crime scene sketches of all criminal cases should be uploaded to the National Criminal Scene Investigation Information System (NCSIIS). However, there are wrong images and low quality sketches frequently being uploaded to NCSIIS, which would make crime scene sketches unable to undertake their tasks. Yet, checking the sketches uploaded to NCSIIS still reamins as a manual work by the police officers. In this paper, we focus on a new problem of crime scene sketches classification. Firstly, a crime scene sketches database was constructed, sampled from NCSIIS. Secondly, an automatic crime scene sketches classification method is proposed based on CNN. A new architecture, namely Crime Scene Sketch Net (CSS-Net) is designed for high accuracy. Experiments are conducted on the database constructed. The experimental results show that the method proposed by this paper is of good performance.

Keywords: Criminal investigation · Crime scene sketch · Image classification · Convolutional Neural Network

1 Introduction

In criminal investigation domain, crime scene sketch establishes a permanent record of items, conditions, and position relationships [14]. It is an effective way to document a crime scene. Sketches can provide an in-depth understanding of the circumstances of crime scene beyond the level of comprehension that can be attained solely by reading a written report or studying photographs [6]. Compared with notes, sketches are more vivid than words. They also have some unique advantages over photos. They can show some details better, such as track of criminal walking. Sketches can eliminate some unnecessary details and pay more attention to the important items which are more relative to the crime [15].

This paper is a student paper

This work is supported by the National Key Research and Development Program (Grant No. 2017YFC0803506), the Ministry of Public Security Technical Research Project (Grant No. 2018JSYJC20), the Opening Project of Shanghai Key Laboratory of Crime Scene Evidence (Grant No. 2017XCWZK18).

Z. Lin et al. (Eds.): PRCV 2019, LNCS 11859, pp. 149–160, 2019.
https://doi.org/10.1007/978-3-030-31726-3_13

And in court, sketches would complement other documenting methods, such as photo, video and report. In addition to these advantages, sketches also play an important role in restoring and reconstructing crime scene.

Due to the importance of crime scene sketch, the Ministry of Public Security of People's Republic of China has established an information system, named National Crime Scene Investigation Information System (NCSIIS), to store and manage these records. And according to regulations, criminal investigators are supposed to draw and upload two types of sketches, one shows the location of crime scene, the other shows details in crime scene. And the result of spot check on the qualification of uploaded sketches shows a pretty pessimistic phenomenon. Lacking of sketches occurred in many cases, would lead to many serious consequences, such as being unable to reconstruct the crime scene and some legal problems in court. In some cases, investigator did upload two images, nonetheless the two images belong to the same class. And plus that there is no such a function which can recognize different types of sketches in the existing information system. Therefore, in a bid to check these uploaded records, there is no other way except manual verification. However, this method is time consuming and labour-intensive. Besides, manual verification cannot verify all records as numerous of sketches flock into the system. In conclusion, solving the problem how to perform automated classification of crime scene sketches is urgently required.

In 2012, the AlexNet which was proposed on ImageNet Large Scale Visual Recognition Challenge (ILSVRC), showed the dawning of Convolutional Neural Network (CNN) [4]. In recent years, it has become a mainstream on ILSVRCs [10]. And the champions that teams with algorithm based on CNN had won, proved that Convolutional Neural Network have the capacity to solve the problem of image classification, especially on the large-scale data sets. This led to a booming of convolutional neural network application study [1,8]. In recent years, Big Data and Artificial Intelligence started to be employed to Public Security, and they made a great success. The application of Biometric Technology has also provided great help cracking criminal cases. However, to the best of author's knowledge, this is first hand-shaking between Convolutional Neural Network and criminal investigation records management. In addition, peculiarity of crime scene sketch makes it very difficult to build a large-scale data set, let alone a publicly available large-scale image datasets. These all make this classification problem challenging.

In this paper, our works are summarized as follows:

- We proposed a new application problem of Convolutional Neural Network. To solve it, we built a crime scene sketches data set with a training and validation set of 53,324 images, and a test set of 10,897 images. These data are collected from the real-life records stored in NCSIIS with manual labeled precisely.
- To solve our problem, we designed our convolutional neural network based on AlexNet. Then we compared its performance with two classic architectures.
- Finally, we measured the performance of our CSS-Net, to indicates the capability of recognizing each categories.

2   Related Works

Because crime scene sketch is confidential, the related work is less than nothing. However the heart of automated classifying crime scene sketch problem lies a classic challenge, image classification. It has been a hot issue in pattern recognition and computer vision for a long time.

Back to 1990s, Yann Lecun et al. firstly used CNN on handwriting digit recognition and achieved a great success on MNIST dataset. Then, due to defects of CNN, the flourish of traditional pattern recognition methods such as Gaussian mixture model, K-means and support vector machine came to image classification domain. They did a good job on solving some simple problems, but in most cases, they were not competent [9]. Then, with the exploding growth of computing power, some disadvantages of deep neural network were compensated, while their benefits were magnified. CNN has a simple network topology, they can spend less training time by sharing weights, and one architecture of CNN could solve more than one classification problems, which made CNN more popular in image classification. Besides, in resent years, many excellent ideas of deep neural network has emerged, like VGG [11], GoogLeNet [13], ResNet [2] and deepID [12]. Hence, a trend of CNN application started.

In general, convolutional neural network has the ability to solve our problem. On account of small number of categories, there is no need to use a deep network structure. Some classic CNNs could competent this work.

3   Crime Scene Sketch

In this section, we focus on two things, what a qualified sketch should be and how to distinguish the different types of sketches. To figure them out, we viewed plenty of official documents and books related to criminal investigation. In China, there is no such a national or professional standard, but rules of drawing and classifying sketches exist in working specifications and textbooks about criminal investigation.

3.1   Sketch Taxonomy

Graph Performance Range. According to performance range of images, crime scene sketches can be divided into three categories. Location Sketch shows the location and surrounding of crime scene, which covers the biggest range. Crime Scene Overview Sketch describes the overall crime scene and it shows the result of criminal investigation including various items, evidence, traces, etc. The third one is Key Parts Sketch, highlight matters and crucial site, which is strongly related to crime. It is the one that covers the smallest range.

Representation of Image. This classification is similar to the one in United States which divide sketches into floor plan (or bird's view) sketch, elevation sketch and the cross-projection (or exploded view) [7]. But in China, there are two more categories in this sorting mode, Stereo View Sketch and Cutaway View Sketch.

- Floor plan is a horizontal top view drawn on the principle of parallel projection. It is for important evidence and objects distributed on the horizontal surface of the scene.
- Elevation sketch shows the vertical projection of the crime scene.
- Cross-projection is a combination of the first two types of scene maps. It shows other façades or tops of the crime scene, on the basis of floor plan sketch.
- Stereo View Sketch can represent the object's shape in three directions (eg. front, top and side) on one projection map, using the methods of angular parallel or center projection.
- Cutaway View Sketch is a special form of Stereo View Sketch. It removes part of object's surface and reflects the internal state of the object

Plotting Scale. In this sorting mode, sketches are divided into two categories, one with a scale, the other without scale. Sketch with scale should be made to scale, but sketch without scale could not. Therefore, only in some serious cases, investigators draw sketch with scale.

In this study, to meet the needs of criminal investigation, sketches are divided into Crime Scene Overview Sketch and Location Sketch, as these two types can cover the compulsory information of crime scene.

3.2   Rules of Uploading Sketch

What should a qualified crime scene sketch look like? In China, a qualified sketch should meet requirements both in format and content. The Ministry of Public Security revised Public Security Crime Scene Investigation Regulations and Sample of Crime Scene Investigation Records dated in October 2015, so as to meet the requirement of revised "Criminal Procedure Law" for crime scene investigation and further standardize the documenting work. In these two documents, rules are that drawing sketches should meet the following requirements:

- Mark the identifier, discovering time and location of the case.
- The location sketch should exactly reflect the location and scope of the scene.
- Crime Scene Overview Sketch should precisely reflect the main objects related to criminal activities, indicating the specific location of the body, traces, physical evidence, and tools for committing crimes.
- Text description should be concise and accurate
- Proper layout with highlighted priority.
- Clear presentation with standardized signs.
- Sketch should indicate the direction, legend (key), drawing date, cartographer and his (or her) organization.

Furthermore, on the conference of National Criminal Investigation Work on December 24, 2014, the Ministry of Public Security presented a series of regulations of criminal investigation, in order to normalize routine for investigating crime scene. In the regulations, a complete crime scene investigation record should cover two types of sketch describing site layout and location in detail. One is Crime Scene Overview Sketch, and the other is Location Sketch. These sketches uploaded into the NCSIIS system should be finished images and meet the requirements mentioned above.

4 Methodology

Convolutional Neural Network usually works in a common way, containing forward propagation and backward propagation. In the forward propagation phase, when images inputs, CNN begins sampling, down sampling, and finally outputs a loss value in training or scores of each categories in test. The loss value shows the distance between predicted results and label. The scores shows the probability that input image belongs to certain categories. Then it turns to backward propagation. It only exists in training process and works for finding the minimum loss value guided by the gradient [9].

The architecture of Convolutional Neural Network usually contains convolutional layer, pooling layer and fully connected layer. Convolutional layer is responsible for sampling, and pooling layer takes charge of down sampling. These two layers undertake the main tasks of CNN. How these layers work would be illustrated in following parts.

In a convolutional layer, there are more than one kernels available. When an image inputs to this layer, kernels slip on this matrix of image pixels in a fixed stride. In every step, a convolutional calculation exists. And it can be expressed as:

$$f(x) = \sigma(x \times W + b) \tag{1}$$

In Eq. (1), assuming $f(x)$ as output, x represents the input, then x times weight matrix W and plus a bias term b, finally put it to a nonlinear activation function $\sigma(x)$. When kernels traverses the whole image, the convolutional layer outputs numbers of feature maps.

Pooling layer usually plays a role in down sampling feature maps output by convolutional layer. Through this layer, the size of feature maps would shrink, but the number of them would stay. In this study, we used max pooling method. It works by sliding windows walking on the feature maps in a fixed stride. On the area covered by kernel, it works as:

$$f(x) = max(x) \tag{2}$$

In Eq. (2), x means the area covered by pooling kernel and this function output the biggest number in this area. It is a traditional approach where adjacent pooling kernels do not overlap during it sliding on feature map. In this study, however, we used overlapping pooling method. It makes the stride less than the size of kernel. When pooling kernel slides on feature maps, adjacent ones would overlap each other. And it has positive effects on reducing error rates and overfitting.

In the end of convolutional neural network, there would be some fully connected layers. They works for turning the matrix of feature maps into a feature vector and finally get a probability distribution P based on the input. As the Eq. (3) shows, the heart of CNN is to perform the operation of multi-layer filtering, reducing the amount of calculation, so as to obtain a mathematical model of feature expression P.

$$P(j) = P[L = l_j | x_j; (\omega, b)] \tag{3}$$

In Eq. (3), x_j represents the input image, l_j means label of it, and function $L(\omega, b)$ shows distance between label and the predicted result of forward propagation. Ideally, the best trained model reaches the point where value of $L(\omega, b)$ is minimized.

5   Experiment

In this study, our goal is to apply CNN to solve our problem, and this problem is not challenging enough to use some complicated architectures. Therefore, we employed classic architectures, LeNet-5 and AlexNet. To fit our data better, we designed a new architecture of CNN based on AlexNet and called it Crime Scene Sketch Net (CSS-Net). The whole experiment were conducted on Caffe [3], a convolutional architecture.

5.1   Data Set

Due to sensitive information involved in sketch, there is no public dataset to use in this study. Our first task was to build a dataset. We collected 71,839 sketches of 32,409 cases occurred in six different provinces from the database of NCSIIS. These sketches were drawn to documented the investigation of real-life cases and uploaded to the information system by criminal investigators. It might seem an easy job by simply downloading the data to get a dataset, but actually it was time-consuming and labor-intensive.

Manual Inspection. On account of lacking supervision, the images below the mark were mixed with the qualified sketches. We needed to scrutinize the data downloaded from the database. Then, 18,515 unqualified images were removed from the data set.

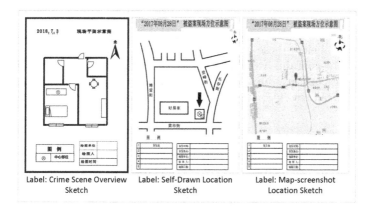

Label: Crime Scene Overview   Label: Self-Drawn Location   Label: Map-screenshot
            Sketch   Sketch   Location Sketch

Fig. 1. Labeled crime scene sketches

Manual Label. In this study, these data should be labeled into two classes, crime scene overview sketch and location sketch, based on the range of grapy performance. Finishing labeling, we found that a huge intra-class variation exists in the location sketches. As known to us all, huge intra-class variation can damage the performance of the classifier. To get a better result, we subdivided the location sketches into two classes by drawing method. One is called Map-screenshot Location Sketch. It considers the screenshot of electronic map as main body of the image to show where the crime occurred. The other is called Self-drawn Location Sketch. It is manually drawn using graphics software. This type of sketch uses symbols to represent the buildings, roads, rivers and so on, to indicate the location and scope of crime scene. Finally we labeled these sketches into three categories, as shown in Fig. 1 (Table 1).

Table 1. The composition of dataset

	Train and validation set	Test set
Crime scene overview sketch	16425	4975
Self-drawn location sketch	8876	3647
Map-screenshot location sketch	28023	2275
Total	53324	10897

Train and Validation Set. Then, we got a dataset containing 16,425 Crime Scene Overview Sketch, 8,876 self-drawn location sketches, and 28,023 map-screenshot location sketches. In this dataset, we randomly sampled 80% of each type of sketches as the training set, and the remaining 20% as the validation set.

Test Set. In order to test the robustness of the trained model, we collected 10,897 new sketches from some provinces different with the six provinces. After examined and labeled, these new data were used as test set.

This dataset contains variable-resolution images, while the architecture of CNN needs a constant input dimension. Consequently, we normalized the sketches to a fixed resolution of 256*256. Finally, we got our crime scene sketch dataset.

5.2 Architecture

In this study, we employed two classic architectures, LeNet-5 and AlexNet. The details of them could turn to the Ref [5] and Ref [4]. Although we got a trained model that can apply to solve our problem, it was not good enough. Therefore, we revised the AlexNet and designed our new architecture. In this section, we will mainly focus on our CSS-Net.

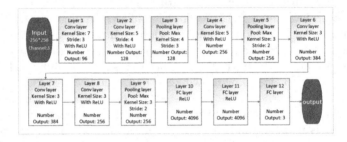

Fig. 2. Architecture of CSS-Net: Conv layer means convolutional layer, FC layer represents fully connected layer

Our CNN has six convolutional layers and three fully connected layers. Different from AlexNet, we added a convolutional layer and set size of input as 256*256 pixels. And for fear of training difficulty growing sharply, we used small convolution kernels to replace a big kernel. The tricks in AlexNet which benefit the training process were retained. However, the data augmentation fell short of lifting accuracy of classification and greatly increased cost of computing resource. Thence, image cropping was fired. Finally, we got a better classifier than classic CNNs. More details are shown as Fig. 2.

6 Results and Analysis

6.1 Compared with Classic CNNs

In this part, we trained our CSS-Net and classic nets of same parameters except the ones mentioned. Details are shown in Table 2.

Table 2. Parameters of training

	CSS-Net	AlexNet		LeNet-5
Crop size	None	227	None	None
Mirror	False	True	False	False
Batch size	128			
lr policy	inv			
base lr	0.0001			

In this table, there are some abbreviations which need to be explained. 'lr policy' means learning rate policy which represents the policy of changing learning rate during training phase. 'base lr' means base learning rate which is the initial value of it. If 'Mirror' was true, data augmentation method of mirror flipping would be used in this net. And during training phase, test on the validation set existed every 1000 iterations. Finally their accuracy made up this following Fig. 3.

As the results show that the rate of convergence on our CSS-Net is faster than classic nets, while LeNet-5 oscillating all the time. Besides, at the end, CSS-Net get a accuracy of 2% better than AlexNet with crop method. Therefore we can figure that CSS-Net performs better on our training set as our net get a higher accuracy and is easy to train.

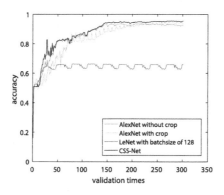

Fig. 3. Accuracy on validation set

To ensure that our trained model was not overfitting, accuracy of test on test set plays a significant role. To figure it out, we tested the models of 250,000 iterations and 300,000 iterations trained on AlexNet and our CSS-Net. The results are shown in following Table 3.

As shown, LeNet-5 lacks the ability to classify crime scene sketches, while AlexNet did a good job on our dataset, and this is the reason for choosing AlexNet to modify. It also shows that the image augmentation methods, image

Table 3. Accuracy on test set

	AlexNet with crop	AlexNet without crop	CSS-Net
250,000 iters	86.5229%	84.5688%	89.8073%
300,000 iters	87.8349%	84.1009%	90.1193%

cropping, benefits on our task. This is behind attributes of crime scene sketches. Rotation, deformation, and image noises are hardly seen in crime scene sketches, while image shifting is very common. Image cropping can fix errors caused by image shifting. It, however, makes the net become more difficult to train. This is why we remove it from CSS-Net. To make up for the loss of it and to make our net easier to train, we replaced a convolutional layer using a big kernel with two layers using small ones, and they did a good job. The performance of trained model could partly meet the requirements of application.

6.2   Performance Analysis

In this part, we focus on characterizing the performance of our model trained on CSS-Net. To make it visible, we draw the ROC (Receiver Operator Characteristic) curve and the PR (Precision-Recall) curve. For this study, we plotted curves of each categories and average of them. For example, in the curve of crime scene overview sketch, we define it as positive case, and remaining categories are defined as negative cases. Finally, we averaged the results of each classes and plotted the average curve.

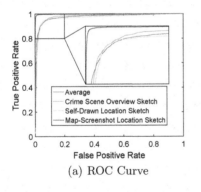

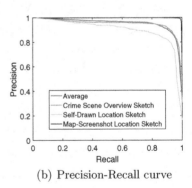

(a) ROC Curve   (b) Precision-Recall curve

Fig. 4. ROC and PR curves of our CNN

In Fig. 4(a), the ROC curves show that performance of distinguishing map-screenshot location sketch with the rest of two types almost reaches the peak. But capability of recognizing the two other classes is in a low level, which stuck the improvement of our net's classification ability. In Fig. 4(b), PR curves suggest that our model works well on our data set, while there is still much room for

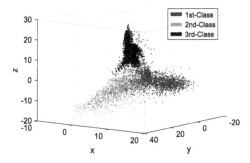

Fig. 5. Distribution of Deep Features: 1st-class represents Crime Scene Overview Sketch, 2nd-class represents Self-Drawn Location Sketch, and 3rd-class represents Map-Screenshot Location Sketch.

improvement, especially for improving capability of recognizing self-drawn location Sketch. Although, in the ROC curve, it is similar to the ability of recognizing crime scene overview sketch.

To show it in a more vivid way, we extracted the deep feature vectors output by the last fully connected layer. Because the number of output equals to number of categories, we can directly plot it on 3-D space. This figure illustrates the spacial distribution of data having experienced forward propagation. From Fig. 5, we can see that the deep features could be distinguished by some decision boundaries, but the degree of classifying difficulty is different. map-screenshot location sketch is the easiest one, while the rest are not discriminative enough. It is behind the results of ROC and PR curves.

7   Conclusion

In this paper, we proposed an application problem of image classification. Then, we built a crime scene sketch dataset and came up with a solution based on convolutional neural network as we called it CSS-Net. Our net performs better than classic ones and can basically meet the requirement of real-life application. But the capability of recognizing self-drawn location sketch and crime scene overview sketch needs to be improved. In this study, our dataset lack a class of negative class to get rid of photos which were usually uploaded as sketches. The number of self-drawn location sketches is not enough. Besides, our architecture is based on AlexNet which is too old. As a result, we will continue this study in two aspects, including expanding the dataset and designing a new architecture with novel technology.

References

1. Acharya, U.R., Oh, S.L., Hagiwara, Y., Tan, J.H., Adeli, H.: Deep convolutional neural network for the automated detection and diagnosis of seizure using EEG signals. Comput. Biol. Med. **100**, 270–278 (2018)

2. He, K., Zhang, X., Ren, S., Sun, J.: Deep residual learning for image recognition. In: Proceedings of the IEEE Conference on Computer Vision and Pattern Recognition, pp. 770–778 (2016)

3. Jia, Y., et al.: Caffe: convolutional architecture for fast feature embedding. In: Proceedings of the 22nd ACM International Conference on Multimedia, pp. 675–678. ACM (2014)

4. Krizhevsky, A., Sutskever, I., Hinton, G.E.: Imagenet classification with deep convolutional neural networks. In: Advances in Neural Information Processing Systems, pp. 1097–1105 (2012)

5. LeCun, Y., Bottou, L., Bengio, Y., Haffner, P., et al.: Gradient-based learning applied to document recognition. Proc. IEEE **86**(11), 2278–2324 (1998)

6. Lyman, M.D.: Criminal Investigation: The Art and the Science. Prentice Hall, Upper Saddle River (2001)

7. Miller, M.T., Massey, P.: The Crime Scene: A Visual Guide. Academic Press, Cambridge (2018)

8. Raghavendra, U., Fujita, H., Bhandary, S.V., Gudigar, A., Tan, J.H., Acharya, U.R.: Deep convolution neural network for accurate diagnosis of glaucoma using digital fundus images. Inf. Sci. **441**, 41–49 (2018)

9. Rumelhart, D.E., Hinton, G.E., Williams, R.J., et al.: Learning representations by back-propagating errors. Cogn. Model. **5**(3), 1 (1988)

10. Russakovsky, O., et al.: Imagenet large scale visual recognition challenge. Int. J. Comput. Vision **115**(3), 211–252 (2015)

11. Simonyan, K., Zisserman, A.: Very deep convolutional networks for large-scale image recognition. arXiv preprint arXiv:1409.1556 (2014)

12. Sun, Y., Wang, X., Tang, X.: Deeply learned face representations are sparse, selective, and robust. In: Proceedings of the IEEE Conference on Computer Vision and Pattern Recognition, pp. 2892–2900 (2015)

13. Szegedy, C., et al.: Going deeper with convolutions. In: Proceedings of the IEEE Conference on Computer Vision and Pattern Recognition, pp. 1–9 (2015)

14. Wade, C., Trozzi, Y.E., Quantico, V.: Handbook of forensic services. US Department of Justice, Federal Bureau of Investigation, Washington, DC (1999)

15. Weston, P.B., Wells, K.M.: Criminal Investigation: Basic Perspectives. Prentice-Hall, Upper Saddle River (1974)

Image-Based Air Quality Estimation

Qin Li[ID] and Bin Xie[✉]

Central South University, Changsha, Hunan, China
{liqin6,xiebin}@csu.edu.cn

Abstract. In this paper, we attempt to estimate the outdoor air quality only using images. To address this problem, we mainly collect an available database of high quality outdoor images. We hope this database will encourage further research on image based air quality estimation. Moreover, we perform comprehensive experiments based on this database. We use different hand-crafted features to analyze the appearance variances of outdoor images in different air quality conditions. Results show that the accuracy of meteorological features is much better than that of traditional hand-crafted features. Moreover, in meteorological features, the extinction coefficient indicating the degree of light intensity attenuated by particles performs best with the accuracy of 64.

Keywords: Air quality estimation · Image database · Hand-crafted features

1 Introduction

The China economy has grown at a fantastic speed recently. The fast development in economy greatly increases the stress on the environment protection. Air pollution is a serious environmental issue that is attracting increasing attention globally. Particulate matters like PM2.5, PM10, and NO2, represent air pollutants that can be inhaled via nasal passages to the throat and even the lungs. Long-term exposure to air pollutants increase the incidence of associated disease in humans. Therefore, it is important to awake the whole society by the air quality estimation to work together in controlling the air pollution.

2 Related Work

To estimate fine-grained, city-wide air quality with limited monitoring stations, there has been much existing literature from several research fields.

Some researchers employ theoretical meteorological emissions models [11,15] for pollutant discharge simulation [3,16,35]. [5] proposed a CMAQ model to simulate PM2.5 formation and its response to precursor emission reductions, which could be used to design effective emissions control strategies for regulatory

---

Qin Li is a student.

© Springer Nature Switzerland AG 2019
Z. Lin et al. (Eds.): PRCV 2019, LNCS 11859, pp. 161–171, 2019.
https://doi.org/10.1007/978-3-030-31726-3_14

applications. [26] proposed a WRF-CHEM model to simulate the meteorological model and air quality, which is a fully coupled online model that enables air quality simulations at the same time as the meteorological model runs, improving its potential for operational forecasts. However, the simulation processes suffer from unreliable pollutant emission data and incomplete theoretical foundations, which leads to low estimation accuracy.

Some researchers adopt statistical methods in a data-driven manner. Artificial neural networks (ANNs) [4,7], multiple linear regression [17], and support vector regression [12,23,27] are commonly used for air quality prediction. Considering the high spatial correlations between different air quality stations, spatiotemporal prediction models have been considered, like the spatiotemporal artificial neural network (STANN) [22], the spatiotemporal support vector regression (STSVR) models [8] and the spatiotemporal stacked autoencoder model [19].

Recently, many studies have focused on air quality estimation via spatiotemporal (ST) heterogeneous urban big data, which refers to the data sets containing spatial, temporal, and category information [6,9,13,34]. The basic assumption is that air quality is considerably influenced by these urban dynamics (e.g., wind, vehicular traffic, and point of interest (POI)). By analyzing the temporal dependency and spatial correlation between urban dynamics data, such as meteorology and traffic, air quality at locations which are not covered by monitoring stations can be estimated. However, These works achieve good results at the cost of time consumption on the complex algorithms. Moreover, the massive sensing data used in these works are difficult to obtain.

With the development of computer vision, use of the outdoor camera is of great interest. Despite the remarkable value, only a few studies have focused on air quality estimation based on image data. Zhang et al. constructed an image database of two view sites, and extract several image features as the robust representation for air quality prediction. By using machine learning methods, they learned an adaptive classifier for air quality estimation [32,33]. Wang et al. chose a view site to collect scene images by a camera. They analyzed a relationship between the concentration of PM2.5 and the degradation of observed images [30]. Liu et. al built a database of outdoor images available for Beijing, Shanghai and Phoenix. They fused image features and other relevant data, such as the position of the sun, date, time, geographic information and weather conditions, to predict PM2.5 [20]. Zhang et. al proposed a haze image database and record the related weather and air quality information at a view site in Hefei [31]. Based on this database, they proposed a novel no-reference image quality assessment (IQA) method for haze images.

3   Our Database

In this paper, we present a database of high quality images in different outdoor scenes, captured regularly for a period of 5 years. The database is called Visual Air Quality Index Database (VAQI-1).

VAQI-1 contains 7649 images in total, which come from 85 different view sites in 26 cities in China. The distribution of view cities is shown in Fig. 1. VAQI-1

Table 1. AQI values, Air pollution levels, colors and Descriptions.

AQI values	Air Pollution level	Colors	Descriptions
0-50	I	Green	No air pollution
51-100	II	Yellow	Air quality is good while a few contaminants exist
101-150	III	Orange	Concentrations of contaminants increase.
151-200	IV	Red	Slight irritations may occur.
201-300	V	Purple	Irritations further deteriorates.
301-500	VI	Maroon	There may be strong irritations and symptoms.

Fig. 1. Distribution of view cities in China

is a comprehensive collection of images under a wide variety of air quality. We adopt the air quality index (AQI) as the ground truth data. AQI is a guideline for reporting air quality, and is divided into six levels indicating the increasing air pollutant concentration (in Table 1). The statistic numbers of VAQI at six air pollution levels are shown in Table 2. Figure 2 shows example outdoor images at different air pollution levels.

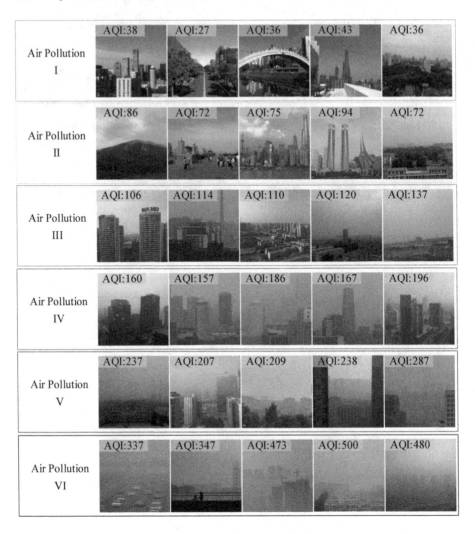

Fig. 2. Example scene images of VAQI-1

3.1 Collection and Annotation

Images of VAQI come from two sources. The first one is an environmental protection project, named Yi Mu Liao Ran [2]. Zou Yi, an organizer of this project, takes an identical photo of a specific site every day by using a smart phone camera and records the corresponding AQI values. He selects the view sites near air quality monitoring stations, which ensures the accuracy of AQI values. With the increase of this project's influence, people from other cities start to follow him. They use smart phone cameras to take photos of specific sites, and send their photos along with AQI values to this project. There have been 5315 outdoor images from 31 view sites in 17 cities. This project has become the main source of VAQI.

Table 2. Statistic numbers of outdoor images in VAQI-1.

Air Quality Category	Number of Outdoor Images
Excellent	2219
Good	2031
Lightly Polluted	1161
Moderately Polluted	706
Heavily Polluted	831
Severely Polluted	701

The second one is MJ weather [1], which is a free weather information query software. It offers a public platform where people can upload real-time images taken by smart phone cameras along with the location and time of photo taking. The corresponding AQI value is obtained from the nearest air quality monitoring station. We select images with the time strictly coinciding with the update time of the nearest monitoring station. We select 9 major cities with serious air pollution. There have been 2334 outdoor images from 54 view sites in these cities, which enlarges the quantity and enriches the site diversity of VAQI.

3.2   Appearance

Outdoor scene appearance is greatly affected by characteristics of atmosphere pollutants like PM10, SO2, NO2 and O3. The characteristics include species, size and concentration. Figure 3 shows the example view site appearances with different AQI values in VAQI-1. With the increase of concentrations on large-scale atmosphere pollutants, the air quality is getting worse, which leads to variances of image features like contrast, transmission, saturation. These features are the main references to air quality estimation.

Water droplets in the air also have an influence on scene appearance, like fog scenes. Appearances of fog is similar with haze. However, unlike the atmosphere pollutants, concentration on water droplets does not affect the air quality. The AQI values of foggy images are always less than 50. Figure 4 shows a comparison of fog and haze appearances. As can be seen, the color of fog is more vivid than haze, and the fog has clearer boundaries. Despite such differences, there is no effective method to distinguish fog and haze based on scene images, which makes the image based air quality estimation more challenging.

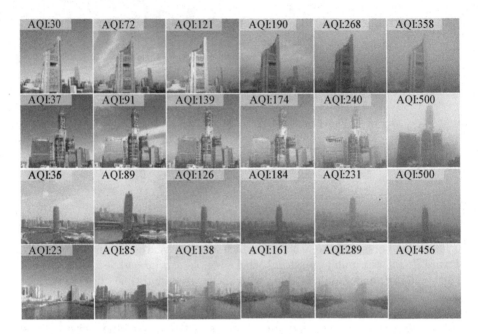

Fig. 3. Example view site appearances with different AQI values

3.3 Diversity

(1) *Site Diversity:* In real life, varieties of air quality occur in any type of sites (e.g., highway, city, farm, nature scene and so on). With the aim to estimate the exact air quality anywhere, we collect outdoor images from almost all types of sites, which provides a wide estimating range of view sites. However, appearances of different sites at the same AQI will have a huge distinction, which also pushes a limit of visual estimation abilities for both human and computers.

(2) *Visual Angle Diversity:* The visual angle is the angle a viewed object subtends at the camera, which includes high angle, flat angle and low angle. The high-angle photography technology is utilized in general outdoor surveillance, which employs the camera look down on a distant viewed object from a high angle. However, there are a lot of outdoor images taken from flat angle and low angle in real life. In general, images from low angle weaken the visual effects of scene imaging, which will affect the visual analysis of air quality (see red box in Fig. 5). Similar, short-distance images also show the incomplete atmosphere information of scenes (see green box in Fig. 5). VAQI-1 contains a certain number of such images, which not only enriches the visual angle diversity, but also increases the difficulty of air quality estimation.

We compare VAQI-1 with existing outdoor air quality databases (see Table 3). As can be seen, VAQI-1 expands both the database size and the number of view

Fig. 4. Example scene appearances of fog and haze with AQI values. [red box] foggy scene appearances. [green box] haze scene appearances. (Color figure online)

sites. Only VAQI-1 is publicly available. Moreover, we will constantly update and maintain VAQI-1 for a long term with the aim to encourage further research on image based on air quality estimation.

4   Image Based Air Quality Estimation

In this section, we attempt to estimate the air quality based on the VAQI-1. Note that the scene appearances with adjacent AQI values are almost the same, which brings difficulty to AQI estimation based on images. Moreover, the diversity of scene and visual angle further increases the estimation difficulty. According to the air pollution level, we divide VAQI-1 into six classes, and then the air quality estimation becomes a six-class classification of air pollution levels. We randomly select half images from each class as the training set and the rest as testing set.

In traditional image classification tasks, the mainly used hand-crafted features are SIFT [10], HOG [29], LBP [29] and color histogram. We attempt to use these features for air quality estimation. Moreover, by analyzing the visual and spectral clues related to the air quality, we also extract several meteorological features:

Fig. 5. Example images of low angle and near distance in VAQI-1. [red box] images of low angle. [green box] images of near distance. (Color figure online)

Table 3. Statistics of databases for image-based air quality estimation.

Database	Number of view sites	Number of outdoor images	Collection period
OAQIS in [33]	2	2000	2014
Database in [30]	1	<500	2013–2014
Database in [31]	1	287	2014
Database in [20]	3	6587	2014–2016
VAQI-1	75	7649	2014-Now

(1) *Medium transmission:* Medium transmission indicates the degree of light intensity attenuated because of the particulate matter scattering. Based on He et al. [14], we compute the dark channel values of each image, and combine the scene imaging model to calculate medium transmission.

(2) *Extinction Coefficient:* Extinction coefficient indicates the scattering degree of the particles in the atmosphere. We compute the value of extinction coefficient based on [18,25].

(3) *Contrast:* Contrast indicates the atmospheric clarity. Outdoor images captured in clear and haze days exhibit different global and local contrast. We compute the contrast according to Root Mean Square (RMS) [24].

(4) *Sky Color:* Sky is the most important cue for weather labeling. A clear sky is blue as air molecules scatter blue light more than other light. Pollution particles scatter long-wavelength light, which makes sky look gray or yellow. We detect the sky region in an image with the method suggested in [21,28]. Then, we extract A and B channels in the LAB color space of the sky region to form a feature vector.

We employ these hand-crafted features and utilize LIBSVM to evaluate their performance based on VAQI-1 (see Table 3). As can be seen, the accuracy of

SIFT, HOG, LBP and color histogram, for air quality estimation is quite low, which shows that the traditional hand-crafted features can not describe the air quality. On the other hand, the accuracy of meteorological features is much better than that of traditional hand-crafted features. However, the sky color is easily effected by the presence of clouds, as the clouds are made of tiny water droplets, making sky look gray or white. Although medium transmission and contrast perform better than sky color, these two features are determined by both the atmospheric clarity and the distance between the objects and the visual sensors, which can not accurately indicate the air quality like extinction coefficient. Extinction coefficient performs best with the accuracy 64%, which shows that this feature gives the best description of air quality (Table 4).

Table 4. The accuracy of air pollution level classification with different hand-crafted features.

Num	Feature	Accuracy
1	SIFT	0.06
2	HOG	0.15
3	LBP	0.19
4	Color histogram	0.20
5	Sky color	0.45
6	Contrast	0.52
7	Medium transmission	0.57
8	Extinction coefficient	0.64

5   Conclusion

In this paper, we attempt to solve a challenging problem: How to estimate outdoor air quality only using outdoor images? The absence of public database is a barrier to solve this problem. Therefore, we build an available database of high quality outdoor images in different view sites, which is labeled by AQI values. To the best of our knowledge, this database is currently the largest for image based air quality estimation. Based on this database, we perform comprehensive experiments by using different hand-crafted features including the traditional features and meteorological features respectively to analyze the appearance variances of outdoor images in different air quality conditions. The results show that the accuracy of meteorological features is much better than that of traditional hand-crafted features. Moreover, in meteorological features, the extinction coefficient indicating the degree of light intensity attenuated by particles performs best with the accuracy of 64%.

Acknowledgement. This work was supported by the National Natural Science Foundation of China (No. 61602520). We also gratefully acknowledge the valuable cooperation of Zou Yi.

References

1. mj weather. http://www.moji.com
2. yi mu liao ran. https://weibo.com/u/1000481815
3. Baklanov, A., et al.: Towards improving the simulation of meteorological fields in urban areas through updated/advanced surface fluxes description. Atmos. Chem. Phys. **8**(3), 523–543 (2008)
4. Chan, K.Y., Jian, L.: Identification of significant factors for air pollution levels using a neural network based knowledge discovery system. Neurocomputing **99**, 564–569 (2013)
5. Chen, J., Lu, J., Avise, J.C., DaMassa, J.A., Kleeman, M.J., Kaduwela, A.P.: Seasonal modeling of pm 2.5 in California's San Joaquin Valley. Atmos. Environ. **92**, 182–190 (2014)
6. Chen, J., Chen, H., Pan, J.Z., Wu, M., Zhang, N., Zheng, G.: When big data meets big smog: a big spatio-temporal data framework for China severe smog analysis. In: Proceedings of the 2nd ACM SIGSPATIAL International Workshop on Analytics for Big Geospatial Data, pp. 13–22. ACM (2013)
7. Cheng, S., Li, L., Chen, D., Li, J.: A neural network based ensemble approach for improving the accuracy of meteorological fields used for regional air quality modeling. J. Environ. Manag. **112**, 404–414 (2012)
8. Cheng, T., Wang, J., Li, X.: The support vector machine for nonlinear spatio-temporal regression. In: 2007 Proceedings of Geocomputation (2007)
9. Devarakonda, S., Sevusu, P., Liu, H., Liu, R., Iftode, L., Nath, B.: Real-time air quality monitoring through mobile sensing in metropolitan areas. In: Proceedings of the 2nd ACM SIGKDD International Workshop on Urban Computing, pp. 15. ACM (2013)
10. Goring, C., Rodner, E., Freytag, A., Denzler, J.: Nonparametric part transfer for fine-grained recognition. In: Proceedings of the IEEE Conference on Computer Vision and Pattern Recognition, pp. 2489–2496 (2014)
11. Guocai, Z.: Progress of weather research and forecast (WRF) model and application in the United States. Meteorol. Mon. **12**, 005 (2004)
12. Hájek, P., Olej, V.: Ozone prediction on the basis of neural networks, support vector regression and methods with uncertainty. Ecol. Inform. **12**, 31–42 (2012)
13. Hasenfratz, D., Saukh, O., Walser, C., Hueglin, C., Fierz, M., Thiele, L.: Pushing the spatio-temporal resolution limit of urban air pollution maps. In: 2014 IEEE International Conference on Pervasive Computing and Communications (PerCom), pp. 69–77. IEEE (2014)
14. He, K., Sun, J., Tang, X.: Single image haze removal using dark channel prior. IEEE Trans. Pattern Anal. Mach. Intell. **33**(12), 2341–2353 (2011)
15. Jeong, J.I., Park, R.J., Woo, J.-H., Han, Y.-J., Yi, S.-M.: Source contributions to carbonaceous aerosol concentrations in Korea. Atmos. Environ. **45**(5), 1116–1125 (2011)
16. Kim, Y., Fu, J.S., Miller, T.L.: Improving ozone modeling in complex terrain at a fine grid resolution: part I-examination of analysis nudging and all PBL schemes associated with LSMs in meteorological model. Atmos. Environ. **44**(4), 523–532 (2010)
17. Li, C., Hsu, N.C., Tsay, S.-C.: A study on the potential applications of satellite data in air quality monitoring and forecasting. Atmos. Environ. **45**(22), 3663–3675 (2011)

18. Li, Q., Li, Y., Xie, B.: Single image based scene visibility estimation. IEEE Access **7**, 24430–24439 (2019)
19. Li, X., Peng, L., Yuan, H., Shao, J., Chi, T.: Deep learning architecture for air quality predictions. Environ. Sci. Pollut. Res. **23**(22), 22408–22417 (2016)
20. Liu, C., Tsow, F., Zou, Y., Tao, N.: Particle pollution estimation based on image analysis. PLoS One **11**(2), e0145955 (2016)
21. Lu, C., Lin, D., Jia, J., Tang, C.-K.: Two-class weather classification. In: Proceedings of the IEEE Conference on Computer Vision and Pattern Recognition, pp. 3718–3725 (2014)
22. Nguyen, V.A., Starzyk, J.A., Goh, W.-B., Jachyra, D.: Neural network structure for spatio-temporal long-term memory. IEEE Trans. Neural Netw. Learn. Syst. **23**(6), 971–983 (2012)
23. Nieto, P.J.G., Combarro, E.F., del Coz Díaz, J.J., Montañés, E.: A SVM-based regression model to study the air quality at local scale in Oviedo urban area (Northern Spain): a case study. Appl. Math. Comput. **219**(17), 8923–8937 (2013)
24. Peli, E.: Contrast in complex images. JOSA A **7**(10), 2032–2040 (1990)
25. Li, Q., Xie, B.: Visibility estimation using a single image. In: Yang, J., et al. (eds.) CCCV 2017. CCIS, vol. 771, pp. 343–355. Springer, Singapore (2017). https://doi.org/10.1007/978-981-10-7299-4_28
26. Saide, P.E., et al.: Forecasting urban PM10 and PM2. 5 pollution episodes in very stable nocturnal conditions and complex terrain using WRF-Chem CO tracer model. Atmos. Environ. **45**(16), 2769–2780 (2011)
27. Sánchez, A.S., Nieto, P.J.G., Iglesias-Rodríguez, F.J., Vilán, J.A.V.: Nonlinear air quality modeling using support vector machines in Gijón urban area (Northern Spain) at local scale. Int. J. Nonlinear Sci. Numer. Simul. **14**(5), 291–305 (2013)
28. Tao, L., Yuan, L., Sun, J.: Skyfinder: attribute-based sky image search. In: ACM Transactions on Graphics (TOG), vol. 28, pp. 68. ACM (2009)
29. Vedaldi, A., Fulkerson, B.: VLFeat: an open and portable library of computer vision algorithms. In: Proceedings of the 18th ACM International Conference on Multimedia, pp. 1469–1472. ACM (2010)
30. Wang, H., Yuan, X., Wang, X., Zhang, Y., Dai, Q.: Real-time air quality estimation based on color image processing. In: 2014 IEEE Visual Communications and Image Processing Conference, pp. 326–329. IEEE (2014)
31. Zhan, Y., Zhang, R., Wu, Q., Wu, Y.: A new haze image database with detailed air quality information and a novel no-reference image quality assessment method for haze images. In: IEEE International Conference on Acoustics, Speech and Signal Processing (2016)
32. Zhang, Z., Ma, H., Fu, H., Liu, L., Zhang, C.: Outdoor air quality level inference via surveillance cameras. Mobile Inf. Syst. **2016**, 10 (2016)
33. Zhang, Z., Ma, H., Fu, H., Wang, X.: Outdoor air quality inference from single image. In: He, X., Luo, S., Tao, D., Xu, C., Yang, J., Hasan, M.A. (eds.) MMM 2015. LNCS, vol. 8936, pp. 13–25. Springer, Cham (2015). https://doi.org/10.1007/978-3-319-14442-9_2
34. Zheng, Y., Liu, F., Hsieh, H.-P.: U-air: when urban air quality inference meets big data. In: Proceedings of the 19th ACM SIGKDD International Conference on Knowledge Discovery and Data Mining, pp. 1436–1444. ACM (2013)
35. Zou, B., Wilson, J.G., Zhan, F.B., Zeng, Y.: Air pollution exposure assessment methods utilized in epidemiological studies. J. Environ. Monit. **11**(3), 475–490 (2009)

Rotational Alignment of IMU-camera Systems with 1-Point RANSAC

Banglei Guan[1,2], Ang Su[1,2(✉)], Zhang Li[1,2], and Friedrich Fraundorfer[3]

[1] College of Aerospace Science and Engineering,
National University of Defense Technology, Changsha, China
suang@nudt.edu.cn
[2] Hunan Provincial Key Laboratory of Image Measurement and Vision Navigation,
Changsha, China
[3] Institute for Computer Graphics and Vision,
Graz University of Technology,
Graz, Austria

Abstract. In this paper we present a minimal solution for the rotational alignment of IMU-camera systems based on a homography formulation. The image correspondences between two views are related by homography when the motion of the camera can be effectively approximated as a pure rotation. By exploiting the rotational angles of the features obtained by *e.g.* the SIFT detector, we compute the rotational alignment of IMU-camera systems with only 1 feature correspondence. The novel minimal case solution allows us to cope with feature mismatches efficiently and robustly within a random sample consensus (RANSAC) scheme. Our method is evaluated on both synthetic and real scene data, demonstrating that our method is suited for the rotational alignment of IMU-camera systems.

Keywords: Rotational alignment · Minimal solution · Pure rotation · IMU-camera calibration

1 Introduction

The fusion of vision and IMU data have been applied to a wide variety of applications, such as structure from motion (SfM) [21] and simultaneous localization and mapping (SLAM) [14]. The accuracy of these applications highly depends on the axis alignment between the IMU and the camera coordinate system [5,6,21]. This paper investigates the problem of IMU-camera calibration. In particular, we are interested in the minimal case, i.e. to compute the rotational alignment of IMU-camera systems exploiting one point correspondence together with rotational angles obtained by, *e.g.* SIFT detector [17]. The novel minimal case solution is significant within a RANSAC scheme, to cope with the outliers of feature matches efficiently and robustly.

The IMU-camera calibration problem has already been addressed by various researchers. A class of approaches use IMU measurements directly and estimate

© Springer Nature Switzerland AG 2019
Z. Lin et al. (Eds.): PRCV 2019, LNCS 11859, pp. 172–183, 2019.
https://doi.org/10.1007/978-3-030-31726-3_15

the calibration parameters as part of visual-inertial sensor fusion by adopting a filter-based approach [13,18,24]. Due to the large number of DOFs, these approaches require a high camera frame rate. Considering that common IMUs output the complete rotation information with respect to the IMU reference coordinate system, IMU-camera calibration is generally regarded as hand-eye calibration regarding the IMU as the hand [3,10,16,19,23]. Hence, the IMU-camera calibration problem can be represented as the hand-eye calibration equation $\mathbf{AX} = \mathbf{XB}$, where $\mathbf{X}$ is the transformation between the IMU coordinate system and the camera coordinate system which consists of a rotational matrix and a translational vector, $\mathbf{A}$ and $\mathbf{B}$ are the relative rigid motions of the camera and the IMU, respectively. Hand-eye calibration problem has already been addressed by many researchers in the past. The traditional methods need recover the camera poses in advance by using a calibration device or a SfM approach [10,25,27]. Recently, some methods avoid requiring prior knowledge of the camera poses and compute the hand-eye calibration directly from feature matches. Heller *et al.* [9] and Ruland *et al.* [20] employ the branch-and-bound algorithm to obtain globally optimal hand-eye calibration by minimizing the residuals in image space. Bender *et al.* [2] perform an in-flight IMU-camera calibration by exploiting a graph optimization framework.

A class of methods are proposed to perform IMU-camera calibration when the motion of the calibrated camera is a pure rotation or can be effectively approximated as a pure rotation. Seo *et al.* [22] solve the rotational matrix between the IMU coordinate system and the camera coordinate system by assuming all the translations to be zero. Hwangbo *et al.* [11] propose a calibration method based on homography transformation of image correspondences. Karpenko *et al.* [12] calibrate the camera and gyroscope system by quickly shaking the camera while pointing it at a far-away object. Guan *et al.* [7] propose minimal case solutions to the rotational alignment of IMU-camera systems using homography constraints, especially only 1.5 point correspondences are required for the pure rotation case. In fact, the assumption that the motion of the camera is a pure rotation is not restrictive in practical environment, because we rotate the camera outside where the scene is far away, the parallax-shift of most objects is hardly noticeable and the calibration method for a pure rotation case can be directly applied to such data. Thus IMU-camera calibration in the pure rotation case has practical relevance.

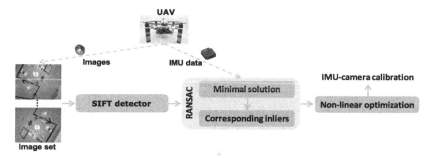

Fig. 1. Overview of the proposed IMU-camera calibration method.

The presented work is an extension of [7] which explores the different minimal case solutions to the rotational alignment of IMU-camera systems. Here, we extend [7] with a novel minimal case solution for the pure rotation case and achieve more accurate calibration result. Figure 1 illustrates the proposed IMU-camera calibration method. Our contributions can be summarized in the following way: (i) We propose to compute the rotational alignment of IMU-camera systems with 1 feature correspondence and the corresponding rotational angles obtained by e.g. the SIFT detector. (ii) Our method adopt the RANSAC [4] to cope with feature mismatches. The proposed minimal case solution is efficient within a RANSAC scheme, because the number of random samples that must be taken to find one outlier free sample depends exponentially on the number of parameters to instantiate one hypothesis. (iii) A non-linear parameter optimization over all image pairs is proposed. Our method not only can compute the rotational alignment of IMU-camera systems using a single image pair, but also can achieve more robust calibration results with multiple image pairs.

The remainder of the paper is structured as follows. We establish basics and notations for homography constraints for a pure rotation case in Sect. 2. In Sect. 3, we derive the minimal case solution by exploiting the rotational angles of the features and describe the non-linear parameter optimization over all image pairs. In Sect. 4, we validate the proposed method experimentally using both synthetic and real scene data. Finally, concluding remarks are given in Sect. 5.

2   Homography Constraints

Assume the intrinsic parameters of camera to be known, a general homography relation between two different views is represented as follows [8]:

$$\lambda \mathbf{x}_j = \mathbf{H} \mathbf{x}_i, \tag{1}$$

where $\mathbf{x}_i = [x_i, y_i, 1]^T$ and $\mathbf{x}_j = [x_j, y_j, 1]^T$ are the normalized homogeneous coordinates of the ideally projected image points in views i and j. $\mathbf{H}$ is the homography matrix and λ is a scale factor.

As shown in Fig. 2, the motion of the camera between views i and j is a pure rotation. $\mathcal{F}_r$ denotes IMU reference coordinate system. The camera coordinate systems of the views i and j are expressed with $\mathcal{F}_c^i$ and $\mathcal{F}_c^j$, respectively. The rotations of $\mathcal{F}_c^i$ and $\mathcal{F}_c^j$ in $\mathcal{F}_r$ can be expressed as $\mathbf{R}_{imu}^i \mathbf{R}_{calib}$ and $\mathbf{R}_{imu}^j \mathbf{R}_{calib}$, respectively. The rotational alignment difference between camera coordinate system and IMU coordinate system is expressed with $\mathbf{R}_{calib}$. The image correspondences between views i and j are related by homography and the homography can be written as:

$$\mathbf{H} = \mathbf{R}_{calib}^T (\mathbf{R}_{imu}^j)^T \mathbf{R}_{imu}^i \mathbf{R}_{calib}. \tag{2}$$

The skew-symmetric matrix $[\mathbf{x}_j]_\times$ is multiplied in both sides of Eq. 1 to further eliminate the unknown scale factor λ:

$$[\mathbf{x}_j]_\times \mathbf{H} \mathbf{x}_i = \mathbf{0}. \tag{3}$$

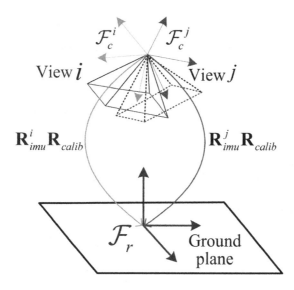

Fig. 2. The relationship between the views i and j.

Since the skew-symmetric matrix $[\mathbf{x}_j]_\times$ is only of rank 2, Eq. 3 only imposes two independent constraints on $\mathbf{H}$. In many situations, the approximate installation relationship between the IMU and the camera can be obtained from hand measurements or device layouts [7]. Thus the rotational relationship between the IMU and the camera $\mathbf{R}_{calib}$ can be represented:

$$\mathbf{R}_{calib} = \hat{\mathbf{R}}_{calib}\mathbf{R}_A, \tag{4}$$

where $\mathbf{R}_A$ is the approximate installation relationship between the IMU and the camera, and $\hat{\mathbf{R}}_{calib}$ is the remaining rotation between the IMU and the camera. Since the remaining rotation angles are small, $\hat{\mathbf{R}}_{calib}$ can be expressed by its first-order expansion:

$$\hat{\mathbf{R}}_{calib} = \mathbf{I}_{3\times3} + [\hat{\mathbf{r}}]_\times, \tag{5}$$

where $\hat{\mathbf{r}} = [\hat{r}_x, \hat{r}_y, \hat{r}_z]^T$ is a three-dimensional vector. Thus Eq. 2 can be reformulated as follows:

$$\mathbf{H} = \mathbf{R}_A^T\hat{\mathbf{R}}_{calib}^T(\mathbf{R}_{imu}^j)^T\mathbf{R}_{imu}^i\hat{\mathbf{R}}_{calib}\mathbf{R}_A. \tag{6}$$

3   IMU-camera Calibration

3.1   1pt-RANSAC Calibration Method

The widely-used SIFT detector not only provides the image coordinates of point correspondence, but also provides the rotational angles and scales of features. Our paper aims at involving the rotational angle of feature into the process to reduce the size of the minimal sample required for IMU-camera calibration. The affine correspondence can be described as a triplet: $(\mathbf{x}_i, \mathbf{x}_j, \mathbf{A})$. The local affine transformation $\mathbf{A}$ is defined as follows [1]:

$$
\mathbf{A} = \begin{bmatrix} a_{11} & a_{12} \\ a_{21} & a_{22} \end{bmatrix} = \begin{bmatrix} \cos(\alpha) & -\sin(\alpha) \\ \sin(\alpha) & \cos(\alpha) \end{bmatrix} \begin{bmatrix} s_x & w \\ 0 & s_y \end{bmatrix}
$$
$$
= \begin{bmatrix} s_x \cos(\alpha) & w\cos(\alpha) - s_y \sin(\alpha) \\ s_x \sin(\alpha) & w\sin(\alpha) + s_y \cos(\alpha) \end{bmatrix}.
\tag{7}
$$

Where the rotational angle α is computed by $(\alpha_j - \alpha_i)$, note that the rotational angles of point correspondence α_i and α_j can be obtained directly from the SIFT detector. s_x and s_y are the scales along axes x and y, respectively. w is the shear parameter. $\mathbf{A}$ is given as the first-order approximation of the related homography matrix for perspective cameras:

$$
a_{11} = \frac{\partial x_j}{\partial x_i} = \frac{h_{11} - h_{31}x_j}{s}, \qquad a_{12} = \frac{\partial x_j}{\partial y_i} = \frac{h_{12} - h_{32}x_j}{s},
$$
$$
a_{21} = \frac{\partial y_j}{\partial x_i} = \frac{h_{21} - h_{31}y_j}{s}, \qquad a_{22} = \frac{\partial y_j}{\partial y_i} = \frac{h_{22} - h_{32}y_j}{s},
\tag{8}
$$

where h_{ij} is the element from the ith row and the jth column of the homography matrix $\mathbf{H}$, $s = x_i h_{31} + y_i h_{32} + h_{33}$ is the projective depth.

Based on Eqs. 7 and 8, we obtain the relationship between the rotational angle of the feature and the corresponding homography matrix:

$$
\frac{a_{11}}{a_{21}} = \frac{\cos(\alpha)}{\sin(\alpha)} = \frac{h_{11} - h_{31}x_j}{h_{21} - h_{31}y_j},
\tag{9}
$$

We further expand Eq. 9 as follows:

$$
\sin(\alpha)(h_{11} - h_{31}x_j) - \cos(\alpha)(h_{21} - h_{31}y_j) = 0.
\tag{10}
$$

Assume one point correspondence $\mathbf{x}_i = [x_i, y_i, 1]^T$, $\mathbf{x}_j = [x_j, y_j, 1]^T$ and the corresponding rotational angle α, obtained by $e.g.$ SIFT detector, to be known. Combining Eqs. 3 and 10, we attain 3 polynomial equations in 3 unknowns $\hat{\mathbf{r}} = [\hat{r}_x, \hat{r}_y, \hat{r}_z]^T$:

$$
f_w(\hat{r}_x, \hat{r}_y, \hat{r}_z) = 0, \quad w = 1, 2, 3.
\tag{11}
$$

The automatic Gröbner basis solver [15] is used to solve the above polynomial equation system. The maximum polynomial degree of Eq. (11) is 2 and there is at most 8 solutions for $\hat{\mathbf{r}}$. This polynomial equation system only needs 140 lines to print out, which leads to an extremely short run-time for the solver. Thus this solver is suitable to perform IMU-camera calibration on smart devices with limited computational power.

In the 1-point RANSAC loop, we obtain the remaining rotation $\hat{\mathbf{R}}_{calib}$ from each solution $\hat{\mathbf{r}} = [\hat{r}_x, \hat{r}_y, \hat{r}_z]^T$ by Eq. 5. The corresponding exact rotation matrix can be retrieved by projecting the matrix to the closest rotation matrix. Then the homography $\mathbf{H}$ for the image features is composed with Eq. 6, and the solution with the maximum number of inliers is selected as the final solution. Finally, the rotational alignment of IMU-camera system $\mathbf{R}_{calib}$ is calculated by Eq. 4.

3.2   Non-linear Parameter Optimization

For each image pair, $\mathbf{R}_{calib}$ and the corresponding inliers can be obtained by 1-point RANSAC calibration method. The rotational alignment between the IMU and the camera is further optimized based on all the inliers in M image pairs. We minimize the total transfer errors of the inliers and the cost function is defined as follows:

$$
\begin{aligned}
\varepsilon &= \min_{\bar{\mathbf{R}}} \sum_{p=1}^{M} \sum_{k=1}^{N_p} \left\| \mathbf{x}_j^k - \mathbf{H}_p \mathbf{x}_i^k \right\| \\
&= \min_{\bar{\mathbf{R}}} \sum_{p=1}^{M} \sum_{k=1}^{N_p} \left\| \mathbf{x}_j^k - g(\bar{\mathbf{R}}, \mathbf{R}_{imu}^p) \mathbf{x}_i^k \right\|,
\end{aligned}
\tag{12}
$$

where $\bar{\mathbf{R}}$ is a three-vector used for optimization which is represented in Euler angles. The initial value of $\bar{\mathbf{R}}$ is set to the mean or median angles of M calibration results. Each image pair p is composed of views i and j. N_p represents the number of inliers and k is the index of the inliers within each image pair. $\mathbf{x}_i^k$ and $\mathbf{x}_j^k$ are the homogeneous image coordinates of the inlier k. $\mathbf{R}_{imu}^p$ denotes the IMU rotation matrices of views i and j. The homography $g(\bar{\mathbf{R}}, \mathbf{R}_{imu}^p)$ is the transformation model within each image pair, which transfers the image coordinate $\mathbf{x}_i^k$ in view i to the corresponding image coordinate $\mathbf{x}_j^k$ in view j.

Considering that there may still be a few outliers existed in the image correspondences, the robust cost function created by Cauchy function is used to reduce the influence of outliers:

$$
\rho(\varepsilon) = \frac{\sigma^2}{2} \log(1 + \frac{\varepsilon^2}{\sigma^2}),
\tag{13}
$$

where the σ parameter of the Cauchy function can be set to the inlier threshold of the RANSAC loop.

4   Experiments

The performance of the proposed IMU-camera calibration method is validated using both synthetic and real scene data. To obtain expressive results, we also compare the proposed calibration method to 1.5pt-GB calibration method and 1.5pt-3Q3 calibration method [7]. These methods are suitable for the rotational alignment of IMU-camera systems in the pure rotation case. For 1.5pt-GB and 1.5pt-3Q3 calibration methods, even though only one of the two available equations from the second point is used, both methods still need sample 2 feature correspondences in the RANSAC loop. When a RANSAC scheme is used to cope with feature mismatches, the necessary number of samples to get an outlier free sample with a chance of 99% and an outlier ratio of 50% is 17 for the 1.5pt calibration method, but the 1pt calibration method only need 7 samples.

4.1   Experiments with Synthetic Data

In the simulation experiments, we assess the calibration error by the root mean square (RMS) of the errors of all trials. The calibration error compares the angle difference between the true rotation and estimated rotation:

$$\xi_{\mathbf{R}} = \arccos((Tr(\mathbf{R}_{gt}\mathbf{R}_{calib}^{T}) - 1)/2), \tag{14}$$

where $\mathbf{R}_{gt}$ denotes the ground-truth rotation and $\mathbf{R}_{calib}$ is the corresponding estimated rotation.

Accuracy with Increasing Rotation. Since the remaining rotation matrix is approximated to the first-order and the higher-order terms are truncated, the proposed method is evaluated with respect to increasing magnitudes of remaining rotation. We choose three approximate installation angles between the IMU and the camera randomly from $-180°$ to $180°$. Three remaining angles between the IMU and the camera ranges from $0°$ to $10°$ at an interval of $1°$. At each remaining rotation magnitude, 10000 independent trials are conducted, and for each test, one image feature correspondence is generated randomly. We report the results on the data points within the first interval of a 5-quantile partitioning[1] (Quintile) of 10000 trials. As shown in Fig. 3, the calibration error of the proposed method increases slowly with increasing magnitudes of remaining rotation. Since all of these methods have utilized a first-order rotation approximation for the remaining rotation matrix, our method has similar accuracy with 1.5pt-GB and 1.5pt-3Q3 calibration methods.

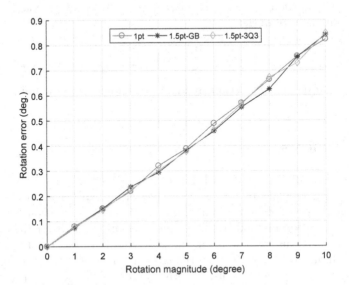

Fig. 3. RMSE for the calibration error with increasing magnitudes of remaining rotation.

---

[1] k-quantiles divide an ordered data set into k regular intervals.

Accuracy with Increasing Image Noise. We synthesize a pinhole camera with zero skew and an unit aspect ratio. The resolution is 800×640 pixels and the principle point is assumed to be at the image center. The focal length is chosen as 600 pixels, so that one pixel corresponds to about $0.1°$. The approximate installation angles between the IMU and the camera are set to $(180°, 0°, -90°)$, and the remaining rotation angles are set to $(1°, 1°, -1°)$. We add a different level of Gaussian noise to the image feature observations. The standard deviation of Gaussian noise is ranging from 0 to 2 pixels at an interval of 0.1 pixel. At each noise level, 10000 independent trials are conducted, and for each test, one image feature correspondence is generated randomly. We also report the results on the data points within the first interval of a 5-quantile partitioning of 10000 trials. As shown in Fig. 4, the calibration error of the proposed method increases almost linearly with the increase of image noise. For image noise of more than 0.4 pixel, our calibration method is slightly more accurate than 1.5pt-GB and 1.5pt-3Q3 calibration methods.

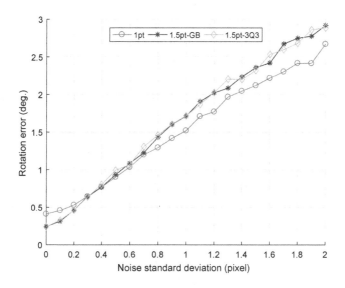

Fig. 4. RMSE for the calibration error with increasing image noise

4.2   Real Scene Data Experiment

We demonstrate the proposed method using a real scene data set under pure rotation, which is acquired with the Pixhawk drone [7], see Fig. 5. The markers are attached to the camera mount and the pose is tracked by a motion capture system consisting of 10 cameras. The marker poses are used as IMU data in the experiments. On the basis of the design of the 3D printed mount, the approximate installation angles between the IMU and the RGB camera are $(113°, 0°, 90°)$. The resolution of camera is 640×480 pixels and the intrinsic parameters are calibrated in advance. The camera is typically looking towards the ground and 81 images under pure rotation are captured.

(a) Pixhawk drone

(b) Sample image

Fig. 5. Pure rotation data set.

In the 1pt-RANSAC calibration step, we consider feasible image pairs for image matching and feature matches are created using SIFT feature matching [17] for each image pair. The inlier threshold is set to 2 pixels and the maximum number of iterations is set to 1000 in the RANSAC procedure. In the subsequent optimization step, the median and mean angle values of the calibration results of all image pairs are chosen as the initial values for non-linear parameter optimization, respectively. However, the optimization using the inliers of all the image pairs converges to the same result for both initializations. The calibration results of the different calibration methods are shown in Table 1. The calibration result of the proposed method is quite consistent with 1.5pt-GB and 1.5pt-3Q3 calibration methods.

Table 1. The calibration results for the pure rotation data set.

Method	Calibration results (degree)
Approximate installation angle	(113.0, 0.0, 90.0)
1pt	(114.3300, 1.1364, 88.6720)
1.5pt-GB	(114.4211, 1.2609, 88.7395)
1.5pt-3Q3	(114.4241, 1.2845, 88.74310)

To evaluate the accuracy of the calibration results as shown in Table 1, a data set of images for a checkerboard is acquired by the Pixhawk MAV. 49 images are randomly taken around the checkerboard and the image poses are computed by OPnP algorithm [26]. The coordinates of the checkerboard corners are measured by the motion capture system. The ground truth of the relationship between the IMU and the camera can be determined directly by combining with the corresponding IMU data: rotational matrix is $(114.1497°, 1.1152°, 88.7120°)$ and translational vector is $(0.0316\,\text{m}, 0.0222\,\text{m}, -0.0638\,\text{m})$ [7].

Then the accuracy of the calibration results is evaluated using the reprojection error, which is the mean distance between the measured image corners and the reprojection of the 3D corner. For comparison, the translational vector between the IMU and the camera is fixed as $(0.0316\,\text{m}, 0.0222\,\text{m}, -0.0638\,\text{m})$. The results of the accuracy evaluation are shown in Table 2. The table shows that the proposed method produces obviously lower reprojection errors than using the approximate installation angles directly, and outperforms 1.5pt-GB and 1.5pt-3Q3 calibration methods in terms of accuracy.

Table 2. The results of the accuracy evaluation

Calibration results	Ground truth	3D printer	1pt	1.5pt-GB	1.5pt-3Q3
Reprojection error (pixel)	1.3495	11.5408	2.5066	2.7785	2.8244

The pose of the RGBD camera can be obtained directly from the IMU data and the calibration result. Thus we reconstruct a common scene using the RGBD camera to verify the calibration result intuitively. The offset of the RGB camera and the depth camera has been calibrated beforehand, which is a pure translation $(0.00\,\text{m}, -0.02\,\text{m}, 0.00\,\text{m})$. The 3D reconstruction results based on the approximate installation angles and the calibration result of the proposed method are shown in Fig. 6. There are many false point clouds around the table and the deviation of the reconstructed line is quite large in the Fig. 6(a). The 3D reconstruction result using our calibration result is significantly better than the 3D reconstruction result using the initial values of 3D printing. This experiment successfully demonstrates the practicability of the proposed calibration method. It also means that it is necessary to calibrate the rotational alignment of IMU-camera systems even though the approximate installation angles is known.

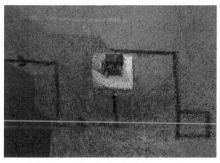

(a) Approximate installation angles   (b) Calibration result of our method

Fig. 6. 3D reconstruction results.

5   Conclusion

In this paper, we show that by exploiting the rotational angles of the features obtained by *e.g.* the SIFT detector, it is possible to calibrate IMU-camera systems with only 1 feature correspondence in the pure rotation case. Our method need fewer point correspondences for IMU-camera calibration as compared to other calibration methods. The novel minimal case solution is useful to reduce the computation time and increase the calibration robustness, when using Random Sample Consensus (RANSAC) to cope with feature mismatches. Furthermore, a non-linear parameter optimization over all image pairs is performed for a more accurate calibration result. The experimental results of both synthetic and real experiments have demonstrated that our method is suited for the rotational alignment of IMU-camera systems.

References

1. Barath, D.: Five-point fundamental matrix estimation for uncalibrated cameras. In: Proceedings of the IEEE Conference on Computer Vision and Pattern Recognition, pp. 235–243 (2018)
2. Bender, D., Schikora, M., Sturm, J., Greniers, D.: Ins-camera calibration without ground control points. In: 2014 Sensor Data Fusion: Trends, Solutions, Applications (SDF), pp. 1–6 (2014)
3. Daniilidis, K.: Hand-eye calibration using dual quaternions. Int. J. Robot. Res. **18**(3), 286–298 (1999)
4. Fischler, M.A., Bolles, R.C.: Random sample consensus: a paradigm for model fitting with applications to image analysis and automated cartography. Commun. ACM **24**(6), 381–395 (1981)
5. Fraundorfer, F., Tanskanen, P., Pollefeys, M.: A minimal case solution to the calibrated relative pose problem for the case of two known orientation angles. In: Daniilidis, K., Maragos, P., Paragios, N. (eds.) ECCV 2010. LNCS, vol. 6314, pp. 269–282. Springer, Heidelberg (2010). https://doi.org/10.1007/978-3-642-15561-1_20
6. Guan, B., Vasseur, P., Demonceaux, C., Fraundorfer, F.: Visual odometry using a homography formulation with decoupled rotation and translation estimation using minimal solutions. In: 2018 IEEE International Conference on Robotics and Automation (ICRA), pp. 2320–2327 (2018)
7. Guan, B., Yu, Q., Fraundorfer, F.: Minimal solutions for the rotational alignment of imu-camera systems using homography constraints. Comput. Vis. Image Underst. **170**, 79–91 (2018)
8. Hartley, R., Zisserman, A.: Multiple View Geometry in Computer Vision. Cambridge University Press, Cambridge (2003)
9. Heller, J., Havlena, M., Pajdla, T.: Globally optimal hand-eye calibration using branch-and-bound. IEEE Trans. Pattern Anal. Mach. Intell. **38**(5), 1027–1033 (2016)
10. Horaud, R., Dornaika, F.: Hand-eye Calibration. Int. J. Robot. Res. **14**(3), 195–210 (1995)
11. Hwangbo, M., Kim, J.S., Kanade, T.: Gyro-aided feature tracking for a moving camera: fusion, auto-calibration and GPU implementation. Int. J. Robot. Res. **30**(14), 1755–1774 (2011)

12. Karpenko, A., Jacobs, D., Baek, J., Levoy, M.: Digital video stabilization and rolling shutter correction using gyroscopes. CSTR **1**, 2 (2011)
13. Kelly, J., Sukhatme, G.S.: Visual-inertial sensor fusion: localization, mapping and sensor-to-sensor self-calibration. Int. J. Robot. Res. **30**(1), 56–79 (2011)
14. Kneip, L., Chli, M., Siegwart, R.Y.: Robust real-time visual odometry with a single camera and an IMU. In: Proceedings of the British Machine Vision Conference (2011)
15. Kukelova, Z., Bujnak, M., Pajdla, T.: Automatic generator of minimal problem solvers. In: Forsyth, D., Torr, P., Zisserman, A. (eds.) ECCV 2008. LNCS, vol. 5304, pp. 302–315. Springer, Heidelberg (2008). https://doi.org/10.1007/978-3-540-88690-7_23
16. Kukelova, Z., Heller, J., Pajdla, T.: Hand-eye calibration without hand orientation measurement using minimal solution. In: Lee, K.M., Matsushita, Y., Rehg, J.M., Hu, Z. (eds.) ACCV 2012. LNCS, vol. 7727, pp. 576–589. Springer, Heidelberg (2013). https://doi.org/10.1007/978-3-642-37447-0_44
17. Lowe, D.G., Lowe, D.G.: Distinctive image features from scale-invariant keypoints. Int. J. Comput. Vision **60**(2), 91–110 (2004)
18. Mirzaei, F.M., Roumeliotis, S.I.: A Kalman filter-based algorithm for IMU-camera calibration: observability analysis and performance evaluation. IEEE Trans. Rob. **24**(5), 1143–1156 (2008)
19. Park, F.C., Martin, B.J.: Robot sensor calibration: solving ax = xb on the Euclidean group. IEEE Trans. Robot. Autom. **10**(5), 717–721 (1994)
20. Ruland, T., Pajdla, T., Krüger, L.: Globally optimal hand-eye calibration. In: Proceedings of the IEEE Conference on Computer Vision and Pattern Recognition, pp. 1035–1042 (2012)
21. Saurer, O., Vasseur, P., Boutteau, R., Demonceaux, C., Pollefeys, M., Fraundorfer, F.: Homography based egomotion estimation with a common direction. IEEE Trans. Pattern Anal. Mach. Intell. **39**, 327–341 (2016)
22. Seo, Y., Choi, Y.J., Lee, S.W.: A branch-and-bound algorithm for globally optimal calibration of a camera-and-rotation-sensor system. In: Proceedings of the International Conference on Computer Vision, pp. 1173–1178 (2009)
23. Tsai, R.Y., Lenz, R.K.: A new technique for fully autonomous and efficient 3D robotics hand/eye calibration. IEEE Trans. Robot. Autom. **5**(3), 345–358 (1989)
24. Weiss, S., Achtelik, M.W., Chli, M., Siegwart, R.: Versatile distributed pose estimation and sensor self-calibration for an autonomous MAV. In: 2012 IEEE International Conference on Robotics and Automation, pp. 31–38 (2012)
25. Zhang, Z.Q.: Cameras and inertial/magnetic sensor units alignment calibration. IEEE Trans. Instrum. Meas. **65**(6), 1495–1502 (2016)
26. Zheng, Y., Kuang, Y., Sugimoto, S., Astrom, K., Okutomi, M.: Revisiting the PnP problem: a fast, general and optimal solution. In: Proceedings of the IEEE International Conference on Computer Vision, pp. 2344–2351 (2013)
27. Zhuang, H., Shiu, Y.C.: A noise tolerant algorithm for wrist-mounted robotic sensor calibration with or without sensor orientation measurement. In: Proceedings of the IEEE/RSJ International Conference on Intelligent Robots and Systems, vol. 2, pp. 1095–1100 (1992)

Bidirectional Adversarial Domain Adaptation with Semantic Consistency

Yaping Zhang[1,2], Shuai Nie[1], Shan Liang[1], and Wenju Liu[1(✉)]

[1] Institute of Automation, Chinese Academy of Sciences, Beijing, China
{yaping.zhang,shuai.nie,sliang,lwj}@nlpr.ia.ac.cn
[2] University of Chinese Academy of Sciences, Beijing, China

Abstract. Unsupervised domain adaptation (DA) aims to utilize the well-annotated source domain data to recognize the unlabeled target domain data that usually have a large domain shift. Most existing DA methods are developed to align the high-level feature-space distribution between the source and target domains, while neglecting the semantic consistency and low-level pixel-space information. In this paper, we propose a novel bidirectional adversarial domain adaptation (BADA) method to simultaneously adapt the pixel-level and feature-level shifts with semantic consistency. To keep semantic consistency, we propose a soft label-based semantic consistency constraint, which takes advantage of the well-trained source classifier during bidirectional adversarial mappings. Furthermore, the semantic consistency has been first analyzed during the domain adaptation with regard to both qualitative and quantitative evaluation. Systematic experiments on four benchmark datasets show that the proposed BADA achieves the state-of-the-art performance.

Keywords: Domain adaptation · GAN · Unsupervised learning

1 Introduction

Deep learning has shown great success in multimedia analysis by learning discriminative representations from massive labeled data [7,9]. However, collecting the well-annotated datasets is exceedingly expensive. A promising alternative is to take full advantage of labeled data from an easily available source domain. Unfortunately, the inevitable domain shifts between the source and target domain limit the generalization of models. To alleviate this issue, recent domain adaptation methods try to align the feature distribution [4,29], which focus on minimizing the distance between the source and target feature domain. However, the feature-level alignment methods suffer two limitations: (1) feature-level alignment is hard to sufficiently transfer knowledge from the source domain to the target domain, due to missing the low-level pixel-space variance, which is critical to the generalization of the model; (2) the measure of feature-level difference fails to consider the semantic consistency during the alignment, and it is difficult to directly observe whether the transferred knowledge is reasonable.

The first author is a student.

© Springer Nature Switzerland AG 2019
Z. Lin et al. (Eds.): PRCV 2019, LNCS 11859, pp. 184–198, 2019.
https://doi.org/10.1007/978-3-030-31726-3_16

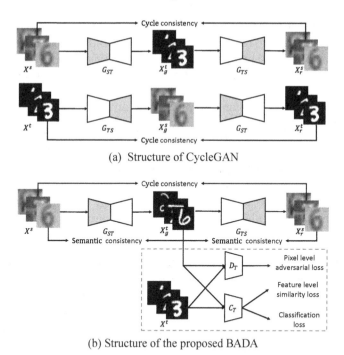

(a) Structure of CycleGAN

(b) Structure of the proposed BADA

Fig. 1. (a) Structure of CycleGAN: Cycle consistency only ensures the reconstruction of original content, where the middle mapping suffers label flipping. For example, the source image $\mathbf{X}^s$ is with label "6", while the transferred target image inconsistently belongs to label "3", hence it cannot be used to train a new target classifier.(b) Structure of the proposed BADA method: a generator G_{ST} that maps source domain images $\mathbf{X}^s$ to adapted target image $\mathbf{X}_g^t$, and an another inverted generator G_{TS} that generates the reconstructed image $\mathbf{X}_r^s$ as if from original source domain, while keeps cycle consistency and semantic consistency. For example, the transferred target image keeps the label "6", and can be used for training a new target classifier C_T. The target discriminator D_T is to distinguish the generated target images $\mathbf{X}_g^t$ from unpaired real target image X^t, which offers the guidance for generators.

Adversarial pixel-level domain adaptation [21] has shown great potential recently, which tries to align the raw pixel-level distribution between two domains. Specifically, pixel-level domain adaptation tries to map images from the source domain to appear as if they were sampled from the target domain, while keeping their original contents. The existing adversarial pixel-level domain adaptation is achieved by learning a unidirectional pixel-level mapping with unpaired images, which must maintain similar foregrounds between two domains to provide training stability.

Cycle-consistent adversarial network (CycleGAN) [28] introduces a pair of bidirectional mappings with cycle consistency to relax the strong assumption that two domains must have similar contents to capture larger domain shifts. The cycle consistency loss ensures that an image translated from one domain to another domain can be reconstructed to original domain. It shows compelling results on unpaired image-to-image translation tasks. However, CycleGAN *cannot* guarantee that the semantic contents are preserved during the translating process. As shown in Fig. 1(a), CycleGAN suffers from random label flipping, that is, *lack of semantic consistency*.

To overcome the shortcoming of CycleGAN in the domain adaptation task, we proposed a novel Bidirectional Adversarial Domain Adaptation (BADA) model. As shown in Fig. 1(b), BADA contains a pair of bidirectional reversible mappings: one generator G_{ST} maps source domain images $\mathbf{X}^s$ to the adapted target images $\mathbf{X}_g^t$, and another inverted generator G_{TS} that reconstructs adapted images back to the source domain, while keep cycle consistency and semantic consistency. The adapted target images $\mathbf{X}_g^t$ not only possess the style of the target domain, but also inherit the labels from the source domain. And thus the adapted target images $\mathbf{X}_g^t$ can be used to learn a supervised target classifier C_T. Furthermore, through the coordination between the pixel-level adversarial loss and the feature-level similarity loss, the target classifier C_T is able to capture both the low-level and high-level shifts between the source domain and target domain. What's more, BADA is under the guidance of a soft label-based semantic consistency constraint, which takes advantage of semantic information during bidirectional mappings and is superior to unidirectional semantic consistency in CyCADA [8] and SBADA-GAN [20]. We summarize our contributions as follows:

- We propose a novel BADA method to jointly consider the pixel-level and feature-level domain adaptation with semantic consistency. The pixel-level adaptation preserves more detail information and is easily visualized, while the feature-level adaptation could capture more high-level domain-invariant representations.
- We propose a soft label-based semantic consistency constraint considering semantic information during bidirectional mappings, which effectively solves the random label flipping problem that is suffered by CycleGAN, and we analyze the semantic consistency with regard to both qualitative and quantitative evaluation for the first time.
- The proposed BADA significantly outperforms the state-of-the-art domain adaptation methods on some benchmark datasets, which shows that the proposed semantic consistency constraint, as well as the joint consideration of the pixel-level and feature-level domain adaptation can improve the domain adaptation ability.

2   Related Work

Existing methods generally aim to reduce domain shifts by minimizing the distance of feature distribution [4,26,29] between the source domain and target domain. The measure of distance can be roughly divided into maximum mean discrepancy (MMD) [2,14], correlation distances [22,23], deep reconstruction loss [6] or an adversarial loss [5,13,25,26]. While there are so many feature-level domain adaption methods, we mainly focus on the MMD-based and adversarial-loss based methods, which are highly related to our work. Maximum Mean Discrepancy (MMD) based methods [2,14] are to learn domain-invariant features by computing the norm of the difference between two domain means. The Deep Adaptation Network (DAN) [14] applies MMD to the feature layers of deep neural networks, effectively inducing a high-level feature alignment. Other methods chose an adversarial loss to measure the domain shifts between the learned features [3,25,26], which introduce an extra domain discriminator to encourage features not being distinguished between two domains. Adversarial loss based methods could be further divided into discriminative methods and generative methods. The adversarial discriminative methods [5,25] consider the feature alignment only, while adversarial generative domain adaptation methods [13,24] try to utilize a weight sharing constraint to learn a joint multi-domains distribution with the reconstruction of target domain. However, the performance of feature-level domain adaptation method is far from purely supervised methods, due to the lack of ability to capture pixel-level domain shifts. Recently, pixel-level domain adaptation methods have shown the huge potential [1,8,17]. Unsupervised Pixel-level Domain Adaptation (PixelDA) [1] adapts the source-domain images to appear as if drawn from the target domain, and achieve surprising results on some unsupervised domain adaptation task. While pixelDA has a strong assumption that the source domain and target domain must share many similar foregrounds limiting larger domain shifts.

In contrast, cycle-consistency loss based network [11,28] shows amazing results on unpaired image-to-image translation by a pair of dual pixel-level mappings, which do not need similar foregrounds and instead simply ensure that the translated images could be reconstructed back to their original domains with identical contents. However, they fails to keep the semantic consistency during the conversion process. Motivated by this, the proposed BADA model considers the unpaired pixel-level translation with a novel semantic consistency constraint for unsupervised domain adaptation. We note that the motivation of CyCADA [8] and SBADA-GAN [20] are similar to ours. However, we solve the label flipping problem from different perspective. Compared to CyCADA and SBADA-GAN, we propose a more effective semantic consistency constraint, where we focus on the bidirectional reversible semantic consistency during the unpaired pixel-level mappings. Furthermore, we combine a simple but effective MMD feature-level domain adaptation method to boost performance. While CyCADA needs an extra discriminator neural network and SBADA-GAN needs to combine the source and target classifier for the final prediction. Moreover, we firstly analyze the semantic consistency, with regard to both qualitative and quantitative evaluation, during the domain adaptation.

3   The Proposed Model

3.1   Formulations

Suppose that there are N^s annotated source-domain samples $\mathbf{X}^s = \{\mathbf{x}_s{}^i\}_{i=0}^{N^s}$ with labels $\mathbf{Y}^s = \{\mathbf{y}_s{}^i\}_{i=0}^{N^s}$ and N^t unlabeled target-domain samples $\mathbf{X}^t = \{\mathbf{x}_t{}^i\}_{i=0}^{N^t}$.

With the well-annotated source data, we could learn an optimized source classifier C_S parameterized θ_{C_S} by minimizing a standard supervised classification loss expressed as:

$$L_{cls}(C_S; \mathbf{X}^s, \mathbf{Y}^s) = E_{(\mathbf{x}_s, \mathbf{y}_s) \sim (\mathbf{X}^s, \mathbf{Y}^s)} \left[-\mathbf{y}_s^\top \log(\sigma(C_S(\mathbf{x}_s; \theta_{C_S}))) \right], \qquad (1)$$

where $\mathbf{y}_s$ is the one-hot vector of the class label, and $\sigma(\cdot)$ denotes the softmax function.

However, the trained source classifier C_S is hard to perform well on the target domain, due to the inevitable shifts across the different domains. Our model is to adapt images from the source domain to appear as if they were drawn from the target domain by learning a discriminative mapping, and then we could use the generated labeled target domain images to train a new target classifier C_T as if the training and test data were from the same distribution. Unfortunately, lack of the paired images, the key semantic content is hard to keep consistent by the unidirectional pixel-to-pixel mapping from the source domain to the target domain. To alleviate this issue, we introduce two reversible mappings: a generator G_{ST} that maps a source domain image $\mathbf{x}_s$ to an adapted target image $\mathbf{x}_t^g = G_{ST}(\mathbf{x}_s)$, and an another inverted generator G_{TS} that makes a target domain image back to the source domain, ending up the same semantic content.

To ensure that learnt pixel-level mappings are semantic consistent between the source and target domain, we introduce four different losses: a *pixel-level adversarial loss* L_{pix} for matching the distributions of two domains in low-level pixel-space; an *feature-level similarity loss* L_{fea} to guide model to capture high-level domain-invariant features; a *cycle consistency loss* L_{cyc} to prevent the learned bidirectional mappings G_{ST} and G_{TS} from contradicting each other [28]; and a *semantic consistency loss* L_{sem} that encourages the consistency of the key discriminative semantic contents during the pixel-level mapping across domains.

Pixel-Level Adversarial Loss. The two generators are augmented by two adversarial discriminators respectively. A target discriminator D_T distinguishes between the real target data $\mathbf{x}_t$ and generated target data $G_{ST}(\mathbf{x}_s)$. In the same way, a source discriminator D_S distinguishes between the real source data $\mathbf{x}_s$ and the generated source data $G_{TS}(\mathbf{x}_t)$. Specifically, for the generator G_{ST}, it tries to map a source domain image to an adapted target domain sample $\mathbf{x}_t^g = G_{ST}(\mathbf{x}_s)$ that cannot be distinguished by its corresponding discriminator D_T , where the discriminator D_T is trained to do as well as possible in detecting generated "fake" target domain image $\mathbf{x}_t^g$. More formally, the generator $G_{ST}(\mathbf{x}_s)$ is trained with D_T by adversarial learning with the loss:

$$L_{adv}(G_{ST}, D_T, \mathbf{X}^s, \mathbf{X}^t) = E_{\mathbf{x}_t \sim \mathbf{X}^t}[\log(D_T(\mathbf{x}_t))] + E_{\mathbf{x}_s \sim \mathbf{X}^s}[\log(1 - D_T(G_{ST}(\mathbf{x}_s)))].$$
$$(2)$$

Likewise, for the generator G_{TS} with the discriminator D_S, we introduce a similar adversarial learning process with the adversarial loss $L_{adv}(G_{TS}, D_S, \mathbf{X}^s, \mathbf{X}^t)$. The pixel-level adversarial loss is defined as:

$$L_{pix} = L_{adv}(G_{ST}, D_T, \mathbf{X}^s, \mathbf{X}^t) + L_{adv}(G_{TS}, D_S, \mathbf{X}^s, \mathbf{X}^t). \qquad (3)$$

Feature-Level Similarity Loss. We also add a feature-level similarity loss to encourage that the high-level features from the adapted target images and the real target images are as similar as possible. The feature-level similarity loss L_{fea} is defined as Eq. 4 based on MMD [2], which is a kernel-based distance function widely used for the feature-level domain adaptation.

$$
\begin{aligned}
L_{fea}(C_T(G_{ST}(\mathbf{x}_s)), C_T(\mathbf{x}_t))) &= \|E_{\mathbf{x}_s \sim \mathbf{X}^s}[\phi(C_T(G_{ST}(\mathbf{x}_s)))] - E_{\mathbf{x}_t \sim \mathbf{X}^t}[\phi(C_T(\mathbf{x}_t))]\|^2 \\
&= E\left[K(C_T(G_{ST}(\mathbf{x}_s)), C_T(G_{ST}(\mathbf{x}_s)))\right] \\
&\quad + E\left[K(C_T(\mathbf{x}_t), C_T(\mathbf{x}_t))\right] \\
&\quad - 2E\left[K(C_T(G_{ST}(\mathbf{x}_s)), C_T(\mathbf{x}_t))\right],
\end{aligned}
\tag{4}
$$

where $K(\cdot, \cdot)$ denotes is a kernel function. In our experiments, we use a linear combination of multiple RBF kernels expressed as:

$$
K(\mathbf{x}, \mathbf{y}) = \sum \eta_n \exp\left\{-\frac{1}{2\sigma_n}\|\mathbf{x} - \mathbf{y}\|^2\right\},
\tag{5}
$$

where η_n and σ_n are the weight and the standard deviation for n-th RBF kernel [2], respectively.

Cycle Consistency Loss. Through the pixel level adversarial learning, ideally, G_{ST} could adapt the images from source domain to the images identically distributed as target domain. However, the adversarial loss alone still cannot guarantee that the contents of original samples could be reconstructed [28]. We hope that the image mapping from the source domain to the target domain should be a reversible process. In other word, the adapted image $G_{ST}(\mathbf{x}_s)$, which is generated by mapping a source domain image $\mathbf{x}_s$ to the target domain, should be able to back to the original image by the reversal mapping G_{TS}, that is $G_{TS}(G_{ST}(\mathbf{x}_s)) \approx \mathbf{x}_s$. Therefore, we impose a cycle-consistency constraint with L_1 normalization operator $\|\cdot\|_1$ as:

$$
\begin{aligned}
L_{cyc}(G_{ST}, G_{TS}, \mathbf{X}^s, \mathbf{X}^t) &= E_{\mathbf{x}_s \sim X^s}\left[\|G_{TS}(G_{ST}(\mathbf{x}_s)) - \mathbf{x}_s\|_1\right] \\
&\quad + E_{\mathbf{x}_t \sim \mathbf{X}^t}\left[\|G_{ST}(G_{TS}(\mathbf{x}_t)) - \mathbf{x}_t\|_1\right].
\end{aligned}
\tag{6}
$$

Semantic Consistency Loss. Although the cycle consistency loss in Eq. 6 can encourage the image mapping cycle to bring the source domain image back to the original image. There is no obvious constraint to ensure that the middle mapping could keep the semantic contents consistent. As shown in Fig. 1(a), the mapping is free to shift the semantic contents, *i.e.* the image of class "3" may be transferred to the image of class "6".

To alleviate this issue, as illustrated in Fig. 1(b), we enforce the middle mapping is semantic consistent. The basis of the semantic consistency is that the mapping from the labeled source domain to the target domain should keep the same class. To evaluate if the generated image $G_{ST}(\mathbf{x}_s)$ is at the same class with the source image $\mathbf{x}_s$, we introduce the pretrained source classifier C_s to do a preliminary inspection.

Given that the pretrained source classifier is noisy for the generated images, we use the output vector $C_S(\mathbf{x}_s)$ of source classier as a soft label vector to encourage that an image to be classified in the same way after mapping as it was before mapping. Due to our bidirectional pixel-level mappings are reversible, both the generated image and the reconstructed image should also keep the same semantics with the original image. Furthermore, we take full advantage of both soft label and hard label to augment semantic consistency during mapping processes, and the semantic consistency loss is defined as follows:

$$
\begin{aligned}
L_{sem}(G_{ST}, G_{TS}, \mathbf{X}^s, C_S) = {} & E_{\mathbf{x}_s \sim \mathbf{X}^s} \left[\| C_S(G_{ST}(\mathbf{x}_s)) - C_S(\mathbf{x}_s) \|^2 \right] \\
& + E_{\mathbf{x}_s \sim \mathbf{X}^s} \left[\| C_S(G_{TS}(G_{ST}(\mathbf{x}_s))) - C_S(\mathbf{x}_s) \|^2 \right] \\
& + L_{cls}(C_S, G_{TS}(G_{ST}(\mathbf{X}^s)), \mathbf{Y}^s).
\end{aligned}
\tag{7}
$$

3.2 Optimization

As shown in Fig. 1(b), the combination of objectives above will encourage a model to learn bidirectional pixel-to-pixel mappings between two domains, while keeping the same discriminative semantic content. By the discriminative pixel-to-pixel mapping from the source domain to the target domain, the generated target images $G_{ST}(\mathbf{x}_s)$ will preserve the label information from the source domain. Furthermore, a new target classifier C_T could be trained on the generated images as if trained on samples drawn from the target domain with minimizing the prediction loss:

$$
L'_{cls}(C_T; G_{ST}(\mathbf{x}_s), \mathbf{Y}^s) = E_{(\mathbf{x}_s, \mathbf{y}_s) \sim (\mathbf{X}^s, \mathbf{Y}^s)} \left[-\mathbf{y}_s^\top \log(\sigma(C_T(G_{ST}(\mathbf{x}_s)))) \right].
\tag{8}
$$

So far, G_{ST}, G_{ST}, D_S, D_T and C_T could be jointly optimized with the total optimization objective as:

$$
L_{DA} = L'_{cls} + L_{pix} + L_{fea} + \lambda_{cyc} L_{cyc} + \lambda_s L_{sem}
\tag{9}
$$

where λ_{cyc} and λ_s are weights that control the interaction of losses to achieve better trade-off between the adaptation and classification. They are trained by an alternative training way in the concurrent sub-processes:

$$
(\hat{\theta}_{G_{ST}}, \hat{\theta}_{G_{TS}}) = \underset{\theta_{G_{ST}}, \theta_{G_{TS}}}{\arg\min} \; L_{DA},
\tag{10}
$$

$$
(\hat{\theta}_{D_S}, \hat{\theta}_{D_T}) = \underset{\theta_{D_S}, \theta_{D_T}}{\arg\max} \; L_{pix},
\tag{11}
$$

$$
\hat{\theta}_{C_T} = \underset{\theta_{C_T}}{\arg\min} \; L'_{cls}.
\tag{12}
$$

where $\theta_{G_{ST}}$, $\theta_{G_{TS}}$, θ_{D_S}, θ_{D_T} and θ_{C_T} denote the parameters of the G_{ST}, G_{TS}, D_S, D_T and C_T respectively. The parameters can be updated by stochastic gradient descent optimization algorithms, like Adadelta [27].

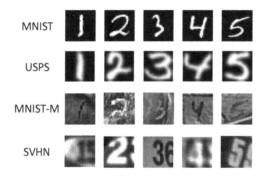

Fig. 2. Dataset samples for our domain adaptation tasks.

4 Experiments

4.1 Datasets

We conduct experiments on 4 widely-used domain adaptation datasets: MNIST [12], USPS [10], MNIST-M [1], SVHN [19], as shown in Fig. 2. The statistics of the datasets are summarized in Table 1. For a fair comparison, we evaluate our algorithm on the 4 common domain adaptation tasks: MNIST → USPS (M → U), USPS → MNIST (U → M), MNIST → MNIST-M (M → M-M), SVHN → MNIST (S → M), using the training set only during training process and evaluating on the standard test sets. The token "→" means the direction from the source domain to the target. The images are all resized to 28 × 28 pixels, and pixels of images are all normalized to $[0, 1]$. And we use grayscaled images for all tasks, except M → M-M task, where MNIST dataset were extended to three channels in order to match the shape of MNIST-M images (RGB images).

4.2 Experimental Setup

Network Architecture. Our network architecture is inspired by the Cycle-GAN [28]. The G_{ST} and G_{TS} use the same generative network architecture [28]. The generative network consists of 3 convolutional blocks, 9 residual blocks, and 3 transposed convolutional blocks. Each convolutional block consists of a convolutional layer followed by instance normalization layer and rectified linear unit (Relu) [18]. The architecture used for the discriminators D_S and D_T is a fully convolutional network with five convolutional layers. The networks used for the classifiers C_S and C_T are composed of 4 convolutional layer followed by instance norm layer with leaky rectified linear unit (Leaky Relu) [15], 2 max-pooling layers, and a fully connected layer.

Training Details. All of our experiments are implemented with Tensorflow, and our implementation code will be released soon. We use the Adadelta optimizer [27] with a minibatch of size 16. Considering the regular adversarial loss suffers from the vanishing gradients problem, we replace the adversarial loss Eq. 3

Table 1. Datasets, "*/*" in columns of "Instances" denotes the number of train/test image pairs.

Dataset	Instances	classes	Image size	Color map
MNIST	60,000/10,000	10	28×28	Gray
USPS	7,291/2,007	10	28×28	Gray
MNIST-M	59,001/9,001	10	32×32	RGB
SVHN	73,257/26,032	10	32×32	RGB

with the least-squares GANs (LSGANs) loss [16], which can generate higher quality samples and perform more stable during the learning process.

Table 2. Accuracies ($mean \pm std$) on unsupervised domain adaptation among MNIST, USPS, SVHN and MNIST-M

Method	Reference	M→U	U→M	M→M-M	S→M
Source Only	ours	0.812	0.751	0.6070	0.6503
Target Only	ours	0.9729	0.9956	0.9545	0.9956
MMD	ICML 2015	0.8110	-	0.7690	0.7110
Domain Confusion	ICCV 2015	0.791 ± 0.005	0.665 ± 0.033	-	0.681 ± 0.003
DSN w/MMD	NIPS 2016	-	-	0.8050	0.7220
CoGAN	NIPS 2016	0.912 ± 0.008	0.891 ± 0.0008	0.620	-
DSN w/DANN	NIPS 2016	0.913	-	0.8320	0.827
DANN	JMLR 2016	0.771 ± 0.018	0.730 ± 0.020	0.7666	0.7385
DRCN	ECCV 2016	0.918 ± 0.0009	0.7367 ± 0.0004	-	0.8197 ± 0.0016
ADDA	CVPR 2017	0.894 ± 0.0002	0.901 ± 0.0008	-	0.760 ± 0.0018
pixel-DA	CVPR 2017	0.959	-	0.982	-
CyCADA	ICML 2018	0.956 ± 0.002	0.965 ± 0.001	0.976 ± 0.002	0.904 ± 0.004
DIFA	CVPR 2018	0.923 ± 0.001	0.910 ± 0.004	0.924 ± 0.001	0.897 ± 0.002
Image2Image	CVPR 2018	0.925	0.908	0.916	0.847
RAAN	CVPR 2018	0.89	0.921	-	0.892
SBADA-GAN	CVPR 2018	**0.976**	0.950	**0.994**	0.761
BADA	Ours	0.9483 ± 0.0008	**0.9689 ± 0.0004**	0.9872 ± 0.0005	**0.9254 ± 0.0012**
BADA without L_{fea}	Ours	0.9531 ± 0.0006	0.9651 ± 0.0019	0.9866 ± 0.0003	0.8498 ± 0.0061

4.3   Comparison with Existing Methods

In this section, we compare the proposed BADA model with different domain adaptation (DA) methods among 4 widely adopted tasks. The compared methods are: (1) MMD [1,14], DSN w/MMD [2], Domain Confusion [24, 25], DANN [5], DRCN [6], CoGAN [13], DSN w/DANN [1,2], ADDA [25], DIFA [26], and RAAN [3], which are feature-level DA methods; (2) pixel-DA [1], Image2Image [17], CyCADA [8] and SBADA-GAN [20], which are pixel-level DA methods. Table 2 presents the unsupervised DA recognition accuracy ($mean \pm std$) over three independent experiments. From Table 2, we can draw the follow observations:

– Firstly, we compare our BADA model with the "Source Only" and "Target Only" model. The "Source Only" and "Target Only" mean that the models are trained only on the source domain or target domain without any domain adaptation, respectively. They can be seen as a lower bound and an upper bound, respectively. We observe that our model achieves much better results than the "Source Only". It's more exciting that our results are much closer to the "Target Only".

– Compared with feature-level methods, our model not only achieves much better performance than MMD [1,14] and DSN w/MMD [2], which use traditional MMD loss [2,14] to minimize the feature-level difference between the source and target domain. But also our model is superior to Domain Confusion, DANN, CoGAN, DSNw/DANN, ADDA, DIFA and RAAN that are based on the feature-level adversarial method. This mainly owes to the proposed BADA model being able to capture the semantic contents transferred from the source domain to the target, by learning a bidirectional discriminative pixel-to-pixel mapping.

– Compared with pixel-level methods, our model outperforms the best competitor, pixel-DA on the M→M-M task, which is also an unsupervised pixel-level domain adaptation model with GAN. However, the pixelDA algorithm assumes that there are similar backgrounds between the source and target domain, which cannot perform well on more difficult S→M task. While our model outperforms the state-of-the-art CyCADA [8] model with a accuracy gap greater than 2.5% on the S→M task. This indicates the advantage of using the bidirectional pixel-level mapping with semantic consistency than the unidirectional pixel-level mapping with content similarity in pixelDA.

– Furthermore, the comparisons with CyCADA and SBADA-GAN also show the superiority of our bidirectional semantic consistency constraint. Although the SBADA-GAN method combines the source and target classifier for final prediction, which achieved the best performance on two tasks, our method outperforms it with accuracy gaps greater than 16.4% on the more difficult S→M task.

4.4   Evaluation on Semantic Consistency

Qualitative Analysis. In order to ensure that the proposed model could learn two semantic consistent mappings, we first visualize the bidirectional mapping results of the model in different tasks. As shown in Fig. 3, the proposed BADA learns a semantic consistent forward mapping from the source domain to the target with an inverted semantic consistent mapping simultaneously.

Quantitative Analysis. Furthermore, we demonstrate the quantitative analysis of the semantic consistency in Table 3. The first three rows represent the accuracy of original source image $\mathbf{x}_s$ on source classifier, generated target image $G_{ST}(\mathbf{x}_s)$ on the adapted target classifier C_T, and the reconstructed source image $G_{TS}(G_{ST}(\mathbf{x}_s))$ on the source classifier C_S, respectively. Accordingly, the last

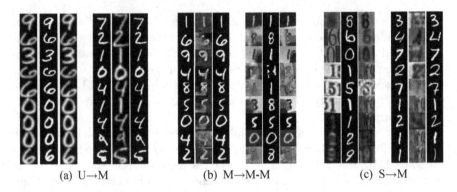

(a) U→M   (b) M→M-M   (c) S→M

Fig. 3. The visualization of pixel-to-pixel mapping: The left triple shows the mapping from the source domain to the target domain and back to the original source domain. The right triple shows the inverted mapping. Each triple consists of the original image (left), the generated image (middle), and the reconstructed image (right).

three rows report the accuracy of target image $\mathbf{x}_t$ on the adapted target classifier, generated source image $G_{TS}(\mathbf{x}_t)$ on the well-trained source classifier C_S, and the reconstructed target image $G_{ST}(G_{TS}(\mathbf{x}_t))$ on the target classifier C_T. We can observe that both the transferred and reconstructed images are recognizable by the corresponding classifiers, which can prove the semantic consistency during our dual pixel-to-pixel mappings. A comparison between the $4th$ row and $5th$ rows in Table 3 shows that the performance of the adapted target images on the source classifier C_S could even nearly equal to the performance of the real target images on the target classifier. It indicates that the well-trained source classifier C_S can be shared with the target domain, while we only need to transfer the target image to the source image by the mapping we have learnt.

Table 3. Qualitative analysis of semantic consistency.

Method	M→U	U→M	M→M-M	S→M
$C_S(\mathbf{x}_s)$	0.9956	0.9729	0.9956	0.9308
$C_T(G_{ST}(\mathbf{x}_s))$	0.9821	0.9640	0.9902	0.8941
$C_S(G_{TS}(G_{ST}(\mathbf{x}_s)))$	0.9868	0.9670	0.9935	0.8721
$C_T(\mathbf{x}_t)$	0.9483	0.9689	0.9872	0.9254
$C_S(G_{TS}(\mathbf{x}_t))$	0.9550	0.9675	0.9907	0.9113
$C_T(G_{ST}(G_{TS}(\mathbf{x}_t)))$	0.9432	0.9663	0.9866	0.9008

4.5   Ablation Study

Effect of Feature-Level Similarity Loss. The feature-level similarity loss L_{fea} is used to encourage the robustness of model. In order to investigate the effect of the feature-level similarity loss in more detail, we develop and evaluate two variations of BADA: BADA without L_{fea} and BADA, while keeping the optimization procedure in the same way. Table 2 shows the performance of two variations on the four widely adopted tasks. We can observe that BADA without L_{fea} has similar performances with BADA in different domain adaptation tasks, but one task on the S→M, where BADA performs much better. We infer that the pixel-level mapping combined with L_{fea} could capture more difficult domain shifts to get higher performance. Furthermore, we visualize the distribution of the target images in task S→M after training on source only and BADA using t-SNE tool respectively. A comparison between Fig. 4(a) and Fig. 4(b) reveals that our semantic consistent pixel-level BADA without L_{fea} still has the ability to learn an adapted classifier for unsupervised target domain. Furthermore, as shown in Fig. 4(b) and Fig. 4(c), the proposed model combined with feature-level similarity loss further boosts the performance.

(a) Source only   (b) BADA without L_{fea} (c) BADA

Fig. 4. The t-SNE visualizations of target domain samples features trained on (a) source only, (b) BADA without L_{fea}, (c) BADA with L_{fea} for the S→M task. We use 1000 test samples to generate the t-SNE plots.

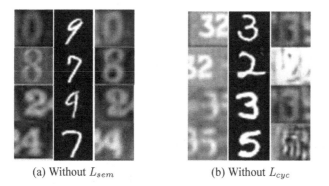

(a) Without L_{sem} (b) Without L_{cyc}

Fig. 5. The domain adaptation results of the proposed BADA without semantic consistency or without cycle consistency. In subfigures (a) and (b), a triple in each row consists of three images: (i) *left* is the source SVHN image; (ii) *middle* is the generated target MNIST image; and (iii) *right* is the reconstructed source SVHN image.

Effect of Consistency in BADA. In this scenario, we verify the importance of the *cycle consistency loss* L_{cyc} and *semantic consistency loss* L_{sem} for our pixel-to-pixel mapping. We developed and assessed two variations of our BADA: no semantic consistency or no semantic consistency, which mean BADA without L_{sem} or without L_{cyc}, respectively, while keeping the other loss satisfied and use the similar optimization. Figure 5 shows the results of the mapping from the source domain to the target domain, and back to the original source domain in pixel-level. When there is no semantic consistency but with cycle consistency, the mapping from the source domain to the target domain suffers the shift of semantic contents, despite the good reconstruction of the original images. Conversely, when there is no cycle consistency but with semantic consistency, the middle mapping could preserve the semantic contents, although, the reconstructed source images are failed to be consistent with the original images. The two cases indicate that both the cycle consistency and semantic consistency contribute to the overall performance of model.

Parameter Sensitive Analysis. In this scenario, we evaluate the sensitiveness of the hyper-parameter λ_{cyc} and λ_{sem} on the performance of unsupervised domain adaptation. In the objective function Eq. 9, λ_{cyc} and λ_{sem} control the contributions of cycle consistency and semantic consistency respectively. Here, we conduct the experiments on the SVHN $\rightarrow$ MNIST task, where 2000 samples randomly selected from target test set as a validation set. Specifically, we explore the different λ_{cyc} and λ_{sem} from $0, 0.5, 1.0, 2.0, 4.0$. As aforementioned, $\lambda_{cyc} = 0$ and $\lambda_{sem} = 0$ indicate the proposed BADA without cycle consistency or without semantic consistency, respectively. The evaluation is conducted by changing one parameter (e.g. $Lcyc$) while keeping the other hyper-parameters fixed. As shown in Fig. 6, both λ_{cyc} and λ_{sem} are important to the overall performance. Note that, when $\lambda_{sem} = 0$, the model performs badly. Thus it indicates that the λ_{sem} plays an essential role in the proposed model.

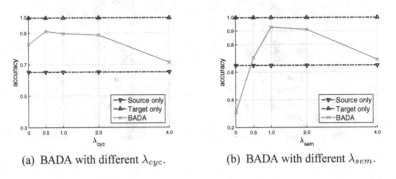

(a) BADA with different λ_{cyc}.   (b) BADA with different λ_{sem}.

Fig. 6. Effect of model parameters (a) λ_{cyc} and (b) λ_{sem} in the proposed BADA.

5   Conclusion

In this paper, we proposed a novel BADA model to adapt the source domain images to appear as if drawn from the target domain by learning a pair of bidirectional pixel-level mappings that keep semantic consistency. BADA is capable to transfer the label information from the source domain to the target domain to learn a good target classifier, meanwhile it is advantaged to adapt the target images to the source domain to share the well-trained source classifier. Comprehensive experimental results on some widely used benchmark datasets show that the proposed BADA method outperforms the state-of-the-art domain adaptation methods with advances on superior visualization and semantic consistency analysis.

References

1. Bousmalis, K., Silberman, N., Dohan, D., Erhan, D., Krishnan, D.: Unsupervised pixel-level domain adaptation with generative adversarial networks. In: Proceedings of the CVPR (2017)
2. Bousmalis, K., Trigeorgis, G., Silberman, N., Krishnan, D., Erhan, D.: Domain separation networks. In: Proceedings of the NIPS (2016)
3. Chen, Q., Liu, Y., Wang, Z., Wassell, I., Chetty, K.: Re-weighted adversarial adaptation network for unsupervised domain adaptation. In: Proceedings of the CVPR (2018)
4. Fernando, B., Habrard, A., Sebban, M., Tuytelaars, T.: Unsupervised visual domain adaptation using subspace alignment. In: Proceedings of the ICCV (2013)
5. Ganin, Y., Ustinova, E., Ajakan, H., Germain, P., Larochelle, H., Laviolette, F., Marchand, M., Lempitsky, V.: Domain-adversarial training of neural networks. J. Mach. Learn. Res. 17(1), 2030–2096 (2016)
6. Ghifary, M., Kleijn, W.B., Zhang, M., Balduzzi, D., Li, W.: Deep reconstruction-classification networks for unsupervised domain adaptation. In: Leibe, B., Matas, J., Sebe, N., Welling, M. (eds.) ECCV 2016. LNCS, vol. 9908, pp. 597–613. Springer, Cham (2016). https://doi.org/10.1007/978-3-319-46493-0_36
7. He, K., Zhang, X., Ren, S., Sun, J.: Deep residual learning for image recognition. In: Proceedings of the CVPR (2016)
8. Hoffman, J., et al.: CyCADA: cycle-consistent adversarial domain adaptation. In: Proceedings of the ICML (2018)
9. Huang, G., Liu, Z., Weinberger, K.Q., van der Maaten, L.: Densely connected convolutional networks. In: Proceedings of the CVPR, vol. 1, p. 3 (2017)
10. Hull, J.J.: A database for handwritten text recognition research. IEEE Trans. Pattern Anal. Mach. Intell. 16(5), 550–554 (1994)
11. Kim, T., Cha, M., Kim, H., Lee, J.K., Kim, J.: Learning to discover cross-domain relations with generative adversarial networks. In: Proceedings of the ICML (2017)
12. LeCun, Y., Cortes, C., Burges, C.: MNIST handwritten digit database, AT&T Labs, February 2010
13. Liu, M.Y., Tuzel, O.: Coupled generative adversarial networks. In: Proceedings of the NIPS (2016)
14. Long, M., Cao, Y., Wang, J., Jordan, M.I.: Learning transferable features with deep adaptation networks. arXiv preprint arXiv:1502.02791 (2015)

15. Maas, A.L., Hannun, A.Y., Ng, A.Y.: Rectifier nonlinearities improve neural network acoustic models. In: Proceedings of the ICML (2013)
16. Mao, X., Li, Q., Xie, H., Lau, R.Y., Wang, Z., Smolley, S.P.: Least squares generative adversarial networks. In: Proceedings of the ICCV. IEEE (2017)
17. Murez, Z., Kolouri, S., Kriegman, D., Ramamoorthi, R., Kim, K.: Image to image translation for domain adaptation. In: Proceedings of the CVPR (2018)
18. Nair, V., Hinton, G.E.: Rectified linear units improve restricted boltzmann machines. In: Proceedings of the ICML (2010)
19. Netzer, Y., Wang, T., Coates, A., Bissacco, A., Wu, B., Ng, A.Y.: Reading digits in natural images with unsupervised feature learning. In: NIPS Workshop on Deep Learning and Unsupervised Feature Learning, vol. 2011, p. 5 (2011)
20. Russo, P., Carlucci, F.M., Tommasi, T., Caputo, B.: From source to target and back: symmetric bi-directional adaptive GAN. In: Proceedings of the CVPR (2018)
21. Shrivastava, A., Pfister, T., Tuzel, O., Susskind, J., Wang, W., Webb, R.: Learning from simulated and unsupervised images through adversarial training. In: Proceedings of the CVPR (2017)
22. Sun, B., Feng, J., Saenko, K.: Return of frustratingly easy domain adaptation. In: Proceedings of the AAAI (2016)
23. Sun, B., Saenko, K.: Deep coral: correlation alignment for deep domain adaptation. In: Proceedings of the ECCV (2016)
24. Tzeng, E., Hoffman, J., Darrell, T., Saenko, K.: Simultaneous deep transfer across domains and tasks. In: Proceedings of the ICCV (2015)
25. Tzeng, E., Hoffman, J., Saenko, K., Darrell, T.: Adversarial discriminative domain adaptation. In: Proceedings of the CVPR (2017)
26. Volpi, R., Morerio, P., Savarese, S., Murino, V.: Adversarial feature augmentation for unsupervised domain adaptation. In: Proceedings of the CVPR (2018)
27. Zeiler, M.D.: Adadelta: an adaptive learning rate method. arXiv preprint arXiv:1212.5701 (2012)
28. Zhu, J.Y., Park, T., Isola, P., Efros, A.A.: Unpaired image-to-image translation using cycle-consistent adversarial networks. In: Proceedings of the CVPR (2017)
29. Zhuo, J., Wang, S., Zhang, W., Huang, Q.: Deep unsupervised convolutional domain adaptation. In: Proceedings of the 2017 ACM on Multimedia Conference. ACM (2017)

A Novel Hard Mining Center-Triplet Loss for Person Re-identification

Xinbi Lv[1], Cairong Zhao[1(✉)], and Wei Chen[2,3]

[1] Department of Computer Science and Technology, Tongji University,
Shanghai 201804, China
zhaocairong@tongji.edu.cn
[2] Shanghai Key Laboratory of Crime Scene Evidence, Shanghai, China
[3] Shanghai Research Institute of Criminal Science and Technology,
Shanghai, China

Abstract. Recently, center loss and triplet loss have proved their effectiveness for person re-identification. However, they have difficulties in making optimizations of the intra/inter-class distance and the cost of computing and mining hard training samples simultaneously. To solve these problems, in this paper, we propose a hard mining center-triplet loss, a novel improved strategy of triplet loss. For one thing, it combines the advantages of center loss and triplet loss aiming at minimizing the intra-class distance and maximizing the inter-class distance. For another thing, it employs hard sample mining strategy on the level of center of class instead of individual sample to mine hard triplets with the purpose to reducing the number of hard triplets for training and further reducing the cost of computing. Finally, the results on two large-scale datasets Market1501 and DukeMTMC-reID show the robustness and efficiency of our method in making optimizations of these problems simultaneously and learning robust feature representation, which also demonstrate that our method outperforms most of existing loss function and achieves better performance for person re-identification.

Keywords: Person re-identification · Hard sample mining · Hard mining center-triplet loss

1 Introduction

Person re-identification (ReID) is a challenging task which aims at matching two pedestrian images from non-overlapping camera views. Because of large appearance variations in illumination, posture, viewpoint, misalignment, and background occlusions, ReID becomes a difficult task, some examples are shown in Fig. 1.

Benefited from the development of deep convolution neural networks (CNNs) [2–6], the current work of ReID is mainly to focus on learning robust feature representation by training an end-to-end CNN directly. There are two key sections of this work including the design of CNN and the design of metric loss function. In the process of the design of CNN, most of excellent methods [7–15] use self-designed CNN to learn discriminative feature representation. In the process of the design of metric loss

© Springer Nature Switzerland AG 2019
Z. Lin et al. (Eds.): PRCV 2019, LNCS 11859, pp. 199–210, 2019.
https://doi.org/10.1007/978-3-030-31726-3_17

function, most of previous methods usually adopt softmax loss to train and optimize their networks for the learning of robust feature representation. However, the methods still have a high error rate to classify samples. To solve this problem, many deep metric loss functions [10–12, 17–23] are proposed to replace softmax loss to make optimizations, which mainly focus on minimizing the intra-class distance and maximizing the inter-class distance for clustering of samples. Typical methods are center loss [17] and triplet loss [10].

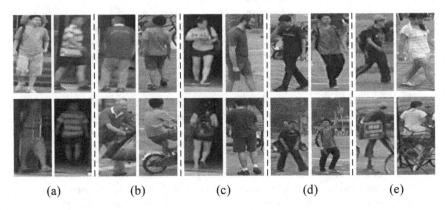

Fig. 1. Some image pairs from the Market1501 [1] dataset. The upper and lower adjacent images have the same identity: (a) variations in illumination. (b) variations in posture. (c) variations in viewpoint. (d) variations in misalignment. (e) variations in background occlusion.

However, center loss and triplet loss still have some shortcomings. Center loss is only designed to pull samples of the same class to their center more closely without the consideration of maximizing the inter-class distance. Triplet loss only requires the inter-class distance larger than the intra-class distance by a predefined margin, without the consideration of minimizing the intra-class distance, which usually results in a relatively large cluster within intra-class. In addition, it has a sharply increasing number of triplets including many negative triplets for training when the dataset is explosive. To deal with the problems of triplet loss, some improved loss functions have been proposed, such as improved triplet loss [11], trihard loss [18], quadruplet loss [12], margin sample mining loss [19], etc. They are better at minimizing the intra-class distance and maximizing the inter-class distance. However, they are suffering from a huge time consuming in mining and training of hard triplets. Thus, the target of metric loss function should be making optimizations of the intra/inter-class distance and the cost of computing and mining hard training samples simultaneously.

Recently, two novel loss functions provide a new idea for us, class-wise triplet loss (CWTL) [24] and triplet-center loss (TCL) [25]. They both successfully attempt to combine the ideas of triplet loss and center loss to solve these three problems. Inspired by them, we propose the hard mining center-triplet loss also with the aim of making optimizations of the intra/inter-class distance and the cost of computing and mining hard training samples simultaneously. It combines with the idea of triplet loss and center loss, which employs hard sample mining strategy on the level of center of class instead of individual sample to calculate triplet loss. Finally, the experimental results show that our method is more efficient than most of other loss functions for ReID. Our main contributions are summarized as follows.

- We propose a novel improved strategy of triplet loss for ReID.
- We propose a hard mining center-triplet loss (HCTL). It can make optimizations of the intra/inter-class distance and the cost of computing and mining hard training samples simultaneously, thereby learns more robust feature representation and achieves better performance than most of existing losses.

2 Related Work

Traditional deep metric learning methods regard ReID as a multiple classification task which usually adopt softmax loss to train and optimize their networks. However, the methods usually result in large clusters in intra-class and heavy overlaps in inter-class, thereby have a high error rate to classify samples. As illustrated in Fig. 2(a). 1, 2 and 3 represent the overlapping areas of different classes.

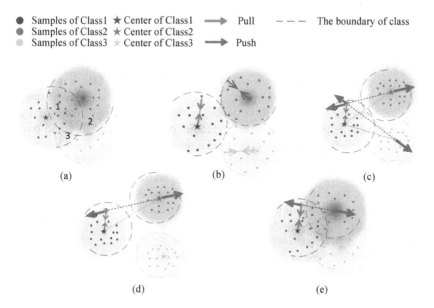

Fig. 2. A visualization illustration of the distributions of samples learned by (a) softmax loss. (b) softmax loss + center loss. (c) softmax loss + CWTL. (d) softmax loss + TCL. And (e) describes the idea of the TCL with hard sample mining.

To improve the performance of ReID, most of deep metric loss functions are proposed. Wen et al. [17] firstly presented the center loss, by learning a center for the same class samples to pull them to their centers. Specifically, the center loss can be formulated as:

$$L_c = \frac{1}{2} \sum_{i=1}^{P*k} \left\| f_i - c_{y^i} \right\|_2^2 \tag{1}$$

where P is the number of classes in mini-batch, K is the number of samples of each class, the c_{y^i} denotes the center features of y^ith class center, f_i denotes the deep features of ith sample.

Since the centers are used with each mini-batch instead of the whole training set, the updating of which is very unstable. It must be under the joint supervision of softmax loss during training process which has a good guider for seeking better class centers. Center loss does not consider how to enlarge inter-class distance and it still has a few overlaps in the inter-class, as shown in Fig. 2(b).

The successful application of facenet [16] in face recognition has led scholars to focus on how to efficiently select the triplets to train the end-to-end network for ReID. Ding et al. [10] made the first attempt at using triplet framework to calculate triplet loss. Triplet loss aims at controlling the intra-class distance less than the inter-class distance by a predefined margin m, which can be computed as:

$$L_{tri} = \sum_{y_a=y_p \neq y_n} a, p, n \ max(d_{a,p} - d_{a,n} + m, 0) \tag{2}$$

where a, p, n denote the anchor, positive and negative in each triplet pair respectively, and m is the margin that is enforced between positive and negative pairs.

However, there are two problems with the classic triplet loss. One is the output of the model may have a relatively large cluster within intra-class samples because the loss only requires the inter-class distance larger than the intra-class distance by the margin m. Another is that the use of large number of negative triplets could produce poor results. Some improved methods have been proposed based on triplet loss to solve the above problems. Concerning the first problem, Cheng et al. [11] optimized the training process of triplet framework by adopting an improved triplet loss which requires to reduce the distance of the pairs from same class less than a margin α (α is much less than m). In terms of the second problem, Hermans et al. [18] proposed the trihard loss which aims at selecting the hardest triplets for training, but mining the hardest triplets was time consuming.

Thus, it is not optimal to only consider the optimizations of the intra/inter-class distance. The optimization for reducing cost of computing and mining of hard samples is also important. Recently, two novel studies have attracted wide attention.

One is Ming et al. [24] proposed the class-wise triplet loss (CWTL) for face recognition. Different from classic triplet loss, it aims to decrease the distance between the anchors and the intra-class centers and enlarge the distance of the anchors to the inter-class centers, by learning the centers of the classes of samples and using them instead of individual samples as the positives and negatives to form the triplets, which can significantly reduce the number of triplets involved in training of model and thus reduce the cost of calculation loss. The CWTL can be formulated as:

$$L_{cwt} = \sum_{i=1}^{p*k} \sum_{l=1, l \neq y^i}^{k} max \left(D \left(f_i, c_{y^i} \right) - D(f_i, c_l) + m, 0 \right) \tag{3}$$

where $D(A, B)$ represents the squared Euclidean distance function denoted as:

$$D(A, B) = \|A - B\|_2^2 \tag{4}$$

As illustrated in Fig. 2(c), the CWTL effectively solves the problems of large clusters within intra-class and heavy overlaps within inter-class.

Another is He et al. [25] proposed the triplet-center loss (TCL) for Multi-View 3D Object Retrieval. Specifically, the proposed TCL can control the distance between the samples and their corresponding center c_{y^i} less than the distance between the samples and their nearest negative center c_l by a margin m. It could be computed as follows:

$$L_{tc} = \sum_{i=1}^{p*k} max \left(D \left(f_i, c_{y^i} \right) - min_{l \neq y^i} D(f_i, c_l) + m, 0 \right) \tag{5}$$

An illustration of the distributions of samples learned by TCL can been seen from Fig. 2(e) to (d).

Inspired by CWTL and TCL, we put forward the hard mining center-triplet loss (HCTL), a novel improved strategy of triplet loss. It can achieve better performance for ReID. The next chapter, we will present our method in detail.

3 Proposed Hard Mining Center–Triplet Loss

For better making optimizations of the intra/inter-class distance and the cost of computing and mining hard training samples simultaneously, we have proposed our method in this chapter. We first describe the design of our loss function in Sect. 3.1, then elaborate the overall CNN model framework and training algorithm of our method in Sect. 3.2. In addition, we compare the advantage of our method with other loss functions in extra Sect. 3.3.

3.1 Hard Mining Center–Triplet Loss Function

Inspired by CWTL and TCL, we propose a metric loss function named hard mining center-triplet loss (HCTL), a novel improved strategy of triplet loss. It aims to learn the centers of the classes of samples and use them instead of individual samples to form the hard triplets. Specifically, we firstly regard the centers of all classes as the anchors in the mini-batch. For each center, we select the hardest positive sample which has the farthest distance to it with the same class label and the hardest negative sample which has the closest distance to it with the different class label. Then we use them to form the hard triplet pair for computing the triplet loss. Our HCTL will control the distance between the center c_p and its farthest positive sample less than the distance between the center c_p and its nearest negative sample by a predefined margin m. In summary, the hard mining center-triplet loss we defined is as follows:

$$L_{hct} = \frac{1}{P}\sum_{p=1}^{p} max\big(max_{1 \leq i \leq k}\big(D\big(c_p, f_{p^i}\big)\big) - min_{l \neq p, 1 \leq l \leq p, 1 \leq j \leq k}\big(D\big(c_p, f_{lj}\big)\big) + m, 0\big)$$

$$(6)$$

where c_p denotes the deep features of pth class center, f_{p^i} denotes the deep features of the ith sample in pth class.

An illustration of the distributions of samples learned by HCTL can been seen in Fig. 3.

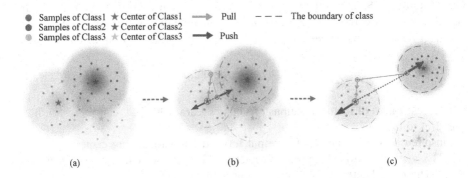

Fig. 3. A visualization illustration of the distributions of samples learned by (a) softmax loss and (c) softmax loss + HCTL. And (b) describes the process of mining the hardest triplets.

3.2   Our Deep Convolutional Neural Network Architecture

The specific network architecture of our proposed method is shown in Fig. 4.

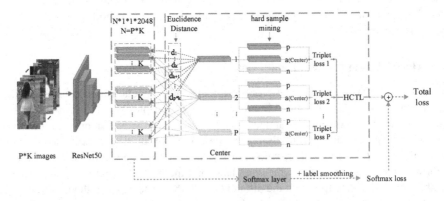

Fig. 4. Proposed deep convolutional neural network

We first use ResNet50 [6] as the base model. In each mini-batch, images are resized into 256×128 pixels as inputs and the 2048-d deep features are extracted through the average pooling layer after the conv5_x layer.

Due to the updating of centers of class is unstable in mini-batch with our HCTL, we also joint it with softmax loss for training. In order to make softmax loss have a better guidance for seeking better class centers, we use the label-smoothing regularization (LSR) [26] to optimize the calculation of softmax loss. Thus, it is divided into two parts and calculated separately HCTL and softmax loss. For the former, the features of centers of classes of training samples are learned by averaging the features of the corresponding classes, then our hard triplets will be mined to compute HCTL by using hard sample mining strategy. For the latter, the deep features will be calculated the softmax loss through an added softmax layer. Finally, we need a hyper-parameter λ to balance HCTL and softmax loss to calculate the total loss, which can be formulated as:

$$L = L_{cls} + \lambda L_{hct} \qquad (7)$$

where L_{cls} denotes the softmax loss, L_{hct} denotes our HCTL, and λ is the weight used to balance the HCTL and softmax loss.

Since the calculation of softmax loss needs an extra softmax layer, we should make optimizations of HCTL and softmax loss separately during back propagation. Finally, Algorithm 1 shows the main procedure of the training by our method.

Algorithm 1. Hard Mining Center-Triplet Loss Training Algorithm

Input: Training samples $\{I_i\}$. Initialized networks parameters $\{\omega\}$. Initialized softmax layer parameters $\{\vartheta\}$ of softmax loss. Hyperparameter λ and learning rate μ. The number of iteration $t \leftarrow 0$.

Output: The networks parameters $\{\omega\}$.

1: while $t \leq T$ do
2:     $t \leftarrow t + 1$;
3:     Calculate deep features of samples f_{p^i} by forward propagation;
4:     Calculate the distance $\max\limits_{1 \leq i \leq K} \left(D\left(c_p, f_{p^i}\right) \right)$, $\min\limits_{\substack{l \neq p, 1 \leq l \leq P, \\ 1 \leq j \leq K}} \left(D\left(c_p, f_{l^j}\right) \right)$
5:     Calculate the total loss $L = L_{cls} + \lambda L_{hct}$
6:     Calculate the $\frac{\partial L_{cls}}{\partial \omega}$, $\frac{\partial L_{hct}}{\partial \omega}$ by back propagation
7:     Update the softmax layer parameters $\{\vartheta\}$ of softmax loss
       $\vartheta^{t+1} = \vartheta^t - \mu^t \cdot \frac{\partial L_{cls}}{\partial \vartheta^t}$
8:     Update the networks parameters $\omega^{t+1} = \omega^t - \mu^t \cdot \frac{\partial L}{\partial \omega^t}$
       $= \omega^t - \mu^t \left(\frac{\partial L_{cls}}{\partial \omega} + \lambda \cdot \frac{\partial L_{hct}}{\partial \omega} \right)$
9: end while

3.3   Compared with Other Loss Functions

We compare the proposed method with the similar methods in optimization of metric loss function. Now most methods adopt softmax loss, center loss, triplet loss or their varieties to optimize network. Different from them, our HCTL makes the first attempt that regards the center of class as the anchor, the farthest positive sample as the positive and the nearest negative sample as the negative, to form a new hard triplet pair for calculating triplet loss.

Specially, if randomly select P classes of samples and then randomly sample K images from each class to form a mini-batch for training, there will be a large set of P*K*(K-1)*(P-1)*K triplets. Since CWTL uses the centers of the classes to represent the global distribution of the classes rather than the individual samples, which only have K-1 triplets for each sample, totally there is a set of P*K*(K−1) triplets to be chosen to train CNN by using CWTL. The design of TCL combines the advantages of trihard loss and center loss. For each sample, TCL only selects the hardest negative center as negative to form the triplet, which have one triplet for each anchor. Finally, P*K triplets will be constructed for one mini-batch, which is same with trihard loss. Far less than neither of them, our HCTL only considers the distance of a center to the farthest intra-class sample and the distance to closest inter-class sample, only P hard triplets are selected in each mini-batch. Thus, our HCTL is more efficient in optimizing the intra/inter-class distance and the cost of computing and mining hard training samples.

In next chapter, we will compare the proposed loss with several simialr loss functions and show improvement performance of our method.

4   Experiments

In this section, we firstly show the processes and the results of the experiments with different loss functions for ReID, then we compare the performance of the proposed method with them.

4.1   Datasets

We conduct experiments on two representative large-scale datasets Market1501 and DukeMTMC-reID [27], respectively.

Market1501 is one of the largest benchmark datasets for ReID, which contains 32,668 images of 1,501 identities from 6 camera views. Each identity is captured by at most six cameras. There are 751 identities in the training set and 750 identities in the testing set.

DukeMTMC-reID is a subset of the DukeMTMC [28] tracking dataset, which contains 36,411 images with 1,812 identities captured from 8 different viewpoints. Specifically, there are 16,522 images with 702 identities for training, 17,661 images with 1,110 identities in gallery, and another 2,228 images with 702 identities in the gallery for query.

4.2 Implementation Details

In our experiments, every 32 images are randomly selected to form a mini-batch for training, which contains 8 identities and each identity has 4 images. For optimization, the standard AMSGrad [29] algorithm is adopted for faster and more robust back propagation and loss convergence. The initial learning rate of softmax loss and the initial learning rate of HCTL are both set to 3e−4. The weight of the hard mining center-triplet loss λ is set to 0.001, and the predefined margin m that control the intra-class distance less than the inter-class distance is set to 0.3.

4.3 Experimental Results and Analysis

We conduct experiments with different loss functions on the standard ResNet50 and evaluate them with rank-1, 5, 10 accuracy and mAP to illustrate the robustness and efficiency of our proposed loss. Classic Triplet stands for the classic triplet loss [10], Quadruplet stands for quadruplet loss [12], OIM stands for Online Instance Matching Loss [22], Cluster loss stands for cluster loss [20], Trihard stands for the trihard loss [18], and Softmax stands for softmax loss with LSR. We also combine ring loss [23], center loss [17], range loss [21], class-wise triplet loss (CWTL), triplet-center loss (TCL), and our hard mining center-triplet loss (HCTL) with Softmax. The results on two datasets are shown in Tables 1, 2 and Fig. 5.

Results Analysis on Market1501. As clearly seen in Table 1, our HCTL gets 73.8% mAP and 88.4% rank-1 accuracy, which outperforms all compared losses, exceeding the 2nd best TCL by 2.1% in rank-1 and 4% in mAP. Compared with softmax loss, adding HCTL could increase accuracy by 6.4% on rank-1 and 10.2% on mAP. Compared with trihard loss, they also increase by 3.7% and 4.8%.

Table 1. Scores of different loss for ReID on Market1501. The best scores are in red.

Method	MAP	Rank-1	Rank-5	Rank-10
Classic Triplet	54.8	75.9	89.6	--
Quadruplet	61.1	80.0	91.8	--
Softmax	63.6	82.0	92.8	95.2
OIM	62.5	83.0	93.1	95.2
Softmax+Ring loss	66.9	83.4	93.5	95.7
Softmax+Center loss	66.4	84.1	94.2	96.3
Softmax+Range loss	66.2	84.4	94.0	96.1
Softmax+CWTL	68.0	85.2	93.6	96.0
Trihard	69.0	84.7	94.2	96.2
Cluster loss	71.5	86.1	95.0	--
Softmax+TCL	69.8	86.3	94.2	96.3
Softmax+HCTL（Our）	73.8	88.4	95.5	97.3

Table 2. Scores of different loss for ReID on DukeMTMC-reID. The best scores are in red.

Method	MAP	Rank-1	Rank-5	Rank-10
Softmax	48.5	68.9	82.4	86.6
Softmax+Center loss	50.0	70.0	83.3	87.6
Softmax+Ring loss	51.3	70.7	83.5	87.0
Softmax+CWTL	52.0	72.2	84.2	88.0
Softmax+TCL	53.2	72.1	84.4	88.6
Softmax+Range loss	54.1	73.3	85.5	89.0
OIM loss	54.6	73.1	85.9	91.5
Trihard loss	57.7	74.5	86.4	89.5
Softmax+HCTL（Our）	55.8	75.2	87.0	90.4

Results Analysis on DukeMTMC-reID. On DukeMTMC-reID, our HCTL also gains the highest rank-1 accuracy and the 2nd best mAP. Although the performance does not improve much compared with trihard loss, fewer hard triplets are mined for training with our HCTL. It has a significantly reduction of the cost of computing and mining hard training samples. Compared with softmax loss, adding our HCTL could increase the rank-1 accuracy and mAP by 6.3% and 7.3%.

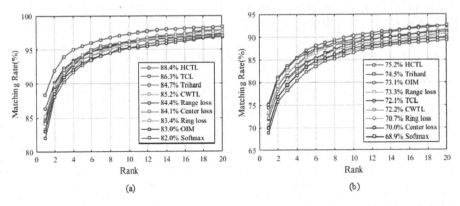

Fig. 5. The CMC curves and rank-1 accuracy on two datasets: (a) Comparison with different loss on Market1501. (b) Comparison with different loss on DukeMTMC-reID.

In summary, compared with excellent loss functions above all, our loss is more efficient in training networks and making optimizations of the intra/inter-class distance and the cost of computing and mining hard training samples simultaneously. It can learn more robust features and achieve better performance than them.

5   Conclusion

In this paper, we firstly reviewed and analyzed the performance of different metric loss function for person re-identification. Inspired by them, we have proposed our hard mining center-triplet loss, a novel improved strategy of triplet loss, which builds the hardest triplet pair for computing loss. It can effectively make optimizations of the intra/inter-class distance and the cost of computing and mining hard training samples simultaneously, thereby enhance learning more robust feature representation. Finally, the experiments on two large-scale datasets Market1501 and DukeMTMC-reID show the robustness and efficiency of our method and demonstrate that our method outperforms most of the state-of-the-art loss functions and achieves better performance for person re-identification. In the future, we would like to verify this effectiveness of our proposed loss on more datasets and models.

Acknowledgement. The authors would like to thank the anonymous reviewers for their critical and constructive comments and suggestions. This work was supported by the China National Natural Science Foundation under Grant No. 61673299, 61203247, 61573259, 61573255.

References

1. Zheng, L., Shen, L., Tian, L., et al.: Scalable person re-identification: a benchmark. In: Proceedings of the IEEE International Conference on Computer Vision, pp. 1116–1124 (2015)
2. Krizhevsky, A., Sutskever, I., Hinton, G.E.: ImageNet classification with deep convolutional neural networks. In: Advances in Neural Information Processing Systems, pp. 1097–1105 (2012)
3. Zeiler, M.D., Fergus, R.: Visualizing and understanding convolutional networks. In: Fleet, D., Pajdla, T., Schiele, B., Tuytelaars, T. (eds.) ECCV 2014. LNCS, vol. 8689, pp. 818–833. Springer, Cham (2014). https://doi.org/10.1007/978-3-319-10590-1_53
4. Simonyan, K., Zisserman, A.: Very deep convolutional networks for large-scale image recognition. arXiv preprint arXiv:1409.1556 (2014)
5. Szegedy, C., Liu, W., Jia, Y., et al.: Going deeper with convolutions. In: Proceedings of the IEEE Conference on Computer Vision and Pattern Recognition, pp. 1–9 (2015)
6. He, K., Zhang, X., Ren, S., et al.: Deep residual learning for image recognition. In: Proceedings of the IEEE Conference on Computer Vision and Pattern Recognition, pp. 770–778 (2016)
7. Li, W., Zhao, R., Xiao, T., et al.: DeepReID: deep filter pairing neural network for person re-identification. In: Proceedings of the IEEE Conference on Computer Vision and Pattern Recognition, pp. 152–159 (2014)
8. Li, S., Liu, X., Liu, W., et al.: A discriminative null space based deep learning approach for person re-identification. In: 2016 4th International Conference on Cloud Computing and Intelligence Systems (CCIS), pp. 480–484. IEEE (2016)
9. Varior, R.R., Haloi, M., Wang, G.: Gated siamese convolutional neural network architecture for human re-identification. In: Leibe, B., Matas, J., Sebe, N., Welling, M. (eds.) ECCV 2016. LNCS, vol. 9912, pp. 791–808. Springer, Cham (2016). https://doi.org/10.1007/978-3-319-46484-8_48
10. Ding, S., Lin, L., Wang, G., et al.: Deep feature learning with relative distance comparison for person re-identification. Pattern Recogn. **48**(10), 2993–3003 (2015)

11. Cheng, D., Gong, Y., Zhou, S., et al.: Person re-identification by multi-channel parts-based CNN with improved triplet loss function. In: Proceedings of the IEEE Conference on Computer Vision and Pattern Recognition, pp. 1335–1344 (2016)

12. Chen, W., Chen, X., Zhang, J., et al.: Beyond triplet loss: a deep quadruplet network for person re-identification. In: Proceedings of the IEEE Conference on Computer Vision and Pattern Recognition, pp. 403–412 (2017)

13. Zhang, X., Luo, H., Fan, X., et al.: AlignedReID: surpassing human-level performance in person re-identification. arXiv preprint arXiv:1711.08184 (2017)

14. Wu, S., Chen, Y.C., Li, X., et al.: An enhanced deep feature representation for person re-identification. In: 2016 IEEE Winter Conference on Applications of Computer Vision (WACV), pp. 1–8. IEEE (2016)

15. Zhao, H., Tian, M., Sun, S., et al.: Spindle Net: person re-identification with human body region guided feature decomposition and fusion. In: Proceedings of the IEEE Conference on Computer Vision and Pattern Recognition, pp. 1077–1085 (2017)

16. Schroff, F., Kalenichenko, D., Philbin, J.: FaceNet: a unified embedding for face recognition and clustering. In: Proceedings of the IEEE Conference on Computer Vision and Pattern Recognition, pp. 815–823 (2015)

17. Wen, Y., Zhang, K., Li, Z., Qiao, Yu.: A discriminative feature learning approach for deep face recognition. In: Leibe, B., Matas, J., Sebe, N., Welling, M. (eds.) ECCV 2016. LNCS, vol. 9911, pp. 499–515. Springer, Cham (2016). https://doi.org/10.1007/978-3-319-46478-7_31

18. Hermans, A., Beyer, L., Leibe, B.: In defense of the triplet loss for person re-identification. arXiv preprint arXiv:1703.07737 (2017)

19. Xiao, Q., Luo, H., Zhang, C.: Margin sample mining loss: a deep learning based method for person re-identification. arXiv preprint arXiv:1710.00478 (2017)

20. Alex, D., Sami, Z., Banerjee, S., et al.: Cluster Loss for Person Re-Identification. arXiv preprint arXiv:1812.10325 (2018)

21. Zhang, X., Fang, Z., Wen, Y., et al.: Range loss for deep face recognition with long-tailed training data. In: Proceedings of the IEEE International Conference on Computer Vision, pp. 5409–5418 (2017)

22. Xiao, T., Li, S., Wang, B., et al.: Joint detection and identification feature learning for person search. In: Proceedings of the IEEE Conference on Computer Vision and Pattern Recognition, pp. 3415–3424 (2017)

23. Zheng, Y., Pal, D.K., Savvides, M.: Ring loss: convex feature normalization for face recognition. In: Proceedings of the IEEE Conference on Computer Vision and Pattern Recognition, pp. 5089–5097 (2018)

24. Ming, Z., Chazalon, J., Luqman, M.M., et al.: Simple triplet loss based on intra/inter-class metric learning for face verification. In: 2017 IEEE International Conference on Computer Vision Workshops (ICCVW), pp. 1656–1664. IEEE (2017)

25. He, X., Zhou, Y., Zhou, Z., et al.: Triplet-center loss for multi-view 3D object retrieval. In: Proceedings of the IEEE Conference on Computer Vision and Pattern Recognition, pp. 1945–1954 (2018)

26. Szegedy, C., Vanhoucke, V., Ioffe, S., et al.: Rethinking the inception architecture for computer vision. In: Proceedings of the IEEE Conference on Computer Vision and Pattern Recognition, pp. 2818–2826 (2016)

27. Zheng, Z., Zheng, L., Yang, Y.: Unlabeled samples generated by GAN improve the person re-identification baseline in vitro. In: Proceedings of the IEEE International Conference on Computer Vision, pp. 3754–3762 (2017)

28. Ristani, E., Solera, F., Zou, R., Cucchiara, R., Tomasi, C.: Performance measures and a data set for multi-target, multi-camera tracking. In: Hua, G., Jégou, H. (eds.) ECCV 2016. LNCS, vol. 9914, pp. 17–35. Springer, Cham (2016). https://doi.org/10.1007/978-3-319-48881-3_2

29. Reddi, S.J., Kale, S., Kumar, S.: On the convergence of adam and beyond (2018)

Kinematic Feature-Based Evaluation Method for Elderly Balance Ability by Using Factor Analysis

Rui Ming[1,2] , Xing-Rong Fan[1(✉)] , and Guoliang Xu[3]

[1] Chongqing Engineering Laboratory for Detection,
Control and Integrated System, Chongqing Technology and Business University,
Chongqing 400067, China
fanxingrong@ctbu.edu.cn
[2] College of Communication and Information Engineering,
Chongqing University of Posts and Telecommunications,
Chongqing 400065, China
[3] Electronic Information and Networking Research Institute,
Chongqing University of Posts and Telecommunications,
Chongqing 400065, China

Abstract. Modeling and assessing balance ability for elderly people is an important and realistic task with a view to assisting them in mobility status, correcting postures and preventing accidental falling. The aim of this study was to develop a novel kinematic feature-based evaluation method for elderly balance ability by using factor analysis. Based on the kinematics, twenty-five feature indicators were first extracted from walking gait data, which were collected by deploying twenty-four monitoring points on the body of the elderly subjects. Then, two main factors were identified by using factor analysis that affect the walking balance ability of the elderly, and the comprehensive evaluation scoring model of the elderly balance ability was constructed. Finally, real data from all the elderly subjects in free walking state were used to validate our method. The results of empirical analysis confirm the validity and usefulness of the proposed method.

Keywords: Evaluation method · Elderly balance ability · Kinematic feature · Factor analysis

1 Introduction

Falling is a major problem of elderly people because it may cause severe injuries and many complications in elderly people. As a result, the side effects can be so debilitating as to accelerate body failure. Besides, the fear from falling may impair the ability to move and maintain balance and posture, which therefore worsen the quality of life significantly. Consequently, it is of great realistic importance to develop a balance

Student as first author. This work was supported by the Natural Science Foundation of Chongqing, China (cstc2018jcyjAX0587) and Scientific research platform open project of Chongqing Technology and Business University (KFJJ2018059).

© Springer Nature Switzerland AG 2019
Z. Lin et al. (Eds.): PRCV 2019, LNCS 11859, pp. 211–222, 2019.
https://doi.org/10.1007/978-3-030-31726-3_18

ability evaluation method for elderly people with a view to assisting them in mobility status, correcting postures and preventing accidental falling.

Early time domain parameters (*e.g.*, swing distance and swing speed) and frequency domain features (*e.g.*, power spectrum) were used to evaluate the elderly balance ability [1]. Then, more characteristic parameters were derived from distance, position, amplitude distribution, area, velocity, power spectrum and vector to analyze the relationship between these parameters and balance ability [2, 3]. However, in the current related work, most parameters are not sensitive to age and reflect static balance characteristics mainly and the lack of research on the effectiveness of gait parameters reflecting balance ability leads to blind and one-sided selection of gait characteristics [4, 5]. Gait symmetry is also an important feature of describing gait, which is closely related to the risk of fall, but is rarely involved in existing research. Therefore, our main interest is to develop a novel kinematic feature-based evaluation method for elderly balance ability by using factor analysis, which help them correct their postures and prevent accidental falling. The main contributions are summarized as follows:

1. Based on the kinematics, we extract twenty-five feature indicators from walking gait data.
2. We identify two main factors from twenty-five feature indicators by using factor analysis, and then establish a comprehensive evaluation scoring model of the elderly balance ability according to the variance contribution rate of the first two factors.
3. We develop a kinematic feature-based evaluation method to quantitatively assess the walking balance ability of the elderly.

This paper is structured as follows. Section 2 gives data description and extraction of feature indicators. Section 3 describes the proposed method. Section 4 present results and discussions, and Sect. 5 summarizes the paper.

2   Data Description and Extraction of Feature Indicators

2.1   Experimental Data

In order to acquire gait experimental data for walking of the elderly, a random sampling test is made by deploying twenty-four monitoring points on the body of the elderly subjects [6]. See the layout of the points indicated in the Fig. 1. The data contains the coordinates of these twenty-four monitoring points of each subject.

Basic Data for Elderly People. The basic data of a total of seventy-nine elderly people are collected, including their Number, Sex, Age, Height, Weight, BMI (Body Mass Index) and Fall times in one year. Table 1 gives the basic data of the elderly people (Samples data from eight elderly people are given).

Walking Gait Data for Each Elderly Subject. The gait data are gathered in the free walking state and contain the coordinates of these twenty-four monitoring points of each elderly subject. Table 2 gives walking gait data for each elderly subject. In Table 2, the first column is Frame sequence, the second column is Time, and starting from the third column, each of the three columns represents the motion coordinates of the monitoring points (x, y, z), for a total of twenty-four monitoring points.

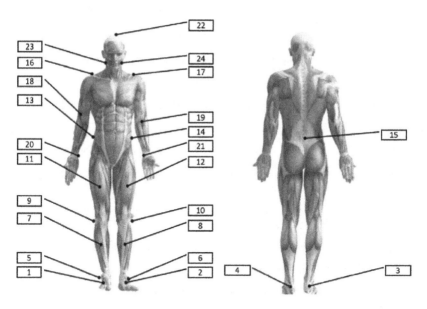

Fig. 1. The layout of the twenty-four monitoring points for the body of the elderly subjects

Table 1. Basic data of elderly people

Number	Sex	Age	Height	Weight	BMI	Fall times in one year
9	Male	66	164.8	73.1	26.91553	0
13	Female	67	151.1	56.1	24.57163	0
26	Female	70	161.9	61.2	23.34843	1
40	Female	64	159.8	61.2	23.96613	0
53	Male	64	162.2	56.5	21.47567	0
61	Female	65	151	57	24.9989	0
67	Female	65	157.5	72.9	29.38776	0
76	Female	64	165.6	61.1	22.28027	0

Table 2. Walking gait data for each elderly subject

Frame sequence	Time	Monitoring point 1			...	Monitoring point 24		
		x	y	z	...	x	y	z
1	0	−400.33051	160.61575	116.47953	...	−148.18779	390.34433	1409.57141
2	0.017	−364.45184	165.86482	118.15626	...	−135.38573	392.40829	1410.90454
3	0.033	−327.4585	171.01143	118.95445	...	−122.67791	394.35785	1412.24402
...	...	...	...	...	...	...	...	...
179	2.967	2342.21289	195.69763	38.71908	...	2155.9812	342.29654	1400.6626
180	2.983	2342.18311	195.49048	38.72082	...	2167.92505	341.19678	1401.2522
181	3	2342.17627	195.40556	38.7226	...	2179.64136	340.27466	1401.95886
...	...	...	...	...	...	...	...	...

2.2   Feature Indicators Extraction Based on the Kinematics

The gait reflects the dynamic posture of human body in free walking state, which follows certain law of motion. Besides, the kinematic parameters of the gait can be expressed by spatial and time parameters, such as swing phase, step size and step stride. Thus, we extract the twenty-five feature indicators from walking gait data based the kinematics. These feature indicators are summarized as follows:

Left Support Phase. Left support phase (TL_{stand}) is the time when the left lower limb is in contact with the ground in a gait cycle, $TL_{stand} = t_{down}^2 - t_{up}^4$, where t_{down}^2 is the landing time of the left toe of the second point and t_{up}^4 is the departure time of the left toe of the fourth point in the gait cycle.

Right Support Phase. Right support phase (TR_{stand}) is the time when the right lower limb is in contact with the ground in a gait cycle, $TR_{stand} = t_{down}^1 - t_{up}^3$, where t_{down}^1 is the landing time of the right toe of the first point and t_{up}^3 is the departure time of the left heel of the third point in the gait cycle.

Left Swing Phase. Left swing phase (TL_{sway}) refers to the swinging time of the left lower limb in the air during a gait cycle, $TL_{sway} = t_{down}^4 - t_{up}^2$, where t_{down}^4 is the landing time of the left heel of the third point in the gait cycle.

Right Swing Phase. Right swing phase (TR_{sway}) refers to the swinging time of the right lower limb in the air during a gait cycle, $TR_{sway} = t_{down}^3 - t_{up}^1$, where t_{down}^3 is the landing time of the right heel of the first point in the gait cycle.

The Cycle of Left Walk. The cycle of left walk (TL_{cycle}) refers to the time period from the landing time of the left lower limb to the next landing time in the walking, $TL_{cycle} = t_{down}^4(N) - t_{down}^4(N-1)$, where $t_{down}^4(N)$ is the landing time of the left heel of the fourth point in the N-th of the gait cycle.

The Cycle of Right Walk. The cycle of right walk (TR_{cycle}) refers to the time period from the landing time of the right lower limb to the next landing time in the walking, $TR_{cycle} = t_{down}^3(N) - t_{down}^3(N-1)$, where $t_{down}^3(N)$ is the landing time of the right heel of the third point in the N-th of the gait cycle.

The Length of Left Step. The length of left step (LL_{step}) refers to the distance between the left heel strike and the opposite heel strike in the walking,
$$LL_{step} = \sqrt{\left(x_{down}^4(N) - x_{down}^3(N-1)\right)^2 + \left(y_{down}^4(N) - y_{down}^3(N-1)\right)^2}.$$

The Length of Right Step. The length of right step (LR_{step}) refers to the distance between the right heel strike and the opposite heel strike in the walking,
$$LR_{step} = \sqrt{\left(x_{down}^3(N) - x_{down}^4(N-1)\right)^2 + \left(y_{down}^3(N) - y_{down}^4(N-1)\right)^2}.$$

The Length of Step Stride of Left Foot. The length of step stride of left foot (LL_{stride}) refers to the coordinate position of the left footprint is the anteroposterior direction

distance of the next footprint on the same side in a gait cycle,
$$LL_{\text{stride}} = \sqrt{\left(x^4_{\text{down}}(N) - x^3_{\text{up}}(N-2)\right)^2 + \left(y^4_{\text{down}}(N) - y^3_{\text{up}}(N-2)\right)^2}.$$

The Length of Step Stride of Right Foot. The length of step stride of right foot (LR_{stride}) refers to the coordinate position of the left footprint is the anteroposterior direction distance of the next footprint on the same side in a gait cycle,
$$LR_{\text{stride}} = \sqrt{\left(x^3_{\text{down}}(N) - x^3_{\text{up}}(N-2)\right)^2 + \left(y^3_{\text{down}}(N) - y^3_{\text{up}}(N-2)\right)^2}.$$

The Step Width. The step width (L_{width}) refers to the distance between the center lines of the feet on both sides of the walk, which is the distance from the center of one side of the footprint to the center of the opposite footprint, $L_{\text{width}} = \left|mx^3_{\text{up}} + b - y^3_{\text{up}}\right|/\sqrt{m^2+1}$, where m and b are constant and can be estimated from the walking gait data.

The Speed of Left-Step. The speed of left-step (VL_{gait}) refers to the distance traveled by the left foot per unit time, $VL_{\text{gait}} = LL_{\text{step}}/TL_{\text{cycle}}$.

The Speed of Right-Step. The speed of right-step (VR_{gait}) refers to the distance traveled by the right foot per unit time, $VR_{gait} = LR_{\text{step}}/TR_{\text{cycle}}$.

Left Walking Rhythm. Left walking rhythm (CL_{gait}) refers to the number of steps of left walking per minute, $CL_{\text{gait}} = 120/TL_{\text{cycle}}$.

Right Walking Rhythm. Right walking rhythm (CR_{gait}) refers to the number of steps of right walking per minute, $CR_{\text{gait}} = 120/TR_{\text{cycle}}$.

Deflection Angle of Left Foot. Deflection angle of left foot (AL_{toe}) refers to the angle between the center line of the left foot and the walking line when walking, $AL_{\text{toe}} = \arctan|(k-m)/(1+km)|$, where k and m are constant and can be estimated from the walking gait data.

Deflection Angle of Right Foot. Deflection angle of right foot (AR_{toe}) refers to the angle between the center line of the right foot and the walking line when walking, $AR_{\text{toe}} = \arctan|(q-m)/(1+qm)|$, where q and m are constant and can be estimated from the walking gait data.

Contralateral Heel to Ground Ratio. Contralateral heel to ground ratio (P_b) refers the elapsed time from the heel strike to the contralateral heel strike in a gait cycle as a percentage of the gait cycle, $P_b = \left(t^4_{\text{down}}(N) - t^3_{\text{down}}(N)\right)/\left(TL_{\text{cycle}}\right)$.

Contralateral Toe Off-ground Ratio. Contralateral toe off-ground ratio (P_f) refers to the elapsed time from the heel strike to the toe off the ground in a gait cycle as a percentage of the gait cycle, $P_f = \left(t^2_{\text{up}} - t^1_{\text{up}}\right)/TL_{\text{cycle}}$.

Double-Feet Support Period. Double-feet support period (S_b) refers to the time when one foot is in contact with the ground during a gait cycle, $S_b = t_{up}^1(N) - t_{down}^4(N) + t_{up}^2(N) - t_{down}^3(N)$.

Swing Amplitude of Left Arm. Swing amplitude of left arm (L_h) describes the height change of the left arm, $L_h = z_{max}^{19}(N) - z_{min}^{19}(N)$.

Swing Amplitude of Right Arm. Swing amplitude of right arm (R_h) describes the height change of the right arm, $R_h = z_{max}^{18}(N) - z_{min}^{18}(N)$.

Swing Frequency of Left Arm. Swing frequency of left arm (TL_h) reflects the number of swings of the left arm in one minute, $TL_h = 60 / (t_{max}^{19}(N) - t_{min}^{19}(N))$.

Swing Frequency of Left Arm. Swing frequency of left arm (TR_h) reflects the number of swings of the right arm in one minute, $TR_h = 60 / (t_{max}^{18}(N) - t_{min}^{18}(N))$.

Head Offset. Head offset ($Bias_{head}$) can indirectly reflect the angle of inclination of the body, but is expressed by two linear equations, $Bias_{head} = \arctan|(k_2 - m)/(1 + k_2 m)|$ where k_2 and m are constant and can be estimated from the walking gait data.

3   Kinematic Feature-Based Evaluation Method

This paper develops a novel kinematic feature-based evaluation method for elderly people's balance ability by using factor analysis. It consists of balance factor selection and factor score computation. We first normalize the indicators' data and then use factor analysis to identify the two main balance factors of the elderly, so the scores of each factor can be calculated. Finally, the comprehensive evaluation scoring model of the elderly balance ability is constructed.

3.1   Elderly Balance Ability Factor Selection and Calculation Method

The factor analysis method explores the basic structure in the observed data by studying the internal dependencies between variables, and uses a few hypothetical variables to represent the data structure between the variables. These hypothetical variables can reflect the main information of many original variables. The original variable is an observable explicit variable, while the hypothetical variable is an unobservable latent variable, also known as a factor.

The twenty-five feature indicators extracted in this paper are the explicit variables we have observed, and the hypothetical variables that need to be merged are the factors of the system. Based on the principle of factor analysis, we select and calculate the balance factor of the elderly, as in Eq. (1):

$$M_i = \alpha_{i1} F_1 + \cdots + \alpha_{im} F_m + \varepsilon_i (m \leq p) \tag{1}$$

where $M_i(i = 1, 2, \cdots, 25)$ is the twenty-five feature indicators we have observed. It can also be written as:

$$
\begin{bmatrix} M_1 \\ M_2 \\ \vdots \\ M_{25} \end{bmatrix} = \begin{bmatrix} \alpha_{11} & \alpha_{12} & \cdots & \alpha_{1m} \\ \alpha_{21} & \alpha_{22} & \cdots & \alpha_{2m} \\ \vdots & & & \vdots \\ & & & \\ \alpha_{(25)1} & \alpha_{(25)1} & \cdots & \alpha_{(25)m} \end{bmatrix} \begin{bmatrix} F_1 \\ F_2 \\ \vdots \\ F_{25} \end{bmatrix} + \begin{bmatrix} \varepsilon_1 \\ \varepsilon_2 \\ \vdots \\ \varepsilon_{25} \end{bmatrix} \tag{2}
$$

As common factors, they are unobservable variables, and their coefficients are called load factors. The special factor ε_i is a part that cannot be included by the first m common factors and is satisfied with Eq. (3).

$$
\begin{aligned}
&E(F) = 0, E(\varepsilon) = 0, Cov(F) = I_m \\
&D(\varepsilon) = Cov(\varepsilon) = diag\left(\sigma_1^2, \sigma_2^2, \cdots, \sigma_m^2\right) \\
&Cov(F, \varepsilon) = 0
\end{aligned} \tag{3}
$$

The factor load is the correlation coefficient between the i-th variable and the j-th common factor, reflecting the relative importance of the i-th variable and the j-th common factor. The greater the absolute value, the higher the correlation.

Data Normalization. First we standardize the raw data. There are twenty-five index variables for factor analysis for a total of 76 evaluation objects, and the value of the j-th index of the i-th evaluation object is a_{ij} $(i = 1, 2, \cdots, 25, j = 1, 2, \cdots, 76)$. Convert each indicator a_{ij} value into a standardized indicator $\tilde{a}_{ij}$, as in Eq. (4):

$$
\tilde{a}_{ij} = \frac{a_{ij} - \overline{\mu_j}}{s_j} \tag{4}
$$

where $\overline{\mu_j}$ and s_j are the sample mean and sample standard deviation for the j-th indicator, respectively. Likewise, each indictor variable is also normalized, as in Eq. (5):

$$
\tilde{x}_j = \frac{x_j - \overline{\mu_j}}{s_j} \tag{5}
$$

Calculate the Correlation Coefficient Matrix R. Correlation coefficient matrix $R = \left(r_{ij}\right)_{25 \times 25}$ has

$$
r_{ij} = \frac{\sum_{k=1}^{25} \tilde{a}_{ki} \cdot \tilde{a}_{kj}}{25 - 1} \tag{6}
$$

where r_{ij} is the correlation coefficient between the i-th index and the j-th index.

Calculate the Elementary Load Matrix. Calculating the eigenvalues of the correlation coefficient matrix R and the corresponding feature vector vectors $u_1, u_2, \cdots, u_{25}$, as in Eq. (7):

$$u_j = \left[u_{1j}, u_{2j}, \cdots, u_{(25)j} \right] \tag{7}$$

Elementary load matrix is obtained, as in Eq. (8):

$$\Lambda_1 = \left[\sqrt{\lambda_1} u_1, \sqrt{\lambda_2} u_2, \cdots, \sqrt{\lambda_{25}} u_{25} \right] \tag{8}$$

Select m Principal Components. According to the elementary load matrix, calculate the contribution rate of each common factor and select m main factors. Rotating the extracted factor load matrix to obtain a matrix, as in Eq. (9):

$$\Lambda_2 = \Lambda_1^m T \tag{9}$$

where Λ_1^m is the first m column of Λ_1, T is an orthogonal matrix, from which the construction factor model, as in Eq. (10):

$$\begin{cases} \tilde{M}_1 = \alpha_{11} F_1 + \alpha_{12} F_2 \cdots + \alpha_{1m} F_m \\ \qquad \vdots \\ \tilde{M}_{25} = \alpha_{(25)1} F_1 + \alpha_{(25)2} F_2 \cdots + \alpha_{(25)m} F_m \end{cases} \tag{10}$$

3.2   Comprehensive Evaluation Scoring Model for Elderly Balance Ability

This paper calculates factor scores by using regression method to find the single factor score function, as in Eq. (11):

$$\hat{F}_j = \beta_{j1} \tilde{M}_1 + \beta_{j2} \tilde{M}_2 + \cdots + \beta_{j25} \tilde{M}_{25} \tag{11}$$

An estimate of the score of the i-th sample point for the j-th factor, as in Eq. (12):

$$\hat{F}_{ij} = \beta_{j1} \tilde{a}_1 + \beta_{j2} \tilde{a}_2 + \cdots + \beta_{j25} \tilde{a}_{25} \tag{12}$$

We can draw

$$\begin{bmatrix} \beta_{11} & \cdot & \beta_{m1} \\ \cdot & \cdot & \cdot \\ \cdot & \cdot & \cdot \\ \cdot & \cdot & \cdot \\ \beta_{1(25)} & \cdot & \beta_{m(25)} \end{bmatrix} = R^{-1} \Lambda_2 \tag{13}$$

Meanwhile,

$$\hat{F}=\left(\hat{F}_{ij}\right)_{25*m}= X_0 R^{-1}\Lambda_2 \tag{14}$$

According to Eqs. (11)–(14), the comprehensive evaluation scoring model can be obtained.

Table 3. Rotated Component Matrix for twenty-five feature indicators

Index	Factor 1	Factor 2
Right support phase	0.887	0.151
Left support phase	0.876	0.022
Right swing phase	0.637	−0.199
Right swing phase	0.500	0.333
The cycle of right walk	0.907	−0.004
The cycle of left walk	0.882	0.242
The length of right step	0.049	−0.422
The length of left step	0.056	−0.610
The length of step stride of right foot	−0.163	0.687
The length of step stride of left foot	−0.423	0.539
Speed of step	−0.536	0.168
Step width	−0.160	−0.056
Walking rhythm	−0.888	−0.100
Deflection angle of right foot	0.037	−0.245
Deflection angle of left foot	−0.085	0.293
Contralateral heel to ground ratio	−0.107	−0.263
Contralateral toe off-ground ratio	0.242	−0.038
Double-feet support period	0.332	0.338
Right foot support period	0.854	0.112
Left foot support period	0.808	0.038
Swing amplitude of right arm	0.121	0.363
Swing amplitude of left arm	0.213	0.192
Swing frequency of right arm	−0.146	−0.535
Swing frequency of left arm	−0.039	−0.277
Head offset	0.043	−0.039

4   Results and Discussion

4.1   Analysis of Elderly Balance Ability Factors and Score Results

Based on the kinematics, we selected two factors to express the overall balance ability. Since the purpose of establishing the kinematic feature-based evaluation method by using factor analysis is not only to identify common factors and to group variables, but more importantly, to understand the meaning of each common factor for further analysis.

Considering that the factor load matrix is not unique, the factor load matrix should be rotated. Here we use the variance maximization method from each of the simplification factor load matrices to maximize the variance of the square of the load associated with each factor. When only a few variables have a higher load on a factor, the interpretation of the factor is the simplest. The results of the factor load matrix are given in Table 3.

As shown in Table 3, the observed factors show that the first factor includes parameters such as the swing phase, the walking period, and the arm swing frequency, which represents the motion state of the elderly. The second factor includes the angle of the foot and the period of support of the two feet, reflecting the change in the center of gravity of the elderly. The comprehensive evaluation system formed by the two factors not only contains twenty-five characteristics, but also eliminates the duplicate information between them, and can effectively evaluate the balance ability of the elderly.

4.2   Elderly Balance Ability Comprehensive Score Results

Model Parameter Result. According to the factor load matrix of rotation, twenty-five feature indicators are divided into different factors according to the contribution rate, and the score function of the two factors composed of twenty-five feature indicators is $F_1 = \alpha_1 M^T$ and $F_2 = \alpha_2 M^T$. Among them, $\alpha_1 = [a_1, a_2, \cdots, a_{25}]$ and $\alpha_2 = [b_1, b_2, \cdots, b_{25}]$ is the weight of twenty-five feature indicators of the first two factor, respectively. Thus, the comprehensive evaluation scoring model can be rewritten as $F = (55.808F_1 + 24.780F_2)/80.588$. From this, we can get the contribution rate of twenty-five feature indicators to the total score. We rewrite the above formula to get $F = \gamma M^T$, where $\gamma = [5.60, 6.10, 4.72, 2.73, 6.34, 5.82, 1.12, 1.22, -2.16, -3.59, -3.86, 1.18, -5.96, 0.44, -0.73, -0.54, 1.43, 1.90, 5.45, 5.68, 0.70, 1.57, -0.15, -0.02, 0.59]$.

The KMO and Bartlett's test of the obtained results (data not shown) show that the KMO value is 0.62, and there is a good correlation between the indicators, indicating that it is indeed suitable for factor analysis.

Besides, it can be observed that the coefficients of the walking rhythm, stride speed, left stride step, right stride step, and left foot declination are negative and their absolute values are large, indicating that the measured statistical values of the corresponding index are smaller.

Comprehensive Evaluation Score Results for Each Sample. In this paper, the balance ability score of each old person is calculated. For the limitation of space, Fig. 2 gives the distribution of their balance ability and Table 4 only gives the comprehensive evaluation score results of 8 elderly people.

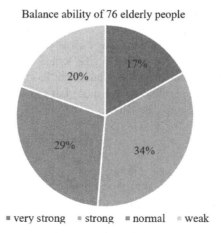

Fig. 2. The distribution of the balance ability of 76 elderly people

Table 4. Comprehensive evaluation score results for some elderly people

No.	Principal component 1	Principal component 2	Total score	Score range of balance ability	Category of balance Ability
53	−2.07	−0.04	−13.99	score ≤ − 7	Weak
26	−1.61	−0.92	−13.22		Weak
9	−0.41	−1.45	−6.62	−7 < score ≤ 0	Normal
76	−1.45	1.20	−6.54		Normal
40	−0.34	0.95	0.23	0 < score ≤ 7	Strong
67	−0.28	0.86	0.42		Strong
61	1.55	−0.84	8.15	7 ≤ score	Very strong
13	2.143	0.67	16.15		Very strong

Based on the comprehensive evaluation score results for each elderly people, the higher the score of the elderly's balance ability, the better their balance ability. According to Table 4, suggestions based on these indicators are: reducing the pace of walking, reducing the step size and the foot angling. Index step width, left step length, contralateral toe off-ground ratio, left arm swing amplitude, biped support period, left swing phase, right swing phase, right single foot support period, left walking period, left support phase, right walk.

Comparative Analysis. Although all real categories of balance ability for 76 elderly people cannot be known which leads to not giving the correct rate of our method, we can give a quantitative analysis. Specifically, after getting the total scores of elderly balance ability, we analyze the factors affecting the balance ability by combining the information from Table 1 in Sect. 2.1.

We come to observe the same points between each class and analyze the common attributes of people with the same balance. First look at people with weak balance ability No. 53 and No. 26 are all women aged 60 and so on. Their BMIs are both higher than 27 and No. 26 has had a fracture. Then, we compare the differences between the different classes and find out the differences. People with lower grades have significantly lower BMI. And the older person is, the worse the balance ability, and the women's balance ability is generally worse than men. In the history of illness, people who are sick and have multiple illness have more fall times and need to walk on the stairs more often while going up the stairs.

5 Conclusion

A kinematic feature-based evaluation method is presented for accessing elderly balance ability by using factor analysis. To the best of authors' knowledge, the presented work is the first to apply factor analysis to medical health care. Based on the kinematics, we extract twenty-five feature indicators from walking gait data, then identify two main factors from twenty-five feature indicators by using factor analysis and then establish a comprehensive evaluation scoring model of the elderly balance ability according to the variance contribution rate of the first two factors.

According to real observed data, the body balance ability can be simulated and compared. The results of empirical analysis confirm the validity and usefulness of the proposed method. Meanwhile, effective recommendations for elderly people with weak balance can be proposed. Furthermore, personalized suggestions can be put forward for each elderly people to improve his balance and prevent falling.

References

1. Kollmitzer, J., Ebenbichler, G.R., Sabo, A., Kerschan, K., Bochdansky, T.: Effects of back extensor strength training versus balance training on postural control. Med. Sci. Sports Exerc. **32**(10), 1770–1776 (2000)
2. Demura, S.I., Kitabayashi, T.: Body-sway characteristics during a static upright posture in the elderly. Geriatr. Gerontol. Int. **8**(3), 188–197 (2010)
3. Cuaya, G., Muñoz-Meléndez, A., Carrera, L.N., Morales, E.F., Quiñones, I., Pérez, A.I., Alessi, A.: A dynamic Bayesian network for estimating the risk of falls from real gait data. Med. Biol. Eng. Comput. **51**(1–2), 29–37 (2013)
4. Lewek, M.D., Bradley, C.E., Wutzke, C.J., Zinder, S.M.: The relationship between spatiotemporal gait asymmetry and balance in individuals with chronic stroke. J. Appl. Biomech. **30**(1), 31–36 (2014)
5. He, H., Chen, Z., Luo, Y.J., Liu, Q., Xu, Y.L.: Multidimensional evaluation model of elderly people based on 3D monitoring points. In: International Conference on Information Technology, Electrical and Electronic Engineering 2019, ITEEE, Sanya, China, 20–21 January 2019, pp. 326–331 (2019)
6. Organizing Committee of Asia and Pacific Mathematical Contest. http://www.saikr.com/vse/apmcm/2018?inc=d6d7a35f1539405935. Accessed 21 Dec 2018

Efficient Automatic Meta Optimization Search for Few-Shot Learning

Xinyue Zheng, Peng Wang$^{(\boxtimes)}$, Qigang Wang, Zhongchao Shi, and Feiyu Xu

AI Lab, Lenovo Research, Beijing 100089, China
{zhengxy7,wangpeng31,wangqg1,shizc2,fxu}@lenovo.com

Abstract. Previous works on meta-learning either relied on elaborately hand-designed network structures or adopted specialized learning rules to a particular domain. We propose a universal framework to optimize the meta-learning process automatically by adopting neural architecture search technique (NAS). NAS automatically generates and evaluates meta-learner's architecture for few-shot learning problems, while the meta-learner uses meta-learning algorithm to optimize its parameters based on the distribution of learning tasks. Parameter sharing and experience replay are adopted to accelerate the architectures searching process, so it takes only 1-2 GPU days to find good architectures. Extensive experiments on Mini-ImageNet and Omniglot show that our algorithm excels in few-shot learning tasks. The best architecture found on Mini-ImageNet achieves competitive results when transferred to Omniglot, which shows the high transferability of architectures among different computer vision problems.

Keywords: Meta-learning · Few-shot learning · Neural architecture search

1 Introduction

Many meta-learning methods [6,16,22] have achieved success in "K-shot, N-way" scenario. In this scenario, each task is a N-classification problem, and the learner only sees K training instances from each class. After training with these training instances, the learner is able to classify new images in the test set. Finn et al. [2] proposed a model-agnostic meta-learning approach (MAML). The key breakthrough is its initialization technology, which allows the learner to repeatedly train on each sampled task and set parameters at the optimal start point. Compared to MAML, which needs to calculate second derivatives in back-propagation, Reptile [12] only uses first-order derivatives with higher efficiency and less computational resource. However, the Reptile algorithm only optimizes meta-learner from the parameters level, and the learner's model is a simple and powerful network structure that are artificially designed. Designing

---

X. Zheng and P. Wang—These authors contributed equally to this work

© Springer Nature Switzerland AG 2019
Z. Lin et al. (Eds.): PRCV 2019, LNCS 11859, pp. 223–234, 2019.
https://doi.org/10.1007/978-3-030-31726-3_19

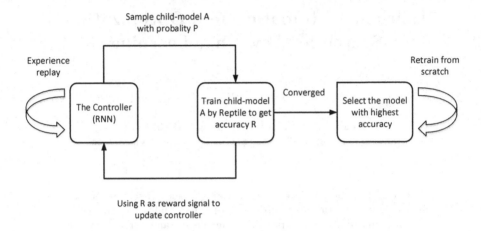

Fig. 1. An overview of efficient automatic meta-learning method

architectures is a time-consuming process which often requires rich expert knowledge and many experimental comparisons. Therefore, we propose a novel joint optimization scheme which combines model-agnostic meta-learning algorithm and automatic architecture design to improve the few-shot learning.

As is shown in Fig. 1, our scheme employs the neural architecture search technique to automate architecture design process. The contributions of each component are listed as follows: the controller is trained with policy to sample the meta-learner's architecture from component library; meta-learner uses Reptile to seek high adaptive initial parameters for different tasks; experience replay and parameter sharing speed up meta-learner search by learning from historical knowledge.

To be specific, our model search method is based on ENAS [13] which improves the efficiency of NAS by allowing parameter sharing among generated model. Figure 1 shows a recurrent network – the controller that outputs variable-length string to define a child model, including configurable model depth, stochastic skip connection, and different combination of convolution cells. The parameters of child model are trained by Reptile [12]. After a period of Reptile training, child model returns the accuracy as reward to evaluate and adjust the controller's architecture-generation policy. To speed up model searching procedure, we apply experience replay to reduce the number of controller interactions with the environment and encourage the controller to fully study its accumulated experience in the changing environment. Ultimately, the controller can optimize its policy and yields the best model architecture. We retrain this model from scratch using Reptile, and it can generalize across tasks with only a small number of gradient steps using few samples on each task.

We make the following contributions:

- We are the first to propose an automatic meta-optimization system by applying neural architecture search technique to meta-learning method.

- A series of experiments show that the joint automatic optimization method can ensure that the training model has rich expression ability and high cross-task generalization ability. On Mini-ImageNet benchmark, it achieves excellent performance with 74.20% accuracy.
- We achieve remarkable meta-learner search efficiency (5-shot with 48 GPU hours; 1-shot with 32 GPU hours). It credits to the incorporation of parameter sharing and experience replay techniques in search process.
- The algorithm shows high transferability among different computer vision problems. The best architecture found on Mini-ImageNet achieves competitive results on Omniglot tasks, and the searched models in 5-shot, 5-way classification are transferable to 1-shot, 5-way scenario.

2 Related Work

2.1 Meta Learning

Meta-learning allows learners to train through a variety of similar tasks, and expects to generalize to previously unseen tasks quickly. There are several ways to realize meta-learning. Memory based methods [11,16] adjust bias by weights update and generate outputs by learning from memories. Santoro et al. [16] make use of external memory introduced by Neural Turing Machine [3] to realize short term memory and build connections between labels and input images, so that latter inputs are able to compare with related images in memories to achieve better predictions. Gradient based methods [1,6] train a LSTM optimizer to learn parameter optimization rules of the learner network. While [1] targets at large-scale classification, [6] is interested in few-shot learning and learns both optimization rules and weight initialization. Recent work such as relation network [20] and matching network [22] employ idea from metric learning. Instead of using artificially designed metrics, it completely utilizes neural networks to learn deep distance metric. Simple Neural Attentive Learner (SNAIL) [10] uses temporal convolution to collect past experience and soft attention to pinpoint specific pieces of details. Object-level representation learning [8] decomposes images into objects, and applies object-level relation learned from source dataset to the target dataset.

Although the existing approaches have achieved impressive results, they either introduce extra parameters which need more storage spaces or bring constraints on the model architecture. MAML [2] is well accepted for its simplicity and model-agnostic. This method learns highly adaptive parameters to initialize the neural network so that only a small number of gradients updates are required for fast learning on a new task. Recently, OpenAI proposes a similar method Reptile [12] which does not require differentiability during the optimization process compared to MAML.

2.2 Neural Architecture Search

Human-designed networks usually only perform specific tasks. An automated method to generate appropriate architecture with adaptive model parameters and hyperparameters for any given tasks is desired. Many hyperparameter optimization methods have been studied [4,7,9,19]. These optimization algorithms are able to select and fine tune the model hyperparameters automatically which surpass human expert-level optimizations. However, they are not flexible and often limited in generating fixed-length configuration for networks.

Recent years evolutionary algorithms and reinforcement learning algorithms have been adopted for neural architecture search and achieved promising performance. Neuro-evolution methods [14,15] use mutation operations to explore large search spaces, which have expensive evaluation cost and need heuristic algorithms. The reinforcement learning approach has higher feasibility and achieves better results. Zoph et al. [23,24] use recurrent network to generate expected "child model", and utilize the accuracy of the child model on the validation set as reward signals to train this RNN. Efficient Neural Architecture Search (ENAS) [13] speeds up the training process by allowing parameter sharing among child models. Another efficient method Differentiable Architecture Search (DARTS) [18] constructs continuous search space and optimizes architecture in a differentiable manner.

3   Method

In meta-learning, learners make progress at task level rather than data point level. For example, MAML [2] takes in a distribution of tasks, where each task is an independent learning problem. In order to lower the loss L_τ on task τ, we need to compute the following formula:

$$\min_{\theta,\mathcal{A}} \sum_\tau L(D_\tau', \theta_\tau') = \sum_\tau L(D_\tau', T(D_\tau, \theta)) \tag{1}$$

where D_τ and D_τ' represent the training set and test set on task τ respectively, the $T(D_\tau, \theta)$ is the training procedure acting on D_τ, and the L_τ is computed on updated parameters θ' with test samples D_τ'. $\mathcal{A}$ represents the model architecture of the meta-learner, and the θ are the model parameters under this architecture. In classic meta-learning setting, $\mathcal{A}$ is fixed and we only optimize θ. In our proposed scheme, $\mathcal{A}$ and θ will be joint optimized with the alternatively training manner.

There are two stages in each meta-optimization search step. First the controller with policy ϕ is trained to sample a architecture $\mathcal{A} = f(\phi, R)$, where R is the reward output by the meta-learner, it is a random value at the first time. Second, using this architecture, the meta-learner is trained with Reptile algorithm. Reptile [12] is the first order of MAML. Using the same principle, it seeks an initialization condition for model parameters which can be fine-tuned easily, so that the trained learner is able to achieve high performance on previously unseen tasks. The score on validation set will be input as reward to the controller based on reinforcement learning. These two stages are alternatively trained until some good architecture candidates are generated. After all search steps finished, we

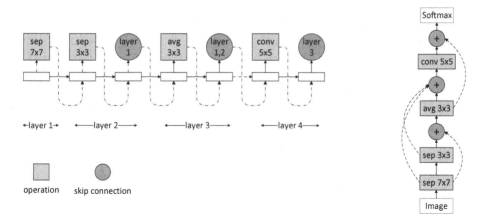

Fig. 2. *Left*: The prediction string made by controller. *Right*: Connect prediction string to build a complete network.

would finally retrain these candidates to obtain the architecture with highest score on the meta-test dataset.

Since the discrete domain search of $\mathcal{A}$ can be transformed into the continuous domain optimization of controller network in our method, the formula (1) can be rewrite as a differential form which can be optimized with end-to-end training:

$$\min_{\theta,\phi} \sum_{\tau} L(D'_{\tau}, \theta'_{\tau}) = \sum_{\tau} L(D'_{\tau}, T(D_{\tau}, \theta)) \tag{2}$$

3.1 Generating Transferable Architecture by Controller

We use LSTM as the controller to generate a variable-length string which specifies the model architecture. The controller receives a randomly initialized variable as input at the very beginning, then the input of time step t is the embedding of the decision sampled from time step $t-1$.

As shown in Fig. 2, the controller aims to generate a four-layer child model architecture. It needs to make two sets of decisions according to the current generation policy: (1) what operations to be applied and (2) which previous layers to be concatenated. There are several available operations: ordinary convolutions, depthwise-separable convolutions, average pooling and max pooling. After selecting the operation, the controller will decide to select the previous skip connection layers. Take layer k as an example, $k-1$ indices of previous layers are sampled, which conduce to $2^{(k-1)}$ possible choice. Corresponding to Fig. 2, at layer $k = 3$, the controller selects the indices $1, 2$, which means the output of layer 1 and 2 are concatenated along depth dimension and sent to layer 4.

3.2 Training Controller with Reinforcement Learning

Policy Gradient. When training the controller, we freeze parameters of the child model and only update controller's policy ϕ (referred to as Algorithm 1). Actions $a_{1:T}$ are the decisions made by the controller's policy in time series: selecting an operand and layers for skip connection. We utilize policy gradient [21] to train the controller to maximize the expected reward $E_{P(a_{1:T};\phi)}[R]$. The traditional policy gradient formula is:

$$\nabla_\phi U(\phi) = \frac{1}{m} \sum_{j=1}^{m} \sum_{t=1}^{T} \nabla_\phi \log P\left(a_t | a_{(t-1):1}; \phi\right) R_j \tag{3}$$

where m stands for the m architectures sampled by the current policy. T denotes the number of predictions made by the controller. R controls the parameter update direction and step size. Equation (3) targets at increasing the generation probability of high reward models and reducing the opposite. We employ the empirical average reward of these m architectures to approximate the policy gradient.

The above method is unbiased but with high variance. As is proposed by [23], we introduce a baseline bl in reward to reduce the variance. bl is defined as the exponential moving average of previous architecture accuracy. By subtracting the baseline, we can understand the improvement of a model compared with an average one.

$$A_j = R_j - bl_j \tag{4}$$

$$\nabla_\phi U(\phi) = \frac{1}{m} \sum_{j=1}^{m} \sum_{t=1}^{T} \nabla_\phi \log P\left(a_t | a_{(t-1):1}; \phi\right) A_j \tag{5}$$

The advantage function (4) helps to update policy parameters (5) with a more specific direction.

Algorithm 1. Automatic architecture search with experience replay.

1: Randomly initialize policy ϕ, input state S_0
2: **for** $j = 1$ to J **do**
3:     Observe S_j, and generate action stream $A_j = a_{1:T}$ to form a child model
4:     Train Child model with **Algorithm 2** on meta-training to get reward R_j
5:     Perform PG to ϕ with this experience (S_j, A_j, R_j)
6:     Store (S_j, A_j, R_j) if $R_j \geq bl$, or with probability $\frac{R_j}{bl}$ into replay buffer M
7:     **if** $j \bmod k == 0$ **then**
8:         **for** $r = 1$ to R **do**
9:             Uniformly sample transition B from M
10:             Update policy parameters ϕ with B
11:         **end for**
12:     **end if**
13: **end for**

Experience Replay. Policy gradient is based on stochastic gradient algorithms. The controller is updated using only one sample architecture generated by the current policy and discards it after a single update. Therefore, the controller tends to forget its past experience which leads to oscillation. We solve this issue by adopting experience replay skills [17]. To perform experience replay, we store transition (S_j, A_j, R_j) in a replay buffer, where A_j stands for the j-th architecture string $a_{1:T}$ selected by the controller, S_j refers to the input state of the controller, and R corresponds to the accuracy computed on the validation set. Since not all experiences are expected to be learned more than once, experience will be stored in the buffer with probability:

$$P_j = \begin{cases} \frac{R_j}{bl}, & R_j \leq bl_j \\ 1, & R_j > bl_j \end{cases} \tag{6}$$

The criterion to measure the importance of transition is its reward R_j, which suggests how good this architecture is compared with current baseline bl_j.

3.3   Training Child Model with Reptile

When training the child model (referred to as Algorithm 2), we freeze the controller's policy parameters ϕ. Child models are required to learn from limited number of images, so we build our work on a scalable meta-learning algorithm Reptile. Assume that $p(T)$ are the distribution probability of tasks, we sample a batch of tasks T from $p(T)$. The standard cross-entropy loss L_{τ_i} denotes the task-specific loss function. In order to make the model parameters θ sensitive, we calculate each task τ_i with k gradient steps on loss L_{τ_i} and get the final parameter vector W_i. Meta-optimization across tasks is performed via Adam algorithm, where $\sum_{i=1}^{N}(W_i - \phi)$ is treated as gradient. Besides, training the child model on the validation set generates accuracy R, which will be returned as the reward to scale gradients of the controller.

Algorithm 2. Reptile at training time.

1: Randomly initialize θ
2: **repeat**
3:    Sample batch of N tasks $T_b \sim p(T)$
4:    **for** each τ_i in T_b **do**
5:        Compute adapted parameters with k gradients step: $W_i = SGD(L_{\tau_i}, \theta, k)$
6:    **end for**
7:    Update $\theta \leftarrow \theta + \alpha \frac{1}{k} \sum_{i=1}^{N}(W_i - \theta)$
8: **until** Convergence
9: **return** Accuracy on validation set as reward R_j

---

4   Experiment

In this section, we evaluate automatic meta-learning method on two important benchmarks: Mini-ImageNet and Omniglot, and compare our results against strong baselines. All of our experiments consider solving K-shot, N-way learning problem. For each task τ_i of K-shot, N-way classification, the learner trains on N related classes each with K examples, we firstly sample N classes from meta-dataset and then select $K + 1$ examples for each class. Then, we split these examples into training and test sets, where training set D_{train} contains K examples for each class and test set D_{test} contains the remaining sample. Take 5-shot, 5-way classification as example, we use 25 examples — 5(images) x 5 (classes) to train the learner and use additional examples to test the model.

4.1   Few-Shot Learning Datasets

Mini-ImageNet is created by randomly sampling 100 classes from ImageNet and selecting 600 examples for each class. Training set has $38,400$ images with 64 classes, test set consists of $12,000$ images with 20 classes, and validation set contains 9600 images with 16 classes.

Omniglot consists of 1623 characters from 50 different alphabets. We randomly select 1200 characters for training and use the remaining character classes for testing. As is proposed by Santoro et al. [16], we augment the dataset with rotations by multiples of 90 degrees. Omniglot was proposed by lake and used in the 2015 Science paper [5].

4.2   Implementation Details

The controller is a one-layer LSTM with 100 hidden units, whose goal is to search 8-layers child models. Operations can be selected from: 3×3, 5×5, and 7×7 convolutions, 3×3, 5×5, and 7×7 depthwise-separable convolutions and 3×3 average pooling and max pooling. We perform experience replay on the controller every 60 steps and 5 transitions each time. A global average pooling is added before the fully connected layer and dropout layers with 0.25 drop rates are added after each layer. These tricks reduce the number of parameters and avoid overfitting during training. We use 1 GPU for 1-2 days to search for top-3 architectures for meta-learner, and each architecture takes 6 GPU hours to retrain from scratch. Table 1 presents parameter settings in the final retrain process.

4.3   Evaluation

As shown in Table 2, Our method achieves competitive results on Mini-ImageNet. In transductive mode, the trained model classifies all the samples in test set at once, so the information is allowed to leak between test samples through batch normalization [12]. As expected, the transductive experiments achieve 74.2% high accuracy on 5-shot 5-way task.

Table 1. Parameters for final-retrain on Mini-ImageNet

Parameters	5-shot 5-way	1-shot 5-way
Adam learning rate	0.005	0.003
Outer iterations	$7K$	$7K$
Outer step size	1	1
Meta batch size	5	5
Inner iterations	8	8
Inner batch size	10	10
Train shots	15	15
Eval. inner iterations	88	50
Eval. inner batch size	10	5

Table 2. Results on Mini-ImageNet

Algorithm	Transduction	5-shot 5-way	1-shot 5-way
MAML [2]	Y	$63.11 \pm 0.92\%$	$48.70 \pm 1.84\%$
Reptile [12]	N	$62.74 \pm 0.37\%$	$45.79 \pm 0.44\%$
Reptile	Y	$66.00 \pm 0.62\%$	$48.21 \pm 0.69\%$
Matching Nets [22]	N	$55.31 \pm 0.73\%$	$43.56 \pm 0.84\%$
Relation Nets [20]	N	$65.32 \pm 0.70\%$	$50.44 \pm 0.82\%$
SNAIL [10]	N	$68.88 \pm 0.92\%$	$\mathbf{55.71 \pm 0.99\%}$
Ours	N	$67.10 \pm 0.90\%$	$48.00 \pm 0.82\%$
Ours	Y	$\mathbf{74.20 \pm 0.32\%}$	$\mathbf{52.43 \pm 1.08\%}$
Ours (Transfer)	N	\	$47.04 \pm 0.52\%$
Ours (Transfer)	Y	\	$51.62 \pm 0.43\%$

Automatic searching process learns directly from the task distribution of dataset, We show it enables some degree of transferability. In experiments, we transfer the model constructed from 5-shot 5-way configuration into 1-shot 5-way for final-retrain. It achieves 51.62% accuracy which still beyond the original Reptile performance on Mini-ImageNet.

Although some methods [10, 20] have achieved competitive performance as ours, our method sacrifices some accuracy in exchange for time and space efficiency. For example, we only select the top3 searched architectures for retrain. If we select top10, or top100 architectures for retrain, the accuracy may be improved. In addition, the network could automatically select the number of layers, the number of feature maps, etc., which is easier than the manual setting to find the most powerful architecture, but this procedure is very time-consuming. What's more, we use the experience replay to encourage learner learning from past experience but reduce the number of times to explore new architectures. Although it greatly improves the efficiency, it reduces the possibility of exploring the best architecture to some extent. Therefore, if we only focus on accuracy, there is a great room for improvement, but we think efficient algorithm with competitive results are more valuable. Compared to the original NAS technology, who takes 32,400-43,200 GPU hours, our algorithm can search for good architectures within 48 GPU hours.

Table 3. Results on Omniglot

Algorithm	Transduction	5-shot 20-way	1-shot 20-way
Matching Nets [22]	N	98.7%	93.5%
1^{st}order MAML [2]	Y	$97.0 \pm 0.1\%$	$89.4 \pm 0.5\%$
MAML	Y	$98.9 \pm 0.2\%$	$95.8 \pm 0.3\%$
Reptile [12]	N	$96.65 \pm 0.33\%$	$88.14 \pm 0.15\%$
Reptile	Y	$97.12 \pm 0.32\%$	$89.43 \pm 0.14\%$
Ours	N	$98.97 \pm 0.12\%$	$95.50 \pm 0.35\%$
Ours (Transfer)	N	$97.95 \pm 0.23\%$	$93.80 \pm 0.18\%$

In Omniglot, we try the distance transfer experiment to test the generalization performance of the searched architecture. Here, we merely transfer the model architecture from Mini-ImageNet, but all the weights will be re-trained from scratch. From Table 3 we find that transferred architecture generalize well to Omniglot problems, even exceeds the accuracy of original Reptile method with transductive setting. So the automatic meta-learning method has been proven not only to achieve within-task generalization, but also cross-task generalization.

Figure 3 shows the experience replay contributes to the understanding of new tasks, and helps the learner to discover better architectures with less computational cost. Note that the y-axis is the moving average of previous architecture

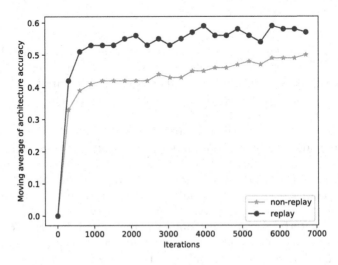

Fig. 3. Training curves for the architecture search procedure: exponential moving average architecture accuracy over 7K iterations.

accuracy, so it only reflects the average value and many architectures can achieve much higher accuracy. Figure 4 shows the good architectures we discovered.

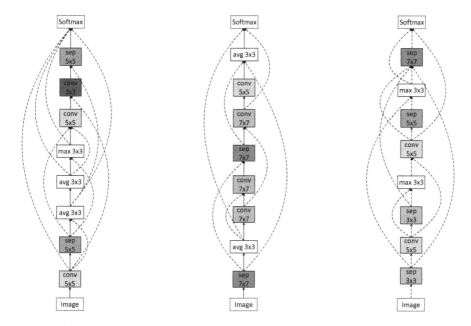

Fig. 4. High accuracy architectures searched by 5-shot, 5-way classification on Mini-ImageNet, and can be transferred to other classification scenes.

5 Conclusion

In this paper, we introduce an efficient automatic meta optimization search for few-shot learning problems. Rich experiments show that the proposed algorithm achieves competitive performance in few-shot learning tasks. Our work has a few key insights. Firstly, the proposed framework is universal because the architecture search will discover scalable architectures for meta-learner, which can be easily nested on any model-agnostic meta-learning algorithm. Secondly, parameter sharing and experience replay techniques greatly save the computational cost and improve the efficiency of our approach. Lastly, We show the within-task generalization and cross-task generalization of the learner's architecture, this transferability is a desirable characteristic and deserves further study.

References

1. Andrychowicz, M., et al.: Learning to learn by gradient descent by gradient descent. CoRR abs/1606.04474 (2016). http://arxiv.org/abs/1606.04474
2. Finn, C., Abbeel, P., Levine, S.: Model-agnostic meta-learning for fast adaptation of deep networks. arXiv preprint arXiv:1703.03400 (2017)

3. Graves, A., Wayne, G., Danihelka, I.: Neural turing machines. CoRR abs/1410.5401 (2014). http://arxiv.org/abs/1410.5401
4. Hazan, E., Klivans, A., Yuan, Y.: Hyperparameter optimization: a spectral approach. arXiv preprint arXiv:1706.00764 (2017)
5. Lake, B.M., Salakhutdinov, R., Tenenbaum, J.B.: Human-level concept learning through probabilistic program induction. Science **350**(6266), 1332–1338 (2015)
6. Ravi, S., Larochelle, H.: Optimization as a model for few-shot learning. In: International Conference on Learning Representations (ICLR) (2017)
7. Li, L., Jamieson, K., DeSalvo, G., Rostamizadeh, A., Talwalkar, A.: Hyperband: a novel bandit-based approach to hyperparameter optimization. arXiv preprint arXiv:1603.06560 (2016)
8. Long, L., Wang, W., Wen, J., Zhang, M., Lin, Q., Ooi, B.C.: Object-level representation learning for few-shot image classification. CoRR abs/1805.10777 (2018). http://arxiv.org/abs/1805.10777
9. Loshchilov, I., Hutter, F.: CMA-ES for hyperparameter optimization of deep neural networks. arXiv preprint arXiv:1604.07269 (2016)
10. Mishra, N., Rohaninejad, M., Chen, X., Abbeel, P.: Meta-learning with temporal convolutions. CoRR abs/1707.03141 (2017). http://arxiv.org/abs/1707.03141
11. Munkhdalai, T., Yu, H.: Meta networks. CoRR abs/1703.00837 (2017). http://arxiv.org/abs/1703.00837
12. Nichol, A., Schulman, J.: Reptile: a scalable metalearning algorithm. arXiv preprint arXiv:1803.02999 (2018)
13. Pham, H., Guan, M.Y., Zoph, B., Le, Q.V., Dean, J.: Efficient neural architecture search via parameter sharing. arXiv preprint arXiv:1802.03268 (2018)
14. Real, E., Aggarwal, A., Huang, Y., Le, Q.V.: Regularized evolution for image classifier architecture search. arXiv preprint arXiv:1802.01548 (2018)
15. Real, E., et al.: Large-scale evolution of image classifiers. arXiv preprint arXiv:1703.01041 (2017)
16. Santoro, A., Bartunov, S., Botvinick, M.: One-shot learning with memory-augmented neural networks. CoRR (2016). http://arxiv.org/abs/1605.06065
17. Schaul, T., Quan, J., Antonoglou, I., Silver, D.: Prioritized experience replay. CoRR abs/1511.05952 (2015). http://arxiv.org/abs/1511.05952
18. Shin, R., Packer, C., Song, D.: Differentiable neural network architecture search (2018)
19. Snoek, J., Larochelle, H., Adams, R.P.: Practical bayesian optimization of machine learning algorithms. In: Advances in Neural Information Processing Systems, pp. 2951–2959 (2012)
20. Sung, F., Yang, Y., Zhang, L., Xiang, T., Torr, P.H., Hospedales, T.M.: Learning to compare: Relation network for few-shot learning. arXiv preprint arXiv:1711.06025 (2017)
21. Sutton, R.S.: Policy gradient methods for reinforcement learning with function approximation. In: Advances in Neural Information Processing Systems, vol. 12, pp. 1057–1063 (1999)
22. Vinyals, O., Blundell, C., Lillicrap, T.P.: Matching networks for one shot learning. CoRR abs/1606.04080 (2016). http://arxiv.org/abs/1606.04080
23. Zoph, B., Le, Q.V.: Neural architecture search with reinforcement learning. arXiv preprint arXiv:1611.01578 (2016)
24. Zoph, B., Vasudevan, V., Shlens, J., Le, Q.V.: Learning transferable architectures for scalable image recognition. arXiv preprint arXiv:1707.07012 (2017)

Visual Odometry with Deep Bidirectional Recurrent Neural Networks

Fei Xue[1(⊠)], Xin Wang[2,3], Qiuyuan Wang[2,3], Junqiu Wang[4],
and Hongbin Zha[2,3(⊠)]

[1] UISEE Technology Inc., Beijing, China
fei.xue@uisee.com
[2] Key Laboraory of Machine Perception, Peking University, Beijing, China
[3] PKU-SenseTime Machine Vision Joint Lab, Beijing, China
{xinwang_cis,wangqiuyuan,zhahb}@pku.edu.cn
[4] Beijing Changcheng Aviation Measurement and Control Institute, Beijing, China
jerywangjq@foxmail.com

Abstract. We propose a novel architecture for learning camera poses
from image sequences with an extended 2D LSTM (Long Short-Term
Memory). Unlike most of the previous deep learning based VO (Visual
Odometry) methods, our model predicts the pose per frame with temporal information from image sequences by adopting a *forward-backward*
process. In addition, we use 3D tensors as basic structures to generate
spatial information. The network learns poses in a *bottom-up* manner by
coupling local and global constraints. Experiments demonstrate that on
the public KITTI benchmark dataset, our architecture outperforms the
state-of-the-art end-to-end methods in term of camera motion prediction
and is comparable with model-based methods. The network generalizes
well on the Málaga dataset without extra training or fine-tuning.

Keywords: Visual Odometry · Motion estimation · Convolutional
Neural Networks · Recurrent Neural Network

1 Introduction

Visual Odometry (VO) estimates camera poses from sequential images by revealing the consistency between consecutive frames. As an essential task in computer
vision, it has been required in areas such as autonomous driving and robot navigation. The last thirty years have witnessed plenty of VO systems [3,4,11]. In
VO, heavy accumulated errors and scale drift would appear if merely two adjacent frames are taken into consideration. Therefore, in order to estimate more
accurate camera poses, most systems leverage the sptio-temporal consistency by

This work was done when Fei Xue was a student in Key Laboraory of Machine Perception, Peking University. The work was supported by the National Key Research
and Development Program of China (2017YFB1002601) and National Natural Science
Foundation of China (61632003, 61771026).

© Springer Nature Switzerland AG 2019
Z. Lin et al. (Eds.): PRCV 2019, LNCS 11859, pp. 235–246, 2019.
https://doi.org/10.1007/978-3-030-31726-3_20

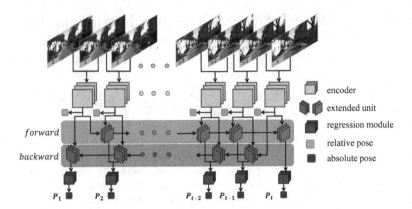

Fig. 1. Our architecture learns camera motion with *forward-backward* process using an extended LSTM. The *bottom-up* prediction experiences two stages with coupled local and global constraints.

introducing temporal sliding windows and building local 3D maps. It could be interpreted as a sequence-to-sequence mechanism, where camera poses can be estimated and refined by exploiting information from previous and later frames.

Traditional VO methods require sophisticated calibration to ensure estimation precision. Learning-based end-to-end approaches, however, can be used to tackle VO problem without such a limitation [10,15,16,18,19,21]. These methods leverage the powerful CNN (Convolutional Neural Network) and RNN (Recurrent Neural Network) to solve the problem by learning from massive training data.

The regular RNN structure adopts only *forward* processes that predicts current poses from previous information, thus may suffer from learning bias and error accumulations when running on long sequences. Moreover, with only the constraint on global poses, these frameworks might suffer from over-smoothness and fail to recover the local irregularities in trajectories such as sharp rotations. In addition, fully connected layers heavily used in such structures are prone to over-fitting and thus hampering the generalization ability of the overall network.

In this paper, we propose a novel end-to-end network that learns camera poses from image sequences by leveraging the Bidirectional Recurrent Neural Networks (BRNN) with extended LSTM units (as shown in Fig. 1). The main contributions include:

- A novel architecture with *forward-backward* processes that can not only predict the pose of current frame using historical information but refine previous poses given newly gained knowledge;
- A two-stage *bottom-up* prediction strategy with coupled local and global constraints, which is able to handle various motion patterns among sequences by extracting motion-sensitive features.

The paper is organized as follows: Sect. 2 reviews related work on traditional and learning-based monocular VO methods, and RNNs. In Sect. 3, we introduce our architecture in detail. Section 4 evaluates the proposed method against the state-of-the-art methods. Section 5 concludes the paper.

2 Related Work

VO has been studied for decades and great progress has been made in recent years. In this section we focus mainly on the relevant studies of monocular VO.

Model-Based VO Methods. Classical methods can be roughly categorized into feature-based and direct methods. Feature-based approaches establish correspondences by matching features between frames, and estimate camera motion through minimizing reprojection error. VISO2 [6] utilizes sparse feature matching between consecutive frames to realize an efficient VO system. ORB-SLAM2 [11] extracts ORB features, builds sparse 3D point clouds, and optimizes both camera poses and maps. Direct methods [3,4], on the other hand, recover poses by directly minimizing photometric error. These methods do not require expensive feature extraction, yet are sensitive to the changing of illumination. DSO [3] alleviates the problem by integrating a full photometric calibration. Both feature-based and direct methods are designed for static scenes and may face problems when they encounter dynamic objects. Meanwhile, they tend to fail in texture-less environments.

Learning-Based VO Methods. Deep learning has been proved useful for various computer vision tasks with impressive efficiency, provided sufficient training datasets. Recently, CNN has been applied to 3D related topics, including depth map prediction [18,19,21]. It has also been utilized in VO/SLAM systems by replacing imperfect components in classic systems, such as depth initialization [17]. There are also end-to-end frameworks directly dealing with VO-related problems. DeepTAM [20] estimates depth and motion from two consecutive images captured by a monocular camera. SfmLearner [21], GeoNet [18] and Depth-VO-Feat [19] recover depth images of scenes and ego-motions from unlabeled sequences with view synthesis as the supervisory signal. UnDeepVO [10] extends the work of SfmLearner to stereo images by adding left-right consistency. DeepVO [15] learns camera poses by combining CNNs and RNNs. It feeds 1D vectors into a regular LSTM to predict pose per frame and builds the loss function over the absolute global poses. ESP-VO [16] extends DeepVO by inferring poses and uncertainties directly in a unified framework. These approaches do not emphasize the backward refinement and ignore the spatial connections of features. In this paper, we aim to tackle VO problem by learning the motion at each time step with the spatio-temporal consistency over the whole sequence.

Recurrent Neural Networks. RNN extends the feed-forward neural networks with loops in connection, hence it is able to process sequential inputs. LSTM [8], a variation of RNN, can deal with the vanishing gradient problem by controlling the flows from input to output. ConvLSTM [14] adopts convolutional

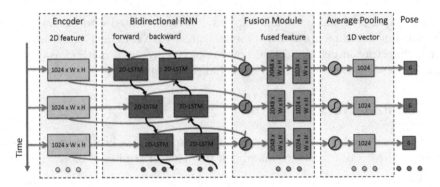

Fig. 2. Pipeline of our model. A 3D tensor is fed to the Bidirectional RNN to provide spatio-temporal information. The outputs of *forward* and *backward* processes are combined and fed into a GAP Layer for further 6DoF pose estimation.

structure as basic operations and accepts 3D tensors as input to preserve the spatial dependence. BRNN (Bidirectional Recurrent Neural Network) [13] is an extension of standard RNN. It defines a reverted direction on the negative time in order to utilize future information. We adopt the BRNN with convolutional LSTM as the basic structure to implement the *forward-backward* VO system.

3   Approach

As shown in Fig. 1, our model receives monocular RGB image sequences as input. High-level features are first extracted from consecutive images with encoders (Sect. 3.1). The feature maps are then fed into the Bidirectional RNNs, experiencing a *forward-backward* operation (Sect. 3.2). Outputs of both *forward* and *backward* processes are concatenated and fused. Finally, 6-DoF poses are produced from the output of global average pooling (GAP) layer. The *bottom-up* learning strategy is adopted using both local and global constraints as loss functions (Sect. 3.3).

3.1   Encoder

We build the encoder upon ResNet34 [7]. ResNet34 is a variation of ResNet with 16 "basicblocks", a 3-channel input layer, an additional GAP layer, and a classifier layer for classification. To consider spatio-temporal information, we replace the 3-channel input layer with a 6-channel convolutional layer to accept two RGB images, discard the last pooling and classier layers, and add two convolutional layers with 3×3 kernel size to produce a 2D feature map with 1024 channels (see Fig. 2). We reserve the form of 3D tensors instead of a conversion to 1D feature vectors so as to keep the information in the spatial domain.

3.2 *Forward-Backward* Process with 2D Convolutional LSTM

As depicted in Fig. 1, the core of our framework is the recurrence module that allows the network to retain the information prior to and following the current frame and update the memory by controlling the *gates* in the spatial domain. A naive solution could be the usage of a vanilla LSTM network such as [15,16]. However, by operating 1D feature vectors, it lacks the ability to maintain spatial information which is indispensable for predicting sequential camera poses. To deal with this problem, we design a new architecture that processes the image flow in *forward-backward* directions by operating 3D tensors to retain the spatial information over the whole sequence.

2D Convolutional LSTM. We utilize the 2D convolutional LSTM made up of a set of structured units spatially distributed in 3D tensors to emphasize the spatial relationship between neighboring pixels. Each regular LSTM unit indexed by (i,j) has an independent hidden state $h_{t,(i,j)} \in R^N$. The operation of an standard GRU (Gated Recurrent Unit) [2] can be described by

$$u_t = \sigma(W_u x_t + U_u h_{t-1} + b_u), \tag{1}$$

$$r_t = \sigma(W_r x_t + U_r h_{t-1} + b_r), \tag{2}$$

$$h_t = (1 - u_t) \odot h_{t-1} + u_t \odot tanh(W_h x_t + U_h(r_t \odot h_{t-1}) + b_h), \tag{3}$$

where u_t, r_t, h_t represent the update gate, reset gate, and the hidden state respectively. σ is the sigmoid function. $\odot$ denotes element-wise multiplication. We use subscript t to refer to an activation at time t. With the same notation but switch the input to 3D tensors, equations governing the 2D-LSTM grid are changed to

$$u_t = \sigma(W_u * x_t + U_u * h_{t-1} + b_u), \tag{4}$$

$$r_t = \sigma(W_r * x_t + U_r * h_{t-1} + b_r), \tag{5}$$

$$h_t = (1 - u_t) \odot h_{t-1} + u_t \odot tanh(W_h * x_t + U_h * (r_t \odot h_{t-1}) + b_h). \tag{6}$$

Here, $*$ denotes the convolution. The output of current unit will be fed into two modules: the next recurrent unit along the time line, and the fusion module associating data from two directions for current absolute pose prediction.

Forward-Backward Process. The pose of current frame can be recovered by accumulating relative poses of previous frames, as shown in Fig. 3(a). However, this strategy leads to error accumulations and non-negligible scale drift. Figure 3(b) shows an improved solution which takes more previous frames into consideration. This is easy to implement by adopting standard unidirectional RNNs, as DeepVO [15] and ESP-VO [16].

In fact, Fig. 3(c) suggests that the current information is also able to refine the previous states. This property can not be fully expressed by a regular LSTM with only *forward* process. Therefore, we introduce a *forward-backward* process by adding an extra *backward* component. Equipped with such a structure, our network will be able to predict current camera poses through the *forward* inference, and refine previous poses via the *backward* process, as illustrated in Fig. 2.

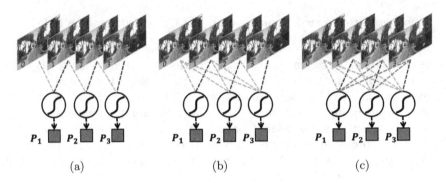

(a)   (b)   (c)

Fig. 3. Learning pose by building consistency over (a) two locally consecutive frames, (b) all previous frames, (c) all frames in the sequence. The blue, green and red lines denote the current, previous and future inputs. (Color figure online)

The outputs from *forward* and *backward* are concatenated before being fed to the fusion module. The fusion model aligns and integrates spatio-temporal information by two convolution layers with a 3×3 kernel to generate 3D tensors of 1024 channels. Finally, the pose is regressed from the immediate output of a GAP layer, in the form of a 6-DoF motion parameters.

3.3   Coupled Local and Global Constraints

Relative poses between two consecutive views are relatively easy to learn due to small motions. But error accumulations and scale drift will severely reduce the accuracy if no additional constraint is provided. Absolute poses with large motions, on the other hand, will be hard to learn through the recurrent module without proper temporal regularization. We propose to learn camera motion progressively in two stages from local to global, with constraints over both the relative and absolute poses respectively, as follows:

$$L_{local} = \frac{1}{t} \sum_{i=1}^{t} ||\hat{p}_{i-1,i} - p_{i-1,i}||_2 + k||\hat{\phi}_{i-1,i} - \phi_{i-1,i}||_2, \tag{7}$$

$$L_{global} = \sum_{i=1}^{t} \frac{1}{i} (||\hat{p}_{0,i} - p_{0,i}||_2 + k||\hat{\phi}_{0,i} - \phi_{0,i}||_2), \tag{8}$$

$$L_{total} = L_{local} + L_{global}. \tag{9}$$

$\hat{p}_{i-1,i}, p_{i-1,i}, \hat{\phi}_{i-1,i}$, and $\phi_{i-1,i}$ represent the predicted and ground-truth relative translation and rotation in three directions, respectively; $\hat{p}_{0,i}, p_{0,i}, \hat{\phi}_{0,i}$, and $\phi_{0,i}$ represent the predicted and ground-truth absolute translation and rotation. L_{local}, L_{global} and L_{total} denote the local, global, and total loss respectively. t is the current frame index in a sequence. k is a fixed parameter for regularizing the rotational and translational errors. It is set to 50 in all our experiments.

Local loss is built on the average relative pose regressed from the output of encoder, which accepts two consecutive images as input. This encourages the network to learn motion-sensitive features at the bottom stage. Global loss is defined on the absolute pose regressed from the fused outputs from *forward* and *backward* processes. With the local constraints at the bottom stage, the recurrence module focuses mainly on temporal consistent motions from the motion-sensitive features instead of raw features, which enhances the system's robustness and improves the accuracy. More importantly, local constraints retain the locality of motions among the sequence since recorded devices cannot be assumed to move at a constant speed especially in sharp turns.

We normalize the local loss by averaging all the relative losses in a local sequence (Eq. 7), while averaging absolute poses with the weight of inverse sequence length in the global context (Eq. 8). This configuration enables our model to leverage the encoded motion-sensitive features in local sequences, meanwhile avoids over-emphasizing relative motions that may lead to decay of global information during long-term localizations.

4 Experiments

We first discuss the implementations in Sect. 4.1 and introduce the benchmarks used in Sect. 4.2. Then, in Sect. 4.3, we compare the four variations of our network, BRNN_lg for Bidirectional RNN (BRNN) plus both local and global constraints, BRNN_g for BRNN plus global constraint, RNN_lg for single directional RNN plus local and global constraints, and RNN_g for RNN plus the global constraint and prove the efficacy of the *forward-backward* and *bottom-up* configurations. Next, we compare the performance of our model on the KITTI dataset [5] against current state-of-the-art learning- and model-based methods in Sect. 4.4. We also show the generalization ability of our network in Sect. 4.5 by testing the network on Málaga dataset [1] with weights trained on the KITTI dataset without any fine-tuning.

4.1 Implementation

Monocular RGB images with size 1080×320 are used for training and testing. We use 7 frames to construct a sequence. At the head of *forward* and *backward* process, the first encoded feature map instead of all-zero/one tensor is used for initialization. In term of prediction, the poses of the first and last frames are only influenced by the *backward* and *forward* processes respectively, as shown in Fig. 1. Both relative and absolute poses are represented as 6-DoF parameters with first 3 for Euler angles and the rest 3 for translation.

We use the PyTorch [12] to build our networks on an NVIDIA 1080 Ti GPU. Adam [9] is adopted as the optimizer in which β_1 and β_2 are set to 0.9 and 0.99, respectively. The networks are trained with a batch size of 4, a weight decay of 10^{-4} for 150,000 iterations in total. The initial learning rate is 10^{-4} and reduced by half every 60,000 iterations.

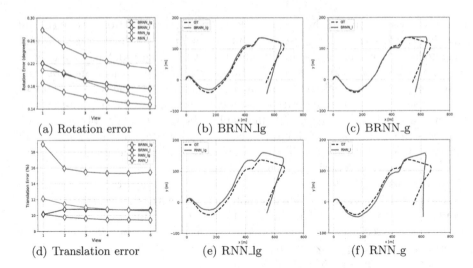

Fig. 4. Rotation and translation errors of four variations of our network on the KITTI dataset [5]. Recovered trajectories on Seq 10 are also illustrated.

4.2   Dataset

KITTI: The KITTI dataset [5] contains 22 sequences of stereo images collected from a moving car in urban and highway environments. The dataset was captured at a relatively low frame rate (10 fps) at the speed up to 90 km/h, and contains many dynamic objects in the urban area, hence is very challenging for monocular VO algorithms. In our experiments, only the left RGB images are utilized and resized to 1080 × 320 for training and testing. As DeepVO [15], Seq 00, 02, 08 and 09 are used for training, and Seq 03–07, 10 are used for evaluation.

Málaga: The Málaga dataset [1] collects data in similar scenes to the KITTI with stereo image sequences at 20 Hz. The rectified left RGB images with 1024 × 768 are used to test the pre-trained networks without fine-tuning. These images are resized to 1080 × 320 to fit in the network pre-trained on KITTI.

4.3   Ablation Study

Figure 4(a) and (d) show the rotation and translation errors on each view of BRNN_lg, BRNN_g, RNN_lg, and RNN_g. In two figures we can observe that (1) The networks with *forward-backward* process (BRNNs) built upon bidirectional LSTM outperform the networks based solely on *forward* process implemented by regular LSTM, especially in term of rotation as shown in Fig. 4(a). (2) The networks learning poses in *bottom-up* steps with both local and global constraints (lg) yield higher accuracy than those built on merely absolute poses. (3) The performance of the network on each image in RNN varies significantly in rotation, and the problem is alleviated in BRNN, which might be caused by spatio-temporal consistency introduced in the bidirectional LSTM units.

Table 1. Estimated rotation and translation errors on the KITTI dataset [5].

Method	Sequence											
	03		04		05		06		07		10	
	t_{rel}	r_{rel}	t_{rel}	r_{rel}	t_{rel}	r_{rel}	t_{rel}	r_{rel}	t_{rel}	r_{rel}	t_{rel}	r_{rel}
VISO2-S [6]	3.21	3.25	2.12	2.12	1.53	1.60	1.48	1.58	1.85	1.91	1.17	1.30
VISO2-M [6]	8.47	8.82	4.69	4.49	19.22	17.58	7.30	6.14	23.61	19.11	41.56	32.99
ORB-SLAM2 [11]	2.28	0.40	1.41	0.14	13.21	0.22	18.68	0.26	10.96	0.37	3.71	0.30
ORB-SLAM2 (LC) [11]	2.17	0.39	1.07	0.17	1.86	0.24	4.96	0.18	1.87	0.39	3.76	0.29
SfmLearner [21]	10.78	3.92	4.49	5.24	18.67	4.10	25.88	4.80	21.33	6.65	14.33	3.30
GeoNet [18]	19.21	9.78	9.09	7.54	20.12	7.67	9.28	4.34	8.27	5.93	20.73	9.04
DeepVO [15]	8.49	6.89	7.19	6.97	**2.62**	3.61	**5.42**	5.82	3.91	4.60	8.11	8.83
ESP-VO [16]	6.72	6.46	6.33	6.08	3.35	4.93	7.24	7.29	3.52	5.02	9.77	10.2
RNN_l	6.13	4.63	5.99	3.81	7.18	3.12	14.53	5.53	4.40	2.53	7.62	3.67
RNN_lg	5.60	3.12	3.91	2.38	6.98	3.08	14.82	5.12	4.82	3.62	7.12	3.57
BRNN_l	5.66	3.38	5.49	2.33	6.82	2.84	19.86	8.23	**3.03**	2.84	7.73	3.83
BRNN_lg	**4.74**	**3.12**	**3.90**	**2.22**	6.02	**2.72**	9.59	**2.38**	5.28	**2.30**	**7.04**	**3.29**

t_{rel} : average translational RMSE (%) on length from 100, 200 to 800m.
r_{rel} : average rotational RMSE ($^{\circ}$/100m) on length from 100, 200 to 800m.

In Fig. 4 we also visualize the predicted trajectories of four networks on KITTI sequence 10 containing intense translations and rotations. It shows that BRNNs with *forward-backward* processes improve the rotation estimation accuracy, especially at sharp turnings (Fig. 4(b)–(e), (c)–(f)), while the joint local global constraint performs better on improving translation (Fig. 4(b)–(c), (e)-(f)).

4.4   Results on KITTI Dataset

We compare our model with previous model-based and learning-based monocular VO approaches on the testing sets of KITTI benchmark used by DeepVO [15] and ESP-VO [16]. The KITTI VO/SLAM error metrics, i.e., averaged Root Mean Square Errors(RMSEs) of the translational and rotational errors, are utilized for all the subsequences of lengths ranging from 100, 200 to 800 m.

We fist compare against learning-based methods DeepVO [15], ESP-VO [16], SfmLearner [21] and GeoNet [18]. As shown in Table 1, in general, all the four variations of our model achieve impressive results, while the networks with *forward-backward* process yield better results on the translation and the networks with *local-global* constraints increase the accuracy of predicted motion. Specifically, our network based on *forward-backward* process with coupled *local-global* constraints achieves up to 50% better performance in terms of rotational errors on almost all sequences. Moreover, our model also reduces the translational errors on most sequences. Sharp turns (approximately 180°) in the two sequences might cause the degeneration of performance.

Additionally, we compare our approach against state-of-the-art classic VO systems, including VISO2 [6] and ORB-SLAM2 (with/without loop closure). In Table 1, our method consistently outperforms monocular VISO2 (VISO2-M) on most of the test sequences in terms of both translation and rotation. ORB-SLAM2 (without LC) achieves impressive results in rotation estimation after aligned with ground-truth due to the lack of scale information. However, it gives relative lower performance compared with our method, especially in complicated

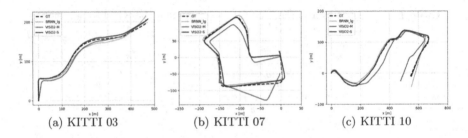

Fig. 5. Ground-truth and trajectories estimated by different methods of Seq 03, 07 and 10 from the KITTI odometry benchmark [5] dataset are illustrated.

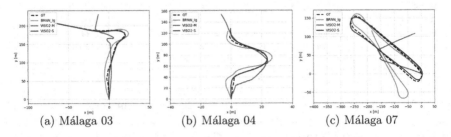

Fig. 6. We compare our model with VISO2-M and VISO2-S on Seq 03, 04 and 07 of the Málaga dataset.

environments (Seq 05, 06, 07). Note that the results produced by our model are vary close to stereo VISO2 (VISO2-S) and ORB-SLAM2 with loop closure (ORB-SLAM2 (LC)), though our network is only a monocular VO system.

Qualitative comparison is illustrated in Fig. 5. Our approach achieves similar performance with other methods on simple motions (Fig. 5(a) and (b)) but yields much better results on complicated motions (Fig. 5(c)) where VISO2-M produces large drift without loop closure.

We intensively test our model in various scenes with diverse motion patterns on sequence 11–21, and the trajectories are presented in Fig. 7. In this case, our network is trained on all the 11 training sequences (00–10) which give sufficient training data to avoid over-fitting and maximize the generalization ability of our networks. Due to a lack of ground-truth on the testing sequences, we rely on the accurate stereo VISO2 as the reference and show the qualitative comparisons of the trajectories recovered by monocular VISO2-M. Figure 7 shows that our model outperforms the VISO2-M in almost all sequences and gives very close performance with VISO2-S.

4.5   Results on Málaga Dataset

We further display the ability of generalization of our network by evaluating on the Málaga dataset [1] without fine-tuning. Figure 6 shows the predicted trajectories of sequence 03, 04 and 07. In this experiment, we test our model against VISO2-M and VISO2-S [6]. Figure 6 demonstrates that our approach performs well on sequences with diverse motion patterns including sharp rotations

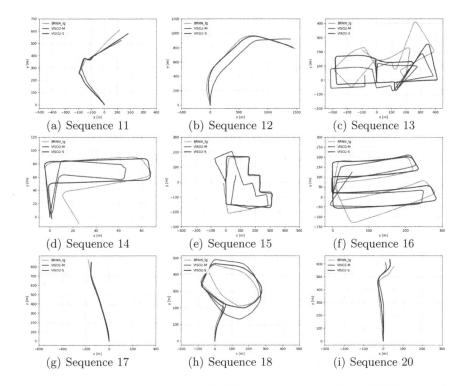

(a) Sequence 11   (b) Sequence 12   (c) Sequence 13

(d) Sequence 14   (e) Sequence 15   (f) Sequence 16

(g) Sequence 17   (h) Sequence 18   (i) Sequence 20

Fig. 7. The predicted trajectories on KITTI sequences 11–20. Stereo VISO2 is used as reference since there are no ground-truth camera poses provided for these sequences.

(sequence 03 and 07), especially outperforms VISO2-M in terms of rotation. The experiment verifies that our model is able to generalize well in totally different urban scenes and camera settings.

5   Conclusion

In this paper, we present an end-to-end neural network to learn camera poses for monocular image sequences. It estimates camera pose at each time step by utilizing information in both *forward* and *backward* processes upon Bidirectional RNNs with extended LSTM units. Additionally, constraints from local to global are coupled to reduce the accumulated error. The network outperforms current state-of-the-art learning-based methods and yields comparable results needless extra scale estimation with model-based approaches on the KITTI dataset. Furthermore, we verify the network's ability to generalize by showing comparable outcomes with current state-of-the-art monocular VO algorithms on the Málaga dataset, without re-training or fine-tuning.

In the future we plan to focus on indoor scenes with more complicated motion patterns. We may also incorporate semantic information for data association, which might improve localization accuracy in texture-less scenes or environments with dynamic objects.

References

1. Blanco-Claraco, J.L., Moreno-Dueñas, F.Á., González-Jiménez, J.: The Málaga urban dataset: high-rate stereo and LiDAR in a realistic urban scenario. IJRR **33**, 207–214 (2014)
2. Cho, K., et al.: Learning phrase representations using RNN encoder-decoder for statistical machine translation. In: ICEMNLP (2014)
3. Engel, J., Koltun, V., Cremers, D.: Direct sparse odometry. TPAMI **40**(3), 611–625 (2018)
4. Engel, Jakob, Schöps, Thomas, Cremers, Daniel: LSD-SLAM: large-scale direct monocular SLAM. In: Fleet, David, Pajdla, Tomas, Schiele, Bernt, Tuytelaars, Tinne (eds.) ECCV 2014. LNCS, vol. 8690, pp. 834–849. Springer, Cham (2014). https://doi.org/10.1007/978-3-319-10605-2_54
5. Geiger, A., Lenz, P., Urtasun, R.: Are we ready for autonomous driving? CVPR, the KITTI vision benchmark suite (2012)
6. Geiger, A., Ziegler, J., Stiller, C.: StereoScan: dense 3D reconstruction in real-time. In: IV (2011)
7. He, K., Zhang, X., Ren, S., Sun, J.: Deep residual learning for image recognition. In: CVPR (2016)
8. Hochreiter, S., Schmidhuber, J.: Long short-term memory. Neural Comput. **9**(8), 1735–1780 (1997)
9. Kingma, D.P., Ba, J.: Adam: a method for stochastic optimization. In: ICLR (2015)
10. Li, R., Wang, S., Long, Z., Gu, D.: UnDeepVO: monocular visual odometry through unsupervised deep learning. In: ICRA (2018)
11. Mur-Artal, R., Tardós, J.D.: ORB-SLAM2: An Open-source SLAM System for Monocular, Stereo, and RGB-D Cameras. T-RO (2017)
12. Paszke, A., Gross, S., Chintala, S., Chanan, G.: Pytorch (2017). https://github.com/pytorch/pytorch
13. Schuster, M., Paliwal, K.K.: Bidirectional recurrent neural networks. TSP **45**(11), 2673–2681 (1997)
14. Shi, X., Chen, Z., Wang, H., Yeung, D., Wong, W., Woo, W.: Convolutional LSTM network: a machine learning approach for precipitation nowcasting. In: NIPS (2015)
15. Wang, S., Clark, R., Wen, H., Trigoni, N.: DeepVO: towards end-to-end visual odometry with deep recurrent convolutional neural networks. In: ICRA (2017)
16. Wang, S., Clark, R., Wen, H., Trigoni, N.: End-to-end, sequence-to-sequence probabilistic visual odometry through deep neural networks. IJRR **37**(4–5), 513–542 (2018)
17. Yang, N., Wang, R., Stückler, J., Cremers, D.: Deep virtual stereo odometry: leveraging deep depth prediction for monocular direct sparse odometry. In: ECCV (2018)
18. Yin, Z., Shi, J.: GeoNet: unsupervised learning of dense depth optical flow and camera pose. In: CVPR (2018)
19. Zhan, H., Garg, R., Saroj Weerasekera, C., Li, K., Agarwal, H., Reid, I.: Unsupervised learning of monocular depth estimation and visual odometry with deep feature reconstruction. In: CVPR (2018)
20. Zhou, H., Ummenhofer, B., Brox, T.: DeepTAM: deep tracking and mapping. In: ECCV (2018)
21. Zhou, T., Brown, M., Snavely, N., Lowe, D.G.: Unsupervised learning of depth and ego-motion from video. In: CVPR (2017)

Fuzzy Control Reversing System Based on Visual Information

Shaofeng Liu[1,2], Yingchun Fan[1], Yuliang Tang[1], Xin Jing[2], Jintao Yao[2], and Hong Han[1,2(✉)]

[1] School of Artificial Intelligence, Xidian University, Xi'an 710071, China
`hanh@mail.xidian.edu.cn`
[2] Shaanxi Key Laboratory of Integrated and Intelligent Navigation,
Xi'an 710071, China

Abstract. Intelligentization of car navigation is an inevitable trend. Visual navigation has the advantages of high precision in short distances and low cost. This paper proposes a fuzzy control reversing system based on visual information. We obtain the trajectory of the rear camera by constructing reversing model of the car. YOLO (You Only Look Once) is used to detect pedestrians and cars appearing in the camera field of view and segment the detected images during the reversing process. The dynamic feature points are removed effectively by the proposed environmental statistical information analysis method. Using visual information to construct constraints to improve the traditional fuzzy control reversing system can provide drivers with accurate driving assistance information and effectively reduce the probability of accidents such as collisions. The experimental results show that the proposed method is effective and feasible.

Keywords: Visual navigation · YOLO · Region segmentation · Fuzzy control · Driving assistance

1 Introduction

In recent years, the development of visual navigation algorithms has provided new ideas for self-driving technology [1–3]. Many excellent algorithms have appeared and been applied to self-driving cars, or driving assistant systems, achieving fruitful results. This paper proposes an intelligent reversing system based on visual information in view of the high accuracy in short distance and low cost of visual navigation.

Fuzzy system has strong robustness and fault tolerance, the use of fuzzy systems for reversing control is a long-term research problem. Halgamuge et al. proposed a hierarchical hybrid fuzzy/crisp system, that can be used for assisting

---

This work is supported by the open fund of Shaanxi Key Laboratory of Integrated and Intelligent Navigation SKLIIN-20180102 and SKLIIN-20180107. This is a student work.

Z. Lin et al. (Eds.): PRCV 2019, LNCS 11859, pp. 247–258, 2019.
https://doi.org/10.1007/978-3-030-31726-3_21

continuous reversing of vehicles with long trailers [4]. Chen et al. used the natural parabolic paths as a suboptimal solution to the shortest distance. They developed a nine-rule controller with fuzzy logic, which can control the truck to follow any feasible trajectories and successfully move into the parking lot even without mathematical system models [5]. However, fuzzy system can only provide the reverse route. If it's to be used in practice, it needs to be combined with other specific information in the environment to avoid people or vehicles that may appear.

In the field of automatic driving or assisted driving, avoiding obstacles is the most critical issue. Especially in the dynamic environment in which the car is traveling, identifying and evading dynamic obstacles quickly and effectively is a major problem that must be solved. Nogami et al. proposed a system that can estimate the moving space for the vehicle, and velocity of the obstacles, and choose another path if the current path is estimated to be not possible [6]. Alvarez et al. developed a method that makes a quadrotor with one single monocular camera to generate collision-free waypoints [7].

In this paper, we propose a fuzzy control reversing system based on visual information. The system directly uses the rear camera of the car to detect pedestrians and cars that may affect the reversing process, and at the same time judges whether the car has the risk of collision or friction. First, we construct the reversing model and analyzed the trajectory of the rear camera. Second, the YOLO network is used to detect pedestrians and cars that appear in the camera field of view and build threat level models. Then the image is divided into three areas: pedestrians, cars and environment. By the proposed environmental statistical information analysis method, cars can be divided into two categories: static and dynamic. The pose of the camera is accurately estimated through the static feature points. Finally, the framework of fuzzy control reversing system based on the visual information is given.

The rest of the paper is structured as follows: Sect. 2 discusses related work in generally two aspects. Section 3 gives the whole pipeline and details of our reversing system, Sect. 4 lists our experiment results.

2 Related Work

A. Semantic SLAM in the Dynamic Environment: The main idea of the semantic SLAM systems work in the dynamic environment is to combine the semantic with geometric information to find dynamic objects and use the stationary parts of the environment to estimate the trajectory and pose of the camera.

DynaSLAM uses Mask R-CNN [8] as the sematic segmentation approach, it can works on monocular, stereo and RGB-D cameras [9]. DynaSLAM eliminates all the potential dynamic targets such as people, vehicle, and animals, combines with more accurate geometric segmentations remove dynamic targets that cannot be judged by semantic information, such as rotating chairs.

DS-SLAM uses SegNet [10] as the semantic segmentation approach. Five parallel threads, feature points tracking, targets semantic segmentation, local mapping, loop closing and semantic octo-tree map creation are running in the system [11]. The system considers people as most possible dynamic targets, whose feature points are made to be outliers. At the same time, the polar constraint is used to remove other dynamic feature points in the environment.

MaskFusion uses Mask R-CNN as the semantic segmentation approach [12]. Authors proposed two strategies to judge whether the objects are moving or not. Firstly, consistence of motion. Secondly, objects interact with people are considered dynamic. Since Mask-RCNN cannot run in real-time, to improve performance, MaskFusion performs semantic segmentation every 5 frames.

B. Vehicle Detection and Distance Estimation: Different moving platforms carrying cameras should also be considered when researching the application of SLAM [13]. At present, the detection and distance estimation of autonomous vehicles are based on the camera installed on the front or the roof of the car to establish a coordinate system. In terms of vehicle detection and distance estimation, Rezaei et al. proposed a monocular-vision-based collision warning system that provides real-time detection of vehicles and the distance. They applied multiple measures to improve the accuracy, including Haar-like features for detection, tail-light segmentation, and feature fusion technics, etc. The system achieved good results under various weather and lighting conditions [14]. Li et al. proposed a pitch angle estimation approach to achieve range measurement. The system is initialized using only a vehicle-mounted camera, and the estimation process doesn't have any cumulative error. They used the adjacent frames captured by the camera to detect optical flow of feature points, then calculated the ego-motion parameters of the camera and optimizes them simultaneously [15]. Kim et al. proposed a real-time lane and vehicle detection system that can be mounted on the self-driving cars. It can provide distance between front vehicle and ego-vehicle [16].

3   Method

3.1   Vision-Based Reversing Model

The simplified model of the car is represented by Fig. 1(a). L is the length of the car, W is the width. Four corners of the car are respectively A, B, C and D. When the car is steering, the front wheels turn, the angle between center axis and the horizontal direction is ϕ, the angle of the front wheels turned is θ, the rear camera of a car is usually installed at the midpoint (x, y). When reversing, the motion of the rear camera is the same as the rear midpoint.

Reversing process is shown in Fig. 1(b). Position of the car at moment t is indicated by the dotted line frame. The car reverses at speed v, and the front wheels turn angle is θ. After the observation interval Δt, the car reaches the solid line frame position. Moving distance of the rear end is r. The angle between

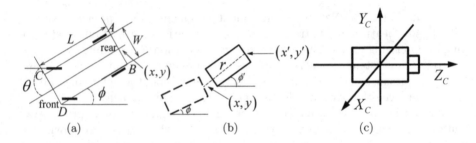

Fig. 1. Reserving model (a) Simplified model (b) Reserving process (c) Coordinate system of the car

the center axis and the horizontal direction is changed from ϕ to ϕ', and the coordinates of the midpoint changed from (x, y) to (x', y').

In practice, the reversing speed is slow, and the value Δt is small. It can be considered that the moving trajectory of the car in this period is a straight-line segment approximately. The calculation expressions for x', y', ϕ' and r are as follows:

$$x' = x + r\cos\phi' \tag{1}$$

$$y' = y + r\sin\phi' \tag{2}$$

$$\phi' = \phi + \theta \tag{3}$$

$$r = v * \Delta t \tag{4}$$

Coordinate system of the camera is shown in Fig. 1(c). When reserving, trajectory of the camera can be decomposed into a rotary motion around the Y_c axis, and translational motions along the optical axis Z_c and X_c.

The rotation matrix of the camera is:

$$R = \begin{bmatrix} \cos(\theta) & 0 & \sin(\theta) \\ 0 & 1 & 0 \\ -\sin(\theta) & 0 & \cos(\theta) \end{bmatrix} \tag{5}$$

The translation matrix of the camera is:

$$t = \begin{bmatrix} r\cos(\phi'), & r\sin(\phi'), & 0 \end{bmatrix} \tag{6}$$

$P_i = [X_i, Y_i, Z_i, 1]^T$ are the coordinates of the space points, and $p_i = [u_i, v_i, 1]^T$ are the coordinates of the projection points on the imaging plane, which satisfy:

$$s_i p_i = KTP_i \tag{7}$$

$$T = \begin{bmatrix} R & t \\ 0^T & 1 \end{bmatrix} \tag{8}$$

where s_i are the scale factors, K is the camera's intrinsic matrix, and T is the camera's extrinsic matrix.

The SURF (Speeded Up Robust Features) [17] algorithm is used in the feature extraction and matching stage, which is one of the best real-time image feature extraction and description algorithms. Since we used a stereo camera in the experiment, the depth information of the matching points can be obtained. Assume that the one pair of matching points are $A = \{P_{a1}, P_{a2}, ..., P_{an}\}$ and $B = \{P_{b1}, P_{b2}, ..., P_{bn}\}$. The external parameter matrix of the camera can be obtained by solving the least squares problem shown below:

$$\min_{R,t} \sum_{i=1}^{N} \|P_{ai} - (RP_{bi} + t)\|^2 \qquad (9)$$

By accurately estimating the external parameter matrix, information such as the front wheels turn angle and the moving distance of car can be derived.

3.2 Real-Time Identification of Obstacles

In the process of reversing, pedestrians or other cars may appear in the rear camera field of view. To avoid collision or friction with these dynamic obstacles, the reversing system is required to make a real-time response by identifying the specific type of obstacles quickly and accurately. Our proposed reversing system uses YOLO network as target detection method. YOLO runs extremely fast, and its faster version can process more than 150 frames per second. YOLO suppresses background error significantly. A general representation of objectives is learnt by YOLO, giving the network strong generalization ability [18,19].

When reversing the car, the rear camera captures a series images of obstacle at different angles and positions if there are dynamic obstacles suddenly move into the rear camera field of view, such as pedestrians or cars. Information available through YOLO includes the center coordinate (x_i, y_i) of the prediction frame of obstacles at different viewing angles, the width w_i of the frame, the height h_i, and the confidence C_i, where i is the number of times the same obstacle is captured. Through the position change of the obstacle prediction frame, the moving direction and speed of the obstacle can be inferred. Key frames are selected out of every three frames to reduce the redundancy of the information, while other frames are discarded. Figure 2 shows the key frame choosing strategy.

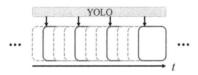

Fig. 2. Choose key frames from the camera frames

Obstacle edge information obtained through YOLO is often imperfect, and the edge of the target is usually fused with environment. In order to effectively ensure the safety of pedestrians and cars, after obtaining the prediction frame of pedestrians, we establish a threat level model of obstacles centering on the prediction frame, increase the width of the prediction frame by half, and the height by 1/4 as a threat area, where the planned route must not pass through. For obstacles that has certain pattern of movement such as cars, the width of the prediction frame is increased by 1/8, and the height is increased by 1/16 as a threat area.

3.3   Detection and Exclusion of Dynamic Obstacle Feature Points

In the process of positioning and mapping of the rear camera, due to too many matching points on the dynamic obstacle, the solution of the formula (9) could be affected, and a large deviation of the camera pose estimation may occur. It is necessary to eliminate the dynamic obstacles captured by the camera [20].

In scenes such as parking lots, the most common dynamic obstacles are pedestrians and cars. YOLO is used to divide the image area into three parts: pedestrian area, car area and environmental area. Feature points within the environment area are considered to be static points. We have agreed that when YOLO detects pedestrian targets, the feature points in the pedestrian detection frames are discarded during the feature point matching process.

The state of cars in the camera field of view can be divided into two types, stationary and moving. We need to find out which car is moving and discard the feature points in its area. A method of key point motion analysis to find static and dynamic feature points in the car area is proposed by Fan et al. [21]. Bayona et al. proposed an algorithm focused on obtaining stationary foreground regions [22], which is based on background difference method and is useful for applications like the detection of abandoned/stolen objects and parked vehicles. However, background difference method and optical flow method commonly used in video surveillance are proved difficult to apply to moving cars.

If the points are stationary, the motion states of these points in the images can be determined as the camera moves. Meanwhile, their motion states should be consistent with each other.

A motion statistical information analysis method is proposed to find dynamic cars. The constraints are constructed by statistical information of the distance and the main direction of matching points in the static environment. The method is as follows:

For two continuous detection frames, the two sets of matching points in the environment area are set to P_1, P_2, and the distance between the matching points is:

$$DIS = \sqrt{\|P_2 - P_1\|} \tag{10}$$

An outlier value is defined as a value that is more than three scaled MAD (median absolute deviations) away from the median. After excluding outliers, the maximum and minimum values in DIS are taken as the upper and lower bounds of the distance constraint, namely:

$$Ubound = max(DIS) \tag{11}$$

$$Dbound = min(DIS) \tag{12}$$

If the distance between more than 90% of the matching points in the car detection frame does not satisfy the following relationship, the car is considered to be dynamic.

$$Dbound \leq DIS_{car} \leq Ubound \tag{13}$$

When the rear camera of the car makes a rotational motion around the axis Y_c or a translational motion along the axis X_c, we count and divide the direction change of matching feature points into 8 directions. As shown in Fig. 3(a), the yellow and blue blocks represent a pair of matching feature points in two continuous frames, where the yellow blocks come from the previous frame, and the arrow indicates the direction change of the matching points. In the statistical process, the direction of the red arrow in the represents the direction change of matching feature points above, and is divided into the sixth area. The direction change of matching feature points in the static environment is counted to determine the main direction of the environment, since they should mostly be the same. If the main directions of car frames are different from the environment, cars in the detection frame are considered to be dynamic.

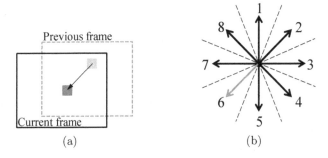

(a)   (b)

Fig. 3. Direction change of the matching feature points in two frames (Color figure online)

When the rear camera of the car makes a translational motion along the optical axis Z_c, direction change of the matching feature points in the environment is directed from periphery to the center of the image, or the opposite. The average value of depth change of the matching feature points d_e in the static environment is calculated, which is the translation distance of the car in direction Z_c, and the evaluation value of depth change d_e in the car detection frame is calculated, if formula (14) is satisfied, the car is considered static, where τ is the empirical value, taking 0.1 in the experiment.

$$\|d_e - d_c\| < \tau * d_e \tag{14}$$

3.4 Obstacle Avoidance and Path Planning

Fuzzy control [23,24] is used to control the process of reversing the self-driving car. The input variable x is the value of the midpoint coordinates of the car tail, ϕ is the angle between the car and the horizontal direction, and the output variable is the front wheel rotation angle θ. Range for each variable is as follows:

$$0 \leq x \leq 100$$
$$-\frac{1}{2}\pi \leq \phi \leq \frac{3}{2}\pi \tag{15}$$
$$-\frac{1}{6}\pi \leq \theta \leq \frac{1}{6}\pi$$

When θ takes a positive value, it means turning the front wheel clockwise, and a negative value means counterclockwise.

After determining the initial position, fuzzy system can obtain the turn angle of the front wheels θ, and the reversing speed is constant. The position and posture information of the next moment can be obtained by (1)–(2), if there is a pedestrian or moving car in the field of view of the rear camera, collision and friction can be predicted by the center of the prediction frame and the threat level model we built. If it happens, the car stops to observe until the danger is lifted. The judgment formula is as follows:

$$\frac{z_i}{f}\sqrt{f^2 + x_i^2 + y_i^2} > \frac{1}{2}(\sqrt{L^2 + W^2} + \frac{z_i}{f}\sqrt{W_i^2 + H_i^2}) \tag{16}$$

where z_i is the depth value of the center of the predicted frame, and (x_i, y_i) is the center coordinate of the predicted frame. L and W indicate the length and width of the car, while W_i and H_i indicate the width and height of the obstacle threat area. If the formula (16) is satisfied, the car can continue to reverse. If not, it indicates that the car has the danger of collision and should stop to observe.

Pedestrians or moving cars in the process of reversing is not considered in the traditional fuzzy reversing system, which leads to great limitation in actual use. The intelligent reversing system fully utilizes information of pedestrians and cars captured by the rear camera, sets constraints with threat of obstacles, and effectively improves the safety of the reversing process. The reversing flow chart is shown in Fig. 4.

4 Experiments

4.1 Reverse Simulation Experiment

We use MATLAB 2018a to simulate the car reversing process. Parameters are as follows: reversing speed is 8 m/s, reversing observation time interval is 0.4 s, car width is 3 m, car length is 6 m, site size is 100 m × 100 m, camera field of view is 140°, camera effective distance is 10 m.

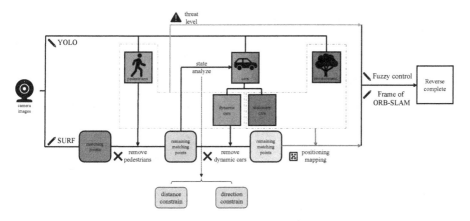

Fig. 4. Vision-based fuzzy control reserving system

Figure 5 shows the results of the reversing simulation experiment. Sub-graphs (a) and (b) show the running diagram of the car and the running trajectory of the rear camera. Sub-graphs (c) and (d) indicate the centroid of the dynamic obstacle with red dots. The red circle is the threat range of the dynamic obstacle. In practice, it is determined by the size of the obstacle frame. The green circle centered on the camera indicates the possible area of car on the next move, and the radius is $\frac{1}{2}\sqrt{L^2 + W^2}$.

Whether the car is parked or not is determined by (16). In the sub-graph (c), a random dynamic obstacle appears in the field of view of the camera. Red dot indicates the center of the detection frame, threat area formed by this obstacle is represented by the red circle. In the simulation process, the radius of the threat area is set to 2m, while in practice, it is determined by the size of the detection frame of the obstacle. When the dynamic obstacle moves to the next position, the system detects that the car is not at risk of collision or friction, and continues to operate, as shown in sub-graph (d).

It can be seen form the simulation results that the path planned by the fuzzy system is smoothing, and when the dynamic obstacles enter the view field of the camera, the system can provide drivers with accurate driving assistance information based on the constrains of the threat level model.

4.2 Detection Results of Feature Points in the Image

The parameters of the stereo camera we used in the experiment are as follows: focal length is 2.1 mm, resolution is 752×480, baseline is 120.0 mm, pixel size is $6.0 * 6.0 \, \mu m$, and camera field of view is $D : 140° H : 120° V : 75°$.

The real experiment site was a parking lot, there are stationary cars, moving cars and pedestrians. Some experimental results are shown in Figs. 6 and 7.

Figure 6 shows the detection and matching of feature points in the presence of pedestrians. Pedestrian areas are marked by the red box, and not used for

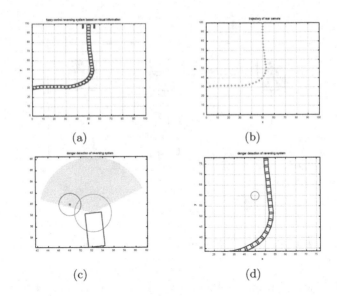

(a)   (b)

(c)   (d)

Fig. 5. Reserving simulation (a) Car operation diagram (b) Trajectory of rear camera (c) Car stops and observes when collision or friction may occur (d) Continue operate when no collision or friction may occur after detection (Color figure online)

(a)   (b)   (c)   (d)

Fig. 6. (a) Match results of SURF (b) Results with YOLO detection and constrains (c) Constructed threat box for the pedestrian (d) Detail comparison of YOLO detection box and the constructed threat box. In the semantic segment process of the YOLO, parts of the pedestrian leaked into the environment. The proposed threat box can encircle the pedestrian effectively. It's necessary to enlarge the detection box, considering the uncertainty of pedestrian movement. (Color figure online)

feature points extraction. It can be seen that some parts of the pedestrian cannot be distinguished from the environment in the YOLO detection and the proposed threat box can encircle the pedestrian entirely.

Figure 7 shows the situation that a moving car enter the view field of the camera. When feature points in the detection frame are not removed, there are many matching feature points on the moving car. Through the analysis of the motion state of the feature points, the matching points on the moving car are deleted effectively whereas the matching points on the static cars are reserved. According to the proportion of the remaining match points to all match points

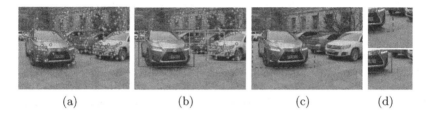

(a)   (b)   (c)   (d)

Fig. 7. Detection results and threat boxes (a) Match results of SURF (b) Results with YOLO detection and constrains, the moving car is marked by red box, static cars by green boxes (c) Constructed threat box for the moving car. (d) Detail comparision of YOLO detection and our threat box (Color figure online)

in the car detection frame, the state of the car can be determined. The moving car is marked by the red frame and static cars by green frames.

5 Conclusion

This paper proposes a fuzzy control reversing system based on visual information. For the typical environment of car reversing, the path is planed by fuzzy system, YOLO is used to identify pedestrians and cars appearing in the rear camera field of view, and segment the image into pedestrians, cars and environment according to the recognition results. To accurately estimate the camera pose, it is necessary to eliminate the dynamic feature points in the image. We agree not to detect the feature points of the pedestrian area, and at the same time, use the feature point motion state analysis to find the moving car. The experimental results show that the proposed method can detect the pedestrians and the dynamic cars effectively, and the constructed threat boxes can provide the driver with accurate driving assistance information to ensure the safety of the vehicles and pedestrians.

References

1. Adams, M., Vo, B., Mahler, R., Mullane, J.: SLAM gets a PHD: new concepts in map estimation. IEEE Robot. Autom. Mag. **21**(2), 26–37 (2014)
2. Häne, C., et al.: 3D visual perception for self-driving cars using a multi-camera system: calibration, mapping, localization, and obstacle detection. Image Vis. Comput. S0262885617301117 (2017)
3. Hee Lee, G., Faundorfer, F., Pollefeys, M.: Motion estimation for self-driving cars with a generalized camera. In: Computer Vision and Pattern Recognition (2013)
4. Halgamuge, S.K., Runkler, T.A., Glesner, M.: A hierarchical hybrid fuzzy controller for real-time reverse driving support of vehicles with long trailers. In: IEEE Conference on Fuzzy Systems, IEEE World Congress on Computational Intelligence (1994)
5. Chen, G., Zhang, D.: Back-driving a truck with suboptimal distance trajectories: a fuzzy logic control approach. IEEE Trans. Fuzzy Syst. **5**(3), 369–380 (1997)

6. Nogami, S., Hidaka, K.: A stereo camera based static and moving obstacles detection on autonomous visual navigation of indoor transportation vehicle. In: IECON 2018–44th Annual Conference of the IEEE Industrial Electronics Society, pp. 5421–5426, October 2018

7. Alvarez, H., Paz, L.M., Sturm, J., Cremers, D.: Collision avoidance for quadrotors with a monocular camera. In: Hsieh, M.A., Khatib, O., Kumar, V. (eds.) Experimental Robotics. STAR, vol. 109, pp. 195–209. Springer, Cham (2016). https://doi.org/10.1007/978-3-319-23778-7_14

8. He, K., Gkioxari, G., Dollar, P., Girshick, R.: Mask R-CNN. IEEE Trans. Pattern Anal. Mach. Intell. (2017)

9. Bescos, B., Fácil, J.M., Civera, J., Neira, J.: DynaSLAM: tracking, mapping, and inpainting in dynamic scenes. IEEE Robot. Autom. Lett. **3**(4), 4076–4083 (2018)

10. Badrinarayanan, V., Kendall, A., Cipolla, R.: SegNet: a deep convolutional encoder-decoder architecture for image segmentation. IEEE Trans. Pattern Anal. Mach. Intell. **39**(12), 2481–2495 (2017)

11. Yu, C., et al.: DS-SLAM: a semantic visual slam towards dynamic environments. In: 2018 IEEE/RSJ International Conference on Intelligent Robots and Systems (IROS), pp. 1168–1174 (2018)

12. Rünz, M., Buffier, M., Agapito, L.: MaskFusion: real-time recognition, tracking and reconstruction of multiple moving objects. In: 2018 IEEE International Symposium on Mixed and Augmented Reality (ISMAR), pp. 10–20 (2018)

13. Camurri, M., Bazeille, S.: Real-time depth and inertial fusion for local slam on dynamic legged robots. In: IEEE International Conference on Multisensor Fusion and Integration for Intelligent Systems (2015)

14. Rezaei, M., Terauchi, M., Klette, R.: Robust vehicle detection and distance estimation under challenging lighting conditions. IEEE Trans. Intell. Transp. Syst. **16**(5), 2723–2743 (2015)

15. Li, B., Zhang, X., Sato, M.: Pitch angle estimation using a vehicle-mounted monocular camera for range measurement. In: 2014 12th International Conference on Signal Processing (ICSP), pp. 1161–1168, October 2014

16. Kim, H., Lee, Y., Woo, T., Kim, H.: Integration of vehicle and lane detection for forward collision warning system. In: IEEE International Conference on Consumer Electronics-Berlin (2016)

17. Bay, H., Tuytelaars, T., Van Gool, L.: SURF: speeded up robust features. In: Leonardis, A., Bischof, H., Pinz, A. (eds.) ECCV 2006. LNCS, vol. 3951, pp. 404–417. Springer, Heidelberg (2006). https://doi.org/10.1007/11744023_32

18. Redmon, J., Farhadi, A.: Yolo9000: better, faster, stronger. In: IEEE Conference on Computer Vision and Pattern Recognition (2017)

19. Redmon, J., Farhadi, A.: Yolov3: an incremental improvement. CoRR, abs/1804.02767 (2018)

20. Danping, Z., Ping, T.: CoSLAM: collaborative visual SLAM in dynamic environments. IEEE Trans. Pattern Anal. Mach. Intell. **35**(2), 354–366 (2013)

21. Fan, Y., Han, H., Tang, Y., Zhi, T.: Dynamic objects elimination in SLAM based on image fusion. Pattern Recognit. Lett. (2018)

22. Bayona, A., SanMiguel, J.C., Martínez, J.M.: Stationary foreground detection using background subtraction and temporal difference in video surveillance. In IEEE International Conference on Image Processing (2010)

23. Kong, S.G., Kosko, B.: Adaptive fuzzy systems for backing up a truck-and-trailer. IEEE Trans. Neural Netw. **3**(2), 211–223 (1992)

24. Kosko, B.: Neural networks and fuzzy systems: a dynamical systems approach to machine intelligence, January 1992

Adversarial Domain Alignment Feature Similarity Enhancement Learning for Unsupervised Domain Adaptation

Jun Zhou[1], Fei Wu[1]([✉]), Ying Sun[1], Songsong Wu[1], Min Yang[1], and Xiao-Yuan Jing[2]

[1] College of Automation, Nanjing University of Posts and Telecommunications, Nanjing, China
zhoujun127@126.com, wufei_8888@126.com, sunyingnupt@163.com, {sswu,yangm}@njupt.edu.cn
[2] School of Computer, Wuhan University, Wuhan, China
jingxy_2000@126.com

Abstract. Unsupervised domain adaptation (UDA) attempts to transfer knowledge learned from labeled source domain to unlabeled target domain. Its main challenge is distribution gap between two domains. Most of works focus on reducing domain shift by domain alignment methods. Although these methods can reduce the domain shift, the samples far from the class center of target domain are still easily misclassified. To solve the problem, we propose a new approach named Adversarial Domain Alignment Feature Similarity Enhancement Learning (AASE). It learns domain invariant features by adversarial game and correlation alignment to reduce the domain gap, and makes these features having better discrimination via joint central discrimination and feature similarity enhancement. AASE makes the learned features have better intra-class compactness and inter-class separability. AASE is evaluated on two datasets, and the results show that AASE has critical improvement in the performance of UDA.

Keywords: Unsupervised domain adaptation · Domain adversarial · Discrimination learning

1 Introduction

Unsupervised domain adaptation [5,18] (UDA) receives wide attention, which focuses on how to transfer learned knowledge from the source domain with the large number of labeled samples to adapt the target domain with unlabeled samples. UDA has different domain distributions, although it has the same task. The main challenge of this knowledge transfer can be called domain shift [25], which refers to the domain distribution discrepancy between the source domain and target domain.

The first author is student.

Z. Lin et al. (Eds.): PRCV 2019, LNCS 11859, pp. 259–271, 2019.
https://doi.org/10.1007/978-3-030-31726-3_22

In recent years, many UDA methods are presented. One kind of typical methods is to reduce the domain shift by learning the domain invariant features, and then utilize the knowledge from the source domain to train the target domain to obtain an adaptive classifier. Following this principle, some previous studies have been proposed to learn domain invariant features with neural networks (Deep Domain Confusion (DDC) [23], Deep Adaptation Network (DAN) [14], Deep Unsupervised Convolutional Domain Adaptation (DUCDA) [28], etc.), by minimizing the distance metric of domain discrepancy, e.g., Maximum Mean Discrepancy (MMD) [15]. Another type of typical methods is to deal with the UDA problem by instance re-weighting, such as [2,4,10], which assumes that even in the shared subspace, some source instances which are irrelated to the target instances still exist. In addition, some studies introduce adversarial learning into UDA (ADDA [22], DANN [5], CoGAN [13], etc.), verifying the advantages of minimizing domain differences relative to traditional methods. Although these methods reduce the domain discrepancy, they do not learn more discriminative features to improve the classification accuracy of the target domain.

Recently, [1] proposed a joint domain alignment and discriminative feature learning (JDDA) method, which reduces the distance between the covariances of source and target domains to align different domains and makes the learned features more discriminative in the common feature subspace.

1.1 Motivation and Contribution

Most of the existing methods, such as DDC, DAN, etc., focus on reducing domain shift but few pay attention to the learning of more discriminative features. Therefore, how to effectively actualize domain alignment and learn more features with stronger discriminating ability is a significant research topic.

A few methods attempt to realize domain alignment and make the learned features more discriminative jointly. [1] is the first method that focuses on effectively and jointly performing domain alignment and discriminate feature learning, but it does not fully utilize the inter-domain and intra-domain relationships, and does not align the different domains well. We design a new UDA approach. The contributions of our study can be summarized as following four points:

1. This is the first UDA approach to effectively joint the adversarial domain alignment, discriminative feature learning and feature similarity enhancement.
2. To reduce the misclassification rate of the edge samples of the target domain class, our approach designs center discriminative loss and feature similarity enhancement loss, which make the domain invariant features have better intra-class compactness and inter-class separability.
3. To maximize the alignment of different domains, we design a dual-channel parameter shared adversarial convolution network. It achieves final domain alignment through the minimax game between the domain classifier and the feature extractor.

4. We conduct extensive experiments of our approach on two authoritative bench-marks, digital identification and office-31. The experimental results verify that our approach can significantly improve the performance of UDA.

2   Related Work

In the classical UDA studies, the methods of processing domain shift attempt to make different domains aligned. Although many metric methods are proposed to measure the similarity of different domain distributions, Maximum Mean Discrepancy (MMD) is the most commonly used in domain adaptation method. [4,6,8] use MMD to reweight the source sample to minimize the discrepancy in source and target domain samples distribution. These methods do not fully use of the feature representations of the source and target domains to make the intra-class samples of the target domain more compact and the inter-class samples more separable.

UDA based on deep learning architecture can link tasks from different domains. In UDA, most methods use deep networks [24] to reduce the domain distribution discrepancy of different domains by learning domain invariant features. In DDC [23], DAN [14] and RTN [16], the authors proposed to link the source data features of deep learning with the target data feature representations, thereby reducing the MMD between the source data feature representation and the target data feature representation. DDC [23] additionally adds an item into loss function to minimize the MMD of the last fully connected layer. And [14] minimizes the MMD of multiple independent fully connected layers. [16] proposed a fusion layer for interaction between multiple feature layers. [28] minimizes the domain difference between the source and target domains projected on second-order correlation statistics. In CORAL [21] and CMD [27], high order moments are used to align the source and target domains in the common feature subspace. These deep domain adaptation studies do not consider the weakly discriminative characteristics of the deep feature representation of class edge samples in the target domain.

In recent years, most of deep domain adaptation methods are based on dual-channel structure to represent the source model and the target model, respectively. The dual-channel non-parametric shared structure is used in [19], and the dual-channel parameter-shared structure is used in [1,23]. Inspired by these deep methods, we design a dual-channel parameter-shared structure as the basis of network. In addition, [7] presents adversarial learning which is proved to be effective, and some researches apply the adversarial learning to the UDA, e.g., DANN [5], ADDA [22], CoGAN [13], which verify that adversarial learning is better than the traditional method. Therefore, we introduce the adversarial learning to design our network based on dual-channel parameter-shared convolution network.

3　Proposed Approach

We design an adversarial dual-channel parameter-shared deep convolutional domain adaptation network, as shown in Fig. 1. The network is mainly composed of three parts: the feature extractor $G_f(\cdot)$ parameterized by Θ_f for high-level feature extraction (v_i^s and v_i^t), label classifier $G_y(\cdot)$ parameterized by Θ_y, and the domain classifier $G_a(\cdot)$ parameterized by Θ_a. In $G_f(\cdot)$, the parameters are shared by two channels. We seek optimal parameter Θ_f that maximizes the domain classification loss, and look for parameter Θ_a which minimizes the loss of domain classification. In addition, we seek the optimal parameter Θ_y to minimize the label prediction loss.

Let $X^s = \{x_i^s\}_{i=1}^{n_s}$ and $X^t = \{x_i^t\}_{i=1}^{n_t}$ denote image sets from the source and target domains, respectively, with $Y^s = \{\tilde{y}_i^s\}_{i=1}^{n_s}$ being the corresponding labels, where $\tilde{y}_i^s \in \{1, ..., C\}$ and C indicates the total number of classes. Here, n_s and n_t separately denote the number of samples in X^s and X^t. x_i^s and x_i^t have the same dimension. Let $\Theta = \{\Theta_f, \Theta_y\}$ denote a collection of parameters, $V_s = \{v_s^i\}_{i=1}^{b} \in \mathbb{R}^{b \times l}$ and $V_t = \{v_t^i\}_{i=1}^{b} \in \mathbb{R}^{b \times l}$ denote the output features of bottleneck layers in the source and target channels, respectively, where b and l separately represent the numbers of neurons in the trained mini-batch and the bottleneck (BN) layers.

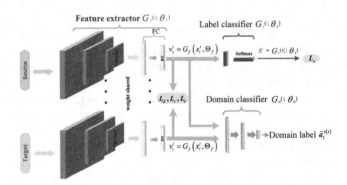

Fig. 1. Overview of the adversarial dual-channel parameter-shared convolutional domain adaptation network. The entire network consists of a feature extractor $G_f(\cdot)$, a label classifier $G_y(\cdot)$, and a domain classifier $G_a(\cdot)$. The domain classifier is connected to the feature extractor through a gradient reversal layer (GRL).

3.1　Domain Adversarial Training

Inspired by DANN [5], we design the adversarial adaptation network to minimize domain discrepancy, i.e., we learn high-level invariant features (v_s^i and v_t^i) from the source and target domains to maximize domain classification loss by training $G_f(\cdot)$, and we train $G_a(\cdot)$ to minimize this loss. In the domain classifier, we manually define the source and target domain labels as $a_i^s = 1$ and $a_i^t = 0$, respectively. Gradient reversal layer (GRL) [5] is introduced in the model to attain a more feasible adversarial training scheme. Given hyperparameter λ and function $f(x)$, the GRL can be termed as $g(f(x), \lambda) = f(x)$, whose gradient is $\frac{\partial}{\partial x} g(f(x); \lambda) = -\lambda \frac{\partial}{\partial x} f(x)$. The outputs of the domain classifier, i.e., $\widehat{a}_i^s$ and $\widehat{a}_i^t$, can be written as follows:

$$\begin{cases} \widehat{a}_i^s = G_a\left(g\left(G_f\left(x_i^s, \Theta_f\right)\right), \Theta_a\right) \\ \widehat{a}_i^t = G_a\left(g\left(G_f\left(x_i^t, \Theta_f\right)\right), \Theta_a\right) \end{cases} \tag{1}$$

In each mini-batch with the size of b, the domain adversarial loss can be defined as follows:

$$L_a = -\frac{1}{b}\sum_{i=1}^{b}\left(a_i^s\log\widehat{a}_i^s + \left(1 - a_i^t\right)\log(1 - \widehat{a}_i^t)\right) \tag{2}$$

3.2 Feature Extraction and Label Classifier Learning

The purpose of our model is to accurately predict the label $\widehat{y}_i^t$ of the target sample x_i^t. The class of the target domain samples in our model is inferred from $\widehat{y}_i^t = G_y(G_f(x_i^t, \Theta_f), \Theta_y)$. To optimize the model, the L_b loss is calculated by the parameter $\Theta = \{\Theta_f, \Theta_y\}$ as follows:

$$L_b\left(\Theta|X^s, Y^s, X^t\right) = L_s + \alpha L_d + \beta L_c + \gamma L_r \tag{3}$$

where α, β and γ are hyperparameters that control the interaction of L_b. The classification loss L_s optimizes the model to predict the output labels we are interested in. In UDA, the L_s loss only works on the source domain, which is the cross-entropy cost loss function of the ground truth class over each source domain sample. This L_s loss function is minimized during training, which is fully described in Eq. (4):

$$L_s = -\frac{1}{n_s}\sum_i^{n_s}\left(y_i^s\log\left(G_y\left(G_f\left(x_i^s, \Theta_f\right), \Theta_y\right)\right) + (1 - y_i^s)\log\left(1 - G_y\left(G_f\left(x_i^s, \Theta_f\right), \Theta_y\right)\right)\right)$$
$$= -\frac{1}{n_s}\sum_i^{n_s}\left(y_i^s\log(\widehat{y}_i^s) + (1 - y_i^s)\log(1 - \widehat{y}_i^s)\right) \tag{4}$$

where $y_i^s \in \mathbb{R}^C$ is the one-hot class label vector of the ith source input, and $\widehat{y}_i^s(\widehat{y}_i^t) \in \mathbb{R}^C$ is the predicted values of $x_i^s(x_i^t)$.

Correlation Alignment. To learn the domain invariant features, CORAL [21] is used to make domain alignment by minimizing the covariance between source and target features. The CORAL loss is defined as the distance between the covariances of the high-level features of source and target domains:

$$L_c = \|C_s - C_t\|_F^2 \Big/ 4l^2 \tag{5}$$

where $\|\cdot\|_F^2$ represents the square of the Frobenius norm. The covariances of the source domain data and the target domain data are described in Eq. (6):

$$\begin{cases} C_t = \frac{1}{b-1}(V_t^T V_t - \frac{1}{b}V_t^T Z V_t) \\ C_s = \frac{1}{b-1}(V_s^T V_s - \frac{1}{b}V_s^T Z V_s) \end{cases} \tag{6}$$

where $Z = 11^T \in \mathbb{R}^{b \times b}$ is an all-one matrix and $1 \in \mathbb{R}^b$ is an all-one column vector.

Feature Similarity Enhancement Loss. To improve the correct classification rate of target domain data that is away from the class center, the feature similarity enhancement [26] term is necessary. It makes full use of the features of the source data and the target data in the shared projection space, which enhances the similarity between the source and target domain data, so that the data of the target domain has better intra-class compactness and inter-class separability. It is expressed as follows:

$$\begin{cases} p_{st}^{ij} = \exp(-\left\|v_s^i - v_t^j\right\|_2^2 /(\sigma_1^2)) \\ p_{tt}^{ij} = \exp(-\left\|v_t^i - v_t^j\right\|_2^2 /(\sigma_2^2)) \end{cases} \tag{7}$$

where p_{st}^{ij} and p_{tt}^{ij} are the similarities of inter-domain and intra-domain samples, respectively. σ_1 and σ_2 are the standard variations of inter-domain and intra-domain samples. In conclusion, the loss function L_r of feature similarity enhancement term is:

$$L_r = \frac{1}{b^2} \sum_{i=1}^{b} \sum_{j=1}^{b} (p_{st}^{ij}\|v_s^i - v_t^j\|_2^2 + p_{tt}^{ij}\|v_t^i - v_t^j\|_2^2) = \frac{1}{b^2}(tr(V_s P_{st} V_t^T) + tr(V_t P_{tt} V_t^T)) \tag{8}$$

where $P_{st}(P_{tt})$ is similarity matrix between inter-domain and intra-domain, and $tr(\cdot)$ denotes the trace.

Center Discriminative Loss. To enable approach learn more easily discriminative features, we design a center discriminative loss. Since training of our method is based on mini-batch, we design batch class center to represent the class center in the training, as shown in Eq. (9):

$$c_k = \frac{\sum\limits_{i=1}^{t} \sum\limits_{j=1}^{b} \delta((\tilde{y}_j^s)^i = k)(v_s^j)^i}{\sum\limits_{i=1}^{t} \sum\limits_{j=1}^{b} \delta((\tilde{y}_j^s)^i = k)} \tag{9}$$

where t represents the current number of iterations and $k \in \{1, ..., C\}$ denotes category. If $(\tilde{y}_j^s)^i = k$, we set $\delta(\cdot)$ to 1, otherwise $\delta(\cdot)$ is 0. The central discriminant loss function is shown as Eq. (10):

$$L_d = \|\max(0, V_c - m_1 11^T)\|_{sum} + \|\max(0, m_2 11^T - D_c)\|_{sum} \tag{10}$$

where m_1 and m_2 are two constraint margins, which are fixed by us as 0 and 100, respectively; $V_c = \{v_c^i\}_{i=1}^b$ and V_s have the same size, and v_c^i represents the distance of the ith depth feature v_s^i from its class center, i.e., $v_c^i = ||v_s^i - c_{\tilde{y}_i^s}||_2^2$. $D_c \in \mathbb{R}^{C \times C}$ denotes the distance between the class centers, i.e., $D_c^{ij} = ||c_i - c_j||_2^2$. Center discriminative loss reduces the distance between the sample and the corresponding class center, and increases the distance between different class centers.

Finally, the overall loss function of our model is:

$$L = L_b + \varphi L_a = L_s + \alpha L_d + \beta L_c + \gamma L_r + \varphi L_a \tag{11}$$

where φ is the trade-off regularizer for the domain classification.

3.3   Optimization with Backpropagation

Our end-to-end model using domain classifier with GRL and feature similarity enhancement term can be optimized by SGD during backpropagation. Specifically, the parameters of our model can be learned by minimizing L_a and maximizing L_b. This procedure can be described as Eqs. (12) and (13).

$$\widehat{\Theta} = (\widehat{\Theta}_f, \widehat{\Theta}_y) = \arg\min L_a(\Theta_f, \Theta_y, \widehat{\Theta}_a) \tag{12}$$

$$\widehat{\Theta}_a = \arg\max L_b(\widehat{\Theta}_f, \widehat{\Theta}_y, \Theta_a) \tag{13}$$

Saddle points in Eqs. (12) and (13) can be found as stationary points of the following stochastic update, where η is the learning rate:

$$\widehat{\Theta} = \Theta - \eta \frac{\partial(L_s + \alpha L_d + \beta L_c + \gamma L_r)}{\partial x_i} \tag{14}$$

$$\widehat{\Theta}_a = \Theta_a - \eta \frac{\partial L_b}{\partial x_i} \tag{15}$$

4   Experiments

We exploit two domain adaptation datasets, Office-31 and Digital Recognition datasets, to verify the effectiveness of our approach. In the following subsections, the paper provides detailed analysis and experimental results of each setting of our approach. And the classification results of our approach on the two datasets are state-of-the-art compared with the results of other advanced methods.

4.1   Datasets

Office-31. Office-31 [20] is a benchmark dataset for computer vision domain adaptation. It includes three image subsets from different domains. The three subsets in the Office-31 contain 4110 images from the common 31 categories: Amazon (A) with 2817 images, DSLR (D) with 498 images, and Webcam (W) with 795 images, respectively. To test the generalization capabilities of different methods, according to the standard task settings [14,23], we evaluate all methods in all six transfer tasks, A→W, A→D, D→W, W→A, D→A, and W→D.

Digital Recognition Dataset. This dataset contains five widely used subsets: Street View House Numbers (SVHN) [17], synthetic digits (syn digits) [5], MNIST [12], MNIST-m [5], and USPS [11]. We focus on four transfer tasks for evaluation as [1,14]: SVHN→MNIST, MNIST→MNIST-m, MNIST→USPS and syn→MNIST.

4.2   Experimental Settings

In experiments, we compare our approach with different advanced related methods on these two datasets. Our AASE is compared with **DDC** [23], **DAN** [14], **DANN** [5], **ADDA** [22], **CMD** [27], **CORAL** [21], **DUCDA** [28], **JDDA** [1], **ResNet** [9] (one baseline method) and **Lenet** [12] (another baseline method).

On Office-31, $G_f(\cdot)$ in our network uses the pre-trained ResNet on ImageNet. We choose the active pool5 output in the last layer of the network as a feature representation of the BN layer and all compared methods utilize the same ResNet-50 setting. However, on the Digital Recognition dataset, we use improved Lenet as $G_f(\cdot)$ of our network. And all input data is resized to 32×32 and converted to the grayscale input. In addition, the domain classifier is composed of three fully connected layers ($fc - 64 - 2$) and is finally connected to a Softmax activation layer.

We use Tensorflow framework to perform our approach and select Adam optimizer in Tensorflow as the optimizer. Due to the small amount of data in Office-31, only FC and scale 5/Block3 in Resnet are updated with a fine-tuned way. For other layers in the network, they are frozen to keep the ability of capturing salient features. In the training process, we set the batch size to 256, i.e., there are 128 samples in each domain. We set the parameters η to be 10^{-4}. We fix the hyperparameter $\varphi = 1.0$ in all experiments. For the hyperparameters α, β and γ, they are determined as 10, 0.02 and 0.03 experimentally. Besides, in $G_a(\cdot)$, we gradually change λ from 0 to 1 using the following schedule [5]: $\lambda_p = 2/(1 + \exp(-\zeta p)) - 1$, where p is the training progress linearly changing from 0 to 1 and ζ is set to 10 for the sensitivity coefficient.

Table 1. The classification results (%) of the Office-31 dataset.

Method	A → W	D → W	W → D	A → D	D → A	W → A	AVG
ResNet	73.1 ± 0.2	93.3 ± 0.2	98.4 ± 0.1	72.6 ± 0.2	55.4 ± 0.1	55.9 ± 0.3	74.7
DDC	73.5 ± 0.3	93.9 ± 0.1	98.5 ± 0.1	74.3 ± 0.4	56.2 ± 0.2	56.4 ± 0.2	75.4
DAN	78.5 ± 0.3	95.5 ± 0.2	98.9 ± 0.1	74.8 ± 0.3	**58.7 ± 0.2**	63.6 ± 0.3	78.3
DANN	72.7 ± 0.3	94.3 ± 0.2	99.3 ± 0.1	74.1 ± 0.5	56.9 ± 0.1	61.4 ± 0.2	76.4
CMD	76.5 ± 0.4	93.3 ± 0.3	99.3 ± 0.2	74.8 ± 0.4	56.7 ± 0.1	61.3 ± 0.2	76.9
CORAL	78.6 ± 0.3	92.9 ± 0.2	99.3 ± 0.1	74.3 ± 0.2	56.1 ± 0.2	62.1 ± 0.2	77.2
DUCDA	79.4 ± 0.3	94.6 ± 0.2	99.6 ± 0.2	76.7 ± 0.3	56.4 ± 0.2	57.7 ± 0.3	77.4
JDDA	82.6 ± 0.4	95.2 ± 0.2	**99.7 ± 0.0**	79.8 ± 0.1	57.4 ± 0.0	66.7 ± 0.2	80.2
AASE	**84.1 ± 0.2**	**96.5 ± 0.2**	99.4 ± 0.2	**81.2 ± 0.1**	58.1 ± 0.1	**67.4 ± 0.3**	**81.1**

Table 2. The classification results (%) on the Digital Recognition dataset.

Method	SVHN $\rightarrow$ MNIST	MNIST $\rightarrow$ MNIST-m	USPS $\rightarrow$ MNIST	syn $\rightarrow$ MNIST	AVG
Lenet	66.9 ± 0.2	63.4 ± 0.2	67.5 ± 0.3	89.4 ± 0.2	71.8
DDC	72.7 ± 0.3	78.2 ± 0.2	76.6 ± 0.2	90.2 ± 0.1	79.4
DAN	78.9 ± 0.2	78.7 ± 0.3	90.3 ± 0.1	76.3 ± 0.2	81.1
DANN	71.3 ± 0.2	77.5 ± 0.3	75.9 ± 0.2	90.3 ± 0.2	78.7
ADDA	73.1 ± 0.2	81.1 ± 0.2	91.7 ± 0.3	96.1 ± 0.3	85.5
CMD	87.2 ± 0.3	86.3 ± 0.2	87.2 ± 0.4	96.3 ± 0.2	89.2
CORAL	90.2 ± 0.2	82.3 ± 0.2	95.9 ± 0.4	96.4 ± 0.2	91.2
DUCDA	92.1 ± 0.3	87.3 ± 0.2	93.7 ± 0.2	96.9 ± 0.3	92.5
JDDA	94.2 ± 0.1	88.4 ± 0.2	97.0 ± 0.2	$\mathbf{97.7 \pm 0.0}$	94.3
AASE	$\mathbf{95.6 \pm 0.1}$	$\mathbf{89.4 \pm 0.2}$	$\mathbf{97.7 \pm 0.2}$	97.4 ± 0.1	$\mathbf{95.0}$

4.3 Results and Analysis

In this paper, we adopt the measure of classification accuracy to evaluate the classification effect of our approach and compared methods. The classification accuracy is the ratio of the correct classification of the test data to the total test data. The UDA classification results on the office-31 dataset based on Resnet-50 are shown in Table 1. To more fully evaluate our approach, we also use the large-scale Digital Recognition dataset to verify the superior classification performance of our AASE in the domain adaptation scene.

In Tables 1 and 2, there are the following observations. First, the classification results of these comparison methods are better than those of baseline methods ResNet and Lenet, revealing that domain adversarial and domain adaptation difference metric learning can improve the performance of UDA. Second, JDDA, as the first method that focuses on effectively and jointly performing domain alignment and discriminate feature learning, performs well among comparison methods. Third, our approach performs the best. Its average classification accuracy is significantly improved by **0.9**% and **0.7**% over JDDA on Office-31 and Digital Recognition dataset, respectively. Compared with JDDA, AASE approach specially considers the intra-domain high-level features and inter-domain high-level features correlation in the shared feature space. Thus, AASE promotes the learning ability of the intra-class compact and inter-class separable features.

In addition, our approach also makes progress in some difficult transfer tasks. For example, data of SVHN is complex while data of MNIST is relatively simple. The sample size of W is even smaller than that of A. However, in transfer tasks SVHN→MNIST and W→A, AASE still shows the best results in Tables 1 and 2. It indicates that AASE has learned transferable feature representations and is suitable for large-scale, small-scale and complex datasets.

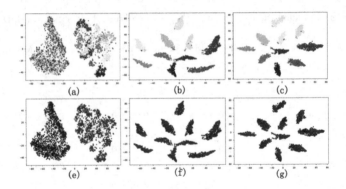

Fig. 2. The t-SNE visualization of the SVHN→MNIST task. In (a)-(c), feature dimensions are set to 2 and each color representing a category. In (e)-(g), red and blue points represent samples of the source and target domains, respectively. (Color figure online)

Predictions Visualization. To better illustrate the effectiveness of our method, we randomly selected 2048 samples with category information and domain information. Then the features of the last layer are embedded into t-SEN [3] for visualization. As shown in Fig. 2, (a)-(c) and (e)-(g) represent visualizations of the initial state, the intermediate state, and the convergence state of category and domain. Observing these graphs, we can see that in the initial stage, the two domains are obviously differently distributed and intra-class samples are intertwined; then, the inter-class feature representations is basically separated and the inter-domain feature representations are basically aligned; in the convergence phase, the inter-class features are obvious distinguished and the domains are perfectly aligned. In simple terms, our model can learn more distinguishing and transferable features.

Table 3. The classification result (%) of the approach variants on the office-31 dataset.

Method	A → W	D → W	W → D	A → D	D → A	W → A	AVG
JDDA	82.6 ± 0.4	95.2 ± 0.2	**99.7 ± 0.0**	79.8 ± 0.1	57.4 ± 0.0	66.7 ± 0.2	80.2
AASE-r	83.5 ± 0.1	95.4 ± 0.2	99.2 ± 0.1	80.6 ± 0.1	57.8 ± 0.1	67.0 ± 0.1	80.6
AASE-a	83.3 ± 0.2	95.7 ± 0.1	99.1 ± 0.2	79.9 ± 0.1	57.5 ± 0.0	66.8 ± 0.1	80.4
AASE	**84.1 ± 0.2**	**96.5 ± 0.2**	99.4 ± 0.2	**81.2 ± 0.1**	**58.1 ± 0.1**	**67.4 ± 0.3**	**81.1**

Table 4. The classification result (%) of the approach variants on the Digital recognition dataset.

Method	SVHN → MNIST	MNIST → MNIST-m	USPS → MNIST	syn → MNIST	AVG
JDDA	94.2 ± 0.1	88.4 ± 0.2	97.0 ± 0.2	**97.7 ± 0.0**	94.3
AASE-r	94.8 ± 0.2	89.0 ± 0.2	97.3 ± 0.0	97.2 ± 0.1	94.6
AASE-a	94.4 ± 0.1	89.1 ± 0.1	97.1 ± 0.1	97.4 ± 0.1	94.5
AASE	**95.6 ± 0.1**	**89.4 ± 0.2**	**97.7 ± 0.2**	97.4 ± 0.1	**95.0**

4.4   Discussion

We evaluate the important components of AASE. We respectively name the version of AASE without Feature Similarity Enhancement as **AASE – a**, the version of AASE without domain adversarial network **AASE – r**. The same experimental setting is given in Sect. 4.2. As shown in Tables 3 and 4, the classification results of the tasks corresponding to JDDA of AASE-a and AASE-r are better than JDDA in most tasks, such as, in the AVG column, AASE-r is higher than JDDA by **0.4%/0.3%**, respectively. In addition, the complete AASE approach performs better than AASE-r and AASE-a methods. Therefore, these analyses indicate that every component of our method is necessary, and the combination of these components has a great help in improving the performance of the UDA method.

5   Conclusion

In this paper, we propose Adversarial Domain Alignment Feature Similarity Enhancement Learning for UDA. It jointly learns domain invariant features and makes these features having better discrimination that leads to better inter-class separability and intra-class compactness. The dual-channel parameter-shared adversarial convolution network realizes the domain alignment by the minimax game between domain classifier and feature extractor. The feature similarity enhancement term makes the samples far from the class center of target domain more easily classified. In addition, experimental results on two widely used datasets demonstrate that AASE outperfroms state-of-the-art UDA methods. Results prove the effectiveness of adversarial domain alignment feature similarity enhancement learning.

Acknowledgments. This work was supported by National Natural Science Foundation of China (No. 61702280), Natural Science Foundation of Jiangsu Province (No. BK20170900), National Postdoctoral Program for Innovative Talents (No. BX20180146), Scientific Research Starting Foundation for Introduced Talents in Nanjing University of Posts and Telecommunications (NUPTSF, No. NY217009), and the Postgraduate Research & Practice Innovation Program of Jiangsu Province (No. KYCX17_0794).

References

1. Chen, C., Chen, Z., Jiang, B., Jin, X.: Joint domain alignment and discriminative feature learning for unsupervised deep domain adaptation. arXiv preprint arXiv:1808.09347 (2018)
2. Chu, W.-S., De la Torre, F., Cohn, J.F.: Selective transfer machine for personalized facial action unit detection. In: IEEE Conference on Computer Vision and Pattern Recognition, pp. 3515–3522 (2013)
3. Donahue, J., et al.: Decaf: a deep convolutional activation feature for generic visual recognition. In: International Conference on Machine Learning, pp. 647–655 (2014)

4. Dudík, M., Phillips, S.J., Schapire, R.E.: Correcting sample selection bias in maximum entropy density estimation. In: Advances in Neural Information Processing Systems, pp. 323–330 (2006)
5. Ganin, Y., et al.: Domain-adversarial training of neural networks. J. Mach. Learn. Res. **17**(1), 2030–2096 (2016)
6. Gong, B., Grauman, K., Sha, F.: Connecting the dots with landmarks: discriminatively learning domain-invariant features for unsupervised domain adaptation. In: International Conference on Machine Learning, pp. 222–230 (2013)
7. Goodfellow, I., et al.: Generative adversarial nets. In: Advances in Neural Information Processing Systems, pp. 2672–2680 (2014)
8. Gretton, A., Smola, A., Huang, J., Schmittfull, M., Borgwardt, K., Schölkopf, B.: Covariate shift by kernel mean matching. Dataset Shift Mach. Learn. **3**(4), 131–160 (2009)
9. He, K., Zhang, X., Ren, S., Sun, J.: Deep residual learning for image recognition. In: IEEE Conference on Computer Vision and Pattern Recognition, pp. 770–778 (2016)
10. Hubert Tsai, Y.-H., Yeh, Y.-R., Frank Wang, Y.C.. Learning cross-domain landmarks for heterogeneous domain adaptation. In: IEEE Conference on Computer Vision and Pattern Recognition, pp. 5081–5090 (2016)
11. Hull, J.J.: A database for handwritten text recognition research. IEEE Trans. Pattern Anal. Mach. Intell. **16**(5), 550–554 (1994)
12. LeCun, Y., Bottou, L., Bengio, Y., Haffner, P.: Gradient-based learning applied to document recognition. Proc. IEEE **86**(11), 2278–2324 (1998)
13. Liu, M.-Y., Tuzel, O.: Coupled generative adversarial networks. In: Advances in Neural Information Processing Systems, pp. 469–477 (2016)
14. Long, M., Cao, Y., Wang, J., Jordan, M.I.: Learning transferable features with deep adaptation networks. arXiv preprint arXiv:1502.02791 (2015)
15. Long, M., Wang, J., Ding, G., Sun, J., Yu, P.S.: Transfer joint matching for unsupervised domain adaptation. In: IEEE Conference on Computer Vision and Pattern Recognition, pp. 1410–1417 (2014)
16. Long, M., Zhu, H., Wang, J., Jordan, M.I.: Unsupervised domain adaptation with residual transfer networks. In: Advances in Neural Information Processing Systems, pp. 136–144 (2016)
17. Netzer, Y., Wang, T., Coates, A., Bissacco, A., Wu, B., Ng, A.Y.: Reading digits in natural images with unsupervised feature learning. In: Neural Information Processing Systems Workshop, pp. 1–9 (2011)
18. Pan, S.J., Yang, Q.: A survey on transfer learning. IEEE Trans. Knowl. Data Eng. **22**(10), 1345–1359 (2010)
19. Rozantsev, A., Salzmann, M., Fua, P.: Beyond sharing weights for deep domain adaptation. IEEE Trans. Pattern Anal. Mach. Intell. **41**(4), 801–814 (2019)
20. Saenko, K., Kulis, B., Fritz, M., Darrell, T.: Adapting visual category models to new domains. In: Daniilidis, K., Maragos, P., Paragios, N. (eds.) ECCV 2010. LNCS, vol. 6314, pp. 213–226. Springer, Heidelberg (2010). https://doi.org/10.1007/978-3-642-15561-1_16
21. Sun, B., Feng, J., Saenko, K. Return of frustratingly easy domain adaptation. In: AAAI Conference on Artificial Intelligence, pp. 2058–2065 (2016)
22. Tzeng, E., Hoffman, J., Saenko, K., Darrell, T.: Adversarial discriminative domain adaptation. IEEE Conference on Computer Vision and Pattern Recognition, pp. 7167–7176 (2017)
23. Tzeng, E., Hoffman, J., Zhang, N., Saenko, K., Darrell, T.: Deep domain confusion: maximizing for domain invariance. arXiv preprint arXiv:1412.3474 (2014)

24. Wu, F., et al.: Intraspectrum discrimination and interspectrum correlation analysis deep network for multispectral face recognition. IEEE Trans. Cybern. 1–14 (2018)
25. Wu, F., et al.: Cross-project and within-project semisupervised software defect prediction: a unified approach. IEEE Trans. Reliab. **67**(2), 581–597 (2018)
26. Wu, F., et al.: Semi-supervised multi-view individual and sharable feature learning for webpage classification. In: The World Wide Web Conference, pp. 3349–3355 (2019)
27. Zellinger, W., Grubinger, T., Lughofer, E., Natschläger, T., Saminger-Platz, S.: Central moment discrepancy (CMD) for domain-invariant representation learning. arXiv preprint arXiv:1702.08811 (2017)
28. Zhuo, J., Wang, S., Zhang, W., Huang, Q.: Deep unsupervised convolutional domain adaptation. In: ACM International Conference on Multimedia, pp. 261–269 (2017)

ADSRNet: Attention-Based Densely Connected Network for Image Super-Resolution

Weiqi Li[1], Yao Lu[1(✉)], Xuebo Wang[1], Xiaozhen Chen[1], and Zijian Wang[2]

[1] Beijing Laboratory of Intelligent Information Technology,
Beijing Institute of Technology, Beijing, China
vis_yl@bit.edu.cn
[2] China Central Television, Beijing, China

Abstract. Densely connected network for Image Super-Resolution (SR) has achieved much better results than most of the other methods owing to its dense connection architecture which can provide more and deeper features for image super-resolution. However, since the dense block accepts the outputs of all previous blocks, it receives a lot of redundant and conflicting information, which results in longer training time and bad super-resolution reconstruction results. To solve this problem, we introduce an attention module into a densely connected network and propose an attention-based densely connected network (ADSRNet) for image super-resolution. With the attention module, our ADSRNet can select more important information and cut off those redundant for image super-resolution from a large number of feature maps by importance ordering. Thus, we can speed up the training of network. Extensive experiments are performed over the datasets Set5, Set14 and BSD100, the qualitatively and quantitatively evaluated results for our proposed ADSRNet are better than ones of some state-of-the-art methods.

Keywords: Super-resolution · Channel attention · Dense connection · Deep neural network

1 Introduction

The image super-resolution task involves increasing the size of a small image while preventing its quality from degrading as much as possible. This task has diverse applications such as surveillance imaging, medical imaging and video enhancement, and the performance of image super-resolution has achieved significant improvement by learning-based SR approaches.

Many learning-based super-resolution methods are emerging recently and achieve better performance compared with previous hand-crafted methods [1–4], such as super-resolution convolutional neural network (SRCNN) [5], deep laplacian pyramid networks (LapSRN) [6], the dense connected convolutional networks (SRDenseNet) [7], deep-recursive convolutional network (DRCN) [8]

© Springer Nature Switzerland AG 2019
Z. Lin et al. (Eds.): PRCV 2019, LNCS 11859, pp. 272–282, 2019.
https://doi.org/10.1007/978-3-030-31726-3_23

etc. However, there are still some neglected problems in these methods. First, most of the network layers only receive the outputs of the previous layer as input but do not utilize features effectively. Second, even if the connection between different layers is established, the network receives too many features to select efficiently, which leads to a lot of information redundancy and conflicting.

To solve these issues, we propose a novel attention-based densely connected super-resolution network to reconstruct a high resolution (HR) image from a low resolution (LR) image. The different channels make different contributions to super-resolution results, in order to select more critical information from a lot of features for image super-resolution, we introduce a new attention module to generate importance weight coefficients. With these weight coefficients, we can guide the subsequent convolutional layer to select the feature maps with the higher weight which are more important. In this way, we can reduce a lot of received features so as to speed up the neural network training time. In addition, some of conflicting features included in those channels with small weight coefficients are cut off so as to improve super-resolution results. Main contributions of our work can be summarized as follows:

(1) We propose a new attention-based densely connected network (ADSRNet) for image super-resolution. Meanwhile, we propose a new dense attention module (DAM) to select important features. The attention module assigns small weight coefficients to the redundant and conflicting features, so as to filter it out and keep important one when features passing through the subsequent convolutional layers.
(2) In our paper, we utilize the ReLU function instead of the Sigmoid function to improve the attention module. With the ReLU function, the difference of features can be well expressed when the features differ greatly, and it can speed up the convergence.

2   Related Work

Image Super-Resolution Based on Neural Network: Dong et al. [5] proposed a neural network for image super-resolution: SRCNN. And in SRCNN, they used a bicubic interpolation to amplify the low resolution image to the target size firstly, then learned the mapping relation from LR to HR images through a three-layer convolution network, and finally outputted a high-resolution image result. To further improve the accuracy as well as speed up the training, a number of CNN models had been proposed since then [8–10]. Kim et al. proposed deeply-recursive convolutional network (DRCN) [8] and VDSR [9]. In DRCN [8], they used more convolutional layers to increase the network receptive fields, in order to avoid excessive network parameters, they used recurrent neural networks. In VDSR [9], they used the residual network for training and speeding up the convergence. Tai et al. proposed deep recursive residual network (DRRN) [10] which used a deeper network structure (52 layers). However, most of the current super-resolution methods can get pleasing results only for limited scale factors, and when the magnification scale is larger, the results by one-step upsampling are unsatisfactory. Lai et al. [6] used a cascading network to learn high-frequency residual details progressively, enabling 8× super resolution. The parameter sharing reduces the computation and improves the computation precision effectively. Tong et al. [7] proposed SRDenseNet utilizing all hierarchical features, interconnecting all layers so that each layer accepts the outputs from all of the previous layers as its extra inputs. The dense connection improves the gradient back propagation, making the network easier to train. Ledig et al. [26] proposed perceptual loss function, they replaced the content loss based on MSE with the loss based on the feature map of VGG network [27]. This network made the generated high-resolution images looked more realistic. Such GAN based model was then introduced in EnhanceNet [28], which combined automated texture synthesis and perceptual loss. [11] introduced the attention module to treat different channels, improving the representation ability of the network.

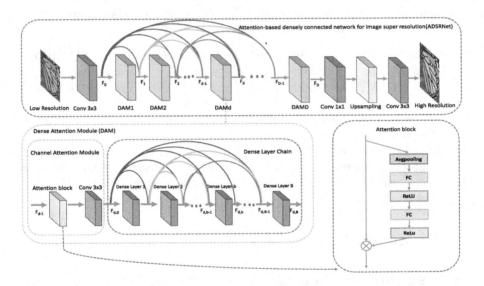

Fig. 1. Neural network structure of our method. The network consists of feature extraction, upsampling and reconstruction section. The figure on the lower left represents our proposed dense attention module (DAM), it consists of a channel attention module and the dense layer chain. DAM is used to extract the high-level features. The figure on the lower right shows the new attention block we proposed. Through the attention block, the feature maps are weighted, and the output channels have different importance.

Attention Module: Recently, the attention module was widely applied to many computer vision tasks [12–20]. Hu et al. [19] proposed the squeeze-and-excitation (SE) block, this block squeezes the original channels, then performs an extraction operation to learn the parameter to establish channel correlation, which is similar to the door mechanism in RNN. The goal is to learn the importance of each channel, enhances the important features and suppresses redundant and conflict-ing features. Woo and Park et al. [20] proposed convolutional block attention module (CBAM), which consists of channel-wise attention and spatial attention. Channel-wise attention allocates resources between channels, and spatial atten-tion adjusts the weight of each position on the feature maps, so that the model can focus on the regions that deserve more attention.

3 Proposed Method

3.1 Network Architecture

The overall architecture of our network is illustrated in Fig. 1. Our network can be divided into four parts: (1) shallow feature extraction, (2) deep feature extraction, (3) upsampling layers, (4) reconstruction layers. In the shallow fea-ture extraction layers, we use one convolutional layer to extract the low-level features. i.e.,

$$F_0 = f_{low}(I_{LR}) \tag{1}$$

where I_{LR} denotes the input low-resolution image, and F_0 denotes the shallow features extracted from I_{LR}, $f_{low}(\cdot)$ denotes the first convolution operation. And then we use the dense attention modules to extract the high-level features:

$$F_d = f_{high}(F_0) \tag{2}$$

where F_d $(d=1...D)$ denotes the output of the d-th dense attention module, D is the number of the dense attention modules, $f_{high}(\cdot)$ represents the operation of the dense attention modules to extract the high-level features. In order to reduce the computational complexity, we use 1×1 convolutional layer to reduce feature map dimensions. For the upsampling and the reconstruction layers, the feature maps are fed into the deconvolutional layers followed by a convolutional layer to generate the HR image.

$$I_{HR} = f_{recon}(f_{up}(F_D)) \tag{3}$$

where F_D denotes the output of the last dense attention module, $f_{up}(\cdot)$ denotes the deconvolution operation, and $f_{recon}(\cdot)$ denotes the reconstruction operation.

3.2 Dense Attention Module

The DenseNet structure was proposed in [21], each dense block accepts the feature maps produced from all previous dense blocks, which will result in too many input channels for the dense blocks. The original dense block use ordinary convolutional layers to extract the features. However, each channel is treated equally in this way, which makes the network just select some feature maps randomly from a large number of feature maps and then feed them to the next convolutional layer. Therefore, the final output feature maps cannot express the important image information well. With our proposed dense attention module,

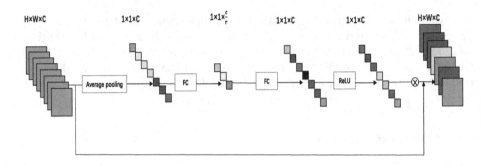

Fig. 2. Structure of our attention block.

the important features will be selected in priority, while unimportant features, such as noise, will be suppressed. We can alleviate the disadvantage of random feature selection in the convolutional layers.

As illustrated in Fig. 1 in the lower left corner, the dense attention module contains a channel attention module (CAM) and a dense layer chain to extract the high-level features. CAM will be stated in Sect. 3.3 Assuming that there are **D** dense attention modules in our network and **B** dense layers in each dense layer chain. An channel attention module produces **k** feature maps, each dense layer chain produces **k** feature maps. In order to achieve multi-level information flow, each dense attention module receives the output of all previous dense attention modules, and each dense layer receives the output of all previous dense layers. The operation of the d-th CAM is formulated as

$$F_{d,0} = f_{att}(F_{d-1}) \tag{4}$$

Where F_{d-1} and $F_{d,0}$ ($d=1...D$) are the input and output feature maps of the d-th channel attention module, $f_{att}(\cdot)$ is the function of CAM. Then, the b-th dense layer in the d-th dense layer chain can be formulated as below.

$$F_{d,b} = f_{d,b}(...f_{d,2}(f_{d,1}(F_{d,0}))...) \tag{5}$$

Where $f_{d,b}(\cdot)$ ($d=1...D$, $b=1...B$) denotes the function of the b-th dense layer in the d-th dense layer chain.

3.3   Channel Attention Module

Inspired by the SENet [19], we design a new channel attention module as illustrated in the lower right corner of Fig. 1. Our CAM consists of two components: attention block and convolutional layer. As shown in Fig. 2. In our attention block, we use the average pooling to get the global information. The feature maps with the size of $1 \times 1 \times C$ are obtained after the average pooling. Extraction operation we proposed is FC-ReLU-FC-ReLU, the final re-calibrated output is also a $1 \times 1 \times C$ weight vector in this way. Then it is multiplied by the original

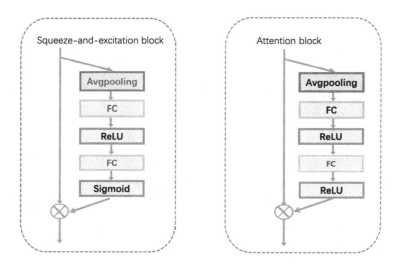

Fig. 3. Difference of squeeze-and-excitation block and our attention block.

feature maps with the size of H × W × C. The convolutional layer followed by the attention block maps the high-dimensional features to the low-dimensional features. With the channel attention module, channels are given different weight coefficients, then we can make better feature selection on feature maps. After the convolutional layer, those channels with higher weights will be preferred, ensuring the redundant features are discarded, thus the expressive ability of network is enhanced.

3.4 Mapping Function

As shown in Fig. 3. In the excitation process of the SENet, the author uses the Sigmoid function to generate weight coefficients. In our paper, we use the ReLU function instead of the Sigmoid function. The Sigmoid function generates weight coefficients between 0 and 1, these coefficients are multiplied by the original feature maps, which makes the value of the original feature maps smaller, and can not distinguish the features well. However, with the ReLU function, the difference of features can be well expressed when the features differ greatly, and it can speed up the convergence.

4 Experiments

4.1 Datasets and Metrics

We train our model in DIV2K [22], which consists of 800 high-quality training images. When using this dataset, we crop the original images firstly, and then use the bicubic interpolation to get the LR images from HR images. For data augmentation, the patches are randomly horizontal flipped and rotated. For

Table 1. Objective comparison

Scale	Method	Set5		Set14		BSD100	
		PSNR	SSIM	PSNR	SSIM	PSNR	SSIM
2×	Bicubic	33.68	0.9304	30.24	0.8691	29.56	0.8435
	SRCNN	36.66	0.9542	32.45	0.9067	31.36	0.8879
	VDSR	37.53	0.9597	33.05	0.9127	31.90	0.8960
	LapSRN	37.52	0.9591	32.99	0.9124	31.80	0.8949
	DRCN	37.63	0.9588	33.04	0.9118	31.85	0.8942
	DRRN	37.74	0.9591	33.23	0.9136	32.05	0.8973
	ADSRNet(OURS)	**38.00**	**0.9597**	**34.32**	**0.9205**	**32.60**	**0.8980**
3×	Bicubic	30.40	0.8686	27.54	0.7741	27.21	0.7389
	SRCNN	32.75	0.9090	29.29	0.8215	28.41	0.7863
	VDSR	33.66	0.9213	29.78	0.8318	28.83	0.7976
	LapSRN	33.82	0.9227	29.79	0.8320	28.82	0.7973
	DRCN	33.82	0.9226	29.76	0.8311	28.80	0.7963
	DRRN	34.03	0.9244	29.96	0.8349	28.95	0.8004
	ADSRNet(OURS)	**34.60**	**0.9257**	**30.24**	**0.8424**	**29.01**	**0.8412**
4×	Bicubic	28.43	0.8109	26.00	0.7023	25.96	0.6678
	SRCNN	30.48	0.8628	27.50	0.7513	26.90	0.7103
	VDSR	31.35	0.8838	28.02	0.7678	27.29	0.7252
	LapSRN	31.54	0.8866	28.09	0.7694	27.32	0.7264
	DRCN	31.53	0.8854	28.02	0.7670	27.23	0.7233
	DRRN	31.68	0.8888	28.21	0.7720	27.38	0.7284
	ADSRNet(OURS)	**32.27**	**0.8890**	**30.81**	**0.8257**	**27.46**	**0.7326**

testing, we use three datasets, dataset Set5 [23], Set14 [2] and BSD100 [24]. Set5 and Set14 are often used for benchmark, BSD100 consists of natural images in the Berkeley Segmentation, these three datasets can test the validity of our model. We evaluate the performance of our ADSRNet by calculating peak-signal-to-noise ratio (PSNR) and structural similarity (SSIM).

4.2 Implementation Details

According to the network structure, we all set the convolution kernel size to 3×3, padding to 1 in the feature extraction layers, and we use 1×1 convolutional layer to reduce feature map dimensions and the network complexity. We observe that when $k = 64$, $B = 7$, $D = 8$, the experimental results are optimal. All our networks are optimized using the Adam optimizer [25] to minimize the L1 loss function. We set learning rate to 0.001 initially and reduced by a factor of 10 per 5 epochs, the training is iterated 14 epochs in total. Our experimental platform is Pytorch framework with NVIDIA GeForce RTX 2080 Ti.

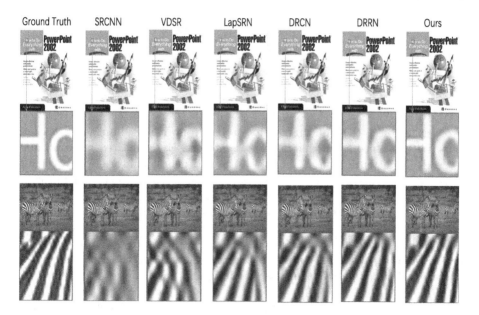

Fig. 4. Qualitative comparison. From left to right is the original image, 4× super-resolution images of SRCNN, VDSR, LapSRN, DRCN, DRRN, and the last one is our result. (1) The first row shows image "ppt3" (Set14 with scale factor ×4) (2) The second row shows image "253027" (BSD100 with scale factor ×4).

Table 2. CAM improves the PSNR on test datasets.

Method	Set5	Set14	BSD100
Network without CAM	31.56	28.36	27.38
Network with CAM (Ours)	32.27	30.81	27.46

4.3 Model Analysis

In order to show the efficiency of our proposed attention module, we compare the iterations of our method with and without the attention module. Different from the 140k iterations network without the attention module, our method only needs 98k iterations to be convergent, which reduces the training time by 30%. As shown in Table 2, our network is also superior to the original method in qualitative comparison.

4.4 Comparisons with the State-of-the-Arts

Our method is also compared with the other networks, we use SRCNN [5], VDSR [9], DRCN [8], DRRN [10], LapSRN [6] to reconstruct HR from LR images. The experiment results of Set 5 [23], Set 14 [2] and BSD100 [24] datasets are shown in Table 1. We can see that our improved network has got a significant improvement over the average PSNR and SSIM compared with the previous network. We give some visual results shown in Fig. 4, images reconstructed using our method are more realistic and have sharpen edges.

5 Conclusion

In order to select the important information from a large number of feature maps, we introduce a new module DAM into densely connected network, and we design an attention-based densely connected neural network ADSRNet for image super-resolution. Our proposed method can speed up the training process and improve the ability of to select features of the network, the effectiveness of proposed method is verified both quantitatively and qualitatively. However, the network is designed to solve the problem of large input dimensions caused by dense connection, and the other structures have not been tested. Therefore, the next research direction is to apply the attention module to the other structures such as ResNet to improve the super-resolution performance.

Acknowledgemet. This work is supported by the National Natural Science Foundation of China (No.61273273), by the national Key Research and Development Plan (No.2017YFC0112001).

References

1. Sun, J., Xu, Z., Shum, H.Y.: Image super-resolution using gradient profile prior. In: 2008 IEEE Computer Society Conference on Computer Vision and Pattern Recognition (CVPR 2008), pp. 24–26, Anchorage, Alaska, USA. IEEE (2008)
2. Zeyde, R., Elad, M., Protter, M.: On single image scale-up using sparse-representations. In: Boissonnat, J.-D., et al. (eds.) Curves and Surfaces 2010. LNCS, vol. 6920, pp. 711–730. Springer, Heidelberg (2012). https://doi.org/10.1007/978-3-642-27413-8_47
3. Chang, H., Yeung, D.-Y., Xiong, Y.: Super-resolution through neighbor embedding. In: Proceedings of the IEEE Conference on Computer Vision and Pattern Recognition (CVPR) (2004)
4. Timofte, R., De Smet, V., Van Gool, L.: Anchored neighborhood regression for fast example-based super-resolution. In: Proceedings of the IEEE International Conference on Computer Vision (ICCV) (2013)
5. Dong, C., Loy, C.C., He, K., Tang, X.: Image super-resolution using deep convolutional networks. IEEE Trans. Pattern Anal. Mach. Intell. **38**(2), 295–307 (2016)
6. Lai, W.-S., Huang, J.B., Ahuja, N. and Yang, M.-H.: Deep Laplacian pyramid networks for fast and accurate super-resolution. In: 2017 IEEE Conference on Computer Vision and Pattern Recognition, CVPR 2017, Honolulu, HI, USA, 21–26 July 2017, pp. 5835–5843 (2017)
7. Tong, T., Li, G., Liu, X., Gao, Q.: Image super-resolution using dense skip connections. In: IEEE International Conference on Computer Vision, ICCV 2017, Venice, Italy, 22–29 October 2017, pp. 4809–4817 (2017)

8. Kim, J., Kwon Lee, J., Mu Lee, K.: Deeply-recursive convolutional network for image super-resolution. In: 2016 IEEE Conference on Computer Vision and Pattern Recognition, CVPR 2016, LasVegas, NV, USA, 27–30 June 2016, pp. 1637–1645 (2016)

9. Kim, J., Kwon Lee, J., Mu Lee, K.: Accurate image super-resolution using very deep convolutional networks. In: 2016 IEEE Conference on Computer Vision and Pattern Recognition, CVPR 2016, LasVegas, NV, USA, 27–30 June 2016, pp. 1646–1654 (2016)

10. Tai, Y., Yang, J., Liu, X.: Image super-resolution via deep recursive residual network. In: 2017 IEEE Conference on Computer Vision and Pattern Recognition, CVPR 2017, Honolulu, HI, USA, 21–26 July 2017, pp. 2790–2798 (2017)

11. Zhang, Y., Li, K., Li, K., Wang, L., Zhong, B., Fu, Y.: Image super-resolution using very deep residual channel attention networks. In: Ferrari, V., Hebert, M., Sminchisescu, C., Weiss, Y. (eds.) ECCV 2018. LNCS, vol. 11211, pp. 294–310. Springer, Cham (2018). https://doi.org/10.1007/978-3-030-01234-2_18

12. Mansimov, E., Parisotto, E., Ba, J.L., Salakhutdinov, R.: Generating images from captions with attention. In: International Conference on Learning Report (ICLR), pp. 1–4, May 2016

13. Wang, F., et al.: Residual attention network for image classification. In: Proceedings of IEEE Conference on Computer Vision Pattern Recognition (CVPR), pp. 3156–3164, July 2017

14. Li, K., Wu, Z., Peng, K.C., Ernst, J., Fu, Y.: Tell me where to look: guided attention inference network. In: CVPR 2018 (2018)

15. Xu, K., et al.: Show, attend and tell: Neural image caption generation with visual attention. In: International Conference on Machine Learning (ICML), pp. 2048–2057, July 2015

16. Chen, L., et al.: SCA-CNN: spatial and channel-wise attention in convolutional networks for image captioning. In: Proceedings of IEEE Conference on Computer Vision Pattern Recognition (CVPR), pp. 5659–5667, July 2017

17. Wang, X., Yu, K., Dong, C., Change Loy, C.: Recovering realistic texture in image super-resolution by deep spatial feature transform. In: Proceedings of IEEE Conference on Computer Vision Pattern Recognitio (CVPR), pp. 606–615, June 2018

18. Xu, H., Saenko, K.: Ask, attend and answer: exploring question-guided spatial attention for visual question answering. In: Leibe, B., Matas, J., Sebe, N., Welling, M. (eds.) ECCV 2016. LNCS, vol. 9911, pp. 451–466. Springer, Cham (2016). https://doi.org/10.1007/978-3-319-46478-7_28

19. Hu, J., Shen, L., Sun, G.: Squeeze-and-excitation networks. In: 2018 IEEE Conference on Computer Vision and Pattern Recognition, CVPR 2018, Salt Lake City, UT, USA, 18–22 June 2018, pp. 7132–7141 (2018)

20. Woo, S., Park, J., Lee, J.-Y., Kweon, I.S.: CBAM: convolutional block attention module. In: Ferrari, V., Hebert, M., Sminchisescu, C., Weiss, Y. (eds.) ECCV 2018. LNCS, vol. 11211, pp. 3–19. Springer, Cham (2018). https://doi.org/10.1007/978-3-030-01234-2_1

21. Huang, G., Liu, Z., Van Der Maaten, L., Weinberger, K.Q.: Densely connected convolutional networks. In: 2017 IEEE Conference on Computer Vision and Pattern Recognition, CVPR 2017, Honolulu, HI, USA, pp. 2261–2269, 21–26 July 2017

22. IEEE Conference on Computer Vision and Pattern Recognition Workshops, CVPR Workshops 2017, Honolulu, HI, USA, 21–26 July 2017. IEEE Computer Society (2017)

23. Bevilacqua, M., Roumy, A., Guillemot, C., Alberi-Morel, M.L.: Low-complexity single-image super-resolution based on nonnegative neighbor embedding. In: British Machine Vision Conference, BMVC 2012, Surrey, UK, 3–7 September 2012, pp. 1–10 (2012)

24. Martin, D.R., Fowlkes, C.C., Tal, D., Malik, J.: A database of human segmented natural images and its application to evaluating segmentation algorithms and measuring ecological statistics. In: ICCV 2001, pp. 416–425 (2001)

25. Kingma, D.P., Ba, J.: Adam: a method for stochastic optimization. arXiv preprint arXiv: 1412.6980 (2014)

26. Ledig, C., et al.: Photo-realistic single image super-resolution using a generative adversarial network. In: 2017 IEEE Conference on Computer Vision and Pattern Recognition (CVPR), pp. 105–114 (2017)

27. Simonyan, K., Zisserman, A.: Very deep convolutional networks for large-scale image recognition. In: International Conference on Learning Representations (ICLR), pp. 2–5 (2015)

28. Sajjadi, M.S., Schölkopf, B., Hirsch, M.: EnhanceNet: single image super-resolution through automated texture synthesis. In: ICCV, pp. 4501–4510 (2017)

Robust and Efficient Visual-Inertial Odometry with Multi-plane Priors

Jinyu Li, Bangbang Yang, Kai Huang, Guofeng Zhang, and Hujun Bao[✉]

State Key Lab of CAD&CG, Zhejiang University,
ZJU-SenseTime Joint Lab of 3D Vision, Hangzhou Shi, China
bao@cad.zju.edu.cn

Abstract. Planes commonly exist in a human-made scene and are useful for robust localization. In this paper, we propose a novel monocular visual-inertial odometry system which leverages multi-plane priors. A novel visual-inertial-plane PnP algorithm is introduced to use plane information for fast localization. The planes are expanded via a reprojection consensus-based way, which is robust to depth estimation error. A novel structureless plane-distance cost is used in sliding-window optimization, which allows to use a small size window while maintaining good accuracy. Together with modified marginalization and sliding window strategy, the computational cost is significantly reduced. Our VIO system is tested on various datasets and compared with several state-of-the-art systems. Our system can achieve very competitive accuracy, and work pretty well on long and challenging sequences. Our system is also very efficient and can perform 30 fps averagely on an iPhone 7 mobile phone with a single thread.

Keywords: Visual inertial odometry · bundle adjustment · Plane priors · Reprojection consensus · Structureless plane-distance cost

1 Introduction

Cameras and IMUs are already very common on smart mobile phones, which are small and cheap, with low power consumption. Hence they are good choices for addressing mobile localization problem in consumer level applications. Recent advances in visual-inertial odometry (VIO) and simultaneous localization and mapping (SLAM) communities have give birth to many successful odometry/SLAM systems like [4,5,8,16,18]. However, these systems either require high computation cost with multiple threads or easily drift in challenging situations.

Human-made scenes generally contain rich planar structures, which can benefit odometry/SLAM. Although some methods [9,21] have been proposed to use

This work was partially supported by NSF of China (Nos. 61822310 and 61672457), and the Fundamental Research Funds for the Central Universities (No. 2018FZA5011). This work was done while Jinyu Li was a PhD student at Zhejiang University.

© Springer Nature Switzerland AG 2019
Z. Lin et al. (Eds.): PRCV 2019, LNCS 11859, pp. 283–295, 2019.
https://doi.org/10.1007/978-3-030-31726-3_24

plane information to aid VIO, the computation cost is obviously increased due to plane extraction and management as well as the increase of optimization complexity. In this paper, we propose a new VIO system which can effectively exploit plane structures in the scene to achieve good tracking results. The key contribution is that we propose a novel VIO approach by exploiting plane information in different modules for robust tracking. Especially, we propose a novel structureless plane-distance cost which can enforce plane constraints in sliding-window optimization without increasing much the computation cost. Thus a very robust and efficient VIO system is achieved, which can perform 30 fps averagely on an iPhone 7 mobile phone with a single thread.

2   Related Works

VIO and VISLAM have been studied over decades. MSCKF [15] is an early filtering-based VIO system. Its state vector contains only a fixed number of the pose states. Observations to the landmarks are marginalized in the update phase, and the overall computational time is bounded. Optimization-based systems like OKVIS [12] generally use marginalization technique to linearize old frames into priors, keeping the size of its sliding window bounded.

However, error accumulation in VIO is inevitable. A SLAM system can leverage loops in the trajectory to reduce error accumulation, achieving better accuracy. PTAM [11], an early visual SLAM system, separates tracking and mapping in two threads. This later became the standard of many state-of-the-art SLAM systems. ORB-SLAM [16] improves PTAM in many aspects, including the use of ORB features, the local mapping with the covisibility graph and the global optimization with the essential graph. VINS-Mono [18] is a successful visual-inertial SLAM system, which also uses sliding-window optimization with marginalization, with a 4-DoF pose-graph map optimization. To achieve realtime performance on a mobile device, its mobile version [13] limits its front-end optimization at 10 Hz.

Another type of systems track camera by minimizing the photometric error directly. Early systems such as LSD-SLAM [5] use dense or semi-dense geometry representation, which can lead to heavy computational cost. DSO [4] used a sparse and direct formulation with sliding window optimization similar to OKVIS, thus improving the performance. Due to the small/smooth movements assumption, direct methods can be prone to rolling-shutter distortions and illumination changes.

SVO [8] is a hybrid odometry system which combines direct sparse tracking with indirect formulation for model optimization. It is highly efficient and is capable of tracking at very high framerate, which can remedy the requirement of slow-smooth movement. Nevertheless, it still suffers from many limitations of direct methods.

Lines and planes can be used for robust tracking in structured environment. Many existing methods, like [9] and [17] simply augment the existing bundle adjustment (BA) with additional structure terms. Since they are built on top of typical systems, they introduce additional cost to the system, making the system obviously heavier. Some methods like StructSLAM [22] assume Manhattan scene, which may not be used in general cases. StructVIO [23] extends Struct-SLAM with inertial measurements, and suffer from similar limitation. Methods like [21] require additional cost to parse planes and can not handle general scenes containing normal objects and planes. In general, there is still a lack of VIO system which can efficiently make use of plane information in a general scene.

3   Visual-Inertial Odometry with Multi-plane Priors

Our framework is illustrated in Fig. 1. Given the input online images and IMU measurements, we first perform feature point tracking on consecutive images and pre-integrate the IMU measurements. We employ a visual-inertial alignment method (Sect. 3.1) to accomplish the initialization. After initialization, the feature point tracking and pre-integration results are sent into the pipeline for localization. We propose a novel visual-inertial-plane PnP (VIP-PnP) to quickly localize the camera pose (Sect. 3.2), which uses information from plane information managed in a local plane map. The output of the VIP-PnP will be integrated with new IMU measurments to get the most up-to-date pose output. After VIP-PnP, the localized frame will be fed into the sliding window, and 3D landmarks are triangulated from newly tracked features. If the last frame in the sliding window is a keyframe, we will do plane expansion via reprojection consensus (Sect. 3.3), and then slide the window, i.e. inserting this new frame and marginalizing the oldest keyframe. A local bundle adjustment is employed, where a novel structureless plane-distance cost is used (Sect. 3.4). If the last frame in the sliding window is not a keyframe, we will directly replace it with the new frame and inherit its IMU measurements. In both cases, the new planes are detected based on the landmarks and added into the local plane map. When there are no planes, all the plane-based modules are disabled, and our system becomes a traditional VIO. Hence our system is still a general purpose VIO which does not fully depend on planes.

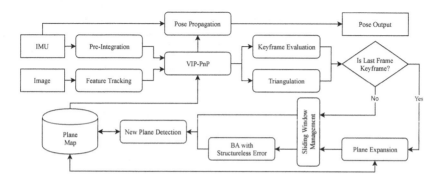

Fig. 1. Pipeline of our visual-inertial odometry with multi-plane priors.

Before describing the algorithm details, we first introduce the convention and major notations for our mathematical formulation. We represent the 3D rotation of image i using Hamiltonian quaternion q_i and use $C(q_i)$ to represent its corresponding rotation matrix. The pose of the device with respect to the world frame is denoted as $^w_b p_i, ^w_b q_i$, and is affixed to the IMU of the device. Camera frame pose $^w_c p_i, ^w_c q_i$ is related to this body frame by rigid extrinsics that can be calibrated beforehand.

We used the pinhole camera model with fixed camera intrinsics K throughout our system. For a landmark point x_k, its projection on camera image I_i will be

$$u_{ik} = \pi_K(C^\top(^w_c q_i)(x_k - ^w_c p_i)), \tag{1}$$

where π_K is the projection function with intrinsics K and the corresponding keypoint for u_{ik} is denoted as $\tilde{u}_{ik}$. We will drop the superscript/subscript and use p_i, q_i, x_k for brevity if the frame is clear from the context.

We use inverse parameterization for our landmarks [3]:

$$x_k = \frac{1}{\lambda_k} C(^w_c q_{\text{ref}(k)}) \cdot \begin{pmatrix} u_k \\ 1 \end{pmatrix} + ^w_c p_{\text{ref}(k)}. \tag{2}$$

The reference frame $\text{ref}(k)$ is the first keyframe observing x_k. u_k is the shorthand for $u_{\text{ref}(k),k}$.

A plane s is parameterized with its normal n_s and its (signed) distance d_s to the origin. A point x on plane s should satisfy $n_s^\top x - d_s = 0$.

3.1 Initialization and Plane Detection

For each input image, we detect keypoints with the Shi-Tomasi keypoint detector [10]. The keypoints are tracked using the KLT feature tracker [14]. The IMU measurements are pre-integrated into relative motion constraints using the method introduced in [7]. Similar to the visual-inertial alignment method from [19], we build a visual-only SfM from initial frames, and then align them with the pre-integrations to solve the initial states.

A plane detection module is responsible for spawning new planes. These new planes are then used for all the tracking and optimization, and will be extended when possible. We used a 3-point RANSAC [6] for plane detection. After each new frame is added into the sliding window, we detect the new planes from all the landmark points in the local map.

3.2 Visual-Inertial-Plane PnP Tracking

Assume there are already P plane models in the local map. For each new image I_i, we perform a visual-inertial-plane PnP (VIP-PnP) tracking to recover its pose. Let $\{x_k : k = 1 \dots M\}$ be the visible landmarks not belonging to any plane, $\{x_{sk} : k = 1 \dots M_s\}$ be the visible landmarks belonging to plane s, r_{IMU} be the IMU propagation error, Ψ and Φ be the inverse of the covariance matrix for keypoint measurement noise and IMU propagation error correspondingly. VIP-PnP is done by solving the following 1-frame bundle adjustment:

$$\underset{^w_b p_i, ^w_b q_i}{\arg\min} \sum_{k=1}^{M} \|u_{ik} - \tilde{u}_{ik}\|_\Psi^2 + \|r_{\text{IMU}}(^w_b p_i, ^w_b q_i)\|_\Phi^2 + \sum_{s=1}^{P}\sum_{k=1}^{M_s} \|u_{i,sk}^\perp - \tilde{u}_{i,sk}\|_\Psi^2 \quad (3)$$

In (3), the projected plane point $u_{i,sk}^\perp$ is obtained by forcing the landmark on the plane. We cast ray from $I_{\text{ref}(k)}$, and find the intersection depth with plane s:

$$\lambda_{sk}^\perp = \frac{n_s^\top C(^w_c q_{\text{ref}(k)})\binom{u_k}{1}}{d_s - n_s^\top {}^w_c p_{\text{ref}(k)}}. \quad (4)$$

Then we compute $u_{i,sk}^\perp$ with this depth enforced. We are solving the BA "as if" there are some points perfectly lying on some planes.

In a typical VIO, depth estimation can be noisy or even degenerated due to small camera translation, especially when the whole sliding window cannot provide sufficient motion parallax. By incorporating plane priors, the depth estimation becomes much more stable, especially when the motion parallax is small. Thus a smooth and robust tracking can be achieved even without maintaining global map and optimization.

3.3   Plane Expansion via Reprojection Consensus

We perform plane expansion when a new keyframe is pushed into the sliding window. A plane can be continuously tracked and refined over time, by keeping expanding new points. Since the triangulation error easily leads to a large error in depth, we use a reprojection consensus-based method for plane expansion. For landmark x_k and plane s, we can re-cast x_k onto the plane s according to (4). The reprojection errors without/with re-casting are computed as:

$$\epsilon_k = \sum_i \|u_{ik}(\lambda_k) - \tilde{u}_{ik}\|^2, \quad \epsilon_k^\perp = \sum_i \|u_{ik}(\lambda_k^\perp) - \tilde{u}_{ik}\|^2. \quad (5)$$

If $\epsilon_k^\perp \leq \max\{\alpha\epsilon_k, \gamma\}$, i.e., the new reprojection error is not greater than a threshold, the x_k is thought to be consistent with plane s, and we add this landmark to the plane. In our experiments, we used $\alpha = 1.2, \gamma = 0.5$.

In order to avoid introducing large error, we do not expand distant points into a local plane area. We represent planes with 12 fan-shaped sectors, 30° each. For a sector τ, its radius r_τ is determined by the currently most distant plane point in it. A new point x_k can be added only if it is within μr_τ distance to the center. We generally set $\mu = 1.2$.

It's worth mentioning that when the motion degenerates, a landmark at arbitrary depth can still be falsely added by the reprojection criteria. However, it also helps to keep the landmark at a reasonable depth. And these false inclusions will be pruned after the depths becoming observable under sufficient translation.

3.4   Sliding-Window Optimization with Structureless Plane-Distance Cost

We utilize a local bundle adjustment (LBA) to refine the camera poses and the landmark points in the sliding window. We keep N image frames in the sliding window. When a new frame comes, we check the parallax of its keypoint matches with respect to the last keyframe. If the parallax exceeds a threshold, we tag the new frame as a keyframe. If the number of matches is below a lower bound, or there have not been any keyframes for the recent T frames, we also mark the frame as a keyframe. After this keyframe evaluation, the new frame will be added into the sliding window. In the following, we assume $I_1, \ldots, I_N$ be the N the frames already in the sliding window, and I_{N+1} be the new one.

We slide the window with marginalization in the following way: If I_N is a keyframe, we first marginalize out I_1 and all keypoints it observes. Then we add I_{N+1} into the sliding window. If I_N is a non-keyframe, we replace it with I_{N+1} directly. The IMU measurements in between are kept and the pre-integration is updated. This particular order is different from systems like VINS-Mono, where they first add the frame, and then perform the marginalization.

As shown in Fig. 2(c–f), if the marginalization is done after the frame insertion, the result marginalization factor will contain an edge to the new frame. Next time, if this frame is not a keyframe, it will be replaced. And this edge must be marginalized again, resulting in a two-way marginalization in VINS-Mono's implementation. In our system, the marginalization is done before the insertion. As a result, the marginalization factor will constrain the oldest $N-1$ frames. No marginalization is required when replacing I_N.

Before marginalizing the oldest keyframe, we marginalize all related landmarks first, which is similar to VINS-Mono. If not, the information matrix for the related landmarks will become dense, which will significantly increase computation cost. For plannar landmarks, we replace them with the following structureless plane-distance cost, which avoids marginalization.

Structureless Plane-Distance Cost. In the core of our local bundle adjustment, we utilize a structureless plane-distance cost. Based on the linear least square triangulation method, we can triangulate a landmark x_k with all its keypoint observations $\{\tilde{u}_{ik}\}$ on images $\{I_i\}$ by constructing matrix A and vector b as:

$$
A_k = \begin{pmatrix} \vdots \\ \tilde{u}_{ikx} r_{i3} - r_{i1} \\ \tilde{u}_{iky} r_{i3} - r_{i2} \\ \vdots \end{pmatrix}, \quad
b_k = \begin{pmatrix} \vdots \\ \tilde{u}_{ikx} p_{i3} - p_{i1} \\ \tilde{u}_{iky} p_{i3} - p_{i2} \\ \vdots \end{pmatrix}. \tag{6}
$$

So x_k can be found by solving $A_k x_k = b_k$. The row vectors r_{ij} are the rows of $KC^\top({}_c^w q_i)$, i.e., $\left(r_{i1}^\top \ r_{i2}^\top \ r_{i3}^\top \right) = [KC^\top({}_c^w q_i)]^\top$. Scalars p_{ij} are the components of $-KC^\top({}_c^w q_i){}_c^w p_i$, $(p_{i1}, p_{i2}, p_{i3})^\top = -KC^\top({}_c^w q_i){}_c^w p_i$. With 2 or more observations that are not degenerated, A_k has more than 4 rows and is a full rank matrix, so we can have the least square solution for x_k.

When there is only one observation $\tilde{u}_{ik}$, or there are insufficient movements in the images, A_k will be ill-conditioned. We use plane information to regularize it: for a landmark x_{sk} belonging to a plane s, we augment the terms in (6) as:

$$A_{sk} = \begin{pmatrix} A_k \\ w_k n_s^\top \end{pmatrix}, \ b_{sk} = \begin{pmatrix} b_k \\ w_k d_s \end{pmatrix}. \tag{7}$$

The augmented row corresponds to the plane constraint $n_s^\top x_{sk} = d_s$, and is weighted by w_k. By augmenting the matrix, the solution to $A_{sk} x_{sk} = b_{sk}$ is regularized by the plane structure. As long as the camera center is not on the plane, A_{sk} is always full-rank. We can then rewrite the closed-form solution of x_{sk} as a function of the related states observing it:

$$x_{sk} = (A_{sk}^\top A_{sk})^{-1} A_{sk} b_{sk} = f(\{^w_b p_i, ^w_b q_i\}, n_s, d_s). \tag{8}$$

Since the landmark x_{sk} should be on the plane, we can minimize the following plane-distance error:

$$r_P(\{^w_b p_i, ^w_b q_i\}, n_s, d_s) = |n_s^\top x_{sk} - d_s|. \tag{9}$$

Although the size of A_{sk} depends on the length of the feature track. $A_{sk}^\top A_{sk}$ and $A_{sk}^\top b_{sk}$ are 3×3 and 3×1. This leads to the efficient evaluation of the cost function and its corresponding Jacobians.

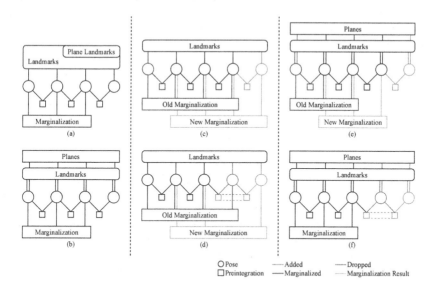

Fig. 2. Structure and marginalization in sliding-window optimization with different strategies: (a) Traditional landmark-only BA; (b) BA with our structureless cost; (c) The oldest-keyframe marginalization process in VINS-Mono; (d) The recent-non-keyframe marginalization process in VINS-Mono; (e) The oldest keyframe is being marginalized in our sliding window; (f) A non-keyframe is being replaced in our sliding window.

Figure 2(a) and (b) illustrate the structure and marginalization in sliding-window optimization. For planar landmarks, we totally remove its original reprojection error terms, and use the structureless cost instead. Given m observations of a landmark, m reprojection error terms are replaced with 1 structureless cost. The state of the plane landmark no longer participate in its corresponding structureless cost. So we can skip these landmarks in the marginalization. Plane parameters are kept fixed during BA. We re-triangulate planar points with refined camera poses after BA, and then update the planes.

4   Experiments

We implemented our system in C++ and use Ceres Solver [1] for solving nonlinear optimization problems. We run our algorithm on public benchmark datasets and evaluate the performance for quantitative results. We also make comparisons with 4 state-of-the-art odometry/SLAM systems: VINS-Mono [18], ORB-SLAM2 [16], SVO2 [8], and DSO [4]. Our system, as a plane-based VIO, will be referred as PVIO in the following.

4.1   Tracking Accuracy and Robustness

We analyze the accuracy of the algorithm by comparing the RMSE of the absolute localization error. We used the suggested configurations from the algorithms, including tuned IMU noise parameters, for the test of VINS-Mono and ORB-SLAM2. The results of SVO2 and DSO on EuRoC dataset are directly from [8]. On TUM dataset, SVO2 performed badly, which always lost quickly. PVIO used the sensor parameters from the specification of datasets, and its sliding window has $N = 8$ frames. Table 1 lists the RMSE of the odometry/SLAM systems on EuRoC [2] and a few results on TUM-VI [20] datasets. The full results on TUM-VI dataset are included in the supplementary material[1].

Accuracy. As shown in Table 1, PVIO has comparable accuracy to VINS-Mono. As for ORB-SLAM, since it does not recover true scale, we scale the camera trajectory and align it with the ground truth, which hence has lower RMSE. SVO2 and DSO are also visual only, whose recovered camera trajectories are also scaled. Despite that, we can still achieve better accuracy on many sequences. We also analyse the error accumulation on several sequences, which are included in the supplementary material due to the limited space. TUM-VI is a challenging dataset, where many sequences contain vigorous movement, and all the sequences are rather long. PVIO still achieves very competitive accuracy.

Robustness. We compare the keyframes involved in the local BA: PVIO has 8 frames, VINS-Mono has 10 frames, while ORB-SLAM2 can have as much as 30 frames. With such a small sliding window, a traditional VIO will easily have

---

[1] http://www.cad.zju.edu.cn/home/gfzhang/projects/SLAM/PVIO/pvio-supp.zip.

Table 1. The RMSE (m) of localization for different algorithms. "+/−Loop" means loop-closure turned on/off. For SVO2, "E+P" means edgelet+prior and "BA" means bundle adjustment. See [8] for the explanations about E+P and BA. For PVIO, "+/−Plane" means with/without plane priors. For the values in parenthesis, the corresponding trajectory is less than 80% complete. × means the trajectory is less than 50% complete (lost). The best results for visual-inertial algorithms are bolded.

Dataset		ORB-SLAM2		SVO2		DSO	VINS-Mono		PVIO	
		−Loop	+Loop	E+P	BA		−Loop	+Loop	−Plane	+Plane
EuRoC [2]	MH_01	0.02	0.03	0.10	0.06	0.05	0.16	0.15	0.19	**0.13**
	MH_02	0.03	0.03	0.12	0.07	0.05	0.18	0.26	**0.16**	0.21
	MH_03	0.17	0.05	0.41	×	0.18	0.20	**0.11**	0.31	0.16
	MH_04	0.15	0.37	0.43	0.40	2.50	0.35	0.37	0.29	**0.29**
	MH_05	0.06	0.04	0.30	×	0.11	0.30	**0.28**	0.79	0.34
	V1_01	0.03	0.03	0.07	0.05	0.12	0.09	0.10	0.10	**0.08**
	V1_02	0.15	0.03	0.21	×	0.11	0.11	0.09	×	**0.09**
	V1_03	(0.49)	0.10	×	×	0.93	0.19	0.18	×	**0.16**
	V2_01	0.03	0.03	0.11	×	0.04	0.09	0.08	0.11	**0.05**
	V2_02	0.15	0.03	0.11	×	0.13	**0.16**	0.17	×	0.20
	V2_03	(0.73)	(0.40)	1.08	×	1.16	0.29	0.37	×	**0.29**
TUM-VI [20]	Room1	×	0.10	×	×	0.06	0.07	**0.07**	1.65	0.26
	Room2	×	0.12	×	×	0.11	0.07	**0.07**	0.12	0.15
	Room3	×	(0.04)	×	×	0.12	0.12	**0.12**	0.18	0.18
	Corridor1	×	×	×	×	5.43	0.59	0.59	×	**0.23**
	Outdoors1	×	×	×	×	×	74.55	81.57	×	**22.26**

robustness problems especially when the motion parallax is insufficient. In contrast, PVIO can still track robustly. We also tried disabling all the plane-related modules. Without using plane priors, PVIO failed to track some sequences on EuRoC dataset, and diverged on almost all long sequences in TUM-VI.

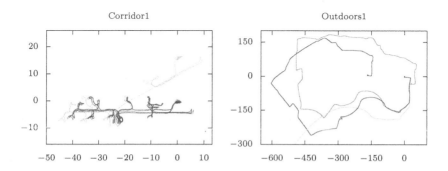

Fig. 3. Trajectories of: — PVIO, — VINS-Mono,   DSO. Axes are in meters.

TUM-VI is a very challenging dataset, where all sequences contain vigorous movement, and many of them are rather long. On almost all sequences, our system successfully tracks the data without lost or divergence. Only VINS-Mono performed better in terms of completeness. DSO diverges occasionally, and the trajectories become completely useless after divergence. ORB-SLAM is almost incapable of running on TUM-VI, which repeatedly gets lost and re-localizes in room sequences, and completely gets lost in other sequences. DSO can only track for few frames, and then fail to continue further.

The Outdoors1 sequence in TUM-VI dataset is a 2656m-long sequence. Figure 3 shows the top-down view of the trajectories from PVIO, VINS-Mono and DSO. Only VINS-Mono and PVIO can get reasonable results in this sequence. PVIO, albeit of being a VIO method, achieving 22.26m RMSE, which is smaller than 1% of the total length. VINS-Mono fails to detect loops in the end, and has significant error accumulation in its orientation estimation. PVIO, on the other hand, successfully takes advantage of the information provided by the ground plane and produces a less distorted trajectory. As a general purpose VIO, plane-priors give PVIO extra robustness, result in good accuracy.

4.2 Efficiency

With the multi-plane priors, the size of the sliding window can be effectively reduced. At the same time, the revisited marginalization strategy and the structureless cost also helped to reduce the computation time. In a canonical system, one can enforce plane constraints by adding additional point-to-plane distance error to the bundle adjustment. We also implemented such bundle adjustment, and name the corresponding VIO system as Ref-VIO. We run VINS-Mono, Ref-VIO and PVIO on the same computer with i7-7700 3.6GHz×4 and 16G memory. We also measure the running time for different parts of the systems. We set the sliding window size of VINS-Mono to 8 frames, and also disable its backend. So three systems have fair competition. Table 2 shows the running time of different components on sequence V1_01_easy.

Table 2. Running time (ms) of VINS-Mono (frontend), Ref-VIO and PVIO.

Module	VINS-Mono	Ref-VIO	PVIO
Keypoint Tracking	8.34	7.42	7.40
Pre-Integration	0.44	0.04	0.04
Plane Management	–	1.04	1.09
Non-Keyframe PnP	17.78	0.93	0.90
Non-Keyframe Marg	0.68	–	–
Keyframe BA	19.18	30.59	19.87
Keyframe Marg	32.91	3.26	2.81
Keyframe Average	60.87	42.35	31.02
All Frames Average	44.72	14.80	13.53

Fig. 4. AR effect on a mobile phone. A virtual "laptop" is placed next to the real one.

As we can see, if we directly use point-to-plane distance in BA, the computation cost will significantly increase. By replacing traditional reprojection error with structureless plane-distance cost, the keyframe BA in PVIO takes almost the same time as the normal BA in VINS-Mono. In the meantime, VINS-Mono uses a 3-frame BA with older frames fixed in its non-keyframe PnP, while PVIO only solves 1 frame, without involving any historical frames. The modified marginalization strategy also significantly reduce the computation time. Summing up all the accelerations, the keyframe processing time of PVIO is only 1/2 of VINS-Mono, and all frames average is taking less than 1/3 of VINS-Mono.

To further verify the efficiency of PVIO, we successfully run PVIO on an iPhone 7 mobile phone. The image is captured at 640×480 (30fps), while IMU is incoming at 100 Hz. The whole system runs in a single thread, and can perform metric tracking and AR on the camera image. The average speed can reach 30fps. Figure 4 shows the AR effect in our demo App.

5 Conclusions and Disscusions

We presented a new robust and efficient VIO system, which exploits multi-plane priors in the tracking and the local mapping. With the design of the structureless plane-distance cost, we can incorporate multi-plane prior constraints into bundle adjustment without introducing much computation cost. Compared to other state-of-the-art systems, our proposed VIO system can get competitive accuracy. Even on long and challenging sequences, our system can track successfully, whereas many other systems fail. Especially, our VIO system is very efficient and requires much less computation cost compared to the complex SLAM systems such as ORB-SLAM and VINS-Mono. Our VIO can perform in real-time even on an iPhone 7 with a single thread. To further improve the robustness and efficiency of our VIO system, we would like to explore the possibilities in using more structure information in the future.

References

1. Agarwal, S., Mierle, K., Others: ceres solver. http://ceres-solver.org
2. Burri, M., et al.: The EuRoC micro aerial vehicle datasets. Int. J. Rob. Res. **35**(10), 1157–1163 (2016)

3. Civera, J., Davison, A., Montiel, J.: Inverse depth parametrization for monocular SLAM. IEEE Trans. Rob. **24**(5), 932–945 (2008)
4. Engel, J., Koltun, V., Cremers, D.: Direct sparse odometry. IEEE Trans. Pattern Anal. Mach. Intell. **40**(3), 611–625 (2018)
5. Engel, J., Schöps, T., Cremers, D.: LSD-SLAM: large-scale direct monocular SLAM. In: Fleet, D., Pajdla, T., Schiele, B., Tuytelaars, T. (eds.) ECCV 2014. LNCS, vol. 8690, pp. 834–849. Springer, Cham (2014). https://doi.org/10.1007/978-3-319-10605-2_54
6. Fischler, M.A., Bolles, R.C.: Random sample consensus: a paradigm for model fitting with applications to image analysis and automated cartography. Commun. ACM **24**(6), 381–395 (1981)
7. Forster, C., Carlone, L., Dellaert, F., Scaramuzza, D.: On-manifold preintegration for real-time visual-inertial odometry. IEEE Trans. Rob. **33**(1), 1–21 (2017)
8. Forster, C., Zhang, Z., Gassner, M., Werlberger, M., Scaramuzza, D.: SVO: semidirect visual odometry for monocular and multicamera systems. IEEE Trans. Rob. **33**(2), 249–265 (2017)
9. Lee, G.H., Fraundorfer, F., Pollefeys, M.: MAV visual SLAM with plane constraint. In: IEEE International Conference on Robotics and Automation, pp. 3139–3144. IEEE, Shanghai, May 2011
10. Shi, J.T.: Good features to track. In: IEEE Conference on Computer Vision and Pattern Recognition, pp. 593–600. IEEE Computer Society Press, Seattle (1994)
11. Klein, G., Murray, D.: Parallel tracking and mapping for small AR workspaces. In: IEEE and ACM International Symposium on Mixed and Augmented Reality, pp. 1–10. IEEE, Nara, November 2007
12. Leutenegger, S., Lynen, S., Bosse, M., Siegwart, R., Furgale, P.: Keyframe-based visual-inertial odometry using nonlinear optimization. Int. J. Rob. Res. **34**(3), 314–334 (2015)
13. Li, P., Qin, T., Hu, B., Zhu, F., Shen, S.: Monocular visual-inertial state estimation for mobile augmented reality. In: IEEE International Symposium on Mixed and Augmented Reality, pp. 11–21. IEEE, Nantes, October 2017
14. Lucas, B.D., Kanade, T.: An iterative image registration technique with an application to stereo vision. In: Proceedings of the 7th International Joint Conference on Artificial Intelligence, IJCAI 1981 , vol. 2, pp. 674–679. Morgan Kaufmann Publishers Inc. (1981)
15. Mourikis, A.I., Roumeliotis, S.I.: A multi-state constraint kalman filter for vision-aided inertial navigation. In: IEEE International Conference on Robotics and Automation, pp. 3565–3572. IEEE, Rome, April 2007
16. Mur-Artal, R., Tardos, J.D.: ORB-SLAM2: an open-source SLAM system for monocular, stereo, and RGB-D cameras. IEEE Trans. Rob. **33**(5), 1255–1262 (2017)
17. Pumarola, A., Vakhitov, A., Agudo, A., Sanfeliu, A., Moreno-Noguer, F.: PL-SLAM: Real-time monocular visual SLAM with points and lines. In: IEEE International Conference on Robotics and Automation, pp. 4503–4508. IEEE, Singapore, May 2017
18. Qin, T., Li, P., Shen, S.: VINS-Mono: a robust and versatile monocular visual-inertial state estimator. IEEE Trans. Rob. **34**(4), 1004–1020 (2018)
19. Qin, T., Shen, S.: Robust initialization of monocular visual-inertial estimation on aerial robots. In: IEEE/RSJ International Conference on Intelligent Robots and Systems, pp. 4225–4232. IEEE, Vancouver, September 2017

20. Schubert, D., Goll, T., Demmel, N., Usenko, V., Stueckler, J., Cremers, D.: The TUM VI benchmark for evaluating visual-inertial odometry. In: International Conference on Intelligent Robots and Systems, October 2018
21. Yang, S., Song, Y., Kaess, M., Scherer, S.: Pop-up SLAM: Semantic monocular plane SLAM for low-texture environments. In: IEEE/RSJ International Conference on Intelligent Robots and Systems, pp. 1222–1229. IEEE, Daejeon,October 2016
22. Zhou, H., Zou, D., Pei, L., Ying, R., Liu, P., Yu, W.: StructSLAM: visual SLAM with building structure lines. IEEE Trans. Veh. Technol. **64**(4), 1364–1375 (2015)
23. Zou, D., Wu, Y., Pei, L., Ling, H., Yu, W.: StructVIO : visual-inertial odometry with structural regularity of man-made environments. arXiv:1810.06796 [cs], October 2018

Contour-Guided Person Re-identification

Jiaxing Chen[1], Qize Yang[1], Jingke Meng[1], Wei-Shi Zheng[1,2(✉)],
and Jian-Huang Lai[1]

[1] School of Data and Computer Science, Sun Yat-sen University, Guangzhou, China
{chenjx228,yangqz,mengjke}@mail2.sysu.edu.cn, wszheng@ieee.org,
stsljh@mail.sysu.edu.cn
[2] Key Laboratory of Machine Intelligence and Advanced Computing,
Ministry of Education, Beijing, China

Abstract. Feature representation is one of the crucial components in person re-identification(re-ID). Recently, local feature has attracted great attention from the re-ID community, and extra visual cues have been well exploited to guide local feature learning, such as pose cues, semantic parsing and *etc*. Besides, the latest research demonstrates that general CNN-based deep models have a bias to texture feature in pattern recognition, but ignore shape-based feature, which has been verified as significant for cross-domain invariance. As far as we know, there is little work focusing on shape-based feature on person re-ID. In this paper, we introduce a new data modality, pedestrian contour, into the re-ID community, which to our best knowledge is the first attempt to utilize contour explicitly in deep re-ID models. We hypothesize that, as an alternative of other exploited visual cues, pedestrian contour could guide deep models to learn robust shape-based feature, with build-in prior information. We propose several contour-guided architectures to explicitly use pedestrian contour, including plain ones and multi-scale one. Extensive experiments have validated the effectiveness of our models. Moreover, we transfer the methodology into a powerful part-based model, Part-based Convolutional Baseline(PCB), and boost the model performance, which verifies the promising prospect of contour-guided models to expand as an auxiliary mechanism in re-ID.

Keywords: Person re-identification · Pedestrian contour · Local feature learning

1 Introduction

Person re-identification(re-ID) aims to search all images of the same pedestrian across different non-overlapping cameras with a given query image, which could intrinsically be seen as a problem of cross-camera pedestrian retrieval. Real-world re-ID is still an extremely challenging task due to large variations of pedestrian pose and camera viewpoint, background clutter, defective person detection, illumination change, and occlusion, *etc*.

Student paper.

© Springer Nature Switzerland AG 2019
Z. Lin et al. (Eds.): PRCV 2019, LNCS 11859, pp. 296–307, 2019.
https://doi.org/10.1007/978-3-030-31726-3_25

Fig. 1. Randomly selected pedestrian images and their extracted contours in Market-1501, DukeMTMC-reID and MSMT17.

Considering the factors above, most existing methods for re-ID focus on either robust feature representation or discriminative distance metric. Deep learning methods [1,14,19,24] currently dominate the re-ID search community. Although deep models have achieved remarkable progress, there is still a gap hindering reliable, real-world application of person re-ID. Many existing deep models for person re-ID typically learn a global full-body embedding [1]. However, the capability of global representation is limited by lack of emphasis on local differences and sensitivity to domain variance and background clutter. Recent improvements in feature representation have mainly been achieved by leveraging local visual cues, which are supposed to be more robust. Either pedestrian pose cue [12,20,21] or semantic parsing [7] has been exploited explicitly as prior guidance for local feature learning.

Since priori information is critical to improving re-ID model performance, here we raise a heuristic question: Is there any other visual cue could help learn robust local feature as a prior guidance? In an end to address this question, in this paper we use pedestrian contour(see Fig. 1) explicitly as an alternative to bounding boxes and semantic parsing in re-ID deep model. To the best of our knowledge, this is the first attempt to leverage contour information explicitly in the community of person re-ID.

Pedestrian contour is vital to identity recognition and many computer vision applications, but yet not received due attention in person re-ID research. Intuitively, human beings recognize different objects fundamentally depending on a shape-based guidance, object contour. Researches in human vision and neuroscience also prove that shape perception is a fundamental component in object recognition. From the perspective of image processing, object contour indicates a transitional area where color and texture change dramatically. Theoretically, contour contains abundant gradient information of color, which has potential to help distinguish different objects.

The latest work [4] takes an insight into how CNN learn deep vision feature. Empirical experiments on ImageNet [3] show that deeply-learned models have a bias to texture-based feature rather than shape-based feature, which is in stark contrast to human behavioural evidence. For example, a cat with an elephant texture is an elephant to CNNs, but still a cat to humans. The different classification strategies inspires authors to carry out further experiments for overcoming texture bias of CNNs. It reveals that deep models learn a long-ranged contour feature show stronger capability of generalization upon domain-shifted or distorted testing samples. A mixture of both texture-based and contour-based embedding is also verified as able to improve performance of image classification and object detection. Nevertheless, it is also be demonstrated that models trained on sole shape-based images perform poorly and struggle in fitting testing samples in the same domain. In the light of the above, it is more reasonable to make use of contour information as auxiliary component to guide domain-invariant local feature learning, instead of processing as an independent modality.

Summarized from the above discussion, we could make several conclusions: First, a feature representation covering both global and local information is a superior pedestrian descriptor. Second, pedestrian contour is an unexploited but potential data modality in future re-ID research, which may be the key to cross-domain generalization. Third, it is notable that existing CNN-based models tend to ignore contour-based feature, so extra prior information for guidance is indispensable for enhancing shape-based learning.

In this paper, we make the first attempt to introduce pedestrian contour explicitly into deeply-based model in person re-ID and put forward several contour-guided deep proposals. Utilizing an off-the-shelf edge detection model, we extract pedestrian contours across several large-scale datasets as advance preparation. Both original pedestrian images and extracted contours are fed as inputs into the convolutional neuron network for feature embedding. We propose several simple but effective architectures to integrate features derived from original images and contours, learning global and contour-guided local features in a unified manner. We not only try to make correlation between different feature branches in a straightforward way, but also take fusion of different scales into consideration and devise a multi-scale schema by hierarchically enhancing their correlation layer to layer. Extensive experiments carried out with no bells and whistles on three datasets(Market-1501, DukeMTMC-reID and MSMT17) have demonstrated the great power of contour-guided models. Surprisingly, even the plain version(see (c) in Fig. 2) outperforms the baseline model by a dramatical margin(Market-1501 by 8.9% in mAP and 5.1% in Rank-1, DukeMTMC-reID by 6.1% in mAP and 2.9% in Rank-1, and MSMT17 by 6.9% in mAP and 6.3% in Rank-1), meanwhile surpassing most of the state-of-the-art. The multi-scale version further boosts the performance slightly.

Furthermore, we also transfer our mechanism into a currently leading re-ID model, PCB, verifying that the proposed methodology is compatible and applicable in the part-based model with performance bonus.

In summary, the contributions of this paper are as follow:

- We exploit pedestrian contour explicitly in deep re-ID model for the first time, since contour is very important in computer vision. Experiments have shown the effectiveness of contour-guided local feature learning, which expectantly might encourage in-depth exploration in this direction.

- We propose several simple but powerful contour-guided architectures for integrating pedestrian contour into a unified framework. Besides the proposed plain versions, the multi-scale model is also devised. Both of them exceed the baseline dramatically, and surpass the current state-of-the-art.
- Our contour-guided mechanism is also applied upon the leading part-based model PCB, and convincingly brings with performance improvement, showing enormous potential to expand.

2   Related Work

Local Feature Learning. The emergence of deep learning greatly advances the development of person re-ID thanks to excellent representation power. Deeply-learned methods transfer the re-ID problem to deep metric learning [1,24], or classification task as a proxy target to learn deep representation [14,19]. Many existing deep models for person re-ID typically learn a global full-body embedding for the input person image in an end-to-end manner [1]. However, for one thing, image-level global feature is not sufficient to holistically depict a pedestrian identity for lack of saliency emphasis on local differences. For another, global representation is prone to background clutter and occlusion. In recent years, strengthening deep global representation by integrating local feature has become a hot topic in person re-identification research. Some works have leveraged extra priori visual information as explicit guidance for learning local feature. Human pose cues(which identifies different types of parts, *e.g.*, arm, shoulder, *etc.*) are utilized to alleviate pose variation and learn part-aligned features [12,20,21]. Besides, some works parse the body into several parts and use probability maps explicitly for pixel-level local saliency weighting [7]. The great significance of prior visual cues has been validated in these works. As a pioneer, we introduce pedestrian contour into deep person re-ID model as an explicit guidance for the first time, and demonstrate the effectiveness empirically.

Contour Related. Edge detection has been well developed in a long term and contour plays a fundamental role in many computer vision areas ranging from traditional tasks such as visual saliency, semantic segmentation, object detection/tracking, motion analysis, medical imaging, and 3D reconstruction [6,16], to modern applications like autonomous driving and image-to-text analysis [2,10]. Precisely localizing contours in image involves visual perception of various levels, which benefits visual image understanding. The latest research [4] has also illustrated contour-based feature learning is beneficial to cross-domain invariance. Nevertheless, there is little focus on contour in person re-ID. In this paper, we hypothesize that pedestrian contour could make deep models pay more attention to contour-based feature and propose several contour-guided architectures.

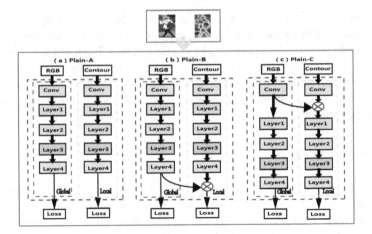

Fig. 2. Our proposed plain architectures. The inputs include original pedestrian images and contours. All plain architectures contain global and contour-guided local feature branches. ⊗ denotes element-wise product. (a) processes different branches independently without any correlation. (b) makes fusion after all feature extraction layers. (c) make fusion after the first convolutional layer.

3   Contour-Guided Architecture

In order to learn a holistic and robust pedestrian descriptor, we propose contour-guided architectures with both global and contour-guided local feature learning branches. We attempt to make fusion on the learning of different data modalities, hoping that the prior distributions of contours could guide the local feature branch to capture something shape-related and learn a domain-invariant embedding. In this work, we use ResNet [5] as the backbones of all proposed contour-guided architectures.

The global feature learning branch that takes original images as inputs, is the same as a standard ResNet. We denote the feature map on the ith layer(see Fig. 2) of this branch as $F_{global}^{(i)}$. As for the contour-guided local feature branch, we firstly feed contours as inputs and the extracted feature map on the ith layer is indicated as $F_{local}^{(i)}$. Then we adopt a straightforward manner to make fusion by operating element-wise product upon 3D feature maps from two feature branches. The feature map after fusion operation could be seen as contour-guided local feature, which is a composite of global feature and contour-based feature. The fusion operation could be formulated as

$$F_{local}^{(i)} = F_{global}^{(i)} \otimes F_{local}^{(i)} \tag{1}$$

where ⊗ denotes the operation of element-wise product.

Theoretically, given an input pedestrian contour with larger value from 0 to 1 in edge pixels, corresponding positions on intermediate feature maps are more likely to be activated in forward propagation and deservedly contain larger

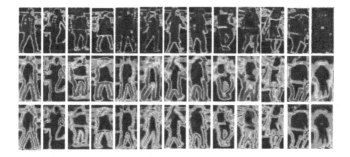

Fig. 3. The first row displays feature maps of global branch. The second row displays feature maps of contour-guided local branch before fusion and the third row corresponds to those after fusion.

values. Thus we take advantage of such intermediate feature maps as weights for contour attention through element-wise product. Furthermore, feature maps shown in Fig. 3 empirically validate our success of guiding the model to capture salient local contour-based features.

3.1 Plain Architecture

We design three plain contour-guided architectures as shown in Fig. 2. All plain versions carry out dual-branch learning and every branch corresponds to an individual loss. In the stage of testing, features from dual branches are concatenated as an integrated feature. The architecture (a) in Fig. 2 is designed to investigate whether features extracted solely from contour have the ability of generalization. The architecture (b) makes fusion after all feature extraction layers, while another schema makes fusion after the first convolution layer. Experiments show the last one is the best solution in the setting of single-scale fusion.

3.2 Multi-scale Architecture

Hierarchical methodology plays an important role in computer vision, which has yielded significant performance in object detection, semantic segmentation, *etc.* Additionally, considering effectiveness of plain architectures fused in different scales, and that making single fusion on a specific scale may not excavate full potential of contour-based guidance, we further propose a multi-scale architecture(as shown in Fig. 4), aiming at fusing contour-guided local features on different scales into an integrated representation.

In the multi-scale version, fusion between original feature and contour-based feature are made from high-resolution to low-resolution, and accumulated layer to layer in a bottom-up pathway. $F_{global}^{(i)}$ makes lateral fusion with $F_{local}^{(i)}$ and the intermediate result will be added back to $F_{local}^{(i)}$ on contour-guided local branch. The multi-scale architecture could be seen as inherent combination of plain architectures that make fusion on different scales and is foreseeable to make

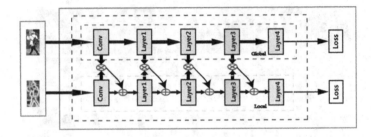

Fig. 4. Our proposed multi-scale architectures. $\otimes$ and $\oplus$ denote element-wise product and plus.

the effect of contour guidance more intensive in a hierarchical way. While testing, F_{global} and F_{local} is concatenated to discriminate pedestrian identifies. Here the fusion operation on ith layer could be reformulated as

$$F_{local}^{(i)} = F_{local}^{(i)} \oplus F_{global}^{(i)} \otimes F_{local}^{(i)} \qquad (2)$$

where $\oplus$ and $\otimes$ denotes element-wise addition and product, respectively.

3.3   Contour-Guided Auxiliary Mechanism

We further transfer our effective methodology to a part-based deep model, PCB [14], demonstrating that our contour-guided method could feasibly serve as an auxiliary mechanism to promote existing state-of-the-art models. We choose ResNet50 as the backbone of PCB model and make slight modification on PCB by applying the architecture(as shown in Fig. 2(c)) on the backbone network. Experiments illustrate that part-based learning and contour-guided mechanism could in fact compensate each other. The contour-guided mechanism shows promising future of combining with other re-ID deep models thanks to simplicity and effectiveness.

4   Experiment

4.1   Datasets and Evaluation Protocol

For performance evaluation, we carry out experiments on three large-scale person re-ID benchmarks: Market-1501 [22], DukeMTMC-reID [23], MSMT17 [17]. We adopt the standard person re-ID setting including the training/test ID split and test protocol on three datasets. Specially, we do not employ validation set of MSMT17 for fairness. For performance measure, we use the cumulative matching characteristic (CMC) and mean Average Precision(mAP) metrics.

4.2 Implementation Details

To extract pedestrian contours, we employ a powerful edge detection model RCF [8]. We implement our contour-guided architectures in the PyTorch framework and conduct a unified parameter setting on three datasets. We leverage the ImageNet-pretrained ResNet as the backbone initialization. All person images are resized to 256×128. In each iteration of training phase, 32 samples form a batch and are forwarded to softmax loss layer. We use AMSGrad optimizer [9] with hyper-parameters $\beta1 = 0.9$ and $\beta2 = 0.999$. We start with fixing all layers of the backbones and solely training the linear classification layer for 10 epochs. Then all layers are trained together for 60 epochs. The initial learning rate of the unified training is set as $3e^{-4}$. After iterating for 20 epochs and 40 epochs, the learning rate will be updated as $1/10$ and $1/100$ of the initial value. To overcome overfitting, we employ a probability of 0.5 to augment training data by means of horizontal flipping and spatial translation.

4.3 Performance Evaluation

Comparisons with Baseline Model. Table 1 compares our contour-guided models against the ResNet50 baseline person re-identification. The structures which make fusion between original images and contours surpass the baseline dramatically. For example, Plain-C improves performance over the baseline model by 8.9%/5.1% in mAP/Rank-1 on Market-1501, 6.1%/2.9% on DukeMTMC-reID and 6.9%/6.3% on MSMT17. The multi-scale one boost the performance further in most situations. With contours as prior guidance information, deep models seems to learn a more robust and generalized feature representation, which verifies our hyphothesis to some extend. However, Plain-A learns original image feature and contour feature separately and degrades a lot. We take an insight of the phenomenon. As shown in Fig. 5, it is harder for contour branch to converge in a classification re-ID model, implying that features individually extracted from contour are not competent enough to fitting complicated pedestrian benchmarks, consistent with the illustration in [4]. So it is appropriate to utilize contour as guidance for learning local features based on global feature.

Table 1. Model performance compared with the baseline model ResNet50. We denote plain architectures in Fig. 2 orderly as Plain-A, Plain-B, Plain-C, and the multi-scale architecture in Fig. 4 as Multi-Scale.

Models	Market-1501				DukeMTMC-reID				MSMT17			
	mAP	R-1	R-5	R-10	mAP	R-1	R-5	R-10	mAP	R-1	R-5	R-10
ResNet50	67.2	85.3	93.8	96.2	58.9	78.3	88.8	91.3	31.1	59.2	74.4	79.9
Plain-A	59.6	81.9	93.2	95.3	49.2	73.0	85.2	88.7	23.2	52.5	67.8	73.9
Plain-B	72.2	88.5	95.8	97.2	60.5	78.8	88.9	91.8	34.4	63.9	77.2	81.8
Plain-C	**76.1**	**90.4**	**96.4**	97.5	65.0	81.2	90.7	93.4	38.0	65.5	78.7	83.6
Multi-Scale	75.7	89.7	96.0	**97.6**	**66.0**	**82.3**	**91.7**	**95.1**	**40.3**	**67.2**	**80.4**	**85.0**

Table 2. Model performance of architectures based on different backbone networks, such as ResNet18, ResNet34 and ResNet50. We denote the ResNet50-based architecture (c) in Fig. 2 as Plain-C-50, and the architecture in Fig. 4 as Multi-Scale-50. The rest are done in the same manner. Specially, Plain-C-50+18 represents the model that use ResNet50 for global branch and ResNet18 for contour-guided local branch.

Models	Market-1501				DukeMTMC-reID				MSMT17			
	mAP	R-1	R-5	R-10	mAP	R-1	R-5	R-10	mAP	R-1	R-5	R-10
ResNet18	60.2	82.0	92.8	95.2	52.9	75.0	86.0	89.2	23.4	51.9	68.1	74.3
Plain-C-18	69.5	88.2	95.5	97.1	58.6	77.9	87.7	90.7	30.3	60.1	73.7	78.8
Multi-Scale-18	69.1	87.3	94.9	96.3	57.9	77.6	87.4	89.9	30.7	60.0	74.1	79.3
ResNet34	68.1	86.3	94.6	96.5	59.1	78.7	88.6	90.9	26.8	55.4	70.8	76.6
Plain-C-34	72.9	89.4	95.9	97.4	62.3	80.0	89.1	91.9	35.1	64.0	77.6	82.3
Multi-Scale-34	72.4	88.2	95.7	97.2	62.1	79.9	89.8	91.9	35.3	64.2	78.3	82.8
ResNet50	67.2	85.3	93.8	96.2	58.9	78.3	88.8	91.3	31.1	59.2	74.4	79.9
Plain-C-50+18	73.0	88.9	96.1	97.2	61.7	79.5	89.0	92.5	34.9	63.4	76.6	81.4
Plain-C-50	**76.1**	**90.4**	**96.4**	97.5	65.0	81.2	90.7	93.4	38	65.5	78.7	83.6
Multi-Scale-50	75.7	89.7	96.0	**97.6**	**66.0**	**82.3**	**91.7**	**95.1**	**40.3**	**67.2**	**80.4**	**85.0**

Effectiveness of Backbone and Feature Selection. Table 2 shows performance of contour-guided models beyond different backbone networks. We apply the architecture (c) in Fig. 2 on the foundation of different backbones. It reveals that either the plain version or the multi-scale version could well generalize remarkable improvement on different backbone networks. Besides, inherent capacity of backbone networks substantially determines competence of contour-guided models. Figure 6 makes a comparison on model performance when testing the multi-scale model with different feature selection(as shown in Fig. 4). The concatenation of global feature and local feature shows overwhelming superiority over individual ones universally, which is regarded as the fusion of common CNN features and contour-guided features.

Performance of Contour-Guided PCB. For the sake of fairness, here we train the standard PCB with the same protocol in our setting. Table 3 shows that the contour-guided mechanism is still effective on PCB model. We could find that contour-guided and part-based learning in fact compensate each other, when comparing PCB-Contour with the other two models. Experiments has proved contour-guided mechanism as simple but useful for expanding and transferring. Notably, plain model also conspicuously surpasses the standard PCB on all benchmarks, showing superiority over the part-based learning.

Comparisons with State-of-the-Art. Table 4 shows the performance of our contour-guided models against the current state-of-the-art. We compares the proposed models with two types of deep models: the global learning ones and pose-guided ones. All of our models including the primitive plain one, surpass the state-of-the-art models. PCB-Contour achieves the best performance on Market-

Table 3. Model comparision between original PCB and our contour-guided models. PCB-Contour represents the contour-guided PCB with a backbone in the same structure of Plain-C.

Models	Market-1501				DukeMTMC-reID				MSMT17			
	mAP	R-1	R-5	R-10	mAP	R-1	R-5	R-10	mAP	R-1	R-5	R-10
Plain-C	76.1	90.4	**96.4**	**97.5**	65.0	81.2	90.7	**93.4**	38.0	**65.5**	**78.7**	**83.6**
PCB	69.1	86.7	94.7	96.4	59.0	79.5	88.4	91.2	33.0	59.9	75.5	80.9
PCB-Contour	**76.7**	**91.2**	96.0	97.4	**68.8**	**82.8**	**91.0**	**93.4**	**39.1**	64.9	77.7	82.6

Table 4. Performance comparision with the state-of-the-art.

Models	Market-1501		DukeMTMC-reID		MSMT17	
	mAP	R-1	mAP	R-1	R-1	mAP
SVDNet [13]	62.1	82.3	56.8	76.7	–	–
AWTL [11]	75.7	89.5	63.4	79.8	–	–
GoogleNet [15]	–	–	–	–	23.0	47.6
GLAD [18]	73.9	89.9	–	–	34.0	61.4
PDC [12]	63.4	84.1	–	–	29.7	58.0
PIE [21]	69.0	87.7	62.0	79.8	–	–
Plain-C	76.1	90.4	65.0	81.2	38.0	65.5
Multi-Scale	75.7	89.7	66.0	82.3	**40.3**	**67.2**
PCB-Contour	**76.7**	**91.2**	**68.8**	**82.8**	39.1	64.9

1501 and DukeMTMC-reID which exceeds global learning and pose-guided competitors by 1%/1.7% and 5.4%/3% in mAP/Rank-1. The multi-scale model is the winner on MSMT17, achieving a performance improvement of 6.3%/5.8% in mAP/Rank-1 over the currently leading models. Contour-guided models taking advantage of both global and contour-guided local learning, empirically demonstrate the huge superiority over conventional global learning methods and pose-guided ones, certifying that contour is a reliable modality to develop in the field of person re-ID.

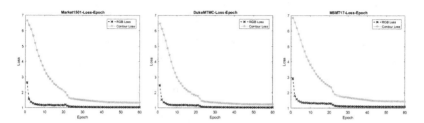

Fig. 5. Loss curves of original RGB image branch and contour-based local branch on architecture (a) in Fig. 2.

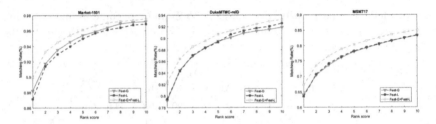

Fig. 6. CMC curves of the multi-scale model when testing with different feature groups. Feat-G and Feat-L denote the feature learned by global branch and local branch shown in Fig. 4. Feat-G+Feat-L means testing with the concatenation of Feat-G and Feat-L.

5   Conclusion

In this paper, we make the first attempt to utilize pedestrian contour explicitly in deep re-ID model. We feed the contours as inputs of deep models, and together with original images form multi-branch architectures. We propose several contour-guided architectures, which not only outperform the baseline model by a large margin, but surpass both of global learning and pose-guided competitors. Empirical experiments have fully demonstrated the great significance of contour-guided learning for robust feature representation. Furthermore, we also apply our methodology on the backbone of a part-based model, PCB. It is revealed that the part-based and contour-guided learning could compensate each other on a unified architecture.

References

1. Ahmed, E., Jones, M., Marks, T.K.: An improved deep learning architecture for person re-identification. In: Proceedings of the IEEE Conference on Computer Vision and Pattern Recognition, pp. 3908–3916 (2015)
2. Berthold, P., Michaelis, M., Luettel, T., Meissner, D., Wuensche, H.J.: Radar reflection characteristics of vehicles for contour and feature estimation. In: 2017 Sensor Data Fusion: Trends, Solutions, Applications (SDF), pp. 1–6. IEEE (2017)
3. Deng, J., Dong, W., Socher, R., Li, L.J., Li, K., Fei-Fei, L.: ImageNet: a large-scale hierarchical image database. In: 2009 IEEE Conference on Computer Vision and Pattern Recognition, pp. 248–255. IEEE (2009)
4. Geirhos, R., Rubisch, P., Michaelis, C., Bethge, M., Wichmann, F.A., Brendel, W.: ImageNet-trained CNNs are biased towards texture; increasing shape bias improves accuracy and robustness. arXiv preprint arXiv:1811.12231 (2018)
5. He, K., Zhang, X., Ren, S., Sun, J.: Deep residual learning for image recognition. In: Proceedings of the IEEE Conference on Computer Vision and Pattern Recognition, pp. 770–778 (2016)
6. Jiang, Z., Yuan, Y., Wang, Q.: Contour-aware network for semantic segmentation via adaptive depth. Neurocomputing **284**, 27–35 (2018)
7. Kalayeh, M.M., Basaran, E., Gökmen, M., Kamasak, M.E., Shah, M.: Human semantic parsing for person re-identification. In: Proceedings of the IEEE Conference on Computer Vision and Pattern Recognition, pp. 1062–1071 (2018)

8. Liu, Y., Cheng, M.M., Hu, X., Wang, K., Bai, X.: Richer convolutional features for edge detection. In: Proceedings of the IEEE Conference on Computer Vision and Pattern Recognition, pp. 3000–3009 (2017)
9. Reddi, S.J., Kale, S., Kumar, S.: On the convergence of Adam and beyond (2018)
10. Rigaud, C., Burie, J.C., Ogier, J.M., Karatzas, D., Van de Weijer, J.: An active contour model for speech balloon detection in comics. In: 2013 12th International Conference on Document Analysis and Recognition, pp. 1240–1244. IEEE (2013)
11. Ristani, E., Tomasi, C.: Features for multi-target multi-camera tracking and re-identification. In: Proceedings of the IEEE Conference on Computer Vision and Pattern Recognition, pp. 6036–6046 (2018)
12. Su, C., Li, J., Zhang, S., Xing, J., Gao, W., Tian, Q.: Pose-driven deep convolutional model for person re-identification. In: Proceedings of the IEEE International Conference on Computer Vision, pp. 3960–3969 (2017)
13. Sun, Y., Zheng, L., Deng, W., Wang, S.: SVDNet for pedestrian retrieval. In: Proceedings of the IEEE International Conference on Computer Vision, pp. 3800–3808 (2017)
14. Sun, Y., Zheng, L., Yang, Y., Tian, Q., Wang, S.: Beyond part models: person retrieval with refined part pooling (and a strong convolutional baseline). In: Ferrari, V., Hebert, M., Sminchisescu, C., Weiss, Y. (eds.) ECCV 2018. LNCS, vol. 11208, pp. 501–518. Springer, Cham (2018). https://doi.org/10.1007/978-3-030-01225-0_30
15. Szegedy, C., et al.: Going deeper with convolutions. In: Proceedings of the IEEE Conference on Computer Vision and Pattern Recognition, pp. 1–9 (2015)
16. Teo, C.L., Fermüller, C., Aloimonos, Y.: A gestaltist approach to contour-based object recognition: combining bottom-up and top-down cues. Int. J. Robot. Res. 34(4–5), 627–652 (2015)
17. Wei, L., Zhang, S., Gao, W., Tian, Q.: Person transfer GAN to bridge domain gap for person re-identification. In: Proceedings of the IEEE Conference on Computer Vision and Pattern Recognition, pp. 79–88 (2018)
18. Wei, L., Zhang, S., Yao, H., Gao, W., Tian, Q.: GLAD: global-local-alignment descriptor for pedestrian retrieval. In: Proceedings of the 25th ACM International Conference on Multimedia, pp. 420–428. ACM (2017)
19. Wu, S., Chen, Y.C., Li, X., Wu, A.C., You, J.J., Zheng, W.S.: An enhanced deep feature representation for person re-identification. In: 2016 IEEE Winter Conference on Applications of Computer Vision (WACV), pp. 1–8. IEEE (2016)
20. Zhao, H., et al.: Spindle Net: person re-identification with human body region guided feature decomposition and fusion. In: Proceedings of the IEEE Conference on Computer Vision and Pattern Recognition, pp. 1077–1085 (2017)
21. Zheng, L., Huang, Y., Lu, H., Yang, Y.: Pose invariant embedding for deep person re-identification. arXiv preprint arXiv:1701.07732 (2017)
22. Zheng, L., Shen, L., Tian, L., Wang, S., Wang, J., Tian, Q.: Scalable person re-identification: a benchmark. In: Proceedings of the IEEE International Conference on Computer Vision, pp. 1116–1124 (2015)
23. Zheng, Z., Zheng, L., Yang, Y.: Unlabeled samples generated by GAN improve the person re-identification baseline in vitro. In: Proceedings of the IEEE International Conference on Computer Vision, pp. 3754–3762 (2017)
24. Zheng, Z., Zheng, L., Yang, Y.: A discriminatively learned CNN embedding for person reidentification. ACM Trans. Multimed. Comput. Commun. Appl. (TOMM) 14(1), 13 (2018)

Robust License Plate Detection Through Auxiliary Information and Context Fusion Model

Ning Wang, Feng Liu$^{(\boxtimes)}$, and Zongliang Gan

Jiangsu Province Key Lab on Image Processing and Image Communications,
Nanjing University of Posts and Telecommunications, Nanjing 210003, China
wangning.amic@foxmail.com, {liuf,ganzl}@njupt.edu.cn

Abstract. License plate detection has wide applications in the intelligent transportation system, while it still remains challenges to improve the robustness under various shooting distance and observation angles. To get better performance, a novel convolutional-neural-network-based method is proposed, which is achieved with auxiliary information and context fusion model. First, the auxiliary information is employed in our framework, which corresponds with resolutions, orientations and shapes of license plates. Specifically, the multiple resolutions are collected through integrating multi-level features of convolution hierarchy. Besides the various scales and ratios, the region proposal network (RPN) with multi-angle anchors and branching structure is applied to generate proper proposals. Second, an effective context fusion model is designed to fully exploit the hidden correlation between license plates and contextual properties. The local and contextual features are independently learned in the dual pathways, which are later joint to form a powerful representation in subsequent layers. Comprehensive experiments on the publicly available datasets confirm the effectiveness of the proposed method.

Keywords: License plate detection · Convolutional neural network · Auxiliary information · Context fusion

1 Introduction

License plate detection plays an important role in intelligent transportation system (ITS), which facilitates wide applications such as vehicle retrieval, traffic control and parking payment. The robustness of license plate detection under different environments, being a crucial component for the whole license plate recognition system. As observed in [1], the main challenges of license plate detection attribute to various resolutions, observation angles and environmental interference. Although numbers of approaches have been proposed, it is still a challenging task to accurately locate license plates in an open environment.

This is a student paper. This work was partially supported by the National Natural Science Foundation of China under Grant 61702278.

© Springer Nature Switzerland AG 2019
Z. Lin et al. (Eds.): PRCV 2019, LNCS 11859, pp. 308–319, 2019.
https://doi.org/10.1007/978-3-030-31726-3_26

In the past two decades, license plate detection has been an active subject in computer vision, a large number of methods are proposed to get robust performance. Zhou et al. [2] build the principal visual word through bag of words model, the local features are joint to find license plate regions. Yu et al. [4] analyze the characteristics of license plates in frequency domain, the wavelet transform and empirical mode decomposition analysis are used for license plate detection. There are some methods following that combining candidate regions and feature analysis to improve detection results. In [5], connection component analysis is used to extract candidate regions and a geometric relationship matrix models the layout of characters. Then the final locations are screened out through genetic algorithm. Panahi et al. [6] perform connected component analysis and random sampling consensus after applying adaptive binarization and block division to gray images. In [7], a line density filter (LDF) based on edge and texture characteristics of license plate is proposed, which unites the similar pixels in each row. Although these methods have made great progress, the detection results of traditional methods are relatively coarse and manually designed features are limited to a certain environment.

In recent years, many researchers focus on convolutional-neural-network-based (CNN) methods to achieve impressive detection results. Kurpiel et al. [13] propose a license plate detection method based on adjacent sub-regions. The input image is segmented into several overlapping sub-regions, each of which gets a confidence score to estimate final results through CNN. In [14], the significance of license plate is enhanced through multi-step preprocessing, then the candidate regions are further screened out through CNN model. Laroca et al. [15] apply the general object detector for license plate detection, which is divided into two consecutive subtasks: vehicle detection and license plate detection. Although this method reduces environmental interference, the false alarms of the multi-step process will propagate in subsequent tasks. The current CNN-based methods rarely take into account license plate's characteristics, which will lead a further improvement to detection performance.

In this paper, we propose a framework for license plate detection under different shooting distances and observation angles. The main contributions are summarized as follows. Firstly, the auxiliary information corresponding to characteristics of license plate is customized in classical Faster R-CNN. We enhance the robustness of small license plates through integrating features of multiple resolutions. Then rotated anchors are adopted in the RPN stage to reduce detection redundancy caused by observation angles. Secondly, focusing on fully exploiting the contextual information of license plate, an effective context fusion model is designed, in which it builds upper and lower branches for powerful representations. The local and contextual correlations are further combined for classification and box regression.

The remainder of this paper is organized as follows. The related works adopted for our method are introduced in Sect. 2. In Sect. 3, the proposed method is introduced in detail. The effectiveness of our method is proved through experiments in Sect. 4. The conclusion of our work is stated in Sect. 5.

2   Related Work

2.1   Deep Learning for License Plate Detection

Comparing to traditional methods with manually designed features, the automatic feature extraction through CNN overcomes the unstable features and environmental interferences to a certain extent. Therefore, some researchers propose CNN-based methods for license plate detection [17–20]. However, a large number of annotated samples are basis for higher performance in deep convolution networks, the generalization ability will inevitably decrease in absence of samples. At present, there are some publicly available datasets, such Brazilian road license plate dataset SSIG [12] and Taiwan's multi-scene license plate dataset AOLP [16]. Abundant samples allow CNN to fit more complex patterns, the data augmentation technology and proper training strategies are also essential to the convolutional neural network.

In the past few years, more and more object detection subjects have adopted deep learning to achieve advanced performance. Girshick et al. [11] first introduce CNN into object detection which achieves impressive improvements compared with traditional methods. Subsequently, a series of CNN-based methods are developed [8–10], there are also many researchers employing such object detection models for license plate detection. Xie et al. [17] propose a multi-directional license plate detection method based on YOLO [9], which detects license plates orderly in two subnetworks. Polishetty et al. [18] propose a heuristic-based method that combining visual significance and deep features. The coarse boundary is extracted by manually designed filters, which is further refined through CNN. Rafique et al. [19] carry out a series of experiments on different detection methods, which provides a feasible work to solve the problem of license plate detection. In [20], the CNN model is used to extract the candidate regions of license plate and the bounding box is refined through horizontal and vertical edge projection. These convolutional-neural-network-based methods prove that automatically extracted features produce more robust performance.

2.2   Available Information for License Plate Detection

The advancement of Faster R-CNN [8], owes a lot to the fact that the region proposal network generates numerous high-quality translation-invariant proposals. For license plate detection task, applying such a multi-category model is not exactly suitable. Since license plates have some special properties and available priors, it is feasible to employ multiple characteristics of license plate in the network to achieve more effective performance. In the actual scene, the angle between license plate and camera often leads a redundant detection region, which is adverse to subsequent recognition. We have noticed that few researchers focus on solving the problem of observation angles, the text detection methods [21,22] can be migrated to establish a suitable bounding box. Furthermore, compared with general objects, license plate normally occupies fewer pixels and its context region is usually fixed in the image, which will provide a wealth of information.

Chen et al. [24] have illustrated that utilizing contextual region has expected effects on small objects. Lin et al. [23] have shown that utilizing the semantic and location information of multi-level feature hierarchies will improve the performance of small object detection. The combination of high and low-resolution features will improve the detection performance for license plates in various resolutions. Therefore, we employ the auxiliary information and context region in Faster R-CNN to solve small targets, multiple angles and interference problems in license plate detection.

3   Proposed Method

In this section, the license plate detection framework is introduced in detail, as shown in Fig. 1. The two-stage network Faster R-CNN is employed as our baseline, which is augmented through auxiliary information and contextual features. Given an input license plate image, the multi-level feature maps in shared convolution are integrated to collect multi-resolution details. The customized orientation and shapes are used in the RPN stage for proposal generation. At last, an effective context fusion model is designed to fully exploit local and contextual features, which forms a comprehensive representation for final results.

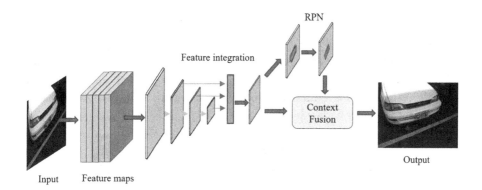

Fig. 1. Overview of proposed framework architecture, which consists of three sequential modules: feature integration, RPN stage and context fusion model.

3.1   Auxiliary Information Enhancement

Due to different shooting distance, the size of license plates vary in a wide range. Aside from license plates with large spatial resolutions, the information representing small license plates is continuously lost in the convolution feature hierarchy. Different from the single-scale feature map exploited in original Faster R-CNN, we reuse the multi-level feature maps to integrate multi-resolution information of license plates, the details are shown in Fig. 2. The multi-level feature

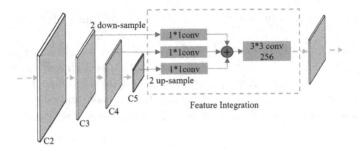

Fig. 2. The detailed architecture of feature integration, which have a comprehensive collection of features at multiple resolutions.

maps $\{C_2, C_3, C_4, C_5\}$ correspond to output of each block in ResNet [3], which have a scaling step of 2 strides from high to low.

In the feedforward network, the bottom-up C_3, C_4 and C_5 are exploited to integrate multi-level features in consideration of the variation range of license plates. In detail, the bilinear interpolation scales C_3, C_5 to the same resolution as C_4, since C_4 has appropriate strides for the multi-scale license plates in image. Then a 1×1 convolution layer unifies channels to the fixed number of 256. Furthermore, the element-wise addition integrates high-level semantics and low-level details into powerful features. At last, the 3×3 convolution layer is used to remove aliasing caused by sampling and refine features. The integrated features are utilized for classification and regression in the following stages.

Classical Faster R-CNN uses horizontal boxes (x, y, w, h) to represent location of objects. However, applying horizontal boxes for multi-directional license plates inevitably leads a redundancy in detection region, as illustrated in Fig. 3.

(a) horizontal bounding box   (b) rotational bounding box

Fig. 3. The illustration of difference between horizontal and rotational detection. The red box denotes the prediction results and the green one denotes the ground truth. (Color figure online)

To handle this problem, a new variable θ is applied to represent the orientation of anchors in the RPN stage. θ is defined as the angle between the longer side of the bounding box and the positive direction of the x-axis. The orientation or its opposite has the same role for the symmetrical structure of license plate. In this paper, we always keep the acute angle to denote the orientation. Finally, the detected license plates are represented by five variables (x, y, w, h, θ).

In addition, the special shape of license plate is taken into account, two convolution layers with similar shapes are applied to efficiently extract features. The original 3×3 convolution layer is replaced by two rectangular layers with size of 5×3 and 3×1, both of which separately slide on each location of the integrated feature map in RPN stage. We concatenate the two 256-dimensional features into 512-dimensional output for proposal generation. The anchor strategy and branch structure in the PRN stage are shown in Fig. 4.

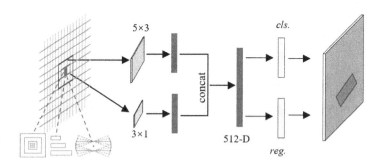

Fig. 4. The anchor strategy and branch structure in the RPN stage. The multiple scales, aspect ratios and angles are used for translation-invariant anchors. The mapped features of each sliding windows are concatenated for proposal generation.

In the RPN stage, a total of 256 anchors are collected in a mini-batch for proposal generation. In order to avoid fewer positive anchors caused by low-quality angles, another strategy is adopted to select positive and negative anchors. (i) The anchors that keep the highest IoU or greater than 0.7 overlapped with the ground-truth are selected as positive samples. (ii) The anchors that keep IoU in the range $[0.3, 0.7]$ within $10°$ differences to the ground-truth are selected as positive samples. (iii) The negative anchors keep the IoU less than 0.3. Considering inaccuracy of using horizontal IoU to select the rotated anchors, a skew IoU algorithm [22] based on triangle partition is applied. The collected anchors will serve as inferences to learn proper proposals for license plates.

3.2   Context Fusion Model

In this subsection, we focus on fully exploiting the local and contextual information to improve the robustness of license plate detection. The proposed method is the first introducing contextual region as supplementary information in license plate detection. Since license plates usually possess distinct texture and fixed backgrounds, it can be considered that contextual region will provide comprehensive features and enhance the capability against environmental interference.

The robustness of classification and box regression will be enhanced through combination with contextual features.

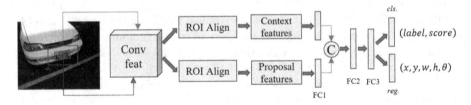

Fig. 5. The architecture of designed context model, which is a dual-path network with multiple layers, the upper blue branch is for context and the lower red branch is for license plate. Features are deeply encoded for final classification and box regression. (Color figure online)

Based on the analysis above, an effective context fusion model is designed to exploit contextual information, as shown in Fig. 5. After proposal generation in the RPN stage, the context regions are extracted from the 4 times of license plate proposal boxes. The ROI align [27] is applied to project the contextual region and proposal onto the multi-scale features which are encoded into fixed dimensions. Subsequently, a fully connected layer (FC1) is used to capture high-level nonlinear representations as well as remove redundancy. Then the learned context and proposal features are concatenated, which are fed into two hidden FCs to mine joint representation of the correlation in local and context. Each fully connected layer follows a non-linearity ReLU, after which the final representations are used for classification and box regression.

In context model, we use horizontal boxes for contextual region to prevent information loss caused by sensitive angles. Since grid splitting has the problem of feature misalignment which will cause a deviation for location regression, the bilinear interpolation is employed in ROI align. Moreover, taking into account the special aspect ratio of license plate, the cropped features are formed into a fixed dimension of 13×4 instead of default 7×7. The learning parameters of upper and lower branches are updated separately in back propagation.

3.3   Loss Function

In the proposed method, the total loss includes two parts: the classification loss $L_{cls}(p_i, p_i^*)$ and regression loss $L_{reg}(t_i, t_i^*)$, which is defined as:

$$L(p_i, p_i^*; t_i, t_i^*) = \frac{1}{N_{cls}} \sum_i L_{cls}(p_i, p_i^*) + \lambda \frac{1}{N_{reg}} \sum_i p_i^* L_{reg}(t_i, t_i^*) \qquad (1)$$

In Eq. (1), L_{cls} employs cross-entropy loss and L_{reg} is defined as $Smooth_{L1}$ loss. The weight λ is 1, the subscript i is the index of anchor in a mini-batch, if the anchor is positive, p_i^* is 1 otherwise it is 0. p_i indicates the probability that anchor i is positive. t_i and t_i^* are 5-dimensional parameterized coordinates defined as:

$$t_x = (x - x_a)/w_a, \; t_y = (y - y_a)/h_a$$
$$t_w = \log(w/w_a), \; t_h = \log(h/h_a) \tag{2}$$
$$t_\theta = \theta - \theta_a + k\pi$$

$$t_x^* = (x^* - x_a)/w_a, \; t_y^* = (y^* - y_a)/h_a$$
$$t_w^* = \log(w^*/w_a), \quad t_h = \log(h^*/h_a) \tag{3}$$
$$t_\theta^* = \theta^* - \theta_a + k\pi$$

where variables x, x^* and x_a are for the predicted, ground-truth and anchor boxes, likewise y, w, h, θ. The integer $k, k \in \mathbb{Z}$ is used to ensure θ within a predefined range of license plate orientations in Eqs. (2) and (3).

4 Experiments

In this section, we first report the experimental datasets and implementation details of the proposed framework. Then a series of experiments are set up to confirm the effectiveness of proposed method. All experiments are implemented on Tesla K40C GPU with 12G memory.

4.1 License Plate Datasets

The Application-Oriented License Plate (AOLP) and SSIG datasets are used in the experiment. The AOLP dataset contains 2049 images of Taiwanese license plates, including three subsets with different difficulties: access control (AC), traffic enforcement (LE) and road patrol (RP). The SSIG dataset is collected on the road, including 6675 images with the size of 1920 × 1080, which contains mutative shooting distance and actual interference. It should be noted that the two datasets are annotated with horizontal boxes, we add angle information through (x, y, w, h, θ) to cover the ground truth. A total of 8000 images are obtained for each dataset through data augmentation, we randomly assigned to 70% for training and the other 30% for testing in the experiment.

4.2 Implementation Details

In the training stage, we adopt the end-to-end strategy to train the proposed framework until it reaches the best performance. The pre-trained resnet-50 is employed as the backbone for feature extraction. The weight decay is set to 10^{-4}. The Adam optimizer [25] with a decreasing learning rate is adopted for total 10^5 iterations. The learning rate maintains 10^{-3} for first 30k iterations and 10^{-4} for another 30k, it remains 10^{-5} to last iteration. In the RPN stage, the proportion of positive and negative anchors is set to 1:1. The basic anchor scales are set in range $\{16, 32, 64, 128, 256\}$, the aspect ratios in $\{2, 3, 4\}$, and the angles in $\{-20°, -10°, 0°, 10°, 20°\}$. For each location on the integrated feature map, a total of $5 \times 3 \times 5$ anchors are generated. The other hyper parameters follow the common settings in original Faster R-CNN.

4.3 Experimental Results

In this subsection, we report comparisons of the performance of our proposed method with other detection methods on SSIG and AOLP datasets. The Precision(P), Recall(R) and F-measure(F) are employed for quantitative assessment. Firstly, we analyze the effectiveness of the proposed method through comparing different models on SSIG dataset, the results are shown in Table 1.

Table 1. Comparison with other detection methods on the SSIG dataset

Model	Feature integration	Rotated anchors	Context fusion	P(%)	R(%)	F(%)
Faster R-CNN [8]				94.10	92.96	93.53
Ma et al. [21]		√		94.74	93.22	93.97
Open ALPR [26]				93.24	91.78	92.50
Part-1	√	√		94.95	94.24	94.59
Proposed	√	√	√	**96.58**	**95.91**	**96.24**

The comparative results in Table 1 show that the proposed method exhibits superior performance to other methods. Compared to RRPN [21] and Open ALPR [26], the auxiliary and contextual information in the license plate detection network facilitate further improvements. To further evaluate the proposed method, we set up another detailed experiment compared with Faster R-CNN [8] and YOLO [9]. As shown in Fig. 6, the proposed model achieves better performance under different environments and IoU thresholds.

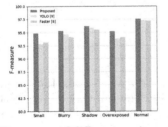

(a) F-measure of different environments   (b) F-measure of different IoU thresholds

Fig. 6. Evaluation of the baselines and proposed method.

In order to prove the effectiveness of the proposed method, we carried out a comparison with other license plate detection methods on the AOLP dataset, as shown in Table 2. It should be noted that the detection results of the second row in Table 2 are quoted from [18]. The multi-directional text detection method [21] are verified on the license plate detection, as shown in the third row. Open ALPR [26] in the fifth row is an open source system. The proposed method has achieved the highest precision and recall on the three subsets.

Table 2. Comparison with other detection methods on the AOLP dataset

Approach	AC			LE			RP		
	P(%)	R(%)	F(%)	P(%)	R(%)	F(%)	P(%)	R(%)	F(%)
Faster R-CNN [8]	98.96	98.89	98.92	96.91	96.66	96.78	95.93	95.14	95.53
Polishetty et al. [18]	98.93	98.87	98.90	98.34	96.81	97.57	96.28	97.43	96.85
Li et al. [20]	98.53	98.38	98.45	97.75	97.62	97.20	95.28	95.58	95.42
Ma et al. [21]	96.81	96.62	96.72	95.70	95.51	95.60	97.32	97.19	97.25
Open ALPR [26]	97.83	98.15	97.99	96.90	97.25	97.07	97.34	97.62	97.48
Proposed	**99.12**	**99.06**	**99.09**	**98.62**	**98.77**	**98.69**	**98.19**	**98.24**	**98.22**

The experiment results on the AOLP dataset demonstrate that the proposed method has competitive results with other methods in the literature. Since the RP subset contains many multi-directional license plates that the proposed method shows a marked improvement over other approaches. Although artificially introducing the auxiliary and contextual information in the network increase additional computation, the time request for testing is averagely 0.76 s per image, which is still at a relatively fast level. The detection examples in Fig. 7 show the superiority of our framework. The example images are partially cropped in the third row.

5   Conclusion

In this paper, we propose an accurate license plate detection framework to solve problems of various scales and observation angles. First, we embed characteristics of license plate in Faster R-CNN to improve the performance. The multi-resolution information is collected through reusing multi-level features. The rotational anchors and branch structure generate suitable proposals for license plate. Moreover, the detection performance is further augmented by utilizing contextual information. Additionally, our framework can also be applied to other region proposal-based methods. Experimental results show that the proposed framework has superior performance in different environments.

Fig. 7. Examples of the detection results.

References

1. Du, S., Ibrahim, M., Shehata, M., Badawy, W.: Automatic license plate recognition (ALPR): a state-of-the-art review. IEEE Trans. Circuits Syst. Video Technol. **23**(2), 311–325 (2013)
2. Zhou, W., Li, H., Lu, Y., Tian, Q.: Principal visual word discovery for automatic license plate detection. IEEE Trans. Image Process. **21**(9), 4269–4279 (2012)
3. He, K., Zhang, X., Ren, S., Sun, J.: Deep residual learning for image recognition. In: IEEE Conference on Computer Vision and Pattern Recognition, pp. 770–778 (2016)
4. Yu, S., Li, B., Zhang, Q., Liu, C., Meng, M.Q.H.: A novel license plate location method based on wavelet transform and EMD analysis. Pattern Recogn. **48**(1), 114–125 (2015)
5. Samra, G.A., Khalefah, F.: Localization of license plate number using dynamic image processing techniques and genetic algorithms. IEEE Trans. Evol. Comput. **18**(2), 244–257 (2014)
6. Panahi, R., Gholampour, I.: Accurate detection and recognition of dirty vehicle plate numbers for high-speed applications. IEEE Trans. Intell. Transp. Syst. **18**(4), 767–779 (2017)
7. Yuan, Y., Zou, W., Zhao, Y., Wang, X., Hu, X., Komodakis, N.: A robust and efficient approach to license plate detection. IEEE Trans. Image Process. **26**(3), 1102–1114 (2017)
8. Ren, S., He, K., Girshick, R., Sun, J.: Faster R-CNN: towards real-time object detection with region proposal networks. In: Advances in Neural Information Processing Systems, pp. 91–99 (2015)

9. Redmon, J., Divvala, S., Girshick, R., Farhadi, A.: You only look once: unified, real-time object detection. In: IEEE Conference on Computer Vision and Pattern Recognition, pp. 779–788 (2016)

10. Liu, W., et al.: SSD: single shot multibox detector. In: Leibe, B., Matas, J., Sebe, N., Welling, M. (eds.) ECCV 2016. LNCS, vol. 9905, pp. 21–37. Springer, Cham (2016). https://doi.org/10.1007/978-3-319-46448-0_2

11. Girshick, R., Donahue, J., Darrell, T., Malik, J.: Rich feature hierarchies for accurate object detection and semantic segmentation. In: IEEE Conference on Computer Vision and Pattern Recognition, pp. 580–587 (2014)

12. Gonçalves, G.R., Silva, S.P.G., Menotti, D., Schwartz, W.R.: Benchmark for license plate character segmentation. J. Electron. Imaging **25**(5), 1–5 (2016)

13. Kurpiel, F.D., Minetto, R., Nassu, B.T.: Convolutional neural networks for license plate detection in images. In: IEEE International Conference on Image Processing (ICIP), pp. 3395–3399 (2017)

14. Selmi, Z., Halima, M.B., Alimi, A.M.: Deep learning system for automatic license plate detection and recognition. In: IEEE International Conference on Document Analysis and Recognition (ICDAR), pp. 1132–1138 (2017)

15. Laroca, R., Severo, E., Zanlorensi, L.A., Oliveira, L.S.: A robust real-time automatic license plate recognition based on the YOLO detector. In: International Joint Conference on Neural Networks (IJCNN), pp. 1–10 (2018)

16. Hsu, G., Chen, J., Chung, Y.: Application-oriented license plate recognition. IEEE Trans. Veh. Technol. **62**(2), 552–561 (2013)

17. Xie, L., Ahmad, T., Jin, L., Liu, Y., Zhang, S.: A new CNN-based method for multidirectional car license plate detection. IEEE Trans. Intell. Transp. Syst. **19**(2), 507–517 (2018)

18. Polishetty, R., Roopaei, M., Rad, P.: A next-generation secure cloud-based deep learning license plate recognition for smart cities. In: IEEE International Conference on Machine Learning and Applications (ICMLA), pp. 286–293 (2016)

19. Rafique, M.A., Pedrycz, W., Jeon, M.: Vehicle license plate detection using region-based convolutional neural networks. Soft Comput. **22**(19), 6429–6440 (2018)

20. Li, H., Wang, P., You, M., Shen, C.: Reading car license plates using deep neural networks. Image Vis. Comput. **72**, 14–23 (2018)

21. Ma, J., Shao, W., Ye, H., Wang, L., Wang, H.: Arbitrary-oriented scene text detection via rotation proposals. IEEE Trans. Multimed. **20**(11), 3111–3122 (2018)

22. He, W., Zhang, X., Yin, F., Liu, C.: Deep direct regression for multi-oriented scene text detection. In: IEEE International Conference on Computer Vision, pp. 745–753 (2017)

23. Lin, T., Dollár, P., Girshick, R., He, K., Hariharan, B., Belongie, S.: Feature pyramid networks for object detection. In: IEEE Conference on Computer Vision and Pattern Recognition, pp. 936–944 (2017)

24. Chen, C., Liu, M.-Y., Tuzel, O., Xiao, J.: R-CNN for small object detection. In: Lai, S.-H., Lepetit, V., Nishino, K., Sato, Y. (eds.) ACCV 2016. LNCS, vol. 10115, pp. 214–230. Springer, Cham (2017). https://doi.org/10.1007/978-3-319-54193-8_14

25. Kingma, D.P., Ba, J.: Adam: a method for stochastic optimization. arXiv preprint arXiv:1412.6980 (2014)

26. OpenALPR: An Open Source Automatic License Plate Recognition Library. https://github.com/openalpr/openalpr

27. He, K., Gkioxari, G., Dollár, P., Girshick, R.: Mask R-CNN. In: IEEE International Conference on Computer Vision (ICCV), pp. 2980–2988 (2017)

PointNet-Based Channel Attention VLAD Network

Rongrong Fan, Hui Shuai[✉], and Qingshan Liu

Jiangsu Key Laboratory of Big Data Analysis Technology,
Nanjing University of Information Science and Technology, Nanjing 211800, China
{frr007,qsliu}@nuist.edu.cn, huishuai13@163.com

Abstract. With the upgrading of application scenarios, computer vision is progressively expanded to 3D. Many methods that process point cloud directly provide a new paradigm for 3D understanding. Most of these methods employ maxpooling to handle the sparsity and disorder of point cloud. However, maxpooling layer extracts the global feature of the entire point cloud without learnable parameters, which is heuristics and insufficient. In this paper, we propose a VLAD enhanced Feature Aggregate Module to aggregate local features adaptively. In addition, a Channel Attention Module is applied to the features to reassemble the elements in high-dimension feature space. The experiments in both classification and segmentation demonstrate that the proposed method can improve the capacity of the baseline to extract more informative features. Specifically, we improve the accuracy from 88.5% to 89.8% for classification in ModelNet40 and improve the accuracy from 78.94% to 82.07% for semantic segmentation in S3DIS.

Keywords: Point cloud · Feature Aggregate Module · Channel Attention Module

1 Introduction

With the upgrading of application scenarios, 3D understanding has received a significant amount of attention in computer vision, especially for automatic driving and drone. Meanwhile, motivated by huge application demand, significant progress has been made in sensor technology and innumerous 3D data is generated by a depth camera, radar, and lidar. Consequently, 3D data has many formats such as voxels, meshes and point cloud owing to the diversity of sensor. Among these different 3D data, the point cloud is characterized by high accurate and easy acquisition. The point cloud is a set of points with sparsity and disorder in 3D Euclidean space and the inherent irregular makes point cloud very different from 2D data. To enable UAVs [1] and unmanned driving [2] to perceive a 3D scene, high-level semantic understanding of 3D data is required. In common with 2D computer vision, the primary tasks for 3D understanding

---

This is a student paper.

© Springer Nature Switzerland AG 2019
Z. Lin et al. (Eds.): PRCV 2019, LNCS 11859, pp. 320–331, 2019.
https://doi.org/10.1007/978-3-030-31726-3_27

are classification and segmentation. However, the input in 2D computer vision is usually images and videos, which are organized in a regular format. Although deep learning [3] has revolutionized many research fields in computer vision, conventional convolutional neural networks are not suitable for the point cloud. Therefore, many methods have been proposed to process point cloud and this paper will focus on the identification of point clouds based on convolutional neural networks. Recently, popular neural networks based methods for point cloud processing can be divided into four categories:

1. Voxel-based convolutional neural networks: These methods transform the point cloud into voxels and then employ 3D convolution neural networks on voxels, such as VoxNet [4] proposed by Maturaba and Scherer. However, the sparsity of the data causes a loss of details. FPNN [5] and Voted3D [6] proposed a special method to deal with the sparsity problem, but convolution is still limited to the sparse voxel. Besides, there are still huge challenges in dealing with large scenes. Some researchers have optimized the network in the data structure. For example, Klokov et al. proposed Kd-Net [7], Wang et al. [8] proposed O-CNN, and Riegler et al. [9] proposed Oct-Net. But sparse 3D data with 3D convolution kernels suffer from computation and memory cost.

2. Multi-view based Convolutional neural networks: Researchers try to process 3D data by referring to 2D data processing methods. For example, rendering 3D data into 2D images from different perspectives [10–12], and then using traditional 2D convolutional neural networks. This paradigm has achieved good results in classification and retrieval thanks to the abstract ability of deep learning. Among them, Su et al. [11] gather the information from multiple views of the 3D object together and turn them into a single compact shape descriptor, which is known as MVCNN. However, multi-view convolutional neural networks are difficult to extend to the segmentation in 3D data. When rendering 3D data, the choice of angle affects the final experimental results. In fact, how to select the angle in this method is also difficult. In addition, rendering the 3D data into 2D data may lose part of the 3D spatial position information, and the data processing process is relatively complicated.

3. Feature-based deep learning network: Fang et al. [13] and Guo et al. [14] convert traditional 3D data into corresponding feature description vectors and then use the fully connected network to obtain the result of classification. Because the features are manually designed, the quality of the features selected directly affects the performance of the network significantly, the process of selecting the original data features will be more complicated.

4. Point cloud based deep learning network: Qi et al. proposed PointNet [15] and PointNet++ [16] to directly deal with the unordered point cloud. These methods are not only convenient but also can preserve the integrity of the point cloud. All points are independently handled to extract local features, sharing multiple multi-layer perceptrons. Maxpooling layer is used to aggregate the global feature from local features because of its permutation invari-

ance. But maxpooling layer has no learnable parameters, which makes this process heuristics and insufficient.

In order to alleviate the weakness caused by the insufficiency of maxpooling layer, we propose the VLAD enhanced Feature Aggregate Module to extract more sufficient global feature and Channel Attention Module to reassemble the elements in high-dimension feature space. The VLAD enhanced Feature Aggregate Module is robust to the order of input points and stores the residuals for each point to the centers in a trainable manner. The Channel Attention Module strengthens the representational power of convolutional layers by enhancing the spatial encoding throughout its feature hierarchy. The architecture of our network is illustrated in Fig. 1 and our contributions are as follows:

1. We develop a convolutional neural network with VLAD enhanced Feature Aggregate Module and Channel Attention modules to extract more informative global feature for 3D point cloud processing in an end-to-end manner.
2. We demonstrate that the limitations of maxpooling layer can be alleviated with some learnable feature aggregate modules robust to the order of points, while the theoretical analysis about the VLAD is provided.
3. We improve the accuracy from 88.5% to 89.8% for classification in Model-Net40 and improve the accuracy from 78.94% to 82.07% for semantic segmentation in S3DIS, which verifies the effectiveness of the proposed method.

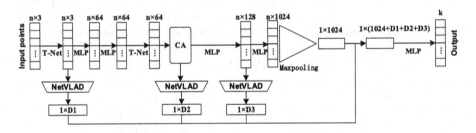

Fig. 1. The architecture of proposed method

2   Related Work

The structure of PointNet is shown in Fig. 2, which can serve as the classification network and segmentation network. In the pointnet framework, multi-layer perceptron (MLP) transforms the 3D coordinate into high-dimensional feature space. Due to the independence of point-wise transform, the point cloud is easy to apply the rigid or affine transformation. Therefore, the T-Net [17] is used for transforming the points adaptively.

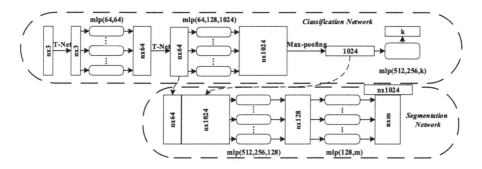

Fig. 2. Structure of PointNet

Formally, given an unordered point set, where an aggregate function can be defined as follows:

$$f(x_1, x_2, ..., x_n) = \gamma(\max_{i=1,...,n} h(x_i)) \tag{1}$$

Where γ and h usually refer to MLPs to transform the features. It can be proved that any continuous aggregate function can be arbitrarily approximated. In this way, points in 3D are transformed into more informative high-dimensional features and the aggregated global feature is robust to the disorder of point cloud. However, there are two problems in the PointNet. (1) When projecting the low dimensional features to high-dimensional features, the surrounding context of the point is not used. Due to this, the network can't capture the contextual features. (2) When using the maxpooling operation, the feature components of different points are used directly to replace the features of the entire input point cloud, resulting in the loss of surface information.

3 Method

3.1 Channel Attention Module

Generally, the importance of different feature components varies a great deal for the final decision. Taking images understanding as an example, an important feature is usually a region where are corners, edges. In PointNet, features are transformed into high-dimension space via MLP while MLP is usually implemented with 1×1 convolution operation. The amount of convolution kernels determines the dimension of the target feature and the components of this feature are supposed to be reassembled for better expression capacity. Inspired by this, we designed a channel-based attention mechanism, called Channel Attention module, referred to as CA. CA module is data-driven processing that enhances representative features and suppresses weaker features. Given a corresponding input, the CA module can be formulated as:

$$X \xrightarrow{CA} Y, X \in R^{N \times D \times C}, Y \in R^{N \times D \times C} \tag{2}$$

Where X is the input, Y is the output, N is the size of the point cloud, D is 1. C is the number of channels. The size of input and output is identical, so the CA module can be embedded into any network easily. The specific operation is shown in Fig. 3. Referring to the idea of Qi et al., in the CA module, we employ the maxpooling operation to retain the most effective features. To obtain the most important channel information, we use a fully connected network for further dimension reducing. The feature information is compressed so that the reserved channel features are more significant. After that, the nonlinearity of the network is increased by the ReLU. Then we use another fully connected network to recover the dimension of the channel with Sigmoid as the activate function. So the number of the channel is the same as the input. Finally, we do the channel weighting and fuse the weighted channel feature with the original features.

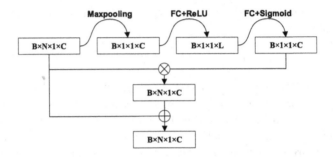

Fig. 3. Channel Attention module

The CA module can rank the importance of the components in the feature and reassemble them, which is an implementation of feature selection in deep learning. In addition, due to the presence of maxpooling in CA module, the global information is fused with local features in an early stage. It ultimately enhances the capability of the network to extract more informative global features.

3.2 NetVLAD Module

Jegou et al. [18] first proposed a local aggregation descriptor vector (VLAD), which is regarded as a simplification of the Fisher kernel. Fisher kernel captures statistical information about the local descriptors aggregated on the image, while VLAD stores the sum of the residuals of each descriptor. Formally, N local image descriptors of $\{x_i\}$ with D given dimension is taken as input, and there are K cluster centers. $\{c_k\}$ are the parameters of VLAD. The description vector V of the output VLAD for the entire image is $D \times K$. For convenience, the vector is written as a $D \times K$ matrix. When used as an image representation, the matrix needs to be converted to a vector and normalized. The (j, k) element of V can be expressed as:

$$V(j, k) = \sum_{i=1}^{N} \alpha_k(x_i)(x_i(j) - c_k(j)) \tag{3}$$

Where, $x_i(j)$ represents the j-th dimension of the i-th descriptor, $c_k(j)$ represents the j-th dimension of the k-th cluster center. $\alpha_k(x_i)$ represents the relationship between x_i and k. Specifically, $\alpha_k(x_i) = 1$ if the cluster is closest to the descriptor; otherwise, $\alpha_k(x_i) = 0$. Intuitively, the D dimension in column k of the vector represents the sum of the descriptor residuals $(x_i - c_k)$ assigned to the cluster c_k. Then, the matrix V is regularized according to the column, converted to a vector, and then regularized.

Inspired by the local aggregate descriptor vector (VLAD) representation, Arandjelovic et al. [19] proposed a new end-to-end convolutional neural network structure that can be used for scene recognition. The main components of this neural network is NetVLAD. NetVLAD is a new universal VLAD layer that excels in image retrieval and location recognition. This network structure can be easily embedded in any CNN framework and can be trained through backpropagation.

The VLAD is discontinuous because of the hard assignment of the descriptors while training through back-propagation requires the module to be differentiable. The problem lies in making VLAD differentiable and Arandjelovic et al. handled this by replacing the hard assignment of descriptors with the soft assignment of descriptors:

$$\overline{\alpha}_k(x_i) = \frac{e^{-\alpha\|x_i - c_k\|^2}}{\sum_{k'} e^{-\alpha\|x_i - c_{k'}\|^2}} \tag{4}$$

The former equation is equivalent to the proximity of other cluster centers, and the weight of the descriptor is assigned to the cluster whose proximity is proportional. The range of $\overline{\alpha}_k(x_i)$ is between 0 and 1, with the highest weight assigned to the nearest cluster center. α is a positive constant that controls the magnitude of the attenuation of the response. It can be noted that this setting is the same as the original VLAD.

By extending the square of equation, the $e^{-\alpha\|x_i\|^2}$ in denominator and the intermolecular can be eliminated:

$$\overline{\alpha}_k(x_i) = \frac{e^{w_k^T x_i + b_k}}{\sum_{k'} e^{w_{k'}^T x_i + b_{k'}}} \tag{5}$$

Among them, vector $w_k = 2\alpha c_k$, scalar $b_k = -\alpha\|c_k\|^2$. Substituting Eq. (5) into Eq. (3), the final form of NetVLAD can be obtained:

$$V(j, k) = \sum_{i=1}^{N} \frac{e^{w_k^T x_i + b_k}}{\sum_{k'} e^{w_{k'}^T x_i + b_{k'}}} (x_i(j) - c_k(j)) \tag{6}$$

Where $\{w_k\}$, $\{b_k\}$ and $\{c_k\}$ are the set of parameters that can be trained in each cluster. Similar to the original VLAD descriptor, the NetVLAD layer aggregates the first-order statistic of the residuals in different parts of the descriptor space, which is weighted by the soft assignment of the descriptors to the corresponding cluster. It is worth noting that the NetVLAD layer has three sets of independent parameters $\{w_k\}$, $\{b_k\}$ and $\{c_k\}$ compared to $\{c_k\}$ of the original VLAD, which is more flexible than the original VLAD. And all parameters of NetVLAD can be obtained automatically. The NetVLAD layer was originally designed to aggregate the local image features known by VGG and AlexNet into the VLAD global descriptor. By sending the local feature descriptor of the point cloud into the neural network, the global representation can also be generated. Descriptor vector can be viewed as a supplement to the max-pooling operation. Besides, it allows end-to-end training and reasoning and can extract global descriptors from a given 3D point cloud. Because of the disorder of the point cloud, the NetVLAD layer needs to be insensitive to the order of the point cloud. In the following proof, it can be concluded that NetVLAD is a symmetric function, that is, it can be applied in the local features to generate global features with permutation invariance.

As shown in Fig. 4, the input of the NetVLAD layer is a high-dimensional feature of the point cloud. It can be obtained by projecting the features with the MLPs. The output is the VLAD descriptor of the input feature. However, the VLAD descriptor is a high-dimensional vector, i.e., a $(D \times K)$ dimensional vector. To alleviate resource conservation, a fully connected layer can be used to compress the $(D \times K)$ vector into a more compact output feature vector, which is then quadraticized to generate the final global descriptor vector.

Fig. 4. NetVLAD layer structure

3.3   Proof of Symmetry of NetVLAD

Pixels of an image have a fixed spatial position, so there is no need to consider the order of input pixels when using filters. However, when it comes to point clouds, the order of points matters. The output of traditional convolutional neural network varies when the order of point cloud changed. Therefore, methods processing points directly must characteristic with permutation invariance. In other words, the points in different orders should produce the same output. In this paper, we use the NetVLAD architecture to get the features of the point cloud because it's symmetrical. The invariance of the NetVLAD layer for the point cloud order is demonstrated below. Given the input point cloud, the MLP independently transforms the input features to another feature space. To prove that NetVLAD is symmetrical, it means the output of the result is irrelevant with the order of the input point cloud.

Proof. Assuming that the characteristics of the input point cloud P are expressed as $\{p'_1, p'_2, \cdots, p'_N\}$, the output of the NetVLAD is $V = [V_1, V_2, \cdots, V_k]$, for $\forall k$, we have

$$V_k = h_k(p'_1) + h_k(p'_2) + \cdots + h_k(p'_N) = \sum_{t=1}^{n} h_k(p'_t) \tag{7}$$

where $V_k(p')$ satisfying

$$V_k(p') = \frac{e^{w_k^T p' + b_k}}{\sum_{k'} e^{w_{k'}^T p' + b_{k'}}}(p' - c_k)$$

Suppose there is another point cloud $\tilde{P} = \{p_1, \cdots, p_{i-1}, p_j, p_{i+1}, \cdots, p_{j-1}, p_i, p_{j+1}, \cdots, p_N\}$, when $\tilde{P}$ are the same as P except for the order of p_i and p_j. So for $\forall k$, we have

$$\tilde{V}_k = h_k(p'_1) + \cdots + h_k(p'_{i-1}) + h_k(p'_j) + h_k(p'_{i+1}) + \cdots$$
$$+ h_k(p'_{j-1}) + h_k(p'_i) + h_k(p_{j+1}) = \sum_{t=1}^{n} h_k(p'_t) = V_k \tag{8}$$

From the former equation, we can draw the conclusion that NetVLAD is symmetrical. Therefore we can use the NetVLAD module to enhance the global feature of the point cloud.

4 Experiments

In this paper, we incorporate the CA module and NetVLAD module into the original PointNet network. The corresponding classification network and segmentation network are designed respectively. The data set of the classification experiment is ModelNet40 [20], and the data set used in the segmentation experiment is S3DIS [21]. The proposed framework is effective both in classification and in segmentation.

4.1 3D Object Classification

The dataset for classification is ModelNet40. It includes 12,311 CAD models, of which 9843 are for training and 2,468 are for testing. The same data used for the PointNet 3D target classification is to evenly sample 2048 points on the mesh surface and normalize them to a unit sphere. During training, training data is augmented by rotating the upper axis and dithering the points by Gaussian noise with zero mean and 0.02 standard deviation. The experimental is conducted on Ubuntu 14.04, and the framework is Tensorflow. Same as PointNet, each experiment has a batch size of 32, the number of input points is 1024, the initial learning rate is 0.001, the learning rate attenuation parameter is 0.7, the step size is 20000 and the optimizer is Adam. PointNet consists of five convolution layers and one maximum pooling layer. In order to verify the validity of the CA module proposed, we embed CA modules in different locations. The results are shown in Table 1:

Table 1. Classification results for different CA module locations

Location	Accuracy avg. class	Accuracy overall
PointNet	85.5	88.5
CONV_1	**86.4**	89.3
CONV_2	85.3	88.4
CONV_3	**86.4**	89.0
CONV_4	85.9	88.9
CONV_5	85.9	88.5
MAX_POOLING	86.2	88.6

When testing the CA module, the data set used is ModelNet40, the setting is consistent with PointNet, the number of input points is 1024, and the dimension reduction factor of the CA channel is 4. It shows that the CA module improves the performance when embedded into most convolutional layers especially the first and third convolutional layer. It can be concluded that the CA module is effective, but the embedding location is sensitive.

Table 2. Classification results for ModelNet40

Methods	Input	# views	Accuracy avg. class	Accuracy overall
SPH	mesh	–	68.2	–
VoxNet	voxel	12	83.0	85.9
Subvolume	voxel	20	86.0	89.2
LFD	image	10	75.5	–
MVCNN	image	80	90.1	–
PointNet (vanilla)	point	–	83.6	87.4
PointNet (baseline)	point	–	85.5	88.5
CA-VLADNet	point	–	86.5	89.8

As we can see in Table 2, compared with previous works, the proposed method achieves better performance. However, there is still a certain gap between the proposed method and the multi-view based method (MVCNN) owing to the information loss in the sampling process. In preprocessing, only 1024 points are sampled from point cloud as the input in the proposed method while a large number of images can be obtained by rendering in MVCNN. It is the lack of geometric details that results in this gab.

4.2   3D Semantic Segmentation

The dataset for semantic segmentation is S3DIS data set. It is a large-scale semantic 3D dataset constructed by Armeni et al. of Stanford University. The data set detected 13 semantic elements, including structural elements (ceiling, floor, wall, beam, pillar, window, and door), common items and furniture (tables, chairs, sofas, bookcases, and planks), and finally type of clutter, each point in the scan is labeled with one of them. The dataset is divided into rooms, and the room is divided into areas of 1 m by 1 m. Each of these points is represented by a 9-dimensional vector from the three-dimensional coordinates XYZ, the color information RGB, and the normalized position of the opposing room (from 0 to 1). During training, 4096 points are randomly extracted from each block randomly, in testing, all points are tested. As mentioned in Armeni et al. [21], training and testing were performed in the k-fold strategy. The batch size is 24, the learning rate is set to 0.001, the learning rate attenuation parameter is 0.5, and the optimizer is Adam. According to Qi et al. [15], the S3DIS data set is divided into 6 regions, and the method of six-fold cross-validation is used. Table 3 shows the six-fold cross-validation results on the S3DIS.

Table 3. Semantic segmentation results for S3DIS

Region	Evaluation	PointNet (baseline)	AC-VLADNet
Region one	IOU	52.86	57.06
	Accuracy	80.82	83.57
Region two	IOU	28.92	34.51
	Accuracy	64.23	73.70
Region three	IOU	54.76	59.20
	Accuracy	83.59	85.99
Region four	IOU	40.06	42.90
	Accuracy	78.55	80.48
Region five	IOU	41.98	43.74
	Accuracy	80.03	80.76
Region six	IOU	47.23	50.99
	Accuracy	78.94	82.07
Average	IOU	47.23	50.99
	Accuracy	78.94	82.07

It can be seen that the IOU and accuracy of each region in this model are higher than that of PointNet. The average IOU of the six regions is about 3.76% higher than the baseline, and the accuracy rate is increased by 3.13%. The result demonstrates that the proposed method is feasible to extract more informative features for semantic segmentation while semantic segmentation rely more on the detail context of the point cloud.

5 Conclusion

We presented a VLAD enhanced PointNet equipped with Channel Attention module for 3D point cloud processing. Both VLAD enhanced Feature Aggregate Module and Channel Attention Module are readily pluggable into any convolutional neural network and trained in an end-to-end manner. Most remarkable of all is that the proposed method aggregate global features with learnable parameters while keeping the robustness to the order of points. The experiments in classification and segmentation verify the effectiveness of the proposed method and the necessity of improving maxpooling to aggregate more informative global features.

References

1. Mozaffari, M., Saad, W., Bennis, M., et al.: A tutorial on UAVs for wireless networks: applications, challenges, and open problems. IEEE Commun. Surv. Tutor. **21**, 2334–2360 (2019)
2. Zhang, X., Gao, H., Guo, M., et al.: A study on key technologies of unmanned driving. CAAI Trans. Intell. Technol. **1**(1), 4–13 (2016)
3. LeCun, Y., Bengio, Y., Hinton, G.: Deep learning. Nature **521**(7553), 436 (2015)
4. Maturana, D., Scherer, S.: VoxNet: a 3D convolutional neural network for real-time object recognition. In: 2015 IEEE/RSJ International Conference on Intelligent Robots and Systems (IROS), pp. 922–928. IEEE (2015)
5. Li, Y., Pirk, S., Su, H., et al.: FPNN: field probing neural networks for 3D data. In: Advances in Neural Information Processing Systems, pp. 307–315 (2016)
6. Wang, D.Z., Posner, I.: Voting for voting in online point cloud object detection. In: Robotics: Science and Systems, vol. 1, no. 3, p. 10.15607 (2015)
7. Klokov, R., Lempitsky, V.: Escape from cells: deep Kd-networks for the recognition of 3D point cloud models. In: Proceedings of the IEEE International Conference on Computer Vision, pp. 863–872 (2017)
8. Wang, P.S., Liu, Y., Guo, Y.X., et al.: O-CNN: octree-based convolutional neural networks for 3D shape analysis. ACM Trans. Graph. (TOG) **36**(4), 72 (2017)
9. Perdomo, O., Otálora, S., González, F.A., et al.: OCT-NET: a convolutional network for automatic classification of normal and diabetic macular edema using SD-OCT volumes. In: 2018 IEEE 15th International Symposium on Biomedical Imaging (ISBI 2018), pp. 1423–1426. IEEE (2018)
10. Qi, C.R., Su, H., Nießner, M., et al.: Volumetric and multi-view CNNs for object classification on 3D data. In: Proceedings of the IEEE Conference on Computer Vision and Pattern Recognition, pp. 5648–5656 (2016)
11. Su, H., Maji, S., Kalogerakis, E., et al.: Multi-view convolutional neural networks for 3D shape recognition. In: Proceedings of the IEEE International Conference on Computer Vision, pp. 945–953 (2015)
12. Su, H., Wang, F., Yi, E., et al.: 3D-assisted feature synthesis for novel views of an object. In: Proceedings of the IEEE International Conference on Computer Vision, pp. 2677–2685 (2015)
13. Fang, Y., Xie, J., Dai, G., et al.: 3D deep shape descriptor. In: Proceedings of the IEEE Conference on Computer Vision and Pattern Recognition, pp. 2319–2328 (2015)

14. Guo, K., Zou, D., Chen, X.: 3D mesh labeling via deep convolutional neural networks. ACM Trans. Graph. (TOG) **35**(1), 3 (2015)
15. Qi, C.R., Su, H., Mo, K., et al.: PointNet: deep learning on point sets for 3D classification and segmentation. In: Proceedings of the IEEE Conference on Computer Vision and Pattern Recognition, pp. 652–660 (2017)
16. Qi, C.R., Yi, L., Su, H., et al.: PointNet++: deep hierarchical feature learning on point sets in a metric space. In: Advances in Neural Information Processing Systems, pp. 5099–5108 (2017)
17. Jaderberg, M., Simonyan, K., Zisserman, A.: Spatial transformer networks. In: Advances in Neural Information Processing Systems, pp. 2017–2025 (2015)
18. Jegou, H., Perronnin, F., Douze, M., et al.: Aggregating local image descriptors into compact codes. IEEE Trans. Pattern Anal. Mach. Intell. **34**(9), 1704–1716 (2012)
19. Arandjelovic, R., Gronat, P., Torii, A., et al.: NetVLAD: CNN architecture for weakly supervised place recognition. In: Proceedings of the IEEE Conference on Computer Vision and Pattern Recognition, pp. 5297–5307 (2016)
20. Wu, Z., Song, S., Khosla, A., et al.: 3D ShapeNets: a deep representation for volumetric shapes. In: Proceedings of the IEEE Conference on Computer Vision and Pattern Recognition, pp. 1912–1920 (2015)
21. Armeni, I., Sener, O., Zamir, A.R., et al.: 3D semantic parsing of large-scale indoor spaces. In: Proceedings of the IEEE Conference on Computer Vision and Pattern Recognition, pp. 1534–1543 (2016)

Multi-scale Deep Residual Network for Satellite Image Super-Resolution Reconstruction

Wen Xu, Chuang Zhang$^{(\boxtimes)}$, and Ming Wu

Beijing University of Posts and Telecommunications, Beijing 100876, China
{xuwen3111,zhangchuang,wuming}@bupt.edu.cn

Abstract. Satellite images are used in all aspects of human life, and the demand for high-resolution satellite images is increasing dramatically as human technology advances. The most straightforward way to improve imaging resolution is to improve hardware design or reduce satellite flight altitude, but at a higher cost and with unbreakable physical limits. Super-resolution reconstruction is a way to improve image resolution. Satellite imagery has a wide imaging range. The scale of the ground target varies greatly and the texture information is diversified, which brings new challenges to the existing image super-resolution technology. A multi-scale residual deep neural network is proposed for the multi-scale characteristics of satellite imagery in this paper. In the middle of the residual body, the series-parallel combined dilated convolution is used to obtain different sizes of receptive fields which can achieve different scale information, and finally generate high-resolution satellite images after pixel shuffle. The experimental results on the Airbus satellite ship image dataset prove the superiority of the proposed algorithm.

Keywords: Super resolution · Satellite images · Multi-scale

1 Introduction

Satellite images are applied in all aspects of human life, and the demand for high-resolution satellite images is increasing rapidly as human technology levels increase. The most straightforward way to improve imaging resolution is to improve satellite-equipped cameras, or to reduce satellite altitude. However, these methods are costly and have unbreakable physical limits, which makes these methods only limited to improve the resolution of satellite imaging systems.

Super-resolution (SR) reconstruction is exactly a way to improve image resolution. SR refers to the recovery of high-resolution (HR) image from its low-resolution (LR) image. SR reconstruction technology is a way to improve image resolution by computer vision method with limited resolution and no change of original hardware. It has the advantages of higher flexibility, short development cycle, low cost and high feasibility comparing to hardware. The obtained HR images have good visual effects, and have important application value in the fields of monitoring equipment, remote sensing images and medical images [1, 2], and have broad commercial, military and

© Springer Nature Switzerland AG 2019
Z. Lin et al. (Eds.): PRCV 2019, LNCS 11859, pp. 332–340, 2019.
https://doi.org/10.1007/978-3-030-31726-3_28

other application prospects, such as object tracking, detection [3], identification and so on. SR can be divided into two types: reconstructing HR image from multiple LR images (VSR) [4] and reconstructing HR image from single LR image [5–7]. Generally, SR using deep learning is always single image super-resolution (SISR). And this paper mainly introduces a SISR deep learning method based on satellite imagery.

Satellite images have a wide range of imaging amplitudes. The scale of ground targets varies greatly and the texture information is diversified, which brings new challenges to existing image SR technology. Satellite images have a wide range of imaging, and the scale of the target is quite different. In a satellite image, objects with large differences may appear at the same time.

In response to the above questions, here we propose a very deep multi-scale CNN-based framework for satellite images based SISR which takes the advantages of skip connections, encoder-decoder architecture, additional dilated convolution layers and pixel shuffle. The input of our framework is a LR satellite image, and the output is its HR version. We observe that it is beneficial to train a very deep model for low-level tasks like denoising, SR and JPEG deblocking [8–11]. The network is composed of multiple layers of convolution and deconvolution operators. As deeper networks tend to be more difficult to train, we further propose to symmetrically link convolutional and deconvolutional layers with multiple skip-layer connections [12], with which the training converges much faster and better performance is achieved. Also, the dilated convolution layers provide different receptive fields for our network which brings multi-scale features.

The remaining content is organized as follows. We provide a brief review of related work in Sect. 2. We present the architecture of the proposed network, as well as training, testing details in Sect. 3. Experimental results and analysis are provided in Sect. 4.

2 Related Work

The concept of SR first appeared in the field of optics. In the field of optics, SR refers to the process of trying to recover data outside the diffraction limit. In 1984, Tsai and Huang [13] first proposed SR reconstruction based on sequence or multi-frame images, and SR reconstruction technology began to receive wide attention. The algorithm before the SR reconstruction technique generates the deep learning method is to treat the image as a signal. It was not until 2014 that various DL-based algorithms were produced. From the algorithm point of view, SR reconstruction can be roughly divided into interpolation-based reconstruction [14], reconstruction-based reconstruction [15] and learning-based reconstruction [16]. The deep learning reconstruction method based on deep learning is a common learning-based SR method. In this section, we will review these approaches.

VDSR [6] proposed by Kim et al. is the first method to introduce global residuals into SR. Since the input LR image and the output HR image are largely similar, that is, the low frequency information carried by the LR image is similar to the low frequency information of the HR image, this part takes a lot of time to train. In fact, we only need to learn the high frequency partial residual between the HR image and the LR image.

The idea of residual network structure is particularly suitable for solving SR problems, which can be said to affect the deep learning SR method.

Upsampling is an indispensable part of SR. The first SR network SRCNN [17] applied convolution layers on the pre-upscaled LR image. It is inefficient because all convolutional layers have to compute on high-resolution feature space, yielding S^2 times computation than on low-resolution space, where S is the upscaling factor. To accelerate processing speed without loss of accuracy, FSRCNN [18] utilized parametric deconvolution layer at the end of SR network, making all convolution layers compute on LR feature space. Another non-parametric efficient alternative is pixel shuffling [19] (a.k.a., sub-pixel convolution). Pixel shuffling is also believed to introduce less checkerboard artifacts than the deconvolutional layer.

Recently, deep convolutional neural networks (DCNNs) have shown their dominance on many visual recognition tasks. Of course, DCNNs have been successfully applied to the task of SISR. Recently, DCNNs based methods have achieved significant improvements over conventional SR methods [8–11]. Among them, Dong et al. proposed SRCNN [17] by firstly introducing a three-layer CNN for Image SR. Then the depth of networks increased to 20 in VDSR [6] and DRCN [20] and 52 to DRRN [21], achieving notable improvements over SRCNN. Network depth was demonstrated to be of central importance for many visual recognition tasks, When He et al. proposed residual net (ResNet [22]), which reaches 1000 layers with residual blocks. Such effective residual learning strategy was then introduced in many other CNN-based image SR methods. Lim et al. [23] built a very wide network EDSR and a very deep one MDSR (about 165 layers) by using simplified residual blocks. The great improvements on performance of EDSR and MDSR indicate that the depth of representation is of crucial importance for image SR.

All of the above mentioned are SR reconstruction of ordinary images. And there are a few super-resolution reconstruction tasks based on deep learning for satellite images. There are several VSR-based and SISR-based remote sensing imagery SR [4] mentioned in Sect. 4. Satellite image-based SR reconstruction still has something to do.

3   Proposed Method

In this section, we mainly describe the proposed network structure. For the multi-scale characteristics of satellite images, combined with the latest super-resolution network, we propose a super-resolution network with multi-scale features for satellite images. In addition to the multi-scale module is specifically designed to deal with multi-scale problems in satellite imagery, the encoder-decoder part is also very helpful to increase the multi-scale information of deep CNNs.

3.1   Symmetric Convolution and Deconvolution

The Peak Signal-to-Noise Ratio (PSNR) on the validation set in RED [24] is reported, which shows that using deconvolution works better than the fully convolutional counterpart. The residual body in our network contains layers of symmetric convolution layers and deconvolution layers except dilation module (see Fig. 1). Skip shortcuts are connected every layer from convolutional feature maps to their mirrored decon-volutional feature maps. The response from a convolutional layer is directly propagated to the corresponding mirrored deconvolutional layer, both forwardly and backwardly. Each convolutional layer and deconvolution layer are followed by a RELU activation. According to EDSR [23], we have abandoned the BN operation which saved us a lot of computing space to increase the depth of the network. In addition, we did not use the pooling operations that are often used in encoder-decoder networks. The reason is that for low-level image restoration, the aim is to eliminate low level corruption while preserving image details instead of learning image abstractions. Different from high-level applications such as segmentation or recognition, pooling typically eliminates the abundant image details and can deteriorate restoration performance.

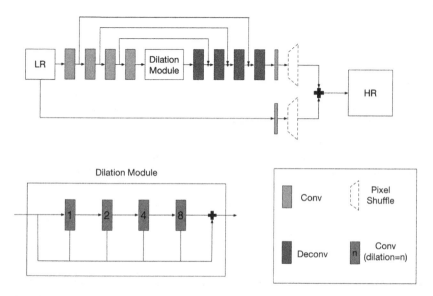

Fig. 1. The overall architecture of our proposed network. Each convolution layer is followed by a ReLU activation.

3.2 Multi-scale Module

Considering the multi-scale nature of satellite imagery, our model specifically adds a multi-scale module that utilizes dilated convolution constructs. As we all known, pooling can reduce the dimension, reduce the number of parameters, and increase the receptive field in many tasks. However, it is not a sagacious idea in super resolution tasks for pooling makes great difficulties in image restoration. So we want to migrate the model of other image task to the image super resolution, and as shown by some state-of-the-art deep learning models [25–27], the convolutional layer can be an ideal alternative to the pooling layer. We use several dilated convolutional layers (also called atrous convolution) and jump connections like D-LinkNet [28] in the central part.

Due to [25], dilated convolution can be stacked in cascade mode (see Fig. 1, Dilation Module). If the dilation rates of the stacked dilated convolution layers are 1, 2, 4, 8, 16 respectively, then the receptive field of each layer will be 3, 7, 15, 31, 63. Due to the size of the feature map after the first half of the 15-layer encoder layers is 32×32, our model uses 3×3 dilated convolution layers with dilation rate of 1, 2, 4, 8, so the feature points on the last layer will see 31×31 points on the first center feature map, which covering almost all part of the feature map. Still, our module takes the advantage of multi-resolution features, and the dilation module can be viewed as the parallel mode.

This dilation module allows the network to obtain different sizes of receptive fields, and will not change the size of the feature map. At the same time, this allows the network to feel different scales of information, making the network more adaptable to satellite image tasks.

3.3   Architecture

The input low-resolution image and the output high-resolution image are largely similar, that is, the low-frequency information carried by the low-resolution image is similar to the low-frequency information of the high-resolution image, and it takes a lot of time to bring this part during training. In fact, we only need to learn the high-frequency partial residual between the high-resolution image and the low-resolution image. The idea of the residual network structure is particularly suitable for solving the super-resolution problem, which can be said to affect the deep learning super-resolution method. Our method also uses this idea. We only trained the high-frequency residual and add the trained residual to the enlarged low-resolution image. After applying the idea of residuals, since the residual image is relatively sparse, many values are small or even zero, which speeds up the training.

Our proposed method extracts all features in the low-resolution stage. According to WDSR [29], we known that it does not affect the accuracy of the SR network, while greatly increasing the speed. A new convolution method called pixel shuffle was proposed in ESPCN [23], also called sub-pixel convolution. This new type of convolution is tailor-made for SR. First get the feature map with the same size as the input image, but the feature channel is $C \times r^2$ after convolution (Where r is the target magnification of the image). And then r^2 channels of each pixel of the feature map are rearranged into an $r \times r$ region corresponding to an $r \times r$-sized sub-block in the high-resolution image. Thus, the feature map of size $H \times W \times C \times r^2$ is rearranged into an HR image of $rH \times rW \times C$. Our model performs pixel-shuffle operations on the LR image and the high-frequency residuals separately and adds them as output.

4   Experiments

4.1   Datasets

Original high-resolution images are from 'Kaggle Airbus Ship Detection Challenge' [30], this competition provides a large number of images which have many images that do not contain ships and many contain multiple ships or only one ship. All the images are satellite images which are around sea. We choose 1000 images to build our super resolution dataset. We use the bicubic interpolation of MATLAB to get a 2 × reduction of low-resolution images. 800 of them are used as training set, 100 as validation set, 100 as test set. The resolution of the high-resolution images is 768 × 768, and the resolution of the low-resolution images is 384 × 384.

4.2   Implementation Details

We use Pytorch [31] to train our model on NVIDIA GTX1080 GPUs. For training, we use the RGB input patches of size 64 × 64 from LR image with the corresponding HR patches. We pre-process all the images by subtracting the mean RGB value of the airbus ship dataset. Before training, we did some data augmentation operations on the data such as random horizontal flips and rotations. We use ADAM optimizer with $\beta1 = 0.9$, $\beta2 = 0.999$, and $\varepsilon = 10^{-8}$ to train our model. We set batch size as 16. The learning rate is initialized as 10^{-4} and halved at every 2×10^5 iterations. We train our networks using L1 loss instead of L2.

4.3   Results

We measure the accuracy with the two most common super-resolution standard Peak Signal to Noise Ratio (PSNR) and structural similarity index (SSIM). We compare our model with other works on the Airbus satellite ship dataset. The following Table 1 gives the performance comparison between our model and other models. And other works include super-resolution construction based on typical neural networks [17, 24, 32], multi-scale model [33] and the satellite images [4, 34].

Table 1. Performance comparison between architectures on the Airbus Satellite Ship Dataset with two standard PSNR (dB) and SSIM for scale 2×.

Networks	PSNR/dB	SSIM
Bicubic	25.10	0.8701
A+ [32]	25.22	0.8778
SRCNN [17]	25.45	0.8812
RED30 [24]	26.03	0.8920
LapSRN [33]	27.89	0.9199
VISR [4]	28.21	0.9308
DMCN [34]	29.87	0.9432
Ours (30 layers)	30.55	0.9610

For each architecture, we measured the average PSNR (dB)/SSIM on the same dataset on the same conditions. We used MATLAB for evaluation. We can see that our method achieves the highest PSNR/SSIM score on the airbus satellite ship dataset. In the experiment, we only used 30 layers. If we deepen our network, we will get better results. In addition, LapSRN [33] gets better result than other dataset, it takes advantage of LapSRN's multi-scale characteristic. This proves that multi-scale features are necessary when doing super-resolution reconstruction on satellite images. At the same time, we also show the qualitative results (see Fig. 2).

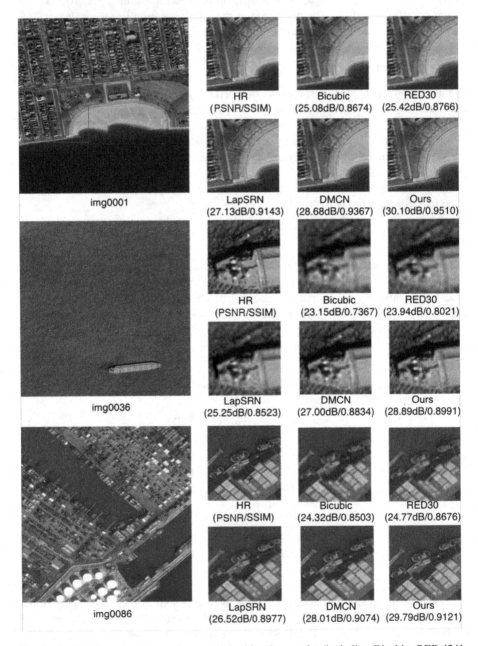

Fig. 2. Qualitative comparison of our model with other works (including Bicubic, RED [24], LapSRN [33], DMCN [34]) on ×2 super-resolution.

5 Conclusion

In this paper, considering the particularity of satellite imagery, multi-scale module is used to improve the adaptability of CNN-based networks to different scales of remote sensing satellite imagery. By combining multi-scale residuals, more accurate high-frequency information such as edges and textures can be obtained. The experimental results on the Airbus ship dataset show that the proposed multi-scale residual deep neural network can effectively enhance the high-frequency information in the reconstructed image, and has better subjective and objective reconstruction quality. Since the paper is mainly aimed at the multi-scale feature of satellite imagery, the proposed methods can also be helped to deal with the multi-scale characteristics of ordinary images.

References

1. Sharon, P., Yehezkel, Y.: Superresolution in MRI: application to human white matter fiber tract visualization by diffusion tensor imaging. Magn. Reson. Med. **45**, 29–35 (2001)
2. Matt, W., Peter, M., Holland, D.A.: Sub-pixel mapping of rural land cover objects from fine spatial resolution satellite sensor imagery using super-resolution pixel-swapping. Int. J. Remote Sens. **27**, 473–491 (2006)
3. Shermeyer, J., Van Etten, A.: The effects of super-resolution on object detection performance in satellite imagery. arXiv preprint arXiv:1812.04098 (2018)
4. Luo, Y., Zhou, L., Wang, S.: Video satellite imagery super resolution via convolutional neural networks. IEEE Geosci. Remote Sens. Lett. **14**(12), 2398–2402 (2017)
5. Bee, L.: Enhanced deep residual networks for single image super-resolution. In: The IEEE Conference on Computer Vision and Pattern Recognition (CVPR) Workshops (2017)
6. Kim, J., Lee, J.K., Lee, K.M.: Accurate image super-resolution using very deep convolutional networks. In: Proceedings of the IEEE Conference on Computer Vision and Pattern Recognition, pp. 1646–1654 (2016)
7. Liu, D.: Robust single image super-resolution via deep networks with sparse prior. IEEE Trans. Image Process. **25**, 3194–3207 (2016)
8. Fan, Y.: Balanced two-stage residual networks for image super-resolution. In: Computer Vision and Pattern Recognition Workshops (CVPRW), pp. 1157–1164 (2017)
9. Tai, Y.: Memnet: a persistent memory network for image restoration. In: Proceedings of the IEEE Conference on Computer Vision and Pattern Recognition, pp. 4539–4547 (2017)
10. Tong, T.: Image super-resolution using dense skip connections. In: 2017 IEEE International Conference on Computer Vision (ICCV), pp. 4809–4817 (2017)
11. Zhang, Y.: Residual dense network for image super-resolution. arXiv e-prints arXiv:1802.08797 (2018)
12. Ronneberger, O., Fischer, P., Brox, T.: U-Net: convolutional networks for biomedical image segmentation. In: Navab, N., Hornegger, J., Wells, W.M., Frangi, A.F. (eds.) MICCAI 2015. LNCS, vol. 9351, pp. 234–241. Springer, Cham (2015). https://doi.org/10.1007/978-3-319-24574-4_28
13. Tsai, R.Y., Huang, T.S.: Multiple frame image restoration and registration. In: Advances in Computer Vision and Image Processing, Greenwich, pp. 317–339 (1984)

14. Batz, M., Eichenseer, A., Seiler, J.: Hybrid super-resolution combining example-based single-image and interpolation-based multi-image reconstruction approaches. In: IEEE International Conference on Image Processing (ICIP), pp. 58–62 (2015)

15. Kim, K.I., Kwon, Y.: Single-image super-resolution using sparse regression and natural image prior. IEEE Trans. Pattern Anal. Mach. Intell. **32**(6), 1127–1133 (2010)

16. Lian, Q.S., Zhang, W.: Super-resolution reconstruction algorithm based on classification of sparse representations of image blocks. J. Electron. **40**(5), 920–925 (2012)

17. Dong, C., Loy, C.C., He, K., Tang, X.: Learning a deep convolutional network for image super-resolution. In: Fleet, D., Pajdla, T., Schiele, B., Tuytelaars, T. (eds.) ECCV 2014. LNCS, vol. 8692, pp. 184–199. Springer, Cham (2014). https://doi.org/10.1007/978-3-319-10593-2_13

18. Dong, C., Loy, C.C., Tang, X.: Accelerating the super-resolution convolutional neural network. In: Leibe, B., Matas, J., Sebe, N., Welling, M. (eds.) ECCV 2016. LNCS, vol. 9906, pp. 391–407. Springer, Cham (2016). https://doi.org/10.1007/978-3-319-46475-6_25

19. Shi, W., Caballero, J., Huszár, F.: Real-time single image and video super-resolution using an efficient sub-pixel convolutional neural network. In: CVPR (2016)

20. Kim, J., Lee, J.K., Lee, K.M.: Deeply-recursive convolutional network for image super-resolution. In: CVPR (2016)

21. Tai, Y., Yang, J., Liu, X.: Image super-resolution via deep recursive residual network. In: IEEE Computer Vision and Pattern Recognition (CVPR). IEEE (2017)

22. He, K., Zhang, X., Ren, S., Sun, J.: Deep residual learning for image recognition. In: CVPR (2015)

23. Lim, B., Son, S., Kim, H.: Enhanced deep residual networks for single image super-resolution. In: IEEE Conference on Computer Vision and Pattern Recognition Workshops (CVPRW). IEEE Computer Society (2017)

24. Mao, X.J., Shen, C., Yang, Y.B.: Image restoration using convolutional auto-encoders with symmetric skip connections. In: NIPS (2016)

25. Fisher, Y., Vladlen, K.: Multi-scale context aggregation by dilated convolutions. arXiv preprint arXiv:1511.07122 (2015)

26. Zhao, H.S., Shi, J.P., Qi, X.J., Wang, X.G., Jia, J.Y.: Pyramid scene parsing network. In: IEEE Conference on Computer Vision and Pattern Recognition (CVPR), pp. 2881–2890 (2017)

27. Fisher, Y., Vladlen, K., Thomas, F.: Dilated residual networks. In: Computer Vision and Pattern Recognition, vol. 1 (2017)

28. Zhou, L., Zhang, C., Wu, M.: D-LinkNet: LinkNet with pretrained encoder and dilated convolution for high resolution satellite imagery road extraction. In: IEEE/CVF Conference on Computer Vision and Pattern Recognition Workshops (CVPRW). IEEE (2018)

29. Yu, J., Fan, Y., Yang, J., et al.: Wide activation for efficient and accurate image super-resolution. In: CVPR (2018)

30. https://www.kaggle.com/c/airbus-ship-detection/data

31. Adam, P., et al.: Automatic differentiation in Pytorch (2017)

32. Timofte, R., De Smet, V., Van Gool, L.: A+: adjusted anchored neighborhood regression for fast super-resolution. In: Cremers, D., Reid, I., Saito, H., Yang, M.-H. (eds.) ACCV 2014. LNCS, vol. 9006, pp. 111–126. Springer, Cham (2015). https://doi.org/10.1007/978-3-319-16817-3_8

33. Lai, W.S., Huang, J.B., Ahuja, N., Yang, M.H.: Deep Laplacian pyramid networks for fast and accurate super-resolution. In: IEEE Conference on Computer Vision and Pattern Recognition (CVPR), Honolulu, USA, pp. 5835–5843 (2017)

34. Xu, W.J., Xu, G.L., Wang, Y., Sun, X., Lin, D.Y., Wu, Y.W.: Deep memory connected neural network for optical remote sensing image restoration. Remote Sens. **10**, 1893 (2018)

CG Animation Creator: Auto-rendering of Motion Stick Figure Based on Conditional Adversarial Learning

Jie Lin$^{(\boxtimes)}$ ⓘ, Jian Cui, Guangming Shi, and Danhua Liu

School of Artificial Intelligence, Xidian University, Xi'an, China
jlin@mail.xidian.edu.cn

Abstract. As an important part of animation production, the existing method for drawing and rendering the CG animated characters according to motion information mostly relays on expensive manual processing. By adopting the conditional adversarial learning, an automatic animation rendering system for geometry structure attribute is proposed, using a deep convolution generative adversarial network called "pix2pixHD". A training database containing a variety of motion stick figure is established for different virtual characters to achieve an end-to-end training system to verify this idea. The trained generator is the desired CG animation creator which shows great performance on visual quality and time efficiency proved by the experimental results.

Keywords: CG animation rendering · Conditional GAN · Deep learning · pix2pixHD

1 Introduction

CG (computer graphics) technology is widely used in the modern film and television animation production industry. It can introduce some virtual characters and special effects to enhance the visual effect through the form of computer-generated animation. In order to achieve a better virtual effect for the generated animation, motion capture technology is usually used in CG animation. After obtaining the motion information of a real human by the sensor, the motion data is rendered to the corresponding virtual carrier, resulting in the desired animation, such as King Kong, Spider-Man, Avatar. Accurately matching the motion data to the virtual images is critical, but the acquirement of motion data is usually costly. The mainstream methods of making CG animation use some professional production software to draw and render the images in the video frame by frame according to the pose of motion. In this process, with the increase of video duration and the complexity of action form, the cycle and costs of animation production will become unacceptable. Therefore, the technology of automatic animation generation with motion stick figures is extremely desired by the film-television industry.

© Springer Nature Switzerland AG 2019
Z. Lin et al. (Eds.): PRCV 2019, LNCS 11859, pp. 341–352, 2019.
https://doi.org/10.1007/978-3-030-31726-3_29

At the same time, how to automatically generate high-quality visual content using the attributes of the real world, and establish interaction between virtual and reality is the ultimate goal of computer graphics. In recent years, deep learning techniques start applying to solve some problems in the field of computer graphics. A sketch-based modeling method of facial expression is proposed in [5] to assist users to get face models quickly. A general framework for style migration is developed in [25] to realize the visual style migration of different images. Google has also opened source the TensorFlow Graphics framework, using computer vision systems to extract scene parameters for 3D graphics modeling [19].

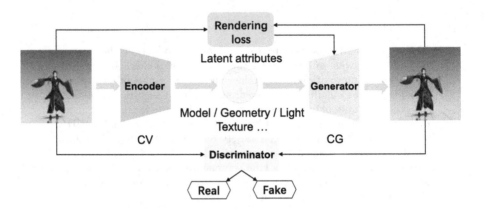

Fig. 1. An adversarial rendering framework based on attribute coding.

Inspired by these works, we explore applying the deep learning technique to automatic animation rendering to resolve the conflict between rendering effect and speed. In this paper, we propose an adversarial framework that extracts object properties from the real world and uses them for CG rendering. We replaced the renderer mentioned in the TensorFlow Graphics framework with a generator and introduced a discriminator for adversarial training (Fig. 1). This makes the overall architecture similar to a VAE-GAN [11], but become more complex. The encoder can extract some hidden attributes of the real world, such as geometry or texture. Then we can render the corresponding virtual scene based on these attributes. Because the distribution of hidden attributes is very complex, we designed a simple animation rendering task to verify the feasibility of this idea from a single geometric attribute. We use a high-resolution semantic generation network called pix2pixHD [22] to establish the mapping relationship between the simple stick figures to animation images and realize fast animation rendering. The automatic animation production can be achieved once the end-to-end training of deep neural network is done. The visual quality of generated animation is quite good based on the metric of SSIM. The experimental results show that this method greatly improves the efficiency of animation rendering without the manual operation. Thus, this method can greatly reduce the cost of animation production and greatly shorten the cycle of anime or movie production.

2   Related Work

Some deep generation models are proposed by previous research work on image and video generation [3,14,20,21], including the popular model of generative adversarial network (GAN) [3], and conditional generative adversarial network (CGAN) [14]. The generator of GAN uses a deep convolution neural network [12,16], which can achieve the super-resolution restoration of a single image and successfully recover the lost high-frequency texture details. The geometry-contrastive generative adversarial network is designed to generate face images according to target expression, based on the geometric information of face [15]. Aiming on the image-to-image translation problems, the models in [7,22] train neural networks with image pairs to learn the mapping relationship between input images and output images. These models can not only generate new images from the object contour, but also generate maps based on satellite remote sensing images, and achieve high-resolution image synthesis using semantic annotation maps. Recently, two interesting research focus on replacing faces and movements. One can transfer one person's motion to another, done by UC Berkeley [2]. The other one is a face changing software based on GAN, named "DeepFake", which has aroused widespread concern [10]. All these works show the potential of GAN on high resolution graphics rendering.

As for the rendering techniques for animation production, a generation model of a 2D animation characters is proposed in [8] for batch generation of head portrait. A progressive structure-conditional generative adversarial networks is designed to generate images with a preset sequence of gestures [4]. Because the preset posture sequence set is extremely simple, it has a large difference with the real model of the human body. Moreover, there is only one dataset used for training which pays more attention to the color change of clothing. Thus, the performance of this model cannot meet the requirement of complex CG animation rendering tasks. To overcome the shortcoming of that model, this paper uses the advanced high-resolution image translation model called pix2pixHD as the ideal renderer to achieves a fast and automatic animation rendering based on motion stick figures. At the same time, we also compare the animation rendering quality at different resolutions with other image translation models like pix2pix [7].

3   Animation Rendering System Based on High-Resolution Conditional Learning Network with Semantic Information

For a rendering task with a stick figure, the geometric structure attribute will be the only variable, and the image will change along the geometric structure dimension, resulting in a specific animation effect. It can achieve a comparable rendering result like frame-by-frame manual calibration. In the proposed model, the process of automatic rendering is divided into three steps. First, we built a full-pose database of animation, matching animation to its structural attributes.

Then, the database is used to train the GAN. Finally, we use the trained generator to achieve automatic rendering of the animation characters based on their stick figures.

3.1 Database Creation for System Training

Database for training can be created in two ways. For the first way, with some professional animation production software such as 3DMAX and MAYA, the animation modeling maps of various poses are used to obtain the virtual characters and the stick figure contains precise information of key points of pose. This method is easy for professional animation companies because they have accumulated a large amount of animated characters and pose stick figure during the animation production in the past. The second way, by capturing the animation images, uses the open source pose extraction framework such as OpenPose [1,24] to locate the key points and obtain the corresponding pose. In this case, OpenPose will be used as an encoder in the rendering system mentioned earlier to obtain geometric properties. This method can be seen as an upgrade to traditional CG motion capture technology, since the trained network can not only complete the rendering of the given pose stick figure, but also realize the production of motion special effects at low cost.

In order to facilitate the experimental operation and comparison with manual animation, the second method is used in the propose model to create four data sets, including 2000 pairs of doll images, 2000 pairs of cartoon images, 8500 pairs of anime images, and 3800 pairs of RPG game character models, respectively. The doll images are with single color and no facial key points in the pose information. The cartoon images and the anime images are rich in color and contains facial information. RPG game characters have a variety of clothing and rich background colors. Through these four data sets, it is possible to effectively demonstrate the rendering capabilities of conditional adversarial learning in different CG animation generation tasks. Figure 2 shows some examples of the data sets constructed in this paper, which are the animation images on the left and the pose images on the right.

3.2 Pix2pixHD for High-Resolution Image Synthesis and Semantic Manipulation

Animation rendering is essentially image generation technology, so the generative adversarial network is usually adopted as the model for animation rendering. The conditional generative adversarial network (CGAN) introduces some conditional constraints to the training of GAN. If both the generator and the discriminator are satisfied to some conditional information C, the constraints can be applied on the generator and discriminator respectively, to guide the image generation. Inspired by CGAN, taking the stick figure of cartoon as the condition information and the extracted structural attribute, we establish a mapping between the pose skeleton and the rendered image by the generator, achieving the automatic

Fig. 2. Examples of four datasets. (Color figure online)

animation rendering in a given pose. The structure of the proposed rendering system is shown in Fig. 3. Because we chose "pose" as the latent variable attribute, the whole pipeline is partially similar to [2]. An end-to-end animation rendering system is constructed by a CGAN model, which makes the training of network easier and more efficient. The stick figure of cartoon directly participates in the training of CGAN. For a better rendering performance, the pix2pixHD framework which is an improved version of CGAN is used as the high-resolution automatic animation rendering model, for the generator and the discriminator. pix2pixHD is a high-resolution image synthesis framework with semantic information, which introduces a new adversarial loss function in CGAN, and adopts multi-scale generator and discriminator [22].

pix2pixHD is based on the image translation model "pix2pix" [7]. Unlike CGAN, the input of generator of pix2pix is not the random noise, but the condition information as an image. In order to manipulate the generation process by the condition information, the training of network is carried out using the true and false data pairs as the input. As shown in Fig. 3, the cartoon image x and the stick figure y in the animation image datasets are used as the training set for network training. Specifically speaking, the pose stick figure y is fed into the generation network G to realize the 2D image filling rendering based on the posture skeleton, acquiring the automatically rendered image $x' = G(y)$. These three datasets are combined into two pairs of data: (x, y) and (x', y), which will be fed into the discriminator for adversarial learning. The network N is used to

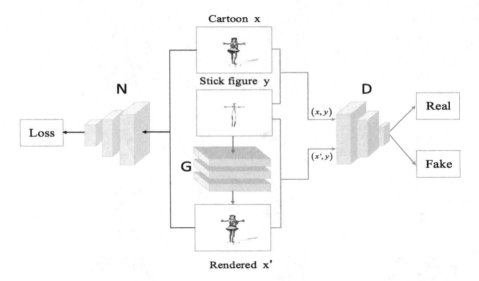

Fig. 3. Automatic animation rendering model, in which the network N calculates the animation rendering error, the network G is generator and D is discriminator.

calculate the loss between the cartoon image x and the rendered image x'. The loss function is:

$$\mathcal{L}_{pix2pix} = \arg \min_{G} \max_{D} \mathcal{L}_{CGAN}(G, D) + \lambda \mathcal{L}_{L1}(G) \qquad (1)$$

where the first term $\mathcal{L}_{CGAN}(G, D) = \mathbb{E}_{x,y}[\log D(x, y)] + \mathbb{E}_y[\log(1 - D(x', y))]$ is the loss of CGAN and the second term of reconstruction error is defined as $\mathcal{L}_{L1}(G) = \mathbb{E}_{x,y}[\|x - x'\|_1]$. The original pix2pix network adopts U-Net [17] as the generator and a patch-based fully convolutional network [13] as the discriminator. In order to improve the visual authenticity and resolution of the generated image, the model of pix2pixHD utilizes a coarse-to-fine generator plus a multiscale discriminator architecture and a robust adversarial learning objective function, which greatly improves the performance of pix2pix. Specifically, pix2pixHD uses a pyramidal network structure to gradually generate more refined images, as shown in Fig. 4 [22]. First, a residual network G1 [6] is trained to generate low-resolution pictures. Then, the generated low-resolution picture's last feature map and the high-resolution stick figure's output feature map are fed into the residual network G2 in the next layer, and a high-resolution picture is generated. At the same time, in order to render more details and realistic textures, the multi-scale discriminators are adopted by pix2pixHD, denoted as D1, D2, as shown in Fig. 4. Thus, the objective function of pix2pixHD with 3 layers is as follows [2,22]:

$$\mathcal{L}_{pix2pixHD} = \arg \min_{G}((\max_{D_1, D_2, D_3} \sum_{k=1,2,3} \mathcal{L}_{CGAN}(G, D_k))$$
$$+ \lambda_{FM} \sum_{k=1,2,3} \mathcal{L}_{FM}(G, D_k) + \lambda_{VGG} \mathcal{L}_{VGG}(x, x')) \qquad (2)$$

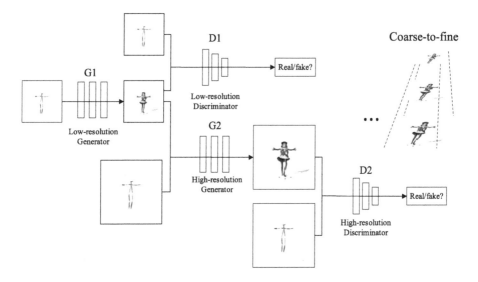

Fig. 4. Schematic diagram of pix2pixHD structure

where the first term $\mathcal{L}_{CGAN}(G, D)$ is the same as in Eq. (1), the second term $\mathcal{L}_{FM}(G, D)$ represents the discriminator feature-matching loss, and the last term $\mathcal{L}_{VGG}(x, x')$ is perceptual reconstruction loss [9], which measures the rendering error of the model with a pre-trained VGGNet [18]. For the training, the generator G produces image with realistic rendering effect as far as possible to induce the discriminator D to judge it as truth, while the discriminator D improves its discriminating ability as far as possible to correctly classify the real images and the rendered images. Ideally, when the game reaches the Nash equilibrium state, the training is completed, and the rendered animation by the generator can be considered to be indistinguishable from the real one.

4   Experimental Results and Analysis

4.1   The Experimental Setups

For animation rendering task, the stick figure is directly fed into the generator as the semantic information of pix2pixHD. The database with four data sets: 2000 pairs of doll images, 2000 pairs of cartoon images, 8500 pairs of anime images, and 3800 pairs of RPG game character models, is used for animation rendering. The image resolution for training is 512×512 and each batch contains 640 images, so as to reduce the memory cost and the computation burden of network training. And when pix2pix is selected as the renderer, the image resolution used for training is reduced to 256×256.

To quantitatively measure the performance of the proposed rendering system, the similarity between the rendered animation and the real animation is compared. We adopt the metric of structural similarity (SSIM) [23] to evaluate the quality of the resulting rendered image. SSIM measures the image similarity from three aspects, i.e., brightness, contrast and structure, which conforms to the human visual system.

4.2 The Similarity Evaluation of Rendered Animation Image

First of all, we show the SSIM results of the rendered images produced by the proposed rendering system, in Table 1. And we also show some rendered images for subjective evaluation, shown in Fig. 5. As can be seen from Table 1, since the SSIM metric reflects the structure and texture of image, it synchronously changes with the visual quality of the rendered image in Fig. 5. The required iteration times for training is related with the size of dataset and the complexity of image. The size of doll and cartoon datasets are smaller than the anime dataset, thus it required more iteration for a comparable quality. The biggest size of anime dataset results in a fast convergence. As for the RPG character dataset, a variety of clothing and rich background colors demands more iteration times for generating an image with good visual quality. At the same time, the comparable experimental data in Table 2 show that the two image translation frameworks can produce similar rendering effects, but pix2pixHD can produce higher resolution images indeed.

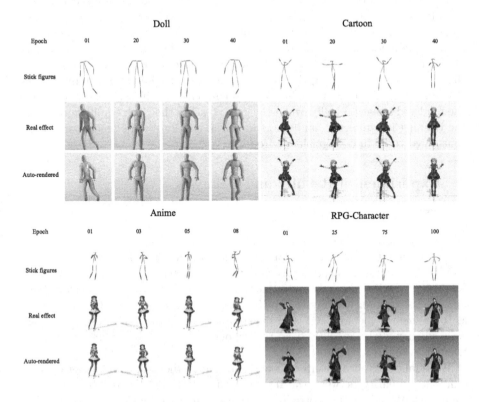

Fig. 5. Auto-rendering results for four datasets. (Color figure online)

Table 1. SSIM variation for four datasets.

Doll	Epoch	01	20	30	40
	SSIM	0.8319	0.9026	0.9414	0.9498
Cartoon	Epoch	01	20	30	40
	SSIM	0.8875	0.9357	0.9784	0.9493
Anime	Epoch	01	03	05	08
	SSIM	0.8459	0.7971	0.8718	0.8843
RPG	Epoch	01	25	75	100
	SSIM	0.8122	0.8943	0.8649	0.9378

Table 2. SSIM comparison of two translation models on Cartoon dataset.

pix2pix [7] (256 × 256)	Epoch	01	20	30	40
	SSIM	0.8733	0.9705	0.9766	0.9775
pix2pixHD [22] (512 × 512)	Epoch	01	20	30	40
	SSIM	0.8875	0.9357	0.9784	0.9493

4.3 The Rendering Loss and Nash Equilibrium of the Model

In all the deep learning methods, the dataset scale is the key. In this subsection, we use VGG-loss [22] and Nash equilibrium state curve to analyze the influence of data set scale and iteration number on animation rendering effect, as shown in Fig. 6. The anime dataset with 8200 image pairs and RPG character with 3800 image pairs are used to obtain the rendering loss and Nash equilibrium curve. In Fig. 6, D_REAL and D_FAKE represent the two components of D cost associated with the classification performance for both "real image pair" and "rendered image pair", respectively. They approximately reflect the Nash equilibrium state of the system. It can be seen from the Fig. 6, the big date size of dataset "anime" brings obvious benefit on convergence speed of loss curve. The rendering system can reach to a good visual effect when the iteration times is about 10 for anime dataset, while near 100 for RPG dataset. The lines D_FAKE and D_REAL trend to reach the equilibrium cost after serval iterations, which implies that upon convergence the good performance of the generator. Also, as we all known, the training of GAN is difficult, and it usually cannot reach to an ideal Nash equilibrium state. So, there is fluctuation on the curve of both loss function and Nash equilibrium trend.

It should be noting that, the size of "RPG character" dataset is not quite big enough, so it takes more iteration number to get a good rendering effect. There is hump on the loss curve at 75-th iteration, the rendered image shown in Fig. 5 has a different appearance of clothing, which shows the imagination ability of the proposed model when it lacks image detail.

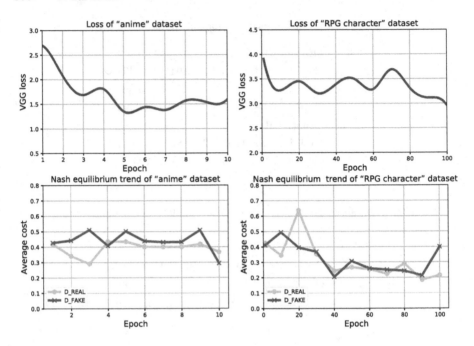

Fig. 6. Nash equilibrium trend and rendering loss. (Color figure online)

4.4   The Time Efficiency of the Automatic Rendering System

In this subsection, we analyze the auto-rendering speed of the model with four sets of action with different duration. In Table 3, the average rendering rate is presented, and the computation resource is a single TITAN Xp GPU. It can be seen that, the time for auto-rendering is about 2–4 times longer than the motion duration. Compared with the traditional manual rendering which usually takes weeks or months, this is a huge leap. If a distributed parallel framework or high-performance computing cluster is used, we believe that a real-time animation rendering can be achieved. Therefore, the automatic rendering of animation is a

Table 3. Automatic rendering speed.

	Motion time (Sec.)	Frame number	Auto-render time (Sec.)	Average rendering rate (frames/Sec.)
Motion 1	40	1000	112	8.93
Motion 2	106	2669	229	11.66
Motion 3	151	3793	342	11.09
Motion 4	285	8523	1178	7.24

revolutionary technique for movie and TV production. This technique will soon be adopted widely in the future.

*The rendered animation demo can be seen online at here: Demo Show : YouKu Video.

Notes: the training data are captured from MikuMikuDance and the Internet. The CG model is Hatsune Miku and Chinese Paladin. They are only used for test case display. The copyright of the animation model is owned by their author.

5 Conclusion

In this paper, the data-driven method of deep learning is used to solve the automatic rendering problem in traditional computer graphics. We build a system which can extract the real object attribute description and use the attribute to quickly render the virtual target to balance the contradiction between rendering speed and quality. The experimental results show that, compared with manual rendering technique, the proposed model can get a comparable visual effect and a very fast speed of rendering. Limited by the acquisition of professional animation database, we have only made a simple attempt in a single geometric attribute dimension (pose). It can be predicted that by selecting different CV systems as encoders, we can achieve changes in other dimensions, such as costumes, appearance, expression, and background. Maybe this work can bring some new inspiration and thinking to the traditional animation industry.

References

1. Cao, Z., Simon, T., Wei, S.E., Sheikh, Y.: Realtime multi-person 2D pose estimation using part affinity fields. In: Proceedings of the IEEE Conference on Computer Vision and Pattern Recognition, pp. 7291–7299 (2017)
2. Chan, C., Ginosar, S., Zhou, T., Efros, A.A.: Everybody dance now. arXiv preprint arXiv:1808.07371 (2018)
3. Goodfellow, I., et al.: Generative adversarial nets. In: Advances in Neural Information Processing Systems, pp. 2672–2680 (2014)
4. Hamada, K., Tachibana, K., Li, T., Honda, H., Uchida, Y.: Full-body high-resolution anime generation with progressive structure-conditional generative adversarial networks. In: Leal-Taixé, L., Roth, S. (eds.) ECCV 2018. LNCS, vol. 11131, pp. 67–74. Springer, Cham (2019). https://doi.org/10.1007/978-3-030-11015-4_8
5. Han, X., Gao, C., Yu, Y.: Deepsketch2face: a deep learning based sketching system for 3D face and caricature modeling. ACM Trans. Graph. (TOG) **36**(4), 126 (2017)
6. He, K., Zhang, X., Ren, S., Sun, J.: Deep residual learning for image recognition. In: Proceedings of the IEEE Conference on Computer Vision and Pattern Recognition, pp. 770–778 (2016)
7. Isola, P., Zhu, J.Y., Zhou, T., Efros, A.A.: Image-to-image translation with conditional adversarial networks. In: Proceedings of the IEEE Conference on Computer Vision and Pattern Recognition, pp. 1125–1134 (2017)

8. Jin, Y., Zhang, J., Li, M., Tian, Y., Zhu, H.: Towards the high-quality anime characters generation with generative adversarial networks. In: Proceedings of the Machine Learning for Creativity and Design Workshop at NIPS (2017)

9. Johnson, J., Alahi, A., Fei-Fei, L.: Perceptual losses for real-time style transfer and super-resolution. In: Leibe, B., Matas, J., Sebe, N., Welling, M. (eds.) ECCV 2016. LNCS, vol. 9906, pp. 694–711. Springer, Cham (2016). https://doi.org/10.1007/978-3-319-46475-6_43

10. Korshunov, P., Marcel, S.: Deepfakes: a new threat to face recognition? Assessment and detection. arXiv preprint arXiv:1812.08685 (2018)

11. Larsen, A.B.L., Sønderby, S.K., Larochelle, H., Winther, O.: Autoencoding beyond pixels using a learned similarity metric. arXiv preprint arXiv:1512.09300 (2015)

12. Ledig, C., et al.: Photo-realistic single image super-resolution using a generative adversarial network. In: Proceedings of the IEEE Conference on Computer Vision and Pattern Recognition, pp. 4681–4690 (2017)

13. Long, J., Shelhamer, E., Darrell, T.: Fully convolutional networks for semantic segmentation. In: Proceedings of the IEEE Conference on Computer Vision and Pattern Recognition, pp. 3431–3440 (2015)

14. Mirza, M., Osindero, S.: Conditional generative adversarial nets. arXiv preprint arXiv:1411.1784 (2014)

15. Qiao, F., Yao, N., Jiao, Z., Li, Z., Chen, H., Wang, H.: Geometry-contrastive generative adversarial network for facial expression synthesis. CoRR abs/1802.01822 (2018)

16. Radford, A., Metz, L., Chintala, S.: Unsupervised representation learning with deep convolutional generative adversarial networks. arXiv preprint arXiv:1511.06434 (2015)

17. Ronneberger, O., Fischer, P., Brox, T.: U-Net: convolutional networks for biomedical image segmentation. In: Navab, N., Hornegger, J., Wells, W.M., Frangi, A.F. (eds.) MICCAI 2015. LNCS, vol. 9351, pp. 234–241. Springer, Cham (2015). https://doi.org/10.1007/978-3-319-24574-4_28

18. Simonyan, K., Zisserman, A.: Very deep convolutional networks for large-scale image recognition. arXiv preprint arXiv:1409.1556 (2014)

19. Valentin, J., Keskin, C., Pidlypenskyi, P., Makadia, A., Sud, A., Bouaziz, S.: TensorFlow graphics: computer graphics meets deep learning (2019)

20. Vondrick, C., Pirsiavash, H., Torralba, A.: Generating videos with scene dynamics. In: Advances in Neural Information Processing Systems, pp. 613–621 (2016)

21. Wang, T.C., et al.: Video-to-video synthesis. arXiv preprint arXiv:1808.06601 (2018)

22. Wang, T.C., Liu, M.Y., Zhu, J.Y., Tao, A., Kautz, J., Catanzaro, B.: High-resolution image synthesis and semantic manipulation with conditional GANs. In: Proceedings of the IEEE Conference on Computer Vision and Pattern Recognition, pp. 8798–8807 (2018)

23. Wang, Z., Bovik, A.C., Sheikh, H.R., Simoncelli, E.P., et al.: Image quality assessment: from error visibility to structural similarity. IEEE Trans. Image Process. **13**(4), 600–612 (2004)

24. Wei, S.E., Ramakrishna, V., Kanade, T., Sheikh, Y.: Convolutional pose machines. In: Proceedings of the IEEE Conference on Computer Vision and Pattern Recognition, pp. 4724–4732 (2016)

25. Zhu, J.Y., Park, T., Isola, P., Efros, A.A.: Unpaired image-to-image translation using cycle-consistent adversarial networks. In: Proceedings of the IEEE International Conference on Computer Vision, pp. 2223–2232 (2017)

Deep Eyes: Binocular Depth-from-Focus on Focal Stack Pairs

Xinqing Guo[2(✉)], Zhang Chen[1], Siyuan Li[3], Yang Yang[2], and Jingyi Yu[1]

[1] ShanghaiTech University, Shanghai, China
{chenzhang,yujingyi}@shanghaitech.edu.cn
[2] DGene Inc., Santa Clara, USA
{xinqing,yyangwin}@udel.edu
[3] École Polytechnique Fédérale de Lausanne, Lausanne, Switzerland
siyuan.li@epfl.ch

Abstract. Human visual system relies on both binocular stereo cues and monocular focusness cues to gain effective 3D perception. In computer vision, the two problems are traditionally solved in separate tracks. In this paper, we present a unified learning-based technique that simultaneously uses both types of cues for depth inference. Specifically, we use a pair of focal stacks as input to emulate human perception. We first construct a comprehensive focal stack training dataset synthesized by depth-guided light field rendering. We then construct three individual networks: a *Focus-Net* to extract depth from a single focal stack, a *EDoF-Net* to obtain the extended depth of field (EDoF) image from the focal stack, and a *Stereo-Net* to conduct stereo matching. We show how to integrate them into a unified *BDfF-Net* to obtain high-quality depth maps. Comprehensive experiments show that our approach outperforms the state-of-the-art in both accuracy and speed and effectively emulates human vision systems.

Keywords: Depth from Focus · Stereo matching · Deep learning · Light field

1 Introduction

Human visual system relies on a variety of depth cues to gain 3D perception. The most important ones are binocular, defocus, and motion cues. Binocular cues such as stereopsis, eye convergence, and disparity yield depth from binocular vision through exploitation of parallax. Defocus cue allows depth perception even with a single eye by correlating variation of defocus blurs with the motion of the ciliary muscles surrounding the lens. Motion parallax also provides useful input to assess depth, but arrives over time and depends on texture gradients.

Computer vision algorithms such as stereo matching [20] and depth-from-focus [12,15] seek to employ binocular and defocus cues which are available

X. Guo and Z. Chen—These authors contribute to the work equally.

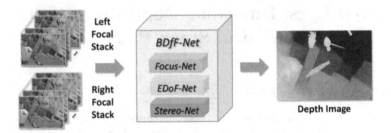

Fig. 1. *BDfF-Net* integrates *Focus-Net*, *EDoF-Net* and *Stereo-Net* to predict high quality depth map from binocular focal stacks.

instantaneously without scene statistics. Recent studies have shown that the two types of cues complement each other to provide 3D perception [6]. In this paper, we seek to develop learning-based approaches to emulate this process.

To exploit binocular cues, traditional stereo matching algorithms rely on feature matching and optimization to maintain the Markov Random Field property. In contrast, depth-from-focus (DfF) exploits differentiations of sharpness at each pixel across a focal stack and assigns the layer with the highest sharpness as its depth. Compared with stereo, DfF generally presents a low fidelity estimation due to limited aperture size. Earlier DfF techniques use a focal sweep camera to produce a coarse focal stack due to mechanical limitations whereas more recent ones attempt to use a light field to synthetically produce a denser focal stack.

Our solution benefits from recent advances on computational photography and we present an efficient and reliable learning-based technique to conduct depth inference from a focal stack pair, emulating the process of how human eyes work. We call our technique binocular DfF or B-DfF. Our approach leverages deep learning techniques that can effectively extract features learned from large amount of imagery data. Such a deep representation has shown great promise in stereo matching [11,28]. Little work, however, has been proposed on using deep learning for DfF or more importantly, integrating stereo and DfF. This is mainly due to the lack of fully annotated DfF datasets.

We first construct a comprehensive focal stack dataset. Our dataset is based on the highly diversified dataset from [13], which contains both stereo color images and ground truth disparity maps. Then we adopt the algorithm from *Virtual DSLR* [26] to generate the refocused images. [26] uses color and depth image pair as input for light field synthesis and rendering, but without the need to actually create the light field. The quality of the rendered focal stacks is comparable to those captured by expensive DSLR camera. Next, we propose three individual networks: (1) *Focus-Net*, a multi-scale network to extract depth from a single focal stack (2) *EDoF-Net*, a deep network consisting of small convolution kernels to obtain the extended depth of field (EDoF) image from the focal stack and (3) *Stereo-Net* to obtain depth directly from a stereo pair. The EDoF image from *EDoF-Net* serves to both guide the refinement of the depth from *Focus-Net* and provide inputs for *Stereo-Net*. We also show how to integrate them into a unified *BDfF-Net* to obtain high-quality depth maps. Figure 1 illustrates the pipeline.

We evaluate our approach on both synthetic and real data. To physically implement B-DfF, we construct a light field stereo pair by using two Lytro Illum cameras. Light field rendering is then applied to produce the two focal stacks as input to our framework. Comprehensive experiments show that our technique outperforms the state-of-the-art techniques in both accuracy and speed.

2 Related Work

Our work is closely related to depth from focus/defocus and stereo. The strength and weakness of the two approaches have been extensively discussed in [21,25].

Depth from Focus. Blur carries information about the object's distance. Depth from Focus (DfF) recovers scene depth from a collection of images captured under varying focus settings. In general, DfF [12,15] determines the depth by analyzing the most in-focus slice in the focal stack. [3] combined focal stack with varying aperture to recover scene geometry. Suwajanakorn *et al.* [23] proposed the DfF with mobile phone under uncalibrated setting. They first aligned the focal stack, then jointly optimized the camera parameters and depth map, and further refined the depth map using anisotropic regularization.

A drastic difference of these methods to our approach is that they rely on hand-crafted features to estimate the focusness, whereas in this paper we leverage the neural network to learn more discriminative features from the focal stack and directly predict the depth at a fraction of the computational cost.

Learning Based Stereo. Depth from stereo has been studied extensively by the computer vision community for decades [20]. Here we only discuss recent methods based on Convolutional Neural Network (CNN).

Deep learning benefits stereo matching at various stages. A number of approaches exploit CNN to improve the matching cost. The seminal work by Žbontar and LeCun [28] computed a similarity score from patches using CNN, then applied the traditional cost aggregation and optimization to solve the energy function. Luo *et al.* [11] speeded up the matching process by using a product layer, and treated the disparity estimation as a multi-class classification problem. [1,18,27] conducted similar work but with different network architecture.

End-to-end network architectures have also been explored. Mayer *et al.* [13] adopted and extended the architecture of the FlowNet, which consists of a contractive part and an expanding part to learn depth at multiple scales. They also created three synthetic datasets to facilitate the training process. Knöbelreiter *et al.* [9] learned unary and pairwise cost of stereo using CNNs, then posed the optimization as a conditional random field (CRF) problem. The hybrid CNN-CRF model was trained in image's full resolution in an end-to-end fashion.

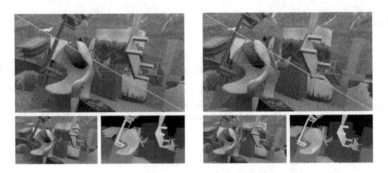

Fig. 2. A binocular focal stack pair consists of two horizontally rectified focal stacks. The upper and lower triangles show corresponding slices focusing at respective depths. Bottom shows the ground truth color and depth images. We add Poisson noise to training data, a critical step for handling real scenes. (Color figure online)

Combining DfF and stereo matching has also been studied, although not within the learning framework. Early work [8] attempted to utilize the depth map from the focus to reduce the search space for stereo and solve the correspondence problem more efficiently. [19] simultaneously recovered depth and restored the original focused image from a defocused stereo pair.

Aforementioned approaches leave the combination and optimization of focus and disparity cue to post-processing. In contrast, we resort to extra layers of network to infer the optimized depth with low computational cost and efficiency.

3   Dual Focal Stack Dataset

With fast advances of the data-driven methods, numerous datasets have been created for various applications. However, by far, there are limited resources on focal stacks. To this end, we generate our dual focal stack dataset based on FlyingThings3D from [13]. Their 3D models and textures are separated into disjointed training and testing parts. In total, the dataset contains about 25,000 stereo images with ground truth disparity. To make the data tractable, we select stereo frames whose largest disparity is less than 100 pixels to avoid objects appearing in one image but not in the other.

Takeda *et al.* [24] demonstrate that in a stereo setup, the disparity and the diameter of the circle of confusion have a linear relationship. Based on above observation, we adopt the *Virtual DSLR* approach from [26] to generate synthetic focal stacks. *Virtual DSLR* requires color and disparity image pair as inputs, and outputs refocused images with quality comparable to those captured from regular, expensive DSLR. The advantage of their algorithm is that it resembles light field synthesis and refocusing but does not require actual creation of the light field, hence reducing both memory and computational load. In addition, their method takes special care of occlusion boundaries to avoid color bleeding and discontinuity commonly observed in brute-force blur-based defocus synthesis.

For binocular focal stack dataset, we evenly separate the scene into 16 depth layers and render a refocused image for each layer. Figure 2 shows two slices from the dual focal stack and their corresponding color and depth images. We further add Poisson noise to both datasets to simulate real images captured by a camera. This turns out to be critical in real scene experiments, as described in Sect. 6. Our final datasets each contain 750 training samples and 160 testing samples, with each sample consisting of 16 differently focused stereo image pair. The resolution of the generated images is 960 × 540, the same as the ones in FlyingThings3D.

4   B-DfF Network Architecture

When designing our network, one general principle is to use deep architecture with small kernels. [22] shows that such a structure is very effective in image recognition tasks. Further, we aim to take an end-to-end approach to predict a depth map.

As already mentioned, the input to the neural network is two rectified focal stacks. To extract depth from defocus and disparity, our solution is composed of three individual networks. We start in Sect. 4.1 by describing the *Focus-Net-Guided*, a multi-scale network that estimates depth from a single focal stack and further enhanced by the extended depth of field images from *EDoF-Net*. Then we combine *Stereo-Net* and *Focus-Net-Guided* in Sect. 4.2 to construct *BDfF-Net* for high quality depth from binocular focal stacks.

4.1   Focus-Net and Focus-Net-Guided for DfF

Motivated by successes from multi-scale networks, we propose *Focus-Net*, a multiscale network to extract depth from a single focal stack. Specifically, *Focus-Net* consists of four branches of various scales. Except for the first branch, other branches subsample the image by using different strides in the convolutional layer, enabling aggregation of information over large areas. Therefore, both the high-level information from the coarse feature maps and the fine details could be preserved. At the end of the branch, a deconvolutional layer is introduced to upsample the image to its original resolution. Finally, we stack the multi-scale features maps together, resulting in a concatenated per-pixel feature vector. The feature vectors are further fused by layers of convolutional networks to predict the final depth value.

An illustration of the network architecture is shown in Fig. 3(a). We use 3 × 3 kernels for most layers except those convolutional layers used for downsampling and upsampling, where a larger kernel is used to cover more pixels. Following [22], the number of feature maps increases as the image resolution decreases. Between the convolutional layers we insert PReLU layer [4] to increase the network's nonlinearity. For the input of the network, we simply stack the focal stack images together along the channel's dimension.

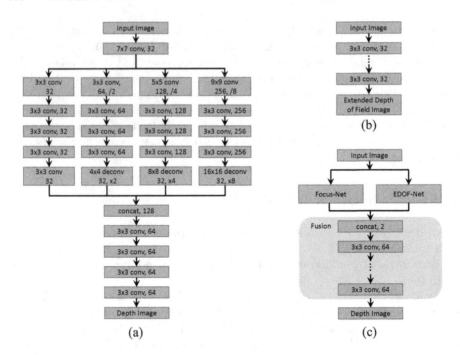

Fig. 3. (a) *Focus-Net* is a multi-scale network for conducting depth-from-focus. (b) *EDoF-Net* consists of 20 layers of convolutional layers to form an extended depth-of-field (EDoF) image from focal stack. (c) Our *Focus-Net-Guided* combines *Focus-Net* and *EDoF-Net* by using the EDoF image to refine the depth estimation.

To further enhance the depth image quality, we set out to extract the EDoF image from the focal stack, and use it to guide the refinement of the depth image. Existing EDoF image extraction methods [10,23] are suboptimal in terms of computational efficiency. Thus, we seek to directly output an EDoF image from a separate network, which we termed *EDoF-Net*. *EDoF-Net* is composed of 20 convolutional layers, with PRelu as its activation function. The input of the *EDoF-Net* is the focal stack, the same as the input of *Focus-Net*, and the output is the EDoF image. With the kernel size of 3×3, a 20 layer convolutional network will produce a receptive field of 41×41, which is larger than the size of the largest blur kernel. Figure 3(b) shows the architecture of *EDoF-Net*.

Finally, we concatenate the depth image from *Focus-Net* and the EDoF image from the *EDoF-Net*, and fuse them by using another 10 convolutional layers. We call the new network *Focus-Net-Guided*, as illustrated in Fig. 3(c).

4.2 Stereo-Net and BDfF-Net for Depth from Binocular Focal Stack

Given the EDoF stereo pair from the *EDoF-Net*, we set out to estimate depth from stereo using another network, termed *Stereo-Net*. For stereo matching, it is

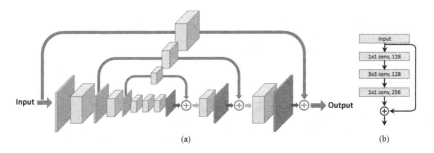

Fig. 4. (a) *Stereo-Net* follows the Hourglass network architecture which consists of the max pooling layer (yellow), the deconvolution layer (green) and the residual module (blue). (b) Shows the detailed residual module. (Color figure online)

critical to consolidate both local and global cues to generate precise pixel-wise disparity.

To this end, we propose *Stereo-Net* by adopting the Hourglass network architecture [16], as shown in Fig. 4. The advantage of this network is that it can attentively evaluate the coherence of features across scales by utilizing large amount of residual modules [5]. The network composes of a downsampling part, an upsampling part and connection layers comprising of residual modules. In this way, the network could both learn a holistic representation of input images and maintain fine structures. Prediction is generated at the end of the upsampling part. One round of downsampling and upsampling part can be viewed as one iteration of predicting, whereas additional rounds can be stacked to refine initial estimates. For *Stereo-Net*, we use two rounds of downsampling and upsampling parts as they already give a good performance. After each pair of downsampling and upsampling parts, supervision is applied using the same ground truth disparity map. The final output is of the same resolution as the input images.

Finally, we construct *BDfF-Net* by concatenating the results from *Stereo-Net*, *Focus-Net-Guided*, and adding 10 more convolutional layers. The convolutional layers serve to find the optimal combination from focus cue and disparity cue.

5   Implementation

Given the focal stack as input and ground truth color/depth image as label, we train all the networks end-to-end. In our implementation, we first train each network individually, then fine-tune the concatenated network with the pre-trained weights as initialization. Because *Focus-Net* and *Focus-Net-Guided* contains multiple convolutional layers for downsampling, the input image needs to be cropped to the nearest number that is multiple of 8 for both height and width. We use the mean absolute error with l_2-norm regularization as the loss for all models.

Following [7], we apply batch normalization after the convolution layer and before PRelu layer. We initialize the weights using the technique from [4]. We employ MXNET as the learning framework and train and test the networks on

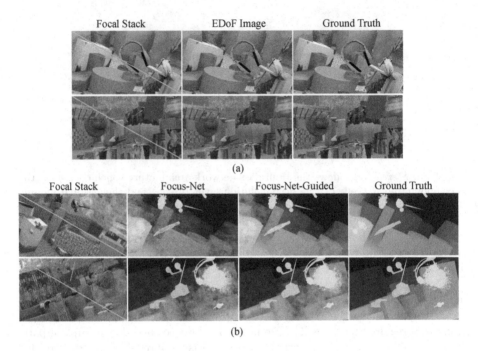

Fig. 5. (a) Results of our *EDoF-Net*. First column shows two slices of the focal stack focusing at different depth. Second and third columns show the EDoF and ground truth image respectively. (b) Comparisons on *Focus-Net* vs. *Focus-Net-Guided*, i.e., without and with the guide of an all-focus image.

a NVIDIA K80 graphic card. We make use of the Adam optimizer and set the weight decay $= 0.002$, $\beta 1 = 0.9$, $\beta 2 = 0.999$. The initial learning rate is set to be 0.001. All the networks are trained for 80 epochs.

6   Experiments

6.1   Extract the EDoF Image from Focal Stack

We train *EDoF-Net* on a single focal stack of 16 slices. Although the network has a simple structure, the output EDoF image features high image quality. Our network also runs much faster than conventional methods based on global optimization: for 960×540 images it runs at 4 frames per second. Figure 5(a) shows the result of *EDoF-Net*. Our experiments also show that it suffices to guide the refinement of depth image and be used as the input of *Stereo-Net*.

6.2   Depth Estimation from Focal Stack

As mentioned in Sect. 4.1, to construct *Focus-Net-Guided*, we first train *Focus-Net* and *EDoF-Net* respectively, then concatenate their output with more fusion

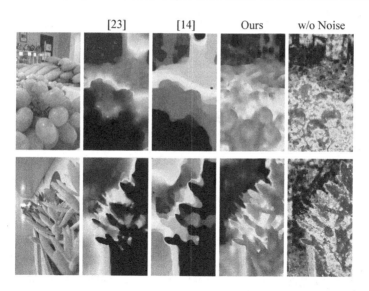

Fig. 6. Comparisons on depth estimation from a single focal stack using our *Focus-Net-Guided* vs. [23] and [14]. *Focus-Net-Guided* is able to maintain smoothness on flat regions while preserving sharp occlusion boundaries. The last column shows Results from *Focus-Net-Guided* trained by the clean dataset without poisson noise. [23] and [14] generate depth value while our *Focus-Net-Guided* generates disparity value, so the colors of the images are inverted. (Color figure online)

layers and train the combination. Figure 5 shows the result of both *Focus-Net* and *Focus-Net-Guided*. We observe that *Focus-Net* produces results with splotchy artifact, and depth bleeds across object's boundary. However, *Focus-Net-Guided* utilizes the EDoF color image to assist depth refinement, alleviating the artifacts and leading to clearer depth boundary. It is worth noting that we also trained a network that has identical structure to *Focus-Net-Guided* from scratch, but the result is of inferior quality. We suspect this is due to the good initialization provided by the pre-trained model.

We compare our DfF results with [23] and [14] using the data provided by the authors of [23]. We select 16 images from their focal stack for DfF. Figure 6 illustrates the results. Our *Focus-Net-Guided* is capable of predicting disparity value with higher quality, while using significantly less time (0.9 s) than [23] (10 min) and [14] (4 s).

Table 1. MAE and running time of models.

	Focus-Net	*Focus-Net-Guided*	*Stereo-Net*	*BDfF-Net*
MAE	0.045	0.031	0.024	0.021
Time (s)	0.6	0.9	2.8	9.7

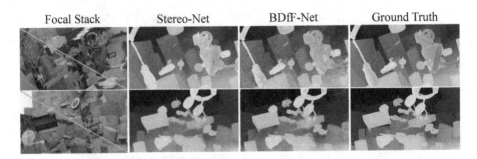

Fig. 7. Comparisons on results only using *Stereo-Net* vs. the composed *BDfF-Net*. *BDfF-Net* produces much sharper boundaries while reducing blocky artifacts.

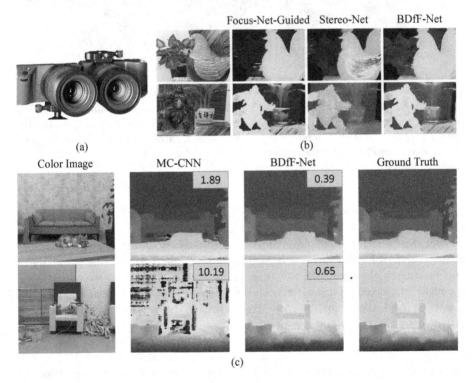

Fig. 8. (a) To emulate our B-DfF setup, we combine a pair of Lytro Illum cameras into a stereo setup. (b) Comparisons of *Focus-Net-Guided*, *Stereo-Net* and *BDfF-Net* on data captured with (a). (c) Comparisons with [29] on data captured with RGB-D camera (on top-right shows MAE of each predicted disparity map). (Color figure online)

We also train the *Focus-Net-Guided* on a clean dataset without Poisson noise. It performs better on synthetic data, but exhibits severe noise pattern on real images, as shown in the last column of Fig. 6. The experiment confirms the necessity to add noise to the dataset for simulating real images.

6.3   Depth Estimation from Stereo and Binocular Focal Stack

Figure 7 shows the results from *Stereo-Net* and *BDfF-Net*. Compared with *Focus-Net-Guided*, *Stereo-Net* gives better depth estimation. This is expected since *Stereo-Net* requires binocular focal stacks as input, while *Focus-Net-Guided* only use a single focal stack. However, *Stereo-Net* exhibits blocky artifacts and overly smoothes boundary. In contrast, depth prediction from *BDfF-Net* features sharper edges. Table 1 describes the mean absolute error (MAE) and running time of all models.

6.4   Real Scene Experiment

We further conduct tests on real scenes. To physically implement B-DfF, we construct a light field stereo pair by using two Lytro Illum cameras, as illustrated in Fig. 8(a). Light field camera contains a microlens array to capture multiple views of the scene, allowing users to perform post-capture refocusing. In our experiment, the two light field cameras share the same configuration including the zoom and focus settings. The raw images are pre-processed using Light Field Toolbox [2]. Finally, we conduct refocusing using shift-and-add algorithm [17] to synthesize the focal stack. Figure 8(b) shows the predicted depth from *Focus-Net-Guided*, *Stereo-Net* and *BDfF-Net*. Results show that *BDfF-Net* benefits from both *Focus-Net-Guided* and *Stereo-Net* to offer smoother depth with sharp edges. The experiments also demonstrate that models learned from our dataset could be transferred to predict real scene depth.

For quantitative analysis, we use a RGB-D camera (Kinect) to collect ground-truth depth. We mount the Kinect on a translation stage and move it horizontally to obtain a stereo pair of color images and disparity images, which we utilize to synthesize dual focal stacks using *Virtual DSLR* [26]. Figure 8(c) compares our *BDfF-Net* with the stereo matching method from [29]. Note that our method produces accurate results in textureless regions while the results from [29] contain large errors. This demonstrates the advantage of our approach, which effectively incorporates both focus and disparity cues in a multi-scale scheme.

7   Discussions and Future Work

Our deepeye solution exploits efficient learning and computational light field imaging to infer depths from a focal stack pair. Our technique mimics human vision system that simultaneously employs binocular stereo matching and monocular depth-from-focus. Comprehensive experiments show that our technique is able to produce high-quality depth estimation orders of magnitudes faster than the prior art. In addition, we have created a large dual focal stack database with ground truth disparity.

Our current implementation limits the input size of our network to be focal stacks of 16 layers. In the future, we will investigate approaches to handle denser focal stack. Further, aside from computer vision, we hope our work will stimulate significant future work in human perception and the nature of human eyes.

Acknowledgements. This work is supported by the National Key Research and Development Program (2018YFB2100500), the programs of NSFC (61976138 and 61977047), STCSM (2015F0203-000-06), and SHMEC (2019-01-07-00-01-E00003).

References

1. Chen, Z., Sun, X., Wang, L., Yu, Y., Huang, C.: A deep visual correspondence embedding model for stereo matching costs. In: ICCV, pp. 972–980 (2015)
2. Dansereau, D., Pizarro, O., Williams, S.: Decoding, calibration and rectification for lenselet-based plenoptic cameras. In: CVPR, pp. 1027–1034 (2013)
3. Hasinoff, S.W., Kutulakos, K.N.: Confocal stereo. IJCV **81**(1), 82–104 (2009)
4. He, K., Zhang, X., Ren, S., Sun, J.: Delving deep into rectifiers: surpassing human-level performance on imagenet classification. In: ICCV, pp. 1026–1034 (2015)
5. He, K., Zhang, X., Ren, S., Sun, J.: Deep residual learning for image recognition. In: CVPR, pp. 770–778 (2016)
6. Held, R., Cooper, E., Banks, M.: Blur and disparity are complementary cues to depth. Curr. Biol. **22**(5), 426–431 (2012)
7. Ioffe, S., Szegedy, C.: Batch normalization: accelerating deep network training by reducing internal covariate shift. In: ICML, pp. 448–456 (2015)
8. Klarquist, W.N., Geisler, W.S., Bovik, A.C.: Maximum-likelihood depth-from-defocus for active vision. In: International Conference on Intelligent Robots and Systems, vol. 3, pp. 374–379 (1995)
9. Knobelreiter, P., Reinbacher, C., Shekhovtsov, A., Pock, T.: End-to-end training of hybrid CNN-CRF models for stereo. In: CVPR, pp. 2339–2348 (2017)
10. Kuthirummal, S., Nagahara, H., Zhou, C., Nayar, S.K.: Flexible depth of field photography. TPAMI **33**(1), 58–71 (2011)
11. Luo, W., Schwing, A.G., Urtasun, R.: Efficient deep learning for stereo matching. In: TPAMI, pp. 5695–5703 (2016)
12. Malik, A.S., Shim, S.O., Choi, T.S.: Depth map estimation using a robust focus measure. In: ICIP, pp. 564–567 (2007)
13. Mayer, N., et al.: A large dataset to train convolutional networks for disparity, optical flow, and scene flow estimation. In: CVPR, pp. 4040–4048 (2016)
14. Moeller, M., Benning, M., Schoenlieb, C.B., Cremers, D.: Variational depth from focus reconstruction. TIP **24**(12), 5369–5378 (2015)
15. Nayar, S.K.: Shape from focus system. In: CVPR, pp. 302–308 (1992)
16. Newell, A., Yang, K., Deng, J.: Stacked hourglass networks for human pose estimation. In: Leibe, B., Matas, J., Sebe, N., Welling, M. (eds.) ECCV 2016. LNCS, vol. 9912, pp. 483–499. Springer, Cham (2016). https://doi.org/10.1007/978-3-319-46484-8_29
17. Ng, R., Levoy, M., Bredif, M., Duval, G., Horowitz, M., Hanrahan, P.: Light field photography with a hand-held plenoptic camera. Stanford Computer Science Technical reports, vol. 2, pp. 1–11 (2005)
18. Park, H., Lee, K.M.: Look wider to match image patches with convolutional neural networks. IEEE Sig. Process. Lett. **24**(12), 1788–1792 (2016)

19. Rajagopalan, A.N., Chaudhuri, S., Mudenagudi, U.: Depth estimation and image restoration using defocused stereo pairs. TPAMI **26**(11), 1521–1525 (2004)
20. Scharstein, D., Szeliski, R.: A taxonomy and evaluation of dense two-framestereo correspondence algorithms. IJCV **47**(1–3), 7–42 (2002)
21. Schechner, Y.Y., Kiryati, N.: Depth from defocus vs. stereo: how different really are they? IJCV **39**(2), 141–162 (2000)
22. Simonyan, K., Zisserman, A.: Very deep convolutional networks for large-scale image recognition. CoRR abs/1409.1556 (2015)
23. Suwajanakorn, S., Hernandez, C., Seitz, S.M.: Depth from focus with your mobile phone. In: CVPR, pp. 3497–3506 (2015)
24. Takeda, Y., Hiura, S., Sato, K.: Fusing depth from defocus and stereo with coded apertures. In: CVPR, pp. 209–216 (2013)
25. Vaish, V., Levoy, M., Szeliski, R., Zitnick, C.L., Kang, S.B.: Reconstructing occluded surfaces using synthetic apertures: stereo, focus and robust measures. In: CVPR, pp. 2331–2338 (2006)
26. Yang, Y., Lin, H., Yu, Z., Paris, S., Yu, J.: Virtual DSLR: high quality dynamic depth-of-field synthesis on mobile platforms. In: Digital Photography and Mobile Imaging XII, pp. 1–9 (2016)
27. Zagoruyko, S., Komodakis, N.: Learning to compare image patches via convolutional neural networks. In: CVPR, pp. 4353–4361 (2015)
28. Zbontar, J., LeCun, Y.: Computing the stereo matching cost with a convolutional neural network. In: CVPR, pp. 1592–1599 (2015)
29. Zbontar, J., LeCun, Y.: Stereo matching by training a convolutional neural network to compare image patches. J. Mach. Learn. Res. **17**(1–32), 2 (2016)

Small Defect Detection in Industrial X-Ray Using Convolutional Neural Network

Long Cheng, Ping Gong[(⊠)], Guanghui Qiu, Jing Wang,
and Ziyuan Liu

Beijing University of Posts and Telecommunications, Beijing 100876, China
{chenglong, pgong, qgh, wjing, lzy700}@bupt.edu.cn

Abstract. It's crucial to ensure the complete reliability of each metallic component in vehicle industry. In the past few years, X-ray testing has been widely adopted in defect detection field. Due to huge production in industry, it's absolutely necessary for manufacturers to employ more intelligent and automated inspection scheme to detect defects efficiently. This study develops an accurate and fast detection method combined with X-ray images using computer vision and deep learning techniques to recognize small defects, mark theirs' area and divide them into different levels according to their sizes. This program modifies the original RetinaNet to adapt to tiny defects. We present a novel data augmentation method aiming to expand the number of defects. Then a multi-scale transform module is designed to generate scale-specific feature map which helps to grade defects better. Experiments show that the proposed method can achieve significant precision improvement over X-ray machine with similarly high recall rate. Both speed and accuracy of this scheme reach practical industrial-service demand.

Keywords: Defect detection · X-ray · Dilated convolution · CNN

1 Introduction

Defect detection is an indispensable part of the aluminum alloy wheel production line, which is usually arranged after casting the wheel. Different from the surface scratches and bumps of the finished product, in this phase we need to detect internal flawed region. These defects, such as bubble, shrink and so on, were born during the casting period. Therefore, X-ray images must be generated by means of an X-ray camera at first. Then X-ray machine can filter a small part of products that are obviously free of any flaws by using light and dark changes between pixels. Despite this, it still need a lot of manpower to screen remaining X-ray images for 24 h all days without rest because of the huge production and the rather low precision of the machine.

At present, with the rapid development of computing power, more and more people focus on deep learning technology. Since deep convolutional neural networks made great progress in ILSVRC2012 [1], convolutional networks quickly reach peak in various computer vision tasks such as image classification, object detection, instance segmentation and so on. A large number of new object detection algorithms [2–5] have been proposed from different optimization perspectives. Meanwhile, traditional image

© Springer Nature Switzerland AG 2019
Z. Lin et al. (Eds.): PRCV 2019, LNCS 11859, pp. 366–377, 2019.
https://doi.org/10.1007/978-3-030-31726-3_31

processing algorithms and plain machine learning methods can hardly satisfy our need in many complex industrial scenarios.

In this paper, we apply RetinaNet [6] with ResNet-101 [7], which achieves start-of-the-art performance in generic object detection task, into the wheel internal defect detection. What's more, to enhance the performance of the model, it has been modified in three aspects.

1.1 Small Defect Data Augmentation

Because the casting process is relatively stable, the cost to collect enough defective wheel samples is enormous. Besides, there are only one or two flaws in the most X-ray images. The proportion of defective areas to the entire image is so small that it's hard for model to learn enough valid information. Therefore, we choose data augmentation method, including copying and pasting small defects in the same image. Specifically, we pull out the defective area at first and paste it into the other position of the hub in the original image. This method can greatly increase the amount of defects.

1.2 Low-Level Features Detection

Deep convolutional networks can extract high-level semantic features of images. However, there are very little small object information remaining in the high-level features due to multiple down-sampling. Thus we add an extra low-level feature as an output layer to improve the detection of small defect and fuse it with the upper-level features to increase its semantic information. Through this strategy, the detection effect for small defects is greatly improved.

1.3 Multi-scale Transform Module

In training and test period, defects are assigned to different feature maps according to their sizes. But for some middle layers, it's hard for model to grade defects clearly due to its insensitivity to objective scale. Thus a multi-scale transform module, called MST for short, is designed to generate scale-specific feature maps. This module consists of a parallel multi-branch architecture in which each branch has different receptive fields with the help of dilated convolutions. The most suitable receptive field is well-designed to match the scale of defects.

Based on this modified RetinaNet, experimental results on the wheel hub X-ray image datasets achieve 5.0 MAP higher than baseline.

2 Related Work

Defect detection methods based on X-ray images normally adopt image processing algorithms. [8] experimented various of traditional methods to identify defects, including Gabor, SIFT, LBP and so on, and at last achieved best result by a simple LBP descriptor with a SVM-linear classifier. [9] applied digital fringes and binary image processing techniques to detect the tiny bump defects.

In recent years, the theory based on CNN is widely adopted in object detection task. RCNN [2], which was proposed in 2014, was the first to detect objects with convolutional networks. Since then, Faster RCNN [3] introduced RPN, which integrated RCNN into an end-to-end model. To overcome slow detection speed of two-stage algorithms, SSD [4] and YOLO [5] was proposed. Afterwards RetinaNet solved the extreme imbalance between easy and hard samples, which achieves start-of-the-art performance in both speed and accuracy.

Referring to these algorithms, defects in the wheel hub can be treated as objects. Thus we adopt modified RetinaNet to make bounding box regression to these objects and locate their positions.

2.1 RetinaNet

Object detection task has been dominated by more accurate two-stage detectors developed by RCNN for a long time. In contrast, one-stage detectors can achieve faster detection speeds, but at the expense of partial precision [10]. RetinaNet expounds the main reason for low precision of one-stage detectors represented by SSD is extreme imbalance over foreground and background. This is caused by the fact that detectors sets too many possible object locations. The imbalance problem is solved by modifying the standard cross entropy in RentinaNet, which down-weights the loss of well-classified samples. In defect detection, the number of defects is so small and defective area accounts for a tiny proportion of the entire image, which leads to an extreme imbalance between positive and negative samples. Thus, RetinaNet is chosen as the basic model. Overview of RetinaNet can be inferred from Fig. 1.

The main innovation of RetinaNet is to modify standard cross entropy to solve the imbalance problem. In one-stage object detection algorithms, in order to accurately cover all targets, numbers of possible candidate locations need to be set. However, only a few candidates match the real object bounding boxes. This imbalance is also evident in defects detection. The imbalance leads to two severe problems: (a) Too many well-classified examples can lead to inefficient training and difficult for model to learn useful information; (b) Easy negatives will overlord training process and result in model degradation. RetinaNet proposed Focal Loss, which reduces the loss of simple samples to focus the model on difficult samples, and add a balance parameter α_t of positive and negative samples. The specific loss expression is shown in (1), where p_t means classified probability of the model.

$$FL(p_t) = -\alpha_t(1 - p_t)^\gamma log(p_t) \tag{1}$$

2.2 FPN

For most detectors based on multi-scale feature layers, the shallow feature maps with more detailed information are mainly responsible for the detection of small targets. However, the shallow features are not good enough due to insufficient semantic information, while the high-level features are just on the opposite. Thus FPN [11] was proposed to solve this problem. FPN exploits pyramidal hierarchy of convolutional

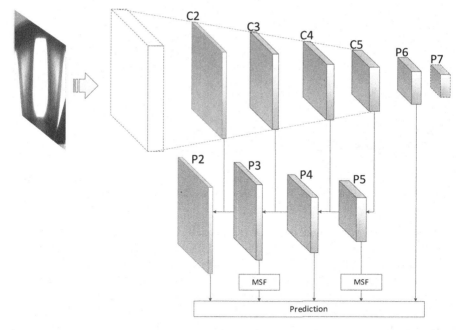

Fig. 1. Overview of modified RetinaNet. The P7 is used as an output layer in original RetinaNet and P2 not. In this paper, P2 is added and P7 is abandoned. The MSF module is added after P3 and P5.

networks to construct feature pyramids, which combines high-level semantic features with low-level pixel features by means of a top-down architecture with up-sampling operations. Through this way, FPN has a perfect effect on targets of different scales, especially on small objects, which is highly suitable for this small defect detection. In RetinaNet, the basic structure applies SSD network with FPN. As in Fig. 1, the layers, including P2, P3, P4, P5, are connected with backbone through FPN mode.

3 Data

3.1 Datasets

In order to establish a standard dataset which is in keeping with actual production, X-ray images are exported from the Dicastal Corporation database. Two representative defects are selected as shown in Fig. 2. Defects are located on wheel spokes and hub respectively, both born in the casting phase. The characteristics of defects can be obviously seen by examples. Tiny defects are too small to distinguish. Moreover, since defects often appear in pieces, a plurality of small defects are treated as a defective object together by a larger bounding box. However, such a defective area contains a lot of unnecessary background information, and the boundary becomes difficult to define, which brings great obstruction to our detection.

 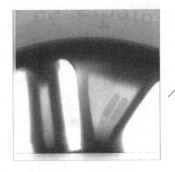 

Fig. 2. Examples of defects. The left one shows a level-3 defect on the spoke and the right shows a level-1 defect on the rim. The right defect is so small that partial enlargement is shown.

A large number of original images were manually screened and marked. All images which are free of defective areas were discarded. Due to the relatively small amount of defects, 1053 defective images were collected finally, including 1288 defect instances. The original size of X-ray images is 1024*1024 pixels. All defects are divided into three grades according to their sizes, namely, level 1, level 2 and level 3. The annotations of dataset are labelled by trained people in the style of COCO [12]. The statistics of training set, validation set and test set are shown in Table 1. More than 80% of defects are in level 1 which are too small to identify.

Table 1. Statics of datasets.

	Sample	Defects	Level 1	Level 2	Level 3
Training	843	1021	830	133	58
Validation	85	108	89	10	9
Test	125	159	132	16	11
Total	1053	1288	1051	159	78

3.2 Metrics

In deep learning, it's common to evaluate the performance of a simple model by means of accuracy, precision, recall, and so on. For a binary classification model, the distribution of labels and predictions can be shown as Table 2.

Table 2. Label and prediction for binary classification.

		Prediction	
		True	False
Label	True	True positive(TP)	False negative(FN)
	False	False positive(FP)	True negative(TN)

Then these metrics can be calculated individually by formulas shown in (2) (3) (4).

$$Accuracy = \frac{TP + TN}{TP + TN + FP + FN} \tag{2}$$

$$Precision = \frac{TP}{TP + FP} \tag{3}$$

$$Recall = \frac{TP}{TP + FN} \tag{4}$$

In the object detection task, it is difficult to measure the performance of a model with above single metric. Thus IOU (intersection over union) is used to indicate the overlap between the detection and the real area, that is, intersection of two regions divided by union. It is considered that the correct result is detected if IOU is greater than 0.5. For a certain category of object, the prediction results can be sorted according to the classification confidence and the corresponding precision and recall can be calculated respectively. Then the area under the P-R curve is AP. For multi-class detection, MAP can be calculated as the mean of AP value for each class. As the most important evaluation metric in the object detection task, MAP can reflect the comprehensive ability of a model in different aspects such as false detection, missing inspection and judgment accuracy.

4 Methods

In this hub defect dataset, the proportion of defective area to whole image is so small that the amount of negative samples is far more than positive ones during training phase. In order to better deal with these problems, we choose to apply the modified RetinaNet as object detection algorithm.

4.1 Data Augmentation

In the raw dataset, there are only one or two defects in most X-ray images so that the total number of positive samples is small. Thus it's necessary to resort to data augmentation technology. The main method adopted is to copy and paste small defects to construct defects artificially. Specifically, the defective instance generates a flawed mask and then it's pasted elsewhere in the same image. One of the processed images is shown in Fig. 3.

At first, use the annotation of an image to extract defective areas as a flawed mask. And then, there is two basic requirements for pasting. The first point is that defects are required to be pasted into hub area and not overlap with others and the second is that the pasted defects should be in harmony with the surroundings. The data augmentation algorithm is outline in Table 3. In X-ray images, the blank area is fully white so the hub area can be directly divided by a simple Image Binarization method. Then randomly select a coordinate point as a candidate center point and calculate the IOU value of the chosen area to other defects. If there is an IOU value greater than threshold, reselect

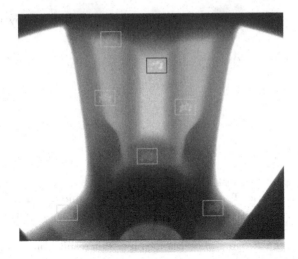

Fig. 3. Example of the data augmentation method. The black box is the original defect and the others in red are generated by data augmentation. (Color figure online)

one. After that, paste the flawed mask with the transparency at 60% to smooth the boundary of defects. Finally, repeat the paste process multiple times, that is N times in Table 3, to generate several defects. Other common data augmentation methods such as horizontal flip, translation and crop are also applied.

Table 3. Data augmentation algorithm for each image.

1: **Input** : An image X with defects set A

2: determine gray hub area $H_x = X < 250$

3: copy A to A_{new}

4: **for** $k = 1,2, \dots, N$ **do**

5:      Randomly choose a center point $x, y \in (0,1024)$, a defect $A_i(x_{1i}, y_{1i}, x_{2i}, y_{2i}) \in A$

6:      calculate pasting area (x_1, y_1, x_2, y_2) according to (x, y) and A_i

7:      **If** $Mean(H_x[x_1:x_2, y_1:y_2]) > 0.9$ and $Max(IOU([x_1:x_2, y_1:y_2], A_{new})) < 0.1$ **then**

8:          $X[x_1:x_2, y_1:y_2] = 0.6 * X[x_1:x_2, y_1:y_2] + 0.4 * X[x_{1i}:x_{2i}, y_{1i}:y_{2i}]$

9:          append (x_1, y_1, x_2, y_2) to A_{new}

10: **end for**

11: update A_{new} to A

4.2 Low-Level Features Extraction

In this dataset, most of the defective area are so small and basically there is no particularly large target. The configuration of generic object detection algorithm doesn't exactly match the hub defect detection. Thus the structure of RetinaNet is modified to adapt to tiny flaw identification.

Due to the intrinsic multi-level structure of deep convolutional network, it's easy to extract features of an image in different levels separately. The original RetinaNet selects three feature layers of the backbone network, including C3, C4 and C5, and then adds two additional convolutional layers P6 and P7. Afterwards the former three feature maps are connected through FPN mode. In this defect detection, the feature layer C2 of backbone, which is a lower layer than C3, is selected as an available feature map and fused with high-level features. The oversized feature layer P7 is removed because there is no such big defective area. Lower convolutional layers have better details for better detection result. The specific network structure is shown in Fig. 1.

4.3 Multi-scale Transform Module

In defect detection task, not only the location of defects needs to be detected accurately, but also defects need to be classified into different grades according to their scales. The common defects are classified into three levels, including level 1, level 2 and level 3. However, the generic detection algorithms are not insensitive to object size so that it is difficult to achieve a good classification effect. Therefore, to deal with scale variation in the defect detection, a multi-scale transform module, called MST for short, is designed elaborately. For different grades of defects, this module consists of a parallel multi-branch architecture aiming to generate scale-specific feature maps.

In the MST module, all branches, which have the same network with dilated convolutions [13], are applied to extract features respectively, while each branch gets different receptive fields with specific dilation rate [14]. Dilated convolutions with dilation rate t_i means to insert $t_i - 1$ zeros between convolutional kernel values, enlarging the filter size without additional parameters and computations. The receptive field of dilated convolution is calculated as (5), where k means the size of convolutional kernel and i means the ith layer.

$$RF_i = RF_{i-1} + (k - 1) * t_i \tag{5}$$

The most effective receptive field is strongly related to the scale of objects. The convolutional branch with smaller receptive field is more suitable for detecting minor defects, while the branch with larger dilation rate can extract the features of severe defects better. Thus, adjusting the receptive field by regulate the dilation rate can help to achieve a better effect on detecting objects of different scales. At last, all the branches features are merged into an integrated feature map as an output. The architecture of the multi-scale transform module is shown in Fig. 4.

In this paper, the multi-scale transform module is arranged over P3 and P5 as shown in Fig. 1 because the defects assigned to the two layers are hard to grade. Specifically, the MST module arranged over P2 is to distinguish level 1 and level 2

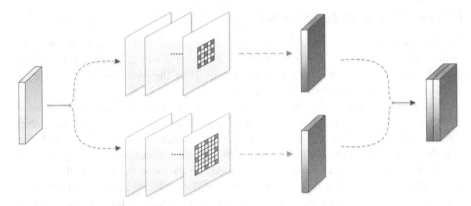

Fig. 4. Structure of the MST module. Each branch consists of several dilated convolutional layers with the same dilation rate while different branches have different dilation rates.

defects and the another one is to distinguish level 2 and level 3. Thus the dilated rates of two MST modules are set to 1,2 and 2,3 respectively. For each branch, the number of dilated convolutional layers is set to 5. What's more, the multi-scale transform module can greatly enrich the extracted features, which helps model identify defects of different grades more accurately [15].

5   Experiments

In this section, experiments are conducted on the hub defect dataset. Considering that the dataset is not big enough to train a complete model like RetinaNet, all following models are pre-trained on the COCO [11] dataset. After that, detectors are trained carefully on the hub dataset described in Sect. 3. Ablation experiments are conducted on the validation set to verify our modification on RetinaNet.

5.1   Implementation Details

We re-implement RetinaNet with ResNet-101 as our baseline method in Keras. The input images are resized to 800*800 pixels. All models used in this article is trained end-to-end in a batch size of 2 on 2 2080TI GPUs with Adam. At First, learning rate start from 0.01 and backbone network is frozen. And then train the whole model with learning rate falling to 0.001. For the evaluation, models are evaluated by MAP described in Sect. 4 (same as VOC [16]) and the threshold is set to 0.5. Other implementation details are as in [1]. The entire training process takes about 10 h excluding pre-training process.

5.2   Ablation Studies

Ablation studies are conducted by keeping other configuration constant and the experimental results are shown in Table 4. The MST module is verified with low-level features modification together.

Table 4. Ablation Studies.

Method	Data Aug	MST	AP@0.5
(a) Baseline	–	–	35.2
(b) Baseline w Data Aug	✔		37.0
(c) Baseline w MST		✔	36.7
(d) Ours	✔	✔	38.4

From the experimental results, the methods used in this paper has greatly improved the performance of RetinaNet on defect detection. Without any other tricks, AP of the model has improved by 3.2 compared to baseline.

Table 5. Comparison with other models.

Method	Backbone	AP@0.5
(a) Faster RCNN	ResNet-101	31.5
(b) Faster RCNN w FPN	ResNet-101-FPN	34.1
(c) RetinaNet	ResNet-101	35.2
(d) RFCN	ResNet-50	33.0
(e) Ours (single scale)	ResNet-101	38.4
(f) Ours (multi scale)	ResNet-101	40.2

5.3   Comparison with Other Models

To further verify the superiority of our modified RetinaNet, we try to compare it with other object detection models. We re-implement Faster RCNN with FPN or not and RFCN [17]. All implementation details are the same as their original papers. From the experimental results in Table 5, it's obviously to find out that our modified RetinaNet is much better than other models. What's more, with multi-scale training/test, AP of our model has improved by 5.0 compared to baseline.

5.4   Comparison with X-Ray Machine

The existing x-ray machine applies image processing technology to detect more than a dozen partial images for each wheel hub. If an image is judged to be defective, all images of the hub will be exported to be determined by well-trained workers. Under such conditions, the X-ray machine can get a high recall rate at 100%. According to historical statistics, the actual defect rate is only about 1%, while images exported by the X-ray machine account for about 35% of the total, including the true defective and false defective samples. Due to the low precision, workers are required to assist in detecting defects in turn all days.

In this paper, our proposed method could guarantee the same high recall rate by lowering the threshold of classification confidence to 0.4 at the expense of partial precision. Even so, all defective samples judged by modified RetinaNet account for about 24% of the total as in Table 6. Compared with the x-ray machine, the workload of workers can be reduced by 31.4%, which greatly improves productivity. What's more, the speed of our model achieves 10 FPS on 1080ti, which can fully reach practical industrial-service demand.

Table 6. Comparison with X-ray machine.

Method	Recall	Precision	(TP + FP)/Total
(a) X-ray machine	100%	2.94%	35%
(b) Our model	99.99%	4.34%	24%

6 Conclusion

In this work, we apply object detection algorithm based on deep learning theory into wheel hub internal defect detection. we choose RetinaNet with ResNet-101, which achieves start-of-the-art performance in generic object detection task, as our baseline. Then apply a novel data augmentation method, extract low-level features and construct a multi-scale transform module to modify RetinaNet to deal with tiny defect detection in small dataset. Experiments show that the modified model we built achieves excellent results in hub defect detection.

References

1. Russakovsky, O., Deng, J., Su, H., et al.: ImageNet large scale visual recognition challenge. Int. J. Comput. Vis. **115**(3), 211–252 (2015)
2. Girshick, R., Donahue, J., Darrell, T., Malik, J.: Rich feature hierarchies for accurate object detection and semantic segmentation. In: CVPR (2014)
3. Ren, S., He, K., Girshick, R.B., Sun, J.: Faster R-CNN: towards real-time object detection with region proposal networks. TPAMI **39**(6), 1137–1149 (2017)
4. Liu, W., et al.: SSD: single shot multibox detector. In: Leibe, B., Matas, J., Sebe, N., Welling, M. (eds.) ECCV 2016. LNCS, vol. 9905, pp. 21–37. Springer, Cham (2016). https://doi.org/10.1007/978-3-319-46448-0_2
5. Redmon, J., Divvala, S.K., Girshick, R.B., Farhadi, A.: You only look once: unified, real-time object detection. In: CVPR, pp. 779–788 (2016)
6. Lin, G.T., Goyal, P., Girshick, R.B., He, K., Dollar, P.: Focal loss for dense object detection. In: ICCV (2017)
7. He, J.K., Zhang, X., Ren, S. Sun, J.: Deep residual learning for image recognition. In: CVPR, pp. 770–778 (2016)

8. Mery, D., Arteta, C.: Automatic defect recognition in X-Ray testing using computer vision. In: WACV (2017)
9. Yen, H., Syu, M.: Inspection of polarizer tiny bump defects using computer vision. In: ICCE (2015)
10. Huang, J., et al.: Speed/accuracy trade-offs for modern convolutional object detectors. In: CVPR (2017)
11. Lin, T.Y., Doll'ar, P., Girshick, R., He, K., Hariharan, B., Belongiev, S.: Feature pyramid networks for object detection. In: CVPR (2017)
12. Lin, T.-Y., et al.: Microsoft COCO: Common Objects in Context. In: Fleet, D., Pajdla, T., Schiele, B., Tuytelaars, T. (eds.) ECCV 2014. LNCS, vol. 8693, pp. 740–755. Springer, Cham (2014). https://doi.org/10.1007/978-3-319-10602-1_48
13. Yu, F., Koltun, V.: Multi-scale context aggregation by dilated convolutions. In: ICLR (2016)
14. Luo, W., Li, Y., Urtasun, R., Zemel, R.: Understanding the effective receptive field in deep convolutional neural networks. In: NIPS (2016)
15. Liu, S., Huang, D., Wang, Y.: Receptive field block net for accurate and fast object detection. In: ECCV (2018)
16. Everingham, M., Gool, L.J.V., Williams, C.K.I., Winn, J.M., Zisserman, A.: The pascal visual object classes (VOC) challenge. IJCV **88**(2), 303–338 (2010)
17. Dai, J., Li, Y., He, K., Sun, J.: R-FCN: object detection via region-based fully convolutional networks. In NIPS, pp. 379–387 (2016)

ODCN: Optimized Dilated Convolution Network for 3D Shape Segmentation

Likuan Qian[1], Yuanfeng Lian[1(✉)], Qian Wei[2], Shuangyuan Wu[1], and Jianbin Zhang[1]

[1] China University of Petroleum-Beijing, Beijing 102200, China
pczebra@outlook.com,
{lianyuanfeng,wsy,zhangjb}@cup.edu.cn
[2] CNPC Beijing Richfit Information Technology Co., LTD.,
Beijing 102200, China
weiqian01@cnpc.com.cn

Abstract. 3D shape segmentation is a vital and fundamental issue in 3D shape analysis tasks, and the multi-view paradigm is one of practical approaches to solve it. The typical multi-view paradigm contains an image-based convolutional neural network (CNN) for effective view-based semantic segmentation. To improve the accuracy of multi-view paradigm, this paper presents a new dilated convolution network called Optimized Dilated Convolution Network (ODCN). We derive a novel network architecture by using the gradient descent with momentum algorithm to minimize some objective functions related to neural network propagation. In addition, the dilated convolution, which increases the resolution of output feature maps without reducing the receptive field of network, is adopted for semantic segmentation. Experimental results verify that the proposed method achieves better performance over other state-of-the-art methods.

Keywords: Dilated convolution · Optimization algorithm · Multi-view · 3D shape segmentation · CNN

1 Introduction

Recently, 3D shape data has experienced explosive growth due to the fast development of AR/VR technology. 3D shape representation of objects in the form of polygonal meshes or point clouds can be easily obtained by using depth sensors on fixed or mobile ends. 3D shape segmentation [1–4] is widely applied in various tasks, including 3D shape analysis [5], texture mapping [6] and shape retrieval [7, 8]. In order to improve the quality of 3D shape segmentation, multi-view approaches [14, 15] have been extensively used. In multi-view segmentation, a set of viewpoints is selected to render 3D model to generate multiple view images, and all the images are fed into a convolutional neural network with shared weights to obtain semantic labeled maps,

---

Student as first author.

Z. Lin et al. (Eds.): PRCV 2019, LNCS 11859, pp. 378–389, 2019.
https://doi.org/10.1007/978-3-030-31726-3_32

then the maps are mapped back to the 3D shape surface. The typical multi-view shape segmentation approach has three challenges: (1) How to select multiple viewpoints so that the selected viewpoints set is able to minimize surface occlusion and completely cover the shape surface. In this paper, a method of shape surface enclosure is proposed, which obtains viewpoints set from all vertices of a tetrahedron surrounding shape surface, and complete coverage of the surface is obtained by rotating angle. (2) Multi-view approaches require semantic segmentation of all input images, but a better network designed for multi-view paradigm is still challenging [9]. This paper proposes a new variant of dilated CNN inspired by recent advance in designing network architecture by unfolding optimization algorithms [27], the proposed OCDN network is constructed based on momentum gradient descent [20]. The idea is motivated by the success of the designed networks [27] for image recognition tasks. (3) Multi-view approaches output confidence maps of each image. When these maps are fused and mapped back to the 3D shape surface, the consistency of shape boundary and occluded part must be guaranteed. In this paper, a conditional random field (CRF) [17] is used to ensure the surface consistent segmentation.

The main contribution of this paper is the Optimized Dilated Convolution Network (ODCN) for 3D shape segmentation, which belongs to multi-view paradigm. The ODCN derives its network architecture according to optimization algorithms, resulting in faster convergence speed. Compared with the most popular deep neural networks (ResNet [11], DenseNet [12]) with the same depth, the ODCN outperforms by accuracy. Dilated convolution [13] is adopted to achieve larger receptive field while maintaining the resolution of network input. It makes the ODCN more applicable for semantic segmentation at the image level and 3D shape segmentation at the mesh level. Experiments demonstrate that the ODCN outperforms other state-of-the-art approaches.

The rest of the paper is organized as follows. Some related work is reviewed in Sect. 2. The proposed ODCN is described in detail in Sect. 3. Section 4 presents and discusses experimental results, and conclusion is drawn in Sect. 5.

2   Related Work

Convolutional Neural Networks. Our work relates to advances in semantic segmentation using dilated convolutions [13, 16]. Dilated convolution increases the receptive field of a CNN without pooling operation. The VGG network [18] was modified by [13], which removed two last pooling and convolution layers, and added dilated convolutions. Yu et al. [16] raised the Dilated Residual Networks (DRN) by adding dilated convolution operations in ResNet. Li et al. [27] derived AGD-Net through Nesterov's accelerated gradient descent algorithm [32], and achieved good performance on the CIFAR dataset.

Optimization Algorithms for Deep Learning. Gradient descent method (GD) [19] obtains the global optimal solution by minimizing the loss function of all training samples, it can be very slow. The stochastic gradient descent algorithm (SGD) uses partial samples to approximate the whole samples, the final solution is often near the global optimum. Gradient descent with momentum (GDM) [20] uses momentum term to offset the fluctuations of the gradient descent, making the algorithm converge faster.

3D Shape Segmentation. Early 3D mesh model shape segmentations rely on artificially designed geometric features (such as surface curvature [21], shape context [22], etc.). Later, CNN was used [1], but this method only operated on hand-designed geometric descriptors in 2D matrices and lacked spatial coherence structure. Kalogerakis et al. [24] proposed a data-driven method for marking meshes by optimizing conditional random field (CRF). Recently, multi-view approaches [2, 14, 25] have been widely used. On the one hand, the cost of 2D image feature descriptors is lower than 3D shape descriptors. On the other hand, semantic segmentation for 2D images is more mature.

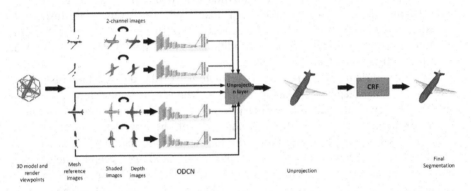

Fig. 1. Pipeline of ODCN framework for 3D shape segmentation.

3   Proposed Method

In this section, we'll introduce the ODCN, a multi-view approach for shape segmentation. Figure 1 presents the pipeline of ODCN framework. The method uses a set of images obtained from multiple viewpoints uniformly placed around the 3D model as input, and the images are segmented into a set of semantic labeling confidence maps by ODCN network. These confidence maps will be integrated and back projected to the shape surface. At last, a surface-based CRF achieves consistent segmentation of the model surface.

3.1   Input

3D shapes may not upright oriented along a consistent axis, so we need to find a tetrahedron that can enclose the surface of the shape. All the vertices of the tetrahedron form a set of observation points, where 24 virtual cameras are located. All the cameras point to the centroid of the 3D mesh model. Then according to the Phong reflection model [26], using perspective projection, four 512×512 shadow grey images are rendered from each camera by rotating 0, 90, 180 and 270 degrees along the axis from the camera to the centroid. In order to improve the accuracy of segmentation, the paper simultaneously generates depth images of 512 × 512 size of the 3D shape while rendering the shadow images. The grayscale image and depth image at the same location will be joined into a single two-channel image that is fed into the image processing module as input of the ODCN network.

Besides the shadow image and depth image, for each camera point, the 3D shape is rasterized into a mesh reference image for storing the ID of the mesh vertex corresponding to each pixel. The correspondence is determined by the proximity from 2D image pixel to the nearest 3D vertices. These mesh reference images are used in the unprojection layer for back projecting the two-channel images to the shape surface (Fig 2).

Fig. 2. Virtual cameras are placed at each vertex of a tetrahedron to render the 3D shape model.

3.2 ODCN Structure

Li et al. [27] raised an assumption: Since the propagation in standard CNN type feedforward neural networks could be summarized as finding the minimum value of an objective function, and optimization algorithms were used to solve the value, the structure of the neural network may be derived during the solving process. They used the gradient descent algorithm to minimize some functions related to the propagation in the feedforward neural networks that the networks have same linear transformation in different layers. Experiments on ImageNet and CIFAR-10 verified their hypothesis. Inspired by their creative works, we try to use gradient descent algorithm with momentum (GDM) [20] to design new network structure.

The GDM is an improved algorithm of gradient descent:

$$\delta_{i+1} = \delta_i - d\delta_i + \beta(\delta_i - \delta_{i-1}) \tag{1}$$

where β is a hyperparameter of momentum term. And the parameter of gradient is set to 1 for simplify. The formula is also vividly called the heavy ball algorithm [23].

In order to link network derivation with optimization algorithms, suppose there is a symmetric positive definite matrix U, let:

$$V = \sqrt{U}, \theta = V\delta \tag{2}$$

One of the objective functions that meets the above assumption [27] is:

$$f(\theta) = \frac{\|\theta\|^2}{2} - \sum_i \Psi_i(\theta) \tag{3}$$

where

$$\Psi_i(\theta) = \begin{cases} \frac{(V_i^T\theta)^2}{2}, & if \ V_i^T\theta > 0, \\ 0, & otherwise \end{cases} \tag{4}$$

for every θ_i in columns of θ, and $\theta_i > 0$, the derivative of the objective function is:

$$d\theta_i = \theta_i - V\Psi(V\theta_i) \tag{5}$$

using (1) to minimize (3), by substituting formula (2) and (5), formula (1) becomes

$$\begin{aligned} \theta_{i+1} &= \theta_i - (\theta_i - V\Psi(V\theta_i)) + \beta(\theta_i - \theta_{i-1}) \\ &= V\Psi(V\theta_i) + \beta\theta_i - \beta\theta_{i-1} \end{aligned} \tag{6}$$

if we replace β by β_1 and β_2, set $\beta_1 = 1, \beta_2 = -1$ and combine with formula (2), we shall get the building block of our ODCN network:

$$\delta_{i+1} = \Psi(U\delta_i) + \delta_i + \delta_{i-1} \tag{7}$$

the function $\Psi(U\delta)$ represents for combination of convolution, batch-normalization (BN) and ReLU. Figure 3 gives the structure of the building block.

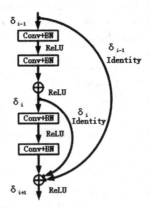

Fig. 3. The building block of ODCN

Inspired by DRN, the paper modifies the above building block by adding dilated convolution to it. Firstly, we use the mentioned building block to replace every block of ResNet-18. Secondly, pooling operations are removed from ResNet-18, and additional convolutional filters are added after the 7×7 convolution. Thirdly, we add 2-dilated convolutions in the fourth groups of convolutional layers, and replaces the fifth groups of ResNet-18 by 4-dilated convolutions. Finally, we apply a different strategy with DRN to overcome the "degridding" problem. Illustrated in Fig. 4, level 7 to level 9 remove residual connection from several additional building blocks, and have different dilated rate by 1,2,5. Since the input two-channel images are 512×512 scale, and level 10 outputs confidence maps of size 64×64,we resize the maps to 512×512 scale through a deconvolution operation of stride 8. The consistent confidence maps produced by ODCN network are back projected to 3D surface using the mentioned above mesh reference images.

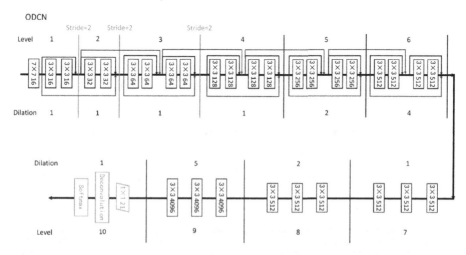

Fig. 4. Architecture of ODCN. Each black frame rectangle is a combination of convolution, BN and ReLU. The whole network is separated into different level for different rate of dilation. Deconvolution is used to resize the feature maps to 512×512.

The unprojection layer projects the confidence maps back to 3D surface. Since the paper doesn't assume that shapes are oriented consistently, there is no need to care about the order of the input images. Mesh reference images preserve pixel-to-vertex information, ensuring that the two-channel images correspond correctly to the shape surface. For each triangle mesh m, the paper specifies its label as l_m, which is the label of all two-channel images mapped to the mesh with the maximum label confidence. It's worth noting that triangular mesh reference may be absent near the edge of the model shape, and occluded portion may be mapped onto the shape contour, making the occluded portion unreliable. A reasonable operation is to use the CRF method to initialize the segmentation of shape edges and occlusion portions. Defining l_m as the initial label of mesh m, if m has no label, set $l_m = 0$. Let M be the set of the whole meshes in 3D surface, a CRF x operating on the surface representation contains a unary factor and a pairwise term:

$$\Psi(x) = \sum_{m \in M} \Psi_{unary}(x_m) + \sum_{(m,n) \in (M,M)} \Psi_{pairwise}(x_m, x_n) \qquad (8)$$

the unary term is set according to the labels produced in the projection layer:

$$\Psi_{unary}(x_m = g) = \begin{cases} 0, \forall g & if \; l_m = 0 \\ 0 & if \; l_m = g \\ \infty & else \end{cases} \qquad (9)$$

the pairwise term measures the label similarity between two neighbor meshes:

$$\Psi_{pairwise}(x_m = g_m, x_n = g_n) = \begin{cases} e^{-d_{m,n}^2} & if \; g_m \neq g_n \\ e^{-(1-d_{m,n})^2} & if \; g_m = g_n \end{cases} \qquad (10)$$

where $d_{m,n}$ represents the geodesic distance between mesh m and mesh n. Distances are normalized to [0,1]. The formula (8) can be solved by mean-field approximation [28].

4   Experimental Setup and Evaluation

In this section, we evaluate the quality of our proposed ODCN framework on two widely-used 3D datasets: PSB and COSEG datasets [29] (Fig. 5).

Fig. 5. Mesh representation of the PSB dataset.

4.1   Datasets and Implementation Details

The PSB dataset contains 11 categories and each contains 20 mesh models. The COSEG dataset is smaller with 8 categories, about 20 mesh models per category. All models in the PSB have water-tight mesh representation with clean topology. Most shapes in COSEG are similarly preprocessed, facilitating use in geometry processing.

The experiments were carried out using a Xeon Bronze 1.7 GHz CPU, powered with a GTX 1080Ti GPU and 16 GB RAM. In each category of PSB and COSEG datasets, we randomly selected 16 models as training sets and 4 models as test sets. We used GDM optimization algorithm with initial learning rate 0.01, batch size 4 and trained for 30000 iterations.

Fig. 6. Representative segmentation results produced by our ODCN framework on PSB dataset. Different categories have different numbers of labels.

4.2 Comparison Between Different Methods

Our shape segmentation approach is compared against (I) the SVM by Chang et al. [30] (II) the CNN method proposed by Guo et al. [1], (III) ShapeBoost proposed by Kalogerakis et al. [24], (IV) ShapePFCN [2] combines image-based fully convolutional networks and surface-based CRF to yield coherent segmentations of 3D shapes.

Taking labeling accuracy as metric, the performance of all above methods on the PSB dataset is shown in Table 1. Labeling accuracy measures the percentage of meshes labeled correctly according to the ground-truth mesh labeling. Our ODCN approach outperforms the best-performing prior work [1] by 0.81% in terms of the average of per-category accuracies. Moreover, our approach obtains significantly higher performance in categories like airplanes, cups, fishes, glasses, octopus, pliers and tables. The best segmentation results on PSB dataset of our approach is shown in Fig. 6. Figure 7 demonstrates the segmentation results on COSEG dataset, and Table 2 gives the numbers of labeling accuracy.

Figure 8 presents the segmentation results of the ground-truth segmentations, along with our approach (ODCN), and two high-performance prior approaches, ShapeBoost and ShapePFCN. It demonstrates that our approach can achieve better segmentation effect on the boundaries of the shapes with complex topology.

Table 1. Precision compare on PSB dataset

	SVM	CNN	ShapeBoost	ShapePFCN	Ours
Airplane	80.43	96.67	96.10	92.50	**97.00**
Bird	81.49	88.35	89.60	86.30	**93.08**
Chair	81.38	**98.67**	98.10	98.10	98.57
Cup	94.11	99.73	94.00	93.70	**99.98**
Fish	87.05	95.64	95.70	95.90	**96.23**
Glasses	95.92	97.60	96.92	96.30	**98.49**
Mech	81.87	95.60	**98.70**	97.90	98.02
Octopus	97.04	98.79	98.26	98.10	**99.11**
Plier	92.04	96.22	95.20	95.70	**96.44**
Table	90.16	99.55	99.45	99.30	**99.79**
Teddy	91.01	98.24	**98.70**	96.50	97.30
Average	88.41	96.82	96.43	95.48	**97.64**

Table 2. Labeling accuracy on COSEG dataset

	Candelabra	Chair	Fourleg	Goblet	Guitar	Iron	Lamp	Vase
Accuracy	95.73	97.82	90.58	95.94	98.30	90.08	97.19	91.13

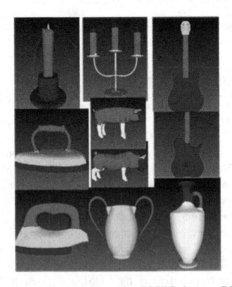

Fig. 7. Representative segmentation results on the COSEG dataset. COSEG dataset is smaller than PSB dataset but has more labels in several categories.

4.3   Analysis of the ODCN

We also evaluated our framework to its alternative degradation variations, to determine the primary source of performance gain. Table 3 shows labeling accuracy on PSB for the following cases: (i) we use ODCN network without "degridding", (ii) we adopt the unary term rather than the entire CRF. Numerical results show that both "degridding" and CRF are responsible for large performance improvement. It also proves the effectiveness of our degridding strategy.

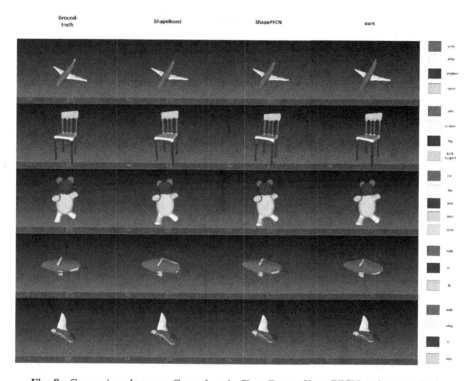

Fig. 8. Comparison between Ground-truth, ShapeBoost, ShapePFCN and our method.

Table 3. Labeling accuracy on PSB dataset for degraded variants of our approach

	ODCN	ODCN without CRF	ODCN without degridding
Airplane	97.00	84.42	71.20
Bird	82.08	78.47	68.80
Chair	98.57	92.25	78.08
Cup	99.99	93.48	87.77
Fish	96.23	80.96	73.92
Mech	98.02	93.66	82.72
Octopus	99.11	97.99	95.82

5 Conclusion

We presented a novel ODCN architecture for 3D shape segmentation. We use a tetrahedron that surrounds the shape surface to obtain multiple viewpoints. The shadow images and depth images rendered from multiple viewpoints are fused and fed to the ODCN network. The ODCN structure design is inspired by the optimization algorithms of deep learning. And dilated convolution is introduced to keep high spatial resolution all the way through the final ODCN output layer. Then, a surface-based unprojection layer aggregates ODCN outputs across multiple views and a CRF improves coherent shape segmentation. Evaluation results show that the ODCN framework has superior performance than prior works on 3D shape segmentation.

The focus of future work is to study whether faster and more stable optimization algorithms can improve the network with better performance. Another issue is to experiment the optimal viewpoint selection method based on viewpoint entropy [31].

Acknowledgments. This work was supported by National Key R&D Program of China (2016YFC0303707).

References

1. Guo, K., Zou, D., Chen, X.: 3d mesh labeling via deep convolutional neural networks. ACM Trans. Graph. **35**(1), 3:1–3:12 (2015)
2. Kalogerakis, E., Averkiou, M., Maji, S., Chaudhuri, S.: 3D shape segmentation with projective convolutional networks. In: Proceedings of the IEEE Conference on Computer Vision and Pattern Recognition, pp. 3779–3788 (2017)
3. Wang, P., Gan, Y., Shui, P.: 3D shape segmentation via shape fully convolutional networks. Comput. Graph. **70**, 128–139 (2018)
4. Shu, Z., et al.: Scribble based 3D shape segmentation via weakly-supervised learning. IEEE Trans. Vis. Comput. Graph. **1**, 1 (2019)
5. Wu, Z., Wang, Y., Shou, R., Chen, B., Liu, X.: Unsupervised co-segmentation of 3D shapes via affinity aggregation spectral clustering. Comput. Graph. **37**(6), 628–637 (2013)
6. Sander, P.V., Snyder, J., Gortler, S.J., Hoppe, H.: Texture mapping progressive meshes. In: Proceedings of the 28th Annual Conference on Computer Graphics and Interactive Techniques, pp. 409–416. ACM (2001)
7. Shalom, S., Shapira, L., Shamir, A., Cohen-Or, D.: Part analogies in sets of objects. In: Proceedings of the 1st Eurographics Conference on 3D Object Retrieval, pp. 33–40 (2008)
8. Zuckerberger, E., Tal, A., Shlafman, S.: Polyhedral surface decomposition with applications. Comput. Graph. **26**(5), 733–743 (2002)
9. He, C., Wang, C.: A survey on segmentation of 3D models. Wirel. Pers. Commun. **102**(4), 3835–3842 (2018)
10. Chen, X., Golovinskiy, A., Funkhouser, T.: A benchmark for 3D mesh segmentation. In: ACM Transactions on Graphics, pp. 73:1–73:12. ACM (2009)
11. He, K., Zhang, X., Ren, S., Sun, J.: Deep residual learning for image recognition. In: Proceeding of the IEEE Conference on Computer Vision and Pattern Recognition, pp. 770–778 (2016)

12. Huang, G., Liu, Z., Van Der Maaten, L., Weinberger, K.Q.: Densely connected convolutional networks. In: Proceedings of the IEEE Conference on Computer Vision and Pattern Recognition, pp. 4700–4708 (2017)
13. Yu, F., Koltun, V.: Multi-scale context aggregation by dilated convolutions. arXiv:1511.07122 (2015)
14. Su, H., Maji, S., Kalogerakis, E., Learned-Miller, E.: Multi-view convolutional neural networks for 3d shape recognition. In: Proceedings of the IEEE International Conference on Computer Vision, pp. 945–953 (2015)
15. Le, T., Bui, G., Duan, Y.: A multi-view recurrent neural network for 3D mesh segmentation. Comput. Graph. **66**, 103–112 (2017)
16. Yu, F., Koltun, V., Funkhouser, T.: Dilated residual networks. In: Proceedings of the IEEE Conference on Computer Vision and Pattern Recognition, pp. 472–480 (2017)
17. Chen, L.C., Papandreou, G., Kokkinos, I., Murphy, K., Yuille, A.L.: Semantic image segmentation with deep convolutional nets and fully connected CRFs. arXiv:1412.7062 (2014)
18. Simonyan, K., Zisserman, A.: Very deep convolutional networks for large-scale image recognition. arXiv:1409.1556 (2014)
19. Bertsekas, D.P.: Nonlinear programming. J. Oper. Res. Soc. **48**(3), 334 (1997)
20. Qian, N.: On the momentum term in gradient descent learning algorithms. Neural Netw. **12**(1), 145–151 (1999)
21. Gal, R., Cohen-Or, D.: Salient geometric features for partial shape matching and similarity. ACM Trans. Graph. **25**(1), 130–150 (2006)
22. Belongie, S., Malik, J., Puzicha, J.: Shape matching and object recognition using shape contexts. IEEE Trans. Pattern Anal. Mach. Intell. **4**, 509–522 (2002)
23. Polyak, B.: Some methods of speeding up the convergence of iteration methods. USSR Comput. Math. Math. Phys. **4**(5), 1–17 (1964)
24. Kalogerakis, E., Hertzmann, A., Singh, K.: Learning 3D mesh segmentation and labeling. ACM Trans. Graph. **29**(4), 102 (2010)
25. Wang, Y., Gong, M., Wang, T., Cohen-Or, D., Zhang, H., Chen, B.: Projective analysis for 3D shape segmentation. ACM Trans. Graph. **32**(6), 192:1–192:12 (2013)
26. Phong, B.T.: Illumination for computer generated pictures. Commun. ACM **18**(6), 311–317 (1975)
27. Li, H., Yang, Y., Chen, D., Lin, Z.: Optimization algorithm inspired deep neural network structure design. arXiv:1810.01638 (2018)
28. Krahenbuhl, P., Koltun, V.: Effcient inference in fully connected crfs with gaussian edge potentials. In: Advances in Neural Information Processing Systems, pp. 109–117 (2011)
29. Wang, Y., Asafi, S., Van Kaick, O., Zhang, H., Cohen-Or, D., Chen, B.: Active co-analysis of a set of shapes. ACM Trans. Graph. **31**(6), 165 (2012)
30. Chang, C.C., Lin, C.J.: LIBSVM: a library for support vector machines. ACM Trans. Intell. Syst. Technol. **2**(3), 27 (2011)
31. Shui, P., et al.: 3D shape segmentation based on viewpoint entropy and projective fully convolutional networks fusing multi-view features. In: The 24th International Conference on Pattern Recognition, pp. 1056–1061 (2018)
32. Nesterov, Y.: A method for unconstrained convex minimization problem with the rate of convergence $0(1/k^2)$. Sov. Math. Doklady **27**(2), 372–376 (1983)

Style Consistency Constrained Fusion Feature Learning for Liver Tumor Segmentation

Yunfeng Liu[1], Xibin Jia[1(✉)], Zhenghan Yang[2], and Dawei Yang[2]

[1] Beijing University of Technology, Beijing, China
hesoyamlyf@emails.bjut.edu.cn, jiaxibin@bjut.edu.cn
[2] Department of Radiology, Beijing Friendship Hospital,
Capital Medical University, Beijing, China
zhenghanyang@263.net, Dawei-yang@vip.163.com

Abstract. Due to diversity among tumor lesions and less difference between surroundings, to extract the discriminative features of a medical image is still a challenging job. In order to improve the ability in the representation of these complex objects, the type of approach has been proposed with the encoder-decoder architecture models for biomedical segmentation. However, most of them fuse coarse-grained and fine-grained features directly which will cause a semantic gap. In order to bridge the semantic gap and fuse features better, we propose a style consistency loss to constrain semantic similarity when combing the encoder and decoder features. The comparison experiments are done between our proposed U-Net with style consistency loss constraint in with the state-of-art segmentation deep networks including FCN, original U-Net and U-Net with residual block. Experimental results on LiTS-2017 show that our method achieves a liver dice gain of 1.7% and a tumor dice gain of 3.11% points over U-Net.

Keywords: Liver Tumor Segmentation · U-Net · Style consistency constraints

1 Introduction

At present, most of the deep learning networks used in biomedical segmentation have a similar structure, viz. encoder-decoder architecture, like a fully convolutional network (FCN) [1] and U-Net [2]. In these encoder-decoder networks, the most important part for segmentation is the skip connection combines the coarse-grained feature mapping from the decoder stage with the fine-grained feature mapping from the encoder stage, which helps recover fine-grained details for determining the region of interested and increasing the accuracy of segmentation.

However, the author of UNet++ [3] thinks the skip connection used in U-Net directly fast-forward high-resolution feature maps from the encoder to the decoder network which will cause a semantic gap, thereby affecting the effect of the feature combination.

In order to make a better combination of features, we introduce a Style Consistency Loss. By reducing the difference of Gram matrix between two features with the Style

---

The first student Yunfeng Liu is Master Degree Candidate.

© Springer Nature Switzerland AG 2019
Z. Lin et al. (Eds.): PRCV 2019, LNCS 11859, pp. 390–396, 2019.
https://doi.org/10.1007/978-3-030-31726-3_33

Consistency Loss, it facilitates improving the semantic similarity. According to our experiments, architecture with the style constraint is effective and achieves the significant performance outperforming that of U-Net.

2 Related Work

The exploration of the segmentation network architecture for medical image has been a focused study. FCN is the first network to use the convolution layer instead of the full connection layer for the pixel level classification, thus solving the problem of image segmentation at the semantic level. Referring to the idea of FCN, U-Net first proposed the encoding and decoding structure which fuse the Fine-grained with Coarse-grained feature through skip connection, thus improving the segmentation accuracy. As an improvement of U-Net, UNet++ use a series of nested, dense skip pathway to connect the encoder and decoder sub-networks which aim at reducing the semantic gap between the feature maps of the encoder and decoder sub-networks. By doing this, UNet++ achieves an average IoU gain of 3.9 and 3.4 points over U-Net. X. Li et al. combined DenseNet [4] with U-Net and proposed H-DenseUnet [5] which achieved very competitive performance on the segmentation results of tumors for liver segmentation even with a single model. These works show that Encoder-decoder architecture has great potential for medical image segmentation.

3 Proposed Method

This section details the general formulation of a Style Consistency Loss and then introduce an instantiation of the model using U-Net.

3.1 Style Consistency Loss

In U-Net, encoder features mainly reflect the details of the image, while decoder features are derived from more abstract information. They are like two pictures that depict the same thing but have different styles. One is realistic, whilst the other is abstract. If we combine them directly, there will be a semantic gap. By reducing the semantic distance between the two features, the model can be better optimized to improve performance.

Referring to the style loss function of neural style transfer [6, 7], we propose a Style Consistency Loss (SC) as:

$$l_{sc} = MSE(G(f_A), G(f_B)) \tag{1}$$

where MSE is mean-square error and G is Gram matrix which defined as follow:

$$G = \frac{1}{WH} \sum_i^{WH} x_i x_i^T = \frac{1}{WH} XX^T \tag{2}$$

therein, taking an image of size W × H, x_i means the location of the image. Gram matrix is exploited to measure the characteristics of the feature at one dimension and the relationship of the feature between the dimensions.

By optimizing the distance of the two features' Gram matrix, the similarity is accordingly improved. Additionally, Gram matrix used in Bilinear CNN [8] for fine-grained visual recognition achieves the state-of-the-art performance on a number of fine-grained datasets. This demonstrates the good ability of Gram matrix in semantic similarity assessment.

3.2 Segmentation Network

According to our experiments, the adopted U-Net consists of an input layer that accepts a 256 × 256 image, an output layer and 6 blocks in the middle (as see Fig. 1). To deal with the semantic gap, we apply the proposed style consistency loss on each pair of features from the encoder and decoder end. The overall loss function for the proposed network is shown as Eq. 3,

$$L_{total} = l_{ce} + \sum_i^n l_{sc_i} \qquad (3)$$

where l_{ce} is the Cross-Entropy Loss for segmentation, l_{sc} is the style consistency loss.

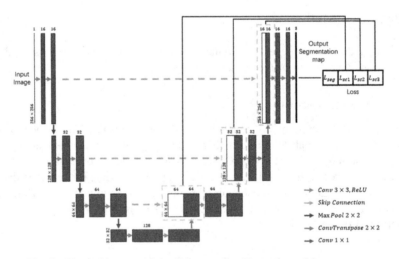

Fig. 1. The architecture of the Segmentation Network used in our paper.

4   Experiments

4.1   Datasets

The Dataset for this study comes from Liver Tumor Segmentation (LiTS) challenge [9], which was collected from 6 medical centers. It consists of 130 training and 70 testing CT scans, meanwhile, the segmentation masks are provided as Nifti.nii files. All ground truth annotations were carefully prepared under the supervision of expert radiologists. Since the challenge no longer provides the test data, we split the training data into two parts: 100 for training and 30 for testing. Due to the limitation of experimental equipment, the network architecture we use is based on 2D convolution. Because the original medical data is 3D data, we slice the 3D medical images into several 2D planes and apply 2D segmentation for each 2D plane. So, the final dataset employed in the paper contains 13419 for 2D training data and 5503 for 2D test data.

4.2   Experiment Settings

We train the network using SGD with size 256×256 and bitch size 1. The network is trained for 10 epochs, the learning rate is set to 0.007, momentum is 0.9 and weight decay is set to 5×10^{-4}.

4.3   Comparison Methods

To verify the effectiveness of the proposed method, three typical networks are used as the comparing methods: FCN8s, U-Net, ResUnet, U-Net + SC.

FCN8s is one version of the original FCN methods, which achieves the best performance in this series.

U-Net is a method based on the encoder-decoder architecture, which used widely in biomedical segmentation.

ResUNet is a residual version of U-Net, we use the original type of residual block with two 3×3 conv instead of the double conv in U-Net.

U-Net + SC is the same architecture with U-Net, except we apply style consistency loss on each skip connection part.

4.4   Evaluation Metrics

Dice is a common Metrics in biomedical segmentation, the equation as follows:

$$Dice = \frac{2 \times truepredict}{groundturth + predict} \tag{4}$$

For the dataset, we used liver dice and tumor dice to verify the methods. separately.

4.5   Results and Analysis

This section details the experiments on Liver Tumor Segmentation (LiTS) datasets. The experiment results are shown in Table 1.

Table 1. Experiment results on Liver Tumor Segmentation (LiTS) datasets

Network	Liver dice	Tumor dice
FCN8s	98.62	11.9
U-Net	97.16	76.15
ResUNet	98.75	78.12
U-Net + SC	*98.86*	*79.26*

As shown in Table 1, our method gains the best performance than the other four methods, which achieves 1.7% liver dice improvement and 3.11% tumor dice improvement on LiTS dataset, compared to UNet without style consistency loss. Specifically, our method obtains 0.11% liver dice improvement and 1.14% tumor dice improvement compared to ResUNet, which demonstrates the effectiveness of the proposed method for the feature combination. U-Net achieves better performance than FCN8s on tumor segmentation but worse on the liver. The reason is that method of feature combination used in FCN8s is superposition, that is not friendly to the small object of the tumor. This is also can be reflected in the Fig. 2.

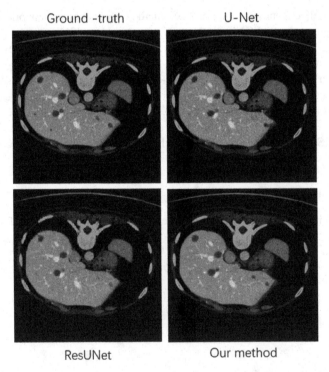

Fig. 2. An example test result. (Color figure online)

Figure 2 shows an example test result, including a comparison of U-Net, ResUNet and Our method. As can be seen, our method gains better performance on both the liver (green mask) and tumor (red mask) segmentation. In addition, because the network is not deep and wide enough, there are some small tumors that can't be identified, but it is enough to prove the superiority of our method.

Figure 3 shows a visualization of feature maps, while the top is the coarse-grained feature maps, and the bottom is the fine-grained feature maps. We can see that comparing traditional U-Net, our method's feature maps work better. In particular, the region of interest of the coarse-grained feature map in our method shows better distinguishability, which is constrained by the consistency of the fine-grained feature map.

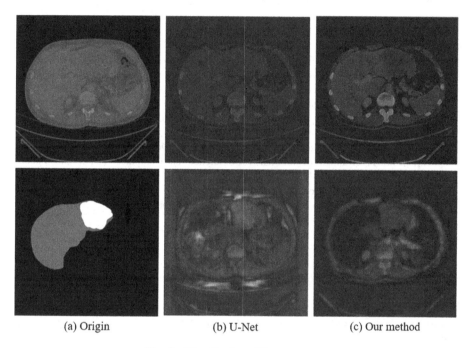

(a) Origin   (b) U-Net   (c) Our method

Fig. 3. Visualization of feature maps.

5 Conclusion

In this paper, we propose a Style Consistency Loss used in U-Net for biomedical segmentation. The proposed loss function is helpful in the feature fusion with increasing similarity in semantics by reducing the difference of Gram matrix between them. The comparison experiment has been done between our proposed U-Net with the style consistency loss with FCN, original U-Net and U-Net with residual block. Our results on the LiTS dataset achieve a liver dice gain of 1.7% and a tumor dice gain of 3.11% points over that with U-Net. This demonstrates our proposed method of improving the segmentation results with more accuracy region determination while taking account of the semantic consistency. In future work, the proposed method will be explored and improved with more clinical liver medical images from the hospital.

Acknowledgement. This work is supported by National Natural Science Foundation of China (No. 61871276), Beijing Natural Science Foundation (No. 7184199), Capital's Funds for Health Improvement and Research (No. 2018-2-2023), Research Foundation of Beijing Friendship Hospital, Capital Medical University (No. yyqdkt2017-25) and WBE Liver Fibrosis Foundation (No. CFHPC2019006).

References

1. Long, J., Shelhamer, E., Darrell, T.: Fully convolutional networks for semantic segmentation. In: IEEE Conference on Computer Vision and Pattern Recognition, pp. 3431–3440 (2015)
2. Ronneberger, O., Fischer, P., Brox, T.: U-Net: convolutional networks for biomedical image segmentation. In: Navab, N., Hornegger, J., Wells, W.M., Frangi, A.F. (eds.) MICCAI 2015. LNCS, vol. 9351, pp. 234–241. Springer, Cham (2015)
3. Zhou, Z., Rahman Siddiquee, M.M., Tajbakhsh, N., Liang, J.: UNet++: a nested u-net architecture for medical image segmentation. In: Stoyanov, D., et al. (eds.) DLMIA/ML-CDS -2018. LNCS, vol. 11045, pp. 3–11. Springer, Cham (2018). https://doi.org/10.1007/978-3-030-00889-5_1
4. Huang, G., Liu, Z., Weinberger, K.Q., van der Maaten, L.: Densely connected convolutional networks. In: Proceedings of the IEEE Conference on Computer Vision and Pattern Recognition, vol. 1, p. 3 (2017)
5. Li, X., Chen, H., Qi, X., Dou, Q., Fu, C.-W., Heng, P.A.: H-DenseUNet: hybrid densely connected UNet for liver and liver tumor segmentation from CT volumes. arXiv preprint arXiv:1709.07330 (2017)
6. Gatys, L.A., Ecker, A.S., Bethge, M.: A neural algorithm of artistic style, pp. 1–16 (2015). arXiv:1508.06576
7. Gatys, L.A., Ecker, A.S., Bethge, M., T.: Image style transfer using convolutional neural networks. In: IEEE Conference on Computer Vision and Pattern Recognition, pp. 2414–2423 (2016)
8. Lin, T.Y., RoyChowdhury, A., Maji, S.: Bilinear CNN models for fine-grained visual recognition. In: Proceedings of the IEEE International Conference on Computer Vision, pp. 1449–1457 (2015)
9. LiTS Homepage. https://competitions.codalab.org/competitions/17094. Accessed 28 Apr 2019

Hierarchical Correlation Stereo Matching Network

Xuliang Chen and Yue Zhou[✉]

Institute of Image Processing and Pattern Recognition,
Shanghai Jiao Tong University, Shanghai, China
{auxlchen,zhouyue}@sjtu.edu.cn

Abstract. Recently, stereo matching from a pair of rectified images has been cast as a supervised learning task using the powerful representation of convolutional neural networks. However, existing methods only utilize last feature maps output from Siamese Networks to compute similarity measurement, which are lack of multi-levels similarity information to construct an informative cost volume. To solve this problem, we propose a hierarchical correlation operation to compute similarity of stereo pairs at multiple levels. In addition, to yield accurate disparity in ill-posed region, we propose a stacked hourglass feature network with dense connections to effectively incorporate context information. Then, hybrid matching cost volume is built leveraging hierarchical correlation features and concatenation features of left and right. 3D CNN encoder-decoder architecture is utilized to regularize the cost volume and regress disparity. Experiments demonstrate that our network achieves competitive performance with state-of-the-art methods on Scene Flow, KITTI 2012, and KITTI 2015 datasets.

Keywords: Stereo matching · Stacked hourglass · Hierarchical correlation · Dense connection

1 Introduction

Stereo matching is a fundamental task in computer vision for sensing depth. Accurately estimating depth of real world scene is crucial to several applications including autonomous driving [10], robotics [14] and 3D scene understanding. The key problem tackled by stereo matching is to find corresponding pixels between left and right rectified images. Given a pixel with coordinate (x, y) in left image, its corresponding pixel in right image can be found at $(x - d, y)$. d is defined as disparity of the pixel(x, y) in left image. After acquiring d, the depth of a pixel in left image can be formulated by $\frac{fb}{d}$, where f refers to camera's focal length and b refers to baseline distance of binocular cameras.

In the recent years, convolutional neural networks have showed significant performance in diverse computer vision tasks such as image classification and

---

X. Chen— Student.

© Springer Nature Switzerland AG 2019
Z. Lin et al. (Eds.): PRCV 2019, LNCS 11859, pp. 397–408, 2019.
https://doi.org/10.1007/978-3-030-31726-3_34

object detection. The first CNN-based stereo matching method proposed by Zbontar and Lecun [20] utilizes powerful ability of CNN to distinguish whether a pair of image patches are matched. This method outperforms contemporary Non-CNN based methods. However, due to lack of context information, it is still a problem for tackling ill-posed region by simply embedding CNN into the conventional stereo matching pipeline. End-to-end CNN model has been applied to dense pixel-wise tasks such as semantic segmentation [6] and pose estimation [11] because it can effectively aggregate global context information to make a prediction. Similar to semantic segmentation, estimating depth is also a dense image-to-image task which can be handled by end-to-end CNN model [1,5,8]. DispNetC [8] proposes a correlation layer to measure similarity about left and right unary features and then form cost volume followed by 2D convolutions to regularize cost volume and regress disparity. GC-Net [5] and PSMNet [1] adopt 3D convolutions to regularize concatenated cost volume over spatial and disparity dimensions thus sufficiently utilizing context information. However, owing to only leveraging deepest unary feature map to construct cost volume, these current methods [1,5,8] are limited by unable to construct a cost volume with multi-levels similarity information.

In this paper, we propose a stacked hourglass feature network with dense connections. The repeated bottom-up and top-down processing in a single hourglass allows network to effectively incorporate global and local features. The dense connections between different hourglasses allow low-level features to flow forward. Therefore, discriminative features are learned for matching cost computation. Based on this, hierarchical correlation is employed to provide comprehensive similarity measurements from low level to high level. Eventually, we can form an informative matching cost volume with both correlation and concatenation manners. 3D CNN aggregation network further regularizes cost volume and regresses disparity. To summarize, our contributions are listed below:

- We propose a stacked hourglass feature network with dense connections. In this way, our network can effectively fuse global and local features thus learning discriminative for matching cost computation.
- We propose a novel hierarchical correlation which contributes to better similarity measurements. In this way, our network can construct a cost volume with rich details.
- Comprehensive experiments demonstrate that our model yields promising performance on Scene Flow, KITTI 2012, and KITTI 2015 datasets.

2   Related Work

The traditional pipeline of stereo matching mainly works on four steps [13]: matching cost computation, cost aggregation, disparity optimization and post processing. In the past, many local [9,21] and global [16] methods have been proposed to improve whole or portions of the four steps in pipeline. However, these classical methods share a weakness relying on hand-crafted features to calculate matching cost and customtized functions to aggregate cost which results in bad performance.

When deep learning comes to stage, the hand-crafted cost computation and regularization functions have been replaced by learnable CNN layers. Zbontar and Lecun propose [20] in which they train a Siamese network to match 9×9 image patches. [7] proposed by Luo et al. computes local matching costs in an efficient way with multi-label classification of disparities. Learnable penalty terms of regularization are proposed by Seki et al. in SGM-Nets [15].

Recently, end-to-end networks have been developed to cover all procedures in stereo matching. Many of these methods yield state-of-the-art performance. Mayer et al. [8] first propose an end-to-end stereo matching network which directly regresses disparity from correlation cost volume. CRL [12] introduces a two-stage strategy to refine disparity estimation from initial disparity through residual learning. Yu et al. [19] propose a novel two-stream neural network where one is for generating cost aggregation proposals and the other one is for aggregation guidance. By explicitly guiding the aggregation procedure using low-level structure information, [19] can handle the ill-posed region very well. GC-Net [5] and PSMNet [1] construct cost volume directly from raw unary features and employ 3D-convolutions to regularize cost volume. 3D-convolutions excel 2D-convolutions because the previous can incorporate context from one more dimension i.e. disparity. Guo et al. [3] proposes group-wise correlation which divides left and right features into groups along channel dimension and compute correlation along groups.

The key insight of stereo matching is to integrate context information which is crucial to predict the disparity in ambiguous regions. In semantic segmentation [6] and pose estimation [11], encoder-decoder architecture with skip connections is useful to fuse global and local features. Inspired by stacked hourglass network for pose estimating [11], we propose a stacked hourglass feature network to extract discriminative features for matching cost computation. To preserve thin structure information, dense connections between different hourglasses are adopted to forward low-level features through shortcut. Based on this effective feature extractor, hierarchical correlation is adopted to measure features similarity from low-level to high-level thus constructing an informative matching cost volume.

3   Approach

In this section, we present the details of our proposed model. Firstly, the whole pipeline of network is described. Secondly, we elaborate each import part of the model. Lastly, output and loss function are explained.

3.1   Network Architecture

The proposed network architecture is illustrated in Fig. 1. In the beginning of the input of Siamese network, a convolution with kernal size 3×3 and stride 2 is

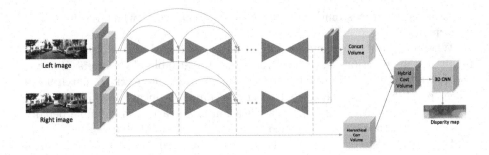

Fig. 1. An overview of the proposed hierarchical correlation stereo matching network. The original left and right image are downsampled to 1/4 resolution of input by consecutive stride convolution and max pooling. Then, stacked hourglass network with dense connections further extracts unary features. For brief display, dense connection is drawn for the first two hourglasses. Hierarchical correlation is implemented among multi-levels features to form hierarchical correlation cost volume. Concatenation volume and hierarchical correlation volume are concatenated to build up hybrid cost volume, which is regularized to regress disparity by 3D CNN.

implemented to downsample raw input image to $\frac{1}{2}$ resolution of original. Before fed into stacked-hourglass feature network, feature maps are further downsampled to $\frac{1}{4}$ size of the input image by max pooling. In addition, several resblocks [4] are inserted after these two downsamplings. Then, we adopt stacked hourglass network to extract unary feature. The stacked hourglass feature network and pre-hourglass modules share weights in both left and right input stream. Each hourglass outputs a unary feature proposal.

For the cost volume construction, by following [3], two kinds of cost volume are adopted to build up the hybrid cost volume. The concatenation volume proposed in [1] is constructed by concatenating the last hourglass outputs of left and right stream. The hierarchical correlation volume is built utilizing intermediate unary features output from stacked hourglass feature network. Two volumes are concatenated to form a 4D hybrid cost volume, which is fed into 3D CNN for regularization.

For cost aggregation, we adopt the stacked 3D hourglass network proposed in [1] to regularize cost volume and regress disparity map.

3.2   Stacked Hourglass Feature Network

According to [11], hourglass architecture has an advantage to extract global semantic information while preserving spatial location which is crucial for matching the ambiguous area. Following the same idea in [11], we design stacked hourglass feature network to extract discriminative features for matching cost computation.

Inner structure of a single hourglass is illustrated in Fig. 2 left. Firstly, in bottom-up sequence, the feature map is downsampled to 1/16 size of input by 4

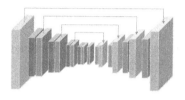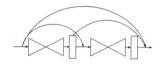

Fig. 2. Left: Inner structure of each hourglass in stacked hourglass feature network. Gray block refers to input feature map. Blue block refers to resblock [4] which don't shrink the resolution of feature maps. Orange block refers to max pooling. Green block refers to nearest neighbor upsampling. The skip connection means that feature map is operated by one resblock and then is fused with the upsampled one by element-wise adding. Right: Dense connections between hourglasses. The rectangle behind each hourglass is the output feature map of corresponding hourglass. (Color figure online)

consecutive modules, each of which consists of a resblock [4] and a max pooling. After reaching the lowest resolution, to fuse adjacent high resolution feature map in bottom-up sequence, nearest neighbor upsampling is implemented followed by element-wise adding. The design of residual block in our hourglass is the same as the one proposed in [11].

The right of Fig. 2 illustrates how we stack hourglasses together. For l_{th} hourglass, its input is the concatenation of input of the first hourglass and preceding hourglasses' outputs, which is denoted as $[X_0, X_1, ..., X_{l-1}]$. The output is fomulated as:

$$X_l = H_l([X_0, X_1, ..., X_{l-1}]),\tag{1}$$

where H_l denotes the l_{th} hourglass mapping function. "$[\cdot]$" denotes concatenation.

In our implementation, the number of hourglasses stacked is 4. The settings of overall residual blocks within the hourglass are the same with 128 channels in input and output. Additional convolution handles the channels of feature map to fit the input size of hourglass after concatenation. At the end of stacked hourglass network ,we implement a 1×1 convolution to reduce the channels of unary feature so as to form a concatenation cost volume with moderate size. The dash lines shown in Fig. 1 refer to intermediate unary feature outputs. Except for the input of first hourglass, the concatenated features after each hourglass are fused by 1×1 convolution to yield intermediate unary feature output.

3.3 Cost Volume

In previous literatures [1,5,8], the cost volume is constructed by only utilizing the last output of Siamese feature network. Limited spatial structure information is provided when feature goes deeper and deeper. It is harmful for matching small object and thin structure.

To solve the issue mentioned above, we propose a novel hierarchical correlation, in which multi-levels features are taken into consideration to calculate similarity. Therefore, similarity computation is more comprehensive than only correlating the last unary feature output.

Correlaiton is implemented on each group of intermediate unary feature output, as shown in Fig. 1. Instead of using the plain correlation [8], group-wise correlation [3] is adopted for constructing more informative correlation cost volume. At each level, the correlation cost volume has the dimension of $[D_{max}/4, H/4, W/4, N_g]$. N_g refers to number of groups. $D_{max}/4$ is the max disparity level corresponding to 1/4 resolution of original input. Eventually, correlation volumes of all levels are concatenated to form the hierarchical correlation cost volume, which has size of $[D_{max}/4, H/4, W/4, N_l \times N_g]$, where N_l refers to number of levels.

The concatenation cost volume is constructed by concatenating the left and the right feature $\mathbf{f}_l$, $\mathbf{f}_r$ output from last hourglass.

$$\mathbf{C}_{concat}(d, x, y, \cdot) = \text{Concat}[\mathbf{f}_l(x, y), \mathbf{f}_r(x - d, y)], \tag{2}$$

where d denotes disparity level. The size of concatenation cost volume can be $[D_{max}/4, H/4, W/4, 2N]$, where N denotes channels of feature map before concatenated.

For constructing hybrid cost volume, two cost volume is concatenated at channel dimension.

3.4   Cost Aggregation Network

In our model, the stacked hourglass network proposed in [1] is adopted to achieve better performance by integrating more context information. But, in our implementation, the shortcut connections within each hourglass proposed in [3] replace

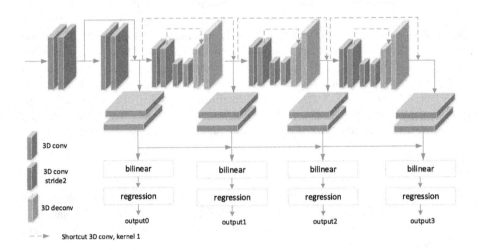

Fig. 3. The architecture of 3D CNN for cost aggregation.

the original shortcut connections between different hourglasses. The whole architecture is illustrated in Fig. 3. For detail, there is a pre-hourglass modules followed by three stacked hourglass networks. pre-hourglass module and each hourglass generate a disparity map prediction. The pre-hourglass module yields initial disparity prediction. The following hourglass networks generate residual features which are added to the previous disparity output for refinement. Four disparity outputs are supervised during training. When running testing, only the last hourglass outputs the disparity prediction.

3.5   Loss Function

For each output module in cost aggregation network, before regressing disparity map, a branch is introduced where two 3D convolutions are conducted to reduce the channels of 4D cost volume into 1. Then, the cost volume is upsampled to size of $H \times W \times D_{max}$. For each pixel, the matching costs for D_{max} different disparity levels are explicitly predicted. Softmax function is applied along the disparity dimension to obtain probability distribution. Soft argmin proposed in [5] is adopted to regress disparity map.

$$\hat{d} = \sum_{d=0}^{D_{max}-1} d \times p_d, \tag{3}$$

where d and p_d denote the disparity level candidate and the corresponding probability.

The loss function for each output branch is defined as:

$$L = \frac{1}{N} \sum_{i=1}^{N} \mathrm{Smooth}_{L_1}(\hat{d}_i - d_i^*), \tag{4}$$

in which,

$$\mathrm{Smooth}_{L_1}(x) = \begin{cases} 0.5x^2, & \text{if } |x| < 1 \\ |x| - 0.5, & \text{otherwise} \end{cases} \tag{5}$$

where, $\hat{d}$ and d^* denote predicted disparity and disparity ground truth. N is the number of labeled pixels. The loss of the whole network is defined as sum of loss of each output branch L_i weighted by its corresponding coefficient λ_i.

$$L = \sum_{i=0}^{3} \lambda_i \cdot L_i \tag{6}$$

4   Experiments

We use three datasets: Scene Flow [8], KITTI 2012 [2], and KITTI 2015 [10] to evaluate our proposed model. In Sects. 4.1 and 4.2, details about datasets and implementation are described. In Sect. 4.3, we have conducted a ablation study to demonstrate the effectiveness of our designs. In Sect. 4.4, we compare our proposed model with the other state-of-the-art methods in KITTI stereo leaderboard.

4.1 Datasets and Metrics

Scene Flow is a large scale synthetic dataset which is generated by computer. it contains 35,454 stereo images for training and 4,370 stereo images for testing. The resolution of each image is $H = 540$ and $W = 960$. Dense and accurate disparity ground truth is provided. The metric used to evaluate Scene Flow test set is end-point error (EPE), which is defined as disparity error averaged in pixels.

KITTI 2015 is a realistic dataset in driving scene. Training set contains 200 stereo images with sparse disparity ground truth which is measured by LiDAR. Testing set contains 200 stereo images without disparity ground truth. The size of each image is 376×1240. In our experiment, 200 training stereo pairs are divided into two parts: 160 for training and 40 for validation. The percentage of erroneous pixels is used to evaluate algorithm. A pixel whose disparity end-point error is larger than 3px and 5% of ground-truth disparity is considered as a erroneous pixel.

KITTI 2012 has the same setting as KITTI 2015, except that there are 194 stereo pairs for training and 195 stereo pairs for testing. In our experiment, 194 training stereo pairs are divided into two parts: 160 for training and 34 for validation. The percentage of erroneous pixels and average end-point error are evaluated on KITTI 2012.

4.2 Implementation Details

We implement our network(HcNet) using PyTorch. Adam optimizer with $\beta_1 = 0.9, \beta_2 = 0.999$ is employed to end-to-end train the network.

During training in Scene Flow, we use random crop for data augmentation. Each image is randomly cropped to 256×512 before fed into the network. The maximum disparity is set to 192 following previous methods [1,5]. We set the batch size to 8 and learning rate to a constant value 0.001 for training 10 epochs on Scene Flow. For testing on Scene Flow, input images are padded on the top to size of 960×576. To supervise the training, loss is only computed at the pixels with ground-truth disparity within the valid range $[0, D_{max})$. The coefficients set in Eq. 6 are 0.5, 0.5, 0.7, 1.0 from λ_0 to λ_3.

For KITTI 2012 and KITTI 2015 dataset, The model pre-trained on Scene Flow dataset is finetuned on KITTI for 300 epochs. The learning rate is set to 0.001 for 200 epochs and reduced to 0.0001 for the rest of 100 epochs. Similarly, random crop is also adopted for data augmentation. For testing on KITTI dataset, input images are padded on the top and the left to size of 1280×384.

The experiment is conducted on four GTX 1080Ti GPUs. It takes almost 20 hours for training on Scene Flow dataset and 5 h for finetuning on KITTI dataset.

4.3 Ablation Study

Using the same cost aggregation network and cost volume construction method, our model has better performance when compared with PSMNet [1] as shown on

Table 1. Ablation study of different model settings. 3px error rate on KITTI 2015 validation set and average end-point error on Scene Flow test set are reported. *Densehg* represents the stack hourglass feature network with dense connections. *Hc* and *Cat* denote to hierarchical correlation volume and concatenation volume. The following number refers to channels of volume. *Base* is the basic 3D CNN architecture in [1]. *Stackhourglass* is the 3D CNN architecture mentioned in this paper.

Model	KITTI 2015 val error(%)	Scene flow EPE(px)
PSMNet-Base [1]	2.097	1.357
Densehg-Cat64-Base	2.087	1.290
Densehg-Hc64-Base	2.090	1.255
Densehg-Hc40-Cat24-Base	2.016	1.291
Densehg-Hc40-Cat24-Stackhourglass	**1.581**	**1.198**

first row and second row in Table 1. For fair comparison, PSMNet [1] is implemented with official code in our experimental condition. It demonstrates that our proposed stack hourglass feature network can yield more effective features for matching.

For evaluating effectiveness of hierarchical correlation, as shown in Tabel 1 from second to fourth row, we have experimented three types of cost volume: volume with only concatenation features, volume with only hierarchical correlation features, and volume with both two features. The model with hybrid cost volume has best performance on KITTI dataset. The model with only hierarchical correlation volume has best performance on Scene Flow dataset.

After replacing the aggregation network with stackhourglass 3D CNN. our model reaches lowest 1.581% 3px error rate on KITTI 2015 validation set.

4.4 KITTI Test Results

In this section, we present qualitative and quantitative test results on KITTI 2012 and KITTI 2015. The model performing best in our ablation experiments is adopted to run the test on KITTI 2012 and 2015.

For KITTI 2015, 200 stereo pairs are tested and the results are submitted to KITTI evaluation server. The results reported by KITTI website are shown in Table 2. Our method outperforms PSMNet [1] 0.22% on D1-all. For qualitative evaluation, some examples are shown in Fig. 4. Compared with PSMNet [1], our model(HcNet) yields more accurate prediction in repeated texture region such as fence and reflective region such as car window.

For KITTI 2012, 195 testing stereo pairs are tested by our model. Results are shown in Table 3. Our model outperforms PSMNet [1] by a large margin. Moreover, compared with GwcNet [3], our method has better performance in reflective region and keeps comparable performance in the whole image. Qualitative results on KITTI 2012 test set are illustrated in Fig. 5.

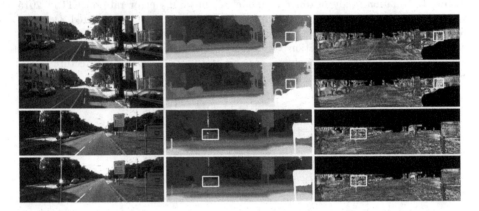

Fig. 4. Results of KITTI 2015 test set. The left column: the left image of stereo pairs. The middle column: disparity estimated by HcNet(ours), PSMNet [1] from top to bottom. The right column: error map of its corresponding disparity prediction on the left side.

Table 2. Comparison with other methods on KITTI 2015 test set.

Method	All(%)			Noc(%)			Time(s)
	D1-bg	D1-fg	D1-all	D1-bg	D1-fg	D1-all	
MC-CNN-acrt [20]	2.89	8.88	3.89	2.48	7.64	3.33	67
DispNetC [8]	4.32	4.41	4.34	4.11	3.72	4.05	0.06
SegStereo [18]	1.88	4.07	2.25	1.76	3.70	2.08	0.6
GC-Net [5]	2.21	6.16	2.87	2.02	5.58	2.61	0.9
PSMNet [1]	1.86	4.62	2.32	1.71	4.31	2.14	0.41
HcNet(ours)	**1.71**	**4.05**	**2.10**	**1.58**	**3.69**	**1.93**	0.48

Table 3. Comparison with other methods on KITTI 2012 test set.

Method	>3px(%)			>5px(%)			Mean error(px)			Time(s)
	Noc	All	Refl	Noc	All	Refl	Noc	All	Refl	
SGM-Net [15]	2.29	3.50	18.97	1.60	2.36	13.55	0.7	0.9	3.8	67
DispNetC [8]	4.11	4.65	18.15	2.05	2.39	9.88	0.9	1.0	2.3	0.06
GC-Net [5]	1.77	2.30	12.80	1.12	1.46	7.99	0.6	0.7	2.0	0.9
PSMNet [1]	1.49	1.89	10.18	0.90	1.15	5.64	0.5	0.6	1.6	0.41
GwcNet [3]	1.32	**1.70**	9.28	0.80	1.03	5.22	0.5	0.5	1.4	0.32
HcNet(ours)	**1.32**	1.71	**8.19**	**0.78**	**1.03**	**4.69**	**0.5**	**0.5**	**1.3**	0.48

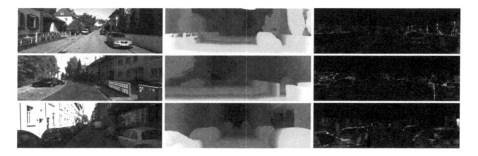

Fig. 5. Qualitative results on KITTI 2012 test set. From left to right: input left image of stereo pairs, disparity estimation, error map.

5   Conclusion

In this paper, we propose a novel hierarchical correlation to measure feature similarity at multi-levels. In this way, informative cost volume can be constructed. We also propose a stacked hourglass feature network with dense connections to effectively incorporate context information. Therefore, discriminative features can be learned for matching cost computation. Experiments show that our model is able to yield robust disparity prediction in ill-posed region. The performance on KITTI 2012 and KITTI 2015 Benchmark is comparable with other state-of-the-art methods. In the future, we are going to explore light weight stereo matching deep network and apply stereo system in other applications such as multiple-object tracking [17].

References

1. Chang, J.R., Chen, Y.S.: Pyramid stereo matching network. In: Proceedings of the IEEE Conference on Computer Vision and Pattern Recognition, pp. 5410–5418 (2018)
2. Geiger, A., Lenz, P., Urtasun, R.: Are we ready for autonomous driving? the kitti vision benchmark suite. In: 2012 IEEE Conference on Computer Vision and Pattern Recognition, pp. 3354–3361. IEEE (2012)
3. Guo, X., Yang, K., Yang, W., Wang, X., Li, H.: Group-wise correlation stereo network. In: Proceedings of the IEEE Conference on Computer Vision and Pattern Recognition (2019)
4. He, K., Zhang, X., Ren, S., Sun, J.: Deep residual learning for image recognition. In: Proceedings of the IEEE Conference on Computer Vision and Pattern Recognition, pp. 770–778 (2016)
5. Kendall, A., et al.: End-to-end learning of geometry and context for deep stereo regression. In: Proceedings of the IEEE International Conference on Computer Vision, pp. 66–75 (2017)
6. Long, J., Shelhamer, E., Darrell, T.: Fully convolutional networks for semantic segmentation. In: Proceedings of the IEEE Conference on Computer Vision and Pattern Recognition, pp. 3431–3440 (2015)

7. Luo, W., Schwing, A.G., Urtasun, R.: Efficient deep learning for stereo matching. In: Proceedings of the IEEE Conference on Computer Vision and Pattern Recognition, pp. 5695–5703 (2016)

8. Mayer, N., et al.: A large dataset to train convolutional networks for disparity, optical flow, and scene flow estimation. In: Proceedings of the IEEE Conference on Computer Vision and Pattern Recognition, pp. 4040–4048 (2016)

9. Mei, X., Sun, X., Dong, W., Wang, H., Zhang, X.: Segment-tree based cost aggregation for stereo matching. In: Proceedings of the IEEE Conference on Computer Vision and Pattern Recognition, pp. 313–320 (2013)

10. Menze, M., Geiger, A.: Object scene flow for autonomous vehicles. In: Proceedings of the IEEE Conference on Computer Vision and Pattern Recognition, pp. 3061–3070 (2015)

11. Newell, A., Yang, K., Deng, J.: Stacked hourglass networks for human pose estimation. In: Leibe, B., Matas, J., Sebe, N., Welling, M. (eds.) ECCV 2016. LNCS, vol. 9912, pp. 483–499. Springer, Cham (2016). https://doi.org/10.1007/978-3-319-46484-8_29

12. Pang, J., Sun, W., Ren, J.S., Yang, C., Yan, Q.: Cascade residual learning: a two-stage convolutional neural network for stereo matching. In: Proceedings of the IEEE International Conference on Computer Vision, pp. 887–895 (2017)

13. Scharstein, D., Szeliski, R.: A taxonomy and evaluation of dense two-frame stereo correspondence algorithms. Int. J. Comput. Vis. 47(1–3), 7–42 (2002)

14. Schmid, K., Tomic, T., Ruess, F., Hirschmüller, H., Suppa, M.: Stereo vision based indoor/outdoor navigation for flying robots. In: 2013 IEEE/RSJ International Conference on Intelligent Robots and Systems, pp. 3955–3962. IEEE (2013)

15. Seki, A., Pollefeys, M.: Sgm-nets: Semi-global matching with neural networks. In: Proceedings of the IEEE Conference on Computer Vision and Pattern Recognition, pp. 231–240 (2017)

16. Sun, J., Shum, H.-Y., Zheng, N.-N.: Stereo matching using belief propagation. In: Heyden, A., Sparr, G., Nielsen, M., Johansen, P. (eds.) ECCV 2002. LNCS, vol. 2351, pp. 510–524. Springer, Heidelberg (2002). https://doi.org/10.1007/3-540-47967-8_34

17. Xu, C., Zhou, Y.: Consistent online multi-object tracking with part-based deep network. In: Lai, J.-H., et al. (eds.) PRCV 2018. LNCS, vol. 11257, pp. 180–192. Springer, Cham (2018). https://doi.org/10.1007/978-3-030-03335-4_16

18. Yang, G., Zhao, H., Shi, J., Deng, Z., Jia, J.: Segstereo: Exploiting semantic information for disparity estimation. In: Proceedings of the European Conference on Computer Vision (ECCV), pp. 636–651 (2018)

19. Yu, L., Wang, Y., Wu, Y., Jia, Y.: Deep stereo matching with explicit cost aggregation sub-architecture. In: Thirty-Second AAAI Conference on Artificial Intelligence (2018)

20. Zbontar, J., LeCun, Y., et al.: Stereo matching by training a convolutional neural network to compare image patches. J. Mach. Learn. Res. 17(1–32), 2 (2016)

21. Zhang, K., Lu, J., Lafruit, G.: Cross-based local stereo matching using orthogonal integral images. IEEE Trans. Circ. Syst. Video Technol. 19(7), 1073–1079 (2009)

An Accurate LSTM Based Video Heart Rate Estimation Method

Mingyun Bian[1,2], Bo Peng[2], Wei Wang[2], and Jing Dong[1,2(✉)]

[1] College of Computer Science, Hunan University of Technology,
Zhuzhou 412007, Hunan, China
mingyun.bian@cripac.ia.ac.cn
[2] Center of Research on Intelligent Perception and Computing,
Institute of Automation, Chinese Academy of Sciences,
Beijing 100190, China
{bo.peng,wwang,jdong}@nlpr.ia.ac.cn

Abstract. Pulse signal is an effective indicator to reflect the physiological and physical state of the human body. There are many heart rate estimation methods in videos and most of them manually design algorithm to modeling noise signal, which is not enough to represent the actual distribution of noise. In this paper, we propose to train a two-layer LSTM to estimate pulse signals because long short-term memory (LSTM) can preserve useful signals by filtering out noise signals upon data-driven. In order to overcome the problem of insufficient heart rate public database, we propose to use quantities of synthetic signals which are generated by the algorithm we designed to pre-train the model and pure periodic signals are filtered from LSTM to calculate the heart rate. Experiential results on the public-domain database show the effectiveness of our proposed method that can be a reference for the heart rate estimation.

Keywords: Pulse signal · LSTM network · Synthetic signal · Heart rate estimation

1 Introduction

Heart rate signal is one of the important signals that reflects the human body condition. Heart rate measurement has many applications [16,23] such as physical condition examination and patient medical monitoring. Methods of pulse estimation are mainly divided into contact methods and non-contact methods. Contact methods are mainly based on contact sensor detection devices, such as electrocardiograph (ECG) [2] and contact photoplethysmography (cPPG) [10]. Although its accuracy in detection is more higher and more stable than non-contract methods, it is inconvenient to take devices around in various scenarios.

This work was partly supported by NSFC (No. 61772529, U1636201 and U1536120) and the National Key Research and Development Program of China (No. 2016YFB1001003).

Z. Lin et al. (Eds.): PRCV 2019, LNCS 11859, pp. 409–417, 2019.
https://doi.org/10.1007/978-3-030-31726-3_35

Non-contact methods have gradually become a research focus because of low cost and easy implementation [3] and mainly based on photoplethysmography (PPG) [5,15,20,23] which can detect subtle color signals changes caused by heart beats from human face regions in videos. In recent years, non-contact pulse estimation methods based on the remote photoplethysmography (rPPG) has attracted increasingly attention, and multiple heart rate estimation algorithms have been proposed [4,8,12,14].

Traditional methods of pulse estimation based on rPPG is mainly to manually design the algorithm to extract the periodic signal or map the color signal into a new space to get a better signal quality and they could not deal with multiple types of noise [9] caused by body motions, illumination changes, camera sensor well. Deep learning methods have been applied in many fields and achieved quite good results, such as machine translation [17] and semantic analysis [6], which mainly require training on huge data while the heart rate estimation public database is still scarce. To solve problems above, we consider learning from signals per frame with a sequential network [13] based on data augmentation we made up for the shortage of the database.

In this paper, we present a novel method by training a sequential network as a signal filter heart rate estimation upon data-driven. Specifically, we design a two-layer LSTM for regression from raw signals after normalization to estimate pulse wave signals and generate a large scale of synthetic heart rate signals which is used to pre-train the LSTM network to prevent over-fitting. We take a part of the public database MMSEHR [24]'s signal into the LSTM network after normalization for the purpose of fine-tuning the LSTM network parameters [18]. By testing on the same public database, our proposed method has better than baseline methods.

The main contributions of this work include: (i) we propose to use LSTM network to filter raw signals with rPPG information and multiply noises to purely periodic pulse wave signals based on data-driven. (ii) We generate quantities of synthetic signals by our designed algorithm to stimulate pulse signals in real scenarios with noises to pre-train the model. (iii) Our proposed method is better than the traditional methods in experiments shows the practicability for heart rate estimation in videos.

2   Related Work

The principle of photoplethysmography for heart rate monitoring is that the periodic contraction and relaxation of the human heart can cause a slight periodic change in facial blood volume. Blood can absorb light signals more easily than skin tissue, and can be reflected and scattered by light. The camera sensor collects a color signal that changes the blood volume of the face, and then processes the color signal to obtain a time-domain signal that changes approximately periodically, and finally converts to the frequency domain to calculate heart rate [15]. Nowadays, PPG technology is extended to the imaging photoplethysmography (iPPG) and remote photoplethysmography (rPPG), they are the related technology with almost the same principles.

Color-Based Methods. In [14], green channel in the raw signal collecting from the skin tends to contain the strongest PPG information compare to red and blue channel and Verkruysse W et al. proved that green channel signals can estimate heart rate. In [4], Poh et al. proposed a approach based on automatic face tracking and blind source separation of color channels signals into independent components. This method can be more robust for the interference of motion during heart rate estimation. Inspired by previous work, the chrominance space analysis (CHROM) method proposed in 2013 [12] mainly focused on the improvement of motion robustness in estimating heart rate. They calculate chrominance feature based on two orthogonal projections of Red-Green-Blue (RGB) space in order to reduce the influence of face motion. Based on previous work, in [8] proposed a plane orthogonal to the skin tone (POS) analysis method is improved by CHROM method using a projection plane orthogonal to the skin tone as pulse extraction based on optical and physiological considerations and assumption of a single light source with a constant spectrum.

The current traditional methods for pulse estimation of video faces based on color space analysis including green channel analysis method, independent component analysis method, chrominance space analysis method, and plane orthogonal to the skin tone analysis method. These methods generally require manual design of signal processing algorithms to extract pure periodic signals.

Motion-Based Methods. In [17], Balakrishnan et al. extracted heart rate from videos by detecting subtle head motion caused by the Newtonian reaction. A combination of frequency filtering and principal component analysis (PCA) can identify the component of motion corresponding to the pulse and then extract peaks of the trajectory to calculate individual beats. Since the method is based on subtle motion and large head movements appear to be common, it results in many limitations in real scenarios.

Deep Learning-Based Methods. There are some methods for heart rate estimation based on deep learning [7,11]. In [19], Hsu et al. proposed to use VGG-16 model to classify 2D Time-Frequency Representations (TFRs) of sequences to estimate the heart rate. We found that Hsu et al. train VGG-16 with thousands of parameters in PPF database containing 5848 samples is far from enough, exposing the problem of data scarcity in deep learning methods. The results of the experiment may depend on the quality of the original signal processing and the number of training samples. The latest representative work is the first end-to-end system for video-based measurement of heart rate by using VGG-style CNN for estimating the physiological signal derivative from the motion representation proposed by [20] and added attention mechanism by using gating schemes [21]. The shortage of their work is estimating heart rate by manually preprocess signals same as traditional methods far enough to eliminate multiply noises in different scenarios.

In summary, existing methods of heart rate detection are mainly based on handcrafted features, and fewer attempts are made to design an end-to-end heart rate estimate. Some methods have their own limitations. For example, some methods need to be based on some lighting or motion assumptions so as to be limited to special application scenarios. Most of methods do not pay attention to the variation of the signal of each frame of videos, but focus on the improvement of signal processing methods.

3 Proposed Approach

Figure 1 gives a diagram for our proposed approach of learning a pulse signal filter based on LSTM network. Generally speaking, we first train the LSTM network model with a large number of time domain synthetic signals, and then normalize the signal extracting from face ROI in real database to fine-tune the pre-trained model. We calculate the heart rate by making the Fast Fourier transform on the filtered signal from model.

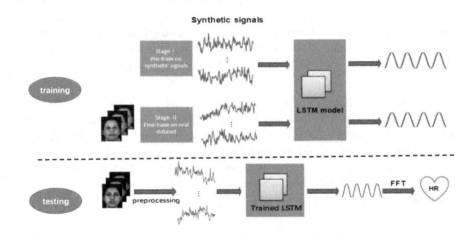

Fig. 1. The framework of our approach.

3.1 Signal Preprocessing

In the whole process of signal preprocessing, we first locate and track facial key points. The green channel signal contains more PPG signals [14], so we extract the green signal of the region of interest (ROI) for normalization. In Fig. 1, we first locate and track the face in the video, then define the ROI using some pre-selected facial landmarks detected by dlib [22] as shown by the bluish region in Fig. 1, finally normalize the G channel signal to a mean of 0 and a standard deviation of 1 extracting from the region of interest of the face in videos.

3.2 LSTM Filtering Model

We designed a two-layer LSTM and dimensions of the hidden state and cell state of each layer are both 128. We believe that LSTM network can be an excellent signal filter after quantities of synthetic noises data training because it can model multiply types of noise in heart rate estimation. The input of the model training is a noisy pulse signal sequence, supervision signal is the corresponding noiseless pulse signal sequence, and the loss function uses the mean square error loss between the prediction sequence and the supervision sequence.

$$L(\theta) = \sum_{t=0}^{N} \left(S_t \left(\theta, x_t \right) - S_t^* \right)^2 \tag{1}$$

where θ is learnable weights and bias parameters in LSTM neural networks. S_t^* represents a noiseless pulse signal, that is a temporal sequence. N represents the length of time series. The optimization method of the model we used is stochastic gradient descent.

3.3 Training Strategy

Training a deep neural network requires thousands of data while collecting a large-scale face videos database containing heart rate signals requires a lot of manpower and financial resources. Therefore, we consider generating a large amount of simulation data for model pre-training. The auxiliary training of a large amount of simulation data can make the model parameters well optimized for the pulse signal de-noising task. A network train only on synthetic data has poor generalization in real scenarios, so we then uses a amount of real data for model fine-tuning. It can effectively improve the generalization ability of the filter model on real data.

There are only 101 video sequences in the MMSE-HR database [8], so we need to design the simulation data generation algorithm to make up for the lack of data. We first use the sine function with a frequency range of [0.4, 3] Hz, corresponding to the heart rate range of [42, 180] bpm, as the basis of the simulation signal. Then we add the random Gaussian noise signals simulating the noise caused by illumination changes and random step signal to the sine signal simulating the noise caused by head motion. The formulation of the simulation signal can be expressed as follow,

$$S = M \sin \left(\omega t + \phi \right) + \sum_{i}^{N} (-1)^{\lceil t_i \rceil} * QStep \left(t - t_i \right) + G(t) \tag{2}$$

where M, Q are the magnitude, while M randomly sampled from [0, 1], Q randomly sampled from [0, 10], and ω corresponding to the frequencies of heart rate limited in [0.4, 3] Hz; $Step(t)$ means the step signal and t_i randomly ranges from [0, 250]; $\lceil . \rceil$ is a round up function and $G(t)$ denotes the Gaussian noise. We generate 3000 simulation signals and we can see an example of sine signals and synthetic signals in Fig. 2. It can be seen that the synthetic signals can approximate simulate real color signals with rPPG information.

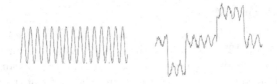

Fig. 2. The sine signal (left) and synthetic signal (right).

4   Experiments

In this section, we (i) analyze and explain the parameter settings in experiments, (ii) compare the proposed method and baseline methods on a public database to analyze advantages of our method and (iii) show the effectiveness of pre-training using synthetic data.

4.1   Experimental Settings

In this paper, we design comparative experiments between traditional methods and our proposed method on public-domain MMSE-HR [24] database, which is widely used on the task of heart rate estimation. For sake of the video alignment in time, we cut the 101 videos in MMSE-HR [24] database into 367 clips of the same length which has 250 frames, the ground-truth heart rate are calculated by real time blood pressure signal measurement provided by this database.

In order to test the effectiveness of our proposed method fairly compare to the GREEN method [14], ICA method [4], CHROM method [12], POS method [8] and the traditional methods are tested directly on the whole databases without training [1]. Our method is based on data-driven, so we randomly divided whole database into 5 folds and trained on four folds and tested on the rest fold, the finally test results we take the arithmetic mean of the results on all test folds. There are many standards for evaluating performance, we use such as the Mean Square Error (MSE), Mean Absolute Error (MAE) and Standard Deviation (std) of heart rate error and Pearson correlation coefficient (ρ) between estimated heart rate and ground-truth heart rate. The formulation of ρ can be expressed as follow,

$$\rho_{x,y} = \frac{E(XY) - E(X)E(Y)}{\sqrt{E\left(X^2\right) - E^2(X)}\sqrt{E\left(Y^2\right) - E^2(Y)}} \tag{3}$$

4.2   Experimental Results

In our experiments, following the test protocol we have mentioned in Experimental Settings, we compare the proposed method with several state-of-the-art methods for estimating the average heart rate given a video with 250 frames from MMSE-HR database [24]. We found in the experiment that the model without pre-training does not converge because the real training data is too small, which indirectly illustrates the importance of data augmentation. In Fig. 3, we can see that the continuous curve of blue is G channel signals after normalization, and the orange dotted line is the waveform obtained after filtering. We can clearly see that the model can eliminate the noise signal after training by large amounts of simulated noise data and our method can be applied to more scenarios generally by learning the distribution of multiple noises.

From Table 1, we can see the results of our method with pre-train shows the best result demonstrating the practical effectiveness of our model and the necessity of pre-trained for optimizing the model. and compare to the best methods with traditional methods we used, our method dropped by 0.2955 on MSE, 1.12 on MAE, 0.2793 on std, and increased by 0.0567 on ρ. Our model can be more stable based on the data-driven and more robust in different scenarios.

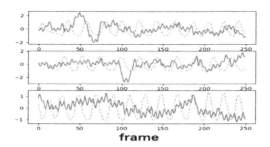

Fig. 3. The waveform after filtering. (Color figure online)

Table 1. The result of experiments on MMSE-HR.

Method	MSE	MAE	std	ρ
GREEN [14]	21.7697	13.53	19.0592	0.302
ICA-Poh [4]	19.0234	11.77	18.1387	0.3471
POS-Wang [8]	14.9463	7.07	14.7692	0.5676
CHROM [12]	10.4503	5.47	10.5009	0.7686
Our method	**10.1548**	**4.35**	**10.2216**	**0.8254**

5 Conclusion and Further Work

Remote heart rate estimation through face videos is a challenging task that the heart rate signals we detect in real scenarios is so weak and it is susceptible to body motion, illumination changes and camera sensors. In this paper, we propose a new regression model for optimally filtering the rPPG signal with noise and achieved good results in our experiments. Based on data-driven, the ability to eliminate noise interference in different scenarios can be effectively trained by supervisory signals. In the future work, we will consider improving our model abilities on larger databases, assisting in training by designing new model architectures to do real time heart rate estimation, and trying to improve the generalization of the model through cross-database testing.

References

1. McDuff, D., Blackford, E.: iPhys: an open non-contact imaging-based physiological measurement toolbox. arXiv preprint arXiv:1901.04366 (2019)
2. Normal ECG: Electrophysiology of the heart (1960)
3. Lewandowska, M., Rumiski, J., Kocejko, T., et al.: Measuring pulse rate with a webcama non-contact method for evaluating cardiac activity. In: 2011 Federated Conference on Computer Science and Information Systems (FedCSIS), pp. 405–410. IEEE (2011)
4. Poh, M.Z., McDuff, D.J., Picard, R.W.: Non-contact, automated cardiac pulse measurements using video imaging and blind source separation. Opt. Express 18(10), 10762–10774 (2010)
5. Hsu, Y.C., Lin, Y.L., Hsu, W.: Learning-based heart rate detection from remote photoplethysmography features. In: 2014 IEEE International Conference on Acoustics, Speech and Signal Processing (ICASSP), pp. 4433–4437. IEEE (2014)
6. Yu, L., Hermann, K.M., Blunsom, P., et al.: Deep learning for answer sentence selection. arXiv preprint arXiv:1412.1632 (2014)
7. Li, X., Komulainen, J., Zhao, G., et al.: Generalized face anti-spoofing by detecting pulse from face videos. In: 2016 23rd International Conference on Pattern Recognition (ICPR), pp. 4244–4249. IEEE (2016)
8. Wang, W., den Brinker, A.C., Stuijk, S., et al.: Algorithmic principles of remote PPG. IEEE Trans. Biomed. Eng. 64(7), 1479–1491 (2017)
9. Lukáš, J., Fridrich, J., Goljan, M.: Digital camera identification from sensor pattern noise. IEEE Trans. Inf. Forensics Secur. 1(2), 205–214 (2006)
10. Naples, M.A., Hampson, D.R.: Pharmacological profiles of the metabotropic glutamate receptor ligands [3H] L-AP4 and [3H] CPPG. Neuropharmacology 40(2), 170–177 (2001)
11. Xu, Z., Li, S., Deng, W.: Learning temporal features using LSTM-CNN architecture for face anti-spoofing. In: 2015 3rd IAPR Asian Conference on Pattern Recognition (ACPR), pp. 141–145. IEEE (2015)
12. De Haan, G., Jeanne, V.: Robust pulse rate from chrominance-based rPPG. IEEE Trans. Biomed. Eng. 60(10), 2878–2886 (2013)
13. Lipton, Z.C., Berkowitz, J., Elkan, C.: A critical review of recurrent neural networks for sequence learning. arXiv preprint arXiv:1506.00019 (2015)
14. Verkruysse, W., Svaasand, L.O., Nelson, J.S.: Remote plethysmographic imaging using ambient light. Opt. Express 16(26), 21434–21445 (2008)
15. Moody, G.B., Mark, R.G., Goldberger, A.L.: PhysioNet: a web-based resource for the study of physiologic signals. IEEE Eng. Med. Biol. Mag. 20(3), 70–75 (2001)
16. Jain, A.K., Nandakumar, K., Nagar, A.: Biometric template security. EURASIP J. Adv. Sign. Process. 2008, 113 (2008)
17. Balakrishnan, G., Durand, F., Guttag, J.: Detecting pulse from head motions in video. In: Proceedings of the IEEE Conference on Computer Vision and Pattern Recognition, pp. 3430–3437 (2013)
18. Zhu, Z., Wu, W., Zou, W., et al.: End-to-end flow correlation tracking with spatial-temporal attention. In: Proceedings of the IEEE Conference on Computer Vision and Pattern Recognition, pp. 548–557 (2018)
19. Hsu, G.S., Ambikapathi, A.M., Chen, M.S.: Deep learning with time-frequency representation for pulse estimation from facial videos. In: 2017 IEEE International Joint Conference on Biometrics (IJCB), pp. 383–389. IEEE (2017)

20. Chen, W., McDuff, D.: Deepphys: video-based physiological measurement using convolutional attention networks (2018)
21. Mobahi, H., Collobert, R., Weston, J.: Deep learning from temporal coherence in video. In: Proceedings of the 26th Annual International Conference on Machine Learning, pp. 737–744. ACM (2009)
22. King, D.E.: Dlib-ml: a machine learning toolkit. J. Mach. Learn. Res. **10**(Jul), 1755–1758 (2009)
23. Allen, J.: Photoplethysmography and its application in clinical physiological measurement. Physiol. Meas. **28**(3), R1 (2007)
24. Zhang, Z., Girard, J.M., Wu, Y., et al.: Multimodal spontaneous emotion corpus for human behavior analysis. In: Proceedings of the IEEE Conference on Computer Vision and Pattern Recognition, pp. 3438–3446 (2016)

Self-supervised Homography Prediction CNN for Accurate Lane Marking Fitting

Yiman Chen[1], Wentao Du[1], Zhiyu Xiang[2]([✉]), Nan Zou[1], Shuya Chen[1], and Chengyu Qiao[1]

[1] College of Information Science & Electronic Engineering, Zhejiang University, Hangzhou, China
{chenyiman,duwentao,znmax,shuya_chen,11831044}@zju.edu.cn
[2] Zhejiang Provincial Key Laboratory of Information Processing, Communication and Networking, Zhejiang University, Hangzhou, China
xiangzy@zju.edu.cn

Abstract. Lane detection is an indispensable part in advanced driving systems. The task is typically tackled with a two-step pipeline: predicting a segmentation of lane markings and fitting the lane markings by a suitable curve model. In this work, we propose a method to optimally fit lane lines by applying a learned perspective transformation, according to the input image. We leverage fundamental computer vision theories and integrate prior geometric knowledge into a deep learning framework, which can be trained in a self-supervised manner. By doing this, we perform multi-lane joint fitting in a realistic top-view space, which is robust against ground-planes slope changes. We tested our model on the CULane dataset. The results show that the proposed fitting method can also improve the location accuracy of lane markings effectively.

Keywords: Self-supervised CNN · Lane marking fitting

1 Introduction

Lane detection is an active topic in autonomous driving research with increasing interests from academic and industrial groups. For self-driving vehicles, it is an important task to identify lanes on the road to ensure that vehicles stay within lane limits while driving, so that to reduce the chance of colliding with other vehicles by crossing lane lines accidentally. Lane markers tell where the passable area is and guide vehicles to find the right way forward. Most lanes are designed to be relatively simple, not only to encourage order but also to make it easier for human drivers to drive at the same speed. However, lane detection is not an easy task due to complex road conditions. Apart from bad weather and lighting conditions, occlusion and degraded markings also affect visibility of lane lines.

With advances of deep learning, recognition tasks such as detection, classification, and segmentation have been solved under a wide set of conditions. Method

---

The first author is a student.

© Springer Nature Switzerland AG 2019
Z. Lin et al. (Eds.): PRCV 2019, LNCS 11859, pp. 418–429, 2019.
https://doi.org/10.1007/978-3-030-31726-3_36

of deep learning has shown considerable promise as a solution to the shortcomings of classic computer vision. However, general CNN for object detection or semantic segmentation only extract features from the original pixel semantics, unable to capture the image pixel spatial relationships. Lanes are kind of things with strong shape priori but less appearance coherence, so spatial relations are very important for lane detection. In this way, putting forward more targeted approaches for lane detection is imperative. Kim et al. [9] propose a method, in which a CNN extracts lane candidate regions and uses the RANSAC algorithm to remove outliers and to perform line fitting. Huval et al. [5] use Overfeat [14] to predict two end-points of a local lane segment in a sliding window and connects these lane segments to get complete lane lines. In [10], a multi-task network guided by vanishing point is designed to jointly handle lane and road marking detection, where a series of post-processing (e.g. point sampling, clustering, lane regression) are required. In AAAI 2018, [13] propose Spatial CNN (SCNN) to output probability maps of lane curves and search position with the highest response. These positions are then connected by cubic splines to generate the final predictions.

The above several methods have in common that they tackle the task of lane detection with a two-step pipeline involving separate feature extraction and model fitting steps. In this work, we focus on the latter stage and propose a simple and practical curve-fitting module, which is a post-processing step in lane detection to get desired prediction. Having estimated the position or probability map, i.e. which pixels belong to lane markings, it is often necessary to line up these pixels. That is to describe them by a parametric expression or a fitting model. Cubic polynomials [11,15], splines [1] or clothoids [3] are some popular fitting models. To better fitting curving lane markings, it is common to convert the original image reference frame into ortho-view (i.e. the top-down view) using a perspective transformation [2] and perform curve fitting there. Typically, we can achieve this conversion by simply multiplying the coordinates from perspective image with a homographic projection matrix. However, the transformation matrix is always calculated once and keeps fixed for all images, which will lead to fitting errors when the relative pose between vehicle and ground plane changes (e.g. by mountain, hilly ground or acceleration/deceleration of vehicles). To alleviate this problem, [12] train a network to output 6 degrees of freedom for a learned perspective transformation matrix. In the field of computer vision, some works have predicted special geometry by network architecture [6,7,16] (e.g. The spatial transformer network (STN) of Jaderberg et al. [6] and the perspective transformer net of Yan et al. [16]). Kendall et al. [7,8] propose a deep learning architecture for 6-DOF camera relocalization.

In this work, we focus on constructing a learned homographic projection matrix to optimally fit lane markings. A self-supervised neural network that can learn an adaptive perspective transformation matrix between the camera and ground is proposed. Unlike in [12] where the lane markings in an image are treated independently, our network is fed with all of the lane markings and trained in a self-supervised manner. Therefore, a better homographic prediction could be achieved. Then the lane markings can be jointly fitted in a more realistic top-view space that is robust against changes of road plane, thanks to this homographic matrix. The experimental results show that our fitting method is able to improve the location accuracy of lane markings effectively.

The remainder of the paper is organized as follows. Section 2 describes procedures of the proposed curve fitting method, followed by experiments and results presented in Sect. 3. Finally, we give the summary of our work in Sect. 4.

2   Methods

The overview of our pipeline is illustrated in Fig. 1. Unlike general task of object detection, in which only bounding boxes are required, lane detection is supposed to get precise prediction of curves. Spatial CNN (SCNN) [13] is adopted to distinguish different lane markings and output probability maps of these lane curves. Having predicted probability maps, lane markings with existence confidence larger than a threshold are kept. Then pixel positions whose probability response are the highest are searched in the map by every some rows. As the post-processing of lane detection, for each lane a curve fitting is required to get a parametric description. Instead of directly connecting these pixel positions by cubic splines in image space like [13], we propose to apply a learned adaptive perspective transformation and fit curves in the projected ground planes. To realize our purpose, a homography prediction network that is able to adaptively estimate the transformation between the camera and the road plane is designed. In this way, the lane fitting is insensitive to the variations of ground-planes.

2.1   Deep Network for Homography Predition

Having estimated which pixels belong to the lane markings by SCNN [13], we are supposed to fit a curve through these pixels to get the parametrization. As a frequently used trick, the lane pixels are first projected into a birds-eye-view representation, in which the lane are ordinarily parallel and their curvature can be accurately fitted with low-order polynomials, not having to resort to higher order polynomials in the original image space. In addition, removing the perspective effects causes lane markings to look parallel regardless of their distance away from the camera. However, due to the fact that the projection operation always employ a fixed transformation matrix, this raises issues when non-flat ground-planes are encountered. In particular, lane points close to the horizon may be projected into infinity, hindering the process of line fitting. To remedy this situation, we train a network to output three crucial factors that affect the perspective transformation: the focal length of camera f, the depression angle θ and the height h at which camera is set. The neural network takes as input the image and is self-supervised trained with a loss function that is tailored to the lane fitting problem.

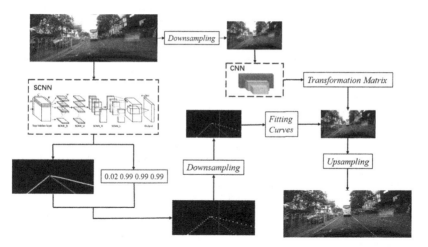

Fig. 1. Overview of the framework. Given an input image, SCNN [13] outputs a probability map and predicts the existence of every lane marking. For each line whose existence probability is larger than 0.5, we search the corresponding map every 20 rows for the pixel with the highest response. Next, we project these lane pixels by a learned homographic projection matrix and perform lane fitting. Finally, the lanes are transformed back to the original image, which are the final predictions.

Transformation Matrix. In our case, the transformation matrix can be derived with prior geometric knowledge and computer vision theories. A full camera model describes the mapping from world to pixel coordinates. It accounts for the following transformations: the rigid body transformation between camera and scene; the perspective projection onto the image plane; the discrete sampling on image plane to obtain the final pixel coordinates.

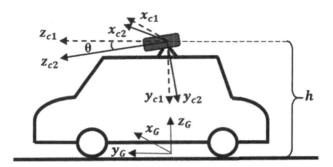

Fig. 2. Transformation from the word to the camera.

See Fig. 2, consider a coordinate system $X_G = (x_G, y_G, z_G)$ attached to the world and another coordinate system $X_c = (x_c, y_c, z_c)$ attached to the camera. The rigid body motion is a kind of transformation that brings a point from the world coordinate system to the camera coordinate system. In a real life scenario, the front facing camera mounted at a certain degrees roll relative to the ground plane. The rigid body motion can be described by a rotation matrix $\mathbf{R}$ and a translation vector $\mathbf{T}$. In this way, the relationship between $\mathbf{X_G}$ and the camera coordinate system without rotation $\mathbf{X_{c1}}$ is:

$$\mathbf{R_1}[x_G, y_G, z_G]^T + \mathbf{T_1} = [x_{c1}, y_{c1}, z_{c1}]^T \tag{1}$$

here $\mathbf{R_1} = \begin{bmatrix} 1 & 0 & 0 \\ 0 & 0 & -1 \\ 0 & 1 & 0 \end{bmatrix}$, $\mathbf{T_1} = [0, h, 0]^T$, h is the height.

Assuming a rotation θ about x-axis between the camera and ground, a new coordinates under frame $\mathbf{X_{c2}}$ can be obtained:

$$
\begin{aligned}
\mathbf{X_{c2}} &= \begin{bmatrix} x_{c2} \\ y_{c2} \\ z_{c2} \end{bmatrix} = \begin{bmatrix} 1 & 0 & 0 \\ 0 & \cos\theta & \sin\theta \\ 0 & -\sin\theta & \cos\theta \end{bmatrix} \begin{bmatrix} x_{c1} \\ y_{c1} \\ z_{c1} \end{bmatrix} \\
&= \begin{bmatrix} 1 & 0 & 0 \\ 0 & \sin\theta & -\cos\theta \\ 0 & \cos\theta & \sin\theta \end{bmatrix} \begin{bmatrix} x_G \\ y_G \\ z_G \end{bmatrix} + \begin{bmatrix} 0 \\ h\cos\theta \\ -h\sin\theta \end{bmatrix}
\end{aligned} \tag{2}
$$

Thus, the transformation between the world and the camera coordinate system with rotation is:

$$
\begin{bmatrix} x_{c2} \\ y_{c2} \\ z_{c2} \\ 1 \end{bmatrix} = \begin{bmatrix} 1 & 0 & 0 & 0 \\ 0 & \sin\theta & -\cos\theta & h\cos\theta \\ 0 & \cos\theta & \sin\theta & -h\sin\theta \\ 0 & 0 & 0 & 1 \end{bmatrix} \begin{bmatrix} x_G \\ y_G \\ z_G \\ 1 \end{bmatrix} \tag{3}
$$

Then, the overall mapping from world coordinates $\mathbf{X_G}$ to pixel coordinates is given by:

$$
z_{c2} \begin{bmatrix} u \\ v \\ 1 \end{bmatrix} = \begin{bmatrix} f_x & 0 & u_0 & 0 \\ 0 & f_y & v_0 & 0 \\ 0 & 0 & 1 & 0 \end{bmatrix} \begin{bmatrix} 1 & 0 & 0 & 0 \\ 0 & \sin\theta & -\cos\theta & h\cos\theta \\ 0 & \cos\theta & \sin\theta & -h\sin\theta \\ 0 & 0 & 0 & 1 \end{bmatrix} \begin{bmatrix} x_G \\ y_G \\ z_G \\ 1 \end{bmatrix} \tag{4}
$$

Assuming $f_x = f_y = f$ and $Z_G = 0$, we can get:

$$
z_{c2} \begin{bmatrix} u \\ v \\ 1 \end{bmatrix} = \begin{bmatrix} f & 0 & u_0 \\ 0 & f & v_0 \\ 0 & 0 & 1 \end{bmatrix} \begin{bmatrix} 1 & 0 & 0 \\ 0 & \sin\theta & h\cos\theta \\ 0 & \cos\theta & -h\sin\theta \end{bmatrix} \begin{bmatrix} x_G \\ y_G \\ 1 \end{bmatrix} \tag{5}
$$

Finally, in this case, the homographic projection 3×3 matrix H is:

$$
\begin{aligned}
H &= \begin{bmatrix} f & 0 & u_0 \\ 0 & f & v_0 \\ 0 & 0 & 1 \end{bmatrix} \begin{bmatrix} 1 & 0 & 0 \\ 0 & \sin\theta & h\cos\theta \\ 0 & \cos\theta & -h\sin\theta \end{bmatrix} \\
&= \begin{bmatrix} f & u_0\cos\theta & -u_0 h\sin\theta \\ 0 & f\sin\theta + v_0\cos\theta & fh\cos\theta - v_0 h\sin\theta \\ 0 & \cos\theta & -h\sin\theta \end{bmatrix}
\end{aligned} \tag{6}
$$

Note that by obtaining the above style homographic matrix, we assume the depression angle θ be the only influential factor among three pose angles. It is reasonable that most of the incorrect projection is caused by the ground slope or pitching angle of vehicle. Fully predicting the whole H in Eq. (6) needs 7 dependent components. Modeling them together as independent output elements of a network is not a good idea since it can be unstable and making the prediction inaccurate. Considering only 3 degrees of freedom in H, it is wise to model it using 3 variables, i.e., f, h and θ.

Network Architecture. The network architecture used in this work is kept intentionally simple for real-time purpose. The network is constructed out of three consecutive blocks of 3×3 convolutions, batch-normalization and ReLUs. Each block is followed by a max pooling layer to decrease the dimension. Two fully-connected layers are added in the end. Figure 3 demonstrates the network architecture that we use in this work. To accelerate the inference process, the network takes RGB images with a reduced size of 128×64 as input and outputs three parameters of transformation. The design of loss function for training this network will be described in the next section.

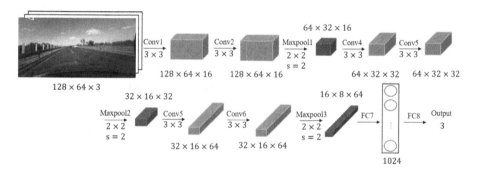

Fig. 3. The network architecture.

2.2 Loss Function and Self-supervised Learning

As explained in the previous section, we apply a learned perspective transformation, conditioned on the input image, in contrast to a fixed transformation. By doing so, the lane fitting is robust against road plane changes and is specifically optimized for better fitting the lanes. In particular, the lane markings are parallel to each other in the birds-eye-view and as such, curve lanes can be fitted by 2nd or 3rd order polynomials. After predicting the parameters of the perspective transformation by the network and generating the final transformation matrix H, lane points are projected to the top-view space for curve fitting.

Curve Fitting. The ground-truth lane points before curve fitting are defined as **P** where each lane pixel is $p_i = [x_i, y_i, 1]^T \in \mathbf{P}$. After transformed by the matrix H, the projected pixel $\boldsymbol{p}'_i = [x'_i, y'_i, 1]^T \in \mathbf{P}'$ is equal to $H\boldsymbol{p}_i$. The least-squares algorithm is then used to fit a group of polynomials $f(y'_i)$ through the transformed pixels $\mathbf{P}'$. The polynomial curves are evaluated at different y-positions, that is, to get the x-position x'^*_i on the fitting line at y-position y'_i of the transformed lane points with $x'^*_i = f(y'_i)$. Gained the fitted points $\mathbf{P}'^*$ with $\boldsymbol{p}'^*_i = [x'^*_i, y'_i, 1]^T \in \mathbf{P}'^*$, we re-project them back to the original image space via the inverse transformation matrix, so that to get: $\boldsymbol{p}^*_i = H^{-1}\boldsymbol{p}'^*_i$ with $\boldsymbol{p}^*_i = [x^*_i, y_i, 1]^T$. Note that the y-positions of the lane points are remain the same while the x-positions are changed through curve fitting. Considering every input image has the same transformation matrix, we jointly fit all the lane curves on one image each time, with the prior that these lanes are parallel to each other. The above process is presented in Fig. 4.

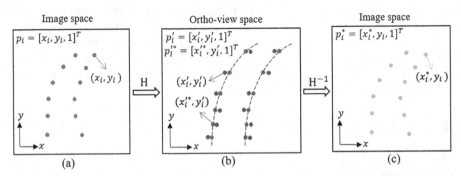

Fig. 4. Illustration of curve fitting. (a) GT points (green) in the original image are projected into ortho-view space by the transformation matrix H. (b) A group of parallel curves are fitted through the transformed points (blue) and evaluate the curves at different heights (red points). (c)The evaluated points are transformed back to the original image space (yellow points). (Color figure online)

Loss Function. In order to train the network for predicting the optimal transformation parameters and produce the learned transformation matrix H for fitting curves in birds-eye-view, we adopt the following loss function. As described before, the given ground-truth lane points $\boldsymbol{p}_i = [x_i, y_i]^T \in \mathbf{P}$ are first projected to: $\boldsymbol{p}'_i = H\boldsymbol{p}_i = [x'_i, y'_i, 1]^T \in \mathbf{P}'$. And then we fit polynomials $f(y') = \alpha y'^3 + \beta y'^2 + \gamma y' + \delta$, for the case of the 3rd order polynomial, through these transformed points. Using the least squares closed-form solution, we can get the coefficients of polynomials:

$$\mathbf{w} = (\mathbf{Y}^T\mathbf{Y})^{-1}\mathbf{Y}^T\mathbf{x}' \tag{7}$$

here, we assume that there is 4 lanes and N lane points on an image in all, thus, $\mathbf{w} = [\alpha, \beta, \gamma, \delta_1, \delta_2, \delta_3, \delta_4]^T$, $\mathbf{x}' = [x'_1, x'_2, \cdots, x'_N]^T$, and

$$\mathbf{Y} = \begin{bmatrix} y'^3_1 & y'^2_1 & y'_1 & 1 & 0 & 0 & 0 \\ y'^3_2 & y'^2_2 & y'_2 & 1 & 0 & 0 & 0 \\ \cdots & & \cdots & & & \cdots & \\ y'^3_N & y'^2_N & y'_N & 0 & 0 & 0 & 1 \end{bmatrix} \tag{8}$$

with $[1\ 0\ 0\ 0]$ is added to the columns following the y-positions (or their power) of points on the first lane, and $[0\ 1\ 0\ 0], [0\ 0\ 1\ 0], [0\ 0\ 0\ 1]$ for the 2nd, 3rd, 4th lane respectively. For images with 3 lanes, we use $[1\ 0\ 0], [0\ 1\ 0], [0\ 0\ 1]$ and so on. In this way, we can get $x_i'^*$ prediction by evaluating the polynomial at each y_i' location as follows:

$$\mathbf{x}'^* = \mathbf{Y} \times \mathbf{w} \tag{9}$$

$$\begin{bmatrix} x_1'^* \\ x_2'^* \\ \cdots \\ x_N'^* \end{bmatrix} = \begin{bmatrix} y_1'^3 & y_1'^2 & y_1' & 1 & 0 & 0 & 0 \\ y_2'^3 & y_2'^2 & y_2' & 1 & 0 & 0 & 0 \\ \cdots & & \cdots & & & \cdots \\ y_N'^3 & y_N'^2 & y_N' & 0 & 0 & 0 & 1 \end{bmatrix} \begin{bmatrix} \alpha \\ \beta \\ \gamma \\ \delta_1 \\ \delta_2 \\ \delta_3 \\ \delta_4 \end{bmatrix} \tag{10}$$

Note that in real traffic situation the fitting lines can be parallel to each other with the same polynomial coefficients except the constant terms δ_i are different, thus the proposed perspective transformation to birds-eye-view space can be reasonable and practical.

Afterwards, the evaluated points are transformed back to the original image space by the inverse matrix: $\boldsymbol{p}_i^* = H^{-1}\boldsymbol{p}_i'^*$, with $\boldsymbol{p}_i^* = [x_i^*, y_i, 1]^T$ and $\boldsymbol{p}_i'^* = [x_i'^*, y_i', 1]^T$. The y-positions are kept unchanged, but the x^*-positions could be supervised by comparing them with the x-positions of ground-truth lane points using a mean squared error criterion, leading to a L2 loss:

$$Loss = \frac{1}{N} \sum_{i=1}^{N} (x_i^* - x_i)^2 \tag{11}$$

In this work, the network is trained involving backpropagation through a least-squares fitting and a loss function for supervision. Since the curve fitting use the closed-form solution of the least squares algorithm, the loss is differentiable and as such, the gradients could be calculated by automatic differentiation. During training process of this homography prediction network, the input (ground truth lane points) itself are also treated as supervised signal in return, therefore it is a self-supervised network.

3   Experiments

3.1   Dataset

In this paper, we adopt the CULane dataset [13] which is a challenging large scale dataset for lane detection task. The dataset incorporates data captured during the day and night time, under various circumstances including urban, rural, and highway scenes. These images have a resolution of 1640×590 and are divided into 88880 for training set, 9675 for validation set, and 34680 for testing set. On each image, the current (ego) lanes and left/right lanes are annotated no matter the lane markings are occluded or unseen.

3.2 Training Setup and Testing

We manually selected 2340 images which have clear parallel lane lines in real life, filtering out those with obviously inaccurate annotations for training. These images are prepared for pre-training with a scaled version of dimension 128×64. The network was trained using Adam optimizer with a learning rate of $1e^{-8}$ and batch size of 5. Our model was implemented on the Tensorflow [4] framework. After training, test was carried out on the testing set. Some qualitative results of homographic projection and fitting are shown in Fig. 5.

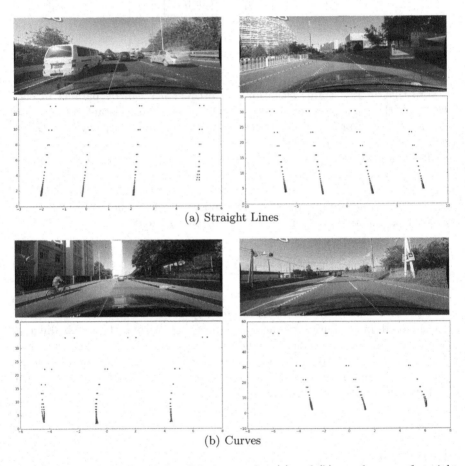

(a) Straight Lines

(b) Curves

Fig. 5. Examples of projection and fitting results. (a) and (b) are the case of straight and curving lane markings, respectively. Original images with lane labels are in the top followed by the projected results in the bottom. (Color figure online)

As shown in Fig. 5, the projection results in testing set are quite satisfactory for both straight lines and curves. Green points are ground truth in test images. They are transformed using the predicted homographic matrix H into blue points on top-view space (at the bottom). Next, a group of parallel lines are fitted through these transformed points and the curves are evaluated at different distances (red points). After that, we project these evaluated points back to the original image space (at the top) as the yellow points represent.

3.3 Evaluation and Results

Since only the x-positions of pixels have changed through projection and curve fitting, we calculate the mean difference of x-value between ground truth and fitted points in image space as follows:

$$error = \frac{1}{N} \sum_{i=1}^{N} |\Delta x| = \frac{1}{N} \sum_{i=1}^{N} |x_{fit} - x_{gt}| \tag{12}$$

Table 1. Errors using three different fitting models (2nd,3rd order polynomial and cubic spline) before and after projection. The units are in pixels.

Error	Normal	Crowd	Hlight	Shadow	Noline	Arrow	Curve	Night	Total
Img_2nd	14.964	17.240	29.054	29.846	41.712	14.491	33.681	20.890	19.584
Proj_2nd	**13.646**	**16.109**	**26.454**	**25.800**	**41.479**	**12.308**	**32.078**	**19.421**	**18.178**
Img_3rd	16.317	18.747	30.778	30.797	43.536	16.347	35.433	21.644	20.804
Proj_3rd	**14.239**	**16.986**	**28.695**	**28.423**	**41.548**	**13.477**	**32.974**	**20.322**	**19.030**
Img_cubic	18.036	20.447	**31.546**	**32.504**	45.006	17.932	35.861	**22.515**	22.203
Proj_cubic	**17.988**	**20.438**	32.145	32.548	**44.829**	18.020	**34.201**	22.527	**22.176**

In Table 1, we compare our proposed fitting method (Proj_xxx) with directly fitting curves in the original image space (Img_xxx) using 2nd,3rd order polynomial or cubic spline fit. The results show that fitting in the projected space leads to superior results.

Table 2. F1-measure values of three different fitting models (2nd,3rd order polynomial and cubic spline).

F1	Normal	Crowd	Hlight	Shadow	Noline	Arrow	Curve	Night	Total
Img_2nd	0.6984	0.5247	0.4729	0.3760	0.2786	0.6533	0.4285	0.4549	0.5178
Proj_2nd	**0.7651**	**0.5970**	**0.4910**	**0.4705**	**0.3006**	**0.7336**	**0.4618**	**0.5013**	**0.5751**
Img_3rd	0.6976	0.5269	0.4774	0.3760	0.2780	0.6680	0.4406	0.4521	0.5175
Proj_3rd	**0.7582**	**0.5892**	**0.4796**	**0.4755**	**0.2952**	**0.7120**	**0.4784**	**0.4954**	**0.5689**
Img_cubic	0.5550	0.3990	0.3801	0.3044	0.2369	0.5142	0.3588	0.3572	0.4079
Proj_cubic	**0.6975**	**0.5368**	**0.4231**	**0.4113**	**0.2564**	**0.6386**	**0.3997**	**0.4321**	**0.5106**

Our proposed fitting module can also directly improve the detection results. Refering to the evaluation approach of SCNN [13], the correct lane predictions are regarded as those whose intersection-over-union (IoU) with GT lanes higher than a threshold. In this paper, we consider $IoU = 0.7$ as a threshold for strict metric of True Positives (TP). Then $\text{F1-measure} = 2 \times \frac{Precicion \times Recall}{Precision + Recall}$ is adopted as the final evaluation indicator, where $Precision = \frac{TP}{TP+FP}$ and $Recall = \frac{TP}{TP+TN}$. As shown in Table 2, no matter what curving models are used, fitting in top-view space has better performance than fitting in images.

Table 3. F1-measure values of the detection by curve fitting under different projections (image only without projection, fixed and predicted projection)

F1	Normal	Crowd	Hlight	Shadow	Noline	Arrow	Curve	Night	Total
Image	0.5550	0.3990	0.3801	0.3044	0.2369	0.5142	0.3588	0.3572	0.4079
Fixed	0.6833	0.5051	**0.4231**	0.3885	0.2455	**0.6425**	0.3830	0.4133	0.4914
Ours	**0.6975**	**0.5368**	**0.4231**	**0.4113**	**0.2564**	0.6386	**0.3997**	**0.4321**	**0.5106**

In Table 3, we compare the values of F1-measure with cubic spline fitting model. Here, lane lines were respectively fitted using no projection, fixed and predicted homographic projection by network. It shows that our method works the better than fitting in image and fitting with a fixed homographic projection, thanks to the adaptive homographic prediction network.

4   Conclusion

In this work, we proposed a self-supervised homographic prediction neural network for optimally fitting the lane curves. To parametrize segmented lanes, we have trained a network to predict the parameters and generate the perspective transformation matrix, conditioned on the image. The neural network takes images as input and is optimized with a custom loss function for lane marking fitting. We jointly fit the transformed coordinate points using a group of parallel lines, which is similar to the situation where lane lines are projected into birds-eye-view. The experimental results show that our proposed method for curve fitting could directly improve the results of lane detection. Besides the application in lane fitting, we can also use the proposed method to determine which lines are parallel to each other in original images or transform lane lines into the bird-view for easier detection. We believe that the learned model for estimating homography projection can inspire more work on the other detection or recognition tasks and demonstrate its wide impact on image understanding.

Acknowledgment. The work is supported by NSFC-Zhejiang Joint Fund for the Integration of Industrialization and Informatization under grant No. U1709214 and NSFC grant No. 61571390.

References

1. Aly, M.: Real time detection of lane markers in urban streets. In: 2008 IEEE Intelligent Vehicles Symposium, pp. 7–12. IEEE (2008)
2. Bertozzi, M., Broggi, A.: Real-time lane and obstacle detection on the gold system. In: Proceedings of Conference on Intelligent Vehicles, pp. 213–218. IEEE (1996)
3. Gackstatter, C., Heinemann, P., Thomas, S., Klinker, G.: Stable road lane model based on clothoids. In: Meyer, G., Valldorf, J. (eds.) Advanced Microsystems for Automotive Applications 2010. VDI-Buch, pp. 133–143. Springer, Heidelberg (2010). https://doi.org/10.1007/978-3-642-16362-3_14
4. Girija, S.S.: Tensorflow: large-scale machine learning on heterogeneous distributed systems. tensorflow. org (2016)
5. Huval, B., et al.: An empirical evaluation of deep learning on highway driving. arXiv preprint arXiv:1504.01716 (2015)
6. Jaderberg, M., Simonyan, K., Zisserman, A., et al.: Spatial transformer networks. In: Advances in Neural Information Processing Systems, pp. 2017–2025 (2015)
7. Kendall, A., Cipolla, R.: Geometric loss functions for camera pose regression with deep learning. In: Proceedings of the IEEE Conference on Computer Vision and Pattern Recognition, pp. 5974–5983 (2017)
8. Kendall, A., Grimes, M., Cipolla, R.: PoseNet: a convolutional network for real-time 6-DOF camera relocalization. In: Proceedings of the IEEE International Conference on Computer Vision, pp. 2938–2946 (2015)
9. Kim, J., Lee, M.: Robust lane detection based on convolutional neural network and random sample consensus. In: Loo, C.K., Yap, K.S., Wong, K.W., Teoh, A., Huang, K. (eds.) ICONIP 2014. LNCS, vol. 8834, pp. 454–461. Springer, Cham (2014). https://doi.org/10.1007/978-3-319-12637-1_57
10. Lee, S., et al.: VPGNet: vanishing point guided network for lane and road marking detection and recognition. In: Proceedings of the IEEE International Conference on Computer Vision, pp. 1947–1955 (2017)
11. Loose, H., Franke, U., Stiller, C.: Kalman particle filter for lane recognition on rural roads. In: 2009 IEEE Intelligent Vehicles Symposium, pp. 60–65. IEEE (2009)
12. Neven, D., De Brabandere, B., Georgoulis, S., Proesmans, M., Van Gool, L.: Towards end-to-end lane detection: an instance segmentation approach. In: 2018 IEEE Intelligent Vehicles Symposium (IV), pp. 286–291. IEEE (2018)
13. Pan, X., Shi, J., Luo, P., Wang, X., Tang, X.: Spatial as deep: spatial CNN for traffic scene understanding. In: Thirty-Second AAAI Conference on Artificial Intelligence (2018)
14. Sermanet, P., Eigen, D., Zhang, X., Mathieu, M., Fergus, R., LeCun, Y.: OverFeat: integrated recognition, localization and detection using convolutional networks. arXiv preprint arXiv:1312.6229 (2013)
15. Smuda, P., Schweiger, R., Neumann, H., Ritter, W.: Multiple cue data fusion with particle filters for road course detection in vision systems. In: 2006 IEEE Intelligent Vehicles Symposium, pp. 400–405. IEEE (2006)
16. Yan, X., Yang, J., Yumer, E., Guo, Y., Lee, H.: Perspective transformer nets: learning single-view 3D object reconstruction without 3D supervision. In: Advances in Neural Information Processing Systems, pp. 1696–1704 (2016)

Scenario Referring Expression Comprehension via Attributes of Vision and Language

Shaonan Wei[1], Jianming Wang[2,3], Yukuan Sun[5(✉)], Guanghao Jin[2,4], Jiayu Liang[2], and Kunliang Liu[2]

[1] School of Electronics and Information Engineering, Tianjin Polytechnic University, Tianjin, China
[2] School of Computer Science and Technology, Tianjin Polytechnic University, Tianjin, China
[3] Tianjin International Joint Research and Development Center of Autonomous Intelligence Technology and Systems, Tianjin Polytechnic University, Tianjin, China
[4] Tianjin Key Laboratory of Autonomous Intelligence Technology and Systems, Tianjin Polytechnic University, Tianjin, China
[5] Center for Engineering Internship and Training, Tianjin Polytechnic University, Tianjin, China
sunyukuan@tjpu.edu.cn

Abstract. Referring Expression Comprehension (REC) is a task that requires to indicate particular objects within an image by natural language expressions. Previous studies on this task have assumed that the language expression and the image are one-to-one correspondence, that is, the language refers to the target region must exist in the current image and then the region with the highest score will be located, no matter whether they match or not. However, in practical applications, REC is required to locate the reference target region from a series of matched, semi-matched and mismatched scene image sequences. It is the 3D version of this challenge that refers to as *Scenario Referring Expression Comprehension (SREC)* in this paper. To accomplish such a task, we made a testset based on the existing real-scenario dataset enhancement, constructed a *Dual Attributes Recursive Retrieve Reasoning Model (DA3R)* for the first time with the Attributes of both images and expressions, and finally verified the feasibility of the method on the testset by assess with three different types of enhanced expression.

Keywords: Scenario · Referring Expression Comprehension · Attributes

The first author of this paper is a student. This work was supported by the National Natural Science Foundation of China (No. 61373104, No. 61405143); the Excellent Science and Technology Enterprise Specialist Project of Tianjin (No. 18JCTPJC59000) and the Tianjin Natural Science Foundation (No. 16JCYBJC42300).

Z. Lin et al. (Eds.): PRCV 2019, LNCS 11859, pp. 430–441, 2019.
https://doi.org/10.1007/978-3-030-31726-3_37

1   Introduction

Referring Expression Comprehension (REC) [8,15,18] is a task that requires to indicate particular objects within an image by natural language expressions, which inputs an image I and its corresponding language expression L, obtains a set of candidate regions $\{O\}$ through image processing and outputs O matching with L. The whole task can be regarded as the process of language expression and target region retrieve matching. Previous work all default that the image and expression are corresponding, so when all subjects $\{O\}$ cannot match with the language expression L, the model will still locate a region with the highest score, which is obviously not conducive to the application. For example, in the scene of visual-and-language based robot navigation, the robot is required to find the target object from the random position of the scene according to the language expression. (The scene here is not represented by a single image or a panoramic image spliced from a set of images, but the scene image sequences, which were collected from different angles of any position in the real environment from the first perspective of a human/robot.) To complete such a practical application, REC must learn to locate the referring target O in a series of matched, semi-matched and mismatched scene image sequences $\{I\}|_{Position \in Scene}$ based on the language expression L. This task is referred as *Scenario Referring Expression Comprehension (SREC)* in this paper (Fig. 1).

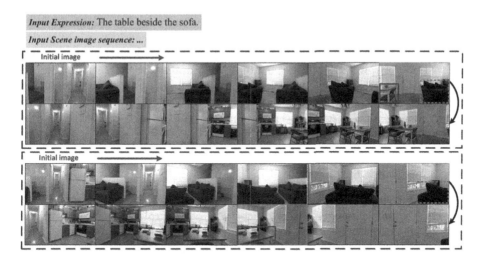

Fig. 1. SREC requires to locate the target region (red-box) by one or more consecutive images in the scene image sequence according to the text expression. (Color figure online)

Despite its impressive achievements, REC has undeniably neglected the relationship between vision and language, which is both "relevant" and "independent". At present, all solutions for REC tied the fate of images and expressions together make the whole process can be regarded as a "one-shot" retrieval matching, but the matched, semi-matched and mismatched relationship between them cannot be determined, which is not conducive to the crossing of REC from 2D images to 3D scenes. To solve such a contradiction and fulfill the task requirements of SREC, this paper constructed a *Dual Attributes Recursive Retrieve Reasoning Model (DA3R)* for the first time with the Attributes of both images and expressions. Firstly, parsing the language expression to get its main instances: "subject", "object" and "relationship" as the Attributes $\{A_L\}$ of the expression. Secondly, the scene image sequences of any position are processed through the traditional object detection method to obtain the Attributes $\{A_O\}$ of the image. Then the Attributes of the two parts are embedded through Word2Vec, and the distance between the two embedded vectors are calculated to get the matching rate $P(A_O|A_L)$. The matching rate is given a range here to solve the problem of agreeing on different statements between the training label and the expression, such as "TV" and "television". When the Attributes in the scene image sequence completely matched the Attributes of expression, finally output the region and the image in which the target is expressed. Otherwise, transform scene image sequence continues to locate the referential target until the key observation positions of the scene is recurred completely and then output the final result.

2   Related Work

With the rapid development of visual and language research in recent years, there are more and more tasks of visual-and-language integration. V2L [22], Image/Text Retrieval [13], VQA [4], Referring Expression [8,15,18] and so on, which all pushing the theoretical research forward to the practical applications. To facilitate the expansion of these tasks to actual scenes, lots of scene datasets and simulators [3,19] are competing to appear, providing convenience for the study of the tasks.

2.1   Image and Text Retrieval

Image and Text Retrieval is to measure the similarity between an image and a piece of text, which is the core algorithm of multiple pattern recognition tasks [9,13]. For example, in the cross-modal retrieval task of image and text [13], when given the query text, it is needed to retrieve images with similar contents according to the similarity of the image and the text; in the Image Caption task [22], given an image, we need to retrieve a similar text based on the image content and further generate a text description of it; in the VQA task [4], it is required to find the content that contains the corresponding answer in the image based on the given text question, and then retrieve the similar text as the predicted answer from the found content. Traditional method extracts multiple local instances contained in the image and text by CNN-LSTM, and then inserts them into a common space to complete the task of retrieval and matching. The process of instance extraction usually requires explicit use of additional object detection algorithms or manual tagging. The processing flow of this task can be regarded as the retrieval and matching process of image instances and language expression instances.

2.2 Referring Expression Comprehension

This task requires both visual features and textual features to comprehend the expressed reference. Modern approaches of REC usually embed the image and its expression into a common space through CNN-LSTM, then the task can be addressed in a retrieval manner, wherein the target region is selected with the minimum distance to the expression in the common space. In the process, object detection can be utilized to obtain a group of candidate regions in the first place [8,10,12,15,18,24]. However, this method focuses on the global information of the image and expression, irrelevant instances will be concerned in the process, and there is always an unbridgeable gap between the image and the text. Therefore, Referring to V2L [22] and VQA [21] using Attributes, the Referring Expression task is trying to use Attributes to replace the global image information and eliminate the semantic gap between images and texts [11,23]. At the same time, more and more attention has been paid on the effect of useless instances in language expression on visual-language tasks, and improvements have been made to methods by analyzing the effect of language expression instances on results [7,14,23].

2.3 Scenario Image Dataset

The scenario image dataset is different from the traditional image sets used by VQA and other tasks. It plays a crucial role in verifying the application of various visual-and-language tasks in reality. At present, there are many virtual and real scene simulators for robot navigation tasks, and the datasets used by these simulators are also applicable to other visual-language tasks. Action Vision Dataset (AVD) [1] is such a small scene real image dataset. In its acquisition process, the sampling points of the scene were firstly obtained discretely with the nearest neighbor distance of 30 cm, which has four nearest neighbors. Then the real scene images were sampled at every angle of 30° for each sampling point, which can simulate the environment seen when the person/robot moves. The datasets used by MINOS [19] and Matterport3D [3] are also real scene images, and the collection process is similar to AVD too, but their sampling points are relatively sparse, which are not as dense as AVD and conform to the motion state in the process of robot movement. In this paper, the SREC testset was obtained by the enhencement of AVD, so that the REC task was extended from the 2D image level to the 3D scene to be more suitable for practical application.

3   Approach

The overall solution to the SREC task in this paper can be seen as a retrieval matching process for the instances of image and language expression. The frame-

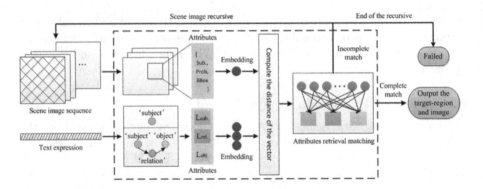

Fig. 2. Architecture of the Dual Attributes Recursive Retrieve Reasoning Model

work, as shown in Fig. 2, consists of three main parts: Expression Attributes Extraction, Image Attributes Extraction, and Attributes Retrieval Matching. The following sections provide a detailed interpretation of each part.

3.1 Scenario Dataset Enhancement

Scenario Dataset is crucial for SREC task. In this paper, Action Vision Dataset [1] was selected as the benchmark of the testset for SREC task, which includes 20,000+ RGB-D images in 9 unique scenes. The collection process is described in Sect. 2.3. Therefore, the dataset can greatly simulate the scene seen by the robot/human movement and restore its 3D structure.

In the AVD dataset, each sampling point P contains 12 consecutive scene images, which will constitute the complete scene observed under the sampling point. In the SREC task, scene images collected at each sampling point are taken as a sequence, then the scene image set $S = \sum_p \{I_{p,n}\}_{n=1}^{12}|_{p \in scene}$. Due to the size of the scene in AVD, the number of image sequences included in each scene is different, but for the entire SREC testset, the number of S is 2062. After that, in order to ensure the integrity of the experiment and verify the influence of observation position on the results, we divided the regions according to its characteristics of each scene. The divison criterion is that all items can be observed by the sampling points in the region, and finally confirmed the central point C of the region to facilitate the experiment. We also enhanced the scene dataset with text expressions, which made the corresponding text expressions for the items and their relations contained in each scene, so as to meet the requirements of the testset for SREC task.

3.2 Expression Attributes Extraction

When the text is expressed as *"Go to the sofa beside the table."* only the main instances *"sofa, beside, table"* transmit all the information, while other non-main instances have no influence on the meaning expressed, but will interfere with the result of the retrieval matching process. So, we extract the main instances as the Attributes from the text expression and use it as a part of DA3R. The process is expressed by the following formula:

$$L = \langle l_1, l_2, l_3, ... \rangle \xrightarrow{parse} A_L = \langle L_{subject}, L_{relation}, L_{object} \rangle \qquad (1)$$

To extract Attributes from text expressions, we use the semantic instance extraction pipeline used in the SPICE metric [2]. SPICE was originally defined as the measurement in image captioning, a sentence was converted into a scene graph by using the Stanford Scene Graph Parser [20], and then the instances of the text expression was extracted from the representation. As this pipeline was originally designed for descriptive captions rather than text expressions in here, so, inspired by Question premises [14], some modifications are made to help extract the main instances of the expression, including disabling pronoun resolution and verb lemmatization, etc. In addition, the SPICE procedure occasionally produces duplicate nodes or object nodes not linked to nouns in the text expression, which we filter out. We also removed the instances like photo, image, scene, house, home, room, etc., because these words refer to the scene image, not the content of the image.

3.3 Image Attributes Extraction

An image usually contains endless information, but for SREC task, the useful infor only occupies a part of it. So, it is essential to obtain the main semantic infor (Attributes) from the image. For previous work, object detection algorithm was generally utilized to extract the Attributes of images [11,23]. In accordance with this idea, this paper makes use of YOLOv3 [17] to implement it.

In order to make the model more generalized for different scenarios, we use the VOC2007 dataset [6] to train the object detection model for the indoor instances. For training there use convolutional weights that are pre-trained on ImageNet [5], then the final weight will be obtained after that, which is used to achieve the object detection and Attributes extraction. When the scene image cross the model, relevant tuples of the target region are usually output like $t = [name, prob, [x, y, w, h]]$, where there is respectively represent of the instance's name, probability and the central coordinate, width and height of the Bounding-Box. For the output tuple, the BBox is particularly important, which can be used to infer the "relationship" between "subject" and "object", see Sect. 3.4 for more detail. After that, the Attributes of the scene image $= \langle t_1, t_2, t_3, ... \rangle_n$ and is ultimately used to matching the text expression Attributes for retrieval. This process can be expressed by the following formula:

$$A_I = \sum YOLO(I_p)|_{p \in sequence \in scene} \qquad (2)$$

3.4 Attributes Retrieval Matching

After the Attributes of the text expression and scene image are extracted, retrieval and matching them is the final and most important process. We embedded them into a common space and calculated their vector distance to get the matching rate. In this process, we need to retrieve t_s and t_o that matched with $L_{subject}$ and L_{object} from the A_I, and then indicate the $I_{relation}$ in the image based on them. If the $I_{relation}$ matchs with $L_{relation}$, the Attributes Retrieval Matching process is completed, finally output the region and the image in which the target is expressed. Otherwise, convert the scene image sequence to augment the A_I until the mission is completed or the scene image sequences of key observation points are fully recursed.

Embedding and Calculation. In order to calculate the matching degree of the Attributes extracted from images and text expressions, Word2Vec [16] was selected to embed them, then calculate the distance of the embedded vectors to obtain their matching rate. Firstly, massive text data is trained to obtain the vector spatial distribution between each word, and then the Attributes of expressions and images are binary embedded through W2V to obtain the corresponding spatial vector representation respectively: $\overrightarrow{v(I)} = [v_{I1}, v_{I2}, v_{I3}, ...]$ and $\overrightarrow{v(L)} = [v_{L1}, v_{L2}, v_{L3}, ...]$. Finally, the matching rate of the two vectors can be evaluated by calculating the cosine value between them. The measurement of matching rate P was implemented by the following formula:

$$P(V_I|V_L) = cosine(V_I|V_L) = \frac{\sum_{k=1}^{n} v_{Ik} v_{Lk}}{\sqrt{\sum_{k=1}^{n} v_{Ik}^2} \sqrt{\sum_{k=1}^{n} v_{Lk}^2}} \tag{3}$$

Process of Comprehension. We already know the expression Attributes $A_L = \langle L_{subject}, L_{relation}, L_{object} \rangle$. Then, firstly, the image Attributes A_I should be retrieved and matched with the $L_{subject}$ and L_{object} to determine the existence of the $I_{subject}$ and I_{object}. If they are both exist in one image, the relation between them will be determined next; if the existence crosses the image, recourse the scene image sequence to augment the A_I until the matching is completed or the sequence is fully recoursed. Secondly, the existence of $L_{relation}$ is to connect $L_{subject}$ and L_{object}, but there are missing the $I_{relation}$ to match with it. Fortunately, from BBOX that existed in the image instance tuples, we can get the center coordinates of the instance in the image, and according to the center coordinates of the $I_{subject}$ and I_{object}, we can get the extension of the relationship between them. For example, the center coordinate of the $I_{subject}$ is located to the left of the I_{object}, then the $I_{relation}$ can be defined as "left", "beside" and "near". In this way, we extend the common positional relationship expressions such as "left", "right", "on", "in", "near" etc., and finally use it to match with $L_{relation}$ to complete the task. It should be specially noted that when the existence of the $I_{subject}$ and the I_{object} are cross images, the determination of the $I_{relation}$ will consider the recursing direction of the view. For example, when the $I_{subject}$ exists in the subsequent image of the I_{object}, the "left" will be determined by the recursion of the image. Finally, we set a threshold value t for each instance of the match, which is the maximum tolerance. And after a lot of tests, we find that $t = 0.8$ is the most suitable here. The result of the final comprehension is represented by the following formula:

$$\theta = argmax \sum P(V_I | V_L) \tag{4}$$

4 Experiments

Before the experiment, we have trained the image Attributes extraction model to ensure the best performance. We have also tested the expression Attributes extraction module and trained the word vector spatial distribution data required by the Attributes embedding. Next, we will verify the reliability of the entire DA3R model for SREC task.

4.1 Single-Sequence Comprehension

Comprehension with any single point scene image sequence is the most direct way to measure the reliability of DA3R and the benchmark for other experiments. The experiment random selects an image in the scenario dataset as the initial one and locates the target referred by the expression around the sequence. We complete the experiment in all image sequences with each text expression

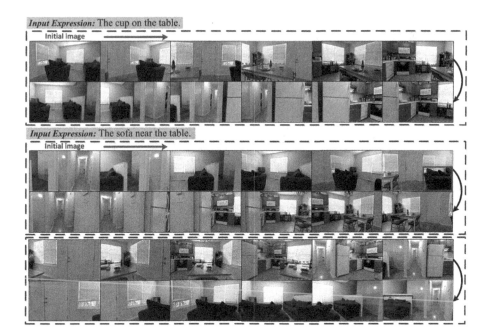

Fig. 3. Above is a partial view of the SSC experiment. The whole test proves the feasibility of DA3R, but the error in the bottom example indicates that the judgment of instances relationship in the scene still needs to be further improved.

corresponded to the scene. For example, in Scene I, there have 1536 scene images, each of which can be used as the initial one to form a sequence of scene images. What we need to do is to locate the reference target in the 1536 image sequences through each expression, and output the relevant regions and image. Figure 3 shows part of the test results.

4.2 Multi-sequences Comprehension

According to the above experiment, it can be seen that the result will be affected by the size of the target and the difference in the position, distance and angle of the observation point [25]. So to make the experiment more completely, it is also necessary to consider find the target in multiple image sequences determined by the key observation points of the scene. Based on the results of the Single-Sequence Comprehension experiment, when the model fails to locate the correct target region, the scene image sequence will be converted according to the key observation points until the task complete, which means that multiple image sequences will participate in the final comprehension of the task. Figure 4 is a partial demonstration of experimental results for Multi-Sequences comprehension.

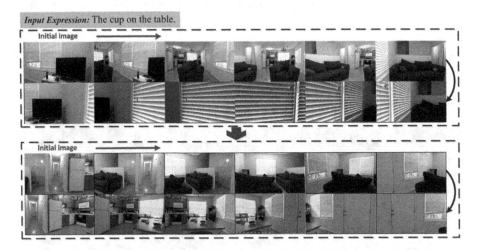

Fig. 4. This is an example of the MSC experiment. The process shows that the target to which the expression refers cannot be found in the initial scene image sequence due to problems such as distance and angle, etc. Then change the sequence based on the key observation point, continue to locate the target region and image.

4.3 Results and Analysis

After the above two groups of experiments, we obtained the corresponding results as shown in Table 1, which is measured against the standard $mIoU$ metric, but with a few changes – when the $IoU \geq 0.5$ for a single test, the result is set to

Table 1. Accuracy of the Single/Multi-Seq. experiments

Experiments	Single-Seq.	Multi-Seq.
Single objective reference (*Eg. The TV in the room.*)	0.84 (10368/12288)	1.00 (12288/12288)
Explicit relationship reference (*Eg. The cup on the table.*)	0.81 (7465/9216)	0.93 (8571/9216)
Implicit relationship reference (*Eg. The sofa near the table.*)	0.57 (5253/9216)	0.68 (6267/9216)

1; otherwise set to **0**. The correct rate **R** is calculated by the following formula. Where **L** is the text expression, **S** is the scene image sequence and **O** is the correct referred region.

$$R = \sum_i \sum_j P(O|L_i, S_j) \tag{5}$$

According to the description of the above two parts, we conducted experiments of Single/Multi scene image sequences. In the process of the experiments, text expressions in the testset were divided into three types, it is separate as "Single objective reference", "Explicit relationship reference" and "Implicit relationship reference". The first one in the sort refers to the expression that only contains the subject. This form of expression is crucial to verify the basic reliability of the model, and we regard it as the benchmark for task completion. The next two are both contained the "subject", "object" and "relationship", but the "relationship" between them is different. For the former, relationship is explicitly expressed, such as "on", "in", "left", "right", etc. But the relationship of the latter is not clear, such as "near", "beside", etc. The whole experiment carried out for the overall scene image sequences by each expression, just as the single objective reference, we have tested 12288 times, the whole process is difficult and time-consuming. So we used a piece of NVIDIA RTX 2080Ti for the training and testing, which greatly saved our precious time, and bringing convenience to the experiment.

Through the analysis of the experiment results in Table 1, we can see that: (1) The result of the Multi-Sequences experiment is better than the Single-Sequence, which can well overcome the influence caused by the distance, position, and angle between the target and the observation points. (2) For the experiments with single objective reference form as the benchmark, due to the target in the test scenes can be detected perfectly (although the accuracy of object detection cannot be 100%, but in the experiments of this paper, the targets contained in the test scenes all can be detected correctly), so if our DA3R model is reliable, the correct rate will be 100%. The experimental results of single objective reference finally verified this point, which further illustrates the reliability of the method in this paper. (3) Results of the explicit relationship test are obviously better than the implicit type, which indicates that the model cannot well complete the determination of fuzzy relationships. Furthermore, it is difficult to identify the relations from the cross-images (as shown in the bottom of Fig. 3), which is the reason for the low accuracy of corresponding experimental results. In general, DA3R model can achieve the basic SREC mission requirements and perform well under some certain experiments, but there are still some issues that require further consideration and resolution.

5   Conclusion

In this paper, contrapose the application of REC in real scenes, the SREC task is proposed, which is required to indicate the relevant image and regions in the scene image sequence through the language expression. To complete such a task, we made a testset based on the existing scenario dataset and constructed a Dual Attributes Recursive Retrieval Reasoning Model. DA3R overcomes the deficiency of the previous REC model that only capable of completing the task under the condition of a single image and corresponding expression, which is able to realize the process of retrieval matching the candidate regions in a set of matched, semi-matched and mismatched scene image sequences. The experimental results showed the reliability of the method and confirmed the influence of different scene observation point on SREC's implement. But in practical applications, we cannot directly obtain the key detection point to complete the acquisition of the scene instance. In future work, the sight of us will locate in the reasoning of the scene position changes and the determination of the cross-image target relationship. We believe that these studies will push the existing visual-language tasks into more and more practical applications and provide more possibilities for our life.

References

1. Ammirato, P., Poirson, P., Park, E., Košecká, J., Berg, A.C.: A dataset for developing and benchmarking active vision, February 2017. https://doi.org/10.1109/ICRA.2017.7989164
2. Anderson, P., Fernando, B., Johnson, M., Gould, S.: SPICE: semantic propositional image caption evaluation. In: Leibe, B., Matas, J., Sebe, N., Welling, M. (eds.) ECCV 2016. LNCS, vol. 9909, pp. 382–398. Springer, Cham (2016). https://doi.org/10.1007/978-3-319-46454-1_24
3. Anderson, P., et al.: Vision-and-language navigation: interpreting visually-grounded navigation instructions in real environments, November 2017
4. Antol, S., et al.: VQA: visual question answering. CoRR abs/1505.00468 (2015). http://arxiv.org/abs/1505.00468
5. Deng, J., Dong, W., Socher, R., Li, L.J., Li, K., Li, F.F.: ImageNet: a large-scale hierarchical image database, pp. 248–255, June 2009. https://doi.org/10.1109/CVPR.2009.5206848
6. Everingham, M., Van Gool, L., Williams, C.K.I., Winn, J., Zisserman, A.: The PASCAL visual object classes challenge 2007 (VOC2007) results. http://www.pascal-network.org/challenges/VOC/voc2007/workshop/index.html
7. Hu, R., Rohrbach, M., Andreas, J., Darrell, T., Saenko, K.: Modeling relationships in referential expressions with compositional modular networks. In: Proceedings of the IEEE Conference on Computer Vision and Pattern Recognition (2017)

8. Hu, R., Xu, H., Rohrbach, M., Feng, J., Saenko, K., Darrell, T.: Natural language object retrieval, November 2015
9. Huang, Y., Wang, W., Wang, L.: Instance-aware image and sentence matching with selective multimodal LSTM, pp. 7254–7262, July 2017. https://doi.org/10.1109/CVPR.2017.767
10. Nagaraja, V.K., Morariu, V.I., Davis, L.S.: Modeling context between objects for referring expression understanding. In: Leibe, B., Matas, J., Sebe, N., Welling, M. (eds.) ECCV 2016. LNCS, vol. 9908, pp. 792–807. Springer, Cham (2016). https://doi.org/10.1007/978-3-319-46493-0_48
11. Liu, J., Wang, L., Yang, M.H.: Referring expression generation and comprehension via attributes. In: The IEEE International Conference on Computer Vision (ICCV), October 2017
12. Luo, R., Shakhnarovich, G.: Comprehension-guided referring expressions, January 2017
13. Ma, L., Lu, Z., Shang, L., Li, H.: Multimodal convolutional neural networks for matching image and sentence. In: 2015 IEEE International Conference on Computer Vision (ICCV), pp. 2623–2631, December 2015. https://doi.org/10.1109/ICCV.2015.301
14. Mahendru, A., Prabhu, V., Mohapatra, A., Batra, D., Lee, S.: The promise of premise: harnessing question premises in visual question answering, May 2017
15. Mao, J., Huang, J., Toshev, A., Camburu, O., Yuille, A., Murphy, K.: Generation and comprehension of unambiguous object descriptions, pp. 11–20, June 2016. https://doi.org/10.1109/CVPR.2016.9
16. Mikolov, T., Chen, K., Corrado, G., Dean, J.: Efficient estimation of word representations in vector space. In: Proceedings of Workshop at ICLR 2013, January 2013
17. Redmon, J., Farhadi, A.: Yolov3: an incremental improvement. arXiv (2018)
18. Rohrbach, A., Rohrbach, M., Hu, R., Darrell, T., Schiele, B.: Grounding of textual phrases in images by reconstruction. In: Leibe, B., Matas, J., Sebe, N., Welling, M. (eds.) ECCV 2016. LNCS, vol. 9905, pp. 817–834. Springer, Cham (2016). https://doi.org/10.1007/978-3-319-46448-0_49
19. Savva, M., Chang, A., Dosovitskiy, A., Funkhouser, T., Koltun, V.: MINOS: multimodal indoor simulator for navigation in complex environments, December 2017
20. Schuster, S., Krishna, R., Chang, A., Li, F.F., Manning, C.D.: Generating semantically precise scene graphs from textual descriptions for improved image retrieval. In: Workshop on Vision & Language (2015)
21. Wu, Q., Shen, C., Wang, P., Dick, A., van den Hengel, A.: Image captioning and visual question answering based on attributes and external knowledge. IEEE Trans. Pattern Anal. Mach. Intell. 40(06), 1367–1381 (2018). https://doi.org/10.1109/TPAMI.2017.2708709
22. Wu, Q., Shen, C., van den Hengel, A., Liu, L., Dick, A.R.: Image captioning with an intermediate attributes layer. CoRR abs/1506.01144 (2015). http://arxiv.org/abs/1506.01144
23. Yu, L., et al.: MAttNet: modular attention network for referring expression comprehension, pp. 1307–1315, June 2018. https://doi.org/10.1109/CVPR.2018.00142
24. Yu, L., Poirson, P., Yang, S., Berg, A.C., Berg, T.L.: Modeling context in referring expressions. In: Leibe, B., Matas, J., Sebe, N., Welling, M. (eds.) ECCV 2016. LNCS, vol. 9906, pp. 69–85. Springer, Cham (2016). https://doi.org/10.1007/978-3-319-46475-6_5
25. Zhu, Y., et al.: Target-driven visual navigation in indoor scenes using deep reinforcement learning, September 2016

Incremental Poisson Surface Reconstruction for Large Scale Three-Dimensional Modeling

Qiang Yu[1,2]([⊠]) [iD], Wei Sui[2], Ying Wang[2], Shiming Xiang[1,2], and Chunhong Pan[2]

[1] School of Artificial Intelligence, University of Chinese Academy of Sciences, Beijing 100049, China
qiang.yu@nlpr.ia.ac.cn
[2] National Laboratory of Pattern Recognition, Institute of Automation, Chinese Academy of Sciences, Beijing 100190, China

Abstract. A novel Incremental Poisson Surface Reconstruction (IPSR) method based on point clouds and the adaptive octree is proposed in this paper. It solves two problems of the most popular Poisson Surface Reconstruction (PSR) method. First, the PSR is time and memory consuming when treating large scale scenes with millions of points. Second, the PSR can hardly handle the incremental reconstruction for scenes with newly arrived points, unless being restarted on all points. In our method, large scale point clouds are first partitioned into small neighboring blocks. By providing an octree node classification mechanism, the Poisson equation is reformulated with boundary constraints to achieve the seamless reconstruction between adjacent blocks. Solving the Poisson equation with boundary constraints, the indicator function is obtained and the surface mesh is extracted. Experiments on different types of datasets verify the effectiveness and the efficiency of our method.

Keywords: Surface reconstruction · Large scale point cloud · Incremental

1 Introduction

Surface reconstruction is a widely studied problem in fields of computer graphics, and is significant for applications such as Augmented Reality (AR), City Digitalization and 3D Printing, *etc.*. Surface reconstruction from point clouds is very challenging since the point clouds obtained from scanning or image based methods are usually unorganized, noisy, data-missing or with misregistration.

With the efforts of researchers, numbers of surface reconstruction methods have been proposed in the last two decades, which can be roughly clustered into two categories, *i.e.*, Computational Geometry (CG) based methods [1,3,6] and Implicit Function Fitting (IFF) based methods [4,8,9]. The CG based methods

© Springer Nature Switzerland AG 2019
Z. Lin et al. (Eds.): PRCV 2019, LNCS 11859, pp. 442–453, 2019.
https://doi.org/10.1007/978-3-030-31726-3_38

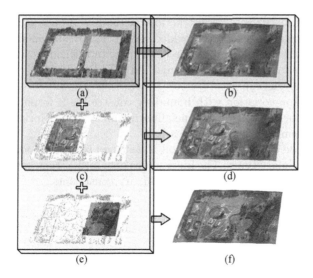

Fig. 1. Our IPSR method can incrementally and seamlessly reconstruct surface meshes from a series of neighboring point cloud blocks. Compared to existent methods (for instance the PSR method), the proposed method does not need to process all points from scratch repeatedly whenever new points are provided. (a) A skeleton point cloud containing two blank regions without points. (b) The reconstruction result of (a). (c) A new inner point cloud block which fills one of the blank regions in (a). (d) The incremental reconstruction result of (c) on the basis of (b). (e) Another new inner point cloud block like (c). (f) The incremental reconstruction result of (e) on the basis of (d).

attempt to directly recover geometry structures from point clouds. These methods are quite fast, but they are essentially local algorithms, and hence can not fill holes and are liable to be affected by noise.

Despite the effectiveness of the IFF based methods, the low efficiency and heavy computational load prevent their applications for large scale scenes. Besides, these methods can only deal with all points simultaneously.

To address the preceding problems, we propose an improved version of Poisson Surface Reconstruction (PSR) [9], called Incremental Poisson Surface Reconstruction (IPSR). Two main modifications are made compared to PSR: (1) Original octree is replaced by an adaptive octree which can be expanded flexibly when new points are provided; (2) Boundary constraints are integrated to Poisson equation, which guarantee the overall implicit function to be seamless. In our method, instead of repairing surface meshes after mesh fusion [5,11,15], the overall implicit function is reconstructed seamlessly in a divided and progressive way (shown in Fig. 1). The underlying mathematical model behind our method is a Poisson equation with well designed boundary constraints.

The main contributions of our method can be summarized as follows:

- An incremental surface reconstruction method is proposed for large scale scenes where point clouds are provided online and area by area. The proposed method is quite flexible and resource saving with the comparable reconstruction accuracy to the original PSR method, which is a popular benchmark of surface reconstruction.
- A novel Poisson equation with boundary constraints is formulated based on the adaptive octree, with which neighboring point cloud blocks can be reconstructed incrementally and seamlessly.
- An octree node classification method is designed to classify octree nodes into inner and boundary types. The inner nodes help reconstruct implicit functions while the boundary nodes provide boundary constraints.

2   Related Work

2.1   Surface Reconstruction

The CG based methods, such as Delaunay triangulation [3], Alpha shapes [6] and Voronoi diagram [1], are early but effective ones for surface reconstruction. These methods directly reconstruct 2D triangles or 3D tetrahedrons by interpolating the whole or subset of points. Thus, they are quite fast and easy to implement. Furthermore, they do not need any prior assumption or auxiliary information about the scene. The main drawback of these methods is that noises and outlier points are taken into consideration during the surface reconstruction process, which will result in seriously bad results when the quality of points is poor.

Afterwards, the IFF based methods have been proposed to improve the robustness of surface reconstruction algorithm. These methods are designed to fit a scalar three-dimensional spacial implicit function or calculate signed distance field to points to represent the model, and then extract the surface as a level set of the implicit function. The implicit functions can be represented as the weighted sum of radial basis functions or piece-wise polynomial functions. The final watertight and manifold mesh will be obtained through marching cubes algorithm [10].

2.2   Poisson Surface Reconstruction

The PSR method is developed under the IFF framework. The main idea of the PSR method is that the implicit function can be estimated as the indicator function (whose value is 1 inside the surface and 0 outside the surface) of the model. The smoothed gradient of the indicator function corresponds to the divergence of normal vector field, which can be approximated by a summation over the oriented points.

We begin by reviewing the PSR method concisely. Let $\mathcal{V} : \mathbb{R}^3 \mapsto \mathbb{R}^3$ be the normal vector field of input oriented points, and $\mathcal{X} : \mathbb{R}^3 \mapsto \mathbb{R}^1$ be the indicator function. Then the problem is formed as a Poisson equation:

$$\Delta \mathcal{X} = \nabla \cdot \mathcal{V}, \tag{1}$$

where $\varDelta$ is the Laplace operator and $\nabla \cdot \mathcal{V}$ represents the divergence of normal vector field $\mathcal{V}$.

The implicit function in the PSR method is represented as the weighted sum of a set of multiresolution Gaussian functions constructed on nodes of the octree. Suppose $\mathcal{F}_i : \mathbb{R}^3 \mapsto \mathbb{R}^1$ is the Gaussian function attached to the i-th node in the octree, and then its value at point $q \in \mathbb{R}^3$ can be represented as

$$\mathcal{F}_i(q) = \mathcal{F}\left(\frac{q - \mathbf{c}_i}{\mathbf{w}_i}\right)\frac{1}{\mathbf{w}_i^3}, \tag{2}$$

where $\mathcal{F} : \mathbb{R}^3 \mapsto \mathbb{R}^1$ is the standardized Gaussian function, $\mathbf{c}_i$ and $\mathbf{w}_i$ are the center and width of the i-th node. Correspondingly, the indicator function and the normal vector field can be represented as

$$\mathcal{X} = \sum_i^n \mathbf{x}_i \mathcal{F}_i = \mathbf{x}^\mathsf{T}\mathbf{F}, \tag{3}$$

$$\mathcal{V} = \sum_i^n \mathbf{v}_i \mathcal{F}_i = \mathbf{v}^\mathsf{T}\mathbf{F}, \tag{4}$$

respectively, where n is the number of octree nodes, $\mathbf{x} \in \mathbb{R}^{n \times 1}$ and $\mathbf{v} \in \mathbb{R}^{n \times 3}$ are the coefficients vectors of indicator function and the divergence of normal vector field respectively, and $\mathbf{F}$ is a column vector of all node functions.

In Eq. (4), $\mathbf{v}_i \in \mathbb{R}^3$ is the vector held by the i-th node in the octree. It is calculated using the normal vectors of the points in the point cloud by the following function

$$\mathbf{v}_i = \sum_{p \in \mathsf{Ng}(o_i)} \frac{1}{\mathsf{Ds}(p)}\, \alpha_{p,o_i}\, p.\mathbf{n}, \tag{5}$$

where p is a point in the point cloud, o_i is the i-th node, $\mathsf{Ng}(o_i)$ is the point set bounded in the $3 \times 3 \times 3 = 27$ neighboring nodes of o_i, $\mathsf{Ds}(p)$ is the point density at p which is estimated as the number of points in its neighborhood [9], α_{p,o_i} is the trilinear interpolation weight of o_i among $2 \times 2 \times 2 = 8$ nearest nodes around p and $p.\mathbf{n}$ is the normal vector held by the point p.

Combined with Eqs. (2), (3) and Eqs. (4), (1) can be reformulated as an linear expression as follows

$$\mathbf{Lx} = \mathbf{v}, \tag{6}$$

where $\mathbf{L} \in \mathbb{R}^{n \times n}$ is the Laplace matrix defined as

$$\mathbf{L}_{i,j} = \left\langle \frac{\partial^2 \mathcal{F}_i}{\partial x^2}, \mathcal{F}_j \right\rangle + \left\langle \frac{\partial^2 \mathcal{F}_i}{\partial y^2}, \mathcal{F}_j \right\rangle + \left\langle \frac{\partial^2 \mathcal{F}_i}{\partial z^2}, \mathcal{F}_j \right\rangle. \tag{7}$$

After obtaining the coefficients vector $\mathbf{x}$, the indicator function can be easily calculated.

However, based on global Poisson equation, the PSR method easily results in over-smoothing of the input points. Another problem is that the PSR method can not deal with out-of-core reconstruction.

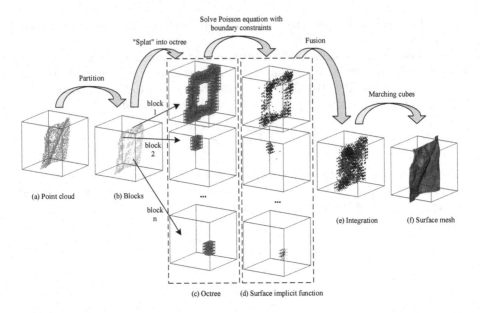

Fig. 2. The pipeline of our IPSR method. (a) The whole point cloud. (b) The partitioned blocks shown in different colors. (c) The parts of octree, on which the Poisson equations with boundary constraints are constructed and then solved. (d) The solved indicator function. We illustrate the indicator function by a series of spheres in 3D space. (e) The integration of the indicator function. (f) The surface mesh extracted from the octree using the marching cubes algorithm. (Color figure online)

2.3   Incremental Surface Reconstruction

Although the PSR method does well in handling noisy data, it suffers from a limitation that all points should be present before performing the surface reconstruction process. Hence, some methods have been proposed to address this problem.

Newcombe *et al.* [12] incrementally constructed a truncated signed distance function (TSDF) using the input points of each scan. Schertler *et al.* [14] incrementally refined the coarse base mesh using field-aligned method. These existing methods have a similar application of reconstructing small models from RGB-D images by indoor scanners.

In contrast, we propose the IPSR method based on the PSR method (and compatible with the SPSR method), which aims at incrementally reconstructing large scale scenes and accepts a series of neighboring but no-overlap-required point clouds.

3   The Proposed Method

In this section, we describe the proposed IPSR method for surface reconstruction from oriented points. Our method is specially designed such that it can perform

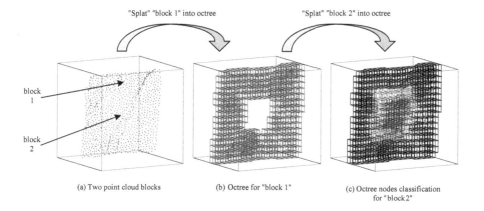

"Splat" "block 1" into octree   "Splat" "block 2" into octree

block
1

block
2

(a) Two point cloud blocks   (b) Octree for "block 1"   (c) Octree nodes classification
                                                                              for "block 2"

Fig. 3. The proposed octree nodes classification method. Left: the input two point cloud blocks, where different colors represents different blocks. Middle: the octree after the reconstruction of the blue block. Right: the new octree when reconstructing the red block. The nodes of categories 1, 2, 3 and 4 are colored in red, yellow, blue and black. The nodes of category 5 are ignored for clarity. (Color figure online)

the reconstruction process in an incremental manner. It is very flexible and resource saving with comparable reconstruction accuracy to the original PSR method.

3.1 Motivation

In the original PSR method [9], the coefficients vector of the indicator function $x \in \mathbb{R}^n$ is obtained by solving Eq. (6), where n is the total number of octree nodes. When the scale of the scene grows, the number of octree nodes become larger accordingly, which makes solving the linear system more time-consuming. Besides, when the scene of points are obtained multiple times, the linear system have to be constructed and solved repeatedly, which is resource wasteful.

Our method aims at reconstructing large scale scene incrementally, such as landscape or urban regions point cloud from the LiDAR on aircraft *etc.*. There are two situations which we pay attention to. First, the points are provided online, that is, one point cloud is provided each time the aircraft flies a line. Thus, we should incrementally reconstruct a series of point clouds from different flight lines. Second, all points are provided offline. In this situation, in order to make the use of our IPSR method, the point cloud should be first partitioned into a series of neighboring blocks. Figure 2 shows the pipeline of our method.

Comparing with the PSR method, the proposed IPSR method in incremental reconstruction mode requires less time and space.

3.2 Point Cloud Partition

When applying the proposed IPSR method to one single large scale point cloud, the whole point cloud needs to be partitioned into a number of blocks of arbitrary size. To make the full use of boundary constraints, we create two conditions to guide the point cloud partition progress.

A good partition should satisfy two conditions:

1. The point density in boundary regions should be as high as possible;
2. The underlying surface in boundary regions should be as smooth as possible.

3.3   Octree Nodes Classification

After dividing the point cloud into different blocks, each block is "splatted" into the octree and a corresponding Poisson equation is constructed on inner nodes while the boundary constraints are imposed on intra nodes. In this subsection, we classify the octree nodes to determine whether they should be taken into the reconstruction. According to the influence from the new coming points, the corresponding octree nodes can be classified into five categories as follows:

1. Nodes that are newly created.
2. Nodes where corresponding normal vector contributions are updated.
3. Nodes that are not included in categories 1 and 2 but the corresponding node functions interact with that of the nodes in categories 1 and 2.
4. Nodes that are not included in categories 1, 2 and 3 but the corresponding node functions interact with that of the nodes in categories 1, 2 and 3.
5. The rest nodes.

Naturally, the coefficients of nodes in the category 1 need to be calculated. In addition, the coefficients of nodes in categories 2 and 3 should be recalculated since the variation of the nodes' normal vector contributions and the corresponding items of the Laplace matrix. The nodes in category 4 are used for boundary constraints, because both their normal vector contributions and their corresponding items of the Laplace matrix keep unchanged during the reconstruction progress for the current block. In the following, we call the nodes in categories 1, 2 and 3 the Poisson nodes, call the nodes in category 4 the boundary nodes and call the nodes in category 5 the unused nodes. An example is given in Fig. 3 to demonstrate the classification results.

3.4   Incremental Reconstruction with Boundary Constraints

The underlying model of the proposed IPSR method is the Poisson equation with boundary constraints.

Let $\mathbf{x}_p \in \mathbb{R}^{n_p \times 1}$ be the coefficients vector of the Poisson nodes, $\mathbf{x}_b \in \mathbb{R}^{n_b \times 1}$ be the coefficients vector of the boundary nodes and $\mathbf{x}_u \in \mathbb{R}^{n_u \times 1}$ be the coefficients vector of the unused nodes, where the n_p, n_b and n_u are number of nodes in corresponding categories. We stack $\mathbf{x}_p$, $\mathbf{x}_b$ and $\mathbf{x}_u$ into a uniform vector $\mathbf{x}$, which is given by:

$$\mathbf{x} = \begin{bmatrix} \mathbf{x}_p \\ \mathbf{x}_b \\ \mathbf{x}_u \end{bmatrix}. \tag{8}$$

Let $\mathbf{x}_b^*$ and $\mathbf{x}_u^*$ denote the true values of $\mathbf{x}_b$ and $\mathbf{x}_u$, which are used as the boundary constraints. Accordingly, the linear system of our IPSR method can be rewritten as:

$$\begin{cases} \begin{bmatrix} \mathbf{L}_p \ \mathbf{L}_b \ \mathbf{L}_u \end{bmatrix} \begin{bmatrix} \mathbf{x}_p \\ \mathbf{x}_b \\ \mathbf{x}_u \end{bmatrix} = \mathbf{v}_p \\ \mathbf{x}_b = \mathbf{x}_b^* \\ \mathbf{x}_u = \mathbf{x}_u^* \end{cases}, \tag{9}$$

where $\mathbf{L}_p \in \mathbb{R}^{n_p \times n_p}$ is the Laplace matrix of the Poisson node functions, $\mathbf{L}_b \in \mathbb{R}^{n_p \times n_b}$ is the pseudo Laplace matrix of the Poisson node functions against the boundary node functions, $\mathbf{L}_u \in \mathbb{R}^{n_p \times n_u}$ is the pseudo Laplace matrix of the Poisson node functions against the unused node functions and thus $\mathbf{L}' = \begin{bmatrix} \mathbf{L}_p \ \mathbf{L}_b \ \mathbf{L}_u \end{bmatrix} \in \mathbb{R}^{n_p \times n}$ is the top n_p rows of the matrix $\mathbf{L} \in \mathbb{R}^{n \times n}$ in Eqs. (6) and (7).

Since the node functions of nodes in category 5 do not interact with that of any nodes in categories 1, 2 and 3, we have:

$$\mathbf{L}_u \equiv \mathbf{0}. \tag{10}$$

By substituting Eq. (10) into Eq. (9), we get:

$$\mathbf{L}_p \mathbf{x}_p = \mathbf{v}_p - \mathbf{L}_b \mathbf{x}_b^*, \tag{11}$$

where $\mathbf{L}_p$ and $\mathbf{v}_p - \mathbf{L}_b \mathbf{x}_b^*$ can be calculated from the normal vector field. It can be seen that $\mathbf{x}_p$ can be easily solved by the methods such as the conjugate gradient algorithm [7].

4   Experiments

In this section, we evaluate our method for incremental surface reconstruction on two datasets. Although there are many new methods such as KinectFusion [12] and field-aligned method [14], the comparison is not shown in this paper because of the limitation of paper space. In addition, our method is mainly designed on top of the PSR method, so we conduct comparative experiments with the PSR method to further demonstrate the capacity of our method.

Two different datasets are employed to evaluate our method. One is that collected from [2], which consists of 4 small point clouds. These point clouds are uniformly sampled from the corresponding MPU models [13] and hence the ground truths can be provided. With the ground truths, this dataset can be used to conduct experiments for quantitative comparison and analysis. For convenience, we name it as the benchmark dataset.

Another is a dataset in which the point clouds are obtained from large scale outdoor scenes such as landscape, hill, valley and buildings. It consists of 6 large scale point clouds without ground truth. For convenience, we name it as the landscape dataset.

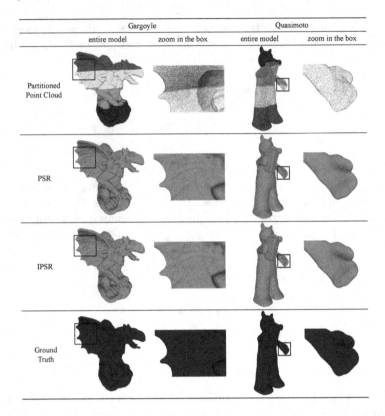

Fig. 4. The surface reconstruction results of point clouds in the benchmark dataset. Different colors indicate points in different blocks. We can see that the results of our method are nearly the same as the ground truths, and the boundary regions are natural and seamless. (Color figure online)

4.1   Reconstruction on Benchmark Dataset

In this subsection, we conduct qualitative and quantitative comparison experiments between our method and the original PSR method on the benchmark dataset. We simply partition the point clouds into several blocks uniformly and set the max depth of octree to 10 for all point clouds, which is deep enough to recover the details.

Qualitative Comparison. The surface reconstruction results of the benchmark dataset are illustrated in Fig. 4 (only two models are shown due to space limitation). We can see that the results of the proposed method are nearly the same as the ground truths. The boundary constraints constructed in Eq. (9) guarantee the seamless transition from one block to another.

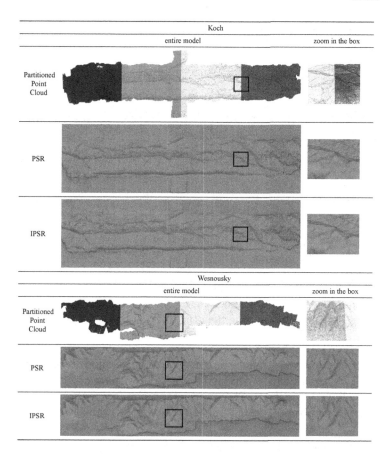

Fig. 5. The incremental surface reconstruction result of point clouds in the landscape dataset. Different colors indicate points in different blocks. (Color figure online)

Quantitative Comparison. To further demonstrate the advantage of our method, we conduct a quantitative comparison to evaluate the reconstruction accuracy of our method and the PSR method. Two metrics in [2] are used to measure the reconstruction accuracy: the distance error and the angle error. This experiment is conducted on the benchmark dataset since it contains ground truth.

As expected, the error values of our method are very close to those of the PSR method. When the octree depth is set to 10, the distance error and the angle error are bounded in 0.1 mm and 5° respectively.

4.2   Reconstruction on Landscape Dataset

In this subsection, we conduct qualitative comparison experiments between our method and the original PSR method on the landscape dataset, and show the

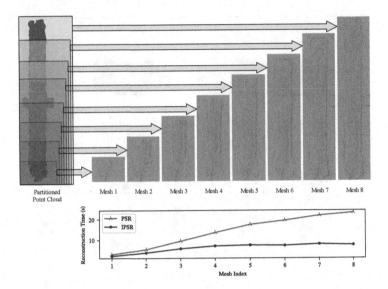

Fig. 6. The result of the incremental reconstruction for the landscape dataset. Our method saves a large amount of time than the PSR method.

great advantages in our incremental reconstruction method. It should be mentioned that this experiment is conducted not to prove that our method can deal with large scale data which the PSR method can not deal with, but to show that our method can perform faster and need less memory than the PSR method.

Reconstruction Result. The surface reconstruction results of the landscape dataset are illustrated in Fig. 5 (only two models are shown due to space limitation). From the reconstruction results we can see that the details are well maintained by our incremental reconstruction method.

Incremental Reconstruction. Under the circumstances that the point cloud of entire scene can not be provided at one time, our method is more profitable than almost all the IFF based surface reconstruction methods for its flexibility and resource saving ability.

The incremental surface reconstruction process is illustrated in Fig. 6.

5   Conclusion

We have proposed an incremental surface reconstruction framework, specially for large scale scenes where the point clouds are provided sequentially. The underlying mathematical model of our method is the Poisson equation with boundary constraints. Comparative experiments on different datasets verify the advantages of our method.

References

1. Amenta, N., Bern, M., Kamvysselis, M.: A new voronoi-based surface reconstruction algorithm. In: Proceedings of the 25th Annual Conference on Computer Graphics and Interactive Techniques, pp. 415–421. ACM (1998)
2. Berger, M., Levine, J.A., Nonato, L.G., Taubin, G., Silva, C.T.: A benchmark for surface reconstruction. ACM Trans. Graph. (TOG) 32(2), 20 (2013)
3. Boissonnat, J.D.: Geometric structures for three-dimensional shape representation. ACM Trans. Graph. (TOG) 3(4), 266–286 (1984)
4. Carr, J.C., et al.: Reconstruction and representation of 3D objects with radial basis functions. In: Proceedings of the 28th Annual Conference on Computer Graphics and Interactive Techniques, pp. 67–76. ACM (2001)
5. Dessein, A., Smith, W.A.P., Wilson, R.C., Hancock, E.R.: Seamless texture stitching on a 3D mesh by poisson blending in patches. In: IEEE International Conference on Image Processing, pp. 2031–2035 (2015)
6. Edelsbrunner, H., Mücke, E.P.: Three-dimensional alpha shapes. ACM Trans. Graph. (TOG) 13(1), 43–72 (1994)
7. Hestenes, M.R., Stiefel, E.: Methods of conjugate gradients for solving linear systems. J. Res. Natl. Bur. Stan. 49(6), 409–436 (1952)
8. Kazhdan, M.: Reconstruction of solid models from oriented point sets. In: Eurographics Symposium on Geometry Processing, p. 73 (2005)
9. Kazhdan, M., Bolitho, M., Hoppe, H.: Poisson surface reconstruction. In: Eurographics Symposium on Geometry Processing, pp. 61–70 (2006)
10. Lorensen, W.E., Cline, H.E.: Marching cubes: a high resolution 3D surface construction algorithm. In: ACM SIGGRAPH Computer Graphics, vol. 21, no. 4, pp. 163–169 (1987)
11. Min, J., Wei, X.: Robust merge of 3D textured meshes (2017)
12. Newcombe, R.A., et al.: KinectFusion: real-time dense surface mapping and tracking. In: 10th IEEE International Symposium on Mixed and Augmented Reality, ISMAR 2011, Basel, Switzerland, 26–29 October 2011, pp. 127–136 (2011)
13. Ohtake, Y., Belyaev, A., Alexa, M., Turk, G., Seidel, H.P.: Multi-level partition of unity implicits. ACM Trans. Graph. 22(3), 463–470 (2003)
14. Schertler, N., Tarini, M., Jakob, W., Kazhdan, M., Gumhold, S., Panozzo, D.: Field-aligned online surface reconstruction. ACM Trans. Graph. 36(4), 77:1–77:13 (2017)
15. Wuttke, S., Perpeet, D., Middelmann, W.: Quality preserving fusion of 3D triangle meshes. In: International Conference on Information Fusion, pp. 1476–1481 (2012)

Deep Voice-Visual Cross-Modal Retrieval with Deep Feature Similarity Learning

Yaxiong Chen[1,2], Xiaoqiang Lu[1], and Yachuang Feng[1(✉)]

[1] The Key Laboratory of Spectral Imaging Technology CAS,
Xian Institute of Optics and Precision Mechanics, Chinese Academy of Sciences,
Xian 710119, China
chenyaxiong2017@opt.cn, luxq666666@gmail.com, yachuang.feng@gmail.com
[2] University of Chinese Academy of Sciences,
Beijing 100049, People's Republic of China

Abstract. Thanks to the development of deep learning, voice-visual cross-modal retrieval has made remarkable progress in recent years. However, there still exist some bottlenecks: how to establish effective correlation between voices and images to improve the retrieval precision and how to reduce data storage and speed up retrieval in large-scale cross-modal data. In this paper, we propose a novel Voice-Visual Cross-Modal Hashing (V2CMH) method, which can generate hash codes with low storage memory and fast retrieval properties. Specially, the proposed V2CMH method can leverage deep feature similarity to establish the semantic relationship between voices and images. In addition, for hash codes learning, our method attempts to preserve the semantic similarity of binary codes and reduce the information loss of binary codes generation. Experiments illustrate that V2CMH algorithm can achieve better retrieval performance than other state-of-the-art cross-modal retrieval algorithms.

Keywords: Cross-modal retrieval · Deep hashing · Deep feature similarity

1 Introduction

Voice-visual cross-modal retrieval has been widely applied in computer vision and natural language processing communities [2,25,26], such as unmanned driving and search engines. The task of voice-visual cross-modal retrieval is to leverage visual images (resp. voices) as the query to retrieve relevant voices (resp. visual images). Because of the heterogeneity of multi-model data, it is difficult for users to find useful information efficiently and quickly. How to solve the heterogeneity problem of multi-model data and how to effectively implement retrieval is a huge challenge for cross-modal retrieval [21].

The first author is a student.

Z. Lin et al. (Eds.): PRCV 2019, LNCS 11859, pp. 454–465, 2019.
https://doi.org/10.1007/978-3-030-31726-3_39

Recently, many deep learning works have been developed to address the issue of the heterogeneity of multi-model data [5,7,19,22]. They generally encode the data of each modality into their own features, and then these features are leveraged to calculate the similarity between voice and image in the common representational space. Although existing voice-visual cross-modal retrieval methods have made some progress, there are still some shortcomings. Firstly, their retrieval features are all real-valued features, which require large storage space and long retrieval time. Secondly, these methods haven't taken full advantage of deep feature relationship between the voice modality and the image modality.

In fact, the hash code of a voice query (resp. image) is more accurately associated with the hash code of related images (resp. voices) if more similarity relationship between images and voices is noticed by humans [4]. Apparently, the above issues would be addressed if we fully associate the voice modality with image modality and hash codes can be leveraged as retrieval features. Motivated by this idea, an adaptive voice-visual cross-modal learning scheme is exploited to generate hash codes by bridging the deep feature similarity relationship between the voice modality and the image modality.

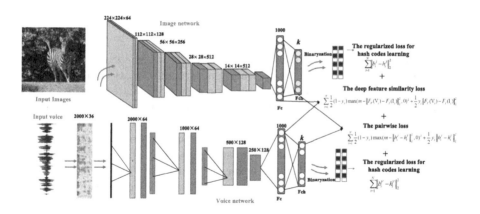

Fig. 1. The overall framework of the proposed V2CMH method.

In this paper, we propose deep voice-visual cross-modal retrieval method, namely *Voice-Visual Cross-Modal Hashing* (V2CMH), to generate hash codes by leveraging deep feature similarity to establish the relationship between voices and images, as illustrated in Fig. 1. To reduce the storage space and accelerate the retrieval speed, we learn hash codes from raw voices and images. Furthermore, the pairwise loss term and the regularized term are proposed to produce more efficient hash codes. To build the relationship between images and voices, V2CMH leverages deep feature representation to learn the semantic similarity relationship of images and voices in the feature space. Moreover, the regularized constraint for voices and images is proposed to reduce the information loss for binary codes generation. Experiments illustrate that V2CMH algorithm can achieve better retrieval performance than other state-of-the-art cross-modal retrieval algorithms.

The contributions of our paper can be summarized into several aspects: (1) A novel voice-visual cross-modal learning framework is proposed to exploit deep feature similarity to solve the problem of insufficient utilization of the semantic relationship between images and voices. To the best of our knowledge, it is the first work to generate hash codes for voice-visual cross-modal retrieval by exploiting high-level semantics similarity. (2) Due to the fact that the information loss of binary codes generation is inevitable, the regularized term is proposed to drive continuous values to approximate discrete values, which can reduce the information loss for binary codes generation. (3) Experimental results show that leveraging deep feature similarity can achieve better search precision than other state-of-the-art cross-modal retrieval algorithms.

2   Prior Work

With the development of multimedia technology, cross-modal retrieval has become a hot issue [9]. And in computer vision, the relationship between vision and voice has been explored recently [13,25].

Non-deep Cross-Modal Retrieval: Some early works focused on *Canonical Correlation Analysis* (CCA) to learn linear transformations to maximize the correlations between two modalities representations. Later, there appears some extensions of CCA. For example, [12] utilized CCA to exploit the relationships between talking face and spoken words. [28] analyzed canonical correlation between image and voice feature matrices though subspace mapping and applied such correlations for clustering on different datasets. In recent years, ranking techniques have attracted wide attention for multimodal problems. [27] presented a novel semi-supervised algorithm named ranking with Local Regression and Global Alignment (LRGA) to learn a robust Laplacian matrix for ranking.

Deep Cross-Modal Retrieval: Recently, many deep learning based models have been put forward to solve multimodal problems. [19] proposed a new deep visual-voice network to explore the multimodal correlates and performed the bi-directional cross-modal retrieval for images and speeches. [24] used the recurrent neural network to predict features of voice from videos and then generated waveforms from the learned features. [5] presented a novel deep neural network model which can acquire rudimentary spoken language through untranscribed voice data with the guiding of contextually relevant visual images. [1] designed a novel voice-visual correspondence learning task with the correspondence between visual and voice as supervised information. [22] presented a new problem, inferring from the voice about the face and vice versa, and introduced the multi-stream dynamic- or static-fusion architecture.

Many existing research on cross-modal voice-visual retrieval focuses on using real-valued feature to perform cross-modal retrieval. Different from these methods, our method not only leverages hash codes to perform cross-modal retrieval, but also establishes the similarity relationship between voices and images in the feature space by exploiting deep feature representation.

3 The Proposed Method

3.1 Problem Definition

Given N pairwise units $\mathcal{P} = \{I_i, V_i\}_{i=1}^N$ and N pairwise labels $\mathcal{Y} = \{y_i\}_{i=1}^N$ where I_i denotes i-th sample in the image modality, V_i denotes i-th sample in the voice modality. $y_i \in \{0, 1\}$, where $y_i = 1$ denotes that image I_i and voice V_j share identical concepts, $y_i = 0$ denotes that image I_i and voice V_j do not share identical concepts. The aim of cross-modal hashing learning is to find two appropriate mapping function $\mathcal{H}_I$: $\mathcal{I} = \{I_i\}_{i=1}^N \rightarrow \{-1, 1\}^{k \times N}$ and $\mathcal{H}_V$: $\mathcal{V} = \{V_i\}_{i=1}^N \rightarrow \{-1, 1\}^{k \times N}$ for the two modalities while maintaining the similarity of cross-modal data in the Hamming space [10,14], where k denotes the length of hash codes.

3.2 Multimodal Architecture

Figure 1 shows the entire network architecture of the proposed deep voice-visual cross-modal hashing framework. The whole system consists of voice branch and image branch. And then the two branches are explained below.

Voice Modeling: Similar to [6], we use a Mel-frequency cepstral coefficients (MFCC) to represent the voice. We use a 16 ms window size with a 5 ms shift between neighbouring frames, specifying 36 filters for the mel-scale filterbank. To take advantage of the computational efficiency, we force every voice spectrogram to the same size. We do this by fixing the spectrogram size at L frames (2000 in our experiments, corresponding to approximately 10 s of voice). We truncate any captions longer than L, and zero pad any shorter voice. The voice model is shown in Fig. 1. The first convolution layer of the voice network leverages filters with the width of one frame across the whole frequency axis. And then the following layers of the voice network is three 1-D dimensional convolution with batch normalization and max-pooling. The last two layers of the voice network are fully connected layers. The respective widths of these convolutional layers are 11, 17 and 19, respectively. All pooling operations exploit 2 strides. These convolutional layers leverage the *Rectified Linear Unit* (ReLU) [23] function as the activation function. The first fully connected layer exploits 1000 nodes, and the activation function of the first fully connected layer is *tanh* function. The second fully connected layer is hash layer, which contains k units and exploits *tanh* function as the activation function. The hash layer can produce k-bits binary-like codes, which can be leveraged to generate k-bits binary codes by the quantization function.

Image Modeling: The configuration of our proposed image model is listed in Fig. 1. Following [19], the convolution architecture of VGG16 is exploited to the backbone of the image model. Then the following layers of the image model are two fully connected layers. To build the relationship between images and voices, the first fully connected layer exploits 1000 nodes, and the activation function is *tanh* function. The second fully connected layer is hash layer, which contains k units and exploits *tanh* function as the activation function. The hash layer can produce k-bits binary-like codes, which can be leveraged to generate k-bits binary codes by the quantization function.

3.3   Joining the Voice and Image Branches

Different from these voice-visual cross-modal feature learning methods [5,19], the proposed method learns hash codes to perform voice-visual cross-modal retrieval. The raw image and voice are mapped into a common Hamming space. Given any image I_i and voice V_i, for image branch, deep hash function $\mathcal{H}$ can be defined as

$$b_i^I = \mathcal{H}_I(I_i) = sign(\tau(F_I(I_i); \theta_I)), \tag{1}$$

where b_i^I denotes k-bits hash codes for image I_i, $F_I(I_i^I)$ denotes deep feature representation for image branch, θ_I denotes the parameters of the hash layer for image branch. τ denotes tanh function. $sign(\cdot)$ denotes the element-wise sign function, *i.e.* $sign(x) = 1$ if $x > 0$, otherwise $sign(x) = -1$. For voice branch, deep hash function can be defined as

$$b_i^V = \mathcal{H}_V(V_i) = sign(\tau(F_V(V_i); \theta_V)), \tag{2}$$

where b_i^V denotes k-bits hash codes for voice V_i, $F_V(V_i)$ denotes deep feature representation in voice branch, θ_I denotes the parameters of the hash layer in voice branch.

Our aim is to find two appropriate mapping function $\mathcal{H}_I$ and $\mathcal{H}_V$ for the two modalities while maintaining the similarity of cross-modal data in the Hamming space [18]. For this aim, the pairwise loss is naturally designed to make matched image and voice as relevant as possible and mismatched image and voice as far away as possible [20]. Based on this purpose, approximate contrastive loss form is exploited as the pairwise loss to avoid collapsed situation [16], the pairwise loss $\mathscr{L}_p$ can be defined as

$$\mathscr{L}_p = \frac{1}{2} y_i H(b_i^I, b_i^V)^2 + \frac{1}{2}(1 - y_i) max(m - H(b_i^I, b_i^V), 0)^2, \tag{3}$$

where $H(b_i^I, b_i^V)$ denotes the Hamming distance between b_i^I and b_i^V, m denotes margin threshold parameter. $max(\cdot)$ denotes maximum function. The first term makes the hash codes of matched image and voice as close as possible, the second term provides the hash codes of mismatched image and voice as far away as possible when the Hamming distance of two hash codes is smaller than margin threshold m.

Directly optimizing the pairwise loss Eq. 3 is infeasible because the computation of the Hamming distance $H(b_i^I, b_i^V)$ needs to thresh deep neural network outputs. Nevertheless, threshing the network outputs may earn it intractable in the network training stage [17]. To solve this issue, a relaxation strategy is adopted to use l_2-norm of binary-like codes to replace the Hamming distance of hash codes, then Eq. 3 is rewritten as

$$\mathscr{L}_p = \frac{1}{2}y_i||h_i^I - h_i^V||_2^2 + \frac{1}{2}(1 - y_i)max(m - ||h_i^I - h_i^V||_2^2, 0)^2, \qquad (4)$$

where $|| \cdot ||_2$ denotes the l_2-norm of the vector. h_i^I denotes hash-like codes of image model, which is the continuous values of the hash layer in image branch. h_i^V denotes binary-like codes of voice model, which is the continuous values of the hash layer in voice branch.

Because binary codes $(+1/-1)$ are relaxed to continuous binary-like codes, we can leverage deep neural network to learn hash-like codes. And then binary-like codes are quantized into binary codes. However, the information loss between binary-like codes and binary codes will increase due to the quantization operation. Inspired by Iterative Quantization (ITQ) [3], a regularizer term is considered to reduce the information loss between binary-like codes and binary codes. The regularizer loss $\mathscr{L}_r$ can be defined as

$$\mathscr{L}_r = ||b_i^I - h_i^I||_2^2 + ||b_i^V - h_i^V||_2^2, \qquad (5)$$

To further learn effective hash codes, the proposed approach leverages deep feature representation to build the relationship between images and voices in the Euclidean space. Because similar deep feature representation can promote similarity learning of hash codes. To preserve the similarity relationship of deep feature representation, the deep feature similarity loss can be define as

$$\mathscr{L}_d = \frac{1}{2}y_i||F_V(V_i) - F_I(I_i)||_2^2 + \frac{1}{2}(1 - y_i)max(m - ||F_V(V_i) - F_I(I_i)||_2^2, 0)^2, \quad (6)$$

where $F_I(I_i^I)$ denotes deep feature representation for image branch, $F_V(V_i)$ denotes deep feature representation in voice branch. The first term makes deep feature representation of matched image and voice as close as possible, the second term provides deep feature representation of mismatched image and voice as far away as possible when the l_2-norm of two deep feature representations is smaller than margin threshold m.

By considering Eqs. 4, 5 and 6, the overall objective function $\mathscr{L}$ of the proposed V2CMH model can be defined as follows:

$$\begin{aligned}
\mathscr{L} &= \mathscr{L}_p + \alpha\mathscr{L}_r + \beta\mathscr{L}_d \\
&= \sum_{i=1}^{N}\{\frac{1}{2}(1 - y_i)max(m - ||h_i^I - h_i^V||_2^2, 0)^2 + \frac{1}{2}y_i||h_i^I - h_i^V||_2^2 \\
&\quad + \alpha(||b_i^I - h_i^I||_2^2 + ||b_i^V - h_i^V||_2^2) + \beta(\frac{1}{2}y_i||F_V(V_i) - F_I(I_i)||_2^2 \\
&\quad + \frac{1}{2}(1 - y_i)max(m - ||F_V(V_i) - F_I(I_i)||_2^2, 0)^2)\},
\end{aligned} \qquad (7)$$

where α and β denote the weighting parameters. The overall objective function in Eq. 7 can be optimized by Adam [11]. During the training stage, $\mathscr{L}_p$ makes the hash codes of matched image and voice as relevant as possible and the hash codes of mismatched image and voice as far away as possible. $\mathscr{L}_r$ can reduce the information loss between binary-like codes and binary codes. $\mathscr{L}_d$ makes deep feature representation of matched image and voice as close as possible and deep feature representation of mismatched image and voice as far away as possible.

4 Experiments

4.1 Dataset and Evaluation Protocols

To prove the effectiveness of the proposed V2CMH method, we exploit two image-voice datasets to compare with other cross-modal retrieval methods. (1) **Mirflickr 25K dataset** [8] contains 25,000 images taken from the "flickr" website. The dataset is a multi-label image dataset, which contains 38 semantic labels. In order to accomplish the cross-modal task of voice and image, we generate voice from semantic tags in text form, and use different speakers to ensure the diversity of speech samples. We construct 50,000 positive and negative image-voice pairs and select 40,000 image-voice pairs as the training set. The rest 10,000 image-voice pairs are chosen as the test and retrieval set. (2) **MS COCO dataset** [15] is a public dataset established by Microsoft team for image recognition, segmentation and image text description tasks. This dataset aims at scene understanding. It mainly intercepts from complex daily scenes. Similarly, we transform form the text of the validation set into speech and build our image-voice database to complete the task of cross-modal retrieval. We construct 81,008 positive and negative image-voice pairs and select 80% image-voice pairs as the training set. The rest 20% image-voice pairs are chosen as the test and retrieval set. The ground-truth neighbors can be given as image-voice pairs that contains the same concepts. According to previous works, two widely metrics are used in this paper: *mean average precision* (mAP) and the precision in top K of the retrieval list (precision@K). If the values of these metric indexes are higher, the performance of the experimental methods is more effective.

4.2 Implementation Detail

The proposed V2CMH approach is implemented by using the open-source KERAS[1] library. The experiments are conducted on workstation with GeForce GTX Titan X GPU, Inter Core i7−5930K 3.50 GHZ CPU and 64G RAM. The objective function Eq. 7 is optimized by exploiting Adam [11] with the learning rate 10^{-3}. The batch size is set to 64. To produce $\{16, 24, 36, 48, 64\}$-bit hash codes, hash code length k is set from 16 to 64 respectively. The initial weights of the image network leverage pre-trained weights. The initial weights of the voice network exploit glorot_uniform distribution. The parameter α is set as 0.1 and

---

[1] https://github.com/fchollet/keras.

Table 1. Comparison of V2CMH-R, V2CMH-D and V2CMH on Mirflickr 25K dataset with mAP for different hash bits

	Constraint	16 bits (mAP)	32 bits (mAP)	48 bits (mAP)	64 bits (mAP)
V → I	V2CMH-D	54.86	55.32	55.78	56.34
	V2CMH-R	55.76	56.18	56.84	57.63
	V2CMH	58.45	59.32	60.11	60.96
I → V	V2CMH-D	58.22	59.27	59.80	60.21
	V2CMH-R	59.58	60.16	60.96	61.73
	V2CMH	62.76	63.53	64.02	64.87

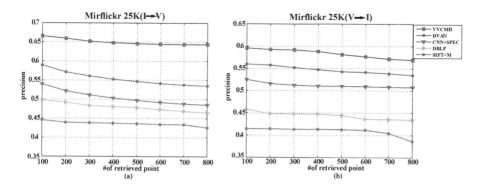

Fig. 2. The retrieval precision within different number of top returned samples with 64 bits on Mirflickr 25K dataset. (a) Using images to retrieve voices. (b) Using voices to retrieve images.

the parameter β is set as 1. The network is trained for 1,000 epoches, or stopped training until the loss does not diminish.

4.3 Evaluation of Different Factors

To measure the effectiveness of the regularized constraint and deep feature similarity in the proposed V2CMH approach, we implement the experiments in following three aspects: Firstly, we use the proposed method without using the regularized constraint to learn hash function (*i.e.* V2CMH-R). Secondly, we use the proposed method without considering deep feature similarity to generate hash codes (*i.e.* V2CMH-D). Thirdly, we exploit the proposed method (*i.e.* V2CMH). Table 1 shows contrastive results of V2CMH-R, V2CMH-D and V2CMH on Mirflickr 25K dataset with different bits. Here, "V → I" represents the case where the query sample is voice and the database is image. "I → V" represents the case where the query sample is image and the database is voice. It is seen from Table 1 that the proposed method can achieve better performance over V2CMH-R or V2CMH-D. For example, for using image to retrieve voice, V2CMH can improve the mAP with 32 bits to 63.53% from 60.16% implemented by V2CMH-R and

59.27% implemented by V2CMH-D. For using voice to retrieve image, V2CMH can improve the mAP with 32 bits to 59.32% from 56.18% implemented by V2CMH-R and 55.32% implemented by V2CMH-D. This is because the proposed method considers the regularized constraint and deep feature similarity to learn more efficient hash functions.

4.4   Method Comparison

To measure the effectiveness of the proposed V2CMH method, we compare our method with SIFT+M, DBLP [5], CNN+SPEC [1], and DVAN [19]. The method SIFT+M means that using SIFT to represent image and using MFCC to represent voice. And then project their own features to a common representational space, which is usually optimized by the pairwise loss that make matched voice-image pairs as relevant as possible and mismatched voice-image pairs as far away as possible. The methods DBLP [5], CNN+SPEC [1], and DVAN [19] were implemented according to the authors' papers. To compare the retrieval performance with those methods, we use the 64 bit hash code.

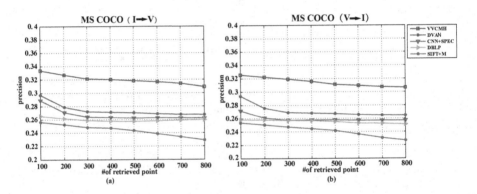

Fig. 3. The retrieval precision within different number of top returned samples with 64 bits on MS COCO dataset. (a) Using images to retrieve voices. (b) Using voices to retrieve images.

Table 2 shows the comparison of experimental results in our proposed V2CMH method and other methods on Mirflickr 25K and MS COCO dataset. We can explicitly observe that: (1) Although contrastive cross-modal retrieval algorithms have achieved good results on four widely metrics, the proposed V2CMH approach can achieve the highest retrieval precision within mean average precision, the highest retrieval precision within top 1 retrieved list, the highest retrieval precision within top 5 retrieved list and the highest retrieval precision within top 10 retrieved list on Mirflickr 25K and MS COCO dataset. (2) The conventional cross-modal retrieval approaches exploiting deep feature can achieve better performance than the identical approaches exploiting hand-crafted feature. For example, for the use of image to retrieve voice, CNN+SPEC can

Table 2. The comparison of experimental results in our proposed V2CMH method and other methods on Mirflickr 25K and MS COCO dataset

Task	Method	Mirflickr 25K				MS COCO			
		mAP	P@1	P@5	P@10	MAP	P@1	P@5	P@10
V → I	SIFT+M	40.71	51.78	50.36	48.57	24.88	32.14	27.13	26.81
	DBLP [5]	45.76	52.18	51.61	50.49	25.04	33.76	32.54	28.26
	CNN+SPEC [1]	51.24	57.66	56.37	54.21	25.41	34.23	32.33	29.79
	DVAN [19]	54.26	63.28	60.45	59.03	28.32	38.23	35.57	29.90
	V2CMH	**57.96**	**67.07**	**66.24**	**65.42**	**31.78**	**41.34**	**40.26**	**38.84**
I → V	SIFT+M	43.64	54.20	52.19	51.56	24.98	32.87	28.09	27.37
	DBLP [5]	48.67	58.46	57.52	55.83	26.23	35.34	34.51	30.48
	CNN+SPEC [1]	52.37	61.81	60.92	59.48	27.77	36.61	34.93	31.24
	DVAN [19]	57.35	67.26	66.96	64.56	28.45	39.12	36.69	32.10
	V2CMH	**64.87**	**72.28**	**71.54**	**70.79**	**32.06**	**41.89**	**40.81**	**39.56**

improve the mAP result on Mirflickr 25K dataset to 52.37% from 43.64% implemented by SIFT+M, For the use of voice to retrieve image, CNN+SPEC can improve the MAP result on Mirflickr 25K dataset to 51.24% from 40.71% implemented by SIFT+M, which demonstrates that deep feature can improve conventional hand-crafted features' performance. (3) For the use of image to retrieve voice on MS COCO dataset, the proposed V2CMH method can improve the mAP result from SIFT+M (24.88%), DBLP (25.04%), CNN+SPEC (25.41%), DVAN (28.32%) to 31.78%. Furthermore, for the use of voice to retrieve image on MS COCO dataset, the proposed V2CMH method can improve the average mAP result from SIFT+M (24.98%), DBLP (26.23%), CNN+SPEC (27.77%), DVAN (28.45%) to 32.06%. This is because V2CMH does not only learn binary representation by exploiting deep feature similarity learning, but also leverage the regularized constraint to enhance binary representation learning.

Figure 2(a) shows the retrieval precision within different number of top returned samples for using images to retrieve voices with 64 bits on Mirflickr 25K dataset. Figure 2(b) presents the retrieval precision within different number of top returned samples for using voices to retrieve images with 64 bits on Mirflickr 25K dataset. Figure 3(a) illustrates the retrieval precision within different number of top returned samples for using images to retrieve voices with 64 bits on MS COCO dataset. Figure 3(b) reflects the retrieval precision within different number of top returned samples for using voices to retrieve images with 64 bits on MS COCO dataset. The results of these four figures further demonstrate the effectiveness of the proposed method.

5   Conclusion

In this paper, we propose a novel cross-modal retrieval method, which can leverage hash codes to implement retrieval for voice and image. The proposed method develop a deep feature similarity idea to establish semantic relationship between voices and images. Furthermore, we design a novel regularized constraint to reduce the information loss of binary codes generation. Extensive experiments demonstrate that the combine of deep feature similarity can achieve better search precision than other state-of-the-art cross-modal retrieval algorithms.

Acknowledgments. We thank all the reviewers and ACs. This work was supported in part by the National Key R&D Program of China under Grant 2017YFB0502900, in part by the National Natural Science Foundation of China under Grant 61702498, in part by the CAS "Light of West China" Program under Grant XAB2017B15. In addition, Y. Chen especially wishes to thank and bless B. Fei on August sixth in the lunar calendar.

References

1. Arandjelovi, R., Zisserman, A.: Look, listen and learn. In: Proceedings of ICCV, pp. 609–617 (2017)
2. Cao, G., Iosifidis, A., Chen, K., Gabbouj, M.: Generalized multi-view embedding for visual recognition and cross-modal retrieval. IEEE Trans. Cybern. **48**(9), 2542–2555 (2018)
3. Gong, Y., Lazebnik, S.: Iterative quantization: a procrustean approach to learning binary codes. In: Proceedings of CVPR, pp. 817–824 (2011)
4. Gu, J., Cai, J., Joty, S., Niu, L., Wang, G.: Look, imagine and match: improving textual-visual cross-modal retrieval with generative models. In: Proceedings of the IEEE International Conference on Computer Vision and Pattern Recognition, pp. 7181–7189 (2018)
5. Harwath, D.: Unsupervised learning of spoken language with visual context. In: Proceedings of Advances in Neural Information Processing Systems, pp. 1858–1866 (2016)
6. Harwath, D., Glass, J.R.: Learning word-like units from joint audio-visual analysis. In: Proceedings of Annual Meeting of the Association for Computational Linguistics, pp. 506–517 (2017)
7. Harwath, D., Recasens, A., Surís, D., Chuang, G., Torralba, A., Glass, J.: Jointly discovering visual objects and spoken words from raw sensory input. In: Ferrari, V., Hebert, M., Sminchisescu, C., Weiss, Y. (eds.) ECCV 2018. LNCS, vol. 11210, pp. 659–677. Springer, Cham (2018). https://doi.org/10.1007/978-3-030-01231-1_40
8. Hodosh, M., Young, P., Hockenmaier, J.: Framing image description as a ranking task: data, models and evaluation metrics. J. Artif. Intell. Res. **47**, 853–899 (2013)
9. Huang, F., Zhang, X., Xu, J., Zhao, Z., Li, Z.: Multimodal learning of social image representation by exploiting social relations. IEEE Trans. Cybern. (2019)
10. Jiang, Q.Y., Li, W.J.: Deep cross-modal hashing. In: Proceedings of CVPR, pp. 3270–3278 (2017)
11. Kingma, D.P., Ba, J.: Adam: a method for stochastic optimization (2015)
12. Li, D., Dimitrova, N., Li, M., Sethi, I.K.: Multimedia content processing through cross-modal association. In: Proceedings of the ACM International Conference on Multimedia, pp. 604–611 (2003)
13. Liang, Z., Ma, B., Li, G., Huang, Q., Qi, T.: Cross-modal retrieval using multi-ordered discriminative structured subspace learning. IEEE Trans. Multimed. **19**(6), 1220–1233 (2017)

14. Liang, Z., Ma, B., Li, G., Huang, Q., Qi, T.: Generalized semi-supervised and structured subspace learning for cross-modal retrieval. IEEE Trans. Multimed. **20**(1), 128–141 (2018)
15. Lin, T.-Y., et al.: Microsoft COCO: common objects in context. In: Fleet, D., Pajdla, T., Schiele, B., Tuytelaars, T. (eds.) ECCV 2014. LNCS, vol. 8693, pp. 740–755. Springer, Cham (2014). https://doi.org/10.1007/978-3-319-10602-1_48
16. Liu, H., Wang, R., Shan, S., Chen, X.: Deep supervised hashing for fast image retrieval. In: Proceedings of CVPR, pp. 2064–2072 (2016)
17. Lu, X., Chen, Y., Li, X.: Hierarchical recurrent neural hashing for image retrieval with hierarchical convolutional features. IEEE Trans. Image Process. **27**(1), 106–120 (2018)
18. Mandal, D., Chaudhury, K.N., Biswas, S.: Generalized semantic preserving hashing for cross-modal retrieval. IEEE Trans. Image Process. **28**(1), 102–112 (2018)
19. Mao, G., Yuan, Y., Lu, X.: Deep cross-modal retrieval for remote sensing image and audio. In: Proceedings of IAPR Workshop on Pattern Recognition in Remote Sensing, pp. 1–7 (2018)
20. Mao, M., Lu, J., Zhang, G., Zhang, J.: Multirelational social recommendations via multigraph ranking. IEEE Trans. Cybern. **47**(12), 4049–4061 (2017)
21. Mueller, M., Arzt, A., Balke, S., Dorfer, M., Widmer, G.: Cross-modal music retrieval and applications: an overview of key methodologies. IEEE Signal Process. Mag. **36**(1), 52–62 (2019)
22. Nagrani, A., Albanie, S., Zisserman, A.: Seeing voices and hearing faces: cross-modal biometric matching. In: Proceedings of CVPR (2018)
23. Nair, V., Hinton, G.E.: Rectified linear units improve restricted Boltzmann machines. In: Proceedings of ICML, pp. 807–814 (2010)
24. Owens, A., Isola, P., McDermott, J., Torralba, A., Adelson, E.H., Freeman, W.T.: Visually indicated sounds. In: Proceedings of CVPR, pp. 2405–2413 (2016)
25. Torfi, A., Iranmanesh, S.M., Nasrabadi, N., Dawson, J.: 3D convolutional neural networks for cross audio-visual matching recognition. IEEE Access **5**, 22081–22091 (2017)
26. Wei, Y., et al.: Cross-modal retrieval with CNN visual features: a new baseline. IEEE Trans. Cybern. **47**(2), 449–460 (2016)
27. Yang, Y., Nie, F., Xu, D., Luo, J., Zhuang, Y., Pan, Y.: A multimedia retrieval framework based on semi-supervised ranking and relevance feedback. IEEE Trans. Pattern Anal. Mach. Intell. **34**(4), 723–742 (2012)
28. Zhang, H., Zhuang, Y., Wu, F.: Cross-modal correlation learning for clustering on image-audio dataset. In: Proceedings of the ACM International Conference on Multimedia, pp. 273–276 (2007)

Exploiting Human Pose for Weakly-Supervised Temporal Action Localization

Bing Zhu, Tianyu Li, and Xinxiao Wu$^{(\boxtimes)}$

Beijing Laboratory of Intelligent Information Technology,
School of Computer Science, Beijing Institute of Technology,
Beijing 100081, People's Republic of China
{zhubing,3120181002,wuxinxiao}@bit.edu.cn

Abstract. Weakly-supervised temporal action localization aims to predict when and what actions occur in untrimmed videos with only video-level class labels. Most current methods make prediction based on global features, while ignoring the classification performance of local descriptions of human body. Additionally, these methods generate incomplete proposals via thresholding, which is too single and crude. To acquire high-quality proposals, we focus on incorporating local information, i.e. human body poses in videos, and propose a noval method called Class Activation and Pose Pattern (CAPP) for weakly-supervised temporal action localization. In our method, action proposals are generated by two modules: a Class Activation Sequence (CAS) module and a Pose Pattern Sequence (PPS) module. The CAS module fuses global features and local features to improve clip-level classification performance and the PPS module adds complementary proposals with high recall via pose pattern clustering. CAPP outperforms the state-of-the-art methods on both the THUMOS-14 and ActivityNet v1.2 datasets, which demonstrates the effectiveness of our method.

Keywords: Temporal action localization · Weakly supervised · Pose estimation

1 Introduction

Temporal Action Localization (TAL) [6,15,24] in untrimmed videos has achieved great progress in the past several years, which is considered as a fully-supervised problem with both class category annotations and temporal interval annotations. However, it is expensive and time-consuming to manually annotate the temporal boundaries of actions. In addition, different from video-level labels, temporal annotations are more subjective. For example, different people have different views on the start and end time when labeling the same action instance. Thus,

---

B. Zhu—Student author.

Z. Lin et al. (Eds.): PRCV 2019, LNCS 11859, pp. 466–478, 2019.
https://doi.org/10.1007/978-3-030-31726-3_40

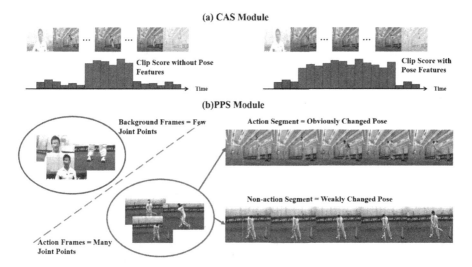

Fig. 1. This figure presents how to utilize pose infromation for weakly-supervised TAL. (a) Add into the network to improve clip level classification. (b) Generate more complete proposals by joint points and pose features.

weakly-supervised TAL methods [13,14,17,20] have been proposed to address these problems, which localize actions with only video-level labels available during training.

Most existing methods of weakly-supervised TAL focus on firstly generating good Class Activation Sequence (CAS) [13,20,25] with global features, and then producing proposals by thresholding on CAS. In these methods, they resort the loss function, such as Outer-Inner-Contrastive (OIC) loss in AutoLoc [17], to improve the video-level classification performance. However, what we need is the classification result of proposals. Detection performance is not only affected by the proposal-level classification, but also affected by the Intersection-over-Union (IoU) of proposals, which can also be regarded as the recall of proposals. The limitations of current methods are reflected in two aspects: (1) Global video features are used to describe scene information for clip-level classification while the action itself is usually ignored, which degrades the detection performance. (2) These methods only set the threshold on CAS to generate proposals, which is simple and unilateral, thus leading to low recall.

To tackle these problems, we try to exploit more information from local regions in the video frames, and propose to use human pose information. Many pose estimation methods [2,10,11] have achieved good performance as they can generate real-time and accuracy human pose joints. However, the high accuracy depends on high resolution frames so that the estimated pose joints in videos are not precise enough. On the other hand, it is still difficult to convert pose joint points into pose features [4,19,23] for classification and the classification performance is much lower than two-stream or C3D features. So we use pose pattern sequence as a complementary module to improve the classification performance of video clips as well as the recall of proposals.

In this paper, we propose a novel method called Class Activation and Pose Pattern (CAPP) for weakly-supervised temporal action localization, which consists of a Class Activation Sequence (CAS) module and a Pose Pattern Sequence (PPS) module. The CAS module fuses global features and local pose features for prediction, and connects the predicted class activation scores in temporal order as CAS. Then we set threshold on CAS to generate proposals, which are named as threshold-based proposals. In the CAS module, pose features improve the recall of threshold-based proposals by boosting the clip-level classification performance, as shown in Fig. 1(a). However, the threshold-based proposals can still not cover large region of action instances. Thus, we take full advantage of human pose joints and design the PPS module to generate high-recall proposals. As shown in Fig. 1(b), we use two selection strategies to remove background frames and segments. In the first selection, we remove frames by the number of human pose joints and compose the remained frames as candidate segments. In the second selection, we consider that poses would change obviously with the human movement. So we cluster the pose features to distinguish between action segments and non-action segments, where the action segments are named as pose-based proposals. Finally, we perform Non-Maximum Suppression(NMS) [12] to combine threshold-based proposals and pose-based proposals for temporally localizing actions.

In summary, the main contributions of this paper are:

(1) We propose exploiting human body poses for weakly-supervised temporal action localization. The estimated poses are newly applied in both proposal generation and feature representation.

(2) We propose a novel method (CAPP), which fuses global features and local features to improve clip-level classification performance and puts forward a clustering method with human pose information to generate high recall proposals.

(3) Our method outperforms the state-of-the-art methods on two challenging datasets, which demonstrate the superiority of our method on exploiting body pose for weakly-supervised temporal action localization.

2   Related Work

Weakly-Supervised Temporal Action Localization. It is essential to develop weakly-supervised TAL models since video label annotation is more easily collected than temporal instance annotation. Wang et al. [20] proposed a framework called UntrimmedNet, consisting of a classification module to perform action classification and a selection module to detect important temporal segments. Nguyen et al. [13] designed a network to identify a sparse subset of key segments associated with target action in a video by an attention module and fuse the key segments through adaptive temporal pooling. Shou et al. [17] proposed a novel Outer-Inner-Contrastive loss to automatically discover the needed segment-level supervision for training a boundary predictor. Paul et al. [14] presented W-TALC with two complimentary loss functions: a Multiple Instance Learning Loss and a Co-Activity Simialrity Loss.

Pose Estimation and Pose-Based Recognition. In recent years, studies in pose estimation have achieved great achievements and many pose estimation methods can generate accuracy human pose joints in real-time speed. Some methods [5][11] adopt the top-down framework. This framework firstly detects human bounding boxes and then applies single person pose estimation on each bounding box. Li et al. [11] proposed joint-candidate SPPE and a global maximum joints association algorithm to estimate poses in crowd scene. On the other hand, bottom-up methods [2,10] detect human pose joints firstly, and then associate detected joints into persons. Kocabas et al. [10] proposed pose residual network to group detected joints in a single shot by considering all the joints together. There have been many pose-based action recognition methods. These methods can be divided into two categories: joint-based methods [19,23] and heatmap-based methods [4]. Joint-based methods extract pose features from pose joints. Yan et al. [23] proposed ST-GCN to use spatial temporal graph convolutional network to automatically extract spatial configuration and temporal dynamics of joints. Heatmap-based methods extract pose features from pose heatmaps which represents the probability of being joints. Choutas et al. [4] proposed colored heatmap to better model the temporal dynamics of human pose.

3   Method

In this section we walk through the pipeline of CAPP, which is illustrated in Fig. 2. The PPS module and the CAS module are introduced in Sects. 3.2 and 3.3, respectively.

Problem Statement. Given a training set of N_v videos $V = \{v_i\}_{i=1}^{N_v}$, each video can be described with a frame sequence $X = \{x_i\}_{i=1}^{N_x}$, where N_x is the frame number. Each video has an action label set $A = \{a_i\}_{i=1}^{N_a}, N_a \geq 1$ and we train models only with the label set A. We also define the set of all the action categories as $S = \{a_j\}_{j=1}^{N_S}$, in which N_S is the number of total categories. During test time, given a test video, we need to predict a set $\Phi = \{\phi = (s_i, e_i, c_i, p_i)\}_{i=1}^{N_\phi}$, where N_ϕ is the number of predicted proposals. s_i and e_i are the start time and end time of the ith proposal, respectively. c_i represents the predicted category and p_i represents the confidence score.

3.1   Feature Extraction

The input of the PPS module is a frame sequence X, and then for each frame we use the CrowdPose network [11] to estimate human poses and obtain a set $P =$

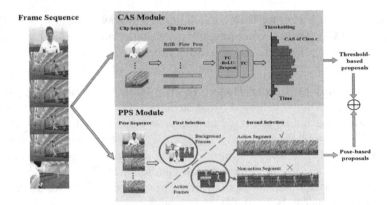

Fig. 2. Method Overview. Our proposed method CAPP contains the PPS module and the CAS module. In the PPS module, we use first selection on pose sequences and generate segments with joints number filtering. Then we use the second selection on segments to remove non-action segments by pose pattern clustering method. In the CAS module, the frame sequence of an input video would be divided as clips, which are used to extract global features and local fetures. Then these features will be fed into our network to generate CAS and predict action class label.

$\{p_\tau\}_{\tau=1}^{N_x}$, with $p_\tau = \{(x_i^j, y_i^j, s_i^j)|i = 1, ..., N_p, j = 1, ..., N_j\}$, where (x_i^j, y_i^j, s_i^j) represents the pose position and confidence score in the τ-th frame, N_p represents the number of persons and N_j represents the number of joints on one person. Then the pose set P is divided into clips and clips are fed into the ST-GCN network [23] to extract pose features. With the interval σ, the pose sequence P can be divided into non-overlap clips with the total clip number $N_c = N_x/\sigma$. The features are denoted as $F_{PPS} = \{f_i\}_{i=1}^{N_c}$, where $f_i \in R^{256 \times 1}$.

The input of the CAS module is a clip sequence with the total clip number $N_c = N_x/\sigma$, which is also generated from the frame sequence X. We use the CrowdPose network and the ST-GCN network to extract local features $f^{pose} \in R^{256 \times 1}$. For global features, we use the I3D network [3] pre-trained on the Kinetics dataset [9] to extract two stream features: $f^{RGB} \in R^{1024 \times 1}$ and $f^{flow} \in R^{1024 \times 1}$. We concatenate global features and local features as the final video encoding, denoted as $F_{CAS} = \{f_i\}_{i=1}^{N_c}$, where $f_i = [f^{RGB}; f^{flow}; f^{pose}]$.

3.2 Pose Pattern Sequence Module

The goal of the PPS module is to propose a noval way for generating action proposals. So we design two selection strategies to select segments which may contain actions.

The First Selection. The first selection utilizes the number of human pose joints. The pose frame p_τ with the human pose joint number J_τ less than threshold θ will be viewed as a background frame. For each untrimmed video X with

N_x frames, we first use the Crowdpose network to extract human pose joints, $p_\tau = \{(x_i^j, y_i^j, s_i^j) | \tau = 1, .., N_x, i = 1, ..., N_p, j = 1, ..., N_j\}$, where (x_i^j, y_i^j, s_i^j) represents the position and confidence score of the jth joint of the ith person in the τth frame. The total joint number J_τ in the τth frame is computed as follows:

$$J_\tau = \sum_{i=1}^{N_p} \sum_{j=1}^{N_j} step(s_i^j, 0.05) \tag{1}$$

where $step(\cdot)$ represents a step function with threshold 0.05. The remaining continuous frames are integrated into segments, denoted as the set $\Phi_{first} = \{\phi_i = (s_i, e_i)\}_{i=1}^{N_{first}}$, where s_i and e_i represent the start time and end time of the ith proposal, respectively.

The Second Selection. In the second selection, based on the characteristic that poses can convey syntax information in a long duration, we suppose that the poses in non-action segments will not change apparently, while poses in action segments will show the apparent trend of change. Then we divide segments into two categories using a clustering method which is named Pose Pattern Clustering, and segments that may contain actions are regarded as proposals.

For each segment in the set Φ_{first}, we extract the corresponding pose features from F_{PPS}, denoted as $F_\phi = \{f_i\}_{i=1}^{N_f}$, where N_f means the number of clip features in the segment ϕ. We compute the distance of clip features as $d_t = \cos(f_1, f_t)$. So the segment can be represented as $D = \{d_t\}_{t=1}^{N_f}$. And for each video, $\Phi_{first} = \{\phi_i = (s_i, e_i, D_i)\}_{i=1}^{N_{first}}$.

As for different segments, N_f is also different, which needs to be scaled for clustering. So we apply linearly interpolation to D, sampling the distance sequence with 16 points, denoted as $D' \in R^{16}$. We name D' as Pose Pattern. Then for all the video sets, we apply clustering to divide segments into two categories according to the results of clustering and denote the segment set that contains actions as pose-based proposals $\Phi_{PPS} = \{\phi_i = (s_i, e_i)\}_{i=1}^{N_{PPS}}$.

3.3 Class Activation Sequence Module

The CAS module fuses global features and local features to generate class activation sequences, and then sets threshold on it to generate proposals.

Prediction and Localization. The two-stream features and pose features are fused for clip-level prediction in weakly-supervised layers and prediction scores are connected in temporal order, then CAS is set with a threshold to generate proposals. Concretely, for each video X, we get its feature set $F_{CAS} = \{f_i\}_{i=1}^{N_c}$, where $f_i = [f^{RGB}; f^{flow}; f^{pose}] \in R^{2304 \times 1}$. Then these features are passed into a weakly-supervised network as follows:

$$X = D(Relu(W_{fc1}[f^{RGB}; f^{flow}; f^{pose}]^T \bigoplus b_{fc1}), k_{dp}). \tag{2}$$

where D represents dropout layer with the dropout rate of k_{dp}. $W_{fc1} \in R^{2304 \times 2304}$ and $b_{fc1} \in R^{2304 \times 1}$ are parameters to be learned in the first fully-connected layer. $\oplus$ represents the element-wise addition operation. X is the fused feature map, and is passed into the second fully-connected layer to compute the class activation score $o \in R^{N_S \times 1}$ where N_S is the number of categories:

$$o = W_{fc2}X \bigoplus b_{fc2}. \tag{3}$$

where $W_{fc2} \in R^{N_S \times 2304}$ and $b_{fc2} \in R^{N_S \times 1}$ are parameters to be learned. The sequence of class activation score o can also be called as class activation sequence $O = \{o_i\}_{i=1}^{N_c}$, which will be used for classification and localization.

To classify the whole untrimmed video X, we select k-max clip-level class activation scores to compute the video-level scores S. The value of k is proportional to video clip length N_c, and computed as follows: $k = max(1, \lfloor \frac{N_c}{p} \rfloor)$, where p is proportional coefficient. We denote the indexes of k-max-scored clips as $ID = \{id_{i,c} | i \in 1, ..., k, c = 1, ..., N_S\}$, then the video-level score S_c for class c is computed as follows: $S_c = \frac{1}{k} \sum_{i=1}^{k} o_{id_{i,c}}$. Finally, the class prediction of the whole untrimmed video is defined by $\{c | S_c > \eta\}_{c=1}^{N_S}$, which indicates that classes whose scores S_c more than threshold η are predicted.

To generate proposals, we set a threshold μ on the class activation sequence, and the continuous clips whose scores are more than μ are connected as proposals. The proposal set $\Phi_{CAS} = \{\phi_i = (s_i, e_i, c_i, p_i)\}_{i=1}^{N_{CAS}}$ need to be predicted, where N_{CAS} is the number of proposals. s_i and e_i are the start time and end time of ith proposal, respectively. c_i and p_i are class label and confidence score of the proposal, respectively.

Loss Function. We use the general Multi Instance Learning (MIL) loss [26] in weakly-supervised object localization and the CAS loss proposed in WTALC [14]. MIL loss is the cross-entropy summation of predicted class score with ground-truth:

$$L_{MIL} = \frac{1}{N_v} \sum_{i=1}^{N_v} \sum_{j=1}^{N_S} -y_{i,j} \log(p_{i,j}) \tag{4}$$

where $y_{i,j} = [y_i^1, ..., y_i^{N_S}]^T$ is the normalized ground-truth vector, and $p_{i,j}$ is the softmaxed video-level class activation scores.

The CAS loss is designed to make non-action and action features far from each other, as well as action features of the same class similar to each other. Given two videos x_m and x_n of the class c, the loss is computed by:

$$L_c^{mn} = \frac{1}{2} \{ max(0, d[f_{m,c}^H, f_{n,c}^H] - d[f_{m,c}^H, f_{n,c}^L] + \delta)$$
$$+ max(0, d[f_{m,c}^H, f_{n,c}^H] - d[f_{m,c}^L, f_{n,c}^H] + \delta) \}. \tag{5}$$

where $f_{m,c}^H, f_{m,c}^L \in R^{2304 \times 1}$ represents the high and low attention weights of video x_m for category c, $d[\cdot, \cdot]$ is the degree of similarity between two features, δ is the margin parameter. Then the total loss for the entire training set can be represented as follows:

$$L_{CAS} = \frac{1}{N_S} \sum_{c=1}^{N_S} \frac{1}{\binom{|S_c|}{2}} \sum_{x_m, x_n \in S_c} L_c^{mn} \tag{6}$$

where S_c is the training subset which contains all videos with label c. The final loss function which is used to learn the weight of the weakly-supervised layer can be represented as follows:

$$L = (1 - \lambda)L_{MIL} + \lambda L_{CAS} + \alpha \|W\|^2 \tag{7}$$

where W represents the weight of the weakly-supervised layers W_{fc1} and W_{fc2}.

3.4   Post Processing

After the PPS module and the CAS module, we can get the set Φ_{PPS} and Φ_{CAS}, while in the Φ_{PPS}, ϕ lacks a class category and a proposal confidence. Since in the CAS module, each video has a video score S_c. If $S_c > \eta$, we set the same label for ϕ in the PPS module.

Score Fusion for Retrieving. To achieve better retrieving performance, for each candidate proposal $\phi = (s, e, c)$, we fuse its class activation score with its video-level score to get the final confidence score p:

$$p = \max(O_c^{(s,e)}) + v \times S_c \tag{8}$$

where $O_c^{(s,e)}$ means the cth class sequence duration from s to e and S_c represents the video-level score for the class c.

Redundant Proposals Suppression. Since our final proposals is composed by Φ_{PPS} and Φ_{CAS}, we need to suppress redundant proposals to obtain higher recall with fewer proposals. We use non-maximum suppression (NMS) [12] algorithm which suppresses redundant results. For each proposal ϕ_a in Φ_{PPS}, if its Intersection-over-Union (IoU) with ϕ_b in Φ_{CAS} is higher than 0.5, we will remove ϕ_b from Φ_{CAS} and add ϕ_a in it. After suppression, we get the final proposal set $\Phi = \Phi_{CAS} = \{\phi_i = (s_i, e_i, c_i, p_i)\}_{i=1}^{N_\phi}$.

4   Experiment

In this section, we experimentally evaluate the proposed method CAPP on two datasets. Firstly we introduce the datasets and metrics in the experiments, then we will give the implementation details and the quantitative results. Following conventions, we use mean Average Precision (mAP) to evaluate the accuracy of video-level classification and weakly detection result. The proposal will be regraded as a correct action instance when it (1) has a high IoU with groundtruth which is more than a preset threshold, and (2) has the same label as groundtruth.

Table 1. Study of effectiveness of parts in CAPP on THUMOS-14 dataset, where the results are reported with mAP with IoU from 0.1 to 0.5.

Method	0.1	0.2	0.3	0.4	0.5
CAS-no pose	55.2	49.6	40.1	31.1	22.8
CAS-pose	57.4	52.7	43.1	33.4	23.8
CAS-pose + PPS	56.5	51.5	42.3	33.5	26.3

4.1 Dataset

THUMOS-14. [8] The temporal action localization task in the THUMOS-14 dataset contains 20 classes. 200 untrimmed videos with video class labels in the validation set are used for training, and 213 untrimmed videos with video class labels in the test set are used for testing. Each video contains at least one action and no more than three classes.

ActivityNet V1.2. [1] The ActivityNet v1.2 dataset contains totally 100 activity classes, 4819 videos in the training set, 2383 videos in the validation set, and 2480 videos in the test set. As in literature, we use the training set for training and the validation set for testing.

4.2 Implementation Details

The I3D features and ST-GCN features are extracted by the released source code. The I3D network is not finetuned and the ST-GCN network is finetuned with 20 class videos of the UCF101 dataset [18]. The weights of the weakly supervised layers are initialized by Xavier method [7]. Our network is trained on a single nvidia GPU using pytorch. On the THUMOS-14 dataset, we use I3D features provided by [14]. On the ActivityNet v1.2 dataset, we extract TSN features by ourselves. When extracting features, we set $\sigma = 8$ in the PPS module and $\sigma = 16$ in the CAS module. In the PPS module, we set $\theta = 9$ for differentiating action frames and background frames. For generating set Φ_{first}, we set inteval as 8 just like σ and at least 24 frames to be a segment. For clustering, we use K-Means algorithm which is implemented by sklearn. In the CAS module, we set $p = 8$ and $\eta = 0$. In the loss function, we set $\delta = 0.5$, $\lambda = 0.5$, and $\alpha = 5 \times 10^{-4}$. For the class activation sequence $O = \{o_i\}_{i=1}^{N_c}$, we set $\mu = \max(O) - (\max(O) - \min(O) \times 0.5$. When fusing score, we set $\upsilon = 0.7$.

4.3 Ablation Study

To evaluate the effectiveness of each part in the PPS module and the CAS module, we demonstrate experiment results by combining each part in Table 1. We can see that "CAS-pose" performs much better than "CAS-no pose" as local information really works by improving the clip level classification with the same

Table 2. Video level classification performance comparisons on THUMOS-14 dataset.

Supervision	Method	mAP
Full	TSN [21]	67.7
Weak	UntrimmedNets [20]	74.2
Weak	W-TALC [14]	85.6
Weak	Ours	**96.2**

Table 3. Detection performance comparisons on THUMOS-14 dataset with state-of-the-art methods, where the results are reported with mAP with IoU from 0.1 to 0.5.

Supervision	Method	0.1	0.2	0.3	0.4	0.5
Full	CDC [16]	-	-	40.1	29.4	23.3
	R-C3D [22]	54.5	51.5	44.8	35.6	28.9
	SSN [24]	60.3	56.2	50.6	40.8	29.1
Weak	UntrimmedNets [20]	44.4	37.7	28.2	21.1	13.7
	Step-by-step [25]	45.8	39.0	31.1	22.5	15.9
	STPN [13]	52.0	44.7	35.5	25.8	16.9
	AutoLoc [17]	-	-	35.8	29.0	21.2
	W-TALC [14]	55.2	49.6	40.1	31.1	22.8
	Ours	**56.5**	**51.5**	**42.3**	**33.5**	**26.3**

threshold on the sequence. While by adding the PPS module, it significantly improves from 23.8 to 26.3 when IoU is 0.5 as we consider that the proposal generated by the PPS module has more recall region than the CAS module. The PPS module can generate more complete proposals. But the results drop down when IoU is 0.1, 0.2 and 0.3, and the possible reason is that the retrieving order has changed after adding the pose-based proposals.

We also perform our framework on the activity classification and present the result on the THUMOS-14 dataset in Table 2. We use only videos from the THUMOS-14 validation set for training and test set for testing. From Table 2, we can see that our method performs significantly better than other state-of-the-art approaches.

4.4   Comparison with the State-of-the-Art Methods

We compare our method with the state-of-the-art methods under both full and weak supervision on the THUMOS-14 and ActivityNet v1.2 datasets, shown in Tables 3 and 4 respectively. Our framework performs much better than other weakly-supervised methods and achieves comparable results compared with fully-supervised methods.

Table 4. Detection performance comparisons on ActivityNet v1.2 dataset with state-of-the-art methods, where the results are reported with mAP when IoU is 0.5, 0.75 and 0.95. The last column Avg. indicates the average mAP for IoU thresholds 0.5:0.05:0.95.

Method	0.5	0.75	0.95	Avg
UntrimmedNets [20]	7.4	3.2	0.7	3.6
Step-by-step [25]	27.3	14.7	2.9	15.6
AutoLoc [17]	27.3	15.1	3.3	16.0
Ours	**28.9**	**16.0**	**3.6**	**16.8**

5   Conclusion

In this paper, we present a noval approach for weakly-supervised temporal action localization. We utilize local information to improve the clip level classification performance, and exploit pose estimation and Pose Pattern Clustering to generate more complete proposals. Experiments on two challenging datasets demonstrate that our method achieves the state-of-the-art results.

Acknowledgement. This work was supported in part by the Natural Science Foundation of China (NSFC) under grants No. 61673062.

References

1. Caba Heilbron, F., Escorcia, V., Ghanem, B., Carlos Niebles, J.: ActivityNet: a large-scale video benchmark for human activity understanding. In: Proceedings of the IEEE Conference on Computer Vision and Pattern Recognition, pp. 961–970 (2015)
2. Cao, Z., Simon, T., Wei, S.E., Sheikh, Y.: Realtime multi-person 2D pose estimation using part affinity fields. In: Proceedings of the IEEE Conference on Computer Vision and Pattern Recognition, pp. 7291–7299 (2017)
3. Carreira, J., Zisserman, A.: Quo vadis, action recognition? A new model and the kinetics dataset. In: Proceedings of the IEEE Conference on Computer Vision and Pattern Recognition, pp. 6299–6308 (2017)
4. Choutas, V., Weinzaepfel, P., Revaud, J., Schmid, C.: Potion: pose motion representation for action recognition. In: Proceedings of the IEEE Conference on Computer Vision and Pattern Recognition, pp. 7024–7033 (2018)
5. Fang, H.S., Xie, S., Tai, Y.W., Lu, C.: RMPE: regional multi-person pose estimation. In: Proceedings of the IEEE International Conference on Computer Vision, pp. 2334–2343 (2017)
6. Gao, J., Yang, Z., Chen, K., Sun, C., Nevatia, R.: Turn tap: temporal unit regression network for temporal action proposals. In: Proceedings of the IEEE International Conference on Computer Vision, pp. 3628–3636 (2017)
7. Glorot, X., Bengio, Y.: Understanding the difficulty of training deep feedforward neural networks. In: Proceedings of the Thirteenth International Conference on Artificial Intelligence and Statistics, pp. 249–256 (2010)

8. Jiang, Y.G., et al.: THUMOS challenge: action recognition with a large number of classes (2014). http://crcv.ucf.edu/THUMOS14/

9. Kay, W., et al.: The kinetics human action video dataset. arXiv Preprint arXiv:1705.06950 (2017)

10. Kocabas, M., Karagoz, S., Akbas, E.: MultiposeNet: fast multi-person pose estimation using pose residual network. In: Proceedings of the European Conference on Computer Vision (ECCV), pp. 417–433 (2018)

11. Li, J., Wang, C., Zhu, H., Mao, Y., Fang, H.S., Lu, C.: CrowdPose: efficient crowded scenes pose estimation and a new benchmark. arXiv Preprint arXiv:1812.00324 (2018)

12. Neubeck, A., Van Gool, L.: Efficient non-maximum suppression. In: 18th International Conference on Pattern Recognition (ICPR 2006), vol. 3, pp. 850–855 IEEE (2006)

13. Nguyen, P., Liu, T., Prasad, G., Han, B.: Weakly supervised action localization by sparse temporal pooling network. In: Proceedings of the IEEE Conference on Computer Vision and Pattern Recognition, pp. 6752–6761 (2018)

14. Paul, S., Roy, S., Roy-Chowdhury, A.K.: W-TALC: weakly-supervised temporal activity localization and classification. In: Proceedings of the European Conference on Computer Vision (ECCV), pp. 563–579 (2018)

15. Richard, A., Gall, J.: Temporal action detection using a statistical language model. In: Proceedings of the IEEE Conference on Computer Vision and Pattern Recognition, pp. 3131–3140 (2016)

16. Shou, Z., Chan, J., Zareian, A., Miyazawa, K., Chang, S.F.: CDC: convolutional-de-convolutional networks for precise temporal action localization in untrimmed videos. In: Proceedings of the IEEE Conference on Computer Vision and Pattern Recognition, pp. 5734–5743 (2017)

17. Shou, Z., Gao, H., Zhang, L., Miyazawa, K., Chang, S.F.: AutoLoc: weakly-supervised temporal action localization in untrimmed videos. In: Proceedings of the European Conference on Computer Vision (ECCV), pp. 154–171 (2018)

18. Soomro, K., Zamir, A.R., Shah, M.: UCF101: a dataset of 101 human actions classes from videos in the wild. arXiv Preprint arXiv:1212.0402 (2012)

19. Tran, K.N., Kakadiaris, I.A., Shah, S.K.: Modeling motion of body parts for action recognition. In: BMVC, vol. 11, pp. 1–12. Citeseer (2011)

20. Wang, L., Xiong, Y., Lin, D., Van Gool, L.: Untrimmednets for weakly supervised action recognition and detection. In: Proceedings of the IEEE Conference on Computer Vision and Pattern Recognition, pp. 4325–4334 (2017)

21. Wang, L., et al.: Temporal segment networks: towards good practices for deep action recognition. In: Leibe, B., Matas, J., Sebe, N., Welling, M. (eds.) ECCV 2016. LNCS, vol. 9912, pp. 20–36. Springer, Cham (2016). https://doi.org/10.1007/978-3-319-46484-8_2

22. Xu, H., Das, A., Saenko, K.: R-C3D: region convolutional 3D network for temporal activity detection. In: Proceedings of the IEEE International Conference on Computer Vision, pp. 5783–5792 (2017)

23. Yan, S., Xiong, Y., Lin, D.: Spatial temporal graph convolutional networks for skeleton-based action recognition. In: Thirty-Second AAAI Conference on Artificial Intelligence (2018)

24. Zhao, Y., Xiong, Y., Wang, L., Wu, Z., Tang, X., Lin, D.: Temporal action detection with structured segment networks. In: Proceedings of the IEEE International Conference on Computer Vision, pp. 2914–2923 (2017)

25. Zhong, J.X., Li, N., Kong, W., Zhang, T., Li, T.H., Li, G.: Step-by-step erasion, one-by-one collection: a weakly supervised temporal action detector. arXiv Preprint arXiv:1807.02929 (2018)
26. Zhu, Y., Zhou, Y., Ye, Q., Qiu, Q., Jiao, J.: Soft proposal networks for weakly supervised object localization. In: Proceedings of the IEEE International Conference on Computer Vision, pp. 1841–1850 (2017)

Combing Deep and Handcrafted Features for NTV-NRPCA Based Fabric Defect Detection

Junpu Wang[1], Chunlei Li[1(✉)], Zhoufeng Liu[1], Yan Dong[1], and Yun Huang[2]

[1] School of Electrical and Information Engineering,
Zhongyuan University of Technology,
Zhengzhou 450007, China
lichunlei1979@sina.com
[2] Xiamen Vision+ Technology Co. Ltd., Xiamen 361006, Fujian, China

Abstract. Fabric defect detection plays an important role in automated inspection and quality control in textile manufacturing. As the textures and defects in fabric images have complexity and diversity, the traditional detection methods show a poor adaptability and low detection accuracy. Low-rank decomposition model that can be used to separate the image into object and background have proven applicable in fabric defect detection. However, how to represent texture feature of the fabric image more effectively is still problematic in this kind of method. Also, in traditional Low-rank decomposition model, we tend to seek the convex surrogate to resolve this model. However, this results in low accuracy and more noises in sparse part. In this paper, a novel fabric defect detection method based on combination of deep global feature and handcrafted local features and NTV-NRPCA is proposed. In this method, image representation ability is well enhanced through fusing the global deep feature extracted by a convolutional neural network and the handcrafted low-level feature masterly. Then, the non-convex total variation regularized non-convex RPCA (NTV-NRPCA) is proposed in which non-convex solution is more approximate to the real solution and non-convex total variation constraint significantly reduces the noises in sparse part. Finally, the defect region is located by segmenting the saliency map generated by the sparse matrix via a threshold segmentation algorithm. The experimental results show that the proposed method improves the adaptability and detection accuracy comparing to the state-of-the-art.

Keywords: Fabric defect detection · Deep-handcrafted feature · RPCA · Total variation · Non-convex

1 Introduction

Fabric defect detection plays an essential role in the process of textile manufacturing, which determines the textiles quality. Currently, fabric defect detection

---

The first author is student.

© Springer Nature Switzerland AG 2019
Z. Lin et al. (Eds.): PRCV 2019, LNCS 11859, pp. 479–490, 2019.
https://doi.org/10.1007/978-3-030-31726-3_41

is conducted visually by human workers in most of the production lines, which results in a low detection rate and is easily influenced by subjective factors of workers. Machine-vision based fabric defect detection can provide objective, stable, reliable performance, and thus has become a research focus. An expectation is that such automated system can deal with different kinds of fabric textures, from the unpatterned fabric images (plain or twill fabrics, as shown in Fig. 1(a)) to patterned fabric images (star-, box-, and dot-patterned fabrics, as shown in Fig. 1(b–d)).

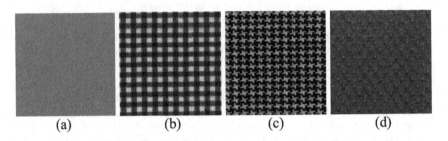

    (a)   (b)   (c)   (d)

Fig. 1. Fabric images: (a) unpatterned fabric. (b) box-patterned fabric. (c) star-patterned fabric. (d) dot-patterned fabric.

Most existing defect detection methods focus on simple plain or twill fabrics, which can be classified into four categories: statistical-based methods [1], frequency analysis-based methods [2], model-based methods [3], and dictionary learning-based methods [4]. These defect detection methods achieve high detection accuracy for the plain and twill fabrics. However, because of the complexity and sophisticated design on patterned fabrics, these proposed methods cannot be extended to detect the patterned fabric defects. Currently, some studies had been conducted on the defect detection for the patterned fabric images, such as motif-based method [5], wavelet-based methods [6], image decomposition method [7], and Elo rating method [8]. However, the above patterned fabric defect detection methods still adopt traditional handcrafted feature descriptor to characterize the fabric images, which cannot efficiently characterize the fabric texture. In addition, these methods adopt template matching technology to localize the defect, detection accuracy depends on precise alignment and a suitable template.

Robust principal component analysis (RPCA), also known as low-rank decomposition model, can divide the image into object and background, have been applied into object detection, image segmentation [9]. For the fabric images, the non-defective background which is macro-homogeneous and highly redundant can be treated as low-rank subspace, defective area which is small and deviates from this subspace can be treated as sparse part, so the low-rank decomposition model is suitable for the fabric defect detection. Some researchers had noticed the superiority of this model in defect detection, a series of related approaches have been proposed and obtain some results [10]. However, considering the case where the test images are contaminated by various noises, among them including Gaussian noise or impulse noise which are also sparse, such sparse noise may be separated into the saliency defect part by low-rank decomposition model. Meanwhile, such RPCA based methods are mainly convex optimization, the solution of them can seriously deviate from the original solution. There is still a long way to go before in the research of defect detection method based on RPCA.

In addition, the performance of the detection method based on RPCA not only depends on construction and solution of the model, but also relies on effective representation of the fabric image. The reason lies in that the effective descriptor can make the background part in a lower dimensional feature subspace, and make the sparse defect farther away from the subspace. In recent years, Convolutional Neural Networks (CNNs) have achieved many successes in visual recognition field. It had been proved that features extracted by using CNNs are highly versatile and often more effective than traditional handcrafted features [11]. Meanwhile, Li et al. [12] asserted that high-level deep feature is complementary to handcrafted low-level feature. Inspired by this, in our work, we will seek to combine the advantages of both deep features and hand-crafted features.

Building on the above analysis, we mainly focus on the improvements of the image representation and RPCA model. Therefore, a Fabric defect detection based on deep-handcrafted feature and non-convex total variation regularized non-convex RPCA (NTV-NRPCA) is proposed in this paper.

The contributions of this paper can be summarized as two folds:

1. A novel fabric image representation method is proposed which can deal with the complex and diverse fabric texture through fusing the high-level deep feature and the low-level handcrafted feature masterly

2. The non-convex total variation regularized non-convex RPCA can not only effectively detect the defect saliency map with less noise, but also improve the solution accuracy.

The remainder of this paper is organized as follows: Sect. 2 presents the specific procedures of the proposed method including the details about deep-handcrafted feature and NTV-NRPCA. In Sect. 3, comprehensively experiments are shown to evaluate the performance of our method in comparison of other state-in-the-art methods. Section 4 summarizes the whole research.

2   Proposed Method

In this paper, a novel fabric defect detection method based on deep-handcrafted feature and NTV-NRPCA is proposed. Firstly, the deep information extracted by a convolutional neural network and some handcrafted low-level contrast information are fused to improve the image representation ability. Then, non-convex total variation regularized non-convex RPCA is constructed, which can not only effectively detect the defect saliency map with less noise, but also further improve the solution accuracy. Finally, the defect region is located by segmenting the saliency map generated by the sparse matrix via a threshold segmentation algorithm. The process can be shown in Fig. 2.

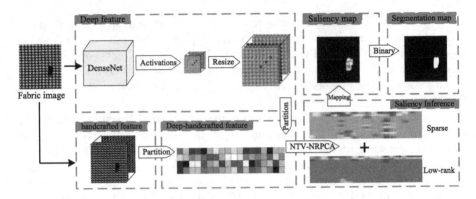

Fig. 2. The flow chart of the proposed method.

2.1 Deep-Handcrafted Feature Extraction

It is well known that an effective feature extractor that can transform the raw images into a suitable internal representation is extremely important and necessary for constructing a pattern recognition or machine learning system. For decade, convolutional neural networks (CNNs) had led to a large volume of astonishing breakthroughs for image classification, location and detection. Actually, CNNs can be deemed to a transferability feature extractor that can automatically learn representative features via a layer-to-layer successive propagation pipeline, the most important is that we do not have to design complicated handcrafted features descriptors which usually depend on knowledge of designer and application scenarios to a great extent. While CNNs are originally inspired by biological neural network, it is a natural choice to build a feature extractor for visual saliency. So, deep features, extracted by CNNs, had been supposed to have a stronger versatility and portability than traditional handcrafted features. Inspired by this, the feature extraction based on CNNs will be performed in this paper.

Unfortunately, there is no public fabric defect datasets that have enough labeled images to support training a new network yet, we only possess a fraction of an unopened datasets. One way to alleviate this problem is transferring a model pretrained over the ImageNet dataset. Since ImageNet contains images of a large number of object categories, extracted features contain rich and distinguishable information. Therefore, we will adopt DenseNet201 [13] as the pretrained model to extract deep features from the input fabric images, because there is a direct connection between any convolutional layer of this network, termed as dense connection. In the adopted network, the feature maps learned by this convolutional layer will be transmitted to all subsequent convolutional layers as input, such structure can realize feature reuse i.e. multiple convolution layer information fusion, that is of great importance to fabric defect detection.

Recognition algorithms based on CNN typically use the output of the last layer as a feature representation. However, the information in this layer is the most sensitive to category-level semantic information and may be too coarse spatially to allow precise localization. This is because multiple levels of convolutional and pooling layers blur the object boundaries. When the task we are interested in is finer-grained, the top layer is not the optimal representation. So feature extracted by the first convolutional layer of DenseNet201 will be considered as the deep feature. Considering the feature map inconsistency caused by convolution and pooling operations, such deep feature maps will be resized to the same size of the input images.

Li et al. [12] proposed that deep features contain sufficient high-level semantic information, but low-level contrast information is insufficient, and it is worth noting that deep high-level features and handcrafted low-level features are complementary. There is no need for too much semantic information in fabric defect detection, we also find the deep-handcrafted hybrid feature could obtain an enhanced result by adding some simple low-level feature in practice. Although low-level features has been obtained by extracting the shallowest convolutional layer in this paper, the extracted low-level features are still relatively insufficient, because the kernel size and stride of initial convolution layer is relatively large in DenseNet201.

Therefore, some handcrafted low-level features including edge and texture information will be extracted as the compensation of deep high-level features. The handcrafted low-level features of fabric images are shown in Table 1. For the edge information, an 18 bin edge direction histogram was used to describe the edges distribution in the image. For the texture information, ten different sub-bands was obtained by computing the three level wavelet transform, then the average absolute value of the coefficients and their standard deviation was computed for each band.

Table 1. Handcrafted low-level features of fabric images.

Edge information	Edge direction values: histogram
Texture information	Coeff. of wavelet transform: mean
	Coeff. of wavelet transform: standard deviation

Then the deep-handcrafted hybrid feature maps are decomposed into small square regions. For each segment R_i, the mean of feature vectors f_i within this segment is treated as the feature of this segment. Finally they will be stacked to form the deep-handcrafted features of this image.

$$F = [f_1, f_2, ..., f_i] \tag{1}$$

2.2 Model Construction

Based on the fact that fabric is woven by warp and weft in a particular way, and the defect breaks this regularity, so the background of a fabric image always can be considered as a highly redundant part which lies in a low dimensional subspace, while the defect is different from the background and usually occupies a relatively small size which implies sparse. Due to the characteristics of background and defects in fabric images, the RPCA could be good at dealing with fabric defect detection, it can be realized through minimizing the following problem:

$$\min_{L,S} \|L\|_* + \gamma \|S\|_1 \quad s.t. \ F = L + S \tag{2}$$

where F is the aforementioned deep-handcrafted feature matrix, L is a low-rank matrix representing the background, S is a sparse matrix indicating the defective object, γ is used to balance the effect of the two items.

However, fabric images are easily contaminated by noise derived from camera sensors and background clutters. At this moment, if we just leverage previous RPCA (2) for saliency inference, defect and sparse noise including Gaussian noise or impulse noise are easily separated into matrix S simultaneously for the reason that they both have the sparse property. Hence, it is meaningful to establish an efficient model to suppress noise in saliency map. A prior knowledge is that the noise in the image is always tiny and can be regarded as pixel-wise discontinuous changes, while the defect is an aggregation of multiple pixels and occupied a fraction of the fabric image. Due to superior performance on suppressing pixel-wise discontinuous changes, preserving the edge information and spatially promoting piece-wise smoothness, total variation regularization [14] is integrated into RPCA to denoising. Such a unit framework, termed as the total variation regularized robust principal component analysis (TV-RPCA), can be formulized via

$$\min_{L,S} \|L\|_* + \gamma \|S\|_1 + \beta \|S\|_{TV} \quad s.t. \ F = L + S \tag{3}$$

Where $\|\cdot\|_{TV}$ is total variation regularization (TV-norm) including anisotropic case and isotropic case, β is a weighting parameter whose role is identical to γ.

However, the above model (3) belongs to a convex optimization problem. The common drawback deriving from such convex relaxation may make the solution seriously deviate from the original solution. Along with the development of non-convex regularization, non-convex optimization had been proved to result in a more accurate estimation. Inspired by this, we will introduce non-convex TV regularization into non-convex RPCA model, termed as the non-convex total variation regularized non-convex RPCA (NTV-NRPCA), it can be realized through minimizing the following problem:

$$\min_{L,S} \|L\|_{w,S_p}^p + \gamma \|S\|_1 + \beta \|S\|_{NTV} \quad s.t. \ F = L + S \tag{4}$$

where $\|L\|_{w,S_p} = \left(\sum_{i=1}^{\min(m,n)} w_i \sigma_i^p \right)^{1/p}$ presents a non-convex relaxation of $rank(\cdot)$ based on Schatten p norm [15] and weighted nuclear norm [16]. $\|S\|_{NTV}$ denotes a non-convex TV regularizations based on the Moreau envelop and minimax-concave penalty [17].

Algorithm 1	Solving NTV-NRPCA by ADMM

Input: Deep-handcrafted features x F; parameter $\gamma > 0, \beta > 0$;

Initialize: $L^0 = S^0 = J^0 = 0, Y_1^0 = F/max(\|F\|_2, \gamma^{-1}\|F\|_\infty)$,$Y_2^0 = 0, \mu^0 = 1.25/\|F\|_2$,$\mu_{max} = \mu^0 10^7$,$\rho = 1.5, k = 0, tol = 3e-4$

while not converged **do**

1. Fix the others and update L by

$$\arg\min_L \xi\left(L, S^k, J^k, Y_1^k, Y_2^k, \mu^k\right)$$
$$= \arg\min_L \frac{1}{\mu}\|L\|_{w,S_p}^p + \frac{1}{2}\left\|L - (F - S^k + \frac{Y_1^k}{\mu^k})\right\|_F^2$$

such subproblem can be solved by Generalized Soft-thresholding (GST) in [18].

2. Fix the others and update S by

$$\arg\min_S \xi\left(L^{k+1}, S, J^k, Y_1^k, Y_2^k, \mu^k\right)$$
$$= \arg\min_S \frac{\gamma}{2\mu}\|S\|_1 + \frac{1}{2}\left\|S - \frac{1}{2}(J^k + F - L^{k+1} + (Y_1^k - Y_2^k)/\mu)\right\|_F^2$$

such subproblem can be solved by Singular Value Thresholding (SVT) in [19].

3. Fix the others and update J by

$$\arg\min_J \xi\left(L^{k+1}, S^{k+1}, J, Y_1^k, Y_2^k, \mu^k\right)$$
$$= \arg\min_J \frac{\beta}{\mu^k}\|J\|_{NTV} + \frac{1}{2}\left\|J - (S^{k+1} + \frac{Y_2^k}{\mu^k})\right\|_F^2$$

such subproblem can be solved by Forward-Backward splitting (FBS) in [20].

4. Update the Lagrange multipliers Y_1, Y_2 and penalty parameter μ by

$$Y_1^{k+1} = Y_1^k + \mu^k(F - L^{k+1} - S^{k+1})$$
$$Y_2^{k+1} = Y_2^k + \mu^k(S^{k+1} - J^{k+1})$$
$$\mu^{k+1} = \min(\mu_{max}, \rho\mu^k)$$

5. Check the stop condition:

$$\|F - L^{k+1} - S^{k+1}\|_F/\|F\|_F < tol$$

6. $k = k + 1$.

end while

Output: The optimal solution S^{k+1}

In order to split the energy, an auxiliary variable $S = J$ will be introduced. Then, its augmented Lagrangian function is

$$\xi(L, S, J, Y_1, Y_2, \mu)$$
$$= \|L\|_{w,S_p}^p + \gamma\|S\|_1 + \beta\|J\|_{NTV} + \langle Y_1, F - L - S\rangle + \langle Y_2, S - J\rangle$$
$$+ \frac{\mu}{2}(\|F - L - S\|_F^2 + \|S - J\|_F^2)$$
$$= \|L\|_{w,S_p}^p + \gamma\|S\|_1 + \beta\|J\|_{NTV} - \frac{1}{2\mu}(\|Y_1\|_F^2 + \|Y_2\|_F^2)$$
$$+ \frac{\mu}{2}(\left\|F - L - S + \frac{Y_1}{\mu}\right\|_F^2 + \left\|S - J + \frac{Y_2}{\mu}\right\|_F^2) \tag{5}$$

Where Y_1 and Y_2 are the Lagrange multiplier matrices, $\langle\cdot\rangle$ represents the inner product, $\|\cdot\|_F$ denotes the Frobenius norm and μ is a positive penalty parameter. The specific sub-problem of the above function can be worked out efficiently. Finally we can obtain the optimal value until reaching the stop condition. The template update scheme is presented in Algorithm 1.

2.3   The Generation and Segmentation of the Saliency Map

According to the above method, let S^{k+1} obtained by the optimal solution to the (3) be the spare component. Saliency score for the i_{th} image block can be obtained by the l_1 norm of the i_{th} column of S^{k+1}.

$$M(R_i) = \left\|S^{k+1}(:,i)\right\|_1 \tag{6}$$

The higher saliency score $M(R_i)$ indicates the image block belongs to the defect with higher probability, the corresponding saliency map M is generated according to the spatial position relation.

Then the following equation will be used to estimate the upper and lower boundary of the automatic thresholding value.

$$T = \mu \pm c \cdot \sigma \tag{7}$$

Where c is a constant, μ and σ are mean and standard deviation of pixel values in the saliency map.

Finally, the segmentation results are given by a binary image $\hat{M}$ to locate the defect regions.

$$\hat{M}(i,j) = \begin{cases} 0, & \mu - c \cdot \sigma < M(i,j) < \mu + c \cdot \sigma \\ 255, & otherwise \end{cases} \tag{8}$$

Where i and j are locations of pixel.

3   Experiments

In this section, we will investigate the effect of the proposed method in this paper. We first introduce implementation details. Then we compare our method with state-of-the-art on the benchmark datasets for performance evaluation.

3.1   Implementation Details

Our experiment is performed in matlab2018b, run on a PC with an i7-8750H CPU and speeded up by a NVIDIA GeForce GTX 1080 GPU. There are two databases will be tested in our experience, one is unpatterned fabric image database set by workgroup on texture analysis of German Research Council [21]. Another one is patterned fabric image database set by Research Associate of Industrial Automation Research Laboratory, Department of Electrical and Electronic Engineering, Hong Kong University. The size of the fabric image is set to 512 pixels × 512 pixels uniformly.

3.2   Comparison with State-of-the-Art

In order to verify the validity and robustness of the proposed method, qualitatively and quantitatively evaluation will be considered on two fabric image benchmarks comparing with several state-of-the-art methods.

Qualitative Evaluations: We compare our method with some visual saliency models, including the histogram of oriented gradient (HOG), the prior guided least squares regression method (PGLSR), and unified method based on low-rank matrix recovery (ULR). The experimental results are demonstrated in Fig. 3. The first column shows the original images. The detection results of HOG [22], ULR [23], PGLSR [24], and our method are listed from the second column to the fifth column.

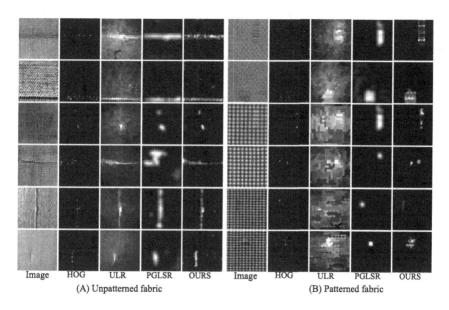

Image   HOG   ULR   PGLSR   OURS   Image   HOG   ULR   PGLSR   OURS
  (A) Unpatterned fabric   (B) Patterned fabric

Fig. 3. Comparison of the detection results using different methods: (A) Detection results for unpatterned fabric image; (B) Detection results for patterned fabric image. The first column is the original image, detection results of HOG, ULR, PGLSR and our method are listed from the second column to the fifth column.

From the Fig. 3, we can conclude that the HOG method is only suitable for the fabric images with simple textures, not for the unpatterned fabric images, because that the results of HOG method have serious noise and defect area suffer from severe dispersion. The ULR method is only suitable for the unpatterned fabric images and a fraction of patterned fabric images, but even so, its detection results is not good enough due to detection results contains a lot of texture information. The PGLSR method could mostly detect defects effectively in the unpatterned and patterned fabric images, but similarities in texture between the background and the defect may lead to inaccurate shape descriptions of the defects. Our method can not only highlight the position of defective regions, but also outline the shape of defects for all types of fabric images.

Quantitative Evaluations: Two criteria, including receiver operating characteristic (ROC) curves and precision-recall (PR) curves, are adopted to perform a comprehensive qualitative evaluation for different methods. Because of the lack of groundtruth images in the unpatterned fabric image database, we only consider the patterned fabric databases for our quantitative evaluation, as shown in Fig. 4.

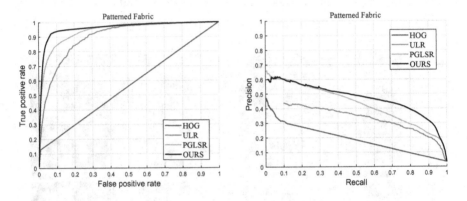

Fig. 4. The quantitative performance of four methods on patterned fabric image database: The left row corresponds to ROC curve, the right row corresponds to PR curve.

It can be noticed that the area under the ROC curve (AUC) of OURS is the largest, which indicates that our proposed method performs better than the other three methods for the patterned fabric datasets. We can see that the PR of our method is higher than the other three methods, which also indicates that our method can achieve the best performance in the four methods.

Table 2. The detection precision (%) of four methods on patterned fabric image database, and the best score is highlighted in bold fonts.

Methods	Fabrics			
	Box-patterned	Dot-patterned	Star-patterned	Average
ULR	71.08	68.32	74.89	71.43
HOG	93.91	84.46	95.23	91.20
PGLSR	92.46	92.30	94.48	93.08
OURS	**97.87**	**96.47**	**97.54**	**97.29**

In order to express that our model can achieve the best results in four methods more intuitively. We will exhibit the detection precision of four methods on patterned fabric image database, the experimental results are shown in Table 2. Statistic data shows that our method is effective and efficient in front of the fabric images including box-, dot- and star-patterned fabric. Besides, it is easy to see that that our method can maintain a high accuracy in average.

4   Conclusion

In this paper, a fabric defect detection algorithm based on deep-handcrafted feature and NTV-NRPCA is proposed. Based on the fact that hand-crafted feature is incapable of characterizing the fabric texture comprehensively, the deep features extracted by a CNN and some handcrafted low-level information are fused to improve the image representation ability. In order to separate the defects, RPCA is adopted to decompose the fabric images into background parts and salient defect parts. Meanwhile, total variation regularization term is integrated into RPCA to prevent defect saliency map from being polluted by noises as much as possible. Besides, non-convex optimization is applied into total variation regularization term and RPCA, which can improve the solution accuracy. The experimental results emphasize that the proposed method is superior to the state-of-the-art methods. Moreover, the proposed method could be extended to detect surface defects of other industrial products such as paper and glass.

Acknowledgements. The authors would like to thank Dr. Henry Y.T. Ngan, Industrial Automation Research Laboratory, Dept. of Electrical and Electronic Engineering, The University of Hong Kong, for providing the database of patterned fabric images. This work was supported by National Nature Science Foundation of China (No. 61772576, U1804157), the Key Natural Science Foundation of Henan Province (No. 162300410338), Science and technology innovation talent project of Education Department of Henan Province (17HASTIT019), the Henan Science Fund for Distinguished Young Scholars (184100510002), Henan science and technology innovation team (CXTD2017091), IRTSTHN (18IRTSTHN013), Program for Interdisciplinary Direction Team in Zhongyuan University of Technology.

References

1. Shi, M., Fu, R., Guo, Y., et al.: Fabric defect detection using local contrast deviations. Multimed. Tools Appl. **52**(1), 147–157 (2011)
2. Tolba, A.S.: Fast defect detection in homogeneous flat surface products. Expert Syst. Appl. **38**(10), 12339–12347 (2011)
3. Li, M., Cui, S., Xie, Z.: Application of Gaussian mixture model on defect detection of print fabric. J. Text. Res. **36**(8), 94–98 (2015)
4. Qu, T., Zou, L., Zhang, Q., et al.: Defect detection on the fabric with complex texture via dual-scale over-complete dictionary. J. Text. Inst. Proc. Abs. **107**(6), 743–756 (2015)
5. Ngan, H.Y.T., Pang, G.K.H., Yung, N.H.C.: Patterned fabric defect detection using a motif-based approach. In: IEEE International Conference on Image Processing. II-33–II-36, IEEE (2007)

6. Ngan, H.Y.T., Pang, G.K.H., Yung, S.P., et al.: Wavelet based methods on patterned fabric defect detection. Pattern Recogn. **38**(4), 559–576 (2005)
7. Ng, M.K., Ngan, H.Y.T., Yuan, X., et al.: Patterned fabric inspection and visualization by the method of image decomposition. IEEE Trans. Autom. Sci. Eng. **11**(3), 943–947 (2014)
8. Tsang, C.S.C., Ngan, H.Y.T., Pang, G.K.H.: Fabric inspection based on the Elo rating method. Pattern Recogn. **51**(4), 378–394 (2016)
9. Peng, H., Li, B., Ling, H., et al.: Salient object detection via structured matrix decomposition. IEEE Trans. Pattern Anal. Mach. Intell. **39**(4), 818–832 (2017)
10. Li, C., Gao, G., Liu, Z., et al.: Fabric defect detection based on biological vision modeling. IEEE Access **6**, 27659–27670 (2018)
11. Mei, S., Jiang, R., Ji, J., et al.: Invariant feature extraction for image classification via multi-channel convolutional neural network. In: 2017 International Symposium on Intelligent Signal Processing and Communication Systems (ISPACS). pp. 491-495, IEEE (2017)
12. Li, G., Yu, Y.: Visual saliency based on multiscale deep features. In: Proceedings of the IEEE Conference on Computer Vision and Pattern Recognition. pp. 5455–5463 (2015)
13. Huang, G., Liu, Z., Van Der Maaten, L., et al.: Densely connected convolutional networks. In: Proceedings of the IEEE Conference on Computer Vision and Pattern Recognition, pp. 4700–4708 (2017)
14. Rudin, L.I., Osher, S., Fatemi, E.: Nonlinear total variation based noise removal algorithms. In: Eleventh International Conference of the Center for Nonlinear Studies on Experimental Mathematics: Computational Issues in Nonlinear Science: Computational Issues in Nonlinear Science, Elsevier North-Holland, Inc. (1992)
15. Nie, F., Huang, H., Ding, C.: Low-rank matrix recovery via efficient schatten p-norm minimization. In: Twenty-Sixth AAAI Conference on Artificial Intelligence (2012)
16. Gu, S., Xie, Q., Meng, D., et al.: Weighted nuclear norm minimization and its applications to low level vision. Int. J. Comput. Vis. **121**(2), 183–208 (2017)
17. Zou, J., Shen, M., Zhang, Y., et al.: Total variation denoising with non-convex regularizers. IEEE Access **7**, 4422–4431 (2019)
18. Zuo, W., Meng, D., Zhang, L., et al.: A generalized iterated shrinkage algorithm for non-convex sparse coding. In: Proceedings of the IEEE International Conference on Computer Vision. pp. 217–224 (2013)
19. Beck, A., Teboulle, M.A.: Fast iterative shrinkage-thresholding algorithm for linear inverse problems. Soc. Ind. Appl. Math. **2**(1), 183–202 (2009)
20. Combettes, P.L., Wajs, V.R.: Signal recovery by proximal forward-backward splitting. Multiscale Model. Simul. **4**(4), 1168–1200 (2005)
21. Workgroup on Texture Analysis of DFG. TILDA Textile Texture Database. http://lmb.informatik.uni-freiburg.de/research/dfg-texture/tilda
22. Li, C., Gao, G., Liu, Z., et al.: Fabric defect detection algorithm based on histogram of oriented gradient and low-rank decomposition. J. Text. Res. **38**(3), 153–158 (2017)
23. Shen, X., Wu, Y.: A Unified approach to salient object detection via low rank matrix recovery. In: 2012 IEEE Conference on Computer Vision and Pattern Recognition, pp. 853–860, IEEE (2012)
24. Cao, J., Zhang, J., Wen, Z., et al.: Fabric defect inspection using prior knowledge guided least squares regression. Multimed. Tools Appl. **76**(3), 4141–4157 (2017)

A Cost-Sensitive Shared Hidden Layer Autoencoder for Cross-Project Defect Prediction

Juanjuan Li[1], Xiao-Yuan Jing[2(✉)], Fei Wu[1], Ying Sun[1], and Yongguang Yang[1]

[1] College of Automation, Nanjing University of Posts and Telecommunications, Nanjing, China
[2] School of Computer, Wuhan University, Wuhan, China
jingxy_2000@126.com

Abstract. Cross-project defect prediction means training a classifier model using the historical data of the other source project, and then testing whether the target project instance is defective or not. Since source and target projects have different data distributions, and data distribution difference will degrade the performance of classifier. Furthermore, the class imbalance of datasets increases the difficulty of classification. Therefore, a cost-sensitive shared hidden layer autoencoder (CSSHLA) method is proposed. CSSHLA learns a common feature representation between source and target projects by shared hidden layer autoencoder, and makes the different data distributions more similar. To solve the class imbalance problem, CSSHLA introduces a cost-sensitive factor to assign different importance weights to different instances. Experiments on 10 projects of PROMISE dataset show that CSSHLA improves the performance of cross-project defect prediction compared with baselines.

Keywords: Shared hidden layer autoencoder · Cost-sensitive learning · Cross-project software defect prediction

1 Introduction

Software defect prediction (SDP) has been a hot research topic in software engineering [23]. Its main goal is to discover defects exist in the software for improving the software quality. The previous research mainly focused on within-project defect prediction (WPDP) [19, 20], mainly using the historical data of one project to train a prediction model and testing the defect tendency of the same project software instance. However, when there is not enough historical data available in the same project, the performance of WPDP becomes significantly worse, and cross-project defect prediction (CPDP) can be considered.

Training a prediction model by using plenty of historical data from other project and predicting defects in a new project instances, is called cross-project defect

---

The first author is a student.

© Springer Nature Switzerland AG 2019
Z. Lin et al. (Eds.): PRCV 2019, LNCS 11859, pp. 491–502, 2019.
https://doi.org/10.1007/978-3-030-31726-3_42

prediction(CPDP) [6, 15]. However, its prediction performance is usually poor, because of the data distribution difference phenomenon between source and target projects, e.g., coding styles, programming language [4]. If the data distribution difference between source project and target project is small enough [8], CPDP model can achieve better results. To solve the problem of data distribution difference in CPDP, several CPDP methods have been developed [6, 15]. However, these methods [4, 8, 15] use the traditional features rather than deep features extracted by deep learning. Such as TCA+ [15], which maps source and target projects into a latent subspace, making the difference of data distribution between source and target projects is minimized. Deep learning has been successfully applied to the field of speech recognition [10] and image classification [1] due to its powerful feature learning capability. Stacked denoising autoencoders model [7] is applied in the field of SDP and proved that the deep features are more promising than the traditional software metric. Furthermore, the shared-hidden-layer autoencoder' method has solved the typical inherent mismatch between the two domains in the field of speech emotion recognition [10, 11].

Besides, class imbalance problem reduces the prediction performance of the CPDP model. That is, the number of defect-free instances is far greater than that of defective instances [2]. Thus the SDP model will more likely to identify defect-free instances. Especially for minority classes, imbalanced distribution is the main reason of poor performance of certain classification models [16]. In this paper, cost-sensitive technique is used to deal with class imbalance problem.

Similar to the idea of transfer learning, a cost-sensitive shared hidden layer autoencoder (CSSHLA) method is proposed for CPDP to solve the data distribution difference problem and the class imbalance problem. It mainly includes two phases: feature extraction stage and classifier learning phase. In the feature extraction stage, we extract a set of deep nonlinear features from the source and target projects by using shared hidden layer autoencoder. In the classifier learning phase, we build a cost-sensitive softmax classifier based on the deep features of source project data.

The main contributions of this paper can be summarized as follows:

1. We propose a shared hidden layer autoencoder for CPDP. It can extract deep feature representations from original features, making the data distribution of source and target projects be more similar in the nonlinear feature subspace to solve the data distribution difference problem. It can also make the instances of same class in source project be more compact.
2. To alleviate the class imbalance problem, we propose a cost-sensitive softmax classification technique. Different misclassification costs are assigned to instances from different class in the model building stage. In this way, the features of defective instances can be better learned.
3. Based on the above two techniques, a cost-sensitive shared hidden layer autoencoder method (CSSHLA) is proposed for CPDP. We evaluate CSSHLA with the baselines on the 10 projects from PROMISE. One conclusion is that we get better results on F-measure and Accuracy than other baselines.

2   Related Work

2.1   Cross-Project Defect Prediction

In recent years, CPDP is a hot topic in software engineering [22]. The most important problem is data distribution difference problem between source and target projects in CPDP. TCA+ [15] is an effective CPDP method that uses transfer component analysis (TCA) to map instance of source and target projects into a common latent subspace, and the difference of feature distributions between the source and the target is small enough. Dynamic cross-company mapped model learning (Dycom) is first used in web effort estimation [13], and transfer learning method Dycom [4] is successfully applied to CPDP, in which 10% of the labeled data comes from the target project in the training process. Log transformations (LT) [3] reduces the data distribution difference by log transformation of the feature values in the source and the target projects, and then aligns the median values of each source project and target project. Training data selection (TDS) [8] selects the most suitable training data related to the test data based on the similarity distance to improve the performance of cross-project defect prediction.

Most of the CPDP methods do not consider the class imbalance problem. In our approach, we consider the class imbalance problem and use cost-sensitive factor to solve the problem.

2.2   Deep Learning

In recent years, deep learning has been successfully applied in many fields because of its powerful feature generation ability, such as speech emotion recognition [9], image classification [1], face recognition [5], etc. Convolution neural network (CNN), deep belief network (DBN) and autoencoder play an important role in deep learning. Wang et al. [17] used DBN to learn the most relevant semantic features from the program's Abstract Grammar Tree (AST) and showed that the deep semantic features are better than the traditional features. Good results are obtained by using DBN to predict the defects for just-in-time defect prediction [21] than without deep feature representation. By integrating the similar feature learning technology and distance measurement learning technology, siamese dense neural network [14] is successfully applied to SDP. The autoencoder has been successfully applied to the field of speech recognition [10]. Some researchers applied autoencoder in the field of defect prediction [7].

Because of the strong feature extraction advantage of deep learning, a deep learning autoencoder method is introduced to solve the CPDP problem in our paper. And the improved autoencoder is used to solve the problem of data distribution difference in CPDP effectively.

3   Proposed Methodology

We design a cost-sensitive shared hidden layer autoencoder (CSSHLA) network, and the overall framework of CSSHLA is shown in Fig. 1. It is mainly summarized as two stages: (1) Data normalization. It makes the source data and target data have same order of magnitude. (2) Training network. The network is composed of feature extraction model and classifier model. Feature extraction model takes the source data and target data as input and outputs their deep features. Classifier model uses the deep source features and its corresponding labels to build a classifier.

Let $x \in \{X_{tr} \cup X_{te}\}$, $X_{tr} = \{x_{tr}^i\}_{i=1}^{N_{tr}} \in R^{N_{tr} \times n}$ and $X_{te} = \{x_{te}^i\}_{i=1}^{N_{te}} \in R^{N_{te} \times n}$ mean feature sets from source and target projects, respectively, and $Y_s = \{y_s^i\}_{i=1}^{N_{tr}}$ is the corresponding labels, where x means X_{tr} and X_{te} scrambled sets, $y_{tr}^i \in \{1, 2\}$, 2 means the number of classes, and n is the number of corresponding data features. N_{tr} and N_{te} refer to the number of instances of source and target projects, and usually N_{tr} is not equal to N_{te}. Let θ_{all} denote a collection of parameters. $y(x^i) \in R^{N_{tr(te)} \times m}$ refers to the feature representations of hidden layer in the autoencoder, where m denotes the number of hidden layer neurons during the autoencoder training.

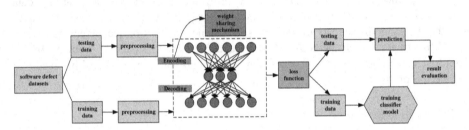

Fig. 1. The overall framework of CSSHLA. It mainly includes three parts: (1) Data normalization stage. Source data and target data can be preprocessed to the same order of magnitude. (2) Feature extraction stage. The source data features and target data features can be better converted into similar data distribution by weight sharing mechanism. (3) Classifier learning stage. The learned source features and its corresponding labels are used to learn a classifier model.

3.1   Data Normalization

We perform data normalization on these features due to the 20 basic metrics used are not the same order of magnitude. We use the 20 basic metrics [12] and min-max data normalization method [18] to convert all the values in the interval from 0 to 1 in this paper. Given feature x, its maximum and minimum values are $\max(x)$ and $\min(x)$, respectively. For each value x_i of the feature x, the normalized value P_i is computed as:

$$P_i = \frac{x_i - \min(x)}{\max(x) - \min(x)} \tag{1}$$

3.2   Feature Extraction Model

In the feature extraction model, we use shared hidden layer autoencoder to extract features. Figure 2 shows the architecture of a basic autoencoder. Figure 3 shows the architecture of shared hidden layer autoencoder, which is an improved version of the basic autoencoder.

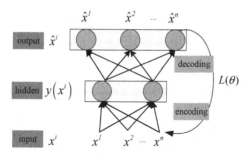

Fig. 2. Architecture of basic autoencoder. First, the original input x^i is mapped to $y(x^i)$. Then $\hat{x}^i$ tries to reconstruct x^i. The reconstruction error loss is expressed as $L(\theta)$.

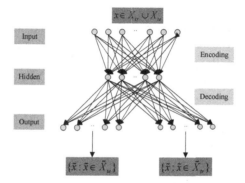

Fig. 3. Architecture of shared hidden layer autoencoder. It mainly includes two stages: (1) Encoding stage. Input data includes source data and target data, which are scrambled into the network to obtain feature representation of the hidden layer. The parameters of the input data adopt the parameter sharing mechanism in this stage. (2) Decoding stage. The feature representation of the hidden layer is decoded to get the reconstructed output data, making that the output data is equal to the input data as much as possible. In this phase, the source data and target data have different parameter settings, respectively.

Autoencoder. Autoencoder means that the output data is equal to the input data as much as possible, and it finds the common deep feature representation from input data. It mainly includes coding phase and decoding phase. Given an input data $x^i \in X_{tr}$, these two phases can be expressed as follows:

$$\text{Encoding phase}: \; y(x^i) = f(w_1 x^i + b_1) \tag{2}$$

$$\text{Decoding phase}: \; \hat{x}^i = f(w_2 y(x^i) + b_2) \tag{3}$$

where $f(\cdot)$ is a non-linear activation function, usually $f(\cdot)$ is sigmoid function, $w_1 \in R^{m \times n}$ and $w_2 \in R^{n \times m}$ are weight matrices, $b_1 \in R^m$ and $b_2 \in R^n$ are bias vectors. $\theta = \{w_1, b_1, w_2, b_2\}$ is included in the autoencoder network parameters, the optimization of parameters is actually to minimize the reconstruction error $L(\theta)$:

$$L(\theta) = \frac{1}{2} \sum_{x^i \in X} \left\| \hat{x}^i - x^i \right\|^2 \tag{4}$$

The implementation of minimizing $L(\theta)$ is achieved through the Adam optimizer during the autoencoder training.

Shared Hidden Layer Autoencoder. To a certain extent, it is similar to autoencoder, except that some improvements have been made in the setting of parameters. In order to solve the data distribution difference problem in CPDP, shared hidden layer autoencoder is used to obtain the advanced deep feature representation of the hidden layer by minimizing the reconstruction error loss $L(\theta_{all})$. $L(\theta_{all})$ loss consists of two parts: $L(\theta_{tr})$ and $L(\theta_{te})$. $L(\theta_{tr})$ is defined as the Euclidean distance between the input source data and the output source data. We add the label information of the source data to make the source data with the same label more compact in the decoding phase. $L(\theta_{te})$ is defined as the Euclidean distance between the input target data and the output target data. $L(\theta_{tr})$ and $L(\theta_{te})$ can be expressed as follows:

$$L(\theta_{tr}) = \frac{1}{2} \sum_{x^i_{tr} \in X_{tr}} \left\| \hat{x}^i_{tr} - x^i_{tr} \right\|^2 + \sum_{\hat{x}^i_{tr} \in X^0_{tr}} \left\| \hat{x}^i_{tr} - \bar{\hat{x}}^i_{tr_0} \right\|^2 + \sum_{\hat{x}^i_{tr} \in X^1_{tr}} \left\| \hat{x}^i_{tr} - \bar{\hat{x}}^i_{tr_1} \right\|^2 \tag{5}$$

$$L(\theta_{te}) = \frac{1}{2} \sum_{x^i_{te} \in X_{te}} \left\| \hat{x}^i_{te} - x^i_{te} \right\|^2 \tag{6}$$

where $\hat{x}^i_{tr}$ refers to the source data features obtained after the decoding phase, $\hat{x}^i_{te}$ refers to the target data features obtained after the decoding phase. X^0_{tr} refers to all the instances in the source project are 0 and X^1_{tr} refers to all the instances in the source project are 1. $\bar{\hat{x}}^i_{tr_0}$ and $\bar{\hat{x}}^i_{tr_1}$ are the mean values of all source project instances labeled 0 and all source project instances labeled 1 after decoding the source project data, respectively.

Combined with the above two formulas, optimizing $L(\theta_{tr})$ and $L(\theta_{te})$ two formulas at the same time, the final objective function can be expressed as:

$$L(\theta_{all}) = L(\theta_{tr}) + rL(\theta_{te}) \tag{7}$$

The network needs to optimize parameter θ_{all}: $\theta_{all} = \{w^1, b^1, w^2_{tr}, b^2_{tr}, w^2_{te}, b^2_{te}\}$. r is a regularization parameter, it can help to regularize the functional behavior of the autoencoder. The goal of this term is to make the source as similar as possible to the distribution of the target by changing the value of r.

3.3   Cost-Sensitive Softmax Classifier Model

To better learn features of minority class, cost-sensitive softmax classifier model is used to alleviate the class imbalance problem by assigning different misclassification costs to instances from different classes in the model building stage. In the trained autoencoder above, the deep feature representations of source data learned from the hidden layer are used to build a classifier.

To calculate the classification loss C, we usually measure the similarity between the real label and the predicted label by using the cross-entropy loss function, which is expressed as follows:

$$C = -\frac{1}{N_{tr}} \sum_{i=1}^{N} \sum_{c=1}^{k} \left(\left(y_s^i \right)_c * \log \left(g(x_s^i) \right)_c \right)$$

(8)

where N_{tr} is the number of source project instances, c refers to class of label, k is number of label class, which is set as 2 in this paper. y_s^i is ground-truth label, $g(x_s^i)$ is the final predicted label, $g(\cdot)$ is softmax activation function.

Table 1. Cost matrix for CSSHLA.

	Actual defective	Actual defect-free
Predict defective	$cost(i,i)$	$cost(i,j)$
Predict defect-free	$cost(j,i)$	$cost(j,j)$

Furthermore, we add the cost-sensitive method to the classifier, so we propose a cost-sensitive softmax classifier. The goal of cost-sensitive learning is to take the cost matrix into consideration and generate a prediction model with minimum misclassification cost. The cost matrix as shown Table 1, $cost(i,j)$ is the cost value $f(c)$ of classifying a instance from the $i-th$ class as the $j-th$ class, a correct classification will be no cost in the cost matrix, that is $cost(i,i) = 0$ and $cost(j,j) = 0$. Because more defective modules should be found, the cost of defective modules should be higher. The setting of the remaining cost value is set according to the works of [24]. $f(c)$ is defined as:

$$f(c) = \begin{cases} \dfrac{N_0}{N_1}, & c = 1 \\ 1, & c = 0 \end{cases}$$

(9)

Based on this, the final cost-sensitive cross-entropy loss can be defined as:

$$C = -\frac{1}{N_{tr}} \sum_{i=1}^{N} \sum_{c=1}^{k} \left(f(c) * \left(y_s^i \right)_c * \log \left(g(x_s^i) \right)_c \right)$$

(10)

where N_0 is the number of the defective instances, N_1 is the number of the defect-free instances. $f(c)$ means the cost of instance of class c.

4   Experiment

4.1   Datasets

In this experiment, we chose 10 projects from the PROMISE repository [12]. Table 2 lists the project name, the number of instances (#instance), the number of defective instances (#defect) and the percentage of defective instances in all instances (%defect).

Table 2. Datasets in our experiment.

Datasets	#instance	#defect	%defect
ant-1.7	745	166	22.28
camel-1.6	965	188	19.48
jedit-3.2	272	90	33.09
log4j-1.0	135	34	25.19
lucene-2.0	195	91	46.67
poi-1.5	237	141	59.49
redaktor	176	27	15.34
synapse-1.0	157	16	10.19
xalan-2.6	885	411	46.44
xerces-1.3	453	69	15.23

4.2   Evaluation Metrics

In order to evaluate the performance of proposed method, the evaluation metrics F-measure and Accuracy are widely used in SDP. As shown in Table 3, they can be defined by the confusion matrix.

Table 3. Confusion matrix.

	Predicted as defective	Predicted as defect-free
True defective	TP	FN
True defect-free	FP	TN

where TP is the number of defective instances that are predicted as defective, FP is the number of defect-free instances that are predicted as defective, TN is the number of defect-free instances that are predicted as defect-free, FN is the number of defective instances that are predicted as defect-free. So F-measure and Accuracy can be defined as:

$$precision = TP/(TP+FP), \; recall = TP/(FP+FN) \qquad (11)$$

$$F\text{-}measure = (2 * precision * recall)/(precision + recall) \qquad (12)$$

$$Accuracy = (TP+TN)/(TP+TN+FP+FN) \qquad (13)$$

4.3 Implementation Detail

In the training process, the CSSHLA model has 4 hidden layers and the number of nodes in each layer is 20-15-10-10-2, where 20 is the dimension of the input data, 2 is the dimension of the data that enters the softmax classifier. Each layer uses rectified linear unit (ReLU) activation function and the setting of layers is empirically obtained. CSSHLA using Adam optimizer performs the parameter optimization of during the training process. The mini-batch is set 64, and the hyper-parameter r is the following: $r \in \{0.1, 0.5, 1, 5, 10, 15\}$, the good results are obtained at $r = 10$.

4.4 Experiment Setup

In this paper, to prove the effectiveness of the proposed method CSSHLA for CPDP, we compare CSSHLA with prior CPDP methods: TCA+ [15], TDS [8], Dycom [4], LT [3] and SHLA(shared hidden layer autoencoder without cost-sensitive). We use 10 projects from PROMISE datasets as our experiments data. And we select one project from 10 projects as target, select one of the remaining nine projects and take their turn as source. We have nine possible combinations for each target project, in total, we have 90 possible CPDP combinations from 10 projects of PROMISE datasets. For example, we chose ant 1.7 as target, and our combination of CPDP is as follows: camel 1.6 - ant 1.7, jedit 3.2 - ant 1.7, camel 1.6 - ant 1.7, log4j 1.0 - ant 1.7, etc.

4.5 Experiment Result and Analysis

Through the above experimental settings, we made a comparison between CSSHLA and baselines(TCA+ , TDS, Dycom, LT, HLA). Tables 4 and 5 present the F-measure and Accuracy performance of CSSHLA compared with the five baselines, respectively. We can see that the average of F-measure of CSSHLA exceeds 5 baseline methods from Table 4, the F-measure values of CSSHLA range from 0.257 to 0.647, and CSSHLA improves F-measure results at least by $0.015 = (0.433-0.418)$. Table 5 shows that CSSHLA gets an average Accuracy of 0.652. Accuracy results in an improvement of at least $0.002 = (0.652-0.650)$.

CSSHLA can effectively solve class imbalance by using cost-sensitive learning technology compared with SHLA. The F-measure and Accuracy of CSSHLA were increased by 0.056 and 0.017, respectively. There are two reasons why our results are better than the baselines: First, to learn more about the features of minority class, we consider the influence of the class imbalance problem on the model learning by assigning different importance weights to different instances. Second, we use the advanced deep features, which are more efficient than traditional features. The results

Table 4. F-measure comparison of CSSHLA model versus 5 baselines.

Target	TDS	TCA+	Dycom	LT	SHLA	CSSHLA
ant-1.7	**0.530**	0.463	0.408	0.447	0.361	0.440
camel-1.6	0.160	**0.321**	0.070	0.260	0.233	0.288
jedit-3.2	0.444	0.510	0.415	**0.532**	0.481	0.530
log4 g-1.0	0.373	0.466	0.428	0.413	0.416	**0.487**
lucene-2.0	0.288	0.530	0.508	0.316	0.492	**0.549**
poi-1.5	0.225	0.596	0.579	0.423	0.611	**0.647**
redaktor	**0.387**	0.235	0.197	0.367	0.223	0.257
synapse-1.0	0.333	0.265	**0.336**	0.097	0.212	0.287
xalan-2.6	0.404	0.481	**0.546**	0.405	0.432	0.533
xerces-1.3	0.345	0.317	0.299	**0.360**	0.291	0.308
Average	0.349	0.418	0.379	0.365	0.377	**0.433**
Improved	0.084	0.015	0.054	0.068	0.056	–

Table 5. Accuracy comparison of CSSHLA model versus 5 baselines.

Target	TDS	TCA+	Dycom	LT	SHLA	CSSHLA
ant-1.7	0.680	0.684	0.674	0.675	0.631	**0.701**
camel-1.6	0.742	0.618	**0.769**	0.722	0.731	0.609
jedit-3.2	0.593	0.663	0.710	0.599	0.702	**0.722**
log4 g-1.0	0.715	0.657	**0.763**	0.726	0.711	0.716
lucene-2.0	0.538	0.621	0.600	0.533	0.621	**0.636**
poi-1.5	0.559	0.576	0.435	0.527	0.611	**0.616**
redaktor	0.579	0.556	0.386	**0.648**	0.361	0.494
synapse-1.0	0.761	0.641	**0.796**	0.643	0.592	0.603
xalan-2.6	0.417	0.591	0.603	0.531	0.582	**0.611**
xerces-1.3	0.714	0.627	0.764	0.757	0.810	**0.815**
Average	0.630	0.623	0.650	0.636	0.635	**0.652**
Improved	0.022	0.029	0.002	0.016	0.017	–

of F-measure and Accuracy of CSSHLA are better than baseline results. According to the evaluation metrics, the proposed method CSSHLA outperform better than baseline methods.

5   Conclusion

In this paper, we present a cost-sensitive shared hidden layer autoencoder (CSSHLA) method for cross-project defect prediction. To solve the problem of data distribution difference in CPDP, we use autoencoder with shared parameter mechanism. It can make the network adapt to source and target projects, and make the distribution of source and target projects more similar to each other by minimizing the reconstruction error loss. Besides, we use cost sensitive learning technology to solve the class imbalance problem. CSSHLA takes into account the different misclassification costs, different weights are assigned to instances of different class. The average values of F-measure and Accuracy of CSSHLA are at least 0.015 and 0.002 better than the baseline methods, respectively. Empirical results show that CSSHLA can achieve better prediction performance than baselines.

Acknowledgements. The work described in this paper was supported by National Natural Science Foundation of China (No. 61702280), Natural Science Foundation of Jiangsu Province (No. BK20170900), National Postdoctoral Program for Innovative Talents (No. BX20180146), Scientific Research Starting Foundation for Introduced Talents in NJUPT (NUPTSF, No. NY217009), and the Postgraduate Research & Practice Innovation Program of Jiangsu Province KYCX17_0794.

References

1. Krizhevsky, A., Sutskever, I., Hinton, G.E.: Imagenet classification with deep convolutional neural networks. In: Advances in Neural Information Processing Systems, pp. 1097–1105 (2012)
2. Boehm, B.W.: Industrial software metrics top 10 list. IEEE Softw. **4**(5), 84–85 (1987)
3. Camargo Cruz, A.E., Ochimizu, K.: Towards logistic regression models for predicting fault-prone code across software projects. In: International Symposium on Empirical Software Engineering and Measurement, pp. 460–463 (2009)
4. Liu, C., Yang, D., Xia, X., Yan, M., Zhang, X.: A two-phase transfer learning model for cross-project defect prediction. Inf. Softw. Technol. **107**, 125–136 (2019)
5. Wu, F., et al.: Intraspectrum discrimination and interspectrum correlation analysis deep network for multispectral face recognition. IEEE Trans. Cybern. 1–14 (2018)
6. Wu, F., et al.: Cross-project and within-project semisupervised software defect prediction: a unified approach. IEEE Trans. Reliab. **67**(2), 581–597 (2018)
7. Tong, H., Liu, B., Wang, S.: Software defect prediction using stacked denoising autoencoders and two-stage ensemble learning. Inf. Softw. Technol. **96**, 94–111 (2018)
8. Herbold, S.: Training data selection for cross-project defect prediction. In: International Conference on Predictive Models in Software Engineering, p. 6 (2013)
9. Hinton, G., et al.: Deep neural networks for acoustic modeling in speech recognition. IEEE Signal Process. Mag. **29**(6), 82–97 (2012)
10. Deng, J., Xia, R., Zhang, Z., Liu, Y., Schuller, B.: Introducing shared-hidden-layer autoencoders for transfer learning and their application in acoustic emotion recognition. In: International Conference on Acoustics, Speech and Signal Processing, pp. 4818–4822 (2014)
11. Deng, J., Zhang, Z., Eyben, F., Schuller, B.: Autoencoder-based unsupervised domain adaptation for speech emotion recognition. IEEE Signal Process. Lett. **21**(9), 1068–1072 (2014)
12. Jureczko, M., Madeyski, L.: Towards identifying software project clusters with regard to defect prediction. In: International Conference on Predictive Models in Software Engineering, p. 9 (2010)
13. Minku, L., Sarro, F., Mende, E., Ferrucci, F.: How to make best use of cross-company data for web effort estimation? In: International Symposium on Empirical Software Engineering and Measurement, pp. 1–10 (2015)

14. Zhao, L., Shang, Z., Zhao, L., Qin, A., Tang, Y.Y.: Siamese dense neural network for software defect prediction with small data. IEEE Access **7**, 7663–7677 (2019)
15. Nam, J., Pan, S.J., Kim, S.: Transfer defect learning. In: International Conference on Software Engineering, pp. 382–391 (2013)
16. Wang, S., Yao, X.: Using class imbalance learning for software defect prediction. IEEE Trans. Reliab. **62**(2), 434–443 (2013)
17. Wang, S., Liu, T., Tan, L.: Automatically learning semantic features for defect prediction. In: International Conference on Software Engineering, pp. 297–308 (2016)
18. Kotsiantis, S.B., Kanellopoulos, D., Pintelas, P.E.: Data preprocessing for supervised learning. Int. J. Comput. Sci. **1**(2), 111–117 (2006)
19. Kim, S., Zhang, H., Wu, R., Gong, L.: Dealing with noise in defect prediction. In: International Conference on Software Engineering, pp. 481–490 (2011)
20. Liu, W., Liu, S., Gu, Q., Chen, J., Chen, X., Chen, D.: Empirical studies of a two-stage data preprocessing approach for software fault prediction. IEEE Trans. Reliab. **65**(1), 38–53 (2016)
21. Yang, X., Lo, D., Xia, X., Zhang, Y., Sun, J.: Deep learning for just-in-time defect prediction. In: International Conference on Software Quality, Reliability and Security, pp. 17–26 (2015)
22. Gao, Y., Yang, C., Liang, L.: Software defect prediction based on geometric mean for subspace learning. In: Advanced Information Technology, Electronic and Automation Control Conference, pp. 225–229 (2017)
23. Yang, Y., et al.: Are slice-based cohesion metrics actually useful in effort-aware post-release fault-proneness prediction? An empirical study. IEEE Trans. Softw. Eng. **41**(4), 331–357 (2015)
24. Li, Z., Jing, X., Wu, F., Zhu, X., Xu, B., Ying, S.: Cost-sensitive transfer kernel canonical correlation analysis for heterogeneous defect prediction. Autom. Softw. Eng. **25**(2), 201–245 (2018)

Person ReID: Optimization
of Domain Adaption Though Clothing
Style Transfer Between Datasets

Haijian Wang[1], Meng Yang[1(✉)], Hui Li[2], and Linbin Ye[1]

[1] Sun Yat-sen University, Guangzhou, Guangdong, China
haijianwang@163.com, yangm6@mail.sysu.edu.cn
[2] Shenzhen University, Shenzhen, Guangdong, China

Abstract. It is manifested that when training and testing models on different datasets, the performance of trained models will severely dropped due to the differences in style of the datasets. In person ReID task, the clothing style is a crucial factor existing in different datasets, which has not been considered in the current research. We proposed a novel approach of Optimization of Domain Adaption Though Clothing Style Transfer (ODA-CST), which includes clothing mask extraction and clothing style transfer. Firstly, we generate the clothing mask by jointly locally extracting clothing and globally detecting the person. Meanwhile, we also organize a clothing mask dataset to improve the model. Our ODA-CST can effectively generate photos with the clothing style transferred, which is the first method that tries to solve the clothing style gap in person ReID task to the best knowledge. The importance of clothing style transfer and the effectiveness of our method are verified by the experiment.

Keywords: Person Re-identification · GAN · Domain Adaption · Style Transfer

1 Introduction

Person re-identification (person ReID) aims to obtain all pictures or videos matching specific targets from the gallery data collected by a large-scale camera network. It has important application prospects in the field of smart city construction such as intelligent security and intelligent monitoring. In recent years, ReID is regarded by academic circles and industry as a critical hot spots in computer vision research.

However, there are still many challenges in the field of person ReID. One of them is the demand for a large amount of training data, which is reflected in the fact that training data is very limited [1, 3, 4], data acquisition is difficult, and data labeling is difficult. In the current mainstream three person ReID datasets [1–4], the number of person IDs and the number of pictures are relatively small. At the same time, there is a widespread problem of domain gaps between different datasets. In other word, the performance of model be seriously reduced when dealing with cross datasets problems.

Student paper.

© Springer Nature Switzerland AG 2019
Z. Lin et al. (Eds.): PRCV 2019, LNCS 11859, pp. 503–515, 2019.
https://doi.org/10.1007/978-3-030-31726-3_43

There are relatively fixed picture style due to the short time span of data collection and limited on the number of cameras in most ReID datasets. So the exited models that cannot adapt to the complex changes under realistic conditions. This results in most of the person ReID models unable to adapt to complex scene changes under realistic conditions.

Therefore, the academic community has begun to try to expand the capacity of datasets through various methods. On the one hand, some new large-scale datasets are constantly proposed including MSMT 17 [9]. On the other hand, GAN [10] can be used to solve learning problems when the annotation data is insufficient, such as unsupervised learning, semi-supervised learning, and so on. Therefore, one of the applications of deep learning in ReID is to use GAN to generate unmarked pedestrian data for data augmentation [11].

The academic community has tried to use GAN to generate images to expand the dataset, mainly to generate images of different poses of the same pedestrian for data augmentation, such as FD-GAN [13], have achieved good results. In addition, Zhong et al. [12] transferred the photos of different cameras for the problem of domain gap, and PTGAN [9] transferred the background style between different datasets, which reduced the domain gap and improved the domain adaptability when training and testing the model on different datasets (Fig. 1).

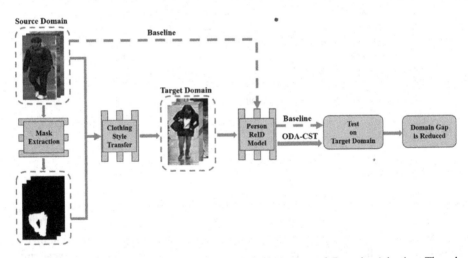

Fig. 1. Overview of the proposed approach of Optimization of Domain Adaption Though Clothing Style Transfer (ODA-CST). We first obtain the mask of the pedestrian clothing through the pedestrian clothing extraction model, and then feed the pedestrian image together with the corresponding clothing mask into the clothing style migration model, and the generated new dataset obtains better performance on the person ReID model than the baseline.

However, most of the related research on the domain gap of person ReID are focused on the domain gap caused by the overall picture environment, background style, lighting conditions. Our proposed method is no longer limited by these factors, but also include differences in the style of pedestrian clothing. The different seasons of different datasets may result in huge differences in the style of dressing, especially when one dataset was collected in winter and the other was collected in summer. However, there is no related research to the best knowledge, which motivates us to explore the clothing style transfer between datasets to reduce the domain gap.

To verify our ideas, we proposed a novel approach of Optimization of Domain Adaption Though Clothing Style Transfer (ODA-CST), which includes clothing mask extraction model and clothing style transfer model. In the model of clothing style transfer, we need the clothing binary mask in the person ReID dataset as a constraint. Unfortunately, there are currently few pedestrian clothing semantic segmentation tags for person ReID datasets. We integrated the existing pedestrian semantic segmentation dataset [14–16] and organized a pedestrian clothing mask extraction dataset in the first stage. This dataset is composed of manually selected pictures with similar pedestrian styles in the image of the person ReID dataset. There are more than 8,000 pedestrian pictures and corresponding clothing masks. Subsequently, based on the framework of CycleGAN [17], we used the pedestrian image and the clothing mask of the person ReID dataset to transfer the clothing style and generate a new dataset with the similar clothing style of the transfer target domain.

Our ODA-CST method is the first method known in the field of person ReID to reduce the domain gap caused by clothing style difference. Experiments have been conducted on benchmark datasets, which shows that the performance was significantly improved compared with the baseline. The accuracy of top-1, top-5, top-10 increased by 1.3%–11.4%, and mAP improved by 1%–3.3%. This also verifies that the clothing style is also one of the crucial factors that cause domain gaps, which has been ignored in the former research. And the clothing style transfer can effectively reduce the clothing domain gap, making the model more adaptable to unseen datasets.

2   Related Works

2.1   Semantic Segmentation of Pedestrian Mask

Pedestrian masks are increasingly being used in person ReID research. Wei et al. [9] used PSPNet [22] for the extraction of the pedestrian mask. Song et al. [14] used the FCN-based model to train on the Baidu People Segmentation Dataset, effectively extracting the pedestrian binary segmentation mask from person ReID datasets.

2.2   Image-to-Image Translation with GAN

GAN [10] is able to generate images that are consistent with the distribution of real data, making itself a widely-used network structure for style transfer. Radford et al. [19] propose DCGAN, which significantly improved the quality of the generated photos and speed up the convergence. Isola et al. [20] proposed a very adaptable and effective image-to-image transfer model called pix2pix, which is able to generate photos of almost every given style corresponding to an input photo.

Zhu et al. [17] proposed CycleGAN without requiring paired photos for training as pix2pix does. Compared with the traditional GAN, it mainly constrains the generated image by a cyclic consistency loss: $G_{YX}(G_{XY}(x)) \approx x$ and $G_{XY}(G_{YX}(y)) \approx y$.

However, the CycleGAN [17] learns is mainly the distribution pattern and global style information of images without any local instance awareness. Direct application of CycleGAN in the ReID task will lead to confusion of the pedestrians and the backgrounds. The quality of the generated picture will be degraded with distraction of identity-related information, which means CycleGAN [17] is not adaptive to the task of local style transfer. At the same time, CycleGAN [17] isn't a promising solution in changing the shape between source and target domain. To solve this problem, Mo et al. [21] optimized CycleGAN and proposed a new InstaGAN model. InstaGAN takes the instance segmentation label and the original image as input, and only converts the instances and keep the background unchanged as possible.

2.3   GAN in Person ReID Research

In the field of person ReID, the current application of GAN in person ReID mainly lie in data augmentation as labeled person ReID data is difficult to obtain. GAN can be applied to generate more unmarked pedestrian images [11]. However, due to the low resolution of images in the person ReID datasets and the insufficient performance of the model itself, the quality of generated pedestrian image is also limited. On the other hand, photos taken with different cameras in the same person ReID dataset have biases in terms of lighting conditions and viewpoints. Zhong et al. [12] performed style transfer between photos taken with different cameras and generated more new images with higher quality. PTGAN [9] process a style transfer among different datasets in order to reduce the bias due to background environment and other factors.

On the other hand, domain gaps of ReID caused by pedestrian pose change [2, 13] attracts more attention. Qian et al. [2] used GAN to generate eight standard pose images of every person, and extracted the features of descendants with different pose. These features were combined with the extracted pose-independent features to obtain the pooled comprehensive features, making the model well adapted to the bias caused by pedestrian pose changes.

3   Implementation

Our proposed ODA-CST method aims to improve the domain adaptability of the person ReID model when training and testing on different datasets by performing clothing style transfer on different datasets. New datasets obtained by style transfer can be used to train the person ReID model to achieve data augmentation effects and adapt the model to the style characteristics of different datasets. We first extract the clothing mask of the person ReID dataset, and then input it into the clothing style transfer model together with pedestrian pictures to generate new pedestrian pictures.

3.1   Clothing Mask Extraction

The extraction model of the clothing mask is the first part of our ODA-CST method, whose extraction accuracy directly affects the model effect of the subsequent part. In order to optimize the CycleGAN [17], we take masks of pedestrian clothing as a constraint for style transfer.

The extraction of the mask requires an extra model. We leverage the pix2pix [20] model as backbone and develop a clothing mask extraction model. Although the semantic segmentation is not included in the common application of pix2pix model, it's found efficient in our task. The original image and the binary mask are regarded as a separate picture style. The model needs paired pictures of the labeled clothing mask and the original pictures. Currently, the datasets of the mainstream person ReID do not have a corresponding pedestrian mask. Therefore, we first train the model by using the pedestrian street image of the Clothing Co-parsing (CCP) dataset [15] and the ATR dataset [16] and the corresponding pixel-level semantic masks (Fig. 2).

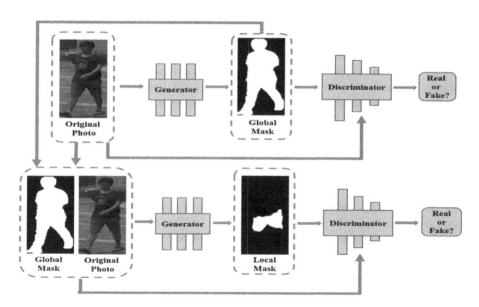

Fig. 2. Model of clothing mask extraction. We first use the pedestrian mask in the paper of Song et al. [22] to train a pedestrian global mask extraction model, then merge each photo with the corresponding global mask, and then extract the local mask based on the framework of the pix2pix model, which is the mask of pedestrian clothing. In this way, we can use the global mask to filter out the background interference and improve the accuracy of the clothing mask extraction.

$$\min_{G} \max_{D} E[\log D(x, G(x)) + \log(1 - D(x, y))] \tag{1}$$

The objective function of the pix2pix [20] model is as follows. As showed in formula (1), the optimization target of pix2pix combines the input x and the generated picture G(x). According to the information of the two pictures, the discriminator D can judge whether the generated picture is related to the input image x, instead of randomly generating a picture that matches the target domain style.

It should be emphasized that if the pix2pix model is used directly to extract the mask of pedestrian clothing, the test results are not stable. For this reason, the clothing mask extraction model need to be improved. We first train the clothing extraction model to extract the global mask, and use these global masks to merge the pedestrian image, covering the pedestrian background in the original image, making the model more sensitive to the pedestrian's body information. The model combines the global mask and then extracts the local clothing mask, which improves the accuracy.

3.2 Clothing Style Transfer

The clothing style transfer model is the second part of our ODA-CST method, which takes good use of the extracted clothing mask to achieve the effective clothing style transfer while keeping the rest of the picture unchanged. In other words, it maintains the overall characteristics (identity-related information) of the pedestrian and can accommodate the style transfer of objects with very large difference on shapes (such as the style transfer between pants and shorts or skirts in this paper).

The InstaGAN [21] is based on this idea to perform the image style transfer with instance awareness. However, the InstaGAN is a style transfer model for multiple instances of a picture. In this task, most of the pedestrian's bounding box images contain only one person, so we only need to transfer one instance of the clothing in an image. Therefore, we adopt the framework of InstaGAN [21] and streamline its structure.

Architecture. Given a set of image pairs (x, a) are fed to the model and obtain another set of (y, b). x is a pedestrian picture and a is its corresponding clothing mask. The generator G uses f_{GX} and f_{GA} to extract the features of x and a respectively, and then inputs them into the image and attribute generator, and then fuses the extracted features with h_{GX} and h_{GA} to generate the migrated images and attributes respectively. The output of h_{GX} is input to the generator g_{GX}, and the output of h_{GA} is input to generator g_{GA}. The formulas for h_{GX} and h_{GA} are as follows.

$$h_{GX}(x, a) = [f_{GX}(x); f_{GA}(a)], \; h_{GA}(x, a) = [f_{GX}(x); f_{GA}(a); f_{GA}(a)] \qquad (2)$$

On the other hand, the discriminator D can encode x and a, and determine whether the picture pair belongs to this field, and h_{DX} is finally input to g_{DX}. Similar to the previous one, the h_{DX} formula is as follows.

$$h_{DX}(x, a) = [f_{DX}(x); f_{DA}(a)] \qquad (3)$$

With the constraint of the attribute feature corresponding to the pedestrian picture, the generator can generate new clothes on the clothing position of the original picture.

Training Loss. According to the InstaGAN model [21], in order to maintain the background while changing the style of the clothes, the loss should be divided into two parts, namely domain loss and content loss. The domain loss is used to constrain the generated image to conform to the characteristics of the target domain, and the content loss is to constrain the generated image to retain the overall content of the image. Specifically, domain loss is the loss of GAN (LSGAN [5]), and content loss includes loss of cycle-consistency (Kim et al. [6]), identity mapping loss (Taigman et al. [7]) and content preserving loss (from InstaGAN [21]), as showed in the bellow.

$$L_{LSGAN} = (D_X(x, a) - 1)^2 + D_X(G_{YX}(y, b))^2 + (D_Y(y, b) - 1)^2 + D_Y(G_{XY}(x, a))^2 \quad (4)$$

$$L_{cyc} = \|G_{YX}(G_{XY}(x, a)) - (x, a)\|_1 + \|G_{XY}(G_{YX}(y, b)) - (y, b)\|_1 \quad (5)$$

$$L_{idt} = \|G_{XY}(y, b) - (y, b)\|_1 + \|G_{YX}(x, a) - (x, a)\|_1 \quad (6)$$

$$L_{ctx} = \|w(a, b') \odot (x - y')\|_1 + \|w(b, a') \odot (y - x')\|_1 \quad (7)$$

Finally, the loss function of the model is as follows.

$$L_{InstaGAN} = L_{LSGAN} + \lambda_{cyc}L_{cyc} + \lambda_{idt}L_{idt} + \lambda_{ctx}L_{ctx} \quad (8)$$

4 Experiment

4.1 Implement Details

In the DukeMTMC-reID dataset, 16,522 bounding boxes of 702 identities are used for training and the rest are included in the testing set. In the Market1501 dataset, the training set contains 12,936 bounding boxes of 751 identities, and the rest 750 identities are included in the testing set. When training the ResNet50 model, we used 4 NVIDIA 1080Ti GPUs and set the batch size to 256 with an initial learning rate of 0.1 (if only one GPU is used, the batch size is set to 64 and the initial learning rate is 0.025). The size of input image is 256×256. Finally, we train the model for 100 epochs. Our network is implemented in PyTorch.

4.2 Clothing Mask Extraction

We used pants and shorts or skirts as winter and summer clothes, and filtered the data of 6000 pants and 2000 shorts or skirts, respectively, and put the corresponding binary masks and original photos to the network for training (Fig. 3).

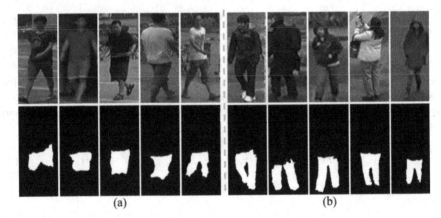

                    (a)   (b)

Fig. 3. (a) Examples of mask extraction in Market1501 dataset. (b) Examples of mask extraction in DukeMTMC-reID dataset. The 1st row presents the original images and the 2nd row presents the results of binary mask of pants or shorts in the images.

To improve the adaptability of the trained model on the person ReID dataset, we first crop the image of the training set and the corresponding clothing binary mask, which is similar to the pedestrian bounding boxes in the person ReID dataset. The advantages includes unify the size of the image in the person ReID, while avoiding the interference caused by the excessive background of the training set. The trained model can realize the clothing mask extraction of the person ReID dataset.

It can be seen that the pix2pix model can complete the extraction task of the pedestrian clothing mask. We applied it to DukeMTMC (data collected in winter) and Market1501 (data collected in summer) datasets for trousers and shorts or skirts masks.

4.3   Clothing Style Transfer

The DukeMTMC dataset [1] was collected in the winter, people mainly wear thick coats, trousers and other clothing, the Market1501 dataset [3] is collected in the summer, people mainly wear T-shirts, shorts or skirts. Reducing the difference in clothing style between different datasets will help reduce the domain gap.

We use InstaGAN model for clothing transfer as it can accommodate style transfer of targets with big differences in shape. Clothing mask and the bounding boxes are the input. The summer dress (pants) and winter clothes (shorts and skirts) of the CCP dataset [15] and ATR dataset [16] are regarded as an individual domain. We tested the pants of the DukeMTMC dataset [1] and the shorts and skirts of the Market1501 dataset [3]. The results are shown in the Figs. 4 and 5.

Fig. 4. Examples of clothing style transfer in DukeMTMC-reID dataset. Direction: from jeans/pants to shorts/skirts, the 1st row presents the original images and the 2nd row presents the generated images.

Fig. 5. Examples of clothing style transfer in Market1501 dataset. Direction: from shorts/skirts to jeans/pants, the 1st row presents the original images and the 2nd row presents the generated images.

We can conclude that clothing transfer has a good effect on these two Person ReID datasets. It's observed that most of the images have obvious clothing transfer effects.

4.4 Tests of Domain Adaption on Transferred Datasets

Quantitative Evaluations. The data of the DukeMTMC dataset [1] and the Market1501 dataset [3] after clothing style transfer are taken as a new dataset, and the ReID model is trained on the new dataset, and then the corresponding test data can be obtained. The baseline for test is a model trained in the source dataset using the ResNet50 [18] model which is common used in person ReID study.

Table 1. Contrast experiment on DukeMTMC and Market dataset. The subscript Market denotes the transferred target dataset Market1501, and the subscript Duke denotes the transferred target dataset DukeMTMC-reID.

Model	Training set	Test set	Top-1	Top-5	Top-10	mAP
Baseline	DukeMTMC	Market1501	37.5	54.6	62.5	15.3
Ours	DukeMTMC$_{Market}$	Market1501	**38.8**	**56.7**	**64.9**	**16.3**
Baseline	Market1501	DukeMTMC	24.3	40.2	47.5	13.2
Ours	Market1501$_{Duke}$	DukeMTMC	**27.1**	**43.0**	**50.2**	**14.7**

Table 2. Contrast experiment on DukeMTMC and CUHK dataset. The subscript CUHK denotes the transferred target dataset CUHK03, and the subscript Duke denotes the transferred target dataset DukeMTMC-reID.

Model	Training set	Test set	Top-1	Top-5	Top-10	mAP
Baseline	DukeMTMC	CUHK03	19.5	42.9	56.6	13.0
Ours	DukeMTMC$_{CUHK}$	CUHK03	**20.4**	**46.5**	**60.1**	12.7
Baseline	CUHK03	DukeMTMC	15.8	27.8	34.4	8.3
Ours	CUHK03$_{Duke}$	DukeMTMC	**23.8**	**38.8**	**45.8**	**11.6**

We apply the model trained on one dataset and the test it on another dataset to observe the adaptability of the model. The mAP and Top-n accuracy is used as a quantitative standard. The adaption of a model trained is positively correlated with the accuracy of test results on another dataset. For fair comparison, we will select the model when the new dataset and the original dataset are trained to achieve the same accuracy on their own test sets. The obtained precision is shown in the Table 1.

From Table 1, we can conclude that the trained ResNet50 [18] model is better able to adapt to the test on the Market1501 dataset by training on the new dataset obtained after the pants of the DukeMTMC dataset are converted to shorts or skirts. At the same time, the trained ResNet50 [18] model is more adaptable to testing on the DukeMTMC dataset [1] by training the new dataset obtained after the shorts or skirts of the Market1501 dataset [3] transferring to pants. The mAP has increased by more than 1%, and the accuracy of top-1, top-5, and top-10 has also increased by 1.3%–2.8%. As shown in the Table 2, it's observed that our purposed ODA-CST method is also outperformed significantly in the contrast experiment on DukeMTMC and CUHK03 dataset. Experimental results of Table 3 demonstrate that our purposed ODA-CST method outperforms other unsupervised methods. Therefore, we can conclude that clothing style transfer are indispensable for improving the transferable ability of ReID models.

Table 3. Performance comparison to other methods.

Model	Training set	Test set	Top-1	mAP
UMDL [23]	Market1501	DukeMTMC	18.5	7.3
Verif + Identif [8]	Market1501	DukeMTMC	25.7	12.8
Ours	Market1501$_{Duke}$	DukeMTMC	**27.1**	**14.7**

Limitation. We notice that due to data bias (e.g., pose, lighting) in the original training set, our generative module tends to be occasionally unstable. As shown in Table 2, we transfer the clothing style from DukeMTMC to CUHK03 and the Top-n accuracy are all improved notably while the mAP accuracy decrease.

4.5 Ablation Study

Comparison. In our purposed ODA-CST method, the key component is the clothing mask extraction model without which the clothing style transfer model will fail. Therefore, we trained the CycleGAN model which can not aware the local clothing features of different domain as the baseline model for comparison. As shown in Fig. 6, our purposed ODA-CST method is found to be able to sense the profile of clothing while the baseline model isn't.

Table 4. Qualitative evaluations of ablation study.

Model	Training set	Test set	Top-1	Top-5	Top-10	mAP
Baseline	DukeMTMC	Market1501	37.5	54.6	62.5	15.3
CycleGAN	DukeMTMC$_{Market}$	Market1501	38.4	56.9	64.9	15.1
Ours	DukeMTMC$_{Market}$	Market1501	**38.8**	**56.7**	**64.9**	**16.3**

(a)DukeMTMC(pants)→Market1501(shorts/skirts)   (b)Market1501(shorts/skirts)→DukeMTMC(pants)

Fig. 6. Ablation study on the effect of clothing style transfer model of our method.

Qualitative Evaluations. Experiment results in Table 4 clearly verifies that the performance of ReID model boost as the effect of clothing transfer improved, which demonstrate it is the clothing style transfer that attribute to the improvement of the ReID model performance.

5 Conclusions

Based on the idea of data augmentation for person ReID datasets, we explored the problem of severe performance degradation of person ReID models in cross-dataset scenarios. By transferring the clothing style between different datasets, we effectively reduce the domain gap between different datasets, so that the person ReID models can more effectively adapt to the style of different datasets, which is useful in unsupervised domain adaptation. In addition, during the experiment, we also integrated a new dataset of pedestrian clothing segmentation mask, and trained a model that can effectively extract the clothing segmentation mask in low-resolution pedestrian image. In the future, we will try to speed up the training process, and try to improve the model so that it can simultaneously transfer both the background and clothing style.

Acknowledgement. This work is partially supported by the National Natural Science Foundation of China (Grant no. 61772568), the Guangzhou Science and Technology Program (Grant no. 201804010288), and the Fundamental Research Funds for the Central Universities (Grant no. 18lgzd15).

References

1. Zheng, Z., Zheng, L., Yang, Y.: Unlabeled samples generated by GAN improve the person re-identification baseline in vitro. In: ICCV 2017 (2017)
2. Qian, X., Fu, Y., Wang, W., et al.: Pose-normalized image generation for person re-identification. arXiv preprint. arXiv:1712.02225 (2017)
3. Zheng, L., Shen, L., Tian, L., Wang, S., Wang, J., Tian, Q.: Scalable person re-identification: a benchmark. In: ICCV 2015 (2015)
4. Li, W., Zhao, R., Xiao, T., Wang, X.: Deepreid: deep filter pairing neural network for person re-identification. In: CVPR 2014 (2014)
5. Mao, X., Li, Q., Xie, H., Lau, R.Y.K., Wang, Z., Paul Smolley, S.: Least squares generative adversarial networks. In: ICCV (2017)
6. Kim, T., Cha, M., Kim, H., Lee, J.K., Kim, J.: Learning to discover cross-domain relations with generative adversarial networks. arXiv preprint. arXiv:1703.05192 (2017)
7. Taigman, Y., Polyak, A., Wolf, L.: Unsupervised cross-domain image generation. arXiv preprint. arXiv:1611.02200 (2016)
8. Zheng, Z., Zheng, L., Yang, Y.: A discriminatively learned CNN embedding for person re-identification. In: TOMM (2016)
9. Wei, L., Zhang, S., Gao, W., et al.: Person transfer GAN to bridge domain gap for person re-identification. In: CVPR (2018)
10. Goodfellow, I., et al.: Generative adversarial nets. In: NIPS 2014 (2014)
11. Zheng, Z., Zheng, L., Yang, Y.: Unlabeled samples generated by GAN improve the person re-identification baseline in vitro. arXiv preprint. arXiv:1701.07717 (2017)
12. Zhong, Z., Zheng, L., Zheng, Z., et al.: Camera style adaptation for person re-identification. arXiv preprint. arXiv:1711.10295 (2017)
13. Ge, Y., et al.: FD-GAN: pose-guided feature distilling GAN for robust person re-identification. In: CVPR (2018)
14. Song, C., Huang, Y., Ouyang, W., Wang, L.: Mask-guided contrastive attention model for person re-identification. In: CVPR (2018)

15. Yang, W., Luo, P., Lin, L.: Clothing co-parsing by joint image segmentation and labeling. In: CVPR (2014)
16. Liang, X., et al.: Deep human parsing with active template regression. TPAMI **37**(12), 2402–2414 (2015)
17. Zhu, J.-Y., Park, T., Isola, P., et al.: Unpaired image-to-image translation using cycle-consistent adversarial networks. arXiv preprint. arXiv:1703.10593 (2017)
18. He, K.M., Zhang, X.Y., Ren, S.Q., Sun, J.: Deep residual learning for image recognition. In: CVPR (2016)
19. Radford, A., Metz, L., Chintala, S.: Unsupervised representation learning with deep convolutional generative adversarial networks. In: ICLR (2016)
20. Isola, P., Zhu, J.-Y., Zhou, T., Efros, A.A.: Image-to-image translation with conditional adversarial nets. In: CVPR (2017)
21. Mo, S., Choy, M., Shin, J.: InstaGAN: instance-aware image-to-image translation. In: ICLR (2019)
22. Zhao, H., Shi, J., Qi, X., Wang, X., Jia, J.: Pyramid scene parsing network. In: CVPR (2017)
23. Peng, P., Xiang, T., Wang, Y., et al.: Unsupervised cross-dataset transfer learning for person reidentification. In: CVPR (2016)

Shellfish Detection Based on Fusion Attention Mechanism in End-to-End Network

Guangyao Li[1,2], Zhenbo Li[1,2(✉)], Chuyue Zhang[1], Yaodong Li[3],
and Jun Yue[4]

[1] College of Information and Electrical Engineering,
China Agricultural University, Beijing 100083, China
{liguangyao,lizb,zcy980416}@cau.edu.cn
[2] National Innovation Center for Digital Fishery, China Agricultural University,
Beijing 100083, China
[3] College of Engineering, China Agricultural University, Beijing 100083, China
lyd980324@cau.edu.cn
[4] School of Information and Electrical Engineering, Ludong University,
Yantai 264025, China
yuejuncn@126.com

Abstract. Object detection has many difficulties and challenges in the agricultural field, mainly due to the lack of data and the complexity of the agricultural environment. Therefore, we built a shellfish dataset containing 3772 images in 7 categories, all of which were manually labeled and verified. In addition, based on the SSD model framework, we used the lightweight MobileNet-v2 classification network to replace the original VGG16 network, and introduced a residual attention mechanism between the classification network and the prediction convolution layer. This could not only lead to a better capture the local features of the images, but also meet the needs of real-time and mobile use. The experimental results show that the performance of our model on the shellfish dataset is better than the current mainstream target detection models. And the verification results achieved an accuracy of 95.38% and a detection speed of 33 ms per picture, indicating that the validity of the model we proposed.

Keywords: Shellfish detection · Attention mechanism · MobileNet-v2 · SSD

1 Introduction

Object detection is an important part of computer vision, and it is of great significance in smart agriculture and human-computer interaction. The traditional object detection algorithm based on manual extraction features has occupied a dominant position for a long time, but it faces the problem of severe redundancy, lack of pertinence and high time complexity of the region selection strategy window of the sliding window. RBG et al. designed the R-CNN [1] framework in 2014 using a combination of convolutional neural networks (CNN) and regional suggestion networks, and replaced the methods

Student Paper.

Z. Lin et al. (Eds.): PRCV 2019, LNCS 11859, pp. 516–527, 2019.
https://doi.org/10.1007/978-3-030-31726-3_44

based on sliding windows and manual design features in traditional object detection. Since then, object detection has made a huge breakthrough.

There are two main targets for the current object detection. One is the method with Region Proposal as the main step, such as R-CNN, SPP-NET [2], Fast-RCNN [3], Faster-RCNN [4]. The other is based on end-to-end regression, such as Yolo [5], Yolo v3 [6] and other models. The former introduces a deep neural network into the object detection, achieving a qualitative leap in accuracy, but does not meet the real-time requirements in terms of speed. The latter uses the idea of regression to directly return the object frame and the object category at this position in multiple positions of the image, which greatly speeds up the detection, but it is difficult to improve in accuracy. The SSD [7] method proposed by Liu et al. combines the Anchor mechanism in Faster R-CNN with the regression idea in YOLO, and returns the regional features of each position of the whole graph through a multi-scale method. This method also achieves good accuracy and speed in the case of low image resolution. However, as the depth of the model deepens, the complexity of the model increases. For example, the number of layers in ResNet [8] has reached 152 layers. So these methods have high computational power requirements for hardware and are difficult to popularize. To this end, researchers have begun to study lightweight networks for better versatility.

In order to meet the needs of the equipment, some lightweight networks have been proposed, the most typical of which are MobileNet [9], SqueezeNet [10], ShuffleNet [11], Xception [12] and so on. Especially the MobileNet uses different convolution kernels for each input channel and uses a smaller convolution kernel of 1x1 to improve accuracy. These lightweight networks are a good solution to the problem of insufficient memory due to the deep depth of the model. However, these networks are faced with a large number of invalid feature maps during the training process. Then, the attention mechanism based on recurrent neural network has entered people's field of vision, which has enabled researchers to have new ideas in the direction of improving object detection efficiency. Wang et al. [13] proposed an Attention-based residual learning approach to improve the performance of stackable rescue attention modules. In addition, the first-ranked SENet [14] network in the ILSVRC 2017 classification project introduces the residual attention network and repeatedly adjusts the network model by weight function to re-weight the information features to achieve better image classification tasks. The introduction of these attention mechanisms further increases the efficiency of object detection.

At present, mainstream object detection algorithms have achieved certain results in academia and industry, and research in the agricultural field is still rare. As an important part of the agricultural economy, marine shellfish have many kinds and complicated characteristics. The traditional human-oriented operation is difficult to meet the market demand. Therefore, the research on shellfish object detection has great significance for the agricultural economy.

In the existing shellfish target recognition, most of them are based on the manual extraction of contour features, using the principle of graphics to identify. For example, Kun et al. [15] proposed an algorithm based on Gabor filter and two-dimensional principal component analysis to extract the characteristics of snail shellfish, which can be used to classify snail shells. Hiroki et al. [16] used a 1-MHz acoustic focus probe to detect shellfish in sediments and then acquired shellfish targets using two-dimensional acoustic imaging techniques. These traditional methods of detection are often inefficient and inaccurate, and studies based on CNNs have not yet been discovered. This is because of the complexity of the agricultural environment and there is currently no corresponding shellfish dataset.

In this paper, we use the basic framework of SSD, combined with MobileNet lightweight network, through the introduction of residual attention mechanism, continuous parameter tuning, and finally achieved good results in the detection accuracy and speed of the shellfish dataset. The shellfish detection effect process is shown in Fig. 1. Our main contributions are as follows:

(1) We built a shellfish dataset by means of our own shooting and web crawling, which included 7 types of 3772 photos. And all the pictures are manually labeled and verified.
(2) Based on the SSD framework, we adopt a lightweight MobileNet-v2 network and introduce a residual attention mechanism to propose a shellfish detection and recognition model. And our method achieves 95.38% accuracy and 32 ms/sheet speed, laying the foundation for intelligent research of shellfish.

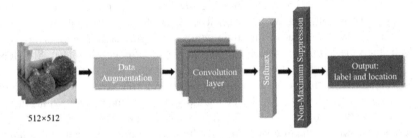

Fig. 1. Shellfish detection framework.

2 Methodology

The CNN can capture the characteristics of the image from the global receptive field to describe the image. However, it is quite difficult to learn a very powerful network. Therefore, the suggestion of attention mechanism can make up for this deficiency very well. In essence, it is to imitate the way humans observe objects, and can gather local features of targets in images to improve detection accuracy.

Therefore, the main idea of our model is based on the SSD model and based on the MobileNet classification network. A residual attention module is introduced between the MobileNet network and the prediction module to strengthen the selected interest area. The overall network framework is shown in Fig. 2. Our approach starts with the relationship between feature channels, explicitly models the interdependence between feature channels, and adopts a new "feature recalibration" strategy to automatically obtain the importance of each feature channel. Then, according to this importance level, the useful features are enhanced and the features that are not useful for the current task are suppressed, so that the feature channel adaptive calibration can be realized. This allows the entire network structure to focus not only on the overall information, but also on the local information. The schematic diagram of introducing the attention residual module is shown in Fig. 3.

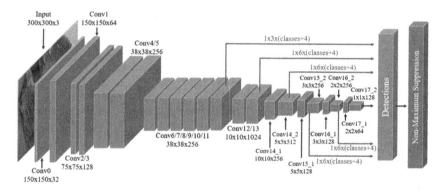

Fig. 2. MobileNet-v2-SSD framework.

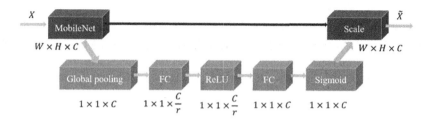

Fig. 3. Framework drawing introducing attention mechanism.

The above figure is interpreted as assuming that the original feature map is $W \times H \times C$, and then globally pooled through $W \times H$ pooled window to get the feature map of $1 \times 1 \times C$. Then use two fully connected layers and one sigmoid layer to output the result. In order to better fit the complex correlation between the channels, when the first fully connected layer is used, the number of neurons C is divided by r for dimensionality reduction, and the second fully connected layer is added to the dimension to return to F. feature. In addition, due to the correlation between the channels, the final output is $1 \times 1 \times C$, where sigmoid is used instead of SoftMax. And our model uses default boxes and loss functions similar to the SSD framework.

Default Boxes. To deal with objectives of different sizes and shapes in images, it is necessary to set prior frames of corresponding scale and proportion according to the network's feature map. The setting of a prior frame is mainly consisting of three parameters: scale, ratio and default box. The specific formula is as follows:

To calculate scale, the size of Default Box in each Feature Map could be calculated as follows:

$$S_k = S_{\min} + \frac{S_{\max} - S_{\min}}{m - 1}(k - 1), \ k \in [1, m] \tag{1}$$

In the formula, the value of $S_{\min}$ is 0.2 and the value of $S_{\max}$ is 0.95, which means the level of the lowest layer is 0.2 and that of the highest layer is 0.5. Different values of

$a_r = 1, 2, 3, 1/2, 1/3$ are respectively applied to calculate the height and width of the Default Box. The height and width could be calculated as follows:

$$w_k^a = S_k\sqrt{a_r}, \quad h_k^a = S_k\sqrt{a_r} \tag{2}$$

In addition, for the case of Ratio = 1, a specific Default Box is added with a scale of $s'k = \sqrt{S_k S_{k+1}}$. As a result, there are 6 different Default Boxes. Set the center of each Default Box to $((i+0.5)/|f_k|, (j+0.5)/|f_k|)$. And $|f_k|$ represents the size of the first feature map $i, j \in [0, |f_k|)$.

Loss Function. The loss function is calculated similar to the loss function in Fast RCNN. The total loss function is the weighted sum of localization loss (LOC) and confidence loss (CONF). The formula is as follows:

$$L(x, c, l, g) = \frac{1}{N}\left(L_{conf}(x, c) + \alpha L_{loc}(x, l, g)\right) \tag{3}$$

In this formula, N is the number of default boxes matching the ground truth box. $x = \{0, 1\}$ is an indicator parameter. And the weighting coefficient α is set to 1 by cross-validation. For CONF, the idea of SoftMax loss is used, defined as follows:

$$L_{conf}(x, c) = -\sum_{i \in Pos}^{N} x_{ij}^p \log(\hat{c}_i^p) - \sum_{i \in Neg} \log(\hat{c}_i^0) \tag{4}$$

Where x_{ij}^p is the identifier of whether the ith default box matches the jth normal data of the category p, and the value is in $\{0, 1\}$. c_i^p is the output of the softmax of the category confidence of the ith default box, $\hat{c}_i^p$ is the confidence level of the background class of the ith default box. *Pos* and *Neg* respectively identify the positive sample set and the negative sample set.

For LOC, Smooth L1 loss mechanism is used, defined as follows:

$$L(x, l, g) = \sum_{i \in Pos}^{N} \sum_{m \in \{cx, cy, w, h\}} x_{ij}^k smooth_{L1}\left(l_i^m - \hat{g}_j^m\right) \tag{5}$$

Because $x_{ij}^k = \{0, 1\}$, the position error could only be calculated for positive samples. It is worth noting that the ground truth g is first encoded to obtain $\hat{g}$, because the predicted value l is also the encoded value. g represent the ground truth box. l indicates the offset of the predicted box from the default box.

3 Experiments

We use dual NVIDIA 1080Ti graphics cards as the computing platform on the Ubuntu 18.04LTS system. This experiment is based on the basic framework of SSD and incorporates lightweight networking and attention mechanisms such as MobileNet. The comparison models we used include Faster R-CNN, Yolo v3, SSD-MobileNet-v1, SSD-inception-v2, and so on. The comparison experiment employs the Object Detection API framework, which provides a nice API interface and rich varieties of object detection models. 2726 original training sets and 565 test sets are used in the experiment, and they are from the same data source. There is no intersection between the data sets and they are relatively independent.

3.1 Dataset

The shellfish dataset contains 3772 pictures in 7 categories. The pictures taken in the field account for about 75%, and those from the network account for about 25%. The 7 categories are scallop, clam, oyster, oncomelania, mussel, razor clam and conch, and the distribution is shown in Fig. 4. Due to the limitations of machine performance, all images are reset to around 500*500 pixels, and the targets in the images are manually labeled according to the Pascal VOC standard. Then the dataset is randomly divided into training set, verification set and test set according to the ratio of 8:1:1. The results of the division are shown in Table 1.

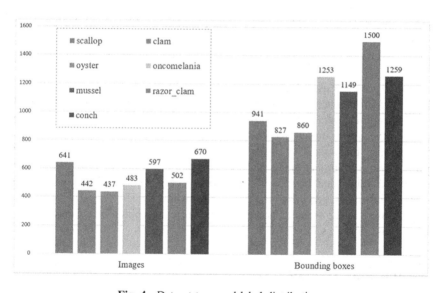

Fig. 4. Dataset type and label distribution.

Table 1. .

Total number	Total spices	Train	Validation	Test
3772	7	2726	481	565

3.2 Data Augmentation

The size and quality of the dataset are critical in deep learning algorithms. On the one hand, a large amount of data could enable the deep learning network to be suitable for complex functions. On the other hand, it could accurately extract the high-level semantic features of data samples. Therefore, in order to make this algorithm more robust to the input in different sizes and shapes, a variety of data augmentation is performed on the images in the dataset, including horizontal flip, random crop and color distortion, randomly sample a patch. Each of the training images randomly samples multiple patches, and the smallest jaccard overlap between objects is: 0.1, 0.3, 0.5, 0.7, and 0.9. This data enhancement operation could increase the number of training samples, and construct more targets of different shapes and sizes, thereby guiding the network to learn more robust features.

3.3 Training Procedure

Before training, the parameters of our model were initialized by a pre-trained model which had been trained on VOC2007 dataset. At the beginning of the training, we randomly weight the image features and use a Gaussian distribution to initialize the weight matrix. The deviation term is a standard normal distribution of 0.0005, and the initial learning rate of the weight is set to 0.0001. In order to improve the training efficiency and make the model converge faster, the Adam gradient descent algorithm is used to train the optimization model. To save training time and speed up the convergence, the experiment uses migration learning to train the deep learning model. First, the parameters of the trained MobileNet classification network are loaded. And then the last classification layer is removed. Finally, the remaining parameter values are assigned to the corresponding parameters in the SSD model.

In training, the values of batch-size, impulse, weight attenuation coefficient, maximum iteration number and initial learning rate are set to 24, 0.9, 0.002, 20000, 0.004, respectively. Then the model is saved once every 5000 iterations, and finally the model with the highest precision is selected. Meanwhile, the Hard-negative mining [17] strategy is used in the training process to enhance the ability of the model to discriminate false positives.

4 Results and Analysis

All of the tests were conducted on our own shellfish dataset. During the evaluation, for each prediction box, the category and the confidence value are first determined according to the category confidence, and the prediction box is filtered out. The prediction boxes with lower confidence threshold is then filtered out. Decode the left prediction frame and get its true positional parameter according to the default box. After decoding, the prediction boxes are arranged in descending order according to its confidence, after which only about 400 of them could be reserved. Finally, the NMS algorithm is performed to filter the prediction boxes with relatively large overlap, and the remaining prediction boxes are the detection result. In order to test the network performance of the integration of attention mechanisms, the result is compared with those by current mainstream object detection methods. Table 2 shows the results of different model methods for shellfish object detection.

Table 2. Comparison of the test results of each model in the Shellfish test library.

Models	Method	Speed (ms)	mAP
Faster RCNN	Resnet50	89	92.59%
	Inception_v2	58	93.09%
Yolo v3	Darknet-53	38	90.94%
SSD	VGG16	40	94.38%
	Inception-v2	42	94.14%
	Mobilenet-v1	30	92.74%
	Mobilenet-v2	31	93.77%
Our model		**33**	**95.38%**

From Table 2 we can see that our model achieved the accuracy of 95.38% on the shellfish dataset. In addition, the object detection based on the end-to-end series of Yolo v3 and SSD series is considerably faster than the region-based Faster R-CNN method. The detection speed of our model is comparable to the lightweight network MobileNet in SSD. And the detection precision scatter plot is shown in Fig. 5.

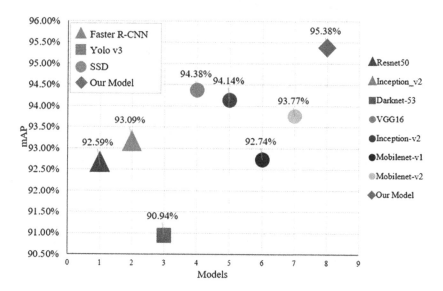

Fig. 5. Shellfish detection accuracy scatter plot.

We can see from Fig. 5 that our model is superior to other models. In order to further better demonstrate the detection performance of the model on each type of shellfish, we give the detection accuracy of each type of shellfish, as shown in Table 3.

Table 3. .

Models	Method	conch	oncomelania	mussel	oyster	razor clam	scallop	clam
Faster RCNN	Resnet50	**98.00**	88.91	87.85	97.67	**98.00**	88.78	88.91
	Inception-v2	96.26	91.36	89.85	**97.87**	95.27	**90.12**	90.91
Yolo v3	Darknet-53	92.00	90.51	91.93	91.83	92.	86.33	91.97
SSD 300*300	VGG16	95.36	92.34	95.07	96.31	96.79	89.33	95.43
	Inception-v2	95.70	93.88	95.49	96.84	96.52	87.07	93.25
	Mobilenet-v1	94.82	93.90	93.85	92.59	96.49	86.83	90.7
	Mobilenet-v2	95.31	94.07	95.22	93.18	96.43	86.41	95.78
Our model		96.75	**95.00**	96.27	97.35	96.98	89.42	**95.89**

The detailed experimental results show that the proposed method of the model is better than the original model, indicating that our improved model improves the penetration capability of the network. The average mAP of our method in shellfish object detection is higher than other methods, although the mAP in some types is not as good as the existing models. For example, the detection accuracy of conch and Razor clam is not as good as Faster R-CNN resnet-50, and the detection accuracy of oyster and scallop is not as good as Faster R-CNN Inception-v2. But this does not affect it's overall mAP. We used the time required to test a single image to evaluate the speed in the experiment. The shorter the time, the faster the detection speed. It could be seen from Table 3 that our method is comparable to SSD MobileNet in speed and is superior in accuracy. Object detection based on the SSD framework could ignore the input size of the image, which means in actual applications, the user can use different camera models to take samples. Replacing the original Vgg16 network with MobileNet lightweight network makes the whole model more portable, laying the foundation for mobile applications such as microcontrollers or mobile phones. The introduction of the attention mechanism is more able to express the local features of the target and improve the detection accuracy. A more intuitive comparison is shown in Fig. 6.

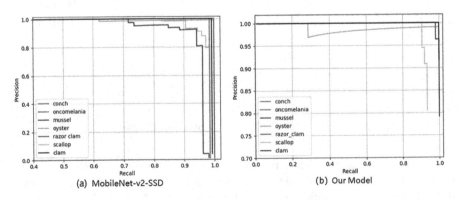

Fig. 6. MobileNet-SSD and our model's precision-recall curve.

It could be seen from Fig. 6 that in the shellfish object detection, the effect of the Precision-Recall graph using only the MobileNet original network is not as good as the effect of adding the residual attention mechanism. To better demonstrate the difference between the better performances in the above two figures, the start values of the recall coordinates in Fig. 6(a) and the precision coordinates in the Fig. 6(b) are respectively set to 0.4 and 0.7. Part of the detection effect is shown in Fig. 7.

Fig. 7. Detection examples on Shellfish test data with our model.

From the pictures of the test we can see that most of the shellfish can still be detected, and can well mark the position of the shellfish target in the picture. However, when the target object is too dense or too large, the false detection rate will increase. This is because the current work is only a macro classification, and it is not classified from fine-grained. This is a work we will do in the later period, which is to detect and classify the characteristics of the smaller particles of the shellfish data.

5   Conclusions and Future Works

In this paper, we mainly do two aspects of work. On the one hand, we made a dataset containing seven kinds of shellfish, and performed a series of object detection tasks on it. On the other hand, based on the MobileNet-v2-SSD framework, we proposed a shellfish object detection model using the residual attention mechanism. It could better show features in the local detail section, and could simplify the training process of the object detection model and shorten the training time. We replaced the original VGG16 network in the SSD with a lightweight MobileNet-v2 classification network and introduced the attention residual mechanism between MobileNet-v2 and the predictive convolutional layer. This can not only better capture the local features of the image, but also meet the needs of real-time and mobile use. Our experimental results show that compared with the current mainstream object detection model, the model with residual attention mechanism has higher accuracy and speed for target recognition. Meanwhile, our work also has some shortcomings, such as high error rate in intensive targets, large targets and similarly shaped shellfish targets. Our future work will further expand the variety and number of shellfish datasets and study the fine-grained classification of images to enable them to be used for more visualization tasks.

Acknowledgements. This work was supported by National Key Research and Development Program of China under Grant 2018YFD0701003.

References

1. Girshick, R., Donahue, J., Darrell, T., Malik, J.: Rich feature hierarchies for accurate object detection and semantic segmentation. In: Proceedings of the IEEE Conference on Computer Vision and Pattern Recognition, pp. 580–587 (2014)
2. He, K., Zhang, X., Ren, S., Sun, J.: Spatial pyramid pooling in deep convolutional networks for visual recognition. IEEE Trans. Pattern Anal. Mach. Intell. **37**, 1904–1916 (2015)
3. Girshick, R.: Fast r-cnn. In: Proceedings of the IEEE International Conference on Computer Vision, pp. 1440–1448 (2015)
4. Ren, S., He, K., Girshick, R., Sun, J.: Faster r-cnn: towards real-time object detection with region proposal networks. In: Advances in Neural Information Processing Systems, pp. 91–99 (2015)
5. Redmon, J., Divvala, S., Girshick, R., Farhadi, A.: You only look once: unified, real-time object detection. In: Proceedings of the IEEE Conference on Computer Vision and Pattern Recognition, pp. 779–788 (2016)
6. Redmon, J., Farhadi, A.: Yolov3: an incremental improvement. arXiv preprint. arXiv:1804.02767 (2018)

7. Liu, W., et al.: SSD: single shot multibox detector. In: Leibe, B., Matas, J., Sebe, N., Welling, M. (eds.) ECCV 2016. LNCS, vol. 9905, pp. 21–37. Springer, Cham (2016). https://doi.org/10.1007/978-3-319-46448-0_2

8. He, K., Zhang, X., Ren, S., Sun, J.: Deep residual learning for image recognition. In: Proceedings of the IEEE Conference on Computer Vision and Pattern Recognition, pp. 770–778 (2016)

9. Howard, A.G., et al.: MobileNets: efficient convolutional neural networks for mobile vision applications. arXiv preprint. arXiv:1704.04861 (2017)

10. Iandola, F.N., Han, S., Moskewicz, M.W., Ashraf, K., Dally, W.J., Keutzer, K.: SqueezeNet: AlexNet-level accuracy with 50x fewer parameters and < 0.5 MB model size. arXiv preprint. arXiv:1602.07360 (2016)

11. Zhang, X., Zhou, X., Lin, M., Sun, J.: ShuffleNet: an extremely efficient convolutional neural network for mobile devices. In: Proceedings of the IEEE Conference on Computer Vision and Pattern Recognition, pp. 6848–6856 (2018)

12. Chollet, F.: Xception: deep learning with depthwise separable convolutions. In: Proceedings of the IEEE Conference on Computer Vision and Pattern Recognition, pp. 1251–1258 (2017)

13. Wang, F., et al.: Residual attention network for image classification. In: Proceedings of the IEEE Conference on Computer Vision and Pattern Recognition, pp. 3156–3164 (2017)

14. Hu, J., Shen, L., Sun, G.: Squeeze-and-excitation networks. In: Proceedings of the IEEE Conference on Computer Vision and Pattern Recognition, pp. 7132–7141 (2018)

15. Wang, H., Zhang, K.: Research on shellfish image classification algorithm based on Gabor features. J. New Industrialization 6, 59–62 (2016). (in Chinese)

16. Suganuma, H., Asada, A., Uehara, Y., Mizuno, K., Yamamuro, M., Okamoto, K.: Detection of shellfish in the sediment by 1-MHz ultrasound: focusing on weak scatter and incident angle. In: 2016 Techno-Ocean (Techno-Ocean), pp. 35–40. IEEE (2016)

17. Shrivastava, A., Gupta, A., Girshick, R.: Training region-based object detectors with online hard example mining. In: Proceedings of the IEEE Conference on Computer Vision and Pattern Recognition, pp. 761–769 (2016)

Multi-branch Structure for Hierarchical Classification in Plant Disease Recognition

Zihao Mao, Jiaming Chen, and Meng Yang[✉]

School of Data and Computer Science, Sun Yat-sen University, Guangzhou, China
maozh3@mail3.sysu.edu.cn, chenjm26@mail2.sysu.edu.cn,
yangm6@mail.sysu.edu.cn

Abstract. Plant disease recognition is a challenging task in agriculture to classify the diseases from the image of plants' leaves, because the plant species and diseases can be various and images of infected leaves may have various appearances and similar structure to normal ones. To solve this problem, hierarchical classification is usually adopted. However, the class information of plant species and diseases has not been yet well exploited. In this paper, we proposed an end-to-end multi-branch hierarchical classification model based on convolutional neural network. Through our designed Select Branch, the proposed model can choose the sub-class from the current cluster iteratively. Meanwhile, a generalized model in hierarchical structure is presented to make the model more scalable for similar classification task. Experiments have been conducted on the benchmark dataset, and the proposed model can achieve better accuracy and be trained much faster than the previous flat classification model.

Keywords: Plant disease recognition · Convolution neural network · Hierarchical classification

1 Introduction

The problem of pests and plant diseases is a long-standing problem in agricultural production. In severe cases, it will cause a huge production reduction. The pests and diseases in the natural environment are complex, and the professional requirements for identifying pests and diseases are high, making prevention and treatment more difficult. How to recognize the disease from the plant leaves and then take appropriate actions is still a challenging problem.

Plant disease recognition is a typical fine-grained few-shot image classification problem. Due to the difficulty of collecting images and make annotations, common datasets are always lacking in images and suffer from imbalanced data problem. The traditional plants disease recognition methods are mainly based

© Springer Nature Switzerland AG 2019
Z. Lin et al. (Eds.): PRCV 2019, LNCS 11859, pp. 528–538, 2019.
https://doi.org/10.1007/978-3-030-31726-3_45

on the morphological features or color features. Rumpf et al. [19] use hyperspectral reflectance features and SVM to classify the plant diseases. Arivazhagan et al. [20] use texture features for automatic detection of plant diseases. These kinds of methods have three main limitations: (1) Few disease classes are included in the dataset, most of the datasets have merely several common diseases of one single species, the recognition usage is limited. (2) Most recognition approaches are based on traditional digital image processing algorithm, the parameters of the algorithm are heavily depended on the data, one set of parameters work well on a specific disease and may perform poorly on other task, even if they are similar. (3) The features are not variable enough, the features of different diseases are diverse but the feature extraction is not adaptive.

A hierarchical structure can handle the fine-grained classification task efficiently. It is a natural way to handle the fine-grained classification task through the hierarchical structure. Traditional flat classification methods neglect the structural information between different classes. A tree-based structure for hierarchical classification is suitable for the inter-relation between classes.

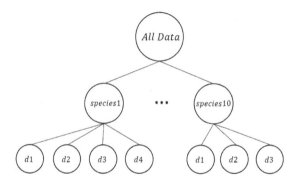

Fig. 1. Tree-based classification structure

A common approach for building hierarchical structure is visual tree [2–4]. In the tree-based classification structure (see Fig. 1), every non-leaf node represents a classifier, every edge from top to bottom represents that the output of the previous classifier is treated as the input of next classifier. However, the simple direct structure has three main disadvantages: (1) The model is not end-to-end. The output of the previous classifier still needs to be sent to the next classifier manually. (2) The number of the classifiers is large. The model consume a large amount of resources (GPU memory etc.). (3) The training process is time-consuming and cumbersome, which is not conductive to online deployment and inference.

In this paper, we proposed an end-to-end multi-branch hierarchical classification model based on deep convolutional neural network. Through our designed Select Branch, the proposed model can choose the sub-class from the current cluster iteratively. Moreover, a generalized model in hierarchical structure is presented to make the model more scalable for similar classification task. The proposed have been evaluated on the benchmark dataset, and experiment results show that the proposed model can achieve better accuracy and be trained much faster than the previous flat multi-class classification model.

Compared with traditional method, our model has three main advantages: (1) the model is light and end-to-end, the training process is less time-consuming and it's easier for deployment and online inference. (2) Using the deep convolutional neural network, the model shares a public low-level feature and each branch in inner-classes have its own high-level feature branch, making the feature extraction more adaptive and efficient. (3) Compared with the flat classification model, our model shows a significant improvement in accuracy by fully consider the inter-relation of different plants species and the training convergence speed is higher.

The rest of this paper is organized as follows. In Sect. 2, we reviews some related works. In Sect. 3, we introduces the proposed model for hierarchical classification. In Sect. 4, we illustrates the result of related experiments. Section 5 provides some conclusions.

2   Related Work

Image classification benefit from the hierarchical structure [3] that can exploit the correlation in different labels. The approaches [1] for building hierarchical structure can be divided into three groups: (1) semantic tree; (2) label tree; (3) visual tree. Researchers like Li et al. [18] constructed image classification dataset like ImageNet based on semantic factors. However, they focus on image classification but did not visualize the hierarchical inter-class relation. Some other researchers use label tree for a better representation. Griffin et al. [5] constructed a binary branch tree to improve visual categorization. Liu et al. [6] constructed a probabilistic label tree for large-scale classification. Bengio et al. [7] built a label-embedding tree for multi-class classification. However, the label tree structure performs poorly on imbalanced data and has low training efficiency. By contrast, visual tree structure with some mechanisms can deal with imbalanced data better. Visual trees constructed by clustering [9–11] produce an efficient hierarchical structure. Lei et al. [10] implemented spectral clustering to construct visual trees. Zheng et al. [12] utilize hierarchical affinity propagation clustering and active learning to build the visual tree. Nister et al. [13] built a vocabulary tree by employing hierarchical clustering.

Recently, the deep Convolutional neural networks (CNN) have achieved great success in image classification [8]. CNN-based multi-class image classification algorithms have received great attention and developed rapidly. Zhu st al. [17] propose the a hierarchical model structure that outputs multiple predictions ordered from coarse to fine along the concatenated convolutional layers corresponding to the hierarchical structure of the target classes. Lin et al. [15] proposed Focal Loss for CNN to deal with imbalanced data by focusing on the hard image samples. By combining powerful feature learning of CNN and visual tree structure, our method can make full use of the inter-relation of labels.

3 Multi-branch Hierarchical Classification Model

3.1 The Inter-relation of Diseases Across Species

We try simple flat classification model on an open source dataset (thoroughly introduced in Sect. 4) provided by AIChallenger PDR[1] (plant disease recognition) competition. The dataset contains 61 classes of pest and disease images. Through the observation of the error samples in the validation stage, we found that the 61-classes flat classification model like ResNet-50 [14] performs poorly on adjacent classes like 'Apple Scab general' and 'Apple Scab serious'. The simple flat classification model do well in cross-species classification but performs poorly in inner-classes distinction like inner diseases of one species and the severity.

(a) "Grape Black Measles (b) "Grape Black Measles
Fungus general"   Fungus serious"

Fig. 2. Grape images from dataset (Color figure online)

Figure 2 shows some different Grape species image samples from PDR dataset, it is obvious that the classification criteria of the severity of the Grape Black Measles Fungus disease mainly lies in size of the infected area.

(a) "Peach Bacterial Spot (b) "Peach Bacterial Spot
general"   serious"

Fig. 3. Peach images from dataset

Figure 2 shows some different Peace species image samples from PDR dataset, it is obvious that the classification criteria of the severity of Peach Bacterial Spot disease mainly lies in the color of the leaves.

---

[1] https://challenger.ai/competition/pdr2018.

From Figs. 2 and 3 we can see that for different species, the criteria for classifying the inner-diseases or severity is different. In order to get higher classification accuracy, it is necessary to first classify the species of the leaves, and then train the inner classifiers for each species, which corresponds with the hierarchical classification.

3.2   Model Architecture

To solve the problem found in Sect. 3.1, we propose our Multi-branch hierarchical classification model based on the ResNet-50 model (Fig. 4).

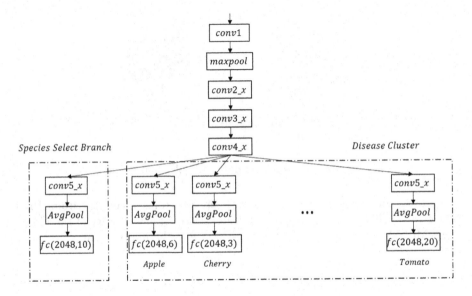

Fig. 4. Multi-branch hierarchical classification model for plant disease recognition

The model has a tree-based end-to-end structure and has specific Clusters and Branches for the plant disease recognition problem introduced in Sect. 1. We modify the feature extraction layer, classification layer and the Loss function of the ResNet. The main idea of the model is to choose the corresponding branch in Disease Cluster according to the classification result of species select branch.

As the network goes deeper, the receptive field of the top-layer pixels is larger. The feature map in bottom-layer carries more texture information while the feature map in top-layer carries more semantic information. We cut off the ResNet branch from conv4_x and make every branch its own con5_x part to build its own semantic classifier because both of the infected area size or the color are semantic level criteria. Every branch shares a public part and also has its inner feature extraction layers to learn different refined features.

In the classification layers, the process is different from flat multi-class classification. Every stage of classification correspond to a pair of branch and cluster. The species select branch trains a 10-class classifier to determine which branch in disease cluster to choose. Based on the result of the species select branch, we pick the corresponding branch in cluster to train inner classifiers and calculate the loss. The results in un-chosen branch are ignored in the calculation of loss function.

Consider the PDR dataset $\{X, Y\}$. $x_i \in X$ is the ith input sample, $y_i \in Y$ is the label of x_i. y_i^s and y_i^d are species-level index label and inner species disease-level index label generated from y_i, respectively. When training our model, The total loss is defined as the sum of the species loss and the selected disease loss. The total loss function can be written as:

$$L(X, Y^s, Y^d) = \sum_{i=1}^{L} \{\text{CEsoftmax}(f_s(X_i), y_i^s) + \text{CEsoftmax}(f_d(X_i), y_i^d)\} \quad (1)$$

where $\text{CEsoftmax}(\cdot)$ represents the Cross-Entropy Softmax Loss. $f_s(X_i)$ is the output of species branch for sample X_i. Similarly, $f_d(X_i)$ is the output of selected disease branch for sample X_i. And L is the number of samples.

3.3   Generalized Model

The exclusive model for plant disease recognition in Sect. 3.2 can be generalized to a general hierarchical classification model.

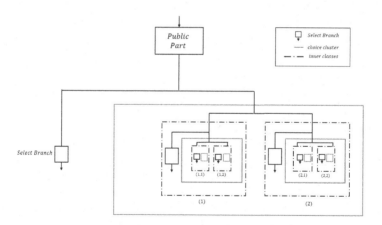

Fig. 5. General multi-branch hierarchical classification model

The generalized model (see Fig. 5) work well for all multi-stage classification problem. Every stage of classification correspond to a pair of Select Branch and choice cluster. Choice cluster is consist of several inner classes in the current stage, every inner classes have their own feature extraction layers and classifiers.

The inner classes are defined as $(n_1, n_2, ..., n_c)$, the cluster level number (or the stage number) c and the chosen inner-class index n_c are defined by the specific task. The lager c means the more refined classification. Similarly, the Select Branch's result determine the choice of branch in the cluster and the loss only counts logits of the chosen branch, the model is still end-to-end.

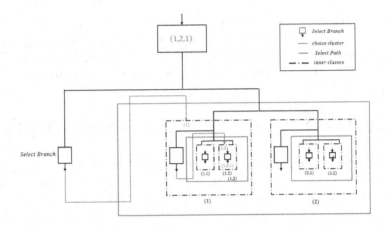

Fig. 6. Data processed in general model

Figure 6 shows the process of classifying a mapped label sample. The $(1, 2, 1)$ is the classes-mapped label of the original flat label. The Select Path shows how the Select Branch choose the branch in current cluster to achieve hierarchical classification.

4   Experimental Results

We evaluate our proposed model on the dataset provided by AIChallenger PDR (plant disease recognition) competition. The dataset has around 50000 photos of plant leaves and these photos are categorized into 61 categories by the format 'species-disease-severity'. These 61 categories are divided into 10 species, 27 diseases (24 diseases were respectively classified into general and serious by severity). Each image contains one leaf occupying main position of the image. The dataset was randomly divided into training set and validation set by a ratio of 7:1.

As shown in Fig. 7, the data distribution is imbalance and the 61 categories need a coarse-to-fine classification. Hierarchical classification is efficient at dealing with such imbalanced, structured data, making it possible to make use of whole imbalanced dataset and obtain higher classification accuracy.

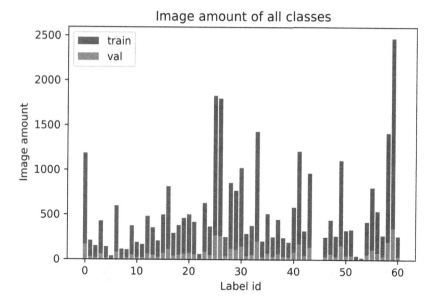

Fig. 7. Statistics of the dataset

In order to prove the utility of our model, we compare the accuracy of the model we proposed in Sect. 3 with some augmentation method and different loss function on PDR dataset. We use 61-classes flat classification with backbone ResNet-50 (pretrained on ImageNet) for baseline. We conduct the experiments on a remote server with 2 Nvidia 1080Ti GPUs. The input image size is 331×331 and batch size is 32. We train the model in Adam optimizer in 30 epoch. The learning rate is $1e-4$ and the weight decay is $1e-4$, we run the validation process after each epoch.

Our model has a faster convergence speed than the baseline model (see Fig. 8) and achieves better training and validation accuracies than the baseline model (see Figs. 9 and 10).

The final validation accuracy Table (see Table 1) shows that the mixup [16] augmentation mechanism and Focal Loss have an improvement on the accuracy of flat classification, indicating that mixup has a effect on anti-overfitting and Focal Loss helps the model to deal with imbalance data. However, when using the mixup and Focal Loss at the same time, the accuracy is even worse than the baseline. We speculate that when linearly blending the input images, the class distribution of the labels were changed, which affects the use of Focal Loss. The experiments on our model shows that our model has higher accuracy and faster training speed than the baseline, better than some common mechanisms like mixup or Focal Loss. Further more, our improvement is structure-based so it can also be combined with similar mechanisms to achieve better performance.

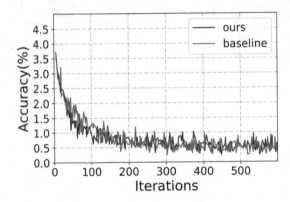

Fig. 8. Training loss of our model (blue) and baseline (red) (Color figure online)

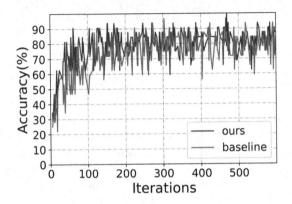

Fig. 9. Training top1 accuracy of our model (blue) and baseline (red) (Color figure online)

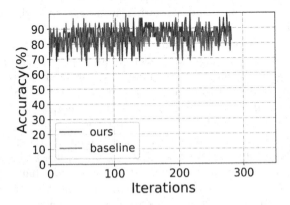

Fig. 10. Validation top1 accuracy of our model (blue) and baseline (red) (Color figure online)

Table 1. Final validation accuracy of different models

Model	Accuracy (%)
ResNet-50 (baseline)	87.6
Baseline + mixup	87.8
Baseline + FocalLoss	88.0
Baseline + mixup + FocalLoss	87.5
Ours	**89.1**

Table 2. Final validation accuracy in ablation study of our model on CIFAR-100

Model	Accuracy (%)
ResNet-50 (baseline)	64.97
Ours	**66.16**

We conduct the ablation study on the CIFAR-100 dataset. The CIFAR-100 dataset has 100 classes containing 600 images each. The 100 classes in the CIFAR-100 are grouped into 20 superclasses. Each image comes with a "fine" label and a "coarse" label, which corresponds with the idea of our two-stage model. The coarse-to-fine classification corresponds with the hierarchical structure of our model. The experimental result (see Table 2) shows that our model works well on similar hierarchical classification problem, making the conclusion more convincing.

5   Conclusion

In this paper, we focus on the plant disease recognition, which is an important application of computer vision to agriculture. It is a challenging task to classify the diseases from the image of plants' leaves, because the plant species and diseases can be various and images of infected leaves may have various appearances and similar structure to normal ones. To address this issue, we proposed an end-to-end multi-branch hierarchical classification model based on deep convolutional neural network. Through our designed Select Branch, the proposed model can choose the sub-class from the current cluster iteratively. Meanwhile, a generalized model in hierarchical structure is presented to make the model more scalable for similar classification task. Experiments results on the benchmark dataset show that the proposed model can achieve better accuracy and be trained much faster than the previous flat multi-class classification model.

Acknowledgement. This work is partially supported by the National Natural Science Foundation of China (Grant no. 61772568), the Guangzhou Science and Technology Program (Grant no. 201804010288), and the Fundamental Research Funds for the Central Universities (Grant no. 18lgzd15).

References

1. Zheng, Y., Fan, J., Zhang, J., Gao, X.: A hierarchical cluster validity based visual tree learning for hierarchical classification. In: Lai, J.-H., et al. (eds.) PRCV 2018. LNCS, vol. 11258, pp. 478–490. Springer, Cham (2018). https://doi.org/10.1007/978-3-030-03338-5_40

2. Fan, J., Zhou, N., Peng, J., Gao, L.: Hierarchical learning of tree classifiers for large-scale plant species identification. IEEE Trans. Image Process. **24**(11), 4172–4184 (2015)

3. Qu, Y., et al.: Joint hierarchical category structure learning and large-scale image classification. IEEE Trans. Image Process. **26**(9), 4331–4346 (2017)

4. Zhou, N., Fan, J.: Jointly learning visually correlated dictionaries for large-scale visual recognition applications. IEEE Trans. Pattern Anal. Mach. Intell. **36**(4), 715–730 (2014)

5. Griffin, G., Perona, P.: Learning and using taxonomies for fast visual categorization. In: Proceedings of IEEE CVPR, pp. 1–8 (June 2008)

6. Liu, T., Tao, D.: Classification with noisy labels by importance reweighting. IEEE Trans. Pattern Anal. Mach. Intell. **38**(3), 447–461 (2016)

7. Bengio, S., Weston, J., Grangier, D.: Label embedding trees for large multi-class tasks. In: Proceedings of NIPS, pp. 163–171 (2010)

8. Zhang, L., Shah, S.K., Kakadiaris, I.A.: Hierarchical multi-label classification using fully associative ensemble learning. Pattern Recogn. **70**, 89–103 (2017)

9. Dong, P., Mei, K., Zheng, N., Lei, H., Fan, J.: Training inter-related classifiers for automatic image classification and annotation. Pattern Recogn. **46**(5), 1382–1395 (2013)

10. Lei, H., Mei, K., Zheng, N., Dong, P., Zhou, N., Fan, J.: Learning group-based dictionaries for discriminative image representation. Pattern Recogn. **47**(2), 899–913 (2014)

11. Marszalek, M., Schmid, C.: Constructing category hierarchies for visual recognition. In: Proceedings of ECCV, pp. 479–491 (2008)

12. Zheng, Y., Fan, J., Zhang, J., Gao, X.: Hierarchical learning of multi-task sparse metrics for large-scale image classification. Pattern Recogn. **67**, 97–109 (2017)

13. Nister, D., Stewenius, H.: Scalable recognition with a vocabulary tree. CVPR **2**, 2161–2168 (2006)

14. He, K., et al.: Deep residual learning for image recognition. In: Proceedings of the IEEE Conference on Computer Vision and Pattern Recognition (2016)

15. Lin, T.-Y., et al.: Focal loss for dense object detection. In: Proceedings of the IEEE International Conference on Computer Vision (2017)

16. Zhang, H., et al.: Mixup: beyond empirical risk minimization. arXiv preprint. arXiv:1710.09412 (2017)

17. Zhu, X., Bain, M.: B-CNN: branch convolutional neural network for hierarchical classification. arXiv preprint. arXiv:1709.09890 (2017)

18. Jia, D., et al.: Imagenet: a large-scale hierarchical image database. In: 2009 IEEE Conference on Computer Vision and Pattern Recognition. IEEE (2009)

19. Rumpf, T., Mahlein, A.K., Steiner, U., et al.: Early detection and classification of plant diseases with support vector machines based on hyperspectral reflectance. Comput. Electron. Agric. **74**(1), 91–99 (2010)

20. Arivazhagan, S., Shebiah, R.N., Ananthi, S., et al.: Detection of unhealthy region of plant leaves and classification of plant leaf diseases using texture features. Agric. Eng. Int. CIGR J. **15**(1), 211–217 (2013)

Author Index

Printed in the United States
By Bookmasters